Mathematical Models for Decision Support

NATO ASI Series

Advanced Science Institutes Series

A series presenting the results of activities sponsored by the NATO Science Committee, which aims at the dissemination of advanced scientific and technological knowledge, with a view to strengthening links between scientific communities.

The Series is published by an international board of publishers in conjunction with the NATO Scientific Affairs Division

A Life Sciences B Physics	Plenum Publishing Corporation London and New York
C Mathematical and Physical Sciences D Behavioural and Social Sciences E Applied Sciences	Kluwer Academic Publishers Dordrecht, Boston and London
F Computer and Systems Sciences G Ecological Sciences H Cell Biology	Springer-Verlag Berlin Heidelberg New York London Paris Tokyo

Series F: Computer and Systems Sciences Vol. 48

Mathematical Models for Decision Support

Edited by

Gautam Mitra

Department of Mathematics and Statistics
Brunel, The University of West London
Uxbridge, Middlesex UB8 3PH, United Kingdom

Co-editors

Harvey J. Greenberg
Freerk A. Lootsma
Marcel J. Rijckaert
Hans J. Zimmermann

Springer-Verlag
Berlin Heidelberg New York London Paris Tokyo
Published in cooperation with NATO Scientific Affairs Division

Proceedings of the NATO Advanced Study Institute on Mathematical Models for Decision Support held in Val d'Isère, France, July 26 – August 6, 1987.

ISBN 3-540-50084-7 Springer-Verlag Berlin Heidelberg New York
ISBN 0-387-50084-7 Springer-Verlag New York Berlin Heidelberg

Library of Congress Cataloging-in-Publication Data. NATO Advanced Study Institute on Mathematical Models for Decision Support (1988:Val d'Isère, France) Mathematical models for decision support/edited by Gautam Mitra; co-editors, Harvey J. Greenberg ... [et al.]. p. cm.—(NATO ASI series. Series F, Computer and systems sciences; vol. 48) "Proceedings of the NATO Advanced Study Institute on Mathematical Models for Decision Support, held in Val d'Isère, France, July 26 – August 6, 1987"—T.p. verso. "Published in cooperation with NATO Scientific Affairs Division." Includes bibliographies.
ISBN 0-387-50084-7 (alk. paper)
1. Decision-making—Mathematical models—Congresses. 2. Decision support systems—Congresses. I. Mitra, Gautam. II. Greenberg, Harvey J. III. North Atlantic Treaty Organization. Scientific Affairs Division. IV. Title. V. Series: NATO ASI series. Series F, Computer and systems sciences ; vol. 48.
QA279.4.N37 1988 658.4'03'4—dc 19 88-30718

Printed in Germany

Printing: Druckhaus Beltz, Hemsbach; Binding: J. Schäffer GmbH & Co. KG, Grünstadt
2145/3140-543210 – Printed on acid-free paper

PREFACE

It is quite an onerous task to edit the proceedings of a two week long institute with learned contributors from many parts of the world. All the same, the editorial team has found the process of refereeing and reviewing the contributions worthwhile and completing the volume has proven to be a satisfying task.

In setting up the institute we had considered models and methods taken from a number of different disciplines. As a result the whole institute - preparing for it, attending it and editing the proceedings - proved to be an intense learning experience for us. Here I speak on behalf of the committee and the editorial team. By the time the institute took place, the papers were delivered and the delegates exchanged their views, the structure of the topics covered and their relative positioning appeared in a different light. In editing the volume I felt compelled to introduce a new structure in grouping the papers. The contents of this volume are organised in eight main sections set out below:

1. Abstracts.
2. Review Paper.
3. Models with Multiple Criteria and Single or Multiple Decision Makers.
4. Use of Optimisation Models as Decision Support Tools.
5. Role of Information Systems in Decision Making: Database and Model Management Issues.
6. Methods of Artificial Intelligence in Decision Making: Intelligent Knowledge Based Systems.
7. Representation of Uncertainty in Mathematical Models and Knowledge Based Systems.
8. Mathematical Basis for Constructing Models and Model Validation.

At the beginning the abstracts appear in a section of their own. This is followed by a review paper that has taken me a long time to prepare. This paper also appears in a section of its own as it is intended to be an overview of the major modelling issues in decision making. The purpose of presenting the material in this order is that by first reading these two sections the readers may gain a fair glimpse of the contents of the remaining six sections of the volume.

It is not possible to stage an institute of this international character without the resource support and goodwill of many parties. I am pleased to acknowledge here the contributions made by many organisations and individuals.

Financial Support The institute was made possible by the main financial grant offered to us by the NATO Scientific Affairs Division. We are grateful to Dr Craig Sinclair, the director of the ASI programme, for the benefit of his advice at all times. He also liaised with other grant giving bodies from NATO countries. As a result National Science Foundation, USA, National Office of Scientific and Technical Investigation, Portugal, Ministry of National Economy, Greece and The Scientific and Technical Research Council of Turkey, provided additional funds to support the attendance of scientists from their respective countries.

Equipment Support I would like to thank particularly Dr E Johnson of IBM, Yorktown Heights, New York, and Mr Sylvain Idy, Digital Equipment Corporation, France for arranging the loan of a number of PC-AT professional micro computers, and a micro VAX computer respectively. The availability of these industry standard work horses gave us the opportunity to mount demonstrations and workshops which would not have been possible otherwise.

Executive Support I have been most fortunate to have the advice and planning support of the members of the committee. Marcel Rijckaert hosted a number of meetings at his university at the planning stage of the institute. Harvey Greenberg, Freerk Lootsma, Marcel Rijckaert and Hans Zimmermann all put in considerable effort to define the structure and contents of the institute. The preliminary proceedings turned out to be voluminous and I was most relieved when the committee members agreed to co-edit the volume and to help in the review and refereeing process.

Administrative Support At administrative level we had the excellent support of Mrs P Denham, who worked tirelessly during the preparation of the Institute. Physical and computer organisation of names, addresses, and papers and responses, were carried out with great care and prepared us well for the event. Dr C Lucas and Dr M Tamiz helped us with the logistics of getting all the documentation together. As a result it was possible to put on a good software exhibition. At the location itself Mrs J Valentine acted as the secretary to the institute. We were very impressed to find how well she worked with Mrs Denham and took over full control of the operation. She dealt with the speakers and the delegates with considerable skill and initiative which went a long way towards the smooth running of the event. After the institute Mrs P Denham took over all the debriefing activities and worked admirably to carry out many chores which were required to complete the volume. Finally, I must thank my wife Dhira for also providing emergency help whenever we had to meet deadlines.

Social Activities To attend an institute held during summer many speakers and participants had to cut short their holidays or embark upon "busman's holidays". For delegates who were accompanied by their families suitable social activities needed to be organised. In this Mrs Ricki Lootsma took the lead and was supported by Mrs Agnes Rijckaert and Mrs Dhira Mitra. They organised many activities in a relaxed yet well thought out fashion. Thus the children remained grouped together, amused and disciplined, and the delegates found places to see or have a drink and a dance, or enjoy the beauty of the mountainside.

Val d'Isère Village We were indeed very lucky to have chosen this mountain village as the venue for the institute. The mayor, Mr Degouey, and head of tourism, Mr Claude Regis, extended a most sincere welcome to the administrative team and the delegates. They invited us to two receptions and helped us whenever we encountered some problem and yet left us to our devices at other times. At the Hotel Sofitel, the principal hotel of our residence, Mrs. Raymond Marret and Mrs Edith Raymonde also showed considerable goodwill and understanding to accommodate many difficult requests that can be expected from a large group of people of varying background and requirements.

In conclusion I would like to thank all the speakers, the delegates and the members of the families who came to the institute for their attendance and for contributing to its success.

Editing this volume and completing the preface brings to an end all the tasks associated with this institute.. We were happy to learn from the delegates attending the institute that they had found the event stimulating and invigorating. I hope readers of this proceedings will find its structure and contents equally valuable and germane to their own field of study and research.

May 1988 - Gautam Mitra, Wentworth, Surrey, United Kingdom

CONTENTS

SECTION 1

ABSTRACTS

LANGUAGE REQUIREMENTS FOR A PRIORI ERROR CHECKING AND MODEL REDUCTION IN LARGE SCALE PROGRAMMING

Johannes J Bisschop, University of Twente, Netherlands

Experience has taught us that several types of errors are made during the construction of large-scale mathematical programming models. One approach is to detect these errors once model results are available, but this approach is unacceptable. Another approach is to try to prevent making errors in large-scale models by identifying them before a solution algorithm is used. This second approach has several merits, but requires that the model builder communicates his knowledge concerning the various model components to a modeling system. The modeling system can then verify if this knowledge is correctly represented, thereby checking for errors. This paper highlights the second approach, and emphasizes the development of special language elements within future modeling languages to allow for a compact but powerful notation for the prevention of errors. Such a notation facilitates the description of domains and ranges for data and models, and can therefore also be used for the a priori reduction of models. Examples of error checking and model reduction are included for illustrative purposes.

A NOTE ON THE REFORMULATION OF LP MODELS

Joaquim Carmona, Economics Faculty of Oporto, Portugal

In the course of writing SIMP, a spreadsheet type LP system, it was necessary to incorporate a procedure to reformulate the models generated in order to reduce the number of constraints/variables in the model. This note describes the ad-hoc way in which this was done, assesses it further and suggests alternatives.

EXPERT SYSTEMS' FRONT END: EXPERT OPINION

Roger M Cooke, Delft University of Technology, The Netherlands

Designers of expert systems have largely ignored the problems at the "front end", namely, problems of evaluating and combining expert opinion. In this contribution some problems associated with the use of expert opinion are reviewed. The basic concepts of expert resolution, calibration and entropy, are set forth. Finally, a theory of weights for convex combinations of expert probability distributions is sketched. The weights are derived from proper scoring rules, and reward both good calibration and low entropy.

A FINANCIAL EXPERT DECISION SUPPORT SYSTEM

Michael A H Dempster and A M Ireland
Dalhousie University, Canada

This paper describes the overall conceptual design for MIDAS, a domain-specific decision support system incorporating expert systems assistance for application, explanation and extension of the results of integrated optimization and simulation models. In the terminology of Kitzmiller and Kowalik [34], MIDAS is a *symbolic-numeric* knowledge based system *deeply-coupled* using object-orientated programming techniques (Fikes and Kehler [23], Stefik and Bobrow [50]). In a clearly *specified domain* such a debt management, a specific expert decision support system such as MIDAS appears to have many advantages. Because the *decision process* for major decisions can be *partly anticipated* or structured, the system can be designed to support it in depth through applicable models.

NATO ASI Series, Vol. F48
Mathematical Models for Decision Support
Edited by G. Mitra

INTERFACES BETWEEN MODELING SYSTEMS AND SOLUTION ALGORITHMS

Arne Stolbjerg Drud, ARKI Consulting and Development A/S, Denmark

Modeling systems provide a bridge between the modeler and his abstract view of a problem and the detailed requirements of most solution algorithms. The paper describes the necessary considerations for designing interfaces for a modeling system that can handle many classes of models, linear as well as nonlinear, and many different algorithms. Both the communication of models from the modeling system and the communication of solution values and messages back are considered.

RELATIONAL DATA MANAGEMENT AND MODELING SYSTEMS: A TUTORIAL

Daniel Dolk, Naval Postgraduate College, USA

Current modeling systems are weak in data manipulation. Relational database management system (RDBMS), on the other hand, afford powerful data handling capabilities. This paper provides an overview of the relational data model and the SQL data manipulation language with examples of how these may be applied to modelling applications. Generalizing from these examples, four ways are suggested in which RDBMS and modeling systems may be integrated.

MODEL MANAGEMENT SYSTEMS FOR OPERATIONS RESEARCH: A PROSPECTUS

Daniel Dolk, Naval Postgraduate College, USA

Technology and concepts are currently available for implementing a model management system (MMS) that does for OR models what a database management system (DBMS) does for data. This paper develops the functional requirements for an MMS in the areas of model description, manipulation, and control. It then shows how the confluence of structured modeling, object-oriented programming, and relational DBMS can facilitate the functions of model description, manipulation, and control, respectively.

MATHEMATICAL PROGRAMMING SOLUTIONS FOR FISHERY MANAGEMENT

Joáo Lauro D Facó, Federal University, Brazil

Regulation and limitation of the quantities of fish captured are most important for ecological and economic reasons. Interacting multispecies fish populations stock regulation models are presented using Optimal Control and solved by a GRG Nonlinear Programming algorithm. Using data of tuna-fish populations from southeastern brazilian coast we present some practical results for fishery management.

A GENERAL NETWORK GENERATOR

M Forster, The Free University of Berlin

In this paper the general network generator GNGEN is presented. GNGEN is based on a modelling language which allows the specification of networks by powerful set algebraic definitions. Arbitrary network structures can be modelled using GNGEN in a simple and concise way. Arc and node data are strictly separated from the definition of the network structure and can be read at generation time from data files. A production and distribution planning problem serves as an example of a typical model formulation using the language.

A CASE STUDY IN THE USE OF MATHEMATICAL MODELS FOR DECISION SUPPORT IN PRODUCTION PLANNING

Manfred Grauer, University of Hagen, West Germany

Initiated by the accident of the 'Seveso-Plant' (Italy 1978) a concept for decision support in production planning for chemical industry under normal and abnormal conditions is presented. This task leads to the necessity to solve an optimal control problem. The corresponding dynamic optimization problem is transformed into an equivalent static nonlinear programming problem under constraints.

The DSS is devoted to control the process of chlorination of phenol with the by-product dioxin. The nonlinear programming package 'OPTIMISER' has been developed by the author for dense problems under constraints and is used to solve the problem.

VALIDATION OF DECISION SUPPORT SYSTEMS

Harvey J Greenberg, University of Colorado, USA

Validation concerns comparison of a model with reality. In this paper we first consider the traditional approaches and then validation as a social process is discussed. We have also examined the role of AI in validation and the scope of using the fuzzy logic in the validation process.

ANALYZE Rulebase

Harvey J Greenberg, University of Colorado, USA

This is a report of the demonstration of ANALYZE with its experimental rulebase to support analysis of linear programming models.

A KNOWLEDGE-BASED SYSTEM FOR PRODUCTION CONTROL OF FLEXIBLE MANUFACTURING SYSTEMS

G W Hintz, RWTH Aachen, West Germany

Due to the changing market demands and under the heavy pressure of competition product life cycles have permanently become shorter. Therefore production companies have to meet requirements of flexibility and efficiency. A central element to deal with this problem are Flexible Manufacturing Systems. In order to use all potentials of an FMS it is necessary to develop dedicated systems for production planning and control (PPC).

In this paper a knowledge based PPC-system is described which combines methods from Operations Research and Artificial Intelligence.

DSS CONCEPTUALIZERS IN O.R: SHOULD YOU APPLY AI?

Gezinus J Hidding, Arthur Andersen & Cie, France

We address the question: "With more and more different problem solving techniques (e.g. AI and OR) available, which one(s) should a DSS designer choose for any specific business problem?" We focus on the conceptualization phase of problem solving, previously not considered in the DSS literature. We have identified a new type of system to support a DSS designer: DSS Conceptualizers. They assist in determining important factors in a problem and in selecting an appropriate model class. We present examples of existing DSS Conceptualizers.

INTERFACING OPTIMIZERS WITH PLANNING LANGUAGES AND PROCESS SIMULATORS

Leon S Lasdon, University of Texas, USA
A D Waren, Cleveland State University, USA
S Sarkar, Execucom Systems Corporation, USA

In optimization-based decision support systems, a key issue is how to interface the model with the optimizer. We examine this question for process simulation models and for models expressed in planning or spreadsheet languages. In this latter case, the widely used IFPS/OPTIMUM system is used as an example. In both instances, reduced gradient formulas are effective in computing derivatives of implicit functions. For real-time process optimization, the degree of integration between process model and solver is also seen to be important.

STRUCTURED MODEL MANAGEMENT

Melanie L Lenard, Massachusetts Institute of Technology, USA

Representing the structured modeling framework as a relational database makes it possible to use a database management system to integrate the data, model, and dialog components of a decision support system. The object-orientated programming paradigm applied to structured modeling suggests the form and structure of the model management component. A prototype model management system is being built to show the feasibility of using this approach to manage at least linear programming models.

FUNDAMENTALS OF STRUCTURED MODELING

Melanie L Lenard, Massachusetts Institute of Technology, USA

Structured modeling [Geoffrion, 1985] is a formal mathematical framework for representing a wide variety of models. It identifies the basic elements of a model and recognizes three levels of structure for capturing the relationships among model elements. Structured modeling is the basis for a proposed modeling language and computer-based modeling environment. The intended benefits are increased productivity, better communication with users, and a means for exploring connections between management science and other model-based disciplines.

FUZZY SET THEORETIC APPROACHES TO NATURAL LANGUAGE IN DECISION SUPPORT SYSTEMS

Weldon A Lodwick, University of Colorado at Denver, USA

The use of fuzzy set theory to implement natural language interfaces with decision support systems (DSS) is explored. Words/phrases such as "very", "more or less", "many", or "few" are inherently ambiguous and a rich part of natural language. A decision support system which incorporates natural language must either eliminate the use of ambiguities or develop methods to transform them into units that can be processed by the computer. A second source of ambiguity arises from natural language description of models, processes, or information that are incomplete but for which results are nevertheless sought.

The problem central to this study is how to interpret natural language input for the computer to perform computations and analyses meaningfully with respect to a DSS. A second problem touched upon is that of translating the results of the computations and analyses in a language that is both "precise" when the results are exact and "ambiguous" when the results are fuzzy. Thus two mapping problems ensue, one from natural language to fuzzy sets and a second from fuzzy sets to natural language. In general, these maps are different.

NUMERICAL SCALING OF HUMAN JUDGEMENT IN PAIRWISE-COMPARISON METHODS FOR FUZZY MULTI-CRITERIA DECISION ANALYSIS

Freerk A Lootsma, Delft University of Technology, Netherlands

We are dealing with the pairwise-comparison methods for solving the typical problem of multi-criteria decision analysis: the ranking and rating of a finite (usually small) number of alternatives under conflicting criteria, by a single decision maker or by a decision-making committee. Our particular concern is the interface with the decision maker: the numerical scaling of the gradations of his comparative judgement. Because the gradations are vague and the decision makers imprecise, we express the judgemental statements in fuzzy numbers with triangular membership functions. We analyze the propagation of fuzziness in multi-level decision making, and we develop a fuzzy preference relation between the alternatives which is practically scale-independent. To illustrate matters, we present some of our results in strategic planning of energy research.

A MULTICRITERIA DECISION PROBLEM WITHIN THE SIMPLEX ALGORITHM

Istvan Maros, Hungarian Academy of Sciences, Hungary

One possible way to reduce the overall computational effort when solving linear programming problems is to try to find a 'good' first feasible solution in Phase-I with the hope that only few iterations will be left for Phase-II. There have been several attempts to achieve this goal with more or less success. The present contribution provides an adaptive procedure which is easily implementable even in LP packages for micro computers and has some favourable characteristics. The problem is regarded as a hierarchical multicriteria decision problem and is solved accordingly.

INTERACTIVE DISTRIBUTION PLANNING

Oli B G Madsen, The Institute of Mathematical Statistics
and Operations Research, Denmark

In this paper we discuss the construction of a decision support system which assists the planner in charge of routing and scheduling tasks at the operational level. The system is implemented on an IBM PC and may be used by companies of any size. The system assists in solving routing problems with one depot and one-depot routing and scheduling problems where time constraints are imposed. The system is interactive, which makes it possible to incorporate usually unquantifiable factors into the solution process and to produce better solutions. The methods are fast and may handle problems with several hundred customers.

MODELS FOR DECISION MAKING: AN OVERVIEW OF PROBLEMS, TOOLS AND MAJOR ISSUES

Gautam Mitra, Brunel University

Models for decision making have a very broad perspective. To understand their context we first consider possible ways of classifying decision problems. Work in the area of soft systems methodology has highlighted the gap between real problems and models. We discuss the scope of traditional management science models. This we follow up with outlines of developments in database technology and the AI methods which have also addressed these problems. The need for unifying these different approaches is briefly considered and some recent work towards this goal is described. We put forward the argument that the extension of the conceptual framework of these models will enable higher productivity in modelling if suitable machine implementations can be found.

A KNOWLEDGEBASE FOR FORMULATING LINEAR PROGRAMS

Frederic H Murphy, Temple University, USA

In this paper we describe some of the characteristics of linear programming models. The properties and modeling alternative are presented in such a way that they can be represented as a knowledgebase in a system for formulating linear programs that uses artificial intelligence techniques.

A KNOWLEDGE-BASED SYSTEM FOR INTEGRATED SOLVING CUTTING STOCK PROBLEMS AND PRODUCTION CONTROL IN THE PAPER INDUSTRY

W Nickels, RWTH Aachen, W Germany

An important problem in the field of production planning and control in the paper industry is the determination of patterns and machine schedules for cutting production rolls into the finished roll and sheet sizes.

In this paper a knowledge based system which works on this problem is described. This sytem is a rule based system and uses the concepts of fuzzy set theory, linguistic variables and approximate reasoning.

CHOICE THEORY AND DATA BASE

James C Moore, William B Richmond and Andrew B Whinston
Purdue University, USA

We view a data base query not as a retrieval process but as a choice process. Using this view, the data base management system assumes the decision making role and the data base is taken to be a set of possible alternatives to the decision problem. The goal of a query is to select the best possible alternative where the criteria for determining the best alternative are based on the user's utility function.

We use a decision model to formulate a lattice data base model, and we discuss the problems of developing choice query algorithms for the model.

EXPERT SYSTEMS: THE STATE-OF-THE-ART

Marcel J Rijckaert, V Debroey, W Bogaerts
Katholieke Universiteit Leuven, Belgium

This paper describes in the first section the essential lines, along which expert systems work. (Knowledge representation, reasoning mechanism, explanation facilities). As advanced issues in expert systems research, the following topics are discussed: real-time systems, expert systems in complex domains, deep and causal knowledge, learning and automated knowledge acquisition, user interface, validation and evaluation.

SOME MATHEMATICAL TOPICS IN THE ANALYTIC HIERARCHY PROCESS

Thomas L Saaty, University of Pittsburgh, USA

The following topics of the Analytic Hierarchy Process (AHP) are briefly covered. Axioms and definitions; the derived scale; reciprocal matrices, eigenvalues, eigenvectors; consistency; composition; functional and structural criteria, rank preservation and reversal; hierarchies and feedback networks, and dependence.

WHAT IS THE ANALYTIC HIERARCHY PROCESS

Thomas L Saaty, University of Pittsburgh, USA

Traditional methods of mathematics and operations research are often dependent on structure, computation, and assumption, requiring the knowledge of an expert. While any technique may have its shortcomings, a decision should be made in an environment relatively free from reliance on sophisticated and opaque procedures. This paper centers around the Analytic Hierarchy Process (AHP), a planning theory which enables decision-makers to deal with tangible and intangible factors together in the same framework, to judge tradeoffs between these factors, and finally to select the best alternatives, allocating resources according to benefits and costs. The AHP provides a practical decision approach to complex issues and problems. These issues are characterized by multiple criteria: ambiquity, risk, conflicting interests, and qualitative and quantitative information. The AHP establishes a framework within which decision makers and their advisors can structure problems and analyze related objectives, issues, and options to arrive at the best possible solution.

STOCHASTIC PROGRAMMING MODELS FOR DEDICATED PORTFOLIO SELECTION

Jeremy F Shapiro, Massachusetts Institute of Technology, USA

The paper begins with a review of deterministic mixed integer programming models for dedicated bond portfolio selection. These models are extended to stochastic programming with recourse models for explicitly analyzing the same bond selection decisions in the face of interest rate and other types of uncertainty. In the process, we introduce a new concept of risk for dedicated portfolios. A numerical example illustrating the stochastic programming approach is extensively discussed.

MATHEMATICAL PROGRAMMING ON MICROCOMPUTERS: DIRECTIONS IN PERFORMANCE AND USER INTERFACE

Ramesh Sharda, Oklahoma State University, USA

This paper provides a summary of linear programming software for microcomputers. Functional differences between various programs are discussed. Recent improvements in user interface, such as spreadsheet modeling and model/matrix generators, are explained. Then the paper reports results of an extensive test of seven LP packages. These results indicate that the PC programs are getting better in terms of speed and accuracy. However, the programs still do not appear to work as claimed when large problems are attempted. Our experimental results indicate that the packages display considerable variability in performance when put through a range of test problems.

AUTOMATED SUPPORT FOR FORMULATING LINEAR PROGRAMS

Edward A Stohr, New York University, USA

Most research in mathematical programming has been concerned with efficient computational algorithms. However, there is increasing interest in developing automated techniques for supporting the modeling process. This paper describes a new kind of interface for formulating linear programming models and explains the inference process used to translate problem specifications in algebraic formulations. The main idea underlying the design of the interface is to change the specification language to a graphical rather than a mathematical notation. The inference process involves the generation of algebraic terms and their subsequent combination into constraint equations. This relies on the syntactic relationships among indices and a knowledge of the physical entities that they represent. An advantage of the approach is that it facilitates the reuse of model components from previous models. The ideas discussed in this paper have been incorporated in a prototype system.

AN INTERACTIVE DSS FOR MULTI OBJECTIVE INVESTMENT PLANNING

J Teghem Jr., Faculté polytechnique de Mons, Belgium
P L Kunsch, Belgonucléaire, Belgium

In the field of Investment Planning within a time horizon, problems typically involve multiple decision objectives and basic data are uncertain. In a large number of cases, these decision problems can be posed as linear programs in which time dependant uncertainties affect the coefficients of objectives and of certain constraints. Given the possibility of defining plausible scenarios on basic data, discrete sets of such coefficients are given, each with its subjective probability of occurence. Moreover, these investment problems very often include some integer variables. The correponding structure is then characteristic for Multi–Objective Stochastic and Integer Linear Programming (MOSILP).

A decision support system (DSS) is designed to obtain at best compromise for such a MOSILP and implemented in a Belgian firm.

Two real world problems analysed with this DSS are first presented. Then the different steps of the mathematical model are described. For the interactive phases a distinction is made between problems with only continuous variables and those with some integer variables; in the last case, an interactive Branch and Bound method has been developed.

AGGREGATION MODELS IN MATHEMATICAL PROGRAMMING

Brigitte M Werners, RWTH Aachen, W Germany

An interactive decision support system is developed which uses fuzzy mathematical programming approaches to model decision problems with multiple objective functions and inexact constraints. In this paper we introduce the procedure of aggregating the objective functions and the constraints. The models which are developed here can be solved efficiently by using standard software tools. The additional information required can be given by the decision maker globally or in a hierarchically structured form.

MATHEMATICAL BASIS FOR DECISION SUPPORT SYSTEMS

James C Moore, William B Richmond, and Andrew B Whinston,
Purdue University, USA

We present a decision Model that incorporates information acquisition where one form of information acquisition can be viewed as executing a series of computer models. The decision model forms a basis for decision support systems on two levels. On the macro level the decision model forms a structure for the optimal use of decision support systems for a given decision problem. On the micro level the decision model provides a basis for the construction of a decision support system. On both levels a decision process is based on the concept of a rational economic agent whose goal is to maximize his/her net payoff from the decision.

THE ENVIRONMENT APPROACH TO DECISION SUPPORT

Clyde W Holsapple and Andrew B Whinston, Purdue University, USA

Decision Support Systems (DSS) must be capable of presenting an integrated representation of diverse types of knowledge to an end user in a manner that is natural to understand and manipulate. In this paper we introduce concepts that would be important in the development of such an integrated environment for DSS type users. A conceptual framework for the environment is presented and its relationship to the internal structure of the DSS problem processor is described. Future research directions are also identified.

MULTIPLE CRITERIA MATHEMATICAL PROGRAMMING: AN UPDATED OVERVIEW AND SEVERAL APPROACHES

Stanley Zionts, State University of New York at Buffalo, USA

An overview of Multiple Criteria Mathematical Programming is presented. Solving problems with more than one objective is considered, and then particularized to mathematical programming problems. Several simple or naive approaches, which are reasonable first approaches to solving such problems, are presented and critiqued; these approaches are shown to have evolved into practical approaches. A number of methods for solving multiple criteria problems are then presented. Examples are given and applications are briefly discussed.

INTERACTIVE DECISION SUPPORT FOR SEMI-STRUCTURED MATHEMATICAL PROGRAMMING PROBLEMS

Hans J Zimmermann, RWTH Aachen, W Germany

We have grown accustomed to viewing problems which are solved as mathematical programming models as being well structured. Often these problems contain vague components for which a crisp and deterministic formulation is actually not appropriate. This is particularly true for problems in multi-objective programming. This paper shows how fuzzy set theory can be used to model and solve this type of problem in a more appropriate way. The structure of an interactive decision support system including facilities to handle vague components, is described and discussed.

PROBABILISTIC AND NON-PROBABILISTIC REPRESENTATION OF UNCERTAINTIES IN EXPERT SYSTEMS

Hans J Zimmermann, RWTH Aachen, W Germany

Expert systems are particularly aimed at situations in which the problems cannot be modeled in a closed analytical way, solved algorithmically, and in which uncertainty plays an important role. The uncertainties involved are of very different nature and require, therefore, different tools for modelling. This paper first tries to trace the origins of uncertainties and to define resulting types of non-deterministic, non-dichotomous structures. It then presents possible theories to model stochastic uncertainties and lexical uncertainties (fuzziness). Possible ways of representing uncertainties in Expert Systems are discussed and available Expert Systems and Tools are mentioned, which already take into consideration uncertainty in their inference engines.

FUZZY SET THEORY - AND INFERENCE MECHANISMS

Hans J Zimmermann, RWTH Aachen, W Germany

Inference Mechanisms play an ever increasing part, in particular in the area of Expert Systems. These systems, however, are directed towards ill-structured problem situations in which the structures cannot be modelled in a deterministic, crisp and dichotomous way. This paper describes the basis and the potential of Fuzzy Set Theory and its application to the area of reasoning under uncertainty. The essentials of fuzzy programming languages, as an implementation of approximate reasoning, are also briefly explained.

SECTION 2:

REVIEW PAPER

MODELS FOR DECISION MAKING : AN OVERVIEW OF PROBLEMS, TOOLS AND MAJOR ISSUES

Gautam Mitra, Brunel University, UK

1. Introduction

Decision making in almost all realms of human endeavour has always been a difficult task. It is also an important task when considered in the context of our social and economic goals and behaviours. We know from history that mathematicians and philosophers have tried to develop theories and models to analyse and describe human behaviour: this naturally encompasses the purpose and nature of human decision making.

Towards the end of the 1940's operations research and management science made great strides, as a result of which a scientific framework for problem solving and decision making emerged. Yet what then seemed to be the alchemy also led to many examples of outstanding failure. Since then a number of information revolutions [SIMON77] and five generations of computer developments [FEIMK83] have taken place. As always we are wiser by such experiences and it is now well accepted that behavioural sciences and computer technology in many ways play as important roles as that of mathematical models for problem solving. During the fifties and sixties, the early days of developments in computer science and management science, these two disciplines evolved closely. Packages and software for management applications were seen to be an important area of research and development for specialists in computer applications. Subsequently OR scientists moved towards algorithmic refinements and mathematical theories whereas equally important issues of productivity, implementation and acceptance fell into neglect. In the meantime computer science developed into information technology with its major focus on commercial computing, and management information systems.

In the mid-eighties again we have seen a convergence of ideas and a breakdown in the barriers between different and somtimes competing disciplines. Scientists with different backgrounds are participating in multi-disciplinary developments. The major contributions have come primarily from two groups: the information processing and the mathematical modelling specialists. The central motivation of course is to create computer (hardware) based tools and products which help us to make better decisions in an expeditious fashion.

NATO ASI Series, Vol. F48
Mathematical Models for Decision Support
Edited by G. Mitra

Diagram 1

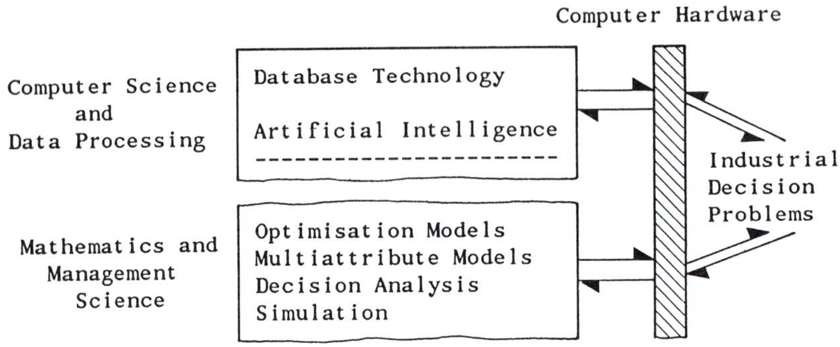

An analysis of recent developments [GEOFF87, BRMYS84, BOHWN81, DOLK86, MITRA86, GREEN87, DMPST87, SHPRO87, LUCAS86] provides further insight. Computer scientists, DP specialists, management scientists, all have been involved in the solution of decision problems. The strict demarcation between these specialisations are becoming less rigid and there is a natural acceptance of complementary contributions from other fields.

Many of us who come from otherwise traditional OR and management science backgrounds need to take into account a particular aspect of decision support tools which has led to the introduction of newly emerging artificial intelligence (AI) methods in a big way. The case is set out below in its essential form. Decision making requires careful gathering and evaluation of facts, ascertaining relative merits of chosen alternatives and reasoning about consequences. In its widest sense mathematics is concerned with manipulation of information, problem representation and arriving at conclusions. This is achieved by reasoning about properties and deriving theorems which relate to a particular problem domain. Thus the mathematical inference procedure which can be based on alternative theories of logic is ideally suited to provide abstract representation as it captures the common denominator for a range of otherwise unrelated problems. In the normal course of events such abstractions only amounted to elegance and completeness until computers were really established as a major gadget in our working and private lives. As early as 1958 Simon, Newell and Shaw [NEWSM63] tried to mechanise inference procedures for problem solving using a computer. The major motivation of this attempt is not just mathematical elegance. Its main outcome may be interpreted as production gains whereby successful application of these approaches gear up and augment our ability for reasoning and problem solving. Thus automation of automation, as discussed by James Martin [JMART84], and knowledge information processing systems as described by Feigenbaum [FEIMK83], in different ways argue the same case that mechanisation and enhancement of human reasoning power is a vital research issue as it encompasses the strategic question of gearing (amplifying) our thinking power.

A fundamental focus of AI research is decision making application. Effective decision making and supporting the decision maker are also the major concern of management science and database technology. These taken together have led to the concept of a decision support system (DSS). DSS is the unifying theme of the present institute yet it is nearly impossible to agree on a formal definition of a DSS. We have therefore introduced in the appendix a working definition of the DSS. The definition takes into consideration feature lists and characteristics advocated by specialists with different perspectives.

The rest of this paper is organised as follows. In section 2 we have described classes of decision problems; a range of contexts in which these problems arise are also considered in this section. In section 3 we analyse the question of model representation of real world problems and highlight the inevitable gaps between reality and models. Established families of quantitative models: optimisation, simulation, and decision theory are considered in their essential form in section 4. There have been a number of developments in database technology: their impact on the problem of decision support is considered in section 5. In section 6 we first present a working definition of an expert system shell. We then provide a detailed discussion of alternative forms of knowledge representation, and the methods of knowledge elicitation. A number of researchers, Brodie et al [BRMYS84], Geoffrion [GEOFF87], have put forward a case for further abstraction and a unified framework for modelling. These topics are discussed in section 7. The importance and scope of man machine dialogue and participative systems design are considered in section 8, and we conclude with a few final remarks in section 9. A working definition of the scope, architecture and focus of decision support systems is set out in the appendix.

2. Classes of Decision Problems

Management scientists have tried to classify decision problems from different perspectives. The best known ones are due to Anthony [ANTNY65], Simon [SIMON65], Phillips [PHILP84] and Jacques [JAQUE82]. They all adopt an organisational viewpoint.

Classification Based on Time Frame

Anthony's classification [ANTNY65] is based on strategic, tactical, and operational decision problems and may be naturally extended to include problems of industrial and process control, Table 1.

Strategic Planning is carried out by top management and the main goal is to acquire and develop productive resources. The time frame of decision making is long five years or more and there is a broad scope of development and growth of the organisation. For large public authorities and super corporations even five years may be too short, and they need to prepare and update strategic plans on seven to ten year time scales. Most of the information is considered in a highly aggregated form and the problem is characterised by high degree of uncertainty concerning the future taking into account both external and internal circumstances.

Tactical Planning is undertaken by the middle managers, it is concerned mainly with efficient resource utilisation and the time horizon of the decisions are shorter around 6 months to 1 year. Decision making is based on moderately aggregated information collated from internal and external sources and there is a reduced level of uncertainty coming mainly from external circumstances. The outcomes of these decisions are more limited in their scope of influencing the organisation's present performance and future development.

Operations Control is focussed on the optimal execution utilising resources which are deployed by the tactical planning exercise. These correspond to well specified clerical or industrial tasks carried out by employees lower down the organisation. The scope of influence at the operations level is narrow, the degree of uncertainty is low; however, the information as required for decision making may be extremely detailed in some specific aspect of the problem.

Industrial Control problems are those where decisions are made and control actions are taken regularly for continued operation of a plant. In the financial sector funds may be transferred or managed against fluctuating exchange rates, interest rates, etc. The

TABLE 1

Problem Characteristics Type	Objectives	Time Horizon	Level of Management Involvement	Scope	Source of Information	Nature of Information	Degree of Uncertainty
Strategic Planning	Resource Acquisition (Development)	Long 5 years	Top	Broad	External and Internal	Highly Aggregate	High
Tactical Planning	Resource Utilization	Medium 6 months - 1 year	Medium	Medium	External and Internal	Moderately Aggregate	Moderate
Operations Control	Optimal Execution	monthly weekly daily?	Low	Narrow	Internal	Detailed in specific Aspects	Low
Monitoring Control of - Industrial Processes - Financial Fund Transfer and Management	Optimal and Robust Execution	daily hourly more frequent	Low + machine support	Narrow	External and Internal	Detailed in specific Aspects	Low

Strategic, Tactical, Operational Decision Problems and Industrial Control Problems

Classification based on Anthony's Framework

Table 2

Basic structure of work in organisations
and associated decision support systems

Time Span	Stratum	Organisational Level	Main Activity	Capabilities Decision Support Syst
50 yrs	VIII	Super Corporation	Shaping Society	
20 yrs	VII	Corporation	Providing overall strategic direction	
10 yrs	VI	Corporate Group of Subsidiaries	Creating strategy and translating it into business direction	
5 yrs	V	Corporate Subsidiary and Top Specialists	Redefining goals and identifying new products and new markets	Articulation of principles guiding goal setting
2 yrs	IV	General Management and Chief Specialists	Creating methods of operation	Selecting from type eg generating new systems
1 yr	III	Departmental Managers and Chief Specialists	Organising programmes and systems of work	Restructuring within fixed structure e.g establishing new criteria
3 months	II	Front Line Managerial Professional & Technical	Generating programmes of work	Altering judgement on a variable within a fixed structure eg"What If?" model
1 day		Office and Shop Floor	Doing Concrete tasks	Judgement within fixed structure eg with information retrieval service

time frame of decision making in this case is daily or hourly and in addition to the optimality consideration one looks for robust decision making.

L Philips [PHILP84] has taken E Jaques' [JAQUE82] analysis of the nature of work as set out in Table 2 and used it to illustrate the same hierarchical structure of decision problems and the scope of decision support tools.

Simon's Taxonomy

Simon [SIMON65] classifies decision problems into two types: programmed and nonprogrammed, which are also referred to as structured and unstructured decisions respectively. This classification is set out in Table 3.

Programmed Decisions can be structured into specific procedural instructions; they can be delegated to the lower echelons of the organisation and do not require extensive supervision. These decision problems occur routinely, repetitively and are normally in the domain of the clerks.

Nonprogrammed Decisions cannot be handled by well established and well defined treatment. Their solution requires considerable creativity, judgemental input and abstract thinking. They are complex and unstructured and are usually dealt with by top managers.

In some sense the two frameworks are not entirely independent of each other. For instance a large number of operations control and industrial control problems are in the nature of structured decision problems. The strategic and tactical planning on the other hand are usually concerned with unstructured problems. However, the boundaries of the structured and unstructured problems and those separated by a time frame are not entirely sharp. For instance a number of scheduling problems such as crew scheduling [MITDA85], vehicle scheduling [CHRST86] are operations control problems. The manual methods of solving these problems, however, require considerable amount of mental abstraction and reasoning skill. It is well known that good human schedulers develop a high degree of specialist skill focussed to their problem and also call upon their experience and intuitions. Some of these are definitely nonprogrammed tasks.

Another important conclusion that emerges from the analysis of this framework can be summarised as follows. If we consider the number of instances of problem solving it becomes obvious, how often we need to solve the problems taken from the different groups. This frequency of problem solving is clearly based on the time frame of these problems themselves. For instance industrial control and operations control problems are solved on hourly, daily, or weekly basis and hence there are

Diagram 2

Table 3

Simon's Taxonomy of Decision Problems

Types of Decisions	Techniques: Conventional	Techniques: Modern
Programmed: Structured Routine Repetitive	1. Clerical Routine 2. Operating Procedures 3. Habit Forming	1. Mathematical Models 2. Electronic Data Processing
Non Programmed: Unstructured Complex Abstract	1. Judgement, intuition creativity 2. Rules of Thumb 3. Executive Training	1. Decision Theory 2. Heuristic Problem Solving 3. Other AI Methods

Programmed = Structured Decisions
They are carried out routinely, repetitively. They can be structured into specific procedural instructions... delegated lower down the strata.

Non Programmed = Unstructured Decisions
They are complex, unique. Do not lend themselves to well defined, treatment requires deep analysis, judgmental input, evaluation of risk.

---

more instances of these than those of tactical planning and strategic planning which are solved on a quarterly or half yearly basis, Diagram 2. Thus the scope for applying computer supported problem solving methodologies is greater with the groups lower down the scale of time span.

It is interesting to note that decision theory approach to problem analysis generally requires that an appropriate structure be imposed on the problem. For this purpose we can derive the following structuring based on the works of Raiffa [RAIFA68] and Keeney and Raiffa [KEERA76]. In this scheme problems are classifed by

(i) single or multiple (group) decision makers,
(ii) time staged problem or otherwise,
(iii) requiring representation of uncertainty or deterministic relations only
(iv) use of single objective or multiple objective.

We notice that (i) and (iv) may require complex evaluation and inference procedures. (ii) requires discounting of the value function and also reasoning about time whereas (iii) is determined by the context of the problem. In section 4 we expand on the modelling aspects of these classes of problems.

These taxonomies (classifications) of decision problems are not without their critics [WINTR80, BKHMP82]. In [HUMPH86] Humphreys takes up the soft systems methodology of Checkland and puts forward the view that instead of asking the question: "what is the problem?" (and what class it belongs to) it is more important to identify: "who is the problem owner?"; (see Checkland [CHECK81]). For problems with little or no structure this is seen to be a valid argument. It also reinforces the view that in such cases applying inference procedures based on knowledge about the problem and use of heuristics is perhaps the only way of analysing and solving such problems. This topic is taken up and expanded in the next section.

These classifications although attractive are less than adequate in many practical situations. This viewpoint can be supported by examples taken from different contexts and illustrated below. For instance, decision problems relating to emergency and hazard management [GASCH86, GASBC86] clearly do not fit well into any of these frameworks. Similar comments apply to problems of medical diagnosis [KOBAT85, SHORT76] and fault diagnosis [KOUKU86, SWABY86]. Performance evaluation [LEMOR81] is yet another example of a decision problem involving multiple decision making units, set in an organisational context, and the problem does not fit the classification scheme. In spite of these criticisms there is a strong case in defence of these classifications. There are many examples such as those in medicine and public transport planning and operation [DAJLM87] [KOAND86] which fit well into these frameworks.

3. Model Representation of Real World Decision Problems

For our purposes a model is an object or a concept used to represent a real situation or an actual (physical) machinery, system, etc. It is presented in a form that is scaled down (physical model) or in an abstract framework that is well understood. A model is a plan for information processing and provides a specification for transforming information: a definition due to Whinston et al [BOHWN81]. Thus a model may be specified in mathematical expressions, in English statements or in computer programs. A mathematical model is an abstract (symbolic/algebraic) representation which is made up of mathematical concepts involving constants, variables, functions, relationships, and restrictions. It is well known that mathematical models form the backbone of all physical sciences. Models have been developed through other forms of abstraction; thus ELIZA [WEIZE66] mimicking a psychiatrist, PARRY [COLWH77] acting the role of a paranoiac and language based industrial controllers [ESHMA81] are early examples of simple linguistic models.

The models which are of immediate interest to us have been classified by the management scientists and the decision analysts [RAIFA68] in three major categories set out below.

Descriptive Models as defined by a set of mathematical relations which simply predicts how a physical, industrial or a social system may behave.

Normative Models constitute the basis for (quantitative) decision making by a superhuman following an entirely rational, that is, logically scrupulous set of arguments. Hence quantitative decision problems and idealised decision makers are postulated in order to define these models.

Prescriptive Models involve systematic analysis of problems as carried out by normally intelligent persons who apply intuition and judgement. Two distinctive features of this approach are uncertainty analysis and preference (or value or utility) analysis.

In order to represent real world problems by means of these models it is necessary to first analyse these problems along the lines discussed in the last section and then discover their underlying structure. This begs the question if a structure exists at all. Whereas early OR analysts accepted and tried to follow such a sequence of logical steps, accumulated wisdom based on many failures led to the emergence of soft systems approach. Stainton [STAIN84] presents this viewpoint in following terms. Very much in the spirit of Simon's taxonomy, the subject of systems (like decision problems) is viewed as either being systematic in nature or as being systemic. The two are distinctly different yet equally worthy of exploration. These two systems paradigms are due to Checkland [CHECK83] who put forward that let R stand for reality and M for the methodology which a human observer might employ to deal with that reality. In this case two possibilities are

I (i) R is systemic: the world contains systems (which we can understand and identify),
(ii) M can be systematic
and

II (i) R is problematical: we cannot know it ontologically (that is as it truly is),
(ii) M can be systemic.

According to Checkland [CHECK81] the important features of paradigm II, as compared with paradigm I, is that it transfers systemicity from the world to the process of inquiry into the world. Thus the paradigm of optimising becomes a paradigm of learning. Traditional analytic approaches (of managements science) based on quantitative models has been rooted in paradigm I. There is an increasing awareness of the inadequacy of paradigm I as we take into consideration the extreme complexity of real world affairs. The methodologies identified in these two paradigms, that is systematic and systemic relate directly to hard systems thinking and soft systems thinking respectively. The former is most effective with well structured problems whereas the latter is best suited to ill structured problems or what has been more aptly described as "messes" [ACKOF74]. Zimmermann [ZIMMR88] suggests that structured and unstructured problems are better described as 'well structured and unstructured' problems.

It is very interesting to note that these unstructured situations or "messes" also provide the natural entry point for artificial intelligence (AI) into the realm of (decision) problem solving. Whinston [BOHWN81] in his discussion of structured and unstructured decision processes presents the perspective of a continuum of problems between two extremes of structure and no structure. His view is that developments in management science has allowed more unstructured problems to be analysed and put into a structured framework. Of course the unstructured problems can be only attacked by adopting

- use of analogy
- problem clarification and redefinition
- formulating general strategy starting from a specialised method
- intuitive approach.

All these are easily seen to be basic tools of AI used in problem solving.

We wish to conclude this section by considering an example which substantiates the arguments put forward so far. It is well known that chess is a board game which calls for both strategy and tactics and moves of rational players are based entirely on an inference mechanism. Thus any move must have a supportable reason. The history of the game which originated in the East does not indicate use of any quantitative model. Yet for the purpose of machine analysis of the game and the generation of supportable moves out of the vast number of alternatives Shannon [SHNON50] introduced a valuation of the pieces (see Table 4). These valuations were then used for position evaluation functions and in lookaheads for tree searches. This in effect captures the essence of the game so well that all introductory text books on how to play chess have adopted this as a means of teaching strategies of opening, middle, as well as end games and evaluating the tactics of positional plays.

Table 4

PIECES	QUEEN	ROOK	BISHOP	KNIGHT	PAWN
VALUE	9	5	3	3	1

4. Established Models: Optimisation, Simulation, Decision Analysis

The well known management science models may be classified into three main categories: constrained optimisation (mathematical programming), simulation (to study queues and other random processes), decision analysis.

From an analytical standpoint there are a few major aspects which influence the nature and applicability of these models to a particular problem area. These are identified as deterministic relations, uncertainty representation and relations, probabilistic event, and preference relations.

– Mathematical Programming (constrained optimisation).

Deterministic constrained optimisation problems with single objective functions are known as mathematical programming models. During the sixties and seventies these evolved to take the central position in the study of decision problems. Until recently most research in mathematical programming has been algorithmic. In this approach deterministic relations (constraints or restrictions) are usually turned into a set of linear or nonlinear equalities. By solving a set of equations, linear or nonlinear, one would satisfy the quantitative restrictions as required by the real life problem. This is equivalent to finding a point in a point set and all linear and nonlinear programming (optimisation) methods incorporate this feature [HADLY65]. Thus the central theme of mathematical programming is to solve a set of equations and to find the extremum of one objective function. The introduction of multiple objective functions compels one to consider preference relations which are discussed in the next subsection. The main issue in mathematical programming is to compute solutions to intractable and difficult problems within a deterministic framework. Over the last decade there has been considerable progress in devising methods and supporting software which process substantial linear and nonlinear programming problems, [MURTG81], [TAMIT87], [MURSN82], [LASDN87].

Integer and mixed integer programming models provide an extremely powerful scheme for problem representation. Recent studies [BLJEL84, WILLM87] show that integer programming representations are connected closely with propositional calculus and predicate calculus and hence to logic programming. We [DALMY88] have also investigated this issue for our own modelling system and have proposed a unified framework for reformulation of problems with logical restrictions and fuzzy relations to zero one mixed integer problems or crisp linear programming problems.

It is true to say that all LP problems of meaningful size can be solved by expending a reasonable amount of computing effort. The situation is different for integer programming methods which continue to present computational difficulty as these take exponential time to solve (as opposed to an average polynomial time for LP problems). Yet the technology of solving optimisation problems has developed much faster than the development of support tools for problem formulation, creating machine readable models and analysing the models and their solutions. In the 60's and 70's special purpose matrix generator computer programs and application languages were created [FOURE83]. The summary position covering more recent developments can be found in [MITRA87].

– Simulation

Mathematical analysis of increasing complexity is applied to study problems of queues or more general situations of randomness. If we assume known statistical distributions and otherwise simple underlying physical systems then a number of analytic results and related (queue) statistics may be derived. Unfortunately the assumptions underpinning such distributions may not be appropriate in a given context and actual sampling may not be possible either. In addition the physical system which is to be investigated may be complex say with multiple stages. As Wagner puts it [WAGNR69] in this case computer simulation is "the only game in town". GPSS, SIMULA and SIMSCRIPT may be cited as three typical languages (for simulation) out of many which were developed for this purpose.

In recent time, however, only SIMSCRIPT has maintained its momentum of development. Simulation is a descriptive tool and is used

(i) to describe a currently existing physical system
or
(ii) to explore a hypothetical system
or
(iii) to design improvements and extensions to an existing facility

The main aim of undertaking a simulation study in (i) and (iii) above is to make tactical and strategic decisions respectively.

Many investigators and system developers Paul [PAULD86], Nance [NANCE84] have recently turned their attention to the question of model specification as an independent task in its own right. Use of computer graphics to present results; WITNESS [WITNS87] and DRAFT [MATHE85] are given considerable importance. Database and data management facilities have also assumed much more prominence. SIMSCRIPT for instance has a procedural language facility which is used to manipulate database and main storage entities and the system is otherwise a powerful application generator.

- Choice, Preference and Decision Analysis.

A wide variety of problems which require choosing, evaluating, planning, allocating resources and assessing risk can all be represented and analysed by applying decision theory. Whereas making choices or deriving preference relations using one criterion involves straight forward scalar comparison and leads to the relatively simple concept of optimality, the situation is naturally more complicated with a multiattribute problem in which it is necessary to compare value vectors and determine trade offs. Recently there has been an enormous upsurge of interest in the problem of multiattribute decision making under certainty as well as uncertainty and most methods essentially employ some way of logically ordering the solutions. The key concept in this context is that of a nondominated set of solutions which is also known as the Pareto optimal set or the efficient frontier. A solution from the Pareto optimal set has the property that no other solution can dominate it. In other words no other solution can be found which is superior in all respects. For a pair of distinct solutions from the set, however, there will be trade off between attributes. Thus one solution will be worse in one given attribute but superior in at least one other. In developing methods to deal with conflicting objectives the major concern is to devise ways of ranking the solutions. Cost benefit analysis [FROST78], indifference mapping [RIVET77], utility theory [FISHB70], outranking relations [ROY73], and hierarchy method [SAATY80], are different approaches to this essentially central problem of ranking the solutions. Lootsma [LOOTS87] has recently extended this work to the area of trade off analysis and resolution of conflicts; he also reports [LOOMV87] a number of recent applications. In multicriteria mathematical programming [ZIONT82] both equation solving and ordering are required. We note that in devising the ranking of the solutions two key concepts of decision theory are always applied: these are concepts of dominance and transitivity. In short the ordering procedure is required to be logically consistent.

Ulvila and Brown [ULBRN82] provide an up-to-date review and a framework of decision analysis based on utility theory. Keeney [KEENY82] has also written an overview of the topic. Phillips [PHILP86] presents the leading issues clearly and summarises the four main principles of coherence in decision making. These are

(i) <u>ordering principle</u> which admits preference, indifference, (but not "I don't know"),
(ii) <u>transitivity principle</u> which may follow from ordering,
(iii) <u>principle of dominance</u>,

(iv) sure–thing principle, which states that preference of A to B should not be influenced by any attribute common to A and B.

Given that probabilities exist and represent uncertain outcomes one can use the expected utility [VNEUM44] or expected monetary value (EMV) as it is variously known to make a choice out of alternatives.

Let $i = 1,2..$ denote decisions and $j = 1,2..$ denote consequences then the expected utility of decision i is given as

$$EU_i = \sum_j p_{ij} u_{ij}$$

where p_{ij} is the probability of consequence j given the decision i and u_{ij} is the return. From an entirely scientific viewpoint the choice is then made by first computing EU_i for all i and then determining

$$\max_i (EU_i)$$

Unfortunately, for reasons discussed in section 3 it is simply not possible to apply any of these three traditional methodologies optimisation, simulation, decision analysis in all domains of decision making. In his plenary address to the TIMS/ORSA meeting at Miami Beach Simon [SIMON86] made a plea that mathematical approaches to problem solving should be extended by taking into account progressively successful techniques of AI. On his part within his framework of structured modelling Geoffrion [GEOFF87] has developed a theory and preliminary implementation which strives to achieve such a goal. Some basic techniques of AI are briefly considered in the next section and in section 6. This is followed up with a discussion of conceptual and structured modelling.

5. Database Technology: Its Role in Decision Support

A practical definition of information and data is provided by Whinston et al [BOHWN87]. In a loose sense "data" is used synonymously with "information": more appropriately data can be used to make inferences and when data is processed it leads to information. An alternative (to management science approach) culture of managerial decision making comes from the development of database technology. In this we use a collection of facts which can be used as basis for reasoning and decision making. Such a collection of data is called a database. Data models are used to construct applications using databases [BRODI84] and the applications are characterised by

- static properties such as objects
- dynamic properties such as operations on objects and relationships
- integrity rules covering objects and operations

Most existing database management systems provide a Data Definition Language (DDL) to specify schemes which define objects, Data Manipulation Language (DML) for writing database programs, and a Query Language (QL) for writing queries.

Brodie [BRODI84] also provides a taxonomy of data models made up of four generations:

1. Primitive data models
2. Classical data models
3. Semantic data models
4. Special purpose models

It is interesting to note that the definition of these four generations are different from those of Gardarin [GARGE84].

The four generations put forward by him are:

(i) The first generation 1950's: sequential files
(ii) The second generation 1960's: direct access files
(iii) The third generation mid-60's to mid-70's: access models and CODASYL [CDSYL71] database standards
(iv) The fourth generation mid-70's to the present: the relational database [CODD70].

Just to highlight the lack of consensus in the IT profession we can cite yet another classification of the four generations by Martin [MARTN84].
The major methods of representing data in databases (classical data models [BRODI84], [DATE81]) are accepted to be

- hierarchical approach: tree structured and extension of sequential files,
- network approach: extension of the hierarchical method,
- relational approach: introduced by Codd [CODD 70] and exploits data relationships.

The relational approach is most recent and has steadily gained in its applicability. In this the end user has a logical view of the database in the form of tables. The data manipulation language needs to specify what information is used and not how (it should process the database to get it). Recently an ANSI standard [ANSI83] has emerged on a normalised SQL data manipulation language.

These developments which have taken place entirely in the Data Processing (DP) profession have put a completely different colour to the use of databases. Instead of assuming the role of an otherwise passive actor and recording/retrieving data, there now are many applications which illustrate the deductive and intelligent components of these database systems. The close connections between relational database and predicate calculus have been discussed by several investigators [GALMN81], [NICOLS82], [MARQE84]. Thus the use of a logic programming language as a host language to a relational database system is a natural choice and has been investigated and adopted by the Japanese [KUNYO82], [MIYA282]. Even without logic programming relational analysis on its own has been used to solve planning and scheduling problems: Minker [MINKR81], Ball et al [DABAL85], Elleby & Grant [ELGRA86], Worden [WORDN86], discuss examples of such applications.

Another paradigm through which database management methods have provided decision support tools can be found in the nearly parallel yet related development of model management systems. In an organisation which has many models and many users the scope of model management is very well appreciated. Palmer and his coworkers in EXXON [BOPAR84] have documented the successful use of database tools to create and manage mathematical programming models, model data, output solutions and reports.

The planning system PLANET [LUCAS86] developed within General Motors provides another example of extensive use of integrated database management and modelling system. Lenard [LENRD86] and Dolk [DOLKN85] have taken this up as a research issue and have discovered important software requirements which lead to a confluence of management science models database technology and AI methods.

6. AI Methods: Knowledge Based (Expert) Systems

Artificial Intelligence (AI) has a broad perspective. In principle AI is concerned with machine analysis and solution of all problems of the "world". Within AI, search theory, pattern recognition, natural language understanding, knowledge representation are, to name a few, themes of major interest [NILSN80], [MCHIE79], [BONET85]. We are, however, interested in a specific area of its application, namely, decision making. We focus our attention on the questions of representation, acquisition, manipulation and utilisation of knowledge as carried out within an Intelligent Knowledge Bases System (IKBS) also called an Expert System (ES). In this section we cover the following four topics germaine to this theme:

- the conceptual and logical framework of an expert system,
- alternative ways of representing knowledge,
- AI planning and reasoning with time,
- alternative ways of representing uncertainty.

– Expert Systems and Expert Systems Shells

An expert system is a computer program which simulates the problem solving behaviour of a human expert in a particular domain of his expertise. Thus an application of an expert system is usually restricted to a specific problem area. In order to simulate the role of an expert the program communicates with the problem owner in a natural way, it is capable of accepting facts and rules supplied to it, it can give advice and it can explain the reasoning by which it arrives at its decisions. Expert systems have been in use now over nearly two decades. MYCIN [SHORT76], INTERNIST/CADUCEUS [POPLE82] in medicine, DENDRAL [FEBUL71] in scientific applications, PROSPECTOR [DUGSH79] in Geology (SEE [JONKR85]). More recently emergency management systems [GASBC86], [GASCH86], are a few of a rapidly growing collection of applications.

In the early days ES were created for a particular application. Subsequently, in the case of MYCIN it was realised that if one removed the problem specific aspect of the program (knowledge base, facts, etc.) then one was left with the essential (or empty) MYCIN: called EMYCIN. As a result another system PUFF was created by introducing new knowledge and facts to EMYCIN. Today we can find [HEWSA86], [HEWTG86] many such generalised tools to construct expert systems: these are called expert systems shells. Rijckaert [RIJCK87] has presented an interesting tutorial on this topic.

In order to explain the nature of expert systems and the role of the expert and the knowledge engineer it is worth investigating how applications are created using these shells.

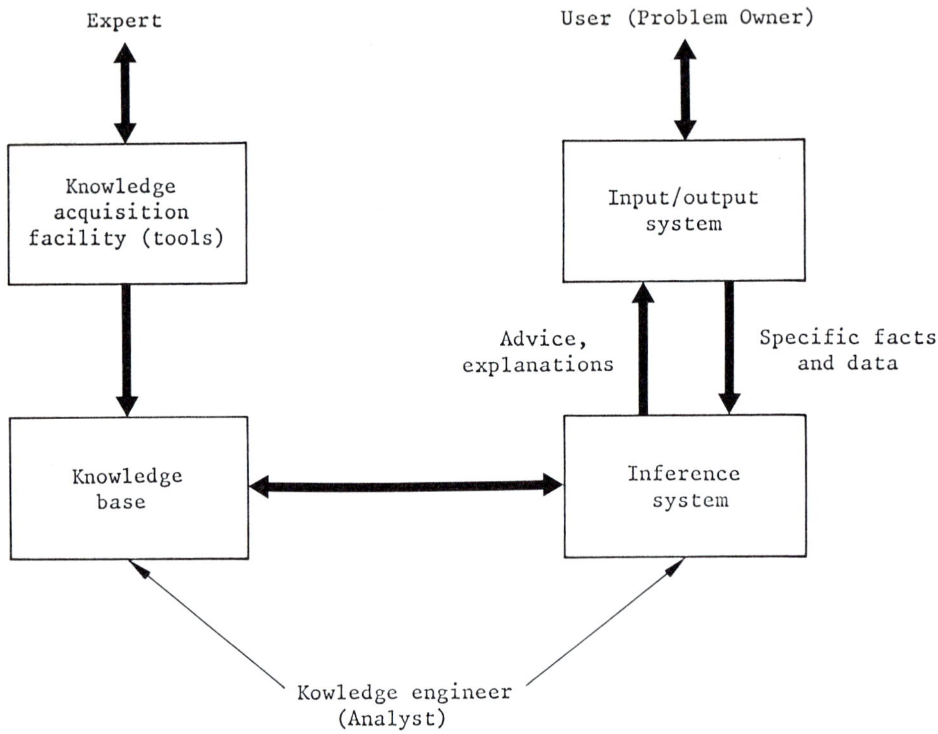

Diagram 3

Essentially we have four parties:

(i) A computer based expert systems shell,
(ii) a domain expert,
(iii) a knowledge engineer (traditionally an analyst),
(iv) a problem owner (traditionally a user).

Diagram 3 is based mainly on the descriptions of Feigenbaum [FEIMK83] and illustrates how these four parties relate to each other. With the help of the ES shell and making use of the knowhow of the domain expert, the knowledge engineer elicitates knowledge and incorporates this in the knowledge base of the system. This in effect is the application development mode of the ES. Subsequently the problem owner presents the ES with specific facts and data: these amount to describing problem instances. The ES program consults the knowledge base and makes inference. It can be used in three forms:

(a) to point out inconsistencies in facts and data presented by the problem owner,
(b) to advise on the course of action to be followed by the problem owner,
(c) to explain the sequence of logical arguments by which it arrived at its conclusions.

Any ES shell therefore includes three specific modules covering knowledge acquisition, inference making and dialogue management. Since all of these work with the knowledge base different ways of representing knowledge is an issue of fundamental importance in ES studies.

- Alternative approaches to knowledge representation

As a part of our discussion covering methods of representing knowledge we first draw an analogy. We would like to claim that the process of knowledge elicitation is comparable with the act of the management scientist discussing with the client's expert the nature of his problem and then creating a computer readable mathematical model. Thus model formulation is synomymous with knowledge representation: a point of view that was put to us by Geoffrion [GEOFF85].

Knowledge representation may be classified in different ways. For instance knowledge can be represented in declarative or procedural forms: these correspond to the classical questions of "knowing what" and "knowing how". A declarative structure can be used only if there is a corresponding rule interpreter. Let P,Q,R stand for three propositions and consider the declared rule $P \wedge Q \rightarrow R$. Then the rule interpreter can use it in any of the following ways.

(a) if P and Q are both true, then R is true,
(b) if P is true R is false, then Q is false,
(c) if the goal is to prove R is true then try to prove P and Q are true.

A procedural representation on the other hand provides a constructive (algorithmic) step by step specification of knowledge in a given domain. Thus a quantity y which takes the value $\sqrt{x}$ (square root of x) can be specified by an algorithmic procedure (say by Newton Raphson method) for computing y as follows.

Procedure SQRT (x,y)

- check if x is non-negative,
- take any value y in the range 0 to x,
- apply the steps of Newton Raphson until convergence to a given accuracy,
- within acceptable tolerance (y.y) is nearly x.

End of Procedure

This and examples of scientific functions such as ln(x), sin(x) in computer libraries, illustrate ways in which we specify and make use of (by making calls in a computer program) procedural representation.

In logic there are formal deductive methods by which exact inferences can be made. These are termed first order logics. There are also much looser forms such as drawing networks, specifying rules through which commonsense reasoning are expressed. Mylopoulous et al [MPLEV84], and Bonnet [BONET85] have provided very compact yet clear descriptions of these alternative methods. Possible ways of representing knowledge are summarised as,

- first order logics,
- semantic networks,
- production rules,
- frames or structured objects

First order logics

Propositional calculus and predicate calculus fall under this category [STOLL61]. Propositional calculus is based on the rules of syntax for forming statements and those of deriving new statements from given statements. Every legal (syntactically correct) statement can essentially assume one of two logical values TRUE or FALSE. The symbols A,B may be used to represent propositions such as "more people watch football than cricket", "sum of all outflows add upto the inflow", etc.

The logical connectives which are used to combine propositions and form statements are shown in Table 5. Table 6 sets out the use and effective definition of these connectives.

TABLE 5

Logical Connective	Symbol
AND	$\wedge$ or &
OR (inclusive)	$\vee$
OR (exclusive)	$\dot{\vee}$
NOT	$\neg$ or ~
IMPLIES	$\Rightarrow$ or $\supset$
EQUIVALENT	$\equiv$

TABLE 6

A	B	$A\wedge B$	$A\vee B$	$A\dot{\vee}B$	$A\Rightarrow B$	$\neg A$	$A\equiv B$
T	T	T	T	F	T	F	T
T	F	F	T	T	F	F	F
F	T	F	T	T	T	T	F
F	F	F	F	F	T	T	T

Three major laws which govern the deductive application of propositional calculus are set out below:

(a) modus ponens which states that if $A\Rightarrow B$ and A is TRUE then B is TRUE also. It is formally stated as

$$(a\wedge(a \Rightarrow b)) \Rightarrow b$$

(b) De Morgan's laws

$\neg (A \wedge B) \equiv \neg A \vee \neg B$

$\neg (A \vee B) \equiv \neg A \wedge \neg B$

(c) Reductio ab absurdum

$A \Rightarrow B \equiv (\neg B \Rightarrow \neg A)$

Propositional calculus fails to express many examples of everyday arguments involving generality and is also inadequate for mathematical reasoning. For instance "every rational number is a real number, 5 is a rational number and hence 5 must be a real number" is a valid argument. Yet the validity of such an argument cannot be established within the framework of the propositional calculus. By introducing a number of new logical notions called *"terms"*, *"predicates"*, *"quantifiers"*, it is possible to extend the use of logic. These and also the ideas of *"formula"* and *"sentence"* are now defined and discussed.

(i) A *term* is either a constant or a variable or an n-tuple of terms,

(ii) A *predicate* is an n-tuple of terms prefixed by a predicate symbol and gives some meaning to the terms (of which it is a predicate).

(iii) Introduce the two *quantifiers*
universal quantifier $\forall$ – for all
existential quantifier $\exists$ – there exists.

(iv) A *formula* is either a predicate or has one of the forms

(R1)	R1$\wedge$R2	R1 $\leftarrow$ R2	
$\neg$R1	R1$\vee$R2	R1 $\leftrightarrow$ R2	QR1

where R1 and R2 are any formulae and Q is a quantifier as in (iii). Here $\leftarrow$ stands for if and $\leftrightarrow$ stands for if and only if (iff)

(v) A *sentence* is a formula in which every occurence of a variable (if any) is within the scope of a quantifier for that variable.

In modern logic programming languages [KOWAL75] such as PROLOG [HOGGR84], [KOWAL81] the concepts of predicate calculus are supported, and knowledge is presented in a declarative form.

Semantic networks

Representation of knowledge to this form was introduced to the field of AI by Quillian [QUILN68] and uses a network structure made up of nodes which represent *concepts, objects* and so on and directed arcs which represent *relations* connecting these. The phrase: "Adam eats apple" can be represented as in diagram 4 or in textual and machine representable form as (eat adam apple). The network can be extended to embed the concepts in their families. Thus if "e" stands for the relation "is an element of" and "s" for the relation "is a subset of" then we can represent the generalisation: humans eat fruit as in Diagram 5.

Diagram 4

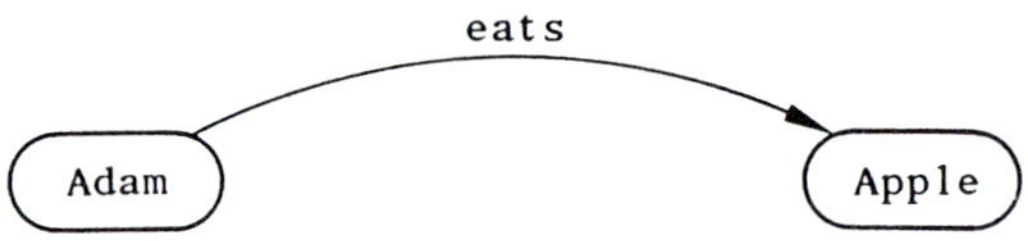

Diagram 5

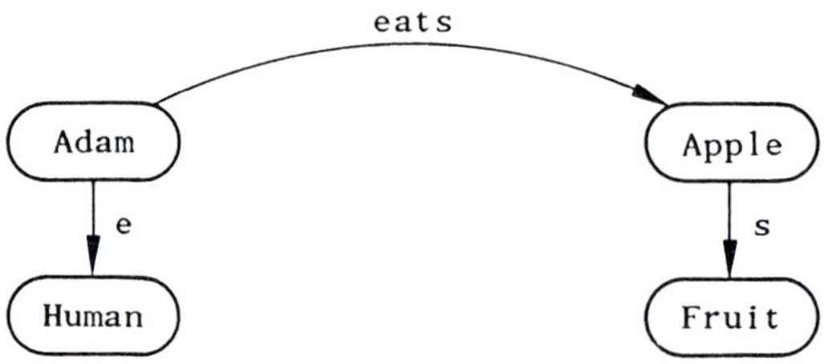

Taxonomies

It is well known that trees (as defined in graph theory) are used extensively in many scientific fields to represent hierarchy of relations or classifications. To represent information in these taxonomical forms it is necessary to introduce other arc types such as 'de' (distinct element of) or 'ds' (distinct subset of). These properties are shown in Diagram 6.

Diagram 6

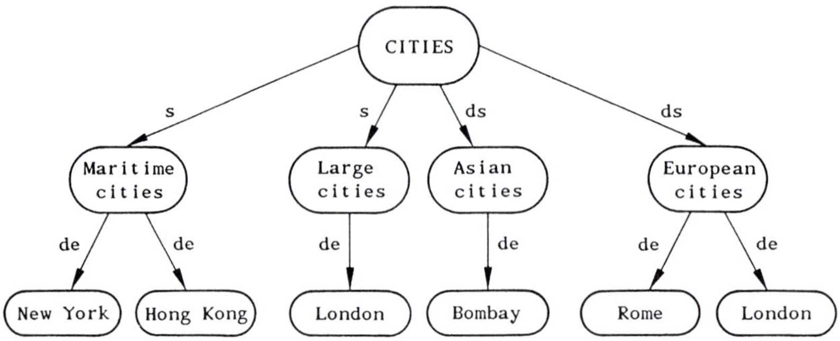

Semantic networks have been used in many ES and PROSPECTOR[DUGSH79] CASNET make extensive use of this particular technique.

Production Rules

A situation and action couple is called a production rule which specifies that whenever a situation to the left is encountered the action to the right (often it is the decision to be taken) is to be performed (recommended) [BONET85],[DUGSH81].

Typical examples taken from the context of kiln control are

IF <the temperature is high> THEN <turn down oxygen flow>

or one of identification in marine biology,

IF <very heavy> and <mamal> and <found in seas> THEN <whale>

are illustrated here.

A system made up of production rules usually has three major components. These are:-

(i) rule base which consists of production rules,

(ii) facts relating to the domain held in a compatible internal format,

(iii) an interpreter of facts and rules.

We notice that the interpreter of facts and rules has many applications. For instance it can be used to do forward chaining to achieve an inference by progressively taking into account facts and interpreting rules. Alternatively, it may work backwards from an achieved goal and work through only the relevant rules (and their facts) which takes it to the target action. The interpreter's mechanism can be used in entirely automated mode to arrive at the final decision or it may work in the analysis/advice giving capacity and the decision reached through a guided dialogue.

Frames and structured-objects

The concept of frames was originally used by Minsky [MINSK75] and this was followed up by frame structured language (FRL) to define and manipulate these. Bonnet [BONET85] presents this as structured objects. A pragmatic definition of frames or structured objects would be that these are complex data structures which also provide different ways of quantifying data items or slots and allows one to define interrelationships, default values, constraints, limits, etc. Bonnet claims that structured objects generalise a number of related ideas such as 'Schemas' used by Bartlett [BARTL32], 'Units' in the KRL language of Winograd [BOBWN77] and 'objects' in the object oriented language such as SMALLTALK [GOLD77]. A number of related concepts and technical notations are used to define structured objects. These are described below.

Aspects or attributes: These are names of properties which characterise the object.

Example: House details in an estate, which contains address, year of construction, current owner's name, type which may be one of the possibilities (detached, semi, bungalow).

Default: This is a value that is assumed for any variable when no specific value is specified.

Prototype: A fully specified structured object which is defined to be the norm or the ideal in relation to which other objects of that category are considered.

Procedures are used to refresh or update structured objects. For instance Date and Time is a structured object and its values may be computed procedurally through leap year etc. Wong et al [BMWNG84] provides an interesting example of updating students records as an example of representing and processing structured objects.

Knowledge elicitation

The methods of acquiring knowledge follow as a natural sequel to the problems of representing knowledge in a knowledge base. Tools for elicitating knowledge from the expert are thus an integral part of an ES since it is best to assume that the expert is not familiar with computer technology and may not even have an explicit model representing his know-how. Michie and Ritchie [RTCHE86] describe a know-how and show-how paradigm by which knowledge is induced. Effectively, they implement ideas of Quinlan and his ID3 system [QUNLN83] whereby the system learns and gathers knowledge by induction taking into account a large number of examples. Applying this method he was able to solve the chess end-game problem (KP-KR) which had previously not been solved by machine. The induction process is described as

> GIVEN: a collection of positive and negative instances (examples) where each instance is the description of an object in terms of a fixed set of attributes.
>
> PRODUCES: an efficient decision tree for differentiating positive and negative instances.

ID3 is designed to work with large numbers of instances. It starts by selecting a small subset of the instances supplied and at each cycle it

(i) forms a decision tree which is correct for the current window,
(ii) finds the exceptions to this decision tree for the other instances,
(iii) constructs a new window from the current window and the exceptions.

This cycle is repeated until a fully consistent decision tree is formed for the instances provided.

AI planning and reasoning with time

AI planning is concerned with the selection and sequencing of actions which achieve a set of desirable goals [NILSN80]. This can be broadly interpreted to cover problems such as job shop scheduling, production planning, maintenance scheduling, in effect all the operational control problems discussed in the time frame classification (see section 2). There are ES shells [SDPLN87] which are developed for this problem. Steel [STEEL87] provides a small yet interesting statement of a situation which essentially captures the time dependency of these problems.

> "I must buy Fred a present. I will go into town by bus. While I am on the bus I will decide what to buy when I arrive. On arrival I will do that."

Grant [ELGRA86] has studied the problem of maintenance scheduling. In an attempt to generalise a method of attack on such problems he suggests [GRANT86] that time should be considered to be a consumable resource, like energy. The STRIPS system due to Nilsson [FKNIL71] is one of the earliest planners and used a representation called STRIPS rules. Fox, in his investigation of the job shop scheduling problem, found that schedulers spent most of their time identifying and measuring constraints. Scheduling methods which are determined mainly by constraint relationships [FOXSM84] thus provide another way of solving these problems. Allen [ALLEN83] outlines essentially four different approaches which are state space method, date based chaining systems, reasoning on time relations and formal logical models. He follows a method of reasoning on time relations and uses a deduction system which is based on constraint propagation. McDermot [MCDER82] has developed a first order temporal logic in order to represent the complexity of time dependence and that of continuous change.

It is interesting to note that these works do not relate to more traditional management science models of time dependent scheduling. Thus representations using acyclic directed graphs, or inductive methods such as that of dynamic programming [BELDR62] are not taken into account in these AI planning methods.

Alternative ways of representing uncertainty

Uncertainty and imprecision naturally appear, either in the data or in the knowledge of the domain expert. A number of alternative methods of representing uncertainty have been introduced in these ES and have led to tremendous controversy as to their appropriateness.

Until the mid seventies uncertainty representation in decision problems was dominated by the Bayesian approach. The arguments in favour of this were as follows. The formal probability methods (the so called objective approach) require a large amount of data to be collected in (particularly) structured forms. Whereas in reality incomplete and unstructured historical data is available in many application domains such as medical diagnosis, geological prospecting, etc. The subjective Bayesian approach takes into consideration information presented simply as judgment, intuition or as practitioners' views. The difficulty of collecting exact information as required in the objective approach is thus avoided and the resulting model uses causal independence which leads to an additive form for the representation of uncertainties. Each term of this additive form has the effect of 'weight of evidence' of that particular component.

This approach is still based on a frequency representation of uncertainty. Spiegelhalter [SPIEG87] outlines four further schools of thought outside probability modelling which are Non-numerical methods, Fuzzy reasoning, Ad-hoc numerical methods *and* Belief functions.

Non-numerical methods

It is argued that qualitative reasoning is adequate for most problems and the use of "endorsements" qualitatively without any numerical weighting should be used. This leads to explicit recognition of quality underlying evidence on which association is made: this is found to be missing in quantitative analysis.

Fuzzy reasoning

Over the last two decades [ZADEH65], [ZIMMR85], [ZIMMR87], fuzzy logic has been developed to represent guarded (hedged) reasoning. Instead of the crisp alternatives (as in classical set theory) of an element belonging to a set or otherwise, fuzzy set theory defines degree of membership of a set. Zadeh claims that [ZADEH83], in many situations instead of introducing "uncertainty" it is natural to use imprecise linguistic terms such as "likely", "very likely", etc., and use a numerical representation (degree of belief) for this imprecision. Consider for instance the production rule stated earlier which may be restated under linguistic hedge (given the expert could not be quite definite) as

IF <the temperature is [*very*] high> THEN <turn down oxygen flow [*slightly*]>.
Let P,R denote propositions and let $\Phi(P),\Phi(R),(0 \leqq \Phi(P),\Phi(R) \leqq 1)$ be defined as possibilities of these propositions. The simple rules for conjunctions and disconjunctions of these possibilities are

$$\Phi(P \wedge R) = \min\,(\Phi(P),\Phi(R)) \qquad \Phi(P \vee R) = \max\,(\Phi(P),\Phi(R))$$

Ad-hoc numerical methods

Early ES shells MYCIN, CASNET, PROSPECTOR used an ad-hoc weighting of evidence called a certainty factor. The combining of evidence was also carried out using arguments taken from fuzzy logic as well as probability theory.

Belief functions

Shafer's work on mathematical theory of evidence [SHAFR76] has led to the use of belief functions which deal with interval valued beliefs. By using probability mass over the set of all subsets of propositions it enables one to 'reserve judgement' over the precise recipient of one's belief. Dempster's rule of combination allows disparate sources of evidence to be put together.

Prade et al [MAPRA86] have developed inference engines which can handle both imprecision and uncertainty. In essence propagating imprecision and uncertainty, developing a method to deal with imprecise rules as well as facts remains the central issue of research in this area.

7. Conceptual and Structured Modelling

A number of investigators have tried to unify alternative approaches to computer representation and modelling of decision problems. Johnson and Kervanou [JONKR88] discuss how the second generation of expert systems may achieve this goal. In the workshop organised by Brodie et al [BRMYS84] the scope of unifying AI methods, database techniques and high level programming languages, was discussed. Whereas the OR specialists are happy to use mathematics as the vehicle to represent and solve models the AI community has been more concerned with the question of elicitating, representing and manipulating knowledge. The major motivation for this considerable intellectual commitment comes from the belief that knowledge representation is the fundamental problem of modelling and knowledge itself is no less than a model of models. The arguments set out here follow Sowa's work [SOWAJ84] which has its roots in cognitive sciences (linguistics, philosophy, psychology) as well as in computer science. After a long series of investigations Sowa has presented a framework which unifies the alternative knowledge representation methods discussed in section 6. Geoffrion has also looked at the problem from a management science perspective. After an extended period of research, which started with the study of model aggregation, he has put forward his scheme which he calls a "structured modelling framework". At a simple level the objective of structured modelling is to capture the three problem solving methodologies of Brodie et al, namely AI, database techniques and high level programming languages, and supplement it with the quantitative management science approach. At a slightly deeper level he itemises eight major aims which we present below in a commentary form. Structured modelling is set out to provide a coherent framework based on a single model representation which can be used equally for managerial communication and mathematical solution. The model representation and solution steps are kept independent. The generality of the framework is extended to encompass optimisation, simulation, markov chains and decision tree models. The components of structured models are designed to be useful in all phases of the model (investigation) life cycle. Many functions, such as ad-hoc query, text handling, are presented in an integrated form.

The components of structured modelling can be introduced in three levels, namely elemental structure, generic structure and modular stucture. A model is viewed as being composed of discrete elements which are defined at this level, or combined out of existing definitions. At this level entity (primitive, compound), attribute, function and tests are introduced. The generic structure aims to capture natural familial positions of the grouped elements. Modular structure deals with hierarchy which is appropriate for a particular context. The structured model is made up of these three structures.

Clearly this work is addressed at the analysts, and aims to be a productivity tool. This claim is supportable if using the same tool kit we can undertake different tasks such as database query, construction and investigation of spreadsheet and optimisation

As we see it there are two major criticisms of this otherwise splendid modelling paradigm. Firstly the overhead of learning and mastering these structures can be considerable. Indeed if productivity gain is a major objective then unless repeated investigation of different models are envisaged, it is questionable if this goal will be achieved. In the second place the work does not take into account considerable development that has taken place in the area of model discourse [GREEN86], [GAINS84]. Addis [ADDIS85] has emphasised the importance of "applied epistemics" in knowledge based systems. He has adopted (from Meredith [MERE66]) the term "applied epistemics" to refer to the techniques and methods of communicating understanding via stored knowledge. No modelling paradigm can any longer ignore the powerful explanation procedure based on mathematical or commonsense reasoning. In structured modelling this aspect of textual explanation is briefly considered but not given a central place.

8. Human Machine Dialogue and Interface Issues

Reductions in cost and the availability of micros as personal or professional work stations have made more people computer literate, and led to substantial developments in methods of man machine communication. In the traditional mould problem owners communicated their problems to the analysts (computer specialists) who in turn interacted with the computer. His role was to obtain an appropriate solution and interpret this to the problem owner. Now-a-days in routine decision support situations, the analyst's role is inessential and the problem owner holds a direct dialogue with the computer through the medium of his DSS application. The development in this field has drawn from psychology, ergonomics and not to mention accumulated experience of computer usage in diverse applications [GAINS84], [KIDDA82]. This field, now called dialogue engineering, has emerged as a professionally challenging and financially rewarding branch of information technology.

A closer examination of the issues reveal many contexts where such dialogues find use. In traditional quantitative models there are two immediate interface requirements: communications of model data and presentation of the solution or results. So at a simple level only these need to be replaced by suitable modern dialogue facilities. Experience has shown that to obtain further support the problem owner may need to interrogate the model and understand the inference made by the solution procedure. Additionally the analyst (we also call him the knowledge engineer) needs to hold discourse with the expert via the system for the purpose of knowledge elicitation (construction of the model). He also creates a framework for the dialogue that takes place between the user and the system. An automatically generated textual and mathematical statement of the model [LUCMT88] is considered to be valuable and is used as a medium of communication amongst the expert, the knowledge engineer and the user.

There are altogether four well known approaches to dialogue management. These are (i) explicit command mode; (ii) menu driven commands; (iii) form filling mode; (iv) natural language method. These are not always employed entirely independent of each other.

..Explicit command mode

In this case, short reserved command words are used to initiate specific actions. Sometimes a command is also qualified by assigning parameters and giving these values.

For instance:

RESERVE, DEP = GAT, ARR = GEN, AIRLINE = XY, DAT = 21 DEC 88, NAME = BLOGG, PRICES = ?, AVAIL = ?

may initiate a place reservation for Mr BLOGG to the flight schedule of the XY airline and report on price and availability.

..Menu Driven Commands

Whereas the explicit command mode may be useful and has the advantage of a fast communication method, it still requires the user to memorise the character sequence making up the command and the possible parameters and their meanings. In an option or menu driven system a set of alternative commands are displayed and does not impose on the user to remember the various commands and their meanings. He can look up options and their meanings (through) a "help" facility and make command choice via a cursor or using a function key or a number. Such a system may be easy to get acquainted with initially but might prove to be slow and irksome to an experienced user.

..Form Filling Mode

In many situations it is convenient to make the data entry reflect as closely as possible the clerical task of completing predefined forms. Form filling is intellectually not demanding and is a structured activity when the context and the nature of the data is progressively pinpointed. In most systems these are introduced for the purpose of defining data or a structured request for action.

..Natural Language Method

Processing, understanding and translating natural languages is a vast field in its own right. Computer interfaces are not necessarily most appropriate or smart if they use natural language communication and it is not essential that natural language forms the major part of a DSS interface. On the other hand to provide explanation and diagnostics to a problem owner and also to support communication between the knowledge engineer and expert team, it is inconceivable not to use the medium of textual narrative and hence natural language. Chomsky [CHOMS65] and Winograd [WINOG72] were the first to bring to the notice of the computer science community the major issues of deep and surface structure meaning and the problem of understanding. Whereas constructing or analysing syntactically correct sentences is not a difficult task, comprehending and communicating meaningful narratives is conceptually, as well as practically, a difficult task. Situations where natural language communication arise due to the very context, such as telex instructions to banks, purchase queries for travel tours, company stocks, life insurance, natural language dialogue is adopted as the most obvious means of supporting the application. A number of such applications are discussed in [PECKH88]. In the field of management information systems INTELLECT [OVUM87] have made considerable progress in supporting natural language dialogue to query user databases.

From a designer's viewpoint a flexible, natural form dialogue reduces the training requirement and the users need to remember commands. Yet it may lead to unnecessary verbose steps in communicating compact and well structured model components and data items. Natural language interfaces for a queuing system [HEIDN72] and that for linear programming [SHEKR73] model specification, although novel in their concept, did not prove to be practical enough to deal with real problems.

Gaines [GAINS84] in his exciting treatise on computer conversation, makes a set of insightful observations. According to him the nature and success of computer dialogue is ultimately determined by the analyst who makes the design which is based on his experience. The computers now provide text, graphics, picture and voice as medium of interaction. Thus users know and think of computers as persons. A good dialogue reduces user's work load and secures the cooperation of the user to validate actions taken under an ambiguous situation. He also believes that the market place determines the style and presentation. On the question of general interface an interesting viewpoint emerges from his discussions. Turing's classic paper [TURIN50] "Can Machines Think" lies at the heart of computer science and algorithm design. Interestingly enough Turing's test for intelligence is based entirely on a scenario of linear interaction between an input device and a man or a machine. Gaines claims "The Turing test may be a reasonable way of rejecting a program designed to simulate a person, but it is not tough enough to be used to accept one". At a pragmatic level the intelligence may not be the issue; instead the analyst's ability to make the computer mimick human behaviour may lead to a credible and useful interface. David Smith, designer of Star user interface [SMITH77] observes that "if everything in a computer system is visible on a display screen, the display becomes reality".

The Alvey program has identified the intelligent front end as a key research theme [BUNSH83]. Their statement of the theme succinctly captures the main requirements and is set out below.

"A front end to an existing software package, for example, a finite element package, or mathematical modelling system, provides a user-friendly interface (a "human window") to packages which without it are too complex and/or technically incomprehensible to be accessible to many potential users. An intelligent front end builds a model of the user's problem through user-orientated dialogue mechanisms based on menus or quasi-natural language, which is then used to generate suitable coded instruction for the package." The construction of such front ends would hopefully narrow the gap between models and the real world of the problem owners. The Japanese fifth generation research also starts from the premise that computers as we know today are not well set up to communicate naturally with humans [FEIMK83]. One major aspect of this research is therefore to improve man machine communication. In concluding discussions relating to the interface issue we observe that the interface and modelling parts of a system do not fall in areas which are sharply separated from each other. In many systems interface and model support to some extent overlap with each other and are together focussed on the particular context of the problem.

9. Concluding Remarks

Decision making is an important real world problem which encompasses our social, industrial and business lives. During the fifties and sixties traditional quantitative models were introduced to address these problems. More recently further contributions from the fields of cognitive sciences, database theory, artificial intelligence, have considerably sharpened these models and have extended their scope.

Many tools have been developed which are based on such models and which use modern information processing machines as vehicles for implementation. The generalisations and abstractions used at the tools level lead to considerable productivity gains in constructing decision support applications. The main focus of decision support applications is to aid the decision maker to make better decisions (by some economic criteria of cost, value, etc) and more effective decisions than he would otherwise make without this support. More often than not there is a gap between the model and the reality yet the very acts of constructing and investigating the model sharpens our understanding of the problem and enhances the quality of decisions which follow.

APPENDIX

Decision support systems: A working definition of their scope, architecture and focus.
..The scope

A decision support system (DSS) is a computer based application system which helps the problem owners to make decisions. The decisions made with the aid of such a DSS are better (by some economic consideration, due to timeliness, or some qualitative criterion such as robustness, etc) than decisions that would be otherwise made without using a DSS. We introduce this as a supportable and a workable design goal for a DSS. Developing a DSS for a particular problem domain, or more specifically tailored to the particular requirement of an organisation, is called "application construction". The software components which are used to construct such domain specific applications are called "tools for constructing decision support applications". These topics are extensively discussed in [SPCAL82], [KNSOM78]. [BOHWN81], [MARTIN84]. In order to emphasise this distinction we cite spread sheet systems, expert systems shells, mathematical programming modelling systems, simulation systems as tools. In contrast a specific system for the discounted cash flow computation for an organisation or a project plan, hazard management, crew scheduling for a bus company or an airline, provide instances of DSS applications. We introduced such a systems tool in section 6 and noted the central place taken by it and also the roles of the additional agents involved in the construction of an application. They are the domain expert, the knowledge engineer (traditionally known as the analyst) and the problem owner (the user). The decision problem that is addressed by such an application is one out of a range of possible problems discussed in section 3. The knowledge engineer and the domain expert work together through the medium of the "tool" to create a particular "DSS application".

..The Architecture

In section 6 we discussed the components of the expert system shell which is a typical application construction tool. Here we set out how such a tool can be utilised to create applications in diverse domains. As shown in diagram A.1 the modules which

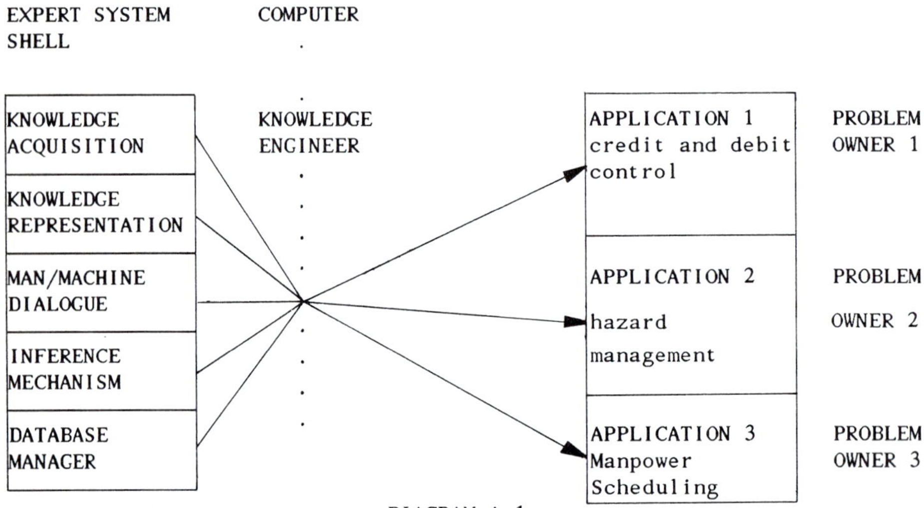

DIAGRAM A.1

support knowledge elicitation, knowledge representation, inference mechanism, dialogue management and database management, may be used in typical applications such as credit and debit control, hazard management, and manpower scheduling problems which have widely different contexts. In the end each application is installed with its own dialogue handler, inference mechanism, facts and knowledge base specific to its own domain.

We discuss a number of different architectures. Although DSS applications are constructed from the same building blocks the resulting systems can have widely different structure. Sowa [SOWAJ84] cites decision support as a major application of AI. He explains a knowledge based application system and its components in the following diagramatic form.

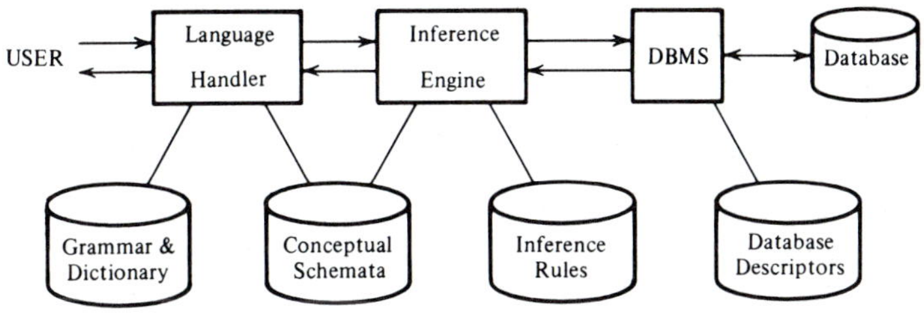

Diagram A.2

Sprague and Carlson [SPCAL82] have discussed this in considerable detail and argue that the exact architecture a DSS assumes is highly domain specific. In some instances the applications are data intensive and in others they are logic intensive. In a third category they may be response time critical. This view is also put forward by Worden [WORDN86] in his analysis of the applications of the knowledge based systems and the blackboard system. Carlson and Sprague describe altogether four alternatives which they call

(i) the network architecture (ii) the bridge architecture
(iii) the sandwich architecture (iv) the tower architecture

respectively.

..Focus of DSS

In seeking support from a DSS application a problem owner may consider in turn the following questions,

(i) does it provide economic (cost) advantage?
(ii) how well does it perform?
(iii) is it robust and reliable?
(iv) is it adaptable?
(v) is it usable? that is does it really help him in solving the problem?

These questions and the answers to them provide a fair outline of the requirements and objectives of an effective DSS.

Simon, in his analysis of this topic, starts with Dewey's observations on problem solving: "What is the problem? What are the alternatives? Which is the best?" He then elaborates on three phases of problem solving which are intelligence, design and choice. The word 'intelligence' here is taken from the military context and stands for information gathering. The main role of a DSS is therefore to aid the problem owner in all these problem solving steps.

REFERENCES

[ACKOF74] Ackoff, R L, Redesigning the future, Wiley, New York, 1974.

[ADDIS85] Addis, T.R., Designing Knowledge Based Systems, Kogan Page, 1985.

[ALLEN83] Allen, J.F., Maintaining knowledge about temporal intervals, Comm. ACM, Vol 26, 1983.

[ANSI83] ANSC X3H3, SQL database language, X3H2-26-15 ANSI Report, 1982.

[ANTNY65] Anthony, R N, Planning and control systems: a framework for analysis, Harvard University, Graduate School of Business Administration, 1965.

[BARTL32] Bartlett, F., Remembering, a study in experimental and social psychology, Cambridge University Press, 1932.

[BELDR62] Bellman, R.E., and Dreyfus, S.E., Applied dynamic programming, Princeton, Univ. Press, 1962.

[BKHMP82] Berkley, D, and Humphreys, P, Structuring of decision problems and the "bias beuristic", Acta Psychologica, Vol 50, 1982.

[BLJEL84] Blair, C E, Jeroslow, R G and Lowe, J K, Some results and experiments in programming techniques for propositional logic, Georgia Institute of Technology, 1984.

[BMWNG84] Borgida, A., Mylopoulos, J., and Wong, H.J.K., Generalisation/Specialisation as a basis for software specification, in [BRMYS84], 1984.

[BOBWN77] Bobrow, D, and Winograd, T, KRL, another perspective, Cognitive Science, Vol. 3, 1977.

[BOHWN81] Bonczek, R H, Holsapple, C W, Whinston, A B, Foundations of decision support systems, Academic Press, 1981.

[BONET85] Bonnet, A, Artificial intelligence: promises and performance, Prentice Hall, 1985.

[BOPAR84] Boudwin, N K, Palmer, K, and Rowland, A J, A model management framework for mathematical programming, Exxon Monograph, John Wiley and Sons, 1984.

[BRMYS84] Brodie, M L, Mylopoulos, J, and Schmidt, J W, (Editors), On conceptual modelling, Springer-Verlag, 1984.

[BRODI84] Brodie, M L, On the developmnent of data models, in [BRYMYS 84], 1984.

[BUNSH83] Bundy, A, Sharpe, B., Uschold, M., and Hendry, N, Intelligent Front End Workshop, Notes of Meeting supplied by Alvey Directorate, 1983.

[CDSYL71] CODASYL Data Base Task Group, Report of the DBTG, ACM New York, 1970.

[CHECK81] Checkland, P B, Systems thinking, systems practice, Chichester, Wiley, 1981.

[CHECK83] Checkland, P B, OR and the systems movement: mappings and conflicts, Journal of the OR Society (GB), Vol 34, 1983.
[CHOMS65] Chomsky, N, Aspects of the Theory of Syntax, MIT Press 1965.

[CHRST86] Christofides, N, Uses of vehicle routing and scheduling system in strategic distribution planning, in [MITRA86], North Holland, 1986.

[CODD70] Codd, E F, A relational model of data for large shared data banks, Comm ACM, Vol 13, No 6, 1970.

[COLWH72] Colby, K M, et al, Artificial panaroia, Artificial Intelligence 3, 1972.

[DABAL85] Dahl, R.W., Ball, M.O., et al, A relational approach to vehicle and crew scheduling in urban mass transit system, in Computer Scheduling of Public Transport 2, J.M. Roussean (Editor), North Holland, 1985.

[DALMY88] Darby-Dowman, K, Lucas, C, Mitra, G and Yadegar, J, Linear, integer, separable and fuzzy programming problems: a unified approach to automatic reformulation, Journal of the OR Society (GB), pp 161-171, 1988.

[DATE81] Date, C J, An introduction to database systems, Addison Wesley, 1981.

[DMPST87] Dempster, M E, An expert financial system manager, this institute, 1987.

[DOLKN85] Dolk, D.R., and Konsynski, B., Model management in Organisations, Information and Management, Vol.9, 1985.

[DOLK86] Dolk, D R, A generalized model management system for mathematical programming, ACM Transactions on Mathematical Software, Vol 12, No 2, 1986.

[DUGSH79] Duda, R, Gaschnig, J, and Hart, P, Model design in the PROSPECTOR consultant system for mineral exploration, in [MCHIE79] 1979.

[DUGSH81] Duda, R, and Gaschnig, J, Knowledge-based expert system come of age, Byte, September, 1981.

[ELGRA86] Elleby, P, and Grant, T, Knowledge based scheduling, in [MITRA86], 1986.

[ESHMA81] Eshragh, F and Mamdani, E H, A general approach to linguistic approximation, in fuzzy reasoning and its applications, Editors Mamdani, E H and Gaines, B R, Academic Press, 1981.

[FEIMK83] Feigenbaum, E A and McCorduck, P, The fifth generation, Addison Wesley, 1983.

[FEBUL71] Feigenbaum, E, Buchanan, B, and Lederberg, J, On generality and problem solving: a case study using the DENDRAL program, in Machine Intelligence, Vol 6, New York, Elsevier, 1982.

[FISHB70] Fishburn, P C, Utility theory of decision making, Wiley, 1970.

[FKNIL71] Fikes, R E, and Nilsson, N J, STRIPS: A new application of theorem proving to problem solving, AI Journal, 1971.

[FOURE83] Fourer, R, Modelling languages versus matrix generators for linear programming, ACM Translations on Mathematical Software, Vol 9, No 2, 1983.

[FOXSM84] Fox, S M, and Smith, S F, ISIS: A knowledge based system for factory scheduling, Expert Systems Journal, Vol. 1, 1984.

[FROST78] Frost, M J, How to use cost benefit analysis in project appraisal, Gower Press, 1978.

[GAINS84] Gaines, B R, and Shaw, M L G, The art of computer conversation, Prentice Hall, 1984.

[GALMN81] Gallaire, H, Minker, J, Nicolas, J M, (Editors), Advances in database theory, Vol 1, Plersurn Press, 1981.

[GARGE84] Gardarin, G and Gelerbeo, E, (Editors) New applications of databases, Academic Press, 1984.

[GASBC86] Gass, S I, Bhasker, S and Chapman, R E, (Editors) Expert systems and emergency management: an annotated bibliography, National Bureau of Standards (US) Publication 728, 1986.

[GASCH86] Gass, S I and Chapman, R E, (Editors) Theory and application of expert systems in emergency management operations, National Bureau of Standards (US) Publication, 717, 1986.

[GEOFF85] Geoffrion, A.M., Private communication at the 12th International Mathematical Programming Symposium, Boston, Massachusetts, 1985.

[GEOFF87] Geoffrion, A M, An introduction to structured modelling, Man. Sci. May 1987.

[GRANT86] Grant, T, An object-orientated approach to AI planning and scheduling, in [MAMEF86], 1986.

[GREEN86] Greenberg, H J, A natural language discourse model to explain linear programming models, Technical Report, University of Colorado, 1986.

[HADLY65] Hadley, G, Nonlinear and dynamic programming, Addison Wesley, 1965.

[HEIDN72] Heidorn, G.E., Natural language inputs to a simulation programming system, Report NPS 55-HD72101A, Naval Postgraduate School, Monetery, USA, 1972.

[HEWSA86] Hewett, J., and Sasson, Z., Expert systems, 1986, USA and Canada, OVUM, UK, 1986.

[HEWTG86] Hewett, J, Timms, S, and d'Aumale, G., Commercial expert systems in europe, OVUM, UK, 1986.

[HOGGR84] Hogger, C J, Introduction to logic programming, Academic Press, 1984.

[HUMPH86] Humphreys, P, Intelligence in decision support, New directions in research in decision making, Edited by B Brehmer et al, North Holland, 1986.

[JAQUE82] Jaques, E, Free enterprise, fair employment, Heinemann, 1982.

[JONKR85] Johnson, L U, and Keravnou, E T, Expert system technology: a guide, Abacus Press, 1985.

[JONKR88] Johnson, L U, and Keravnou, E T, Expert Systems Architecture, Kogan Page, 1988.

[KEENY82] Keeney, R L, Decision analysis: an overview, Opns Res, Vol 30, 1982.

[KEERA76] Keeney, R L and Raiffa, H, Decisions with multiple objectives, preferences and value trade offs, John Wiley, 1976.

[KGOLD77] Kay, A, and Goldberg, A, Personal dynamic media, Computer, Vol. 10, 1977.

[KIDDA82] Kidd, A L, Man-machine dialogue design, British Telecom Research Report, Martelsham, 1982.

[KNSCM78] Keen, P G W, and Scott-Morton, M S, Decision support system: an organizational perspective, Addison Wesley, 1978

[KOAND86] Kohout, L J, Anderson, J, et al, Formalization of clinical management activities for a knowledge-based clinical system, Proceedings, American Association for Medical Systems and Informatics, Washington DC, 1986.

[KOBAT86] Kohout, L J, et al, A knowledge-based decision support system for use in medicine, in [MITRA86], North Holland, 1986.

[KOUKU86] Koukoulis, C, A frame based method for fault diagnosis, in [MAMEF86], UNICOM-Technical Press 1986.

[KOWAL75] Kowalski, R.A., Predicate logic as a programming language, Proceedings of IFIP-74, North Holland, 1975.

[KOWAL81] Kowalski, R.A., PROLOG as a logic programming language, Proc AICA, Congress, PAVIA, Italy, 1981.

[KUNYO82] Kunifuji, S, Yokota, H, PROLOG and relational data bases for fifth generation computer systems, in [NICOLA82], 1982.

[LASDN87] Lasdon, L, Optimization and decision support, this institute, 1987.

[LENRD86] Lenard, M L, Representing models as data, Journal of Management Information Systems, Vol 2, 1986.

[LEMOR81] Lewin, A Y and Morey, R C, Measuring the relative efficiency and output potential of public sector organizations: an application of data envelopment analysis, Journal of Policy Analysis and Information Systems, Plenum Press, Vol 5, No 4, Dec 1981.

[LOOMV88] Lootsma F.A., Mensch, T C S and Vos, F A, Multi-criteria analysis and budget allocation with applications in energy R&D planning: A feasibility study, EEC, Concept Report, 1988.

[LOOTS87] Lootsma, F A, Trade-off analysis and the resolution of conflicts, International Workshop in Decision Support Systems, Moscow, 1987.

[LUCAS86] Lucas, J, PLANET: Expert system/Mathematical programming applied to strategic decisions, presented to TIMS XXVII, Gold Coast, Australia, 1986.

[LUCMT88] Lucas, C and Mitra, G, Computer assisted mathematical programming modelling system: CAMPS, Computer Journal, 1988.

[MAMEF86] Mamdani, A and Efstathiou, J E, (Editors), Expert systems and optimization in process control, UNICOM-Technical Press, 1986.

[MARKW79] Markowitz, H M, SIMSCRIPT, in J Belzer, A G Holzman, and A Kent (Editors), Encyclopedia of Computer Science and Technology, Marcel Dekker, New York, 1979.

[MARTN84] Martin, J, An information systems manifesto, Prentice Hall, 1984.

[MARQE84] Marque-Pucheu, G., et al, Interfacing PROLOG and relational database management systems, in [GARGE84], 1984.

[MATHE85] Mathewson, S C, Simulation program generators: code and animation on a PC, Journal of OR Society (GB), Vol 36, 1985.

[MCDER82] McDermott, D., A temporal logic for reasoning processes and plans, cognitive science, Vol 6, 1982.

[MCHIE79] Michie, D., Expert systems in microelectronic age, Edinburgh University Press, 1979.

[MERED66] Meredith, P., Instruments of communication: An essay on scientific writing, Pergamon Press, 1966.

[MINKR81] Minker, J, Relational data models for scheduling, in Computer Assisted Analysis and Model Simplification, Editors, Greenberg, H J, and Maybee, J S, Academic Press 1981.

[MINSK75] Minsky, M., A framework for representing knowledge, in P. Winston (Editor) Psychology of Computer Vision, McGraw Hill, 1975.

[MITDA85] Mitra, G and Darby-Dowman, K D, CRU-SCHED - A computer based bus crew scheduling system using integer programming, Computer Scheduling of Public Transport 2, Edited by J M Rousseau, North Holland, 1985.

[MITRA86] Mitra, G (Editor), Computer assisted decision making: expert system decision analysis, mathematical programming, North Holland 1986.

[MITRA87] Mitra, G (Guest Editor), Mathematical Programming Modelling Systems, two volumes, Special Issue IMA Journal of Mathematics in Management, 1987.

[MIYAZ82] Miyazaki, N., A data sublanguage approach to interacting predicate logic languages and relational data bases, Tech. Memo No. 1, ICOT, Tokyo (Japan), 1982.

[MURSN82] Murtagh, B.A., and Saunders, M.A., A projected Lagrangian algorithm and its implementation for sparse nonlinear constraints, Math. Prog. Study, Vol 16, 1982.

[MURTG81] Murtagh, B A, Advanced linear programming: computation and practice, McGraw Hill, 1981.

[NANCE84] Nance. R E, Model development revisited, working paper, Computer Science Department, Virginia Polytechnic Institute, 1984.

[NEWSM63] Newell, A and Simon, H A, GPS, A program that simulates human thought, in Computers and Thought, Edited by E A Feigenbaum, McGraw Hill, 1963.

[NICOL82] Nicolas, J.M., Logical bases for data bases, workshop preprints, Toulouse (France), 1982.

[NILSN80] Nilsson, N.J., Principles of artificial intelligence, Tioga Publishing Co., 1980.

[OVUM87] Ovum report on: Commercial applications of natural language understanding, OVUM, UK, 1987.

[PAULD86] Paul, R J and Doukidis, G I, Further developments in the use of artificial intelligence techniques which formulate simulation problems, Journal of the OR Society (GB), Vol 37, 1986.

[PECKH88] Peckham, J., Recent developments and applications of natural language understanding, UNICOM Seminar report series, Kogan Page, UK, 1988.

[PHILP84] Phillips, L D, Decision support for managers, managerial challenge of new office technology, Editors, Otway, H J, and Peltu, M, Butterworths, 1984.

[PHILP86] Phillips, L D, Decision analysis and its application in industry, in [MITRA86], 1986.

[POPLE82] Pople, H., Heuristic methods for imposing structure on ill-structured problems; the structuring of medical diagnosis, in Artificial Intelligence in Medicine, P. Szolovits (Editor), Westview Press, Boulder, Colorado, 1982.

[QUILN68] Quilian, M.R., Semantic memory, in Semantic Information Processing, M. Minsky (Editor), MIT Press, 1968.

[QUNLN83] Quinlan, J.R., Learning efficient classification procedures and their application to chess and games, in Machine learning an AI approach, Michalski, R.S., et al (Editors), Tioga Press, 1983.

[RAIFA68] Raiffa, H, Decision analysis, introductory lectures on choices under uncertainty, Addison Wesley, 1986.

[RIJCK87] Rijckaert, M, Debroey, V, Bogaerts, W, Expert systems: State-of-the-art and advanced issues, this institute, 1987.

[RIVET77] Rivett, B H P, Policy selection by structural mapping, Proceedings Royal Society, London A, 1977.

[ROY73] Roy, B, How outranking relations help multicriterion decision making, Proceedings multicriterion decision making, South Carolina Press, 1973.

[RTCHE86] Ritchie, I C, Knowledge acquisition by computer induction, in [MITRA86], 1986.

[SAATY80] Saaty, T L, The analytic hierarchy process, McGraw Hill, 1980.

[SDPLN87] Systems Designers Ltd., PLANIT final report (developed under Alvey program), 1987.

[SHAFR76] Shafer, G., A mathematical theory of evidence, Princeton University Press, 1976.

[SHEKR73] Shen, S N T, Krulee, G K, Solving linear programming problems stated in English by computer, Proceedings ACM 73, 299-303, 1973.

[SHNON50] Shannon, C E, Programming a computer to play chess, Scientific American, Feb, 1950.

[SHORT76] Shortliffe, E, MYCIN: computer based medical consultations, American Elsevier, 1976.

[SHPRO87] Shapiro, J.F., Optimization models for bond portfolio selection, this institute, 1987.

[SIMON65] Simon, H A, The shape of automation for men and management, Harper and Row, 1965.

[SIMON77] Simon, H A, What computers mean to man and society, Science, Vol 195, March 1977.

[SIMON86] Simon, H A, Two heads are better than one: the collaboration between artificial intelligence and operations research, plenary address, TIMS/ORSA meeting, Miami Beach, October 1986.

[SMITH77] Smith, D C, Pygmallion: A computer program to model and simulate creative thought, Birkhauser, BASEL, 1977.

[SOWAJ84] Sowa, J F, Conceptual structures: Information processing in mind and machine, Addison Wesley, Reading, MA, 1984.

[SPCAL82] Sprague, R H, and Carlson, E D, Building effective decision support systems, Prentice Hall, 1982.

[SPIEG87] Spiegelhalter, D.J., Synthesis of AI and Bayesian methods in medical expert systems, in Interaction Between Statistics and AI, R. Phelps (Editor), Unicom-Technical Press, 1987.

[STAIN84] Stainton, R S, Applicable systems thinking, European Journal of Operational Research, Vol 18, 1984.

[STEEL87] Steel, S., Tutorial notes, AISB-87 Tutorial, 1987.

[STOLL61] Stoll, R.R., Sets, logic and axiomatic theories, Freeman and Company, 1961.

[SWABY86] Swabey, M, Use of deep and shallow knowledge in electronics diagnosis, in [MAMEF 86], UNICOM-Technical Press 1986.

[TAMIT87] Tamiz, M and Mitra G, Construction and testing of large scale linear programming system exploiting sparsity, monograph to be published, 1987.

[TATE86] Tate, A., Knowledge-based planning systems, in [MAMEF86], 1986.

[TURIN50] Turing, A M, Can a machine think: Computing machinery and intelligence, MIND, 1950, Reprinted in Computers and Thought, Edited by E A Feigenbaum and J Feldman, McGrawhill, 1963.

[ULBRN82] Ulvila, J W and Brown, R V, Decision analysis comes of age, Harvard Business Review, Sept - Oct, 1982.

[VNEUM44] Von Neumann, J and Morgenstern O, Theory of games and economic behaviour, Princeton University Press, 1944.

[WAGNR69] Wagner, H M, Principles of Operations Research with Applications to Managerial Decision, Prentice Hall, 1969.

[WEIZE66] Weizenbaum, J, ELIZA, a computer program for the study of natural language communication between man and machine, CACM, Vol 9, 1966.

[WILLM87] Williams, H P, Linear and integer programming applied to the propositional calculus, Systems Research and Information Science, Vol 2, 1987.

[WINTR80] Von Winterfeldt, D., Structuring decision problems for decision analysis, Acta Psychologica, Vol 45, 1980.

[WINOG72] Winograd, T., Understanding natural language, Academic Press, 1972.

[WITNS87] WITNESS, Simulation product, ISTEL, Redditch, Worcestershire, UK, 1987.

[WORDN86] Worden, R, Blackboard systems, in [MITRA86], 1986.

[ZADEH65] Zadeh, L A, Fuzzy sets, Information and Control, Vol 8, 1965.

[ZADEH83] Zadeh, L A, The role of fuzzy logic in the management of uncertainty in expert systems, Fuzzy Sets and Systems, Vol II, 1983.

[ZIMMR85] Zimmermann, H J, Fuzzy set theory and its applications, Kluwer-Nijhoff, 1985.

[ZIMMR87] Zimmermann, H J, Fuzzy sets, decision making and expert systems, Kluwer, 1987.

[ZIMMR88] Zimmermann, H J, Private communication, April 1988.

[ZIONT82] Zionts, S, Multiple criteria decision making: an overview and several approaches, working paper No 454, School of Management, State University of New york, Buffalo, 1982.

SECTION 3:

MODELS WITH MULTIPLE CRITERIA AND SINGLE OR MULTIPLE DECISION MAKERS

NUMERICAL SCALING OF HUMAN JUDGEMENT IN PAIRWISE-COMPARISON METHODS FOR FUZZY MULTI-CRITERIA DECISION ANALYSIS

F.A. Lootsma
Faculty of Mathematics and Informatics
Delft University of Technology
P.O. Box 356, 2600 AJ Delft, Netherlands

1. INTRODUCTION

We are concerned with the multi-criteria problem of how to choose the best item from a finite set of alternatives. We face such a decision problem when we want to attain a goal, and when none of the alternative tools for attaining it seems to be perfect. In general, we consider the alternatives from various viewpoints, and we estimate how well they enable us to attain the goal. Briefly speaking, we estimate the relative importance of the criteria, and we express it in numerical weights. Similarly, we estimate the relative importance of the alternatives under each of the criteria separately. Lastly, we aggregate the weights to obtain a final score for each alternative. With this information, we are in a position to rank and rate the alternatives, and to select the best compromise.

The formulation of performance criteria in an actual decision problem is a complicated process. Usually, we start with a top-down approach: we formulate criteria via logical arguments, using previous experiences in similar situations. Usually, these criteria have the advantage of being generally accepted, but they are ineffective in a particular decision problem if they do not make a distinction between the alternatives under consideration. The second approach, bottom up, is triggered by striking properties of the alternatives themselves. The criteria so obtained are typically ad hoc, but they may be highly relevant in the actual decision problem. The formulation of criteria is not necessarily finished now. It may happen that they are reformulated or dropped during the decision process, and that new criteria emerge as a result of the on-going deliberations.

Today, many decision problems are not solved by a single decision maker but by a committee of decision makers with conflicting views on the alternatives to be considered, the criteria to be used, and the weights to be assigned. The decision makers were hopefully selected on the basis of their ability to judge the alternatives with respect to the goal to be attained. Nevertheless, the weights of their judgemental statements will vary with their power, knowledge, and prestige.

In summary, we are entangled in a clew of criteria, alternatives, and decision makers, which is not easy to unravel. Our objective is to bring some structure in the decision process by the elicitation of the

NATO ASI Series, Vol. F48
Mathematical Models for Decision Support
Edited by G. Mitra

(hidden) preferences and ambitions of the decision makers, possibly followed by the calculation of a compromise solution.

At several stages of the decision process, we are in fact running up against the question of how to weigh a finite number of stimuli: the criteria, the alternatives under a certain performance criterion, or the decision makers themselves. The assignment of weights to a number of stimuli is not an easy task; those who ever attended a wine-tasting party will immediately understand this. In the present paper, we will concentrate on pairwise-comparison methods, where the stimuli under consideration are presented in pairs to a decision maker who is requested to express his preference for one of the two or his indifference between them. The subsequent, mathematical analysis of the judgemental statements will produce the weights, estimates of the (deeply hidden) values of the stimuli.

We illustrate the procedure with an example which is due to our experiences in the Directorate-General XII (Energy) of the European Commission in Brussels. We were requested to study the allocation of a research budget to various non-nuclear energy research programs. This is typically a portfolio problem (see also Légrády et al. (1984), Lockett et al. (1986), and Lootsma et al. (1986)): we apply multi-criteria decision analysis to obtain final scores for the alternatives (the research programs), and we use the final scores in a knapsack problem to find a research portfolio with maximum weight subject to certain budget constraints. It should be noted that the example will only show the technical merits of pairwise-comparison methods within the framework of multi-criteria analysis. The underlying data (criteria, alternatives, the judgemental statements generated in an initial phase of the project) are obsolete now, so that the example is given here as a basis for discussion rather than to illustrate effective or ineffective handling by the Commission.

The organization of the paper is as follows. We start with a brief description of the illustrative example just mentioned. Next, we shall be dealing with the pairwise-comparison methods. We use the example to show that the weights of the criteria and the final scores of the alternatives are sufficiently scale-independent for practical purposes. Because the comparative judgement is imprecise, we turn to a pairwise-comparison method where the judgemental statements are expressed in fuzzy numbers. We employ a simplified procedure to calculate the fuzzy final scores of the alternatives. This procedure will also show the propagation of fuzziness in a multi-level decision problem. The analytical results enable us to understand how fuzziness is controlled by the scale parameter γ and the degree of fuzziness α in the original judgements. We will finally develop a fuzzy preference relation between the alternatives which is practically scale-independent.

2. *THE ILLUSTRATIVE EXAMPLE*

In the seventies and eighties, many countries made substantial budgets available for research and development in the energy sector, particularly for those technologies which are beyond the scope of industrial research in the private oil and gas companies. These budgets were accordingly allocated to promising, complementary technologies such as nuclear, solar, geothermal, and wind energy, where the social and economic benefits are expected to emerge, perhaps not on a short term, but hopefully within one or two decades. The effort of national authorities was further complemented by an international authority such as the Commission of the European Community, who devoted considerable amounts of money to energy research in cases where Community action was felt to be appropriate.

On the basis of our experiences with the Energy Research Council in the Netherlands, in a project set up to advice the government on the allocation of a national research budget to various energy research programs (see Légrády et al. (1983), Lootsma et al. (1986)), we have been invited by the Directorate-General XII (Energy) of the European Commission to carry out a feasibility study of a similar nature. The objective is, first, to assess a number of non-nuclear programs as to their suitability for Community action (there is a separate budget for nuclear energy), and next, to use the scores in order to find an allocation with maximum benefits. In the present paper we only consider the assessment of the following research programs (with their budget in million ECU):

1. Solar Energy (mainly photovoltaic cells)	35.5 MECU
2. Geothermal Energy (hot water and steam)	21.0
3. Energy Saving (heat pumps, fuel cells)	26.5
4. New Energy Vectors (synthetic fuels, liquified coal)	10.0
5. Biomass Energy (from waste, forestry, and crops)	20.0
6. Solid Fuels (coal transportation and combustion)	20.0
7. Hydrocarbons (oil and gas)	15.0
8. Wind Energy (generators, grid connections)	18.0
Total Budget	166.0 MECU

These alternatives were the objects of study in the initial phase of the project. They have been assessed on the ground of their ability to enhance

1. Security of Energy Supply (by diversification)
2. Energy Efficiency (in energy production and use)
3. Social Acceptability (by reduced risks)
4. Innovation-based Industry (by improved competitive position)
5. Long-term Energy Management (by renewable energy, delayed depletion)
6. Environmental Protection
7. International Cooperation (using economies of scale)
8. European Independence Policy (by reduced imports)
9. Support of Weakly Developed Regions.

With these performance criteria, the eight alternatives have been judged by seven decision makers. The results provoked vivid discussions as well as a substantial reformulation of alternatives and criteria. Such a course of events is not surprising. Multi-criteria analysis enables the decision makers to operate with the criteria, and in many cases it is the first time that they have an opportunity to do so. Hence, addition, deletion and/or reformulation of criteria and alternatives is a frequently returning step in the decision process.

Because the present paper concentrates on methodological aspects such as numerical scaling of comparative judgement, scale independence of weights and scores, fuzzy models for imprecise judgement, and fuzzy preference relations, we employ the results of the initial phase to illustrate our theoretical work, notwithstanding the course of events in the feasibility study.

3. *PAIRWISE COMPARISONS*

In a method of pairwise comparisons (David (1963), Saaty (1980), Roy (1985)) stimuli are presented in pairs to a decision maker. The basic experiment is the comparison of two stimuli S_i and S_j by a single decision maker who is requested to express his preference (if any) for one of the two. We assume that the stimuli S_i have respective values V_i $(i=1,\ldots,p)$ on a numerical scale such that $\Sigma V_i = 1$. The purpose of the experiments is to estimate these values. Usually, the decision maker is requested to estimate the preference ratio V_i/V_j, and in order to assess it we use a category scale instead of a real magnitude scale. The conversion is straightforward, requiring only that the responses be restricted to a set of categories with a narrative degree of preference. Thus, the decision maker is merely asked to choose one of the qualifications

indifference
weak (mild, moderate) preference
strong preference
very strong (dominant) preference,

or a threshold between two adjacent qualifications if he hesitates between them. We are particularly interested now in the *interface* with the decision maker: the numerical scale associated with the above *gradations* of his judgement. Let us introduce a quantitative scale with echelons e_n, $-6 \leq n \leq 6$, corresponding to the gradations as follows:

e_6 very strong (dominant) preference for S_i
e_5 dominance threshold towards S_i
e_4 strong preference for S_i
e_3 commitment threshold towards S_i
e_2 weak (mild, moderate) preference for S_i
e_1 indifference threshold towards S_i
e_0 indifference between S_i and S_j
e_{-1} indifference threshold towards S_j
e_{-2} weak (mild, moderate)preference for S_j
....
e_{-6} very strong (dominant) preference for S_j.

We take the symbol e_n to stand for the numerical value of the n-th gradation. For $n \geq 0$, we now use a result which is well-known in psychological measurement (Roberts (1980)): the difference $e_{n+1}-e_n$ must be greater than or equal to the smallest perceptible difference, which is proportional to e_n. Our model for a numerical scale is accordingly based on the relation

```
Euro-Calculations

Member 1

=========+
 FOR     |  Compare the impact of the following pairs of CRITERIA and
 OFFICE  |  mark the appropriate box or box boundary.
USE ONLY |
         |              | has      |      has       |   has    |
         |              | SOMEWHAT | ABOUT EQUAL    | SOMEWHAT |
         |      | has   | HIGHER   |  impact as     | LOWER    |  has     |
   +----+|      | MUCH  | impact   +-----+   +-----+ impact   |  MUCH    |
1-4|   1||      | HIGHER|  than          | |         than     |  LOWER   |
   +----+|      | impact +----------+    | |   +-----------+  impact   |
         |      | than            |    | |   |                than     |
         |      +-------------+   |    | |   |    +--------------------+
         |  DOMINATES         |   |    | |   |    |    is DOMINATED by
56 78    |  ---------------+  |   |    | |   |    |  +-----------------
|| ||    |                 |  |   |    | |   |    |  |
YY YY    |                 Y  Y   Y    Y Y   Y    Y  Y
   +===+                   +--+---+---+--+---+---+--+
4- 3| 2 |  Innovation-based I  |  |  |X|  |  |  |  |  Social Acceptabili
   +===+                   +--+---+---+--+---+---+--+
2- 7| 2 |  Energy Efficiency   |  |  |X|  |  |  |  |  Enhancement of Int
   +===+                   +--+---+---+--+---+---+--+
6- 3| 6 |  Environmental Prot  |X|  |  |  |  |  |  |  Social Acceptabili
   +===+                   +--+---+---+--+---+---+--+
2- 9| 1 |  Energy Efficiency   |  |  |  X  |  |  |  |  Support of Weakly
   +===+                   +--+---+---+--+---+---+--+
8- 7| 4 |  Independence Polic  |  |X|  |  |  |  |  |  Enhancement of Int
   +===+                   +--+---+---+--+---+---+--+
3- 5|-4 |  Social Acceptabili  |  |  |  |  |  |X|  |  Long-term Contribu
   +===+                   +--+---+---+--+---+---+--+
7- 4|-2 |  Enhancement of Int  |  |  |  |  |X|  |  |  Innovation-based I
   +===+                   +--+---+---+--+---+---+--+
1- 8|-1 |  Security of Energy  |  |  |  |  X  |  |  |  Independence Polic
   +===+                   +--+---+---+--+---+---+--+
7- 3|-1 |  Enhancement of Int  |  |  |  |  X  |  |  |  Social Acceptabili
   +===+                   +--+---+---+--+---+---+--+
5- 9| 4 |  Long-term Contribu  |  |X|  |  |  |  |  |  Support of Weakly
   +===+                   +--+---+---+--+---+---+--+
9- 6|-6 |  Support of Weakly   |  |  |  |  |  |  |X|  Environmental Prot
   +===+                   +--+---+---+--+---+---+--+
1- 9| 1 |  Security of Energy  |  |  |  X  |  |  |  |  Support of Weakly
   +===+                   +--+---+---+--+---+---+--+
6- 4| 6 |  Environmental Prot  |X|  |  |  |  |  |  |  Innovation-based I
   +===+                   +--+---+---+--+---+---+--+
1- 7| 2 |  Security of Energy  |  |  |X|  |  |  |  |  Enhancement of Int
   +===+                   +--+---+---+--+---+---+--+
5- 2| 4 |  Long-term Contribu  |  |X|  |  |  |  |  |  Energy Efficiency
   +===+                   +--+---+---+--+---+---+--+
```

Figure 1. Pairs of criteria presented in random order. Member 1 of the decision-making committee is requested to express his comparative judgement by a cross in the appropriate box or on the vertical line separating two adjacent boxes. The numbers, encoded in the left-hand column by an analyst, designate the gradations chosen by Member 1.

$$e_{n+1} - e_n = \epsilon\, e_n,$$

where ϵ stands for a constant which does not depend on n. It follows easily that

$$e_{n+1} = (1+\epsilon)e_n = (1+\epsilon)^2 e_{n-1} = \ldots\ldots = (1+\epsilon)^{n+1}.$$

The echelons can obviously be found on a discrete scale *with geometric progression*. Substituting $\exp(\gamma) = (1+\epsilon)$, we write

$$e_n = \exp(\gamma n),$$

where $\gamma > 0$ represents the *scale parameter*. This expression can also be used if n is a negative integer. Let us now take r_{ijk} to denote the numerical value of the judgement expressed by decision maker k in the basic experiment just mentioned. We have

$$r_{ijk} = \exp(\gamma\, \delta_{ijk}) \;,$$

where δ_{ijk} is an integer, $-6 \leq \delta_{ijk} \leq 6$, designating the gradation which has been chosen by decision maker k in the comparison of the stimuli S_i and S_j. Many experiments have been conducted by Légrády et al. (1984), Kok et al. (1985), Lootsma et al. (1986) to find workable values for the scale parameter γ. In practice, we use a *normal* scale (with $\gamma = 1/2$) and a *stretched* scale (with $\gamma = 1$), in order to identify scale-independent properties. These scales will also be used in section 6.

The preference for S_i with respect to S_j is typically a *linguistic variable* (Zadeh (1973), Zimmermann (1987)). The qualifications (gradations) just mentioned, constituting the *term set* of *linguistic values*, consist of a *primary term* (preference, or importance, impact,...) that can be enlarged by a so-called *modifier* (weak, strong, very strong) expressing the intensity of feelings. Linguistic values are usually modelled as fuzzy numbers. A particular model with triangular membership functions will be the subject of the sections 7-9. In order to prepare the ground we concern ourselves with the above crisp (non-fuzzy) model in the sections 3-6.

The practical question of how to elicit the preferences of the decision makers should not be overlooked. We have used questionnaires of the type which is shown in Figure 1. Pairs of stimuli (criteria in the given situation) are presented to Member 1, who is requested to put a cross, either in the box which he prefers, or on the line separating two boxes if he finds himself on a threshold. The numbers, encoded by an analyst in the column on the left-hand side, designate the gradations chosen by Member 1.

4. *CALCULATION OF THE STIMULUS WEIGHTS*

Let us now turn to the calculation of the stimulus weights. In general, we are dealing with a decision-making committee, and we have to allow for the possibility that some members sometimes abstain from giving their opinion. That is the reason why we employ *logarithmic regression* instead of the eigenvector method (Saaty (1980)). We let D_{ij} stand for the set of decision makers who judged S_i versus S_j. We have r_{ijk} to denote the estimate of V_i/V_j given by decision maker k. Now we could approximate the vector $V = (V_1, \dots, V_p)$ by the normalized vector $\bar{v}$ which minimimizes

$$\sum_{i<j} \sum_{k \in D_{ij}} (\ln r_{ijk} - \ln v_i + \ln v_j)^2 . \tag{1}$$

The members of a committee, however, are usually different in power, prestige, knowledge, and experience. We may take into account their relative position by assigning weights to each of them. In international negotiations, for instance, the weights of national representatives could be derived from national data such as the GNP or the population size. In what follows, we shall be assuming that the k-th decision maker has a normalized weight d_k, and instead of (1) we minimize

$$\sum_{i<j} \sum_{k \in D_{ij}} (\ln r_{ijk} - \ln v_i + \ln v_j)^2 d_k =$$

$$= \sum_{i<j} \sum_{k \in D_{ij}} (q_{ijk} - w_i + w_j)^2 d_k , \tag{2}$$

where $q_{ijk} = \ln r_{ijk} = \gamma \delta_{ijk}$ and $w_i = \ln v_i$. The normal equations (optimality conditions) associated with the minimization of (2) are given by

$$w_i \sum_{\substack{j=1 \\ j \neq i}}^{p} \Big(\sum_{k \in D_{ij}} d_k \Big) - \sum_{\substack{j=1 \\ j \neq i}}^{p} \Big(\sum_{k \in D_{ij}} d_k \Big) w_j = \sum_{\substack{j=1 \\ j \neq i}}^{p} \sum_{k \in D_{ij}} q_{ijk} d_k ,$$

because $q_{jik} = -q_{ijk}$. With the additional notation

$$G_{ij} = \sum_{k \in D_{ij}} d_k$$

$$Q_{ij} = \sum_{k \in D_{ij}} q_{ijk} d_k$$

implying

$$G_{ij} = G_{ji} \text{ and } Q_{ij} = -Q_{ji} ,$$

the system (2) can be rewritten as

$$w_i \sum_{\substack{j=1\\ j\neq i}}^{p} G_{ij} - \sum_{\substack{j=1\\ j\neq i}}^{p} G_{ij}\, w_j = \sum_{\substack{j=1\\ j\neq i}}^{p} Q_{ij} \,. \tag{3}$$

These equations are dependent (they sum to the zero equation). Taking the vector $\bar{w}$ to denote a particular solution of (3), we can write the components of the general solution as $\bar{w}_i + \eta$, and we approximate V_i by

$$\bar{v}_i = \exp(\bar{w}_i+\eta) / \sum_{i=1}^{p} \exp(\bar{w}_i+\eta) = \exp(\bar{w}_i) / \sum_{i=1}^{p} \exp(\bar{w}_i) \,. \tag{4}$$

Obviously, normalization is sufficient to remove the additive degree of freedom in solutions of (3). Let us now use the property that we are working on numerical scales with geometric progression. We can write

$$Q_{ij} = \gamma\, \Delta_{ij},$$

$$\Delta_{ij} = \sum_{k\in D_{ij}} \delta_{ijk}\, d_k,$$

and substitute this expression into (3) to obtain

$$w_i \sum_{\substack{j=1\\ j\neq i}}^{p} G_{ij} - \sum_{\substack{j=1\\ j\neq i}}^{p} G_{ij}\, w_j = \gamma \sum_{\substack{j=1\\ j\neq i}}^{p} \Delta_{ij} \,. \tag{5}$$

Introducing $\bar{w}(\gamma)$ to denote a particular solution of (5) for arbitrary γ, we can immediately write $\bar{w}(\gamma) = \gamma\, \bar{w}(1)$. Obviously, a general solution of (5) has components

$$\gamma\, \bar{w}_i(1) + \eta, \quad i=1, \ldots, p \,,$$

and we approximate V_i by

$$\bar{v}_i(\gamma) = \exp[\gamma\, \bar{w}_i(1)] / \sum_{i=1}^{p} \exp[\gamma\, \bar{w}_i(1)] \,, \tag{6}$$

an expression which immediately shows that the rank order of the $\bar{v}_i(\gamma)$ does not depend on γ. Moreover, the experiments by Légrády et al. (1984) and Lootsma et al. (1986) demonstrate that the $\bar{v}_i(\gamma)$ are not very sensitive to the scale parameter γ when it varies over the range of values (including 1/2 and 1) that seems to be acceptable in the social sciences. This will also be demonstrated in section 6.

It is important to note that the system (5) has an *explicit* solution if the comparisons are *complete*, that is, if every decision maker expressed his judgement about each pair of stimuli. Then $G_{ij} = 1$, and (5) reduces to

$$(p-1)w_i - \sum_{\substack{j=1 \\ j\neq i}}^{p} w_j = \gamma \sum_{\substack{j=1 \\ j\neq i}}^{p} \Delta_{ij} , \tag{7}$$

or, equivalently (since $\Delta_{ii} = 0$),

$$p\, w_i - \sum_{j=1}^{p} w_j = \gamma \sum_{j=1}^{p} \Delta_{ij} .$$

Because we have at least one degree of freedom, we may stipulate that the components of w sum to zero, whence

$$\bar{w}_i(\gamma) = \gamma\left(\frac{1}{p} \sum_{j=1}^{p} \Delta_{ij}\right) \overset{\text{def}}{=} \gamma\, \rho_i .$$

and

$$\bar{v}_i(\gamma) = \exp(\gamma\rho_i) / \sum_{i=1}^{p} \exp(\gamma\rho_i) . \tag{8}$$

If the decision makers have equal weights $d_k = 1/N$, where N stands for the total number of decision makers, we obtain

$$\rho_i = \frac{1}{pN} \sum_{j=1}^{p} \sum_{k=1}^{N} \delta_{ijk} ,$$

$$\exp(\gamma\, \rho_i) = \sqrt[pN]{\prod_{j=1}^{p} \cdot \prod_{k=1}^{N} r_{ijk}} ,$$

implying that we simply have to calculate and to normalize the geometric row means in the tableau of comparative judgements; see also Barzilai et al.(1987) who demonstrate under reasonable consistency axioms that the stimulus weights can only be found by the calculation of geometric means, not by the eigenvector method of Saaty (1980).

The $\bar{v}_i(\gamma)$ computed by (6) or (7) represent the weights assigned to the stimuli by a group of decision makers. An interesting by-product of the method is that stimulus weights assigned by individual members can be calculated by the minimization of

$$\sum_{i<j} (\ln r_{ijk} - \ln v_i^{(k)} + \ln v_j^{(k)})^2 \tag{9}$$

for separate values of k. In many situations these weights focus the discussions on the critical issues. It is typically the purpose of pairwise comparison methods to reveal hidden controversies and to guide the decision makers towards a joint conclusion.

5. *AGGREGATION AND FINAL SCORES*

It is customary in multi-criteria analysis to subdivide the decision problem and to distinguish a number of decision levels. At the first level, we compare the performance criteria, that is, we present pairs of criteria, and for each pair we ask a decision maker to decide whether the two criteria have the same impact in the given situation or, if not, to judge their relative impact. The decision maker is supposed to use the familiar qualifications (indifference, weak or strong preference, dominance) to express the gradations of his judgement. The estimated preference ratios are obtained by assigning numerical values (scale values) to these qualifications on the geometric scale with parameter γ. Thereafter we apply logarithmic regression to approximate the values of the respective criteria (the so-called criterion weights) by quantities $\bar{c}_i(\gamma)$ computed according to formula (6) or (8). We follow the same mode of operation at the second decision level, where we compare the alternatives under each of the performance criteria separately. Thus, working under the i-th criterion, we present an arbitrary pair of alternatives to the decision maker, and we ask him to express his preference (if any) for one of the two via the familiar qualifications. We put these qualifications on a geometric scale with the same value for the parameter γ as at the first decision level. Thereafter, we compute approximate weights $\bar{a}_{ij}(\gamma)$ for the respective alternatives under criterion i, again via the logarithmic regression procedure just sketched.

Lastly, we have to *aggregate* the results in order to obtain final scores for the alternatives under consideration. We argue as follows (see also Lootsma (1985, 1987)). Consider the alternatives A_j and A_k under criterion C_i. The calculated weights $\bar{a}_{ij}(\gamma)$ and $\bar{a}_{ik}(\gamma)$ are not unique, but the ratio

$$\frac{\bar{a}_{ij}(\gamma)}{\bar{a}_{ik}(\gamma)},$$

representing the relative weight of A_j with respect to A_k under C_i, is unique when there is exactly one degree of freedom in the system (5), and this is usually the case. Suppose now that the calculated criterion weights $\bar{c}_i(\gamma)$ are equal (and normalized so that they sum to unity). An appropriate measure for the *overall relative weight* of A_j with respect to A_k would then be given by the geometric mean

$$\prod_i \left(\frac{\bar{a}_{ij}(\gamma)}{\bar{a}_{ik}(\gamma)}\right)^{\bar{c}_i(\gamma)} .$$

On the other hand, we take the ratio of the final scores $\bar{s}_j(\gamma)$ and $\bar{s}_k(\gamma)$ to represent the overall relative weight of alternative A_j with respect to A_k, so that

$$\frac{\bar{s}_j(\gamma)}{\bar{s}_k(\gamma)} = \prod_i \left(\frac{\bar{a}_{ij}(\gamma)}{\bar{a}_{ik}(\gamma)}\right)^{\bar{c}_i(\gamma)} .$$

Finally, we propose to maintain this relation, even if the $\bar{c}_i(\gamma)$ are not equal (but still normalized). Thus, an appropriate model for the final score $\bar{s}_j(\gamma)$ would be given by the geometric mean

$$\prod_i (\bar{a}_{ij}(\gamma))^{\bar{c}_i(\gamma)} . \tag{10}$$

Using first-order approximations we can easily derive

$$\prod_i (\bar{a}_{ij}(\gamma))^{\bar{c}_i(\gamma)} = \exp[\sum_i \bar{c}_i(\gamma) \ln \bar{a}_{ij}(\gamma)] \cong$$

$$\cong 1 + \sum_i \bar{c}_i(\gamma) \ln \bar{a}_{ij}(\gamma) \cong 1 + \sum_i \bar{c}_i(\gamma)[\bar{a}_{ij}(\gamma)-1] = \sum_i \bar{c}_i(\gamma)\, \bar{a}_{ij}(\gamma).$$

Moreover, by the arithmetic-geometric mean inequality, it must be true that

$$\prod_i(\bar{a}_{ij}(\gamma))^{\bar{c}_i(\gamma)} \leq \sum_i \bar{c}_i(\gamma)\, \bar{a}_{ij}(\gamma),$$

implying that the quantities (10) are in general not normalized. Hence, using *normalized geometric means* we can formulate the *aggregation rule*

$$\bar{s}_j(\gamma) = \prod_i (\bar{a}_{ij}(\gamma))^{\bar{c}_i(\gamma)} / \sum_j \prod_i(\bar{a}_{ij}(\gamma))^{\bar{c}_i(\gamma)} . \tag{11}$$

To simplify the calculations, however, we mostly employ the *approximate aggregation rule*

$$\bar{s}_j(\gamma) = \sum_i \bar{c}_i(\gamma)\, \bar{a}_{ij}(\gamma) , \tag{12}$$

so that we only have to compute *inner products* (this is a familiar rule in multi-criteria analysis, intuitively used because it is transparent and convenient). Numerical experience has shown that the differences between the results of (11) and (12) are negligible.

In sec. 3, we found that scale transformations from one geometric scale to another do not produce rank reversal in a *single-level* comparison of stimuli. In *multi-level* decision making, however, where we compare decision criteria (level 1) and alternatives under each of the criteria separately (level 2), rank preservation of the final scores cannot be guaranteed. This is due to the aggregation rules (11) and (12).

Even on a single level, however, the vexing problem of rank preservation has not completely been solved. Saaty and Vargas (1984), for instance, were concerned with three methods for approximating the V_i, starting from a given matrix of preference ratios so that the effect of scale transformations is ignored. They demonstrate that the results of the eigenvalue method (Saaty (1980)), the least-squares method, and our logarithmic regression method may indeed exhibit rank reversal in simple cases where it should clearly not occur. The observation that the calculated rank order is method-dependent may also be found in Légrády et al. (1984) who compared the results of logarithmic regression and the Bradley-Terry method. And let us finally point at the unresolved complications of adding or dropping a stimulus: approximating the values of the remaining stimuli one may also run up against the phenomenon of rank reversal (Saaty, private communication).

Disaggregation is appealing when the decision makers find it difficult to assess or to trust the criterion weights. Usually, they have more confidence in the weights of the alternatives under the respective criteria. Sometimes, they do not even hesitate to carry out a *holistic* exercise and to establish final scores by pairwise comparisons of the alternatives without looking at specific properties. Then the $\bar{a}_{ij}(\gamma)$ and the $\bar{s}_j(\gamma)$ of formula (12) are known, and we can find the $\bar{c}_i(\gamma)$ by solving the quadratic-programming problem

$$\text{minimize} \qquad \sum_j \{\bar{s}_j(\gamma) - \sum_i c_i \, \bar{a}_{ij}(\gamma)\}^2$$

$$\text{subject to} \qquad \sum_i c_i = 1, \; c_i \geq 0.$$

In many cases, however, the problem does not have a unique solution (B. Bhola, Delft University of Technology, private communicaton). This reduces the attractiveness of the approach.

6. *NUMERICAL RESULTS*

Let us now turn to the illustrative example briefly described in section 2. Table 1 displays, first of all, the scales that we discussed: the normal scale (γ=1/2) that we employ directly in our applications, and the stretched scale (γ=1) employed to demonstrate the users that the scale sensitivity of pairwise-comparison methods remains within reasonable limits, although the numerical values of strong and very strong preference increase rapidly with γ. Moreover, we show the widely used scale of Saaty (1980). Next, we exhibit the weights and the rank order of the criteria, as well as the final scores and the rank order of the alternatives. In many applications, we have observed that our normal scale and the scale of Saaty yield practically the same results. The reader will also see it here. Rank reversal of the alternatives does occur in the transition from the normal to the stretched scale, a phenomenon which is due to the transformation of the criterion weights and to the subsequent aggregation procedure.

In table 2, we address the question of whether the criteria with small weights (enhancement of social acceptability, innovation-based industry, or international cooperation, and support of weakly developed regions) can be dropped. Obviously, the five remaining criteria are sufficient to explain the final scores. There is practically no difference between the scores and the rank order of the alternatives in Table 1 and Table 2.

In what follows, we continue with the normal scale. Table 3 exhibits the results per member: the individual criterion weights and the individual final scores (at least as far as possible), and also the joint results with equal weights assigned to the members of the group. Obviously, the opinions diverge considerably. Such a phenomenon will always trigger vivid discussions.

7. PAIRWISE COMPARISONS AND FUZZY NUMBERS

The method described so far has a particular draw-back. Each decision maker is supposed to choose at most one qualification (indifference, weak or strong preference, dominance) to estimate his preference ratio. Mostly, however, he realizes that *several* qualifications are more or less appropriate because his feelings as well as the qualifications themselves are vague. He could model his judgement by assigning *credibilities* to each of the respective qualifications: real numbers between 0 and 1 expressing his belief, and not necessarily summing up to 1 because of the vagueness of definition (see Figure 2). An alternative modus operandi is to choose the most credible qualification, as well as left-hand and right-hand spreads indicating the range of credibility. This is in fact the proposal of Van Laarhoven and Pedrycz (1983) who used *fuzzy estimates* of the preference ratios. For reasons of simplicity, they expressed the ratio estimates by fuzzy numbers with *triangular membership functions*, and they modified the algebraic rules of Dubois and Prade (1980) to simplify the subsequent calculations.

In the present paper, we follow their ideas. Thus, in order to model the *linguistic value* assigned to the preference ratio, we introduce the fuzzy number $\tilde{r}$ with a triangular membership function characterized by three parameters: the *modal value* r_m to locate the top (with value 1), and two values, the *lower value* r_ℓ and the *upper value* r_u, to locate the basis of the triangle. The arithmetic operations on two fuzzy numbers $\tilde{r} = (r_\ell, r_m, r_u)$ and $\tilde{t} = (t_\ell, t_m, t_u)$ can now easily be written in terms of these parameters. For addition and subtraction we have

$$(r_\ell, r_m, r_u) + (t_\ell, t_m, t_u) = (r_\ell + t_\ell, r_m + t_m, r_u + t_u) ,$$

$$(r_\ell, r_m, r_u) - (t_\ell, t_m, t_u) = (r_\ell - t_u, r_m - t_m, r_u - t_\ell) .$$

These operations are exact, both in the parameters and in the shape of the membership function, when we follow the familiar fuzzification

SCALES		NORMAL ($\gamma=\frac{1}{2}$)		STRETCHED ($\gamma=1$)		SAATY (1980)	
	INDIFFERENCE	$\exp(0) = 1$		$\exp(0) = 1$		1	
SCALE	WEAK PREFERENCE	$\exp(2\gamma) \approx 2.7$		$\exp(2\gamma) \approx 7.4$		3	
VALUES	STRONG PREFERENCE	$\exp(4\gamma) \approx 7.4$		$\exp(4\gamma) \approx 54.6$		5	
	DOMINANCE	$\exp(6\gamma) \approx 20.1$		$\exp(6\gamma) \approx 403.4$		7	
	SECURITY OF ENERGY SUPPLY	22.0	1	33.5	1	20.4	1
	ENERGY EFFICIENCY	10.5	5	7.6	5	11.4	5
WEIGHTS	SOCIAL ACCEPTABILITY	5.6	7	2.2	7	6.2	7
AND RANK	INNOVATION-BASED INDUSTRY	8.8	6	5.3	6	9.5	6
ORDER OF	LONG-TERM CONTRIBUTION	14.7	3	15.0	3	14.9	3
CRITERIA	ENVIRONMENTAL PROTECTION	18.7	2	24.3	2	16.0	2
	ENHANCEMENT INT. COOP.	3.9	9	1.0	9	4.5	9
	INDEPENDENCE POLICY	12.1	4	10.2	4	12.4	4
	SUPPORT WEAKLY DEV. REGIONS	3.9	8	1.0	8	4.6	8
	SOLAR ENERGY	15.0	2	13.3	2	15.3	2
FINAL	GEO THERMAL ENERGY	8.1	6	3.6	6	9.3	6
SCORES	ENERGY SAVING	29.1	1	48.4	1	24.0	1
AND RANK	NEW ENERGY VECTORS	7.4	8	3.4	7	8.4	8
ORDER OF	BIOMASS ENERGY	7.9	7	3.3	8	9.0	7
ALTERNATIVES	SOLID FUELS	10.6	4	10.1	3	11.3	4
	HYDRO CARBONS	9.1	5	8.2	5	9.6	5
	WIND ENERGY	12.7	3	9.7	4	13.2	3

Table 1. Weights and rank order of criteria, final scores and rank order of alternatives, obtained from one single collection of comparative judgements encoded on three distinct scales.

	SCALES	NORMAL ($\gamma=\frac{1}{2}$)		STRETCHED ($\gamma=1$)		SAATY (1980)	
	INDIFFERENCE	exp(0) = 1		exp(0) = 1		1	
SCALE	WEAK PREFERENCE	exp(2γ) ≈ 2.7		exp(2γ) ≈ 7.4		3	
VALUES	STRONG PREFERENCE	exp(4γ) ≈ 7.4		exp(4γ) ≈ 54.6		5	
	DOMINANCE	exp(6γ) ≈ 20.1		exp(6γ) ≈ 403.4		7	
WEIGHTS	SECURITY OF ENERGY SUPPLY	29.1	1	38.8	1	27.6	1
AND RANK	ENERGY EFFICIENCY	13.2	5	8.0	5	14.8	5
ORDER OF	LONG-TERM CONTRIBUTION	17.7	3	14.3	3	18.8	3
CRITERIA	ENVIRONMENTAL PROTECTION	25.2	2	28.9	2	23.2	2
	INDEPENDENCE POLICY	14.8	4	10.0	4	15.6	4
	SOLAR ENERGY	13.4	2	11.8	2	13.8	2
FINAL	GEOTHERMAL ENERGY	7.8	6	3.4	6	9.2	6
SCORES	ENERGY SAVING	31.9	1	50.6	1	26.0	1
AND RANK	NEW ENERGY VECTORS	6.6	7	2.6	7	7.7	7
ORDER OF	BIOMASS ENERGY	6.5	8	2.5	8	7.7	8
ALTERNATIVES	SOLID FUELS	11.6	4	10.7	3	12.3	4
	HYDRO CARBONS	9.9	5	8.9	5	10.3	5
	WIND ENERGY	12.3	3	9.5	4	13.0	3

Table 2. Weights and rank order of leading criteria, final scores and rank order of alternatives, also obtained from the collection of comparative judgements underlying the results of Table 1.

RESULTS ON NORMAL SCALE (γ=½) CRITERIA AND ALTERNATIVES	INDIVIDUAL MEMBERS OF THE GROUP 1	2	3	4	5	6	7	8	GROUP
SECURITY OF ENERGY SUPPLY	5.4	39.0	16.2	22.6	26.0	13.9	--	25.8	22.0
ENERGY EFFICIENCY	5.4	8.2	25.3	11.6	1.6	17.4	--	--	10.5
SOCIAL ACCEPTABILITY	3.5	6.6	3.8	3.4	1.6	13.9	--	7.4	5.6
INNOVATION-BASED INDUSTRY	6.7	7.4	7.4	12.9	2.5	6.4	--	15.7	8.8
LONG-TERM CONTRIBUTION	16.4	6.6	16.2	16.2	4.9	13.9	--	22.8	14.7
ENVIRONMENTAL PROTECTION	49.8	5.3	18.1	3.8	50.6	15.5	--	15.7	18.7
ENHANCEMENT INT. COOPERATION	2.2	1.9	2.5	7.4	2.3	6.4	--	3.1	3.9
INDEPENDENCE POLICY	7.5	22.4	7.4	16.2	8.5	8.9	--	6.5	12.1
SUPPORT WEAKLY DEV. REGION	3.1	2.7	3.1	5.9	2.0	3.7	--	3.1	3.9
SOLAR ENERGY	28.1	13.1	8.7	7.9	--	12.1	--	17.3	15.0
GEOTHERMAL ENERGY	4.7	10.6	5.2	7.1	--	7.6	--	7.9	8.1
ENERGY SAVING	23.7	33.2	45.5	25.4	--	32.3	--	14.7	29.1
NEW ENERGY VECTORS	3.6	7.0	5.1	11.9	--	5.5	--	11.1	7.4
BIOMASS ENERGY	12.1	8.2	4.0	6.4	--	7.1	--	6.9	7.9
SOLID FUELS	3.0	7.9	14.6	15.1	--	12.9	--	9.0	10.6
HYDRO CARBONS	1.9	10.1	11.9	18.9	--	7.7	--	12.4	9.1
WIND ENERGY	22.9	9.9	5.0	7.2	--	14.8	--	20.6	12.7

Table 3. Weights of criteria and final scores of alternatives, assigned by individual members and by the group of equally-weighed decision makers.

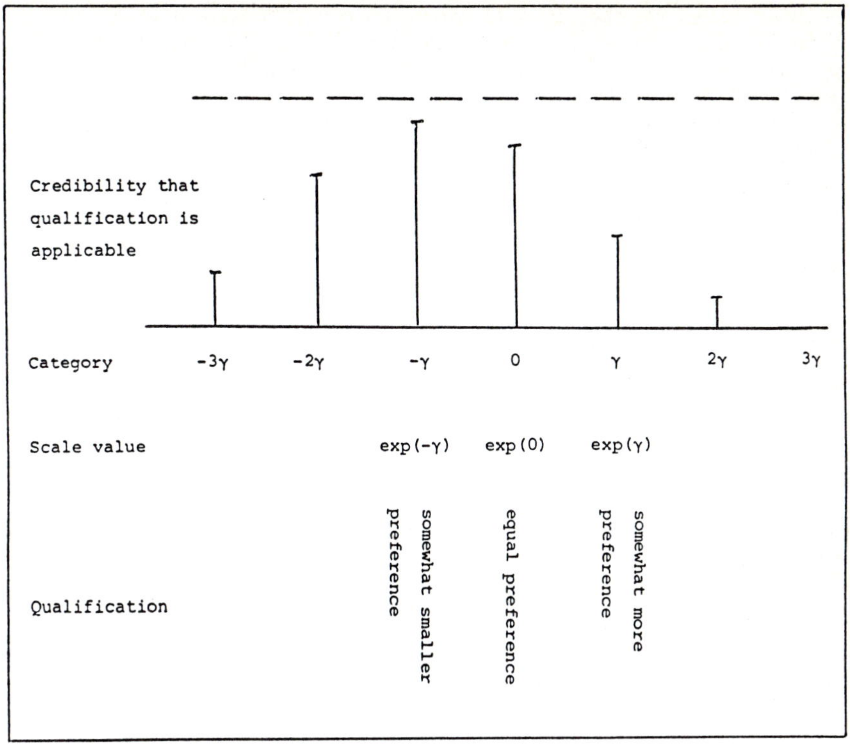

Figure 2. Credibilities of judgemental qualifications, not necessarily summing up to 1 because of vagueness of definition.

principles based on the max and min operators. Multiplication and division are also exact in the parameters, but not necessarily in the shape of the membership function. With a negligible error, however, we can write

$$(r_\ell, r_m, r_u) \times (t_\ell, t_m, t_u) = (r_\ell t_\ell, r_m t_m, r_u t_u) ,$$

$$(r_\ell, r_m, r_u) \,/\, (t_\ell, t_m, t_u) = (r_\ell/t_u, r_m/t_m, r_u/t_\ell) ,$$

provided that $t_\ell > 0$. Finally, if the parameters of $\tilde{r}$ are positive, we may introduce the logarithm $\tilde{q} = \ln \tilde{r}$, approximately written as

$$(q_\ell, q_m, q_u) = (\ln r_\ell, \ln r_m, \ln r_u) .$$

Let us now return to the basic experiment of section 3, where decision maker k expresses his preference for S_i with respect to S_j. His judgement, the fuzzy estimate of V_i/V_j, is modelled as

$$\tilde{r}_{ijk} = (r_{ijk\ell}, r_{ijkm}, r_{ijku}),$$

and its logarithm as $\tilde{q}_{ijk} = \ln \tilde{r}_{ijk}$ such that

$$q_{ijk\ell} = \ln r_{ijk\ell}, \text{ etc.}$$

We shall be assuming that the weights d_k of the respective decision makers are crisp (non-fuzzy), for reasons to be explained at the end of this section. Then G_{ij} is also crisp, but we have to deal with the fuzzy quantities

$$\tilde{Q}_{ij} = \sum_{k \in D_{ij}} \tilde{q}_{ijk} \, d_k .$$

Basically, Van Laarhoven and Pedrycz (1983) propose to approximate the values V_i of the respective stimuli S_i by fuzzy numbers $\tilde{v}_i$, also with triangular membership functions. The procedure is as follows. Let $\tilde{w}_i = \ln \tilde{v}_i$, generalize (3) so that

$$\tilde{w}_i \sum_{\substack{j=1 \\ j \neq i}}^{p} G_{ij} - \sum_{\substack{j=1 \\ j \neq i}}^{p} G_{ij} \tilde{w}_j = \sum_{\substack{j=1 \\ j \neq i}}^{p} \tilde{Q}_{ij} \qquad (13)$$

and calculate the lower, modal and upper values of $\tilde{w}_i$ from the linear systems

$$w_{im} \sum_{\substack{j=1\\j\neq i}}^{p} G_{ij} - \sum_{\substack{j=1\\j\neq i}}^{p} G_{ij}\, w_{jm} = \sum_{\substack{j=1\\j\neq i}}^{p} Q_{ijm} \tag{14}$$

$$w_{i\ell} \sum_{\substack{j=1\\j\neq i}}^{p} G_{ij} - \sum_{\substack{j=1\\j\neq i}}^{p} G_{ij}\, w_{ju} = \sum_{\substack{j=1\\j\neq i}}^{p} Q_{ij\ell} \tag{15a}$$

$$w_{iu} \sum_{\substack{j=1\\j\neq i}}^{p} G_{ij} - \sum_{\substack{j=1\\j\neq i}}^{p} G_{ij}\, w_{j\ell} = \sum_{\substack{j=1\\j\neq i}}^{p} Q_{iju} \tag{15b}$$

Obviously, the modal values appear separately in the system (14) only. Because $Q_{ijm} = -Q_{jim}$ and $G_{ij} = G_{ji}$, we can show that the equations sum to the zero equation. Hence, a solution to (14) has at least one (additive) degree of freedom. We have a similar result for the lower and upper values, to be solved jointly from the system (15): because $Q_{iju} = -Q_{ji\ell}$ and $Q_{ij\ell} = -Q_{jiu}$, the equations sum to the zero equation, so that a solution of (15) has at least one (additive) degree of freedom.

In general, the systems (14) and (15) have exactly one additive degree of freedom each. Hence, a fuzzy approximation to the values V_i of the respective stimuli S_i, $i = 1, \ldots, p$, is represented by the triples

$$(\exp(\bar{w}_{i\ell}+\zeta),\ \exp(\bar{w}_{im}+\eta),\ \exp(\bar{w}_{iu} + \zeta)), \tag{16}$$

where η and ζ are the degrees of freedom in solutions of (14) and (15). To enforce uniqueness, we normalize the above quantities according to the proposal of Boender (see Boender et al. (1987)). This is not a trivial operation. To clarify matters we consider an arbitrary collection of fuzzy numbers

$$(y_{i\ell},\ y_{im},\ y_{iu}),\quad i = 1, \ldots, p\ .$$

Multiplying these by the inverse of their sum we obtain the *normalized* numbers

$$(z_{i\ell},\ z_{im},\ z_{iu}) \stackrel{\text{def}}{=} \left(\frac{y_{i\ell}}{\sum_{i=1}^{p} y_{iu}},\ \frac{y_{im}}{\sum_{i=1}^{p} y_{im}},\ \frac{y_{iu}}{\sum_{i=1}^{p} y_{i\ell}} \right),\quad i=1,\ldots,p$$

which obviously have the properties

$$\sum_{i=1}^{p} z_{im} = 1\ ,$$

$$\left(\sum_{i=1}^{p} z_{i\ell} \right) \cdot \left(\sum_{i=1}^{p} z_{iu} \right) = 1\ .$$

Hence, in order to normalize a fuzzy approximation to the respective stimuli, the degrees of freedom η and ζ must be chosen to satisfy

$$\sum_{i=1}^{p} \exp(\bar{w}_{im} + \eta) = 1 ,$$

$$\left(\sum_{i=1}^{p} \exp(\bar{w}_{i\ell} + \zeta)\right) \cdot \left(\sum_{i=1}^{p} \exp(\bar{w}_{iu} + \zeta)\right) = 1 ,$$

whence

$$\exp(\eta) = \left(\sum_{i=1}^{p} \exp(\bar{w}_{im})\right)^{-1} ,$$

$$\exp(\zeta) = \left(\sum_{i=1}^{p} \exp(\bar{w}_{i\ell}) \cdot \sum_{i=1}^{p} \exp(\bar{w}_{iu})\right)^{-1/2} .$$

In summary, and here we deviate from the original proposal of Van Laarhoven and Pedrycz (1983), we approximate the values V_i of the respective stimuli S_i, $i = 1, \ldots, p$, by the normalized fuzzy approximations $(\bar{v}_{i\ell}, \bar{v}_{im}, \bar{v}_{iu})$ such that

$$\begin{aligned} \bar{v}_{i\ell} &= \exp(\bar{w}_{i\ell}) \, . \, \exp(\zeta) , \\ \bar{v}_{im} &= \exp(\bar{w}_{im}) \, . \, \exp(\eta) , \\ \bar{v}_{iu} &= \exp(\bar{w}_{iu}) \, . \, \exp(\zeta) . \end{aligned} \tag{17}$$

The proposed method still has two short-comings. First, the triple $(\bar{v}_{i\ell}, \bar{v}_{im}, \bar{v}_{iu})$ obtained in the above manner does not necessarily satisfy the order relations

$$\bar{v}_{i\ell} \leq \bar{v}_{im} \leq \bar{v}_{iu} , \tag{18}$$

so that it does not always represent a fuzzy number with triangular membership function. Second, the decision makers have to supply much more information than in the non-fuzzy case, and they are not always willing to do so. As a matter of fact, this obstacle is also presented by the methods of Wagenknecht and Hartmann (1983), and Buckley (1985), both designed for the same type of problems in multi-criteria analysis (the deficiencies of these methods are extensively discussed in Boender et al. (1987)). Although we cannot rigorously prove that (18) is always satisfied, we are able to establish (18) under simplifying assumptions.

The analysis (section 8) shows that violations of (18) are unlikely in practical circumstances.

The crucial step in our method of fuzzy pairwise comparisons is to solve a system of linear equations with crisp coefficient matrix and fuzzy right-hand side (the systems (14) and (15)). The coefficients G_{ij} are not fuzzy indeed because the weights of the decision makers were supposed to be crisp. From a practical viewpoint, it would make sense to introduce fuzzy weights $\tilde{d}_k$, possibly obtained by pairwise comparisons of the decision makers. Solving the resulting linear systems with fuzzy coefficients and right-hand side elements constitutes an open problem, however, so that we restrained ourselves to crisp weights d_k.

8. *ANALYSIS UNDER SIMPLIFYING ASSUMPTIONS*

The responses of the decision makers are in fact limited to a finite number of categories (indifference, weak or strong preference, dominance). Hence, the non-fuzzy estimates r_{ijk}, written as

$$r_{ijk} = \exp(\gamma\ \delta_{ijk}) \ ,$$

are also restricted to a finite, usually small, set of values ($\delta_{ijk} = 0, \pm 1, \ldots, \pm 6$). Boender et al. (1987) observed that the fuzzy estimates $\tilde{r}_{ijk}$ (the linguistic values) are subject to similar limitations. Mostly, they exhibit a particular form of symmetry: the three parameters of the respective membership functions can be written as

$$\left.\begin{aligned} r_{ijk\ell} &= \exp[\gamma\ (\delta_{ijk} - \alpha_{ijk})] \ , \\ r_{ijkm} &= \exp[\gamma\ \delta_{ijk}] \ , \\ r_{ijku} &= \exp[\gamma(\delta_{ijk} + \alpha_{ijk})] \ , \end{aligned}\right\} \tag{19}$$

with positive, integer-valued spread α_{ijk}. The membership functions of the associated $\tilde{q}_{ijk}$ are accordingly isosceles triangles. What simplifies matters even more is the observation that we can reasonably set all α_{ijk} to a common spread α: equal to 1 (a common spread of one scale step upwards and downwards) if the decision makers choose (after some hesitation) exactly one gradation for each pair of stimuli, and equal to 2 (two scale steps upwards and downwards) if they also assign positive credibilities to the adjacent qualifications. In many practical situations it is reaonable to assign even higher values to the common or uniform degree of fuzziness α.

In the case that (19) holds we attempt to solve the equations (13) in terms of fuzzy $\tilde{w}_i$ with the same type of symmetry as the $\tilde{q}_{ijk}$. Observing that

$$q_{ijku} - q_{ijkm} = q_{ijkm} - q_{ijk\ell} = \gamma\, \alpha_{ijk} ,$$

we write

$$w_{iu} - w_{im} = w_{im} - w_{i\ell} = \gamma\, \beta_i \tag{20}$$

with positive spread β_i. The modal values w_{im} are solved from the system (14) to yield a particular solution $\bar{w}_{im}(\gamma)$, and the general solution $\bar{w}_{im}(\gamma) + \eta$, i = 1, ..., p. Subtracting (15a) from (15b) we find that the β_i satisfy the system

$$\beta_i \sum_{\substack{j=1\\j\neq i}}^{p} G_{ij} + \sum_{\substack{j=1\\j\neq i}}^{p} G_{ij}\, \beta_j = \sum_{\substack{j=1\\j\neq i}}^{p} \sum_{k\in D_{ij}} \alpha_{ijk}\, d_k . \tag{21}$$

Now, restricting ourselves to the situation that the spreads α_{ijk} are equal to a uniform spread α, we reduce (21) to

$$\beta_i \sum_{\substack{j=1\\j\neq i}}^{p} G_{ij} + \sum_{\substack{j=1\\j\neq i}}^{p} G_{ij}\, \beta_j = \alpha \sum_{\substack{j=1\\j\neq i}}^{p} G_{ij} . \tag{22}$$

Assuming that $\beta_i = \beta$, i = 1, ..., p, a reasonable assumption in the given situation, we can immediately conclude from (18) that $\beta = \alpha/2$. This is an extremely simple result, which also explains the success of Van Laarhoven's and Pedrycz' method (1983). They propose to solve the systems (14) and (15) directly, although the resulting solution may violate the order relations (18). Violations are unlikely, however, because in practical applications the systems (15) and (21) are perturbations of (22). A fuzzy approximation to the value V_i of the stimulus S_i is now given by the triple

$$(\exp(\bar{w}_{im}(\gamma) + \zeta - \alpha\gamma/2),\ \exp(\bar{w}_{im}(\gamma) + \eta),\ \exp(\bar{w}_{im}(\gamma) + \zeta + \alpha\gamma/2)),$$

and the normalized approximation can be written in the form

$$\tilde{v}_i(\gamma) = \frac{\exp(\bar{w}_{im}(\gamma))}{\sum_{i=1}^{p} \exp(\bar{w}_{im}(\gamma))} (\exp(-\alpha\gamma/2),\ 1,\ \exp(\alpha\gamma/2)). \tag{23}$$

We may clearly take the factor

$$\bar{v}_{im}(\gamma) \overset{\text{def}}{=} \frac{\exp(\bar{w}_{im}(\gamma))}{\sum_{i=1}^{p} \exp(\bar{w}_{im}(\gamma))} \tag{24}$$

to be the non-fuzzy estimate of V_i when fuzziness in human judgement is ignored (see formula (4)). The fuzzy factor represented by the triple

$$(\exp(-\alpha\gamma/2),\ 1,\ \exp(\alpha\gamma/2)) \tag{25}$$

makes it a fuzzy estimate. Formula (23) may be applied when the degree of fuzziness is of the same order of magnitude for all judgements, or when the decision makers agree that the fuzziness of practically all judgements is below a certain, acceptable degree. Usually, we distinguish the following cases.

a) *No fuzziness*. The decision maker chooses exactly one gradation for each comparative judgement. We model this by setting α to 0.

b) The decision maker is *semantically crisp*. He rejects any adjacent gradation on the current scale, but he might assign positive credibilities to more than one gradation on a finer scale with new echelons. We model this by setting α to 1.

c) *Shaded judgement*. The decision maker assigns positive credibilities to the adjacent gradations, but he rejects the gradations two or more scale steps upwards and downwards. An appropriate model is to set α to 2.

d) *Categorical fuzziness*. The decision maker assigns positive credibilities to adjacent categories of judgement. In choosing weak preference, for instance, he may also consider the choice of indifference or strong preference. We model this by setting α to 4.

Substitution of these values into (19) yields an effective tool for a simple form of sensitivity analysis. No additional information, such as lower and upper values of the estimated preference ratios, is required. We only ask the decision makers to estimate their uniform degree of fuzziness, or to estimate a degree which overestimates the fuzziness of practically all judgements. Obviously, the approximations to the respective V_i will exhibit half that degree of fuzziness, a remarkable result because one might have expected that the number p of stimuli or the G_{ij} would affect the fuzziness of the calculated weights $\tilde{v}_i$. The above, analytical results for the simple situation with uniform spread of the fuzzy estimates $\tilde{r}_{ijk}$ do not confirm this. The practical consequences are obvious: one can only reduce the fuzziness of the calculated weights by additional pairwise comparisons with smaller spreads. Otherwise, increasing the G_{ij} will be ineffective.

9. *PROPAGATION OF FUZZINESS*

Let us now return to the multi-criteria decision problem. Suppose that we have used pairwise comparisons to obtain fuzzy approximations

$$\tilde{c}_i(\gamma) = \bar{c}_{im}(\gamma)\ (\exp(-\alpha\gamma/2),\ 1,\ \exp(\alpha\gamma/2))$$

$$\tilde{a}_{ij}(\gamma) = \bar{a}_{ijm}(\gamma)\ (\exp(-\alpha\gamma/2),\ 1,\ \exp(\alpha\gamma/2)) \tag{26}$$

to the values of the criteria and to the values of the alternatives under the respective criteria. Fuzzifying (12) and following the algebraic rules of Van Laarhoven and Pedrycz (1983) we obtain the fuzzy final scores

$$\tilde{s}_j(\gamma) = \sum_i \bar{c}_{im}(\gamma)\ \bar{a}_{ijm}(\gamma)\ (\exp(-\alpha\gamma),\ 1,\ \exp(\alpha\gamma)). \tag{27}$$

We can alternatively write $\tilde{s}_j(\gamma)$ as the triple

$$(\bar{s}_{j\ell}(\gamma),\ \bar{s}_{jm}(\gamma),\ \bar{s}_{ju}(\gamma)) ,$$

where $\bar{s}_{jm}(\gamma)$ stands for the modal value given by

$$\bar{s}_{jm}(\gamma) = \sum_i \bar{c}_{im}(\gamma)\ \bar{a}_{ijm}(\gamma) ,$$

and where the lower and upper values are

$$\bar{s}_{j\ell}(\gamma) = \bar{s}_{jm}(\gamma)\ \exp(-\alpha\gamma) ,$$

$$\bar{s}_{ju}(\gamma) = \bar{s}_{jm}(\gamma)\ \exp(\alpha\gamma) .$$

We can now easily see the propagation of fuzziness in hierarchical decision making. When there is a uniform degree of fuzziness α in the original ratio estimates, we have a uniform degree $\alpha/2$ in the calculated weights of the criteria (decision level 1) and the alternatives (level 2), see formula (26). Aggregating the results to obtain final scores for the alternatives, we add the degrees of fuzziness at the respective levels, see formula (27).

Let us finally apply the results of this section to the illustrative example of section 2. We take the crisp final scores of the energy research programs (Table 1) to calculate fuzzy final scores via formula (27) for varying degrees of fuzziness α. Table 4 presents the outcomes on the normal scale (γ=1/2).

10. *FUZZY PREFERENCE RELATIONS*

Do these fuzzy final scores enable us to distinguish the alternatives from each other? We might draw the triangles and check whether the overlap is sufficiently small to identify the best alternative (see also Baas and Kwakernaak (1977)). We could, alternatively, calculate the

FUZZINESS / ALTERNATIVES	SEMANTICALLY CRISP $\alpha=1$			SHADED JUDGEMENT $\alpha=2$		
	exp(-½)	1	exp(½)	exp(-1)	1	exp(1)
SOLAR ENERGY	(9.1	15.0	24.7)	(5.5	15.0	40.8)
GEOTHERMAL ENERGY	(4.9	8.1	13.3)	(3.0	8.1	22.0)
ENERGY SAVING	(17.7	29.1	48.0)	(10.7	29.1	79.1)
NEW ENERGY VECTORS	(4.5	7.4	12.2)	(2.7	7.4	20.1)
BIOMASS ENERGY	(4.8	7.9	13.0)	(2.9	7.9	21.5)
SOLID FUELS	(6.4	10.6	17.5)	(3.9	10.6	28.8)
HYDROCARBONS	(5.5	9.1	15.0)	(3.3	9.1	24.7)
WIND ENERGY	(7.7	12.7	20.9)	(4.7	12.7	34.5)

Table 4. Fuzzy final scores of the alternatives, on the normal scale ($\gamma=1/2$), under varying degrees of fuzziness in the original comparative judgements: Semantically crisp ($\alpha=1$), only one gradation with positive credibility. Shaded judgement ($\alpha=2$), adjacent gradations also with positive credibilities.

ratio of the final scores of two alternatives, j and k say, and compute its logarithm, a fuzzy number represented by the triple

$$\left(\ln\left(\frac{\bar{s}_{j\ell}(\gamma)}{\bar{s}_{ku}(\gamma)}\right), \quad \ln\left(\frac{\bar{s}_{jm}(\gamma)}{\bar{s}_{km}(\gamma)}\right), \quad \ln\left(\frac{\bar{s}_{ju}(\gamma)}{\bar{s}_{k\ell}(\gamma)}\right)\right) =$$

$$= \left(\ln\left(\frac{\bar{s}_{jm}(\gamma)\exp(-\alpha\gamma)}{\bar{s}_{km}(\gamma)\exp(\alpha\gamma)}\right), \ \ln\left(\frac{\bar{s}_{jm}(\gamma)}{\bar{s}_{km}(\gamma)}\right), \ \ln\left(\frac{\bar{s}_{jm}(\gamma)\exp(\alpha\gamma)}{\bar{s}_{km}(\gamma)\exp(-\alpha\gamma)}\right)\right) =$$

$$= \ln\left(\frac{\bar{s}_{jm}(\gamma)}{\bar{s}_{km}(\gamma)}\right) + (-2\alpha\gamma, \ 0, \ 2\alpha\gamma) \ . \tag{28}$$

In order to decide whether $\bar{s}_{jm}(\gamma)/\bar{s}_{km}(\gamma)$ differs significantly from 1, we check whether the triangle corresponding to (28) straddles the origin in a balanced manner or not. Figure 3 explains our definition of the straddle with respect to the origin: it is the ratio of the shaded areas under the triangular membership function. So, for the fuzzy number (28), the straddle is given by

$$S_{jk}(\gamma) = \frac{(2\alpha\gamma - |\ln(\bar{s}_{jm}(\gamma)/\bar{s}_{km}(\gamma))|)^2}{(2\alpha\gamma)^2 + 2(2\alpha\gamma)|\ln(\bar{s}_{jm}(\gamma)/\bar{s}_{km}(\gamma))| - \ln^2(\bar{s}_{jm}(\gamma)/\bar{s}_{km}(\gamma))} \tag{29}$$

In order to show that formula (29) is practically independent from γ, we first recall that the ratio of two crisp final scores (see section 5) is defined by

$$\frac{\bar{s}_{jm}(\gamma)}{\bar{s}_{km}(\gamma)} = \prod_i \left(\frac{\bar{a}_{ijm}(\gamma)}{\bar{a}_{ikm}(\gamma)}\right)^{\bar{c}_{im}(\gamma)} \ .$$

We invoke (6) to write

$$\ln\left(\frac{\bar{v}_j(\gamma)}{\bar{v}_k(\gamma)}\right) = \gamma[\bar{w}_j(1) - \bar{w}_k(1)] \ ,$$

which shows that the logarithm of the ratio of any pair of stimulus weights is linear in γ. Because the alternatives j and k are also stimuli (at the second decision level) we have

$$\ln\left(\frac{\bar{a}_{ijm}(\gamma)}{\bar{a}_{ikm}(\gamma)}\right) = \gamma[\bar{b}_{ijm}(1) - \bar{b}_{ikm}(1)] \ ,$$

and this result can immediately be used to yield

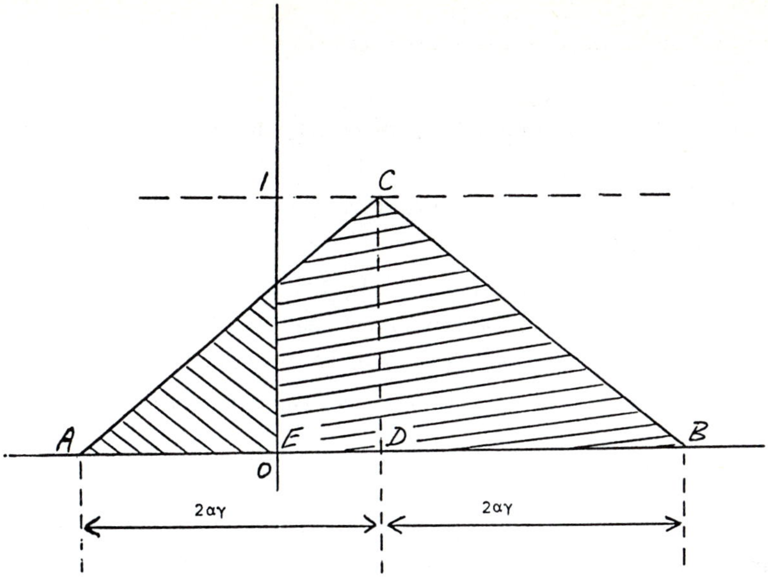

$A = \ln\left(\frac{\bar{s}_{jl}(\gamma)}{\bar{s}_{ku}(\gamma)}\right)$ $D = \ln\left(\frac{\bar{s}_{jm}(\gamma)}{\bar{s}_{km}(\gamma)}\right)$ $B = \ln\left(\frac{\bar{s}_{ju}(\gamma)}{\bar{s}_{kl}(\gamma)}\right)$

E = origin

Figure 3. Straddle of origin by triangular membership function. The ratio of the shaded areas is $(AD-ED)^2/(AD^2 + 2AD.ED - ED^2)$. Obviously, $0 \leq$ straddle ≤ 1, and a small (large) value of the straddle indicates a small (large) amount of overlap of the triangles corresponding to $(\bar{s}_{jl}(\gamma), \bar{s}_{jm}(\gamma), \bar{s}_{ju}(\gamma))$ and $(\bar{s}_{k\ell}(\gamma), \bar{s}_{km}(\gamma), \bar{s}_{ku}(\gamma))$.

$$\ln\left(\frac{\bar{s}_{jm}(\gamma)}{\bar{s}_{km}(\gamma)}\right) = \gamma \sum_i \bar{c}_{im}(\gamma) \, [\bar{b}_{ijm}(1) - \bar{b}_{ikm}(1)] \, ,$$

an expression which is practically linear in the scale parameter γ because the $\bar{c}_{im}(\gamma)$ vary slowly with it. Hence, the straddle $S_{jk}(\gamma)$ of (29) is a *practically scale-independent* measure for the distinction between the alternatives j and k.

We take the complement $P_{jk}(\gamma) = 1 - S_{jk}(\gamma)$ to express our fuzzy preference for one of the two alternatives. So, if $P_{jk}(\gamma) \cong 0$, we are practically indifferent between them, and if $P_{jk}(\gamma) \cong 1$, there is a clear preference for the alternative with the highest modal value.

For a number of research programs in our illustrative example, Table 5 exhibits the preference values, both on the normal scale (γ=1/2) and on the stretched scale (γ=1), when the decision makers admit that their comparative judgements are shaded (α=2). Obviously, energy saving is highly preferred with respect to the other programs, irrespectively of the scale.

11. *BUDGET ALLOCATION*

As soon as final scores for each of the alternatives (the research programs listed in section 2) have been accepted for further decision making, we consider the existing allocation of the budget (166.0 MECU) as well as possible reallocations. We assume that drastic changes from one budget period to the next cannot be made. Furthermore, to focus the discussions on the critical issues, we restrict ourselves to a small number of possible cost levels for each research program. The *current level* will be referred to as the 100% level, and the associated benefits are the final scores just obtained. In the example which is shown in Table 6 we have taken the final scores from our experiments with the normal scale (see Table 1).

Possible deviations from the current level are to be determined by the decision makers. In the example of Table 6, we have shown cost levels at 60%, 80%, 120% and 140% of the current level. The crucial problem now is to decide how the benefits will vary. It is well known that results of a research project are rather sensitive to the budget allocated to it. A small reduction may lead to cuts in travel and communication so that the research team becomes isolated from the scientific community. A small increase may enable the project leader to attract the qualified people who are just needed to obtain significant results. Of course, these effects of budget variations will not automatically emerge. Good research management is required to reap the benefits from an increased budget level, for instance. Nevertheless, we feel that the benefits will vary *nonlinearly* with the costs, and to simplify matters we start off by assuming that they vary *quadratically*. Table 6 accordingly shows benefits at 36%, 64%, 144% and 196% of the current level.

The problem of maximizing the total benefits can easily be formulated as an integer-programming problem with zero-one variables x_{jk}, indicating

ENERGY RESEARCH PROGRAMS AND THEIR MODAL VALUES	ENERGY SAVING 29.1 (if $\gamma=\frac{1}{2}$) 48.4 (if $\gamma=1$)	SOLAR ENERGY 15.0 13.3	WIND ENERGY 12.7 9.7
SOLAR ENERGY 15.0 (if $\gamma=\frac{1}{2}$) 13.3 (if $\gamma=1$)	0.71 0.70		
WIND ENERGY 12.7 9.7	0.79 0.78	0.27 0.27	
BIOMASS ENERGY 7.9 3.3	0.95 0.94	0.70 0.73	0.59 0.63

Table 5. Preference relations between energy research programs on the normal scale ($\gamma=1/2$) and on the stretched scale ($\gamma=1$), when all comparative judgements are shaded ($\alpha=2$). N.B.: a preference value close to 0 indicates indifference, a value close to 1 indicates a strong preference for the program with the highest modal value.

BENEFITS AND COSTS / RESEARCH PROGRAMS		POSSIBLE DEVIATIONS		CURRENT LEVEL	POSSIBLE DEVIATIONS	
	BENEFITS COSTS (MECU)	36% 60%	64% 80%	100% 100%	144% 120%	196% 140%
SOLAR ENERGY	BENEFITS COSTS (MECU) BENEFITS/MECU	5.4 21.3 0.25	9.6 28.4 0.34	15.0 35.5 0.42	21.6 42.6 0.51	29.4 49.7 0.59
GEOTHERMAL ENERGY	idem	2.9 12.6 0.23	5.2 16.8 0.31	8.1 21.0 0.39	11.7 25.2 0.46	15.9 30.2 0.53
ENERGY CONSERVATION	idem	10.5 15.9 0.66	18.6 21.2 0.88	29.1 26.5 1.10	41.9 31.8 1.32	57.0 37.1 1.54
NEW ENERGY VECTORS	idem	2.7 6.0 0.45	4.7 8.0 0.59	7.4 10.0 0.74	10.7 12.0 0.89	14.5 14.0 1.04
BIOMASS ENERGY	idem	2.8 12.0 0.23	5.1 16.0 0.32	7.9 20.0 0.40	11.5 24.0 0.47	15.5 28.0 0.55
SOLID FUELS	idem	3.8 12.0 0.32	6.8 16.0 0.43	10.6 20.0 0.53	15.3 24.0 0.64	20.8 28.0 0.74
HYDROCARBONS	idem	3.3 9.0 0.37	5.8 12.0 0.48	9.1 15.0 0.61	13.1 18.0 0.73	17.8 21.0 0.85
WIND ENERGY	idem	4.6 10.8 0.43	8.1 14.4 0.56	12.7 18.0 0.71	18.3 21.6 0.85	24.9 25.2 0.99

Table 6. Benefits and costs of research programs at the current budget level and at predetermined, lower or higher levels. The benefits are supposed to vary quadratically with the costs. Encircled is the solution to the problem of maximizing the total benefits subject to a budget constraint (166.0 MECU), each research program being supported at one of the five levels.

whether the j-th research program should be supported at the k-th cost level, yes or no. There is one budget constraint, and a logical constraint for each research program stipulating that exactly one of the cost levels should be chosen. The solution may be found encircled in Table 6. It is not surprising that programs with high benefits per MECU should have been identified for increased financial support!

We realize, of course, that these results may depend on the scaling of the judgemental statements and on the presumed cost/benefit relationship of research programs. An extensive sensitivity analysis is required to find stable results. Otherwise, we have to tell the decision makers that their problem cannot completely be solved by the above methodology.

Acknowledgement. It is a pleasure to thank Mr. F. Vos and Ir. T.C.A. Mensch (Delft University of Technology, Faculty of Mathematics and Informatics) for their excellent support during the project described in the present paper. I am also indebted to drs. F. van Scheepen (EEC, Brussels) for the successful coordination of work.

REFERENCES AND LITERATURE

[1] Baas, S., and Kwakernaak, H., Rating and Ranking of Multiple-Aspects Alternatives using Fuzzy Sets. Automatica 13, 47-58, 1977.

[2] Barzilai, J., Cook, W.D., and Golani, B., Consistent Weights for Judgements Matrices of the Relative Importance of Alternatives. To appear in Operations Research Letters, 1987.

[3] Boender, C.G.E., Graan, J.G. de, and Lootsma, F.A., Multi-Criteria Decision Analysis with Fuzzy Pairwise Comparisons. To appear in Fuzzy Sets and Systems, 1987.

[4] Buckley, J.J., Fuzzy Hierarchical Analysis. Fuzzy Sets and Systems 17, 233-247, 1985.

[5] David, H.A., The Method of Paired Comparisons. Griffin, London, 1963.

[6] Dubois, D., and Prade, H., Fuzzy Sets and Systems: Theory and Applications. Academic Press, New York, 1980.

[7] European Community, Non-Nuclear Energy R and D Programme. Directorate-General XII. Commission of the European Community. Wetstraat 200, B-1049 Brussels, Belgium, 1986.

[8] Kok, M., and Lootsma, F.A., Pairwise-Comparison Methods in Multi-objective Programming, with Applications in a Long-term Energy-planning Model. European Journal of Operational Research 22, 44-55, 1985.

[9] Laarhoven, P.J.M. van, and Pedrycz, W., A Fuzzy Extension of Saaty's Priority Theory. Fuzzy Sets and Systems 11, 229-241, 1983.

[10] Légrády, K., Lootsma, F.A., Meisner, J., and Schellemans, F., Multi-criteria Decision Analysis to aid Budget Allocation. In M. Grauer and A.P. Wierzbicki (eds.), Interactive Decision Analysis. Springer, Berlin, 164-174, 1984.

[11] Lockett, G., Hetherington, B., and Yallup, P., Modelling a Research Portfolio using AHP, a Group Decision Process. R&D Management 16, 151-160, 1986.

[12] Lootsma, F.A., Performance Evaluation of Non-linear Optimization Methods via Pairwise Comparison and Fuzzy Numbers. Mathematical Programming 33, 93-114, 1985.

[13] Lootsma, F.A., Modélisation du Jugement Humain dans l'Analyse Multicritère au moyen de Comparaisons par Paires. To appear in the Revue Francaise d'Automatique, d'Informatique et de Recherche Opérationelle, 1987.

[14] Lootsma, F.A., Meisner, J., Schellemans, F., Multi-criteria Decision Analysis as an Aid to Strategic Planning of Energy Research and Development. European Journal of Operational Research 25, 216-234, 1986.

[15] Roy, B., Méthodologie Multicritère d'Aide a la Décision. Collection Gestion, Economica, Paris, 1985.

[16] Saaty, Th.L., The Analytic Hierarchy Process, Planning, Priority Setting, Resource Allocation. McGraw-Hill, New York, 1980.

[17] Saaty, Th.L., and Vargas, L.G., Inconsistency and Rank Preservation. Journal of Mathematical Psychology 28, 205-214, 1984.

[18] Wagenknecht, M., and Hartmann, K., On Fuzzy Rank-Ordering in Poly-optimization. Fuzzy Sets and Systems 11, 253-264, 1983.

[19] Zadeh, L.A., Fuzzy Sets. Information and Control 8, 338-353, 1965.

[20] Zimmermann, H.J., Fuzzy Sets, Decision Making, and Expert Systems. Kluwer, Dordrecht, The Netherlands, 1987.

SOME MATHEMATICAL TOPICS IN THE

ANALYTIC HIERARCHY PROCESS

Thomas L Saaty University of Pittsburgh

1. Introduction

Decisions involving several criteria and alternatives need a correct procedure to combine weights to make tradeoffs and select the best alternatives. There are two parts to the problem, both of which need proof. The first is how to generate judgments and associate numbers with them, and the second is how to combine these numbers in a meaningful way to get an answer.

One needs a theory to justify transforming qualitative judgments to unique numbers that make it possible to trade off the alternatives which ordinarily would have different numerical values and rankings under each criterion. Of course one must have a valid set of weights and rankings for the criteria themselves. This situation is even more complex when the decision involves a hierarchic structure of several levels involving objectives, criteria, sub-criteria, and alternatives.

In other words one cannot assign an arbitrary set of numbers to any of the components of the decision structure and still hope to obtain a valid outcome. Some people argue that the whole process of decision making is so unstructured and so amorphous that it is no use trying to be precise. They say "participant satisfaction" should be the main concern. Thus one observes in the literature that some individuals think it is a simple matter of ingenuity supported with mathematical terminology to improvise ways to generate numbers that please people. Different sets of arbitrary numbers are likely to produce different decisions. If a decision support theory is to be meaningful there must be uniqueness in the representation of judgments, the scales derived from these judgments, and the scales synthesized from the derived scales.

Although convincing others about one's qualitative preferences involves the politics of persuasion and wheeling and dealing, how one's judgments are treated by a decision theory to determine the best alternative is not a political or behavioral process; it is a science of scaling based on mathematics, philosophy and psychology. It is also a science of both careful and faithful representation of the problem capable of capturing its complexity and dependencies.

The Analytic Hierarchy Process (AHP) is a general theory of measurement. It is used to derive ratio scales for the elements in a hierarchy from both discrete and continuous

NATO ASI Series, Vol. F48
Mathematical Models for Decision Support
Edited by G. Mitra

paired comparisons. These comparisons may be expressed in some existing scale or in the fundamental scale of the AHP used to express relative strength of preference concerning some common property of the elements in question. The AHP has a special concern with departure from consistency, its measurement, and on dependence within and between the groups of elements of its structure. It has found its widest applications in multicriteria decision-making, planning and resource allocation, and in conflict resolution. In its general form the AHP is a nonlinear framework for carrying out both deductive and inductive thinking without use of the syllogism by taking several factors into consideration simultaneously and allowing for dependence and for feedback, and making numerical tradeoffs to arrive at a synthesis or conclusion.

This paper presents some of the more recent and interesting results of the AHP in dictionary style and is intended to serve as a brief but comprehensive reference.

2. Axioms and Definitions [6]

Three principles guide one in problem solving using the AHP (Saaty [4]): decomposition, comparative judgments, and synthesis of priorities.

The decomposition principle is applied by structuring a simple problem with elements in a level independent from those in succeeding levels, working downward from the goal in the top level, to criteria bearing on the goal in the second level, followed by subcriteria in the third level, and so on, from the more general (and sometimes uncertain) to the more particular and concrete. Saaty makes a distinction between two types of dependence which he calls functional and structural. The former is the familiar contextual dependence of elements on other elements in performing their function whereas the latter is the dependence of the importance or priority of elements on the priority itself and number of other elements. Absolute measurement, sometimes called scoring, is used when it is desired to ignore structural dependence between elements while relative measurement is used in the alternative case.

The principle of comparative judgments is applied to construct pairwise comparisons of the relative importance of elements in some given level with respect to a shared criterion or property in the level above giving rise to the kind of matrix encountered above and its corresponding principal eigenvector.

The third principle is that of synthesizing the priorities. In the AHP priorities are synthesized from the second level down by multiplying local priorities by the priority of their corresponding criterion in the level above, and adding for each element in a level according to the criteria it affects. (The second level elements are multiplied by unity, the weight of the single top level goal.) This gives the composite or global priority of that element, which is then used to weight the local priorities of the elements in the level below compared to each other with it as the criterion, and so on to the bottom level.

Four axioms govern the Analytic Hierarchy Process and utilize the notion of paired comparisons as a primitive.

Let A be a finite set of n elements called alternatives. Let Z be a set of properties or attributes with respect to which elements in A are compared. We will refer to the elements of Z as criteria. A criterion is a primitive.

We perform binary comparisons on the elements in A according to a criterion in Z. Let $>_C$ be a binary relation on A representing "more preferred than" with respect to a criterion C in Z. Let $\sim_C$ be the binary relation "indifferent to" with respect to a criterion C in Z. Hence, given two elements $A_i, A_j \in A$, either $A_i >_C A_j$ or $A_j >_C A_i$ or $A_i \sim_C A_j$ for all $C \in Z$. We use $A_i \geq_C A_j$ to indicate more preferred or indifferent. A given family of binary relations $>_C$ with respect to a criterion C in Z is a primitive.

Let B be the set of mappings from A x A to R^+ (the set of positive reals). Let f:Z -> B. Let $P_C \in f(C)$ for $C \in Z$. P_C assigns a positive real number to every pair $(A_i, A_j) \in A \times A$. Let $P_C(A_i, A_j) \equiv a_{ij} \in R^+$, $A_i, A_j \in A$. For each $C \in Z$, the triple $(A \times A, R^+, P_C)$ is a <u>fundamental</u> or <u>primitive</u> scale. A fundamental scale is a mapping of objects to a numerical system.

Definition: For all $A_i, A_j \in A$ and $C \in Z$

$$A_i >_C A_j \quad \text{if and only if } P_C(A_i, A_j) > 1,$$

$$A_i \sim_C A_j \quad \text{if and only if } P_C(A_i, A_j) = 1.$$

If $A_i >_C A_j$ we say that A_i dominates A_j with respect to $C \in Z$. Thus P_C represents the intensity or strength of preference for one alternative over another.

<u>Axiom 1 (the Reciprocal Axiom)</u>. For all $A_i, A_j \in A$ and $C \in Z$

$$P_C(A_i, A_j) = 1/P_C(A_j, A_i).$$

This axiom says that the comparison matrices we construct are formed of paired reciprocal comparisons, for if one stone is judged to be five times heavier than another, then the other must perforce be one fifth as heavy as the first. It is this simple but powerful relationship that is the basis of the AHP.

Let $A = (a_{ij}) \equiv (P_C(A_i, A_j))$ be the set of paired comparisons of the alternatives with respect to a criterion $C \in Z$. By the definition of P_C and Axiom 1, A is a positive reciprocal matrix. The object is to obtain a scale of relative dominance (or rank order) of the alternatives from the paired comparisons given in A.

We will now show how to derive the relative dominance of a set of alternatives from a pairwise comparison matrix A. Let $R_{M(n)}$ be the set of (n x n) positive reciprocal matrices $A = (a_{ij}) \equiv (P_C(A_i, A_j))$ for all $C \in Z$. Let $[0,1]^n$ be the n-fold cartesian product of [0,1] and let $\psi: R_{M(n)} \to [0,1]^n$ for $A \in R_{M(n)}$, $\psi(A)$ is an n-dimensional vector whose components lie in the interval [0,1]. The triple $(R_{M(n)}, [0,1]^n, \psi)$ is a derived scale. A derived scale is a mapping between two numerical relational systems.

An important aspect of the AHP is the idea of consistency. If one has a scale for a property possessed by some objects and measures that property in them, then their relative weights with respect to that property are fixed. In this case there is no judgmental inconsistency (although if one has a physical scale and applies it to objects in pairs and <u>then</u> derives the relative standing of the objects on the scale from the pairwise comparison matrix, it is likely that inaccuracies will have occurred in the act of applying the physical scale and again there would be inconsistency). But when comparing with respect to a property for which there is no established scale or measure, we are trying to derive a scale through comparing the objects two at a time. Since the objects may be involved in more than one comparison and we have no standard scale, but are assigning relative values as a matter of judgment, inconsistencies may well occur. In the AHP consistency is defined in the following way, and we are able to measure inconsistency.

Definition. The mapping P_C is said to be consistent if and only if

$$P_C(A_i,A_j)P_C(A_j,A_k) = P_C(A_i,A_k) \text{ for all } i,j,k$$

Similarly, the matrix A is consistent if and only if $a_{ij}a_{jk} = a_{ik}$ for all i,j, and k.

We now turn to the hierarchic axioms, 2, 3, and 4, and related definitions.

In a partially ordered set, we define $x < y$ to mean that $x < y$ and $x \neq y$. y is said to cover (dominate) x. If $x < y$ then $x < t < y$ is possible for no t. We use the notation $x^- = \{y | x \text{ covers } y\}$ and $x^+ = \{y | y \text{ covers } x\}$, for any element x in an ordered set. Let H be a finite partially ordered set. Then H is a hierarchy if it satisfies the conditions:

a) There is a partition of H into sets L_k, $k = 1, \ldots h$ for some h where $L_1 = \{b\}$, b a single element.

b) $x \in L_k$ implies $x^- \subseteq L_{k+1}$ $\quad k = 1,\ldots,h-1$.

c) $x \in L_k$ implies $x^+ \subseteq L_{k-1}$ $\quad k = 2,\ldots,h$.

The notions of fundamental and derived scales can be extended to $x \in L_k$, $x^- \subseteq L_{k+1}$ replacing C and A respectively. The derived scale resulting from comparing the elements in x^- with respect to x is called a local derived scale or the local priorities for the elements in x^-.

Definition. Given a positive real number $\rho \geq 1$, a nonempty set $x^- \subseteq L_{k+1}$ is said to be ρ-homogeneous with respect to $x \in L_k$ if for every pair of elements $y_1, y_2 \in x^-$, $1/\rho \leq P_C(y_1,y_2) \leq \rho$. In particular the reciprocal axiom implies that $P_C(y_i,y_i) = 1$.

<u>Axiom 2 (the Homogeneity Axiom)</u>. Given a hierarchy H, $x \in H$ and $x \in L_k$, $x^- \subseteq L_{k+1}$ is ρ-homogeneous for $k = 1,\ldots,h-1$.

Homogeneity is essential for meaningful comparisons, as the mind cannot compare widely disparate elements. For example, we cannot compare a grain of sand with an orange according to size. When the disparity is great, elements should be placed in separate clusters of comparable size, or in different levels altogether.

Given $L_k, L_{k+1} \subseteq H$, let us denote the local derived scale for

$y \in x^-$ and $x \in L_k$ by $\psi_{k+1}(y/x)$, k=2,3,...,h-1. Without loss of generality we may assume that $\sum_{y \in x^-} \psi_{k+1}(y/x) = 1$. Consider the matrix $\psi_k(L_k/L_{k-1})$ whose columns are local derived scales of elements in L_k with respect to elements in L_{k-1}.

Definition. A set A is said to be <u>outer dependent</u> on a set Z if a fundamental scale can be defined on A with respect to every $C \in Z$.

The process of relating elements (e.g. alternatives) in one level of the hierarchy according to the elements of the next higher level (e.g. criteria) expresses the dependence (what is called <u>outer dependence</u>) of the lower elements on the higher so that comparisons can be made between them. The steps are repeated upward in the hierarchy through each pair of adjacent levels to the top element, the focus or goal.

The elements in a level may also depend on one another with respect to a property in another level. Input-output of industries is an example of the idea of inner dependence, formalized as follows:

Definition. Let A be outer dependent on Z. The elements in A are said to be <u>inner dependent</u> with respect to $C \in Z$ if for some $A_1 \in A$, A is outer dependent on A_1.

<u>Axiom 3</u>. Let H be a hierarchy with levels $L_1, L_2, \ldots, L_h$. For each L_k, k = 1,2,...,h-1,

(1) L_{k+1} is outer dependent on L_k,

(2) L_{k+1} is not inner dependent with respect to all $x \in L_k$,

(3) L_k is not outer dependent on L_{k+1}.

<u>Axiom 4 (the Axiom of Expectations)</u>.

$$Z \subset H - L_h, \quad A = L_h$$

This axiom is merely the statement that thoughtful individuals who have reasons for their beliefs should make sure that their ideas are adequately represented in the model. All alternatives, criteria and expectations (explicit and implicit) can be and should be represented in the hierarchy. This axiom does not assume. People are known at times to harbor irrational expectations and such expectations can be accommodated.

Based on the concepts in Axiom 3 we can now develop a weighting function. For each $x \in H$, there is a suitable weighting function (whose nature depends on the phenomenon being hierarchically structured):

$w_x : \bar{x} \to [0,1]$ such that $\sum_{y \in \bar{x}} w_x(y) = 1$.

Note that h=1 is the last level for which $\bar{x}$ is not empty. The sets L_i are the levels of the hierarchy, and the function w_x is the priority function of the elements in one level with respect to the objective x. We observe that even if $\bar{x} \neq L_k$ (for some level L_k), w_x may be defined for all of L_k by setting it equal to zero for all elements in L_k not in x.

The weighting function is one of the more significant contributions towards the application of hierarchy theory.

<u>Definition</u>: A hierarchy is complete if, for all $x \subset L_k$, $x^+ \subset L_{k-1}$.

We can state the central question:

<u>Basic Problem</u>: Given any element $x \in L_\alpha$, and subset $S \subset L_\beta$, $(\alpha < \beta)$, how do we define a function $w_{x,S} : S \to [0,1]$ which reflects the properties of the priority functions on the levels L_k, $k = \alpha, \ldots, \beta - 1$. Specifically, what is the function $w_{b,L_h} : L_h \to [0,1]$? In less technical terms, this can be paraphrased thus: Given a social (or economic) system with a major objective b, and the set L_h of basic activities, such that the system can be modeled as a hierarchy with largest element b and lowest level L_h.

What are the priorities of the elements of any level and in particular those of L_h with respect to b?

From the standpoint of optimization, to allocate a resource to the elements any interdependence may take the form of input-output relations such as, for example, the interflow of products between industries. A high priority industry may depend on flow of material from a low priority industry. In an optimization framework, the priority of the elements enables one to define the objective function to be maximized, and other hierarchies supply information regarding constraints, e.g., input-output relations.

We now present the method to solve the Basic Problem.

Assume that $Y = \{y_1, \ldots, Y_{m_k}\} \subset L_k$ and that $X = \{x_1, \ldots, x_{m_{k+1}}\} \subset$

L_{k+1}. Without loss of generality we may assume that $X = L_{k+1}$, and that there is an element $v \in L_k$ such that $y_i \in v$.

Then consider the priority functions

$$w_v : Y \rightarrow [0,1] \text{ and } w_{y_j} : X \rightarrow [0,1] \quad j = 1, \ldots, m_k .$$

Construct the priority function of the elements in X with respect to v, denoted w, w: X → [0,1], by

$$w(x_i) = \sum_{j=1}^{m_k} w_{y_j}(x_i) w_v(y_j), \quad i = 1, \ldots, m_{k+1}$$

It is obvious that this is no more than the process of weighting the influence of the element y_j on the priority of x_i by multiplying it with the importance of x_i with respect to z.

The algorithms involved will be simplified if one combines the $w_{y_j}(x_i)$ into a matrix B by setting $b_{ij} = w_{y_j}(x_i)$. If one further sets $w_i = w(x_i)$ and $w_j' = w_v(y_j)$, then the above formula becomes

$$w_i = \sum_{j=1}^{m_k} b_{ij} w_j \qquad i = 1, \ldots, n_{k+1}$$

Thus, one may speak of the priority vector w and, indeed, of the priority matrix b of the (k+1)st level; this gives the final formulation

$$w = Bw'$$

The following is easy to prove:

<u>Theorem</u>. Let H be a complete hierarchy with largest element b and h levels. Let B_k be the priority matrix of the kth level, k = 1, ..., h. If w' is the priority vector of the pth level with respect to some element v in the (p-1)st level, then the priority vector w of the qth level (p<q) with respect to v is given by:

$$w = B_q B_{q-1} \ldots B_{p+1} w'$$

Thus, the priority vector of the lowest level with respect to

the element b is given by:

$$w = B_h B_{h-1} \ldots B_2 b_1$$

if L_1 has a single element, $b_1 = 1$. Otherwise, b_1 is a prescribed vector. We note that the pairwise comparison process takes into consideration nonlinearities. Such nonlinearities are captured by the composition weighting process.

Network Systems

Often alternatives depend on criteria and criteria on alternatives and there should be a cycle connecting the two which is more accurately studied with the network feedback approach. The AHP has been generalized to deal with feedback as shown below, although people generally prefer to simplify and arrange their thinking in terms of a linear hierarchy even if the answers are only approximate.

A network is a set of nodes (each of which consists of a set of elements) and a set of arcs which indicate the order of interaction among the components. The priorities of the elements in each node are components of the principal eigenvector of the matrix of pairwise comparisons of the relative impact of these elements with respect to an element or node with which they interact. The interaction is indicated by an arc of the network. All such eigenvectors define what is known as a supermatrix of impact priorities. By weighting the eigenvectors corresponding to each component by the priority of that component in the system, the supermatrix is transformed into a stochastic matrix. The limiting impact priorities are obtained by computing large powers of this matrix. Formally we have:

Definition: A partially ordered set S is a network system if

a) There is a partition of S into sets C_k, $k = 1, \ldots, s$

b) There is an ordering on C_k, $k = 1, \ldots, s$ such that

$x \subseteq C_k$ implies either x^- or x^+ is in C_{k_j} for some k_j or both $x^- \subseteq C_{k_j}$, $x^+ \subseteq C_{k_j}$ for one or more k_j.

c) For each $x \in S$, there is a suitable weighting function

$$w_x : x^- \to [0,1] \text{ such that } \sum_{y \in x^-} w_x(y) = 1$$

and for $C_k \subseteq S$, $k = 1, \ldots, s$ there is a weighting function

$$w_{(k)} : C_k^- \to [0,1]$$

where $\bar{C}_k = \{C_h \mid C_k \text{ covers } C_h\}$.

We shall now turn to the calculation procedures for the weights and for the inconsistency index.

3. The Eigenvalue Problem

Since this author developed the Analytic Hierarchy Process using the principal eigenvector and compared it with other methods already in use, several other people have suggested these very methods and a few new ones. Old ones are: the method of least squares, logarithmic least squares, weighted least squares and so on; new ones are about variations on the eigenvalue process.

It should be noted that any method that yields nonunique solutions such as the method of least squares is not a good contender. We are aware of various arguments given in favor of one or the other of these methods. For several reasons we believe that the eigenvector is the only procedure to use. Recall that a decision theory must put its house in order before it can help people make choices. Thus if one method leads to a different rank order than another, we must examine the underlying problems and show which approach really addresses all the problems that arise.

The reader might reflect on the following problem. Given two irregular objects, a small one and a large one, how many copies of the small object can be combined to make the larger one? Conversely, into how many parts equal to the smaller object can the larger object be decomposed?

In theory these two questions should yield the same answer, particularly when the comparison involves tangible objects. In practice, the problem requires considerable work by the individual and as he applies himself he is likely to settle for the easier problem of combining copies of the smaller object to make the larger one and not bother with the converse to check on the answer. Even after deep reflection, when the elements being compared are intangibles for which no method of measurement is available, the comparisons are not likely to give the same answer in any case. The individual will usually settle for synthesizing copies of the smaller element to make up the larger one. Thus, by habit, people find it easier to ask for the dominance of the larger object over the smaller than to answer the opposite. Besides, people do not seem to care about whether the general problem of the equivalence of dominating and dominated has an answer and how best to obtain it. Since the two results can in fact differ considerably, and since it is the purpose of a decision theory to measure people's preferences rather than legislate corrections that do not get incorporated into people's thinking to make an impact, the derived scale of measurement should only represent what is given and not what some philosopher or analyst thinks should be or what he thinks is desired from a technical standpoint. If he insists on making the correction, the result may distort the outcome even though the individual believes that he has done his best to represent the problem as he perceives it.

The right eigenvector solution is the correct way to derive a scale from dominance judgments. (A proof of this fact is given below.) To this vector corresponds a left eigenvector. Left and right eigenvectors are reciprocals when the matrix is consistent but they can also be reciprocals when it is not. In general if the matrix is inconsistent it can be written as the elementwise product of a consistent matrix and a reciprocal perturbation matrix. Xu Shubo proved that left and right eigenvectors are reciprocals if and only if the row sums of the perturbation matrix are the same as corresponding column sums.

Information contained in the left eigenvector can be used to measure consistency and hence to decide on whether the information is sufficiently reliable for making a decision. If we write $a_{ij} = (w_i/w_j)\varepsilon_{ij}$ and also $a_{ij} = (v_j/v_i)\theta_{ij}$ where w and v are the right and left eigenvectors respectively, ε and θ are the corresponding perturbation matrices, then we have:

$$\frac{\lambda_{max}-n}{n-1} = -1 + \frac{1}{n(n-1)} \sum_{i<j}\left[\left(\frac{w_j v_j}{w_i v_i} \quad \varepsilon_{ij}\theta_{ij}\right)^{\frac{1}{2}} + \left(\frac{w_j v_j}{w_i v_i} \; \varepsilon_{ij}\theta_{ij}\right)^{-\frac{1}{2}}\right]$$

Some have assumed that the problem of left and right eigenvector relation should be written off by adopting a procedure that essentially ignores the presence of left and right eigenvectors. One simply assumes that they are always reciprocals of one another, artificially forcing the equivalence of the concepts of "dominating" and "dominated." As we already said, such symmetry does not exist in the judgment of people and assuming it dilutes the accuracy of what they express through dominance. However, the answer does not take into account inconsistency in general <u>because the reciprocal relation between left and right eigenvectors does not imply the consistency of the judgment matrix</u>.

It is precisely because of inconsistency that the two answers in general are not the same, and the right eigenvector is used to capture dominance. As we have seen above, the product of left and right eigenvectors puts a bound on inconsistency and the need to improve it to obtain a valid decision. Consistency is the most critical criterion because the greater the inconsistency of a matrix and the closer its entries to being randomly chosen, the less is the reliability of its information content. In decision making the object is not so much to approximate judgments by mathematically minimizing differences as to determine if the information is sufficiently reliable so that a decision can be based on it. One must then compute the priorities in such a way as to capture the dominance expressed in the judgments. It seems to us that the eigenvector is a descriptive rather than a normative approach to the problem.

The foregoing argument shows that the eigenvector captures the way people in fact represent their preferences and does not legislate by an optimization criterion what should be best for them to do. Now for the proof that the eigenvector captures dominance when the matrix is inconsistent.

If $A = (a_{ij})$, $a_{ij} > 0$, $i,j = 1,\ldots, n$, Perron proved that A has a real positive eigenvalue λ_{max} (called the principal eigenvalue of A) that is unique and $\lambda_{max} > |\lambda_k|$ for the remaining eigenvalues of A. Furthermore the principal eigenvector $w = (w_1,\ldots, w_n)$ that is a solution of $Aw = \lambda_{max} w$ is unique to within a multiplicative constant and $w_1 > 0$, $i = 1,\ldots, n$. We can make the solution w unique through normalization. We define the norm of the vector w, $||w|| = we$ where $e = (1,1,\ldots,1)^T$, e^T is its transpose, and to normalize w we divide it by its norm. We shall always think of w in normalized form. My purpose here is to show how important the principal eigenvector is in determining the rank of the alternatives through dominance walks.

There is a natural way to derive the rank order of a set of alternatives from a pairwise comparison matrix A. The rank order of each alternative is the relative proportion of its dominance over the other alternatives. This is obtained by adding the elements in each row in A and dividing by the total over all the rows. However A only captures the dominance of one alternative over each other in one step. But an alternative can dominate a second by first dominating a third alternative and then the third dominates the second. Thus, the first alternative dominates the second in two steps. It is known that the result for dominance in two steps is obtained by squaring the pairwise comparison matrix. Similarly dominance can occur in three steps, four steps and so on, the value of each obtained by raising the matrix to the corresponding power. The rank order of an alternative is the sum of the relative values for dominance in its row, in one step, two steps and so on averaged over the number of steps. The question is whether this average tends to a meaningful limit.

We can think of the alternatives as the nodes of a directed

graph. With every directed arc from node i to node j (which need not be distinct), is associated a nonnegative number a_{ij} of the dominance matrix. In graph-theoretic terms this is the intensity of the arc. Define a k-walk to be a sequence of k arcs such that the terminating node of each arc except the last is the source node of the arc which succeeds it. The <u>intensity of a k-walk</u> is the product of the intensities of the arcs in the walk. With these ideas, we can interpret the matrix A^k: the (i,j) entry of A^k is the sum of the intensities of all k-walks from node i to node j.

<u>Definition</u>: The dominance of an alternative along all walks of length $k \leq m$ is given by

$$\frac{1}{m}\sum_{k=1}^{m}\frac{A^k e}{e^T A^k e}$$

Observe that the entries of $A^k e$ are the row sums of A^k and that $e^T A^k e$ is the sum of all the entries of A^k.

<u>Theorem</u>: The dominance of each alternative along all walks k, as $k \to \infty$ is given by the solution of the eignvalue problem $Aw = \lambda_{max} w$.

<u>Proof</u>:

Let

$$s_k = \frac{A^k e}{e^T A^k e}$$

and

$$t_m = \frac{1}{m}\sum_{k=1}^{m} s_k$$

The convergence of the components of t_m to the same limit as the components of s_m is the standard Cesaro summability. Since

$$s_k = \frac{A^k e}{e^T A^k e} \to w \text{ as } k \to \infty$$

where w is the normalized principal right eigenvector of A, we have

$$t_m = \frac{1}{m}\sum_{k=1}^{m}\frac{A^k e}{e^T A^k e} \to w \text{ as } m \to \infty$$

The essence of the principal eigenvector is to rank alternatives according to dominance in terms of walks. The well-known logarithmic least squares method (LLSM): find the vector $v = (v_1, \ldots, v_n)$ which minimizes the expression

$$\sum_{i,j=1}^{n} \left(\log a_{ij} - \log \frac{v_i}{v_j} \right)^2$$

sometimes proposed as an alternative method of solution, obtains results which coincide with the principal eigenvector for matrices of order two and three, but deviate from it for higher order and can lead to rank reversal. In a certain application in ranking five teachers, the eigenvector ranking was D, B, C, A, E; whereas the LLSM solution ranked them as B, D, C, A, E.

The LLSM minimizes deviations over all the entries of the matrix. The principal eigenvector does not attempt to minimize anything, but maximizes information preserved from all known relations of dominance.

The solution is obtained by raising the matrix to a sufficiently large power then summing over the rows and normalizing to obtain the priority vector $w = (w1, \ldots, wn)$. The process is stopped when the difference between components of the priority vector obtained at the kth power and at the (k+1)th power is less than some pre-determined small value.

An easy way to get an approximation to the priorities is to normalize the geometric means of the rows. This result coincides with the eigenvector for $n \leq 3$. A second way to obtain an approximation is by normalizing the elements in each column of the judgment matrix and then averaging over each row.

We would like to caution the reader that for important applications one should only use the eigenvector derivation procedure because approximations can lead to rank reversal in spite of the closeness of the result to the eigenvector. It is easy to prove that for an arbitrary estimate x of the priority vector

$$\lim_{k} \frac{1}{\lambda_{max}^{k}} A^{k} x = cw$$

where c is a positive constant and w is the principal eigenvector of A. This may be interpreted roughly to say that if we begin with an estimate and operate on it successively by A/λ_{max} to get new estimates, the result converges to a constant multiple of the principal eigenvector.

A simple way to obtain the exact value (or an estimate) of λ_{max} when the exact value (or an estimate) of w is available in normalized form is to add the columns of A and multiply the resulting vector with the vector w. The resulting number is λ_{max} (or an estimate). This follows from

$$\sum_{j=1}^{n} a_{ij} w_j = \lambda_{max} w_i$$

$$\sum_{i=1}^{n} \sum_{j=1}^{n} a_{ij} w_j = \sum_{j=1}^{n} \left(\sum_{i=1}^{n} a_{ij} \right) w_j = \sum_{i=1}^{n} \lambda_{max} w_i = \lambda_{max}$$

The problem is now, how good is the principal eigenvector estimate w? Note that if we obtain $w = (w_1, \ldots, w_n)$ by solving this problem, the matrix whose entries are w_i/w_j is a consistent matrix which is our consistent estimate of the matrix A. The original matrix A itself need not be consistent. In fact, the entries of A need not even be transitive; i.e., A_1 may be preferred to A_2 and A_2 to A_3 but A_3 may be preferred to A_1. What we would like is a measure of the error due to inconsistency. It turns out that A is consistent if and only if $\lambda_{max} = n$ and that we always have $\lambda_{max} \geq n$. This suggests using $\lambda_{max} - n$ as an index of departure from consistency. But

$$\lambda_{max} - n = -\sum_{i=2}^{n} \lambda_i; \quad \lambda_{max} = \lambda_1,$$

where λ_i, i = 1, ..., n are the eigenvalues of A. We adopt the average value $(\lambda_{max}-n)/(n-1)$, which is the (negative) average of λ_i, i=2, ..., n (some of which may be complex conjugates).
It is interesting to note that $2(\lambda_{max}-n)/n-1$ is the variance of the error incurred in estimating a_{ij}. This can be shown by writing

$$a_{ij} = (w_i/w_j)\,\varepsilon_{ij},\quad \varepsilon_{ij} > 0 \text{ and } \varepsilon_{ij} = 1 + \delta_{ij},\quad \delta_{ij} > -1.$$

and substituting in the expression for λ_{max}. It is δ_{ij} that concerns us as the error component and its value $|\delta_{ij}| < 1$ for an unbiased estimator. Normalizing the principal eigenvector yields a uniques estimate of a ratio scale underlying the judgments.

The consistency index of a matrix of comparisons is given by C.I. = λ_{max} -n/n-1. The consistency ratio (C.R.) is obtained by comparing the C.I. with the appropriate one of the following set of numbers each of which is an average random consistency index derived from a sample of size 500 of randomly generated reciprocal matrix using the scale 1/9, 1/8, ..., 1, ...8, 9 to see if it is about 0.10 or less (0.20 may be tolerated but not more). If it is not less than 0.10 study the problem and revise the judgments.

n	1	2	3	4	5	6	7	8	9	10
Random Consistency Index (R.I.)	0	0	.58	.90	1.12	1.24	1.32	1.41	1.45	1.49

Why Tolerate 10% Inconsistency? The priority of consistency to obtain a coherent explanation of a set of facts must differ by an order of magnitude from the priority of inconsistency which is an error in the measurement of consistency. Thus on a scale from zero to one, inconsistency should not exceed .10 by very much. Note that the requirement of 10% should not be made much smaller such as 1% or .1%. The reason is that inconsistency itself is important, for without it new knowledge which changes preference order cannot be admitted. Assuming all knowledge to be consistent contradicts experience which requires continued adjustment in understanding. Thus the objective of developing a wide ranging consistent framework depends on admitting some inconsistency.

This also accounts for why the number of elements compared should be small. If the number of elements is large, their

relative priorities would be small and error can distort these priorities considerably. If the number of items is small and the priorities are comparable a small error does not affect the order of magnitude of the answers and hence the relative priorities would be about the same. For this to happen, the items must be less than ten so their values on the whole would be over 10% each and hence remain relatively unaffected by 1% error for example.

The consistency index for an entire hierarchy is defined by

$$C_H = \sum_{j=1}^{h} \sum_{i=1}^{n_{i_{j+1}}} w_{ij} \mu_{i,j+1}$$

where $w_{ij} = 1$ for $j = 1$, and $n_{i_{j+1}}$ is the number of elements of the (j+1)st level with respect to the ith criterion of the jth level.

Let $|\bar{C}_k|$ be the number of elements of $\bar{C}_k$, and let $w_{(k)(h)}$ be the priority of the impact of the hth component on the kth component, i.e., $w_{(k)(h)} = w_{(k)}(C_h)$ or $w_{(k)} : C_h \to w_{(k)(h)}$. If we label the components of a system along lines similar to those we followed for a hierarchy, and denote by w_{jk} the limiting priority of the jth element in the kth component, we have

$$C_S = \sum_{k=1}^{s} \sum_{j=1}^{n_k} w_{jk} \sum_{h=1}^{|\bar{C}_k|} w_{(k)(h)} \mu_k(j,h)$$

where $\mu_k(j,h)$ is the consistency index of the pairwise comparison matrix of the elements in the kth component with respect to the jth element in the hth component.

4. Rank Preservation and Reversal

In what follows we need two abstract concepts from systems theory to deal with what P. Selznick [9] called structural-functional analysis. These are the dual concepts of form and activity or of structure and function encountered frequently in the analysis of decisions when using AHP. Function generally is understood to be a criterion or property that can be used to describe behavior or change in a system. The structure of a system is the number and arrangement of its parts to perform a function. E. Nagel [1] defined the functions of a system as those observed consequences, produced by a change in a state variable, that cause it to adapt or adjust provided that the variations preserve the system in a particular state. J. Piaget [2] defined structure as a set of parts or forms that relate together in a specific order to perform a function.

Clearly we often need to distinguish between the functions performed by the elements of a system and the structural aspects of the system. Structural aspects, such as the number of elements and their actual measurements under each criterion, are not reflected in information about the relative importance of the elements in performing various functions. As we have seen in the previous section, this functional importance always is affected by structural information when relative measurement is used.

Here is another example of a structural criterion. Suppose an investment in stocks is made according to the priority of that sector of the economy to which each stock belongs. It is essential that the priorities of sectors be modified according to the relative number of stocks in each sector. Otherwise, an important sector with a large number of stocks would distribute a small priority to each stock, resulting in a higher priority of investment being assigned to stocks belonging to less important sectors. Here the number of elements in each sector must be considered as a structural criterion. With relative measurement, we can see that structural and functional information are inextricably linked. The functional criteria depend on structural information; and the latter can be used effectively for making decisions only with structural criteria that amount to transformations of the priorities of the functional criteria.

The mathematics of this subject of structural criteria is found in reference [8].

REFERENCES

1. Nagel, J., "A Formalization of Functionalism," in Logic without Metaphysics, New York: Free Press, 1956.

2. Piaget, J., Structuralism, New York: Harper and Row, 1968.

3. Saaty, R., "The Analytic Hierarchy Process: What It Is and How It Is Used," J. Math. Mod., Special Issue on the Analytic Hierarchy Process, 1987.

4. Saaty, T., The Analytic Hierarchy Process, McGraw-Hill, 1980.

5. Saaty, T., Decision Making for Leaders, University of Pittsburgh, 322 Mervis Hall, Pittsburgh, PA 15260, revised edition 1986.

6. Saaty, T., "Axiomatic Foundation of the Analytic Hierarchy Process," Management Science, Vol. 32, No. 7, July 1986.

7. Saaty, T. and L. Vargas, "Stimulus-Response with Reciprocal Kernels: The Rise and Fall of Sensation," Journal of Mathematical Psychology, Vol. 31, No. 1, March, 1987.

8. Saaty, T., "Rank Generation, Preservation, and Reversal in the Analytic Hierarchy Decision Process," Decision Sciences, Vol. 18, No. 2, Spring 1987.

9. Selznick, P.,"Foundations of the Theory of Organizations," American Sociological Review, Vol. 13, 1948.

WHAT IS THE ANALYTIC HIERARCHY PROCESS?

Thomas L Saaty

University of Pittsburgh

1. Introduction

In our everyday life, we must constantly make choices concerning what tasks to do or not to do, when to do them, and whether to do them at all.

Many problems such as buying the most cost effective home computer expansion, a car, or house; choosing a school or a career, investing money, deciding on a vacation place, or even voting for a political candidate are common everyday problems in personal decision making. Other problems can occur in business decisions such as buying equipment, marketing a product, assigning management personnel, deciding on inventory levels or the best source for borrowing funds. There are also local and national governmental decisions like whether to act or not to act on an issue, such as building a bridge or a hospital, how to allocate funds within a department or how to vote on a city council issue.

All these are essentially problems of choice. In addition they are complex problems of choice. They also involve making a logical decision. The human mind is not capable of considering all the factors and their effects simultaneously. People solve these problems today with seat of the pants judgments or by mathematical models based on assumptions not readily verifiable that draw conclusions that may not be clearly useful.

Typically individuals make these choices on a reactive and frequently unplanned basis with little forethought of how the decisions tie together to form one integrated plan. This whole process of deciding what, when, and whether to do certain tasks is the crux of this process of setting priorities. The priorities may be long-term or short-term, simple or complex.

NATO ASI Series, Vol. F48
Mathematical Models for Decision Support
Edited by G. Mitra

Some organization is needed. This organization can be obtained through a hierarchical representation. But that is not all. Judgments and measurements have to be included and integrated. A procedure which satisfies these requirements is the Analytic Hierarchy Process (AHP). The mathematical thinking behind the process is based on linear algebra. Until recently its connection to decision making was not adequately studied. With the introduction of home computers basic linear algebra problems can be solved easily so that it is now possible to use the AHP on personal computers. The AHP differs from conventional decision analysis techniques by requiring that its numerical approach to priorities conform with scientific measurement. By this we mean that if appropriate scientific experiments are carried out using the scale of the AHP for paired comparisons, the scale derived from these should yield relative values that are the same or close to what the physical law underlying the experiment dictates according to known measurements in that area. The Analytic Hierarchy Process is of particular value when subjective, abstract or nonquantifiable criteria are involved in the decision.

With the AHP we have a means of identifying the relevant facts and the interrelationships that exist. Logic plays a role but not to the extent of breaking down a complex problem and determining relationships through a deductive process. For example, logic says that if I prefer A over B and B over C, then I must prefer A over C. This is not necessarily so (consider the example of soccer team A beating soccer team B, soccer team B beating soccer team C and then C turning around and beating A, and not only that, the odds makers may well have given the advantage to C prior to the contest based on the overall records of all three teams) and the AHP allows such inconsistencies in its framework.

A basic premise of the AHP is its reliance on the concept that much of what we consider to be "knowledge" actually pertains to our instinctive sense of the way things really are. This would seem to agree with Descartes' position that the mind itself is the first knowable principle. The AHP therefore takes as its premise the idea that it is our conception of reality that is crucial and not our conventional representations of that reality by such means as statistics, etc. With the AHP it is possible for practitioners to assign numerical values to what are essentially abstract concepts and then deduce from these values decisions to apply in the global framework.

The Analytic Hierarchy Process is a decision making model that aids us in making decisions in our complex world. It is a three part process which includes identifying and organizing decision objectives, criteria, constraints and alternatives into a hierarchy; evaluating pairwise comparisons between the relevant elements at each level of the hierarchy; and the synthesis using the solution algorithm of the results of the pairwise comparisons over all the levels. Further, the algorithm result gives the relative importance of alternative courses of action.

To summarize, the AHP process has eight major uses. It allows the decision maker to: 1) design a form that represents a complex problem; 2) measure priorities and choose among alternatives; 3) measure consistency; 4) predict; 5) formulate a cost/benefit analysis; 6) design forward/backward planning; 7) analyze conflict resolution; 8) develop resource allocation from the cost/benefit analysis.

For the pairwise comparison judgments a scale of 1 to 9 is utilized. This is not simply an assignment of numbers. The relative intensity of the elements being compared with respect to a particular property becomes critical. The numbers indicate the strength of preference for one over the other. Ideally, when the pairwise comparison process is begun, numerical values should not be assigned, rather the comparative strengths should be verbalized as indicated in the table below of the fundamental scale of relative importance that is the basis for the AHP judgments.

2. The Scale

Pairwise comparisons are fundamental in the use of the AHP. We must first establish priorities for the main criteria by judging them in pairs for their relative importance, thus generating a pairwise comparison matrix. Judgments used to make the comparisons are represented by numbers taken from the fundamental scale below. The number of judgments needed for a particular matrix of order n, the number of elements being compared, is n(n-1)/2 because it is reciprocal and the diagonal elements are equal to unity. There are conditions under which it is possible to use fewer judgments and still obtain accurate results. The comparisons are made by asking how much more important the element on the left of the matrix is perceived to be with respect to the property in question than the element on the top of the matrix. It is important to formulate the right question to get the right answer.

The scale given below can be validated for its superiority over any other assignment of numbers to judgments by taking one of the two illustrative matrices given below and inserting instead of the numbers given numbers from another scale that is not simply a small perturbation or constant multiple of our scale. It will be found that the resulting derived scale is markedly different and does not correspond to the known result.

TABLE 1

THE FUNDAMENTAL SCALE

Intensity of Importance on an Absolute Scale	Definition	Explanation
1	Equal importance.	Two activities contribute equally to the objective.
3	Moderate importance of one over another.	Experience and judgment strongly favor one activity over another.
5	Essential or strong importance.	Experience and judgment strongly favor one activity over another.
7	Very strong importance.	An activity is strongly favored and its dominance demonstrated in practice.
9	Extreme importance.	The evidence favoring one activity over another is of the highest possible order of affirmation.
2,4,6,8	Intermediate values between the two adjacent judgments.	When compromise is needed.
Reciprocals	If activity i has one of the above numbers assigned to it when compared with activity j, then j has the reciprocal value when compared with i.	
Rationals	Ratios arising from the scale.	If consistency were to be forced by obtaining n numerical values to span the matrix.

When the elements being compared are closer together than indicated by the scale, one can use the scale 1.1, 1.2, ..., 1.9. If still finer, one can use the appropriate percentage refinement.

There are various ways of carrying out measurement and in particular pairwise comparisons. When the elements being compared share a measurable property such as weight, they can be measured directly on an absolute scale and pairwise comparisons become unnecessary. However if one were to use the AHP and forms ratios of these weights (resulting in a consistent matrix) then solving for the principal eigenvector, gives the same result obtained by normalizing the numbers. It is rare that numbers should be used in this way. It is almost always the case that measurements only represent some kind of arithmetical accuracy which does not reflect the actual judgment or value that an individual would assign to the numbers to reflect the satisfaction of his needs. In some situations habituation and familiarity may cause people to use the numbers as they are. It must be understood that they should be able to justify how these numbers correspond to their own judgment of the relative intensity of importance.

There are times when people use their judgments to estimate numerical magnitudes. They should do so by comparing them. Otherwise, numbers or ranges of numbers can be arranged into intensity equivalence classes and then compared either by directly using representative numbers from each range, or indirectly by comparing them qualitatively according to intensity. For example, numbers in the millions, billions or trillions may mean the same thing to an individual who is either unfamiliar with very large numbers or does not know what these values apply to or if known, there may still be no way to incorporate in one's judgment or understanding the significance of their magnitudes. Here we need to remember that the reason for a hierarchic structure is to decompose complexity in stages to enable us to scale its smallest elements gradually upwards in terms of its largest elements. If it were possible to assign meaningful numerical values to the smallest elements, there would be no need for the elaborate process of careful decomposition.

Thus the question remains as to how responsive can individual judgments be to make it possible to discriminate between elements sharing a property or properties sharing a higher property. One of the axioms of the AHP relates to how disparate the elements are allowed to be.

In making paired comparisons, the accuracy of the judgments and hence also the derived scale may be improved by ordering the elements according to rank in descending or ascending order. In addition one may compare the largest element with the smallest one first, or alternatively, take the middle element as the basis of the comparisons.

One problem then in teaching people to use the AHP is first to specify qualitative intensities of judgment and feeling that facilitate spontaneous response without elaborate prior training and second to associate appropriate linguistic designations with these expressions. Finally, numerical scale values must in turn be associated with these verbal expressions that lead to meaningful outcomes and particularly in known situations can be tested for their accuracy. Small changes in the words (or the numbers) should lead to small changes in the derived answer.

Finally we use consistency arguments along with the well-known work of Fechner in psychophysics to derive and substantiate the scale and its range.

In 1860 Fechner considered a sequence of just noticeable increasing stimuli. He denotes the first one by s_o. The next just noticeable stimulus by

$$s_1 = s_o + \Delta s_o = s_o + \frac{\Delta s_o}{s_o} s_o = s_o(1+r)$$

having used Weber's law.

Similarly

$$s_2 = s_1 + \Delta s_1 = s_1(1+r) = s_o(1+r)^2 \equiv s_o \alpha^2$$

In general

$$s_n = s_{n-1}\alpha = s_o \alpha^n \quad (n = 0,1,2,\ldots)$$

Thus stimuli of noticeable differences follow sequentially in a geometric progression. Fechner felt that the corresponding sensations should follow each other in an arithmetic sequence occurring at the discrete points at which just noticeable differences occur. But the latter are obtained when we solve for n. We have

$$n = (\log s_n - \log s_o)/\log \alpha$$

and sensation is a linear function of the logarithm of the stimulus. Thus if M denotes the sensation and s the stimulus, the psychophysical law of Weber-Fechner is given by

$$M = a \log s + b, \quad a \neq 0$$

We assume that the stimuli arise in making pairwise comparisons of relatively comparable activities. We are interested in responses whose numberical values are in the form of ratios. Thus b = 0, from which we must have $\log s_o = 0$ or $s_o = 1$, which is possible by calibrating a unit stimulus. The next noticeable response is due to the stimulus

$$s_1 = s_0 \alpha = \alpha$$

This yields a response $\log \alpha / \log \alpha = 1$. The next stimulus is

$$s_2 = s_o \alpha^2$$

which yields a response of 2. In this manner we obtain the sequence 1,2,3,.... For the purpose of consistency we place the activities in a cluster whose pairwise comparison stimuli give rise to responses whose numerical values are of the same order of magnitude. In practice, qualitative differences in response to stimuli are few. Roughly, there are five distinct ones as listed above with additional ones that are compromises between adjacent responses. The notion of compromise is particularly observable in the thinking judgmental process as opposed to the senses. This brings the total up to nine which is compatible with the order of magnitude assumption made earlier.

Now we examine the impact of consistency on scaling. The conscious mind absorbs new ideas by contrasting them through scanning or through concentration and analysis to understand how they are similar to familiar ideas. They are also related to current or future activities and applied to concrete situations to test their compatibility with what is already believed to be workable.

The ideas may be accepted as a consistent part of the existing understanding or they may be inconsistent with what is already known or accepted. In that case the system of understanding and practice is extended and adjusted to include the new ideas.

Growth implies such expansion. If the adjustment of old ideas to accommodate a new one is drastic, then the inconsistency caused by the new idea is great and may require considerable adjustments in the old ideas and beliefs whose old relations may no longer be intuitively recognizable and may call for a new theory or interpretation if at all possible. But such major changes cannot be made every hour, every day or even every week because it takes time to interpret and assimilate relations. Thus inconsistency arising from exposure to new ideas or situations can be threatening, unsettling and painful. Our biology has recognized this and developed for us ways to filter information in such a way that we usually make minor adjustments in what we already know when we are exposed to a new idea or better that we absorb new ideas by interpreting them from the vantage point of already established relations. Thus our emphasis on consistency exceeds our desire for exposure and readjustment. As a result maintaining consistency is considered to be a higher priority of importance than changing. Yet the latter is considered to be also an important concern. One conclusion is that our preoccupation with consistency differs by one order of magnitude from our preoccupation with inconsistency - a split of 90% and 10%.

In addition, in order to maintain their identity, the significance of old ideas must be visibly greater than the adjustments we bring into them because of exposure to the new. In other words, the 90% effort to maintain consistency can at best be divided among a few entities (at most 9) each of which would receive emphasis or priority of the order of 10% in the understanding so that slight readjustment would not change the old relations significantly. If one were to compare homogeneous objects one would not need a scale whose range extends beyond 9.

Before moving on to elaborate decision examples let us illustrate the use of the scale in two elementary examples. These are neither decision nor hierarchical examples. Those will come later below. These examples are to demonstrate that the AHP scheme for assigning measures works. It will be seen that even though a person may not have an idea of the final numerical value by making the comparisons according to his everyday knowledge the derived answer appears to be very reasonable. The first illustration below asks the individual to provide judgments as to which of the seven drinks listed in the matrix is consumed more in the United States, and how strongly more. In the second example he is asked to compare seven foods according to his idea of the relative amount of protein in each. In both cases what is desired is the relative percentage that each has as part of the total for the seven drinks or the seven foods. In both cases we have given the derived estimate and the actual results taken from statistical sources. What is important here is that the judgments were provided by very average people who had no idea of the true answer.

Drink Consumption in the U.S.	Coffee	Wine	Tea	Beer	Sodas	Milk	Water
Coffee	1	9	5	2	1	1	1/2
Wine		1	1/3	1/9	1/9	1/9	1/9
Tea			1	1/3	1/4	1/3	1/9
Beer				1	1/2	1	1/3
Sodas					1	2	1/2
Milk						1	1/3
Water							1

Note that the lower triangular half of this matrix is not given. Those entries are the reciprocals of the entries in the upper triangular half and it is not necessary to show them, although of course they enter in the calculations. The derived scale representing the priorities (or relative values) is obtained by solving for the principal eigenvector of the eigenvalue problem $Aw = \lambda_{max} w$ where A is the matrix of judgments.

The derived scale based on the judgments in the matrix is:

Coffee	Wine	Tea	Beer	Sodas	Milk	Water
.177	.019	.042	.116	.190	.129	.327

with a consistency ratio of .022.

The actual consumption (from statistical sources) is:
.180 .010 .040 .120 .180 .140 .330

In the second example an individual gives judgments as to the relative amount of protein in each food.

Protein in Foods	A	B	C	D	E	F	G
A: Steak	1	9	9	6	4	5	1
B: Potatoes		1	1	1/2	1/4	1/3	1/4
C: Apples			1	1/3	1/3	1/5	1/9
D: Soybean				1	1/2	1	1/6
E: Whole Wheat Bread					1	3	1/3
F: Tasty Cake						1	1/5
G: Fish							1

Here the derived scale and actual values are:

Steak	Potatoes	Apples	Soybean	Whole Wheat Bread	Tasty Cake	Fish
.345	.031	.030	.065	.124	.078	.328
.370	.040	.000	.070	.110	.090	.320

with a consistency ratio of .028.

3. Absolute and Relative Measurement

Cognitive psychologists [1] have recognized for some time that there are two kinds of comparisons, absolute and relative. In the former an alternative is compared with a standard in memory developed through experience; in the latter alternatives are compared in pairs according to a common attribute. The AHP has been used to carry out both types of comparisons resulting in ratio scales of measurement. We call the scales derived from absolute and relative comparisons respectively absolute and relative measurement scales. Both relative and absolute measurement are included in the IBM PC compatible software package Expert Choice [2].

Let us note that relative measurement is usually needed to compare criteria in all problems particularly when intangible ones are involved. Absolute measurement is applied to rank the alternatives in terms of the criteria or rather in terms of ratings or intensities of the criteria such as excellent, very good, good, average, below average, poor and very poor. After setting priorities on the criteria (or subcriteria, if there are some) pairwise comparisons are also performed on the ratings which may be different for each criterion (or subcriterion). An alternative is evaluated, scored or ranked by identifying for each criterion or subcriterion, the relevant rating which describes that alternatives best. Finally, the weighted or global priorities of the ratings, one under each criterion corresponding to the alternative, are added to produce a ratio scale score for that alternative. If desired, in the end, the scores of all the alternatives may be normalized to unity.

Absolute measurement needs standards, often set by society for convenience, and sometimes has little to do with the values and objectives of a judge making comparisons. In completely new decision problems or old problems where no standards have been established, we must use relative measurement to identify the best one among the alternatives by comparing them in pairs.

It is clear that with absolute measurement there can be no reversal in the rank of the alternatives if a new alternative is added or another one deleted. This is desirable when the importance of the criteria, although independent from the alternatives according to function, meaning or context does not depend on their number and on their priorities as it does in relative measurement. In the latter if for example, the students in a certain school perform badly on intelligence tests, the priority of intelligence which is an important criterion used to judge students, may be rescaled by dividing by the sum of the paired comparison value of the students, a transformation carried out through normalization. The priority of each other criterion is also rescaled according to the performance of the students. Thus the criteria weights are affected by the weights of the alternatives.

It is worth noting that although rank may change when using relative measurement with respect to several criteria, it does not change when only one criterion is used and the judgments are consistent. It can never happen that an apple which is more red than another apple becomes less red than that apple on introducing a third apple in the comparisons. It would be counter-intuitive were that to happen. However, when judging apples on several criteria, each time a new apple is introduced, a criterion that is concerned with the number of apples being compared changes as does another criterion concerned with the actual comparisons of the apples. Such criteria are called structural. The way they participate in generating the final weights differs from the traditional way in which the other criteria, called functional, do [4].

Let us now illustrate both types of measurement in decision making.

4. Examples of Relative and Absolute Measurement

Relative Measurement:Reagan's Decision to Veto the Highway Bill

Before President Reagan vetoed the Highway Bill, a high budget bill to repair roads and provide jobs in the economy in the U.S., we predicted that he would veto it by constructing two hierarchies, one to measure the benefits and the other the costs of the possible alternatives of the decision and taking that with the highest benefit to cost ratio. The public image of Ronald Reagan had been tarnished since the "Iran-Contra" affair. His leadership abilities for the remainder of his term were being questioned. He looked at this Bill (a very popular bill with the public) as an opportunity to improve his own and his party's image. We imagined that he subconsciously went through something organized along the lines shown here to make the decision. Because of space limitation we will simply present the hierarchies and the results.

BENEFITS HIERARCHY

Goal:	Best Decision			
Criteria:	Political Image (.634)	Efficiency (.157)	Employment (.152)	Convenience (.057)
Alternatives:	Veto for Modification (.607)		Sign Bill (.393)	

In the benefits hierarchy Mr. Reagan's political image has by far the greatest weight followed by employment, the creation of 800,000 jobs if the bill were to pass.

COSTS HIERARCHY

Goal:	Best Decision				
Criteria:	Political Image (.524)	Energy (.062)	Construction (.312)	Maintenance (.041)	Safety (.061)
Alternatives:	Veto for Modification (.518)		Sign Bill (.482)		

In the costs hierarchy Mr Reagan has his political image foremost on his mind with the construction cost of $86 billion a fairly distant second. The benefit to cost ratios of the alternatives from the two hierarchies are: Veto Bill for Modification .607/.518 = 1.172, Sign Bill .393/.482 = .815. Thus Veto for Modification was the preferred outcome. In order to modify the bill, President Reagan vetoed it, then sent it back to Congress with a strong message to them to modify it and resubmit.

One thing we need to mention here is that the two alternatives must be compared in a separate matrix with respect to each criterion and the resulting derived scales are each weighted by the priority of the corresponding criterion and summed for each alternative to obtain the overall priority shown for that alternative. For example, in the benefits hierarchy the derived scales and the weights of the criteria may be arranged and composed as follows.

	Political Image (.634)	Efficiency (.157)	Employment (.152)	Convenience (.057)	Composite Weights
Modify Bill	.89	.10	.10	.20	.607
Sign Bill	.11	.90	.90	.80	.393

Note for example that the composite weight:

$$.607 = .89 \times .634 + .10 \times .157 + .10 \times .152 + .20 \times .057$$

A final comment here is that the AHP has a more elaborate framework to deal with dependence within a level of a hierarchy or between levels [3], but we will not go into such details here.

Absolute Measurement:Employee Evaluation

The problem is to evaluate employee performance. The hierarchy for the evaluation and the priorities derived through paired comparisons is shown below. It is then followed by rating each employee for the quality of his performance under each criterion and summing the resulting scores to obtain his overall rating. The same approach can be used for student admissions, giving salary raises, etc. The hierarchy can be more elaborate, including subcriteria, followed by the intensities for expressing quality.

Goal:	Employee Performance Evaluation					
Criteria:	Technical (.061)	Maturity (.196)	Writing skills (.043)	Verbal skills (.071)	Timely work (.162)	Potential (personal) (.466)
Intensities:	Excell. (.604)	Very (.731)	Excell. (.733)	Excell. (.750)	Nofollup (.731)	Great (.750)
	Abv.Avg. (.245)	Accep. (.188)	Average (.199)	Average (.171)	OnTime (.188)	Average (.171)
	Average (.105)	Immat. (.081)	Poor (.068)	Poor (.078)	Remind (.081)	Bel.Av. (.078)
	Bel.Av. (.046)					

Alternatives:

1) Mr. X	Excell	Very	Average	Excell.	OnTime	Great
2) Ms. Y	Average	Very	Average	Average	Nofollup	Average
3) Mr. Z	Excell	Immat.	Average	Excell.	Remind	Great

Let us now show how to obtain the total score for Mr. X:

$$.061 \times .604 + .196 \times .731 + .043 \times .199 + .071 \times .750 + .162 \times .188 + .466 \times .750 = .623$$

Similarly the scores for Ms. Y and Mr. Z can be shown to be .369 and .478 respectively.

It is clear that we can rank any number of candidates along these lines.

REFERENCES

1. Blumenthal, A.L., <u>The Process of Cognition</u>, Prentice-Hall, Englewood Cliffs, 1977.

2. Expert Choice, Software Package for IBM PC, Decision Support Software, 1300 Vincent Place, McLean, VA 22101.

3. Saaty, Thomas L., <u>The Analytic Hierarchy Process</u>, McGraw-Hill, 1981.

4. Saaty, Thomas L., "Rank Generation, Preservation, and Reversal in the Analytic Hierarchy Decision Process", <u>Decision Sciences</u>, Vol. 18, No. 2, Spring 1987.

AN INTERACTIVE DSS FOR MULTIOBJECTIVE INVESTMENT PLANNING

J. TEGHEM Jr.
Faculté polytechnique de Mons
9, rue de Houdain,
7000 MONS (Belgium)

P.L. KUNSCH
Belgonucléaire
Rue du Champ de Mars, 25
1050 BRUXELLES (Belgium)

1. INTRODUCTION

In the field of Investment Planning within a time horizon, problems typically involve multiple decision objectives and basic data are uncertain. In a large number of cases, these decision problems can be written as linear programming systems in which time dependent uncertainties affect the coefficients of objectives and of several constraints. Given the possibility of defining plausible scenarios on basic data, discrete sets of such coefficients are given, each with its subjective probability of occurrence. Moreover, these investment problems very often include some integer variables. The corresponding structure is then characteristic for Multi-Objective Stochastic and Integer Linear Programming (MOSILP).

A decision support system (DSS) is designed to obtain best compromise solutions for such a MOSILP. It is presently implemented in a Belgian firm.

Initially, it was developped to deal with energy systems planning with continuous variables. Two real world problems have been analysed :

a) Dispersed power system planning (see [10])

In a Third World Country, small isolated communities, with no industrial activities and far removed from the grid are initially supplied entirely with Diesel generators. The clear sky conditions are favourable to the adoption of solar generators with a large energy storage capability. The problem consists in comparing the merits of a particular type of thermodynamic electrosolar system with the traditional Diesel generators and in defining a planning schedule for their possible introduction.
A model is set up to represent the electricity production system and the dynamic implementation of either diesel or solar generators.
The two first objectives to decide on this implementation can be easily defined :

- the total production costs, discounted at the start of the time horizon;
- the outside expenses measuring the dependance with regard to the outside world.

NATO ASI Series, Vol. F48
Mathematical Models for Decision Support
Edited by G. Mitra

The third objective deals with the uncertainties affecting several production constraints. Its definition is based in some limitations affecting the production engines :

- Diesel generators can experience diesel fuel scarcity (external embargo, governmental control, ...) for which plausible forecasts are given by the experts.
- Solar generators require a minimum level of insolation. Historical data on covered days are available for the specific site.

These limitations on energy production introduce uncertainties in the right hand side (RHS) of several constraints. The third objective is then introduced as explained in section 3 : it represents the safety of energy supply, based on availability of fuel and reliability of insolation.

b) Optimal use of the nuclear fuel (see [5])

Conventional nuclear reactors (Ligh Water Reactors, LWR) are fuelled with uranium enriched in the fissile isotope U-235. The fuel is irradiated during about three years in the reactor. After its unloading, it still contains about 96% of fissile materials. Therefore from an efficiency point of view it is quite profitable to recycle the burnt fuel. First fissile products have to be eliminated. This operation is called reprocessing, and can be carried out in only few plants in Europe. Moreover it increases the variable costs in nuclear electricity production. Becausė in the present days, natural uranium is still very abundant there is no strong economic incentive to practice recycling and it is often preferred to store the burnt fuel. However in the long term, recycling meets the objectives of energetic independance and of safety of supply, because most countries have to import their uranium. Moreover the country with a nuclear programme might think about the opportunity to develop its own recycling technology, also because of the positive impact on nuclear industry (employment and know-how).

This decision problem has been analysed in a linear model with the four following objectives : production cost of nuclear electricity; importation volume of natural uranium; commercial balance ; employment in nuclear industry. Two important parameters in the evaluation of costs are the price of natural uranium and the cost of reprocessing. They are taken into account by means of scenarios.

Thanks to those examples the methodology applied in the DSS is now well established. This approach can be applied to other fields like management and finance ; for instance, it is presently used to treat a portfolio selection model which is naturally a multi-objective problem : the objectives may be the expected return, the dividend yield, the sensibility of the portfolio to changes in different exogeneous variables like the Gross National Product, the inflation rate, ...

In the course of further developments the method and it computerized tools have been extended to non linear objective functions and modified to be able to accept discrete variables in the structure of the problem.

This DSS is interactive so that at each phase the decision maker's preferences are taken into account to construct a best compromise. To demonstrate the potentialities of this method and to make it more easily accessible micro-computer versions of the DSS will be issued in a close future.

2. THE PROBLEM

The following problem of MOSILP is considered :

$$\text{"min"} \quad z_k = c^k.X \qquad k=1,\dots,K$$
$$X\varepsilon D = \{X \mid TX \leqq d, x_j \geqq 0 \text{ for } j\varepsilon N_1, \; x_j \text{ integer} \geqq 0 \text{ for } j\varepsilon N_2\}$$

where c^k and (T,d) are "discrete random variables" ; more precisely

- Each linear objective function depends on S different scenarios, each of them being affected by a subjective probability ; let c^{ks} (s=1,...,S) be the possible values of c^k and p_s the subjective probability of scenario s. (The scenarios are possibly different for each objective : see [11] ; to simplify the notations, this case is not considered here).
- some elements of the constraints are uncertain ; let (T^r, d^r) (r=1,...,R) be the possible outcomes of matrix (T,d) and q_r the corresponding probability.

Three methods are integrated in the DSS :

- STRANGE is specially designed for the continuous case MOSLP ($N_2=\emptyset$) ; let us note that in the basic paper [11] describing this method, uncertainties are considered only in the RHS of the constraints as it often the case in real applications (see [5,10]) ; nevertheless STRANGE can be extended without difficulties to uncertainties in the LHS too.

- RB-STRANGE is an extension of STRANGE to the case of non linear objective functions : the Miller's method (see [16]) is applied using piece-wise linear functions in an extended version of the simplex method called "Restricted Basis" (RB) ; see [3] for details.

- STRANGE-MOMIX is developed for the mixed integer case($N_2 \neq \emptyset$).
  The presence of integer variables in a MOLP structure introduces supplementary difficulties to both the characterization of the efficient solutions (see [12]), and to the interactive work (see [13]). MOMIX is a new interactive method for MOILP (see [14]) ; if in addition uncertainties are present in the problem, MOMIX is to be combined with STRANGE to treat the general MOSILP problem.

In the three methods, the way to manage the uncertainties and to determine a first compromise is identical ; it is briefly described in section 3. The interactive phases of STRANGE and STRANGE-MOMIX are described in sections 4 and 5 respectively. Some conclusions about the DSS are presented in section 6.

3. THE ASSOCIATED DETERMINISTIC PROBLEM AND THE FIRST COMPROMISE

3.1. The uncertainties are managed in two steps :

(a) each situation (k,s) is defined as a criterion to take into account the different scenarios affecting the K objectives

(b) a supplementary criterion, noted z_{K+1}, is created to penalize the violations of the constraints.

An associated deterministic problem is then obtained

$$\text{(1)} \quad \text{"min"} \begin{cases} z_{ks} = c_{ks}X & k=1,\ldots,K\ ;\ s=1,\ldots,S \\ z_{K+1} = \sum_{r=1}^{R} q_r\, b_r\, W_r \\ Z \in D_1(Z) \end{cases}$$

with $Z \equiv (X, V^r, W^r)$, $r=1,\ldots,R$

$$D_1(Z) = \{Z \geqq 0 \mid T^r X + V^r - W^r = d^r \quad r=1,\ldots,R\ ;\ x_j \text{ integer for } j \in N_2\}$$

and where b_r is a vector of penalties.

Remark Criterion z_{K+1} is scenario dependent but to unify the notations, we note $z_{K+1,s} = c_{K+1,s} Z \equiv z_{K+1}$ for all $s=1,\ldots,S$.

Of course, in the following only one couple $(K+1,s)$ must be considered at each step of the method.

3.2. For each of the criteria z_{ks}, the corresponding individual optimization problem is solved and an optimal solution $\tilde{Z}^{ks}$ is determined. This provides an ideal point of components

$$M_{ks}^{(1)} = z_{ks}(\tilde{Z}^{ks}) \qquad k=1,\ldots,K+1,\ s=1,\ldots,S$$

and a pay-off table given by the values

$$z_{ks}(\tilde{Z}^{\ell t}) \qquad k,\ell=1,\ldots,K+1;\ s,t=1,\ldots,S$$

If $\tilde{Z}^{\ell t}$ is not a unique solution for the optimization of criterion $z_{\ell t}$, a special technique (see [11]) is used to avoid ambiguity and to ensure the unicity of the pay-off table. This pay-off table provides a worst value

$$m_{ks}^{(1)} = \max_{(\ell t)} z_{ks}(\tilde{Z}^{\ell t}) \qquad k=1,\ldots,K+1;\ s=1,\ldots,S$$

thus the worse value of z_{ks} in the pay-off table, and some normalizing weights $\Pi_{ks}^{(1)}$, defined by

$$\Pi_{ks}^{(1)} = \frac{\alpha_{ks}^{(1)}}{\sum_{k=1}^{K}\sum_{s=1}^{S}\alpha_{ks}^{(1)} + \alpha_{K+1}^{(1)}} \qquad k=1,\ldots,K+1;\ s=1,\ldots,S$$

where

$$\alpha_{ks}^{(1)} = \frac{m_{ks}^{(1)} - M_{ks}^{(1)}}{m_{ks}^{(1)}} \cdot \frac{1}{\| c_{ks} \|} \qquad \begin{matrix} k=1,\ldots,K+1 \\ s=1,\ldots,S \end{matrix}$$

These weights are measuring the importance of the distances in the objective space to the ideal point. They have a different role and meaning that the weights used to aggregate the objectives into single objective. Other approaches can be used without restriction to determine these weights (see [4]).
Further a minimax optimization is performed to determine the first compromise $\tilde{Z}^{(1)}$:

$$\left[\begin{array}{ll} \min \delta & \\ \sum_{s=1}^{S} p_s \, (c_{ks}.Z - M_{ks}^{(m)}) \, \Pi_{ks}^{(m)} \leq \delta & k=1,\ldots,K+1 \\ Z \in D_1(Z) \; ; \; m=1 & \end{array}\right.$$

This problem corresponds to the use of a Tchebytchef norm. According to Bowman [2], the obtained compromise is certainly efficient in case of an unique solution for (2). Otherwise, a special technique (see [11]),-corresponding to the use of a generalized Tchebytchef norm (see [9])- has to be applied in order to find an efficient first compromise.

Remark. This approach belongs to the large family of methods using the ideal point concept. They have been developed by several authors ([1] [7] [15],[9],...)

4. THE INTERACTIVE PHASES OF STRANGE

If the decision-maker is satisfied with the compromise $\tilde{Z}^{(m)}$ $(m \geq 1)$ and the set of values $z_{ks}^{(m)} = z_{ks}(\tilde{Z}^{(m)})$, the procedure stops.

Otherwise, he will be asked to indicate

- a criterion $(ks)^*$ to be improved
- eventually, a lower limit $\Lambda_{(ks)}^*$ of the value of $z_{(ks)}^{(m+1)*}$

STRANGE will explore the consequences of such an improvement for the decision-maker.
A parametric LP problem is considered,

- introducing in problem (2) the parametric constraint

$$c^{(ks)*}.Z = M_{(ks)*}^{(1)} + \lambda \, (m_{(ks)*}^{(1)} - M_{(ks)*}^{(1)}) \qquad \Lambda \leq \lambda \leq \lambda_0$$

where λ_0 and Λ are given respectively by

$$M_{(ks)*}^{(1)} + \lambda_0 (m_{(ks)*}^{(1)} - M_{(ks)*}^{(1)}) = z_{(ks)*}^{(m)}$$

$$M_{(ks)*}^{(1)} + \Lambda \, (m_{(ks)*}^{(1)} - M_{(ks)*}^{(1)}) = \Lambda_{(ks)*}$$

- setting $\Pi_{(ks)*}^{(1)} = 0$ so that $(ks)^*$ is removed from the minimax calculation.

Using a dual simplex technique, the optimal solution $Z_{m+1}(\lambda)$ to this new problem is found. The sequence of bounds $\Lambda = \lambda_n \leqq \lambda_{n-1} \leqq \dots \leqq \lambda_1 \leqq \lambda_0$ corresponding to the stable intervals for the optimal bases is determined ; for each criterion (ℓt) a piecewise linear function $z_{\ell t}(Z_{m+1}(\lambda))$ is obtained. These functions are represented graphically (see Fig.1) so that the decision maker can assess the complete range of variations of all criteria when criterion $(ks)^*$ is changing. He can answer a lot of questions about the relative gains or losses, elasticity coefficients, etc... ; he will be able to give, on good grounds, an acceptable level $\tilde{\lambda}$ of improvement corresponding to a new compromise :

$$\tilde{Z}^{(m+1)} = Z_{m+1}(\tilde{\lambda})$$

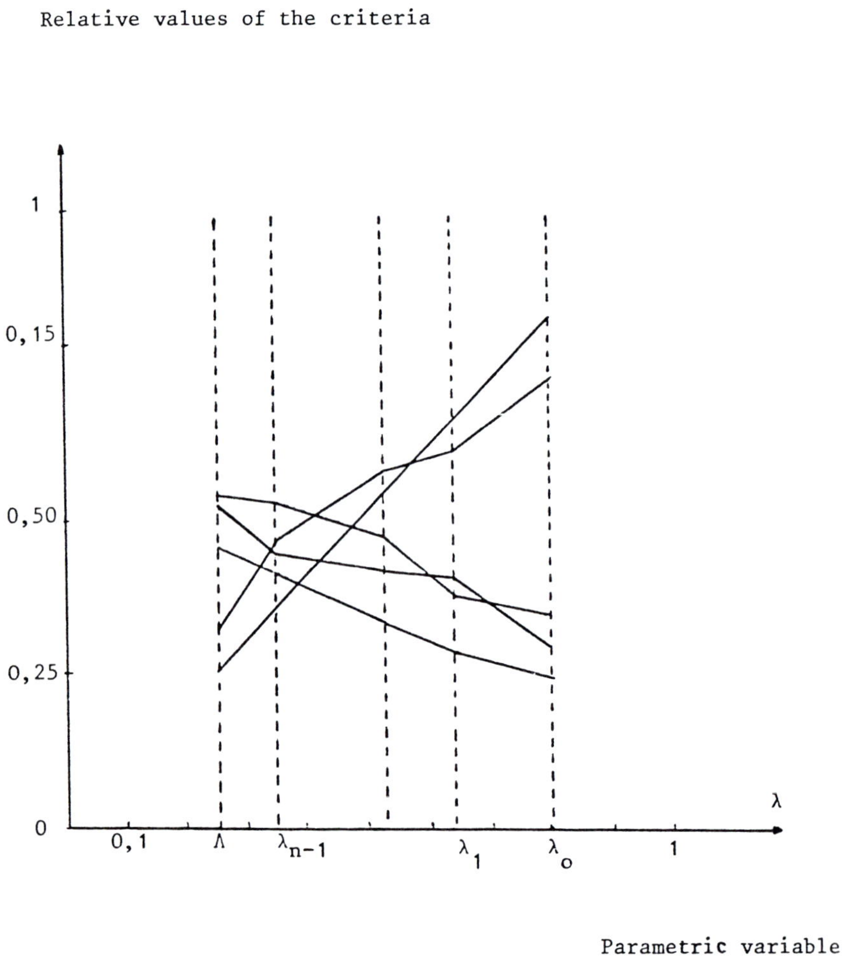

Fig.1. An interactive phase of STRANGE

5. THE INTERACTIVE PHASES OF MOMIX.

In the presence of integer variables, the parametric analysis developed for the interactives phases of STRANGE, is not suitable from a theoretical point of view. Moreover its generalization would be quite impossible to implement for pratical application. It is the reason why the interactive phases of MOMIX is based on a different approach using a Branch and Bound tree (like in [6]).

This interactive Branch and Bound includes two steps :
- the first step (a "depth first" progression in the tree) leads to the determination of a first good compromise;
- the second step (a backtracking procedure) confirms the degree of satisfaction achieved by the decision-maker or it finds a better compromise if necessary.

5.1. For $m \geq 1$, let $\tilde{Z}^{(m)}$ the mth compromise, let be $z_{ks}^{(m)}$ the values of criteria and $[M_{(ks)}^{(m)}, m_{ks}^{(m)}]$, $\Pi_{ks}^{(m)}$ respectively the variation interval and the weight of criterion ks at this m^{th} iteration.
The decision-maker has to choose at each iteration, the criterion $\ell_{(m)}(1) \in \{ks, k=1,\ldots,K+1;\ s=1,\ldots,S\}$ he is willing to improve in priority : a new constraint is then introduced :

$$D^{(m+1)} \equiv D^{(m)} \cap \{Z \mid z_{\ell_m(1)} < z_{\ell_m(1)}^{(m)}\},$$

further the variation intervals $[M_{ks}^{(m+1)}, m_{ks}^{(m+1)}]$ and the weights $\Pi_{ks}^{(m+1)}$ are updated on the new feasible set $D^{(m+1)}$.
The new compromise $\tilde{Z}^{(m+1)}$ is obtained by the resolution of problem (2).
The first branch of this interactive tree is described in figure 2.

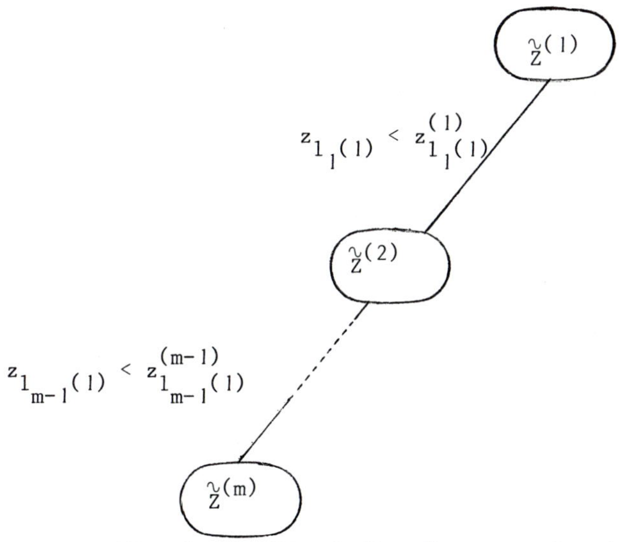

Fig. 2. The "depth first" progression in MOMIX.

Differents tests allow to terminate this first step.

Fathoming tests : the node (m+1) is fathomed if :

(a) $D^{(m+1)} = \emptyset$

(b) $m_{ks}^{(m+1)} - M_{ks}^{(m+1)} \leqq \varepsilon_{ks} \qquad \forall \; (ks)$

(c) the vector $\hat{Z}$ of the incumbent values (values of the criteria for the best compromise already determined) is preferred to the new ideal point (of components $M_{ks}^{(m+1)}$)

Stopping tests : the first step of the procedure is stopped if

(d) More than q successive iterations do not bring an improvement of the incumbent point Z

(e) More than Q iterations have been performed.

The paramaters ε_{ks}, q and Q are fixed in the agreement with the decision.

5.2. It can be hoped that the appropriate choice of the criterion $z_{\ell_m}(1)$ has been made so that at the end of the first step, a good compromise has been found.
Nevertheless it is worth examining some other parts of the tree to confirm the decision-maker's satisfaction. The complete tree is generated in the following manner : at each level, K+1 subnodes are introduced by successively adding the constraints :

1°) $z_{\ell_m(1)} < z^{(m)}_{\ell_m(1)}$

2°) $z_{\ell_m(2)} < z^{(m)}_{\ell_m(2)} \; ; \; z_{\ell_m(1)} \geqq z^{(m)}_{\ell_m(1)}$

.

.

.

K+1) $z_{\ell_m(K+1)} < z^{(m)}_{\ell_m(K+1)} \; ; \; z_{\ell_m(k)} \geqq z^{(m)}_{\ell_m(k)} \qquad k=1,\dots,K$

where $\ell_m(k) \in \{ks \mid k=1,\dots,K+1 \; ; \; s=1,\dots,S\}$ is a set of K+1 criteria -only one scenario being chosen for each objective- They are ordered according to the priorities of the decision-maker. In this way the feasible regions of the K+1 subnodes form a partition of the feasible region of the preceding node in the tree.
The usual backtracking procedure is applied; yet it seems unnecessary to explore the whole tree. Indeed the subnodes $k>\bar{K}$ of each branching correspond to a simultaneous relaxation of those criteria $\ell_m(k)$, $k\leqslant\bar{K}$, the decision-maker wants to improve in priority ; therefore these subnodes do almost certainly not bring any improved solutions. In practice $\bar{K}$ could be equal to 2 or 3.

The fathoming tests a), b) and c) are again applied in this second step ; each time a node is not fathomed, problem (2) is resolved to determine a new compromise. The stopping tests d) and e) - with possibly a choice of new values for the parameters q and Q - limit the number of iterations in this backtracking procedure.

6. SOME CONCLUSIONS

The three methods integrated in the DSS address a large scope of multi-objective investment planning problems, including non linearity of functions, integer variables and uncertainties. The measurement of risk resulting in not satisfying several uncertain constraints is made possible by using an additional criterion. The value of this criterion within its variation range gives a useful measure of risk. This technique is not only mathematically meaningful but it largely contributes to a better understanding of uncertainties as practical applications have shown [5,10].
The scenario approach is also favourably perceived by the users, as mean values and dispersions of results are easily apprehended. All three methods exposed here have the considerable advantage of requiring easy-to-answer questions and comparisons to the users.

This interactive DSS has been first implemented on a mainframe VAX computer and it has been used real world problems (see section 1). For smaller problems and with the aim of a larger diffusion, micro-computer versions are being developed. STRANGE is already available on PC micro-computers as a user friendly, menu-driven decision tool. Its interactive phases make extensive use of graphical techniques.

REFERENCES

[1] R. BENAYOUN et.al.
"Linear Programming with multiple Objective Functions : step method (Stem)". Math.Progr. 1,2 (1971), 366-375

[2] V.J. BOWMAN
"On the relationship of the Tchebytcheff Norm and the efficient frontier of multiple-criteria objectives" in H. Thiriez, S. Zionts (Eds), Multiple criteria Decision Making (Springer-Verlag, Berlin, 1976) pp. 76-85

[3] C. DELHAYE, T. d'HAUCOURT, J. TEGHEM Jr., P. KUNSCH
"Strange on Micro", submitted for publication (1987)

[4] M. KOK
"The interface with decision-makers and some experimental results in interactive multiple objective programming methods" European Journal of Operations Research 26, 1 (1986) , 65-82

[5] P. KUNSCH, J. TEGHEM Jr.
"Nuclear fuel cycle Optimization using Multi-Objective Stochastic Linear Programming", European Journal of Operations Research, 31 (1987), 240-249

[6] O. MARCOTTE, R. SOLAND
"An interactive branch-and-bound algorithm for multiple criteria optimization", Management Science, 32, 1 (1986), 61-75

[7] B. ROY
"A conceptual framework for a prescriptive theory of decision-aid" in Stan M.K., Zeleny M (Eds), Multiple criteria decision making, TIMS studies in the Mn.Sc., vol.6 (1977), North Holland.

[8] R. SLOWINSKI, J. TEGHEM Jr.
"Fuzzy vs. Stochastic approaches for multi-objective linear programming under uncertainty" submitted for publication (1987)

[9] R.E. STEUER, E.U. CHOO
"An interactive method weighted Tchebytcheff Procedure for multiple objective programming" Math. Progr. 26(1983), 326-344

[10] J. TEGHEM Jr., P. KUNSCH
"Multi-objective decision making under uncertainty, an example for power system", in : Chankung, Haimes Eds, "Decision making with multiple objective", Springer-Verlag (1985), 443-456

[11] J. TEGHEM Jr., D. DUFRANE, M. THAUVOYE, P. KUNSCH
"STRANGE : an interactive method for multi-objective linear programming under uncertainty", European Journal of Operations Research 26,1 (1986), 65-82

[12] J. TEGHEM Jr., P. KUNSCH
"Complete characterization of efficient solutions for Multi-objective Integer Linear Programming", Asia-Pacific Journal of Operations Research, 3, 2,(1986), 95-108

[13] J. TEGHEM Jr., P. KUNSCH
"Interactive method for multi-objective integer linear programming" in : M. Grauer et al., Eds, "Large Scale Modelling and Interactive Decision Analysis", Springer-Verlag (1986) 75-87

[14] J. TEGHEM Jr., P. KUNSCH
"MOMIX : an interactive method for mixed integer linear programming" submitted for publication (1987)

[15] A.P. WIERZBICKI
"The use of reference objectives in multiobjective optimization" in G. FANDEL, T. GAL (Eds), Multiple criteria Decision Making Theory and Applications (Springer-Verlag, Berlin, 1980), pp. 468-486

[16] W.I. ZANGWILL
"Non linear programming" Prentice Hall (1967)

MULTIPLE CRITERIA MATHEMATICAL PROGRAMMING: AN UPDATED OVERVIEW AND SEVERAL APPROACHES

Stanley Zionts
Alumni Professor of Decision Support Systems
State University of New York at Buffalo
Buffalo, New York 14260 USA

1 INTRODUCTION

Multiple Criteria Decision Making (MCDM) refers to making decisions in the presence of multiple, usually conflicting, objectives. Multiple criteria decision problems pervade all that we do and include such public policy tasks as determining a country's policy developing a national energy plan, as well as planning national defense expenditures, in addition to such private enterprise tasks as new product development, pricing decisions, and research project selection. For an individual, the purchase of an automobile or a home exemplifies a multiple criteria problem. Even such routine decisions as the choice of a lunch from a menu, or the assignment of job crews to jobs constitute multiple criteria problems. All have a common thread--multiple conflicting objectives.

In this study, we discuss some of the important aspects of solving such problems, and present some methods developed for solving multiple criteria mathematical programming problems and discrete alternative models. We also discuss some applications of the methods.

In multiple criteria decision making there is a decision maker (or makers) who makes the decision, a set of objectives that are to be pursued, and a set of alternatives from which one is to be selected.

1.1 Goals, criteria, objectives, attributes, constraints, and targets: their relationships

In a decision situation we have goals, criteria, objectives, attributes, constraints, and targets, in addition to decision variables. Although goals, criteria, and targets have essentially the same dictionary definitions, it is useful to distinguish among them in a decision making context.

Criterion. A criterion is a measure of effectiveness of performance. It is the basis for evaluation. Criteria may be further classified as goals or targets and objectives.

Goals. A goal (synonymous with target) is something that is either achieved or not. For example, increasing sales of a product by at least 10% during one year over the previous is a goal. If a goal cannot be or is unlikely to be achieved, it may be converted to an objective.

NATO ASI Series, Vol. F48
Mathematical Models for Decision Support
Edited by G. Mitra

Objective. An objective is something to be pursued to its fullest. For example, a business may want to maximize its level of profits or maximize the quality of service provided or minimize customer complaints. An objective generally indicates the direction desired.

Attribute. An attribute is a measure that gives a basis for evaluating whether goals have been met or not given a particular decision. It provides a means for evaluating objectives.

Decision Variable. A decision variable is one of the specific decisions made by a decision maker. For example, the planned production of a given product is a decision variable.

Constraint. A constraint is a limit on attributes and decision variables that may or may not be stated mathematically. For example, that a plant can be operated at most twelve hours per day is a constraint.

1.2 Structuring an MCDM situation

Most problems have, in addition to multiple conflicting objectives a hierarchy of objectives. For example, according to Manheim and Hall (1967), the objective for evaluating passenger transportation facilities serving the Northeast Corridor of the U.S. in 1980 was "The Good Life." This superobjective was subdivided into four main objectives:

1. Convenience
2. Safety
3. Aesthetics
4. Economic Considerations

These in turn are divided into subobjectives, and so on forming a hierarchy of objectives.

Some of the objectives, such as economic considerations, have attributes that permit a precise performance measurement. Other, such as aesthetics, are highly subjective. Not wanting to convert the word subjective to a noun, we may, therefore, have a <u>subjective</u> objective. Further, the number of objectives may be large in total.

To adequately represent the objectives, we must choose appropriate attributes. Keeney and Raiffa (1976) indicate five characteristics the selected attributes of the objectives should have:

1. Complete: They should cover all aspects of a problem.
2. Operational: They can be meaningfully used in the analysis.
3. Decomposable: They can be broken into parts to simplify the process.
4. Nonredundant: They avoid problems of double counting
5. Minimal: The number of attributes should be kept small.

I recommend that at most the magic number of about 7 (see Miller, 1956) objectives be used. Such a limitation tends to keep a problem within the realm of operationality. What happens if there are more than about 7 objectives? First, use constraints to limit outcomes of objectives about which you are sure or about which you feel comfortable about setting such limits. Since constraints <u>must</u> be satisfied at any price, you should not make constraints "too tight." Further, it is useful to check whether feasible alternatives still exist after adding each constraint or after adding a few constraints. An alternative is to treat some of the objectives as goals or targets. We attempt to satisfy the goals. If we can't, we treat them as objectives. We try to get as close to achieving them as possible. We shall go into the idea of doing this mathematically later. Structuring a problem properly is an art, and there is no prescribed way of setting up objectives, goals and constraints.

1.3 A scenario of management decision making

A scenario of management decision making is generally assumed by most academicians:

1. A decision maker (DM) makes a decision.
2. He chooses from a set of possible decisions.
3. The solution he chooses is optimal.

To criticize the scenario, the decision maker, if an individual (as opposed to a group), seldom makes a decision in a vacuum. He is heavily influenced by others. In some instances groups make decisions. Second, the set of possible decisions is not a given. The set of solutions must be generated. The process of determining the set of alternatives may require considerable effort. In many situations, the generation of alternatives was important as the choice mechanism for choosing an alternative.

What is meant by an optimal solution? Since it is impossible to simultaneously maximize all objectives in determining a solution, a more workable definition is needed. A typical definition of optimality is not particularly workable: An optimal decision is one that maximizes a decision maker's utility (or satisfaction. In spite of the limitations of the decision scenario, it is widely used; its limitations are hopefully recognized.

2 SOME MATHEMATICAL CONSIDERATIONS OF MULTIPLE CRITERIA DECISION MAKING

The general multiple criteria decision making problem may be formulated as follows:

$$\begin{aligned} &\text{"Maximize"} \quad F(x) \\ &\text{subject to:} \quad G(x) \leq 0 \end{aligned} \tag{1}$$

where x is the vector of decision variables, and F(x) is the vector of objectives to be "maximized". In some cases it will be convenient to have an intervening vector y where F(x) = H(y(x). For example, y may be a vector of stochastic objectives which is a function of x. In that case, H would be a vector function of the stochastic objectives.

In some cases F will have some components that are ordinal. Attributes such as quality and convenience of location may only be measurable on an ordinal scale. Further, some objectives may be measured only imperfectly. The word maximize is in quotation marks because maximizing a vector is not a well-defined operation. We shall define it in several ways in what follows.

The constraints $G(x) \leq 0$ are the constraints that define the feasible solution space. They may be stated explicitly and if mathematical be either linear or nonlinear. Alternatively, the alternatives may be stated implicitly by listing them as discrete members of a set. Even though such a set is nonconvex, it is convenient to work with the convex hull of the solutions that generate a convex set.

The formulation of the multiple criteria decision making problem (1) is one that I believe includes virtually all of the approaches developed, as well as the various multiple criteria problems. It is clearly too general, because only very specific forms of problem (1) can be solved optimally in practice using quantitative models. A linear version of problem (1) is as follows:

$$\begin{array}{ll} \text{"Maximize"} & Cx \\ \text{subject to:} & Ax \leq b \end{array}$$

$x_j \geq 0$, if needed, may be included in the constraints $Ax \leq b$. This particularization of problem (1) is one on which a substantial amount of study has been made. It is referred to as the multiple objective linear programming problem (MOLP) because it is a linear programming problem with multiple objectives. The following theorem is found in several places in the multiple criteria literature.

Theorem: Maximizing a positive weighted ($\lambda > 0$) sum of objectives $\lambda' F (= \sum_i \lambda_i F_i)$ over a set of feasible solutions yields a nondominated solution.

The theorem does not say that for every nondominated solution there exists a set of weights for which the nondominated solution maximizes the weighted sum. As we shall see, that need not be the case.

The second problem that we consider is the discrete alternatives problem. Though it is not a mathematical programming problem, we shall consider it anyway. It is the problem of choosing the best alternative from a discrete set of alternatives. Mathematically, we want to:

$$\begin{array}{ll} \text{"Maximize"} & F(d) \\ \text{subject to:} & d \varepsilon D \end{array}$$

where d is a decision and D is the set of possible decisions. Examples of this problem are the purchase of a house or car. For the purchase of a house, D is the set of houses available that satisfy the buyer's constraints. The decision d that is chosen in some sense maximizes the buyer's objectives F(d). With discrete alternatives, even if we are able to conceive of convex combinations of alternatives, we are generally unable to realize them in practice. We cannot blend (or take an average of) a Tudor house at 136 Elmwood Street, and a Ranch house at 3550 Maple Road and come up with a Tuanch house at 1843 (the average) Mapwood Street. Nonetheless, it may still be useful to consider "blends" or convex combinations of discrete alternatives. Further "plotting" discrete alternatives generates a number of discrete points, rather than convex regions of feasible solutions. (The set of convex combinations of a set of discrete solutions is the convex hull of the corresponding solutions points.)

2.1 The objective functions

Let us now consider the objective functions more carefully. The objective functions may all be assumed to be maximized, without loss of generality, because any objective that is to be minimized can be minimized by maximizing the value of its negative. Accordingly, we shall henceforth refer to objectives to be maximized.

What do we do if we have any goals or targets (as defined earlier)? If they all are simultaneously achievable, we simply add constraints that stipulate the specified value be met and not consider them further. Thus, the achievement of the goals if transformed into an admissible solution satisfying all of the constraints. There is an interesting duality between objectives and constraints, in that the two are closely related.

If the goals are not simultaneously achievable, simply adding constraints as above will lead to no feasible solution to the problem. What must be done in such a situation is to relax some of the goals, or to change goals to objectives as described earlier: to minimize the difference between the goal and the outcome. The idea is to find a solution that is "close" to the goal.

What do we mean by "maximize"? Unlike unidimensional optimization, we want to simultaneously maximize several objectives. Generally that cannot be done. We may define "maximize" in two ways. From a general perspective, one workable definition of "maximize" is to find all nondominated solutions to a problem.

Definition: Dominance

Solution 1 dominates solution 2 if $F(x_1) \geq F(x_2)$ with strict inequality holding for at least one component of F.

A solution is said to be nondominated if no other solution dominates it, i.e. no other solution is at least as good as it in every respect and better than it in at least one respect. The concept seems eminently reasonable. By finding all nondominated solutions, one can presumably reduce the number of alternatives. However, for many problems, the number of nondominated alternatives may still be too large to help narrow the choice of alternatives.

It is useful to represent sets of nondominated solutions graphically, particularly when there are two objectives. Consider a set of discrete alternatives for which there are two objectives, both of which are to be maximized. (See Figure 1.) The set of nondominated solutions consist of solutions A, B, D, F, H, J, and K. Solutions C, E, and G are dominated, respectively, by D, F, and H (or J). Were we to consider the set of convex combinations of these solution points, a "blend" of solutions A and D would dominate B, and a "blend" of D and H would dominate F. A nondominated solution, in two dimensions, represented as in Figure 1, has no solutions "northeast" of it.

An example of a a convex set of nondominated solutions may be seen in Figure 4 a few pages ahead.

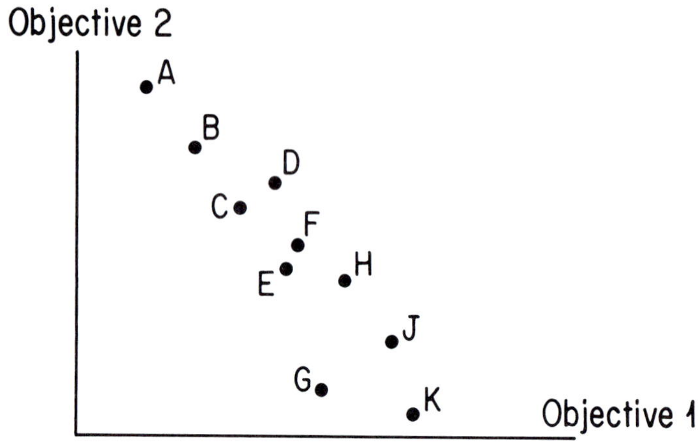

Figure 1 A Discrete Alternatives Example

There may be some instances where we don't want to eliminate dominated solutions. For example, a dominated solution may be sufficiently close to a nondominated solution that we may decide to make a choice based on some secondary criteria not used in the analysis. We may then very well choose the dominated solution based on the secondary criteria. Alternatively, some of the objectives may not be measurable precisely. In such a situation we may not want to exclude dominated alternatives from further analysis. As an example of the first type, suppose a prospective automobile purchaser is choosing among cars on the basis of price, economy, sportiness, and comfort. Suppose further that a foreign-made car appears somehow to be the best choice, but that there is a domestically produced automobile that is its equal in all respects except that the price is slightly higher. The decision maker may nonetheless decide to purchase the domestic automobile because of its better availability of spare parts. In the second instance, suppose that the purchaser is considering two domestically-produced automobiles. We assume as before that the cars are the same for all criteria but one--price. Car A has a lower list price than Car B. However, in the purchase of most automobiles, one can obtain discounts. On haggling with dealers, our purchaser may subsequently find that he can purchase Car B for less than Car A. Hence, if he had excluded Car B because of dominance (on the basis of list price), he would have made a mistake.

The reader may feel that in the first case we should have added spare parts availability to our criteria. Though this could have been done, we may generally use criteria such as this as secondary to resolve close cases. Similarly, it can be argued in the second example that the price variable is transaction price and not list price. Therefore, our selected car is not dominated. Nonetheless, it is difficult to accurately measure transaction price, prior to an automobile purchase transaction.

Another definition of "maximize" is that a decision maker wishes to maximize his utility, as measured by a utility function: a function of the objectives that gives a scalar measure of performance.

Definition: Utility Function

A utility function is a scalar function $u(F(x))$ such that x_1 is preferred to or is indifferent to x_2 if and only if $u(F(x_1)) \geq u(F(x_2))$.

Because of our statement of problem (1), we have at an optimal solution (for any feasible change) the value of the utility function remains the same or decreases. For some multiple criteria methods, we either estimate a utility function u or approximate it locally. In such cases, we use the function or its approximation to identify a most preferred solution.

2.2 A typology of multiple criteria decision making models

Quite naturally, different writers have proposed different decision making typologies. My typology consists of two main dimensions:

1. The nature of outcomes--stochastic versus deterministic.
2. The nature of the alternative generating mechanism--whether the constraints limiting the alternatives are explicit or implicit.

These dimensions are indicated in tabular form in Figure 2. The left-hand column includes the implicit constraint models. When the constraints are nonmathematical (implicit or explicit), the alternatives must be explicit. One of a list of alternatives is then selected. The decision analysis problem is included in the implicit constraint category. When the constraints are mathematical and explicit, then the alternative solutions are implicit and may be infinite in number if the solution space is continuous and consists of more than one solution. Problems in the explicit constraint category are generally regarded as multiple criteria mathematical programming problems.

	Implicit Constraints (Explicit Solutions)	Explicit Constraints (Implicit Solutions)
Deterministic Outcomes	Choosing Among Deterministic Discrete Alternatives or Deterministic Decision Analysis	Deterministic Mathematical Programming
Stochastic Outcomes	Stochastic Decision Analysis	Stochastic Mathematical Programming

Figure 2 A Typology of Multiple Criteria Decision Methods

More dimensions may be added to the typology. In addition to implicit constraints versus explicit constraints, and deterministic outcomes versus stochastic outcomes, we can identify other dimensions as well. We may classify the number of decision makers as a dimension: one decision maker versus two decision makers versus three or more decision makers. We may classify the number of objectives, the nature of utility functions considered, as well as the number of solutions found (one solution versus all nondominated solutions). I have chosen only two dimensions because they seem to be the most significant factors for the problems we consider.

In our presentation we consider only deterministic problems: mathematical programming problems and discrete alternative problems. In virtually all of the work on multiple criteria decision making, the spirit of the model employed is not necessarily to determine the best decision (though that is of course desirable!), but to help the decision maker in arriving at his decision. This is what Roy (1977) refers to as "decision aid." It is also what Keeney and Raiffa (1976) refer to as "getting your head straightened out." Before we consider some of the methods in detail, we present two mathematical programming examples. The first is useful in illustrating come concepts; the second will be used in various forms to illustrate the methods. (We earlier gave a graphical representation of a discrete alternative example.)

2.3 Two examples

Consider the following problem, which we shall refer to as Example 1:

$$\begin{aligned}
\text{Maximize} \quad & f_1 = -x_1 + 2x_2 \\
& f_2 = 2x_1 - x_2 \\
\text{subject to:} \quad & x_1 \leq 4 \\
& x_2 \leq 4 \\
& x_1 + x_2 \leq 7 \\
& -x_1 + x_2 \leq 3 \\
& x_1 - x_2 \leq 3 \\
& x_1, x_2 \geq 0
\end{aligned}$$

For this example, x_1 and x_2 are the decision variables, and f_1 and f_2 are the objectives. A plot of the feasible solutions is shown in Figure 3, the maximum solutions indicated (e for f_1, and b for f_2) for each of the objectives. In that figure, we have also identified all of the feasible extreme point solutions as 0 and a through e and h. In Figure 4 we have plotted the values of the objective functions for this problem. Each of the feasible solutions in Figure 3 has a corresponding point in Figure 4. For example, solution b represented as $x_1 = 4$ and $x_2 = 1$ has objective function values $f_1 = -2$ and $f_2 = 7$ and is so plotted in Figure 3. The nondominated solutions are shown as the broken line b, c, d, e. An optimal solution will be found along that line, because any point not on that line is either dominated (below and/or to the left in Figure 4) or infeasible (above and/or to the right in Figure 4).

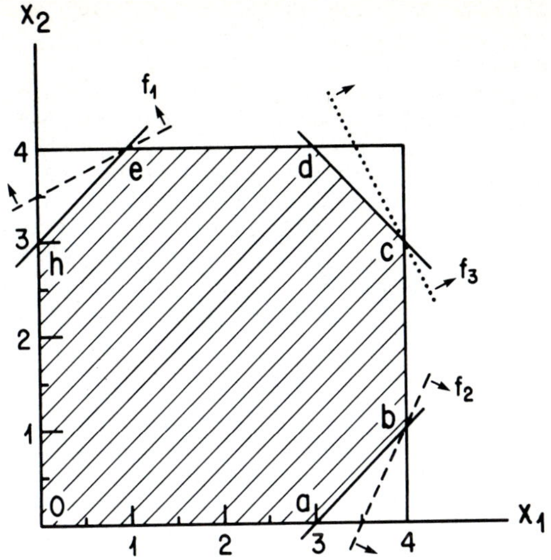

Figure 3 The Feasible Region of Example One and the Two Objectives f_1 and f_2

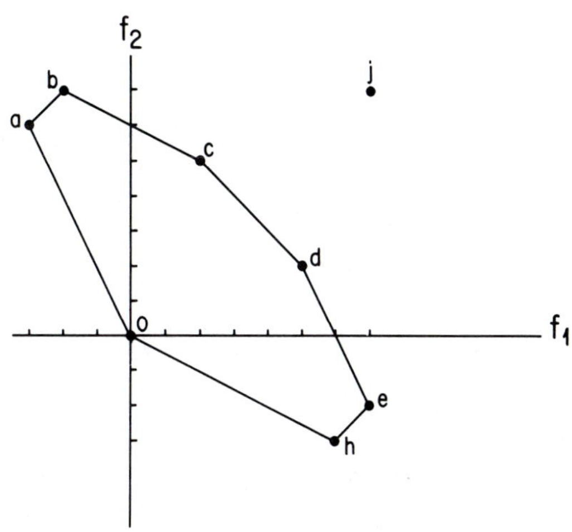

Figure 4 A Plot of the Solutions of the First Example Problem in Objective Function Space: In Terms of the Values of the Objective Function

Since x_1 and x_2 are the decision variables, a graph in terms of x_1 and x_2 (Figure 3) is a graph in decision or activity space. Variables f_1 and f_2 are the objectives; a graph in terms of f_1 and f_2 (Figure 4) is a graph in objective function space. For discrete alternative problems, we cannot normally plot decision variables, because they don't exist. Our example consists of two variables and two objectives. Usually the number of variables is much greater than the number of objectives. We may make the first example more complicated by adding a third objective: $f_3 = 2x_1 + x_2$. See the cross-hatched line in Figure 3. The objective function f_3 is maximized at point c; the plot of the feasible solutions in decision variable space does not change otherwise. To make a plot in objective space with three objectives, we would have to add a third dimension to Figure 4. Rather than do that, we first reconsider Figure 4 with two objectives. Denoting as a weighted objective function $\lambda_1 f_1 + \lambda_2 f_2$, we can see that (assuming without loss of generality $\lambda_1 + \lambda_2 = 1$) for $\lambda_1 > 2/3$ solution e is optimal. For $\lambda_1 = 2/3$ both solutions d and e (as well as the solutions on the line between them) are optimal. For $1/2 < \lambda_1 < 2/3$, solution d is optimal. Similarly, for $1/3 < \lambda_1 < 1/2$, solution c is optimal, and for $0 < \lambda_1 < 1/3$, solution b is optimal. Because $\lambda_2 = 1 - \lambda_1$, we could plot the regions along a straight line. Adding a third objective gives us a weighted objective function $\lambda_1 f_1 + \lambda_1 f_2 + \lambda_3 f_3$. Now using the restriction $\lambda_1 + \lambda_2 + \lambda_3 = 1$ or $\lambda_3 = 1 - \lambda_1 - \lambda_2$ and eliminating λ_3 we may draw the regions in which each solution is optimal. We call the corresponding space the weight space. See Figure 5 where we read off the values of λ_1 and λ_2 and compute $\lambda_3 = 1 - \lambda_1 - \lambda_2$. The solutions with $\lambda_3 = 0$ (i.e., $\lambda_1 + \lambda_2 = 1$) are still valid; they appear along the line $\lambda_1 + \lambda_2 = 1$. Other solutions are indicated accordingly.

We now consider a more complicated example, Example 2.

$$2x_1 + x_2 + 4x_3 + 3x_4 \leq 60 \qquad (\text{slack } x_5)$$

$$3x_1 + 4x_2 + x_3 + 2x_4 \leq 60 \qquad (\text{slack } x_6)$$

$$x_1, x_2, x_3, x_4 \geq 0$$

Three objectives are to be maximized:

$$u_1 = 3x_1 + x_2 + 2x_3 + x_4$$

$$u_2 = x_1 - x_2 + 2x_3 + 4x_4$$

$$u_3 = -x_1 + 5x_2 + x_3 + 2x_4$$

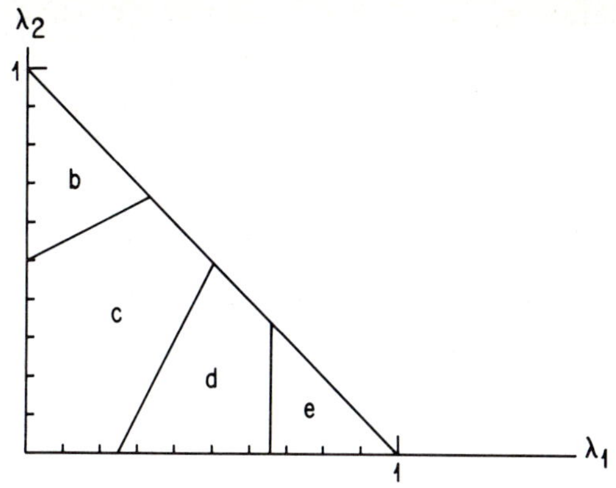

Figure 5 A Plot Indicating the Values of λ_1 and λ_2 ($\lambda_3 = 1 - \lambda_1 - \lambda_2$)

The problem has nine basic feasible solutions. The values of the decision variables and the objective functions are given below (all omitted variables are zero):

1. $x_1 = 18$, $x_3 = 6$, $u_1 = 66$, $u_2 = 30$, $u_3 = -12$
2. $x_4 = 20$, $x_6 = 20$, $u_1 = 20$, $u_2 = 80$, $u_3 = 40$
3. $x_2 = 15$, $x_5 = 45$, $u_1 = 15$, $u_2 = -15$, $u_3 = 75$
4. $x_2 = 6$, $x_4 = 18$, $u_1 = 24$, $u_2 = 66$, $u_3 = 66$
5. $x_1 = 12$, $x_4 = 12$, $u_1 = 48$, $u_2 = 60$, $u_3 = 12$
6. $x_2 = 12$, $x_3 = 12$, $u_1 = 36$, $u_2 = 12$, $u_3 = 72$
7. $x_3 = 15$, $x_6 = 45$, $u_1 = 30$, $u_2 = 30$, $u_3 = 15$
8. $x_1 = 20$, $x_5 = 20$, $u_1 = 60$, $u_2 = 20$, $u_3 = -20$
9. $x_5 = 60$, $x_6 = 60$, $u_1 = 0$, $u_2 = 0$, $u_3 = 0$

The first six solutions are nondominated, the last three are dominated. Figure 6 indicates which solutions are adjacent extreme point solutions of which other solutions (i.e., they differ by precisely one basic variable).

In order to plot the problem solutions in activity space we need to plot a 4-dimensional graph! More reasonable is plotting the objectives in three dimensions. However, instead we present the plot for the weights λ_1 and λ_2 (and λ_3) as we did for Example 1. See Figure 7.

Any solutions which have a common edge in Figure 7 are adjacent. (See Figure 6.) However, some solutions are adjacent (e.g., 3 and 4), yet do not have a common edge.

Solution	is adjacent to Solutions
1	5, 6, 7, 8
2	4, 5, 7, 9
3	4, 6, 8, 9
4	2, 3, 5, 6
5	1, 2, 4, 8
6	1, 3, 4, 7
7	1, 2, 6, 9
8	1, 3, 5, 9
9	2, 3, 7, 8

Figure 6 Adjacency of Basic Feasible Solutions of Example 2

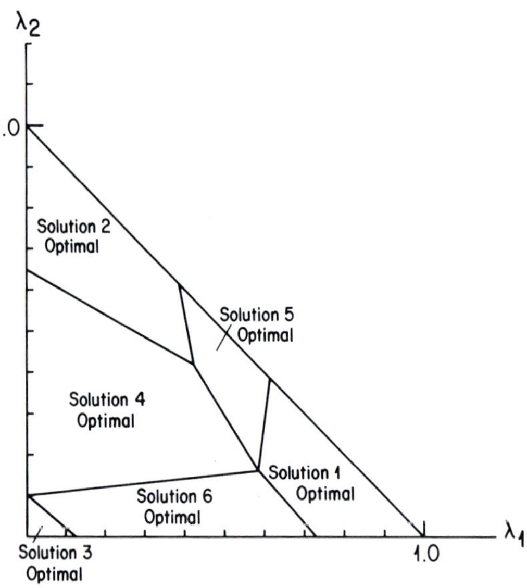

Figure 7 A Plot of Values and the Corresponding Optimal Solutions

For discrete alternative problems, we may plot the points, as we did in Figure 1, in the objective function space. If we consider the convex hull (set of convex combinations) of all such points, we may also construct a weight space for the problem. We cannot, as we indicated earlier, construct a decision space for such problems.

3 SOME NAIVE METHODS OF SOLVING MULTIPLE CRITERIA MATHEMATICAL PROGRAMMING PROBLEMS

There are several naive methods for solving multiple criteria mathematical programming problems. They are simple in concept, though generally not very good. They were early approaches to the problems, and have evolved into current approaches. We shall first consider multiple criteria linear programming problems.

3.1 Setting levels of all objectives

The first of the naive methods to be considered is that of specifying or setting levels of all objectives, and then solving for a feasible solution. The approach is to specify a vector of objectives d such that Cx = d. The object then is to find a feasible solution to the set of constraints:

$$Cx = d$$
$$Ax \leq b, \; x \geq 0$$

The problem can be solved as a linear programming problem, and there are three possible outcomes as illustrated in Figure 8 for a two-objective problem. The feasible region is indicated. The three possible outcomes are as follows:

a. No feasible solution
b. A dominated solution
c. A nondominated solution.

These are illustrated in Figure 8. If the objectives are set too high, there is no feasible solution (e.g., point a). If the objectives are not set high enough, a feasible solution that is dominated (e.g., solution b) will be found. Almost certainly one of these two outcomes will occur. Only in rare circumstances would simply selecting a vector d yield an efficient (or nondominated) solution. Given two points such as a and b, we can sometimes use a line search for a nondominated solution on the line segment connecting them (e.g., line segment ab; the nondominated solution on the line segment between them is point e). That this does not necessarily happen is illustrated by feasible point k and infeasible point h; there is no efficient point on the line segment joining them.

Even if we had a method for finding all efficient solutions, we would still not necessarily know which solution is best. Methods that set levels of all objectives but overcome some of the limitations include goal programming and a method that has been developed by Wierzbicki (1980). These are discussed in later sections. See also the step method (Benayoun _et al_. (1971).

3.2 Setting minimal levels of all but one objective

A second naive approach is to set minimum levels for all but one objective and to maximize the remaining objective. Mathematically this amounts to solving a linear programming problem of the following form:

$$\begin{aligned} \text{Maximize} \quad & C_1x \\ \text{subject to} \quad & C_2x \geq d_2 \\ & C_3x \geq d_3 \\ & C_px \geq d_p \\ & Ax \leq b, \quad x \geq 0 \end{aligned}$$

where $d_2,\ldots.,d_p$ are the minimum levels of objectives $2,\ldots,p$ and $C_1,C_2,\ldots.,C_p$ are the p objective function vectors. We have chosen to

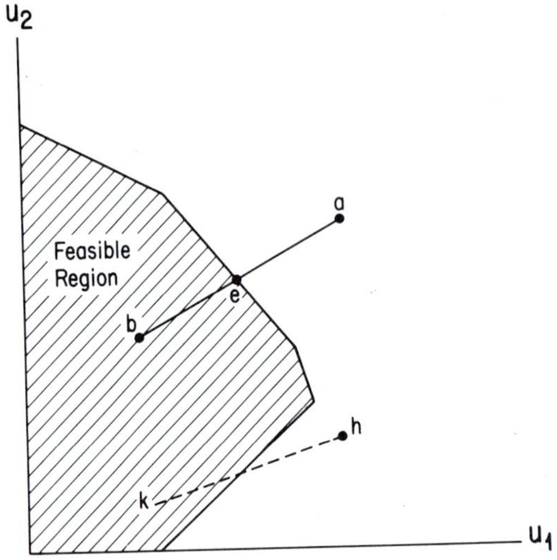

Figure 8 A Graph of a Simple Two Dimensional Example

maximize the first objective without loss of generality. The result will certainly be a nondominated solution*. For our example problem of Figure 3 there are infinitely many solutions along the line segments bc, cd, and de. Presumably, one (or more) of these solutions is preferred to the others. Which of these solutions is not preferred by the decision maker? That is not clear. A method that employs this approach has been developed by Haimes and Hall (1974).

3.3 Finding all efficient extreme point solutions

Multiple Objective Linear Programming (MOLP) to find all nondominated or efficient solutions has been widely proposed as another approach. The concept of vector maximum and its early consideration by researchers (see for example, Charnes and Cooper, 1961) has been around for a long time. Only in the early 1970s was it considered seriously as a computational procedure. Evans and Steuer (1973) and Yu and Zeleny (1975) generated and solved problems of several sizes to obtain all nondominated extreme point solutions. The results were not good, except for two-objective problems for which parametric programming may be used. Basically, the methods consider the linear programming problem:

$$\begin{aligned} \text{Maximize} \quad & \lambda' Cx \\ \text{subject to:} \quad & Ax = b \\ & x \geq 0 \end{aligned}$$

where the vector of weights $\lambda > 0$. For every nondominated extreme point solution, there exists a convex cone in λ space, that is a cone for which $\lambda'(C_N - C_B{}^{-1}N) \leq 0$, using the usual linear programming notation (C_N and

*Ralph Steuer has pointed out that solutions to such problems may be in some cases weakly dominated, though such solutions may be avoided.

C_B are the nonbasic and basic partitions, respectively, of C. N is the complement of B with respect to A.) The λ-space shown in the various figures of the text is the intersection of all cones with the constraint $\Sigma\lambda_j = 1$. The methods for finding all nondominated extreme point solutions essentially enumerate the convex cones. The idea was that all efficient solutions could be computed, and the decision maker could choose from them. Since there are in general far too many, the approach is not workable in practice. Steuer's contracting cone method, described in a later section, partially overcomes the problems.

3.4 Using weights to combine objective functions

The idea of using weights seems to be an attractive one. It involves averaging or blending the objectives into a composite objective and then maximizing the result. The difficulty is in specifying weights. It is incorrect to say that if the weight for one objective is larger than that of another, that the first objective is more important than the second and vice versa. The weights depend upon the units in which the objectives are measured. For example, equal weights have a rather unequal effect if objectives are to maximize GNP measured in billions of dollars and to maximize the fraction of the population who are above the poverty level as measured by a number between zero and one. The second objective will in that case have virtually no effect. The Zionts-Wallenius method (considered below) extends and uses this approach.

4 OVERCOMING THE PROBLEMS OF THE NAIVE APPROACHES

Several of the naive approaches have appealing characteristics, which no doubt led to their development. To overcome some of the problems with the methods, further development was done on these methods. We now describe the results.

4.1 Goal programming

The concept of goal programming, effectively a method for setting all objectives, was introduced by Charnes and Cooper (1961) and extended by Ijiri (1965) and Lee (1972), among others. Goal programming involves the solution of linear programming problems (although other mathematical programming forms such as integer programming have also been formulated in a goal programming context) with several goals or targets. Generally, goal programming assumes a linear constraint set of the (matrix) form $Ax = b$, $x \geq 0$ where x is the vector of decision variables. Denoting an objective as $c_i x$, there are several possible forms, all of which can be rewritten as $h_i \leq c_i' \leq u_i$ where h_i is the desired lower bound on objective i, and u_i is the desired upper bound. The bound constraints are not "hard" in that they may be violated. First add variables s_i and t_i and rewrite the bound constraints as

$$c_i'x - s_i \leq u_i , \qquad i = 1,\dots,p$$

$$c_i'x + t_i \geq h_i , \qquad i = 1,\dots,p$$

where p is the number of objectives or goals. Now using matrix notation with $c_i = (c_{i1}, c_{i2}, \ldots, c_{ip})'$, $s = (s_1, s_2, \ldots, s_p)'$, $t = (t_1, t_2, \ldots, t_p)'$, $k = (k_1, k_2, \ldots, k_p)'$, $q = (q_1, q_2, \ldots, q_p)'$, $u = (u_1, u_2, \ldots, u_p)'$ and $h = (h_1, h_2, \ldots, h_p)'$ we wish to

$$\begin{array}{ll} \text{Minimize} & k's + q't \\ \text{subject to:} & Cx - s \leq u \\ & Cx + t \leq h \\ & Ax = b \\ & x, s, t \geq 0 \end{array}$$

where k and q are vectors of weights to measure the violations of the bound constraints. If desired, several different s and t variables may be used for each goal with different values of k and q as well as upper bounds on the s and t variables. The effect of this is to allow for piece-wise linear, nonlinear penalties in the failure to achieve goals. As outlined, the relationships yield convex sets. For more information on these nonlinearities and others as well as nonconvex nonlinearities, see Charnes and Cooper (1977).

Instead of minimizing a weighted sum of deviations from goals, goal programming may be used to minimize the maximum deviation from a set of goals. This is done by changing the formulation by adding the constraints

$$q_i s_i \leq z$$

$$k_i t_i \leq z$$

and changing the objective to minimize z. The effective objective then is to minimize $(\max\{q_i s_i, k_i t_i\})$, the maximum weighted deviation from a goal.

Another variation of goal programming employs preemptive priorities instead of numerical weights. Let some subset of weights have much greater values than another subset of weights so that any finite multiple of the weights of the latter set is always less than any of the weights of the former set. The effect is to first minimize the weighted sums for the highest preemptive priority group. Then constraining that weighted sum to be equal to its minimum value, the next highest preemptive priority group sum is minimized, and so on, for as many preemptive priority groups as there may be.

Where goal programming falls flat is in the selection of the goals as well as the specification of the weights, that is the vectors k and q. The selection of goals should not be a difficult problem, although it is important for the decision maker to be aware of tradeoffs which face him. The weights must be selected by the user, and goal programming does not have much to say about the choice of weights. About the only device that is offered in terms of weights is preemptive priorities, which we have already considered. Nonetheless, goal programming has been fairly widely used in practice because of the ease of specifying a goal vector, and the ease of understanding what is going on. We consider Example 2 as a goal programming problem, where our objective is to minimize the absolute sum of deviations below the goal values (66, 80, 75). For example, the solution (60, 75, 75) would have a value of $|66-60| + |80-75| + |75-75|$ or 11.

The formulation is as follows:

$$\text{Minimize} \quad t_1 + t_2 + t_3$$

$$\begin{aligned}
\text{subject to:} \quad 3x_1 + x_2 + 2x_3 + x_4 + t_1 & \geq 66 \\
x_1 - x_2 + 2x_3 + 4x_4 + t_2 & \geq 80 \\
-x_1 + 5x_2 + x_3 + 2x_4 + t_3 & \geq 75 \\
2x_1 + x_2 + 4x_3 + 3x_4 & \leq 60 \\
3x_1 + 4x_2 + x_3 + 2x_4 & \leq 60 \\
x_1, x_2, x_3, x_4, t_1, t_2, t_3 & \geq 0
\end{aligned}$$

The optimal solution to the above problem is $x_2 = 6$, $x_4 = 18$, $t_1 = 42$, $t_2 = 14$, $t_3 = 9$ (all other variables are zero), or $u_1 = 24$, $u_2 = 66$, $u_3 = 66$. Changing the objective function to minimize $3t_1 + t_2 + t_3$ changes the solution to $u_1 = 66$, $u_2 = 30$, $u_3 = -12$, to illustrate another set of weights.

If we now add to the formulation $t_1 \leq z$, $t_2 \leq z$, and $t_3 \leq z$ and change the objective to minimize z we have an example of minimizing the maximum deviation from each goal. We obtain the solution $x_1 = 4.86$, $x_2 = 5.01$, $x_3 = 2.88$, $x_4 = 11.24$, $t_1 = t_2 = t_3 = t_4 = z = 29.40$, or $u_1 = 36.6$, $u_2 = 50.6$, and $u_3 = 45.6$.

We now illustrate the use of preemptive priorities. Let us assume that our first priority is to get u_1 to 50, our second priority is to get u_2 to 50, and our third priority is to get u_3 to 50.

We formulate the problem as follows:

$$\text{Minimize} \quad P_1t_1 + P_2t_2 + P_3t_3 \qquad (P_1 >> P_2 >> P_3)$$

$$\begin{aligned}
3x_1 + x_2 + 2x_3 + x_4 + t_1 & \geq 50 \quad (u_1 \geq 50) \\
x_1 - x_2 + 2x_3 + 4x_4 + t_2 & \geq 50 \quad (u_1 \geq 50) \\
-x_1 + 5x_2 + x_3 + 2x_4 + t_3 & \geq 50 \quad (u_2 \geq 50) \\
2x_1 + x_2 + 4x_3 + 3x_4 & \leq 60 \\
3x_1 + 4x_2 + x_3 + 2x_4 & \leq 60 \\
x_1, \ldots, x_4, t_1, t_2, t_3 & \geq 0
\end{aligned}$$

(>> means much greater than)

The optimal solution to the problem is $u_1 = 50$, $u_2 = 50$, $u_3 = 13.65$ ($x_1 = 11.88$, $x_2 = 1.18$, $x_3 = 2.24$, and $x_4 = 8.71$). The procedure is that we first minimize P_1t_1. When we achieve its minimum (here zero), we fix P_1t_1 at that value and minimize P_2t_2. Once we have found that minimum, we fix both P_1t_1 and P_2t_2 at their minima, and minimize P_3t_3, and so on.

4.2 Scalarizing functions and the method of Wierzbicki

Wierzbicki (1980) has developed a method which may be thought of as a method for setting levels of all objectives. It assumes that all objectives are to be maximized, and employs a scalarizing function to find an efficient solution. Referring to our naive version, the chosen levels of objectives are almost certainly infeasible or dominated. The scalarizing method or reference point approach, as it also is called (see Kallio, Lewandowski, and Orchard-Hays, 1980) finds the closest efficient solution to the chosen point. It is intended to be used in a simulation-type mode by the decision maker.

Although there are a wide variety of scalarization functions that could be used, one that seems quite effective is one which can be represented in a linear programming context. Let u_i be the target level for objective i. The objective is to maximize

$$\left\{ \min \left\{ \rho \min_i \{C_i x - u_i\} \, , \, \sum_i (C_i x - u_i) \right\} + \varepsilon \, (C_i x - u_i) \right\}$$

where the parameter $\rho \geq p$ the number of objectives and ε is a nonnegative vector of small positive numbers. This objective function is achieved by a similar representation to that in goal programming for the minimization of the maximum deviation from a set of goals. Here, however, we maximize the minimum of (1) a constant times the minimum overachievement of a goal, and (2) the sum of overachievements of goals, averaged together with a weighted overachievement of goals. As in the case of goal programming, the function and parameters are somewhat arbitrary. However, the purpose of this method is to be used as an efficient solution generator, one that can be used to generate a sequence of efficient solution points. It is rather similar to goal programming and has been programmed to solve problems having as many as 99 objectives with as many as 1000 constraints.

4.3 Steuer's contracting cone method

Steuer's Contracting Cone Method (Steuer and Schuler (1976) and Steuer and Wallace (1978), see also Steuer (1977 and 1986)) is a refinement to the generation of all nondominated solutions that generates only a relatively small number of nondominated extreme point solutions. It does this by selecting a convex cone in space that is large initially and includes sets of weights corresponding to many nondominated extreme point solutions. Rather than generating all of them, however, he generates only a _very_ small number of extreme point solutions, and questions the decision maker regarding their relative attractiveness. He then uses the responses to contract the cone. When the cone becomes sufficiently small, the method generates all of the nondominated extreme point solutions in the cone for final consideration by the decision maker.

Assuming that there are p objectives, Steuer's method generates 2p + 1 trial solutions each time. The vectors generated* are:

	Values in General	Initial Values
λ_1	= the first extreme vector	(1,0,0,...,0)
λ_2	= the second extreme vector	(0,1,0,...,0)
⋮	⋮ ⋮	
λ_p	= the pth extreme vector	= (0,0,0,...,1)
λ_{p+1}	$= 1/p\ (\lambda_1 + \lambda_2 + \dots + \lambda_p)$	$= (1/p, 1/p, 1/p, \dots, 1/p$
λ_{p+2}	$= (\lambda_2 + \lambda_3 + \dots + \lambda_{p+1})/p$	$= (1/p^2, r, r, r, \dots, r)$
λ_{p+3}	$= (\lambda_1 + \lambda_3 + \lambda_4 + .. + \lambda_p + \lambda_{p+1})/p$	$= (r, 1/p^2, r, r, \dots, r)$
λ_{p+4}	$= (\lambda_1 + \lambda_2 + \lambda_4 + .. + \lambda_p + \lambda_{p+1})/p$	$= (r, r, 1/p^2, r, \dots, r)$
⋮		
λ_{2p+1}	$= (\lambda_1 + \lambda_2 + \dots + \lambda_{p-1} + \lambda_{p+1})/p$	$= (r, r, r, \dots, r, 1/p^2)$

where $r = (p + 1)/p^2$

The first p vectors are the extreme vectors of the cone, the p + 1st is the mean or center of gravity of the first p vectors, and each of the others is the mean or center of gravity of p-1 extreme vectors and the p + 1st vector. For each of the weights λ, a linear programming problem is solved maximizing $\lambda'Cx$, and the decision maker is presented with the 2p + 1 solutions. (All these solutions may not be different.) He is asked to choose which of the solutions he likes most, or if he is ready to look at all of the extreme point solutions in the cone. In the latter case, all extreme point solutions in the cone are found and presented to the decision maker for a final choice. Otherwise, the cone is contracted about the selected extreme point solution. The first p vectors (the extreme vectors) for the next iteration are the vectors corresponding to the chosen solution, say λ_q, and the average of that vector with each of the (first) p extreme vectors from the previous iteration.

---

*Instead of using zeros in the vector, we use some sufficiently small positive numbers. However, for simplicity of presentation we use zeros here.

$$\lambda'_i(i=1,\ldots,p) = .5\lambda_i + .5\lambda_q$$

The prime indicates the new trial weights. The remaining p + 1 vectors are found from $\lambda'_1,\ldots,\lambda'_p$ as λ_{p+i}, $i = 1,\ldots,p + 1$ are found from $\lambda_1,\ldots,\lambda_p$.

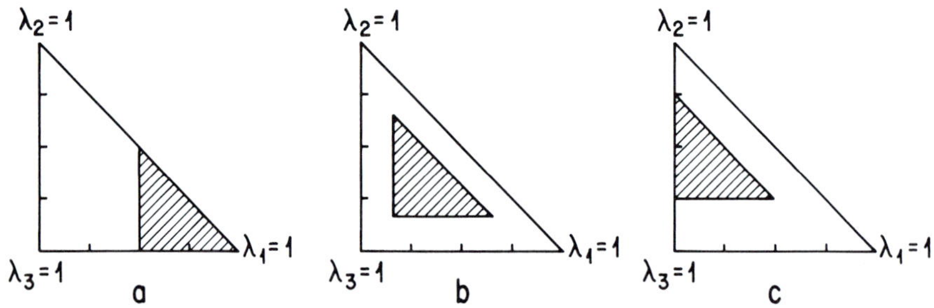

Figure 9 An Illustration of the Three Cases of Contracting Cones in Weight Space for the Case of Three Objectives

(The larger cone is the cone generated by the previous set of weights, and the smaller or shaded cone is the cone generated by the new set of weights)

Case a The solution corresponding to $\lambda_1 = 1$, $\lambda_j = 0$ $(j \neq 1)$, is preferred.

Case b The solution corresponding to $\lambda_j = 1/p$, $j = 1,\ldots,p$, is preferred.

Case c The solution corresponding to $\lambda_1 = 1/p^2$, $\lambda_j = (p + 1)/p^2$, $j \neq 1$ is preferred.

The process is repeated until the decision maker asks for all efficient solutions defined in a cone to make a final decision. The effect of contracting the cone is to reduce the volume of the cone to $(1/2)^p$ of what it was prior to the contraction. This fraction could be adjusted to a larger or smaller fraction, if desired. To illustrate how the cone contracts as we've described, consider a three objective problem. Figure 9 illustrates such a cone section with $\lambda_1 + \lambda_2 + \lambda_3 = 1$. If we contract the cone about one of the original p extreme vectors (e.g., λ_1), we have the diagram shown in Figure 9a. If we contract the cone about the center of gravity (the mean -- λ_4), we have the diagram shown in Figure 9b.

Finally, if we contract the cone about one of the off-center solutions (e.g., λ_5), we have the diagram shown in Figure 9c.

The procedure is appealing, but heuristic in nature. It does not necessarily always find the optimal solution. However, regarding performance, Steuer and Schuler (1976) report favorable experience in applications to a forestry management problem.

4.4 The Zionts-Wallenius method

The Zionts-Wallenius (1976, 1983) method for multiple objective linear programming uses weights. In that framework a numerical weight (arbitrary initially) is chosen for each objective. Then each objective is multiplied by its weight, and all of the weighted objectives are then summed. The resulting composite objective is a proxy for a utility function. (The manager need not be aware of the combination process.) Using the composite objective, solve the corresponding linear programming problem. The solution to that problem, an efficient solution, is presented to the decision maker in terms of the levels of each objective achieved. Then the decision maker is offered some trades from that solution, again only in terms of the marginal changes to the objectives. The trades take the form, "Are you willing to reduce objective 1 by so much in return for an increase in objective 2 by a certain amount, an increase in objective 3 by a certain amount, and so on?" The decision maker is asked to respond either yes, no, or I don't know to the proposed trade. The method then develops a new set of weights consistent with the responses obtained, and a corresponding new solution. The process is then repeated, until a best solution is found.

The above version of the method is valid for linear utility functions. However, the method is extended to allow for the maximization of a general but unspecified concave function of objectives. The changes to the method from that described above are modest. First, where possible the trades are presented in terms of scenarios, e.g., "Which do you prefer, alternative A or alternative B?" Second, each new nondominated extreme point solution to the problem is compared with the old, and either the new solution, or one preferred to the old one is used for the next iteration. Finally, the procedure terminates with a neighborhood that contains the optimal solution. Experience with the method has been good. With as many as seven objectives on moderate-sized linear programming problems (about 300 constraints) the maximum number of solutions is about ten, and the maximum number of questions is under 100.

We describe the general concave (GC) version in more detail. The linear problem form may, of course, be solved as a special case, though the GC method does not reduce to the linear method in that case.

We repeat the formulation of the problem for convenience.

$$\begin{aligned} &\text{Maximize} && g(Cx) \\ &\text{subject to:} && Ax \leq b, \quad x \geq 0 \end{aligned}$$

The underlying concave utility function g is assumed to have continuous first derivatives. We present the algorithm as a sequence of steps.

1. Choose an arbitrary vector of weights, $\lambda > 0$.
2. Solve the linear programming problem

$$\begin{aligned} &\text{Maximize} && \lambda' Cx \\ &\text{subject to:} && Ax \leq b, \quad x \geq 0 \end{aligned}$$

The result is a nondominated extreme point solution x^*. If this is the first time through this step, go to step 3. Otherwise, ask whether solution x^* is preferred to the old x^* solution. If yes, discard the old solution and go to step 3. If no, replace x^* by x^0 and go to step 3.

3. Find all adjacent efficient extreme point solutions to x^* consistent with prior responses. If there are none, drop the oldest set of responses and repeat step 3. Otherwise go to step 4.

4. (This step is simplified over what is used. See Zionts and Wallenius (1983).) Ask the decision maker (DM) to choose between x^* and an adjacent efficient extreme point solution. Do not repeat any questions previously asked. If the objective function values of the solutions are too close, or if x^* was preferred to an adjacent solution, ask the decision maker about the tradeoffs between the two solutions. The DM may indicate which solution he prefers, or indicate that he cannot choose between the two. If he prefers no alternatives or tradeoffs go to step 5. Otherwise mark a solution preferred to x^* as x^0 and go to step 6.

5. If all previous responses have been deleted, stop; if the decision maker does not like any tradeoffs from x^*, the optimal solution is x^*. Otherwise, to find the optimal solution, the method terminates and a search method (not part of this method) must be used to search the facets. If the procedure does not stop in which case previous responses have not been deleted, delete the oldest set of responses and go to step 3.

6. Find a set of weights $\lambda > 0$ consistent with all previous responses. If there is no feasible set, delete the oldest response and repeat step 6. When a feasible set of weights is found, go to step 2.

To find the adjacent efficient extreme points in step 3, consider the tradeoffs offered $(w_{1j},\ldots,w_{pj})$ by moving to the adjacent extreme point solution j. Then, consider the following linear programming problem:

$$\text{Maximize} \quad \sum_{i=1}^{p} w_{ik}\lambda_i$$

$$\text{subject to:} \quad \sum_{i=1}^{p} w_{ij}\lambda_i \leq 0 \qquad j \in N, \quad j \neq k \qquad \text{(A)}$$

$$\lambda_i \geq 0 \qquad i = 1,\ldots,p$$

where N is the set of nonbasic variables corresponding to solution on x^*. No convex combination of tradeoffs dominates the null vector, for otherwise solutions x^* would not be efficient.

<u>Definition</u>: Given two efficient extreme point solutions x_a and x^*, solution x_a is an adjacent efficient extreme point solution of x^* if and only if all convex combinations of x^* and x_a are efficient solutions.

<u>Theorem</u>: The optimal solution to problem (A) is zero if and only if solution k offering the tradeoff vector $w_{1k},\ldots,w_{pk}$ is not an efficient vector of the set of vectors w_j, $j \in N$. (For a proof see Zionts and Wallenius (1976).)

<u>Corollary</u>: If problem (A) has a positive infinite solution, then solution k offering the tradeoff vector $w_{1k},\ldots,w_{pk}$ is an efficient vector of the set of vectors w_j, $j \in N$.

The method does not explicitly solve problem (A) for every value of k. What it does is to choose one value of k at a time and to solve (A) for that value of k. At each iteration, a sequence of tests for other values of k are made which in general eliminate solving problems for other values of k.

As an example of the method, we consider Example 2. As a "true" set of weights we use $\lambda_1 = .58$, $\lambda_2 = .21$, and $\lambda_3 = .21$. Our solution procedure begins with $\lambda_1 = \lambda_2 = \lambda_3 = 1/3$. Refer to Figure 7 for further insight.

The initial solution is solution 4. First the decision maker is asked to compare solutions 4 and 2, he should prefer 4. Considering 4 versus 5, he should prefer 5. Considering 4 versus 6, he should prefer 4. A consistent set of weights is $\lambda_1 = .818$, $\lambda_2 = .182$, $\lambda_3 = 0$, and the new solution* is solution 1. The decision maker is asked to choose between 1 and 5; he should prefer 5. A set of consistent weights is .594, .160, .246. They yield solution 5. A final question is asked: between 5 and 2. Since he should prefer 5, there are no further questions to ask; solution 5 is optimal.

The Zionts-Wallenius method is extended to integer programming in Zionts (1977), which is extended, implemented, and tested in Villareal (1979) and Ramesh (1985). See also Karwan, Zionts, Villareal, and Ramesh (1985).

The Zionts-Wallenius method has been used by several organizations and has met with success. For example, Wallenius, Wallenius, and Vartia (1978) describe an application to macroeconomic planning for the Government of Finland. They used an input-output model of the Finnish economy with four

---

* We don't use zero weights: λ_3 would be equal to some sufficiently small positive number.

objectives chosen by the Finnish Economic Council chaired by the Prime Minister. The objectives were:

1. the percentage change in gross domestic produce
2. unemployment
3. the rate of inflation as measured by consumer prices
4. the balance of trade.

They first tried using the Geoffrion, Dyer, and Feinberg (1972) approach using an improvement prescribed by Dyer (1973). Although the method worked, the users found the estimation of the marginal rates of substitution difficult. Then the Zionts-Wallenius method was used. Results were obtained that were quite satisfactory.

One criticism of the Zionts-Wallenius approach is that if the underlying utility function is nonlinear, at termination we may not always have an optimal solution. (For an underlying linear utility function, the procedure gives an optimal solution.) However, the termination of the procedure indicates when this does occur. In such instances, we will have an extreme point solution that is preferred to all adjacent efficient extreme point solutions. A search procedure will then have to be used to find the optimal. See, for example, Deshpande (1980). Further refinements may be found in Breslawski (1986).

4.5 The Geoffrion, Dyer, and Feinberg method

The next mathematical programming method to be discussed, that of Geoffrion, Dyer, and Feinberg (1972), is in the spirit of a weighting method. However, it is a gradient type of method that allows for a nonlinear problem. The method begins with a decision that satisfies all of the constraints. Then information is elicited from the decision maker indicating how he would like to alter the initial levels of the various objectives. More specifically, he is asked to indicate how much of a reference criterion he is willing to give up in order to gain a fixed amount on one of the other criteria. The responses are elicited for every criterion except the reference criterion.

To illustrate, suppose that one has three objectives:

1. to maximize return on investment;
2. to maximize growth in sales;
3. to minimize borrowing.

Given a starting feasible solution and taking return on investment as our reference criterion, the decision maker would be asked two questions to consider from that solution:

1. What percentage growth in sales must you gain in order to give up a 1% return on investment?

2. What decrease in borrowing must you achieve in order to give up a 1% return on investment?

His responses can be used to determine the direction of change in objectives most desired.

That direction is then used as an objective function to be maximized, and the solution (the new solution) maximizing the objective is found. Then a one-dimensional search is conducted with the decision maker from the previous solution to the new solution. The decision maker is asked in a systematic manner to choose the best decision along that direction. Using the best decision as a new starting point, a new direction is elicited from the decision maker as above and the process is repeated until the decision maker is satisfied with the solution.

We now give an example of the Geoffrion, Dyer, and Feinberg method. If we were to assume a linear utility function, and provide correct tradeoff information, the method requires only one iteration. If we assume a nonlinear utility function or consider a linear utility function and do not provide correct tradeoff information, more iterations are required. We choose to assume a nonlinear utility function. We use example two; our utility function is

$$\text{Maximize} \quad U = -(u_1 - 66)^2 - (u_2 - 80)^2 - (u_3 - 75)^2$$

The constraints are as before.

We start with the solution $u_1 = u_2 = u_3 = x_1 = x_2 = x_3 = x_4 = 0$ ("true" objective function value -16,381). The partial derivatives are

$\frac{\partial U}{\partial u_1} = -2(u_1 - 66)$, $\frac{\partial U}{\partial u_2} = -2(u_2 - 80)$, and $\frac{\partial U}{\partial u_3} = -2(u_3 - 75)$. For the initial solution the vector of partial derivatives is 132, 160, 150, normalized as .299, .362, .339. We solve the linear programming problem using this set of weights to combine objectives. From Figure 7 we see the solution with that set of weights is solution 4 (24 66 66). We then choose the best solution on the line segment between (0 0 0) and (24 66 66) which is (24 66 66) (with true objective function value -2041). We find this by searching along the line segment between the two solutions. The new normalized objective function vector at (24 66 66) is .646 .215 .138, and the solution for that set of weights is solution 5 (48 60 12). The maximum solution is (26.6 63.8 61.2) on the line segment between the two solutions (See Table 1). The new normalized objective function vector at that point is .646 .215 .138, and the maximizing solution for that set of weights is solution 5 (48 60 12). The maximum solution on the line segment between (26.6 63.8 61.2) and (48 60 12) is (27.4 63.7 59.5) (with true objective function value -1999). At this point we begin to alternate between maximizing solutions four and five until the solution converges. The first few solutions and the optimum are summarized in Table 1. The optimal solution is approximately $x_1 = 1.5$, $x_2 = 5.25$, $x_4 = 17.25$ with objective function values (27.0 65.25 59.25).

An application of the method to the operation of an academic department on a university campus is described based on data from the 1970-1971 operations of the Graduate School of Management, University of California, Los Angeles. A linear programming model of the problem was developed and used to formulate annual departmental operating plans. Six criteria for evaluation were stated, including number of course sections offered at various levels, the level of teaching assistance used, and faculty involvement in various nonteaching activities. The decision variables under the control of the department were the number of course sections offered at different levels, the number of regular and temporary faculty hired, and the number of faculty released from teaching. The starting point for the analyst was the previous year's operating position, and the resulting solution suggested an important reallocation of faculty effort from teaching to other activities. The method was used without significant difficulty, and the results were adopted by the department, according to the article.

TABLE 1

	Solution			Objective Function Value	Maximizing Solution		
1	0	0	0	-16,381	24	66	66
2	24	66	66	- 2,041	66	30	-12
3	26.6	63.8	61.2	- 2,005	48	60	66
4	27.4	63.7	59.5	- 1,999	24	66	66
5	27.0	64.0	60.3	- 1,993	48	60	12
6	27.34	63.94	59.52	- 1,992.15	24	66	66
7	27.092	64.093	60.002	- 1,991.8	48	60	12
.							
.							
.	27.0	65.25	59.25	- 1,986.6	(24 / 48)	(66 / 60)	(66 / 12)

The problems with the method are asking the user to evaluate the gradient and asking the user to choose a solution along a line segment in the search procedure.

5 SOME HYBRID APPROACHES

We next consider two hybrid methods, methods that include one or more of the ideas of the naive approaches in their implementation.

5.1 The visual interactive method

Several methods have been developed in reaction to some of the problems associated with earlier approaches. The first of these to be discussed is the visual interactive method developed by Korhonen and Laakso (1986). The method may be thought of as a blend of the Wierzbicki, the Zionts-Wallenius, and the Geoffrion, Dyer, and Feinberg methods, tied together by computer graphics on a microcomputer. It works as follows: (I have taken a bit of poetic license in describing the method).

1. Have the decision maker choose a desired level of each objective that he would like to obtain. This is like goal programming or Wierzbicki's approach. Then using a variation of the Wierzbicki approach, project this solution onto the efficient frontier, and designate the efficient solution as the incumbent solution.

2. Present the incumbent solution to the decision maker, and ask him to specify a new set of desired levels of each objective function that he would now like to achieve. Call this the desired solution, and construct a vector from the incumbent solution to the desired solution (in objective function space). Let that vector have infinite length, thereby extending through and beyond the desired solution.

3. Analogous to step one, project the vector constructed in step two onto the efficient frontier. The projection constitutes a piecewise-linear function along the efficient frontier. In terms of each objective, as we move along the projection, accordingly, the objectives change in a piecewise-linear manner. Use simple computer graphics to show the changes that occur. See Figure 10.

4. Have the user do a line search (using the computer) along the projection to find his most preferred solution along the projection. As the user moves the cursor along the piecewise-linear segments, the screen displays the values for all of the objective functions. Designate the solution found as the incumbent solution, and go to step 2. If the incumbent solution remains the same, stop. An optimal solution has been found.

The computer implementation is on an IBM-PC and involves the representation of the objectives as piecewise continuous straight line functions. A different color is used for each objective. Some experimentation with the method is described by the authors, and the empirical results with the method to date appear to be reasonable. The method is particularly attractive because of its implementation on a popular microcomputer, the IBM PC.

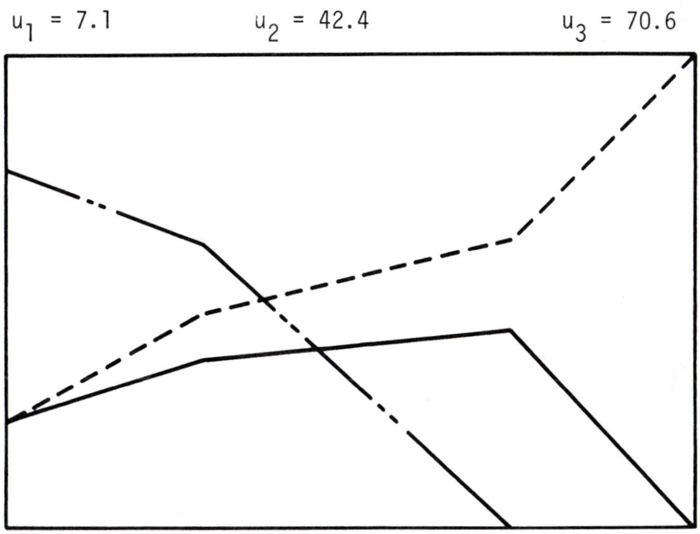

Figure 10 An Example of the Display in the Visual Interactive Method

5.2 A Pareto race

Based on the above approach, Korhonen and Wallenius (1987) have developed an approach that they call a Pareto Race. It continues in the tradition of Korhonen and Laakso, and is almost a video game. It combines the above ideas with the ideas of exploring all nondominated solutions, in the sense that the method explores a subset of nondominated solutions, as directed by the user. It may be used to solve a linear programming problem and involves having the decision maker, in a rough sense, explore the efficient frontier by "driving" around on it, thus the similarity to a video game.

In the case of two objectives, the corresponding efficient frontier may be thought of as one dimensional, and in the case of three objectives, the corresponding efficient frontier may be thought of as two dimensional, but for four or more objectives, the efficient frontier may be thought of as three dimensional or higher. (It is always one dimension less than the number of objectives.) Accordingly, except for two or three objective problems, it is not possible to represent the efficient frontier in a manner that may be visually represented on a plane. (The representation of a three dimensional problem on a plane may be thought of in terms of the weight space illustrated earlier.) Accordingly, the Pareto race uses bar graphs to represent the value of each objective. As the user moves around on the efficient frontier, the bar graphs (in color) change.

Using the analogy of "driving" around the frontier, the approach has certain functions that perform the movement along the frontier. These functions provide certain controls for the user (I use some poetic license in describing these functions; the authors describe these functions somewhat differently):

1. Provide movement in a preset direction. This corresponds to a unit movement along a projection described in the visual interactive method.

2. Increase or decrease the speed. This involves changing the stepsize of a unit movement in step one.

3. Change the minimum level of an objective. It may be set to a given value, or allowed to be free.

4. Change the direction of the path along the efficient frontier. Increase the component of a particular objective.

As with the visual interactive method, the Pareto Race has been implemented on an IBM PC/1 microcomputer. It is easy to use, and has been well received. The authors provide an illustration to a problem and several other applications.

Although the idea of the method and the way in which it is possible to move around the efficient frontier are interesting and worthwhile, the value of the method is greatly enhanced by the computer implementation and the graphics used.

5.3 A discrete alternatives method

A method that has proved successful for solving the discrete alternatives problem is one developed by Korhonen, Wallenius and Zionts (1984) and Koksalan, Karwan, and Zionts (1984). See also Chung (1986). What we present here is an abbreviated version of the first reference. The authors assume a single decision maker who has an implicit quasi-concave increasing utility function of objectives.

The idea is to consider the convex hull of the solution points, and the convex set that it represents. By reference to Figure 1 and the solution points contained therein, observe that the extreme points of the convex hull of the solutions (including the origin O) are solutions O, A, D, H, J, and K. As stated earlier, though solutions B and F are nondominated, they are dominated by convex combinations of solutions (B by A and D, F by D and H).

The method proceeds as follows:

1. Choose an initial set of weights for the objectives. (In the absence of anything better, having scaled the solutions so that the maximum and minimum obtainable for each objective is one and zero, respectively, choose the weights for each objective the same.)

2. Identify the solution that maximizes the weighted sum of objectives (by enumeration) and designate the maximizing solution as the incumbent solution.

3. Using the incumbent solution as a reference solution, identify all of the adjacent efficient solutions to the incumbent solution. Ask the decision maker to compare the incumbent solution with an adjacent efficient solution. Whichever is less preferred is eliminated, and a convex cone is constructed as a result of the choice. Eliminate any solutions that are dominated by the new convex cone. (See below for an explanation of the convex cones.)

4. When an adjacent efficient solution is preferred to the incumbent solution, the adjacent solution becomes the incumbent. Go to step 3. When no adjacent efficient solutions are preferred to the incumbent, the incumbent solution is optimal.

The procedure eliminates solutions from consideration as a result of comparisons (any solution less preferred than another solution may be eliminated), and as a result of cone dominance. What cone dominance does is to construct a cone as a consequence of one solution being preferred to another. Let the preferred solution be solution A, and the less preferred solution be solution B. (More generally, there may be several solutions _all_ preferred to another.) The authors prove that solution B is preferred to any solution in the cone (or halfline) emanating from B in the direction away from A, and consequently to any solutions dominated by the cone. See Figure 11.

The method uses a linear proxy utility function (the weights) to generate solutions. This does not mean that the underlying utility function must be linear. As a result of solutions being eliminated, solutions that are convex dominated may be most preferred.

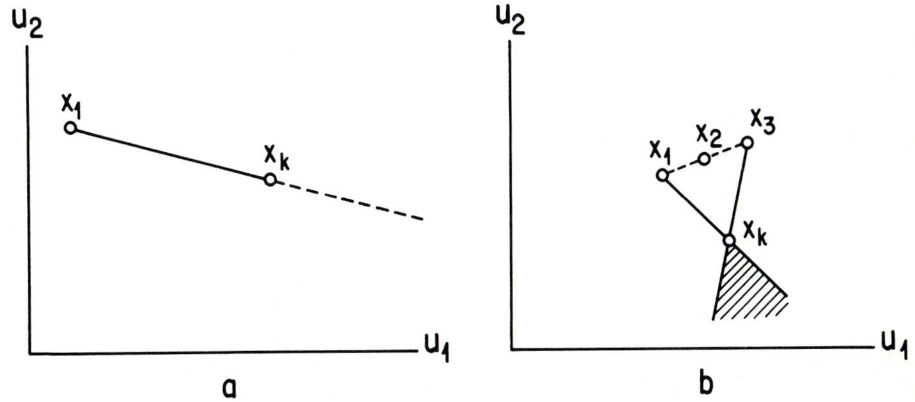

Figure 11 _Some Illustrations of Cone Dominance_

Chung describes an application of a derivative of this approach to a home purchase problem. He also has developed general proxy utility functions, and has the method choose the proxy utility function at each stage as a function of its apparent fit.

6 CONCLUSION

This presentation was designed as a brief introduction to the multiple criteria decision problem, with emphasis on the multiple objective linear programming problem. It includes a selection of methods from the plethora of those developed and presented in the literature. Our treatment was of necessity brief. I have included the methods I believe are important as developments or as stepping stones in the development of methods. For further information on what was presented, refer to the references. For additional information on these methods and new developments in the field, refer to the various journals in management science and decision support systems.

I have been working actively in the area of multiple criteria decision making over twenty years, with a short respite after my earliest work. I can honestly say that, from my perspective, the challenges in the field today are far greater than they have ever been. The computer technology is enabling us to come up with such approaches as numbers 6 and 7. I am sure that we will come up with even more powerful approaches. The problems that we study become even more difficult. We are currently studying the group decision problem, because of its importance and difficulty, and its relationship with other important problems.

The critical issue regarding all of the methods of multiple criteria decision making is in the eating, so to speak, or in the application. The literature is replete with methods that have been developed and published, but have never been used to solve problems. Lest we think that is a blemish, we should reserve judgment until an appropriate later date. We shall see that these methods and methods yet to be developed are used and will be used.

REFERENCES

1. Benayoun, R., de Montgolfier, J., Tergny, J., and Larichev, O., "Linear Programming with Multiple Objective Functions: Step Method (STEM)," Mathematical Programming, 1, 1971, 615.

2. Breslawski, S., A Study in Multiple Objective Linear Programming, Unpublished Doctoral Dissertation, School of Management, State University of New York, Buffalo, New York, 1986.

3. Charnes, A. and Cooper, W. W., Management Models and Industrial Applications of Linear Programming, John Wiley and Sons, New York, 1961.

4. Charnes, A. and Cooper, W. W., "Goal Programming and Multiple Objective Optimization - Part 1," European Journal of Operations Research, 1, 1977, 39.

5. Chung, H. W., Investigation of Discrete Multiple Criteria Decision Making and an Application to Home Buying, Unpublished Doctoral Dissertation, School of Management, State University of New York, Buffalo, 1986.

6. Deshpande, D., Investigations in Multiple Objective Linear Programming-Theory and an Application, Unpublished Doctoral Dissertation, School of Management, State University of New York at Buffalo, 1980.

7. Dyer, J., "A Time-Sharing Computer Program for the Solution of the Multiple Criteria Problem," Management Science, 19, 1973, 349.

8. Evans, J. P. and Steuer, R. E., "Generating Efficient Extreme Points in Linear Multiple Objective Programming: Two Algorithms and Computing Experience," in Cochrane and Zeleny, Multiple Criteria Decision Making, University of South Carolina Press, 1973.

9. Geoffrion, A. M., Dyer, J. S. and Feinberg, A., "An Interactive Approach for Multicriterion Optimization with an Application to the Operation of an Academic Department," Management Science, 19, 1972, 357.

10. Haimes, Y. Y., and Hall, W. A., "Multiobjectives in Water Resources Systems Analysis: The Surrogate Worth Trade Off Method," Water Resources Research, 10, 1974, 615.

11. Ijiri, Y., Management Goals and Accounting for Control, North-Holland Publishing Co., Amsterdam, and Rand McNally, Chicago, 1965.

12. Kallio, M., Lewandowski, A., and Orchard-Hays, W., "An Implementation of the Reference Point Approach for Multiobjective Optimization," Working Paper No. 80-35, International Institute for Applied Systems Analysis, Laxenburg, Austria, 1980.

13. Karwan, M. H. Zionts, S., Villareal, B., and R. Ramesh, "An Improved Interactive Multicriteia Integer Programming Algorithm," in Haimes, Y. Y. and Chan Kong, V., Decision Making with Multiple Objectives, Proceedings, Cleveland, Ohio, 1984, Lecture Notes in Economics and Mathematical Systems, Vol. 242, Springer-Verlag, (Berlin), 1985, pp. 261-271.

14. Keeney, R. L. and Raiffa, H., Decisions with Multiple Objectives Preferences and Value Tradeoffs, John Wiley and Sons, New York, 1976.

15. Koksalan, M., Karwan, M. H., and Zionts, S., "An Improved method for Solving Multicriteria Problems Involving Discrete Alternatives," IEEE Transactions on Systems, Man, and Cybernetics, Vol. 14, No. 1, January 1984, 24-34.

16. Korhonen, P. J., and Laakso, J., "A Visual Interactive Method for Solving the Multiple Criteria Problem," European Journal of Operational Research, 24, 1986, 277-287.

17. Korhonen, P. J., and Wallenius, J., A Pareto Race, Unpublished Paper, Helsinki School of Economics, 1987. Forthcoming in Naval Research Logistics.

18. Korhonen, P., Wallenius, J., and Zionts, S., "Solving the Discrete Multiple Criteria Problem Using Convex Cones," Management Science, 30, 11, 1984, 1336-1345.

19. Lee, S. M., Goal Programming for Decision Analysis, Auerbach, Philadelphia, 1972.

20. Manheim, M. L., and Hall, F., "Abstract Representation of Goals: A Method for Making Decisions in Complex Problems," in Transportation: A Service, Proceedings of the Sesquicentennial Forum, New York Academy of Sciences American Society of Mechanical Engineers, New York 1967.

21. Miller, G., "The Magical Number Seven Plus or Minus Two: Some Limits on Our Capacity For Processing Information," in Psychological Review, 63, 1956, 81.

22. Ramesh, R., Multicriteria Integer Programming, Unpublished Doctoral Dissertation, Department of Industrial Engineering, State University of New York at Buffalo, 1985.

23. Roy, B., "Partial Preference Analysis and Decision Aid: The Fuzzy Criterion Concept," in Bell, D. E., Keeney, R. L. and Raiffa, H., eds., Conflicting Objectives in Decisions, International Series on Applied Systems Analysis, John Wiley and Sons, 1977, 442.

24. Steuer, R. E., "Multiple Objective Linear Programming with Interval Criterion Weights," Management Science, 23, 1977, 305.

25. Steuer, R. E., Multiple Criteria Optimization Theory, Computation, and Application, John Wiley and Sons, New York, 1986

26. Steuer, R. E., and , A. T., An Interactive Multiple Objective Linear Programming Approach to a Problem in Forest Management, Working Paper No. BA2, College of Business and Economics, University of Kentucky, 1976.

27. Steuer, R. E., and Wallace, M. J., Jr., "An Interactive Multiple Objective Wage and Salary Administration Procedure," in Lee, S. M., and Thorp, C. D., Jr., Eds., Personnel Management A Computer-Based System, Petrocelli, New York, 1978, 159.

28. Villareal, B., Multicriteria Integer Linear Programming, Doctoral Dissertation, Department of Industrial Engineering, State University of New York at Buffalo, 1979.

29. Wallenius, H., Wallenius, J., and Vartia, P., "An Approach to Solving Multiple Criteria Macroeconomic Policy Problems and an Application," Management Science, 24, 1978, 1021.

30. Wierzbicki, A. P., "The Use of Reference Objectives in Multiobjective Optimization," in G. Fandel and T. Gal (Eds.), Multiple Criteria Decision Making Theory and Application, Springer-Verlag, New York, 1980.

31. Yu, P. L. and Zeleny, M., "The Set of All Nondominated Solutions in the Linear Cases and a Multicriteria Simplex Method," Journal of Mathematical Analysis and Applications, 49, 1975, 430.

32. Zionts, S., "Integer Linear Programming with Multiple Objectives",Annals of Discrete Mathematics, 1, 1977, 551.

33. Zionts, S. and Wallenius, J., "An Interactive Programming Method for Solving the Multiple Criteria Problem," Management Science, 22, 1976, 652.

34. Zionts, S. and Wallenius, J., "An Interactive Multiple Objective Linear Programming Method for a Class of Underlying Nonlinear Utility Functions," Management Science, 29, 1983, 519.

SECTION 4:

USE OF OPTIMISATION MODELS AS DECISION SUPPORT TOOLS

LANGUAGE REQUIREMENTS FOR A PRIORI ERROR CHECKING AND MODEL REDUCTION IN LARGE-SCALE PROGRAMMING

Johannes J Bisschop

1. Introduction.

Whenever we formulate a mathematical programming model in support of solving some real-world problem, we must be able to write down a complete model specification. Until the introduction of modeling languages, we could only use a personal notation consisting of algebraic statements together with English commentary for additional explanation. This "modeler's form" was then translated into an "algorithm's form" by means of a computer program, usually referred to as a model generator. The model generator generated the input for the solution algorithms, so that the underlying mathematical program could be solved on the computer. During this translation phase, however, errors were introduced and changes in a model over time were not always registered in both representations (see [5]). This has been a source of trouble for many model builders. During an extensive and complex modeling exercise at the Development Research Center of the World Bank (see [2]), there were at one point in time two model generators for the same large-scale model due to change of personnel. This unusual situation taught us an interesting lesson, since both generators turned out to have mistakes and some of these mistakes were only detected because the results of the two generators were not identical. In addition, the domains of definition for both the equations and variables were specified differently in the two generators, resulting finally in correct models, but of different size. Some redundant equations and null variables were eliminated in one generator, but not in the other. A similar situation occurred during a team effort at Shell Research in Amsterdam to develop an experimental refinery model. Even though the model representation had passed by each member of the team several times, subsequent error checking using the computer revealed several mistakes that were not discovered before. In addition, both the number of constraints and variables were reduced by approximately 50% following a careful domain analysis again using the computer (see [1]). Similar experiences have been informally voiced by others in the field, which tells us that even experienced modelers can make errors or generate non-compact models. It also tells us that the reliability of large-scale model representations is inherently low, unless explicit error checking has taken place. It is of course true that there are excellent tools which analyze linear programs and diagnose any algorithmic results. The reader is referred to ANALYZE, which is a computer assisted analysis system for linear programming models [7]. Such a system is based on a different philosophy, namely the detection of errors and insight into the model after the algorithm has been employed. The approach emphasized in this paper is to detect errors before

NATO ASI Series, Vol. F48
Mathematical Models for Decision Support
Edited by G. Mitra

an algorithm has been called. Both approaches complement each other, because if the a priori detection of certain errors does not, or cannot take place, then the a posteriori analysis is pertinent.

The main benefit of a priori checking is that certain well-defined errors cannot occur anymore. This certainly adds to the reliability of the model representation, since some errors may not be discovered in any other way. The main cost is that the model builder must indicate every error that needs to be checked. This requires a lot of time, ingenuity and a firm belief that any kind of mistake imaginable will in fact be made. The main benefits of analyzing a priori the domain of definition of equations and variables are reduced computation times and tighter models. In some instances, the tighter formulation may be the only one that fits a particular machine/algorithm configuration. The main cost is again human time required for the determinations of tight formulations. Based on our experience of improving the quality of large models one thing seems clear at this point. The benefits cannot be altered, but the costs associated with both error checking and model reduction are too high for most practical purposes, and must come down. Only then can it become an integral part of model building with the resulting increase in reliability and compactness. By introducing special language components for error checking and model reduction in future modeling languages this cost/benefit ratio will come down. The purpose of this paper is to indicate how this might be done.

In Section 2 we characterize the type of errors that are typically made in large-scale model representations. This is followed by a brief discussion of domain analysis for model reduction in Section 3. In Section 4 suggestions are made for future modeling languages to deal with the issues raised in Sections 2 and 3. The conclusion of this paper is stated in Section 5.

2. Error in Large-Scale Models.

In order to get a feel for the type of errors that can be made in the mathematical representation of large-scale models, the following three categories can be distinguished.

The first kind of errors that one might encounter in model descriptions are the so-called symbolic errors. They are essentially spelling and referencing mistakes. For instance, if identifiers such as labels, parameter names, equation names and variable names are spelled incorrectly, they may be viewed as new identifiers which is not the intention of the model builder. Whenever an identifier name in a model is indexed with several indices, and the order in which they are referenced is permuted, the name may refer to nonexistent information. This, again, is not the intention of the model builder. Experience has shown that this type of error occurs frequently in large model descriptions, and that the model builder tends to overlook them while inspecting a model description.

Domain and range errors form the second kind of errors that one might distinguish in model descriptions. These errors are essentially an incomplete or inconsistent specification of domain and range definitions of data, equations and unknowns. Let us look at a few examples. One example is the situation where data values are out of range (e.g. input-output coefficients are not between -1 and 1). Another example is the situation where the explicit relationship between two or more data items is not satisfied (e.g. the lower bound on the use of a component in a blend is not less than or equal to the upper bound on the use of this component). A third example is the situation where the elements of an index are not properly represented in a data specification (e.g. each material in a refinery production model has an associated density, but one or more materials are missing in the density specification table). The consistency errors frequently occur during updates of the model or the underlying data. The arrival of a crude at a refinery, for instance, may have an effect on the (re)allocation of tanks, on the permissible set of processes within the refinery model, on the registration of new materials etc. It is then easy to forget to register one of the resulting changes. Domain and range errors in model representations are difficult to detect while reading. This is mostly due to the size and the complexity of a complete model representation.

The third category of errors that one might distinguish consists of formulation errors. These errors are essentially dimensional errors, unit scaling errors, and construction errors. Dimensional errors are made when the underlying dimensions of identifiers do not match in an algebraic expression. Such errors occur frequently in complex technical models describing some physical or chemical reality. Unit scaling errors are made in an algebraic expression when the dimensions are correct, but the units do not match. Consider the last example in the previous paragraph. Even when all data updates resulting from the arriving crude are made, it still may be that the amount of the arriving crude is entered in tons instead of thousands of tons. Construction errors are the most difficult of the formulation errors to detect a priori. They are part of legal expressions with no dimensional or unit scaling errors. The reason why they are construction errors is that they represent a reality that is not intended by the model builder. Consider the example of a raw material balance written in words as "the use of raw materials is equal to the import of raw materials" and written in algebraic terms as

```
SUM( p , a(cr,p,t) * z(p,i,t) )  =  v(cr,i,t) .
```

The indices cr, i, t, and p refer to crude oils, plants, time periods and processes respectively. The unknown z represents production levels, and the data items a and v refer to process input-output coefficients and imports respectively. This expression seems perfectly all right, but contains a construction error which was unintended. The convention for process input-output tables is to represent input coefficients as negative numbers and output coefficients as positive numbers. The correct material balance should have read in words as "the use of raw materials (stated negatively) plus the import of raw materials must balance". In algebraic terms it should have been written as

```
SUM( p , a(cr,p,t) * z(p,i,t) )  +  v(cr,i,t)  =  0  .
```

Such construction errors are subtle, which makes them hard to discover beforehand. A model builder cannot always take the required distance from the constructed model, and therefore tends to overlook this type of errors.

Even though all three types of errors are made and thereby negatively influence the reliability of large-scale model representations, a methodology for systematically transferring the responsibility for avoiding errors to a modeling system can make a drastic improvement. This will be discussed in Section 4.

3. The Reduction of Large-Scale Models.

Whenever each individual variable and constraint in a model description has its own name it is straightforward to indicate which equations must be generated and which variables are part of each constraint. In the event that symbolic names are used to refer to GROUPS of constraints and variables, however, it is not possible to know which individual members of each group are to be generated unless this is explicitly indicated in the model statement.

Large-scale models invariably contain groups of constraints and variables, which implies that the model builder must specify the domain of definition for each group. If a model builder is not careful in the specification of domains, then several things may happen. The worst that can happen, is that meaningless constraints and variables are permitted, thereby altering the intended meaning of the model. This type of misspecification is usually discovered when the model results are obtained. Less troublesome are incorrect domain specifications that lead to the generation of redundant variables and/or constraints. In that case the intended model statement is conceptually correct, but the presence of the redundant constraints and variables causes an unnecessary increase in the size of the generated model. If this increase is in terms of just a few percentages, it does not hamper the solution process. If, on the other hand, the model becomes quite a bit larger, then it is not efficient anymore to let the solution algorithm discover these redundancies. In that case careful domain determination ought to be an explicit part of the model description. Such careful domain specification becomes even indispensable when the reduced model barely stays within the limits of a particular machine.

There are several situations in which model reductions can be obtained.

A first reduction can be achieved by eliminating the trivial null variables and null equations. Whenever the coefficients in a group of linear constraints in nonnegative variables are themselves nonnegative, and the corresponding right hand side contains one or more zero values, then the constraints with zero right hand side are redundant and can be eliminated. The reason for this is that in every feasible solution of the model the value of the variables will be zero. That is why these variables can also be eliminated from any other constraints in the model.

A second reduction can be accomplished by using only those portions of the underlying database that are relevant for a particular model run. If, for instance, the database contains reference to materials that are not available for particular model periods, then any constraint or variable that references that material in these model periods should not be generated. In general there are no clear cut rules as to how one might find these run-specific limitations, and the model builder must use his or her own ingenuity to find such information. In practice, most reductions are obtained by clever use of the database underlying the constraints and variables.

A third way to reduce the model is to recognize when a constraint contains only one variable. By not generating such a constraint, and instead replacing it with a simple upper or lower bound on the variable, one has reduced the number of regular constraints in the model. The simple upper and lower bounds are usually easier to handle for the solution algorithm than the regular constraints.

It should be noted at this point that traditionally mathematical programming models are reduced only after they have been offered to the solution system, and not at the time of formulation. In some sense this is to be preferred, since the model builder does not have to worry about any reductions ([4], [8] and [11]). On the other hand, sloppy formulations without proper domain specification can lead either to erroneous models, or to models that are even too large for the solution system at hand. It is also such that run-specific domain restrictions can lead to model reductions that could not be realized by a solution algorithm. The main intuitive reason for this is that reduction at the level of the model specification can be based on insight into the application, while this information is essentially lost at the lower level of the algorithm.

4. Language Requirements for Error Detection and Model Reduction.

Even though we cannot expect 100% error-free representations of models, we can make drastic improvements in the reliability of large-scale model representations by systematically transferring the responsibility for detecting mistakes to the modeling software. In addition, we can make model formulations tight by proper domain definitions of both equations and variables. These activities are time consuming, and lie on the peripheral of model building. In order to obtain the benefits but at a low cost, any future modeling language for large-scale mathematical programming problems must offer extensive and easy-to-use facilities to make both error checking and domain analysis an integral part of model building.

What facilities are we talking about? In answering this question we will follow the order of topics described in Sections 2 and 3.

4.1 Language Requirements for the Detection of Symbolic Errors.

As we noted in Section 2, symbolic errors are essentially spelling and referencing mistakes. Misspelling of identifiers can be eliminated by requiring that every identifier be declared before it is used anywhere in the model statement. The misspelling of labels (that are used for the identification of numbers etc.) can be eliminated by careful domain specification of each algebraic construct defined over label sets. If A(i,j,k) is declared as 3-dimensional data defined over the label sets i, j and k, with A containing floating point numbers, then any such number can only be described via three labels in the proper order. The system must check for the correct spelling of labels and the correct ordering of these label sets or subsets thereof when any reference to A is made.

The modeling language GAMS is an example of a modeling language which provides facilities for the checking of symbolic errors, but only under stringent conditions (see [3], [9] and [10]). All label sets that can be checked by that system must be constant sets, i.e., sets that are constructed as an explicit list of labels with no subsequent changes made to this list. This means that lists of labels defined in a different manner, say via some algebraic definition involving other sets, cannot be used for domain checking purposes. In practice, this turns out to be a limitation, since explicit construction of label sets can be quite lengthy, while algebraic constructs are compact and more meaningful to anyone reading the model. The reasoning used by the GAMS development team was that domain checking involving label sets should be performed cheaply at compile time. If there would be a separate algebra for label sets within a modeling language, however, then extensive domain checking at compile time is still possible even if label sets are defined algebraically in terms of other sets. Only in the event that algebraic definitions contain extensive reference to other data which is determined elsewhere in the model may one have to resort to domain checking at execution time.

4.2 Language Requirements for the Detection of Domain and Range Errors.

Domain and range errors require special attention, since the model builder must give directives to the modeling system for each error that must be checked.

Let us first look at the domain of one construct. If numbers and/or labels are defined over label sets, then it must be possible to state compactly a variety of properties associated with such a domain. A typical example is the question whether every label in the set appears in the construct, and how frequently. A process input-output table, for instance, should contain all raw and intermediate materials at least once with an associated negative value, and all intermediate and final materials at least once with an associated positive value. In addition, each process name should occur exactly once. Besides being able to express these simple domain properties in a compact fashion, there must also be expression power for the definition of complicated domain conditions. Once all this domain knowledge has been defined for a particular construct, it is the task of the system to automatically verify whether the conditions that are imposed remain satisfied during the model execution phase.

Let us now look at the range of one construct. Without much effort the model builder must be able to state whether the range of a construct consists of numbers, labels, booleans etc. In the case of numbers, it must be possible to state compactly whether numbers are integer, floating, rational, binary, etc., together with simple bounds on the integer, floating and rational values. In the case of labels, it must be possible to state compactly which labels are in the permitted range.

Besides these simple conditions, it must also be possible to define more complicated conditions to describe the range of one construct. Once all this knowledge has been defined once, it is the task of the system to automatically verify whether the conditions that are imposed remain satisfied during the model execution phase.

Next consider relations between domains and ranges of particular constructs in the model. As we saw in Section 2, several consistency errors can only be expressed as relations between domains and ranges that must be true. The language must have a strong power of expression to state such knowledge, which the modeling system must check automatically throughout the execution stage. In practical models these functional relationships can be quite complex. It is therefore desirable that a future modeling language is a non-procedural one, where complicated relationships can be stated as a collection of short definitions. The modeling system will then take care of the procedural part by determining how and in what order these definitions should be applied. In that way the modeling system serves as an expert system for the detection of errors.

The above requirements are not easy to put in a language, and deserve further study. GAMS is an example of a modeling facility that can be used for data consistency checking, but often in a round-about way (see [1]). The dollar operator permits a powerful conditional statement on either domains or ranges, but such a statement must be repeated every time the model builder wants it to be evaluated. In addition, GAMS does not offer special facilities for simple ranges, simple conditions on the occurrence of labels in constructs, or an expert-like system for the definition of complex functional relationships between domains and ranges.

4.3 Language Requirements for the Detection of Formulation Errors.

The formulation errors that result from non-matching dimensions or non-matching units within algebraic expressions can be eliminated completely once the modeling system offers extensive facilities for dimensional analysis. This means that for every algebraic construct dimensions can be declared, and that the system checks the consistency of dimensions automatically. Whenever units do not match, the system can automatically make the appropriate scaling of data so that the units always match. This will alleviate a burden on the model builder who must frequently integrate data from different sources.

The formulation errors that result from pure construction errors (see Section 2) are the most difficult ones to detect beforehand. A clear and easy-to-grasp language for the description of data and model statements is important here, because a person other than the model builder may then be able to detect some of the construction errors. Additional help may come from inspecting some of the model equations at the individual equation level. This would have resolved the error in the example of the raw materials balance equation of Section 2. At some point, however, we will not detect any more errors beforehand. Whenever model results are questionable at that point, further diagnosis with systems such as ANALYZE are needed.

The requirement of a clear and easy-to-grasp language for the description of data and model statements is vague. What is 'clear and easy-to-grasp'? Further research in the area of modeling languages and systems may shed some light on this question. A few guiding principles can be borrowed from fourth generation programming languages: separate issues in different modules, use a functional language to get rid of procedural aspects, simplify input and output definitions, etc. Consider again the GAMS system. This modeling system does provide a notation for the structuring of algebraic constructs, but there are several areas where its power to express is poor or even insufficient. Consider scheduling problems with a rolling horizon, complex combinatorial problems, problems with constructs that contain many subscripts etc. Further research in the area of modeling languages is certainly necessary, and will eventually result in a wider applicability of mathematical programming as a tool for the solution of large-scale problems.

4.4 Language Requirements for the Reduction of Models.

If there is a good functional language for the detection of domain and range errors, then it can function at the same time as a good language for the reduction of models. Model reduction is obtained by restricting the domain of definition of equations and variables. As was stated in Section 3, certain model reductions are performed by some of the solution algorithms. This is the preferred mode of operation, but for some large-scale models a priori reduction still remains necessary. In that case, the language should also offer the facilities to act as an expert system for model reduction. Short definitions pertaining to domains must be possible. These domains can be mutually dependent, in which case a logically consistent evaluation of the definitions must take place.

Consider a multi-period refinery planning model with a preferred planning option. A typical model run consists of trying to obtain a solution that is as close as possible to the initial directives of the planner. In such a model run large portions of the model are not to be generated, but these portions can differ tremendously from experiment to experiment. Indicating the appropriate domains of definition for materials and processes is quite complex, but may be straightforward with the use of recursive definitions. In these definition materials are selected on the basis of processes and processes are selected on the basis of materials. Just specifying these functional relationships should be sufficient. The modeling system should then determine, based on the initial directives of the planner, how these mutually recursive definitions should be evaluated and what their impact is on the model to be generated.

At this point we may observe that current modeling languages have not been designed around the prevention of errors or the construction of compact models. At our Technical University we are currently looking at these and other issues in order to design a next generation modeling language with improved expression power when compared with currently available modeling languages.

5. Summary and Conclusions.

In this paper we have considered the topics of error detection and model reduction in large-scale programming models. It does not seem that error detection should be part of a model description, since it distracts from the intent of the model statement, namely presenting a modeler's vision of a part of the real-world. A similar statement can be made about model reduction, since most algorithms contain reduction schemes.

Despite these two observations, practical experience with large models has indicated that these models contain many specification errors, and that, as a result, explicit detection of these errors ought to be part of the total model statement. Similarly, there are applications where the structure of the model changes from experiment to experiment, and model reduction should be an integral part of the model statement.

Without error detection, a large-scale model representation containing many pages of data, data transformations, and constraints cannot be considered reliable. If mistakes are found, then they are only discovered after a current version of the model fails to produce acceptable solutions. This is a rather roundabout and costly way to detect errors in a model description.

On the basis of experience with large-scale models we argue for special language requirements to be part of future modeling languages in support of both error detection and model reduction.

The following distinction between error types has been made.

I. Symbolic errors
- -- spelling errors
- -- referencing errors.

II. Domain and Range Errors
- -- single domain errors
- -- single range errors
- -- consistency errors.

III. Formulation Errors
- -- dimensional errors
- -- unit scaling errors
- -- construction errors.

Any modeling language and system designed around avoiding these errors will also provide a notation for the reduction of models, since model reduction is nothing more than being able to specify domains of definition for symbolic equations and variables.

In the paper several suggestions concerning language requirements are made, and can be summarized as follows.

I. Require the declaration of each identifier.
II. Develop a separate algebra for label sets.
III. Develop the language modular and functional.

IV. Provide facilities for structural domain properties.
V. Provide facilities for range indication.
VI. Implement global domain setting and checking.
VII. Design the language as a functional language.
VIII. Provide dimensional analysis.
IX. Allow for automatic unit scaling.

This list is by no means an exhaustive list of suggestions for future modeling languages for mathematical programming. It does emphasize, however, those requirements that will help a model builder in improving the overall reliability of large-scale model descriptions. These and other issues play an important role in our current research which centers around the design of a next generation modeling language for the description of large-scale mathematical programming models.

References.

[1] Bisschop, J., "Model Reduction and Error Checking in Large-Scale Linear Programming Applications", to appear in Special Issue of IMA Journal of Management Mathematics, 1987.

[2] Bisschop, J., Candler, W., Duloy, J. and O'Mara, G., "The Indus Basin Model: A Special Application of Two-Level Linear Programming", Mathematical Programming Study, vol. 20 (1982), pp. 30-38.

[3] Bisschop, J. and Meeraus, A., "On the Development of a General Algebraic Modeling System in a Strategic Planning Environment", Mathematical Programming Study, vol. 20 (1982), pp. 1-29.

[4] Brearly, A.L., Mitra, G., and Williams, H.P., Analysis of Mathematical Programming Models Prior to Applying the Simplex Algorithm, Mathematical Programming, Vol. 8 (1975), pp. 54-83.

[5] Fourer, R., "Modeling Languages Versus Matrix Generators for Linear Programming", ACM Transactions on Mathematical Software, Vol 9, No 2 (1983) pp. 143-183.

[6] Goodman, G.M., "Post-Infeasibility Analysis in Linear Programming", Management Science, Vol. 25, No. 9 (1979) pp. 916-922.

[7] Greenberg, H.J., "A Functional Description of ANALYZE: A Computer-Assisted Analysis System for Linear Programming Models", ACM Transactions On Mathematical Software, Vol. 9 (1983), pp. 18-56.

[8] IBM Corporation, Mathematical Programming System Extended, MPSX/370, Reference Manual, SM19-1095-1, 1976.

[9] Kendrick, D. and Meeraus, A., GAMS : An Introduction, (Draft version of a book), Development Research Department, The World Bank, 1985.

[10] Meeraus, A., "An Algebraic Approach to Modeling", Journal of Economic Dynamics and Control, vol. 5 (1983), pp.81-108.

[11] Telgen, J., Redundancy and Linear Programs, Ph.D. Dissertation, Mathematisch Centrum, Amsterdam, 1979.

A NOTE ON THE REFORMULATION OF LP MODELS

(For NATO ASI on Mathematical models for decision support)

JOAQUIM CARMONA

Lecturer

Economics Faculty of Oporto, Portugal

1. INTRODUCTION

One of the advantages of spreadsheet type modelling systems (including the MP or MP dependent ones) is that there is no separation between model generation and report writing; the user defines a report and in the process imbeds the model in it.

SIMP CARMONA [1], CARMONA and JONES [21]) is a spreadsheet type interface to an LP optimiser created from the MPCODE program developed by LAND and POWELL [4] in the sixties. It works by accepting "formulae", not only of the usual form: "cell=expression", but also of the forms: "cell=<expression","cell>=expression" (and "cell=MAX expression" and "cell=MIN expression"). At time of calculation empty cells are regarded as variables in an LP problem, and formulae as constraints. Calculation results in the empty cells being filled up. SIMP runs on "standard" IBM PCs with colour monitors.

MPCODE uses no factorization techniques (although it is based on a reduced basis version of the simplex algorithm); the number of rows and columns of the problems the system could solve was quite limited - 200 rows, 160 columns and an 80 x 80 maximum size of the reduced basis in the version built for SIMP. Although small, this number seemed in principle big enough for the experimental purposes envisaged for SIMP.

NATO ASI Series, Vol. F48
Mathematical Models for Decision Support
Edited by G. Mitra

2. WHY REFORMULATE

When a system is used in which there is a separation between model generation and report writing, frequently information (averages, subtotals, even inventory variables) is left for the report writer to derive. Not so in spreadsheet systems - much of this information is embodied in the report, and is used in the definition of the model as imbedded in the report through formulae. As a result, the size of the problems tend to be remarkably inflated. In SIMP's case, the modeller's convenience became an acute difficulty for the optimizer: in the initial versions of the system, even rather small problems became (due to such "redundant" information) too big to be solved.

To overcome the difficulty, it was necessary to equip SIMP with a reformulation routine. The alternatives of modifying the optimiser or of using another one were not judged feasible, or attractive in the context (mainly time scale) of the project of which SIMP was a part. The implication, therefore, is not that problems should be automatically reformulated before being solved, and still less that the way this was done in SIMP is the best way to do it. The way it was done in SIMP, although having the (then essential) qualities of being simple and hence worked quickly and effectively, is quite obviously not the best one in some respects.

3. METHOD OF REFORMULATION

Faced with a list of constraints, SIMP goes through it and, each time it finds an equality constraint, uses it to eliminate the first variable of that constraint from all other constraints. That constraint, as a rule, is retained separately to be used after optimization to calculate the value of the variable. It may have to be replaced in the LP problem by another constraint to guarantee the non-negativity of the variable which was discarded from the problem. As a result, the problem which is solved has as many variables less as there were originally equality constraints, or may have at most that many less constraints, or has no equality constraints, or has more non-zero matrix elements and is therefore a lot less sparse.

How well this procedure works is illustrated by the results presented in the following table, which lists the number of proper constraints, upper bounds and variables, before and after reformulation, in five problems, A, B, C, D and E. A, B, C and D can be found in WILLIAMS [5] (they are respectively Food Manufacturing, Factory Planning, Manpower Planning and Curve Fitting problems); E is a gasoline blending problem which can be found in DARBY-DOWMAN, LUCAS and MITRA [3].

TABLE 1

Dimension of problems before and after reformulation.

	BEFORE			AFTER		
PROBLEM	CONSTR	UB	VARIAB	CONSTR	UB	VARIAB
A	115	12	165	65	0	66
B	99	107	236	116	48	89
C	66	24	94	35	23	39
D	38	0	62	37	0	23
E	73	0	71	23	0	20

(Annex A lists the Food Manufacturing model - report and formulae, i.e. before reformulation - and the MPCODE problem generated after reformulation).

4. PROCEDURE ASSESSMENT

Although these results are reasonably good, and were satisfactory for the purpose required, there are some points about the procedure which obviously seem less than ideal. They evolve from the choice of the first variable which appears in an equality constraint as the one to eliminate from the problem.

If that variable is upper bounded, replacing it by a linear combination of other variables will result in the upper bound becoming a proper constraint. Preferably other non-bounded variables in the equality constraint should be used.

In an equality constraint with non-negative right-hand side, in which all variables but one have negative coefficients, the variable with positive coefficient is the best candidate to be eliminated from the problem. There is then no need to replace the equality constraint by another constraint to ensure the non-negativity of the variable that is eliminated, and that constraint can simply be dropped. In fact it would seem sensible to completely eliminate this type before all others.

If one of the variables in an equality constraint appears in far less other constraints than the other variables, eliminating it will be simpler and will also not increase the number of non-zero elements in the matrix so much.

(1) CARMONA, J [1985]
Towards effective support of optimization modelling.
PhD Thesis.
Department Management Systems and Sciences, Hull University.

(2) CARMONA, J and JONES, C [1986]
SIMP's User Guide.
Working Paper 12.
Department Management Systems and Sciences, Hull University.

(3) DARBY-DOWMAN, K and LUCAS, C and MITRA, G [1984]
Computer assisted modelling of linear, integer and separable programming problems.
Technical Report TR/08/84.
Department Mathematics and Statistics, Brunel University.

(4) LAND, A H and POWELL, S [1973]
FORTRAN codes for Mathematical Programming: linear, quadratic and discrete.
John Wiley & Sons.

(5) WILLIAMS, H P [1984]
Model building in mathematical programming.
John Wiley & Sons.

Interfaces Between Modeling Systems and Solution Algorithms.

by

Arne Stolbjerg Drud
ARKI Consulting and Development A/S
Bagsvaerdvej 246 A
2880 Bagsvaerd
Denmark

1. INTRODUCTION.

Until recently, a modeler needed to know many details about solution algorithms, in the following referred to a 'solvers', especially about cumbersome input and output formats, and model building was consequently rather skill intensive and expensive. Although computer times often are quoted as a measure of the effort involved in a modeling exercise, the manpower to implement and debug a model is usually much more costly. Better algorithms has for some time not been the key to cheaper modeling, but rather systems that could manage the model building process. As a result of this demand, several so called modeling systems have emerged over the last years, see e.g. Bisschop and Meeraus [3], Fourer [8,9], and Geoffrion [10].

A modeling system is for the purpose of this paper a computer system that accepts a user friendly representation of a model, translates it into a form acceptable to a solver, invokes the solver, and translates the output of the solver back into a form that can be interpreted by the modeler. The model representation will usually be mathematical and the modeling system will also have extended data manipulation facilities, but this is not important for the purpose of this paper. The important point is that solvers are not part of the modeling system itself: they are merely utility systems that the modeling system communicates with, usually developed by some independent party. The modeling system must therefore communicate in two directions: with the modeler and with the solvers, see fig. 1. A good modeling system must make both communications easy, i.e. the interface to the modeler must be

NATO ASI Series, Vol. F48
Mathematical Models for Decision Support
Edited by G. Mitra

oriented towards the needs of a modeler, and the interface to the solvers must be oriented towards the needs of the solvers.

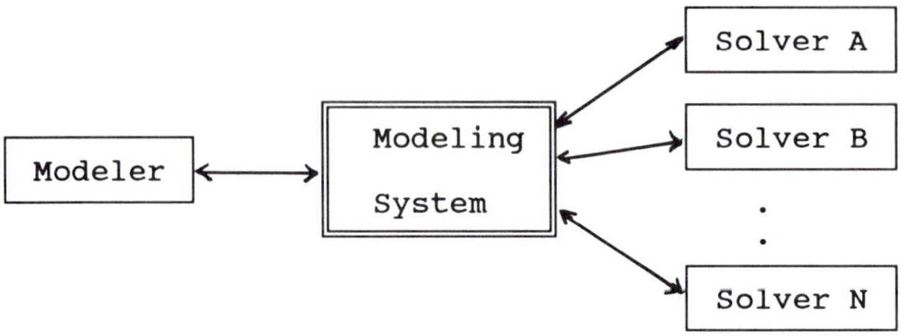

FIGURE 1: The communication channels surrounding a modeling system.

The main concern of this paper is the interfaces between the modeling system and the solvers. It is, however, important to understand the modeling environment and the input to the modeling system, so section 2 describes this component. Section 3 discusses the varying requirements of different solvers, and section 4 touches on the issues of model reformulation, i.e. translation of the model formulated by the modeler into a mathematically equivalent model that is better suited for a particular solver. Section 5 discusses interfaces in general with emphasis on the communication from the modeling system to the solver, section 6 describes the special issues involved in communicating nonlinearities, and section 7 is concerned with the information flowing back, and especially with mechanisms for translating error messages produced by a solver into a format that can be interpreted by the modeler. Section 8 contains some concluding remarks and speculations about the future. The discussion is wherever possible kept at a general level. When practical examples are needed they are throughout the paper chosen from the modeling system GAMS, see Kendrick and Meeraus, 1987.

2. THE MODELING ENVIRONMENT.

The purpose of a modeling system is to help a modeler build models faster and cheaper. The main tool as seen by the modeler is a language that allows him to concentrate on model formulation without being concerned with practical details of solvers; the modeling system takes care of the necessary translations onto the proper formats. The ultimate goal, as seen by this author, is that people with only a marginal knowledge of solution algorithms should be able to formulate and solve models reliably using a modeling system.

The challenge to the designer of a modeling system comes from the fact, that there are many different types of models, and one solver will not be able to solve them all. Table 1 shows the classes of models currently recognized by or planned for the modeling system GAMS, and Table 2 shows the solvers that are available today, permanently or experimentally. The number of solvers that handle more or less the same model classes may seem excessive. But there are good reasons. Some of the LP systems, such as APEX IV and MPSX/370, are only available on some of the machine on which GAMS is available. And the large number of NLP algorithms is used to increase the overall reliability of nonlinear modeling: if one solver fails then it is straight forward to try another.

TABLE 1: Classes of mathematical models and their implementation status in GAMS

Name	Explanation	Status
LP	Linear Program	standard
MIP	linear Mixed Integer Program	standard
RMIP	Relaxed Mixed Integer Program	standard
NLP	Non-Linear Program	standard
DNLP	Discontinuous Non-Linear Program	standard
NET	Linear NETwork	not implemented
GNET	Generalized NETwork	not implemented
NLNET	Non-Linear NETwork	experimental
NLMIP	Non-Linear Mixed Integer Program	experimental

Note, that a model can move from one model class to another by a marginal change in formulation, at least as seen by many modelers. The implementation of a model change that is considered marginal by a modeler should of course require a minimum amount of work, and the representation of the models, as seem by the modeler, must therefore be very similar. However, the marginal change in the model may require a completely new solver, and it is therefore important that the modeling system maintains an model representation that is independent of both solver and model class. All transformations must be performed internally in the modeling system.

3. CHARACTERISTICS OF SOLUTION ALGORITHMS.

We have argued that a modeling system must translate models from a common, algorithm independent format into the formats required by various solvers (solution algorithms), and it is therefore important to look at these formats.

Most commercial Linear Programming systems use a common input format, the MPS-tape. The output formats are, however, rather different, both because file formats are machine specific, and because of subtle differences, for example in the definitions of signs of marginals.

Algorithms for nonlinear models are less standardized, and there is hardly any common elements in their inputs. Some algorithms use sparse representations of the Jacobian of the constraints and need the sparsity pattern as input; some algorithms require nonlinear equations and/or variables to appear before linear ones; some require the objective function to be treated specially and others treat it the same way as a constraint. The nonlinearities are usually defined through a black-box subroutine, but the formats vary: the calling sequence is different; some systems require the complete function to be defined and others only the nonlinear components, and this component may be defined differently across systems; and derivatives are handled in different ways. Further details can be found in Brooke et.al. [4], that gives a comparison of the interface facilities available in four nonlinear programming algorithms.

TABLE 2: Solvers connected to GAMS and the model classes they can handle. The parenthesis around DNLP means that the solver tries to solve the model as if all functions were continuously differentiable.

Name	Model classes	Reference
BDMLP	LP, RMIP	none
APEX IV	LP, RMIP, MIP	[16]
MPSX/370	LP, RMIP, MIP	[17]
Sciconic	LP, RMIP, MIP	[18]
XMP/ZOOM	LP, RMIP, MIP	[14]
MINOS 5	LP, RMIP, NLP, (DNLP)	[15]
CONOPT	LP, RMIP, NLP, (DNLP)	[7]
GRG2	LP, RMIP, NLP, (DNLP)	[13]
NPSOL	LP, RMIP, NLP, (DNLP)	[11]
NLPNETG	NLNET	[1]

Another important characteristic of a solver is whether it is a subroutine that can be changed or it is a self contained (unmodifiable) system at the operating system level. Most LP systems are self contained systems and most NLP systems are modifiable collections of subroutines. The implications of these differences will be discussed in section 5.

The large variability in the input requirements and formats of all these algorithms and the assumption that a modeling system should interface several algorithms makes the design of the interfaces rather challenging. How can we minimize costs by using common software components to create variable output?

4. MODEL REFORMULATIONS.

The model formulated by the modeler is usually translated faithfully into the format required by the solver. There are cases, however, where this may be very inefficient. The following model is a good example:

$$\min \quad z = x1 + x2$$

$$\text{s.t.} \quad x1 = f1(y)$$
$$x2 = f2(y)$$

and network or generalized network constraints on y.

If f1 and f2 are nonlinear functions then this model is a general nonlinear programming model with two nonlinear constraints. If x1 and x2 are substituted out, however, we have a nonlinear network model for which efficient special purpose algorithms are available, e.g. Ahlfeld et.al. [1]. It is often argued that the modeler should formulate his model with tricks like this in mind to utilize the facilities of the available solvers. This is, however, quite contrary to our belief that model formulation should not be a job for algorithm experts but for subject experts, and models should be formulated to be easy for humans to understand.

Reformulation of models creates a new complexity in the interface. In the model above, x1 and x2 and the dual variables associated with the eliminated constraints must be computed based on the solution values for y. Furthermore, all error messages relating to a reformulated model must be translated into messages relating to the original model.

Reformulation is currently absent from most modeling systems. The GAMS modeling system performs a limited amount of reformulation, and further research along these lines are in progress, see Drud [6].

5. INTERFACE MECHANISMS.

As mentioned in section 3, solvers can be of two types: modifiable subroutines and unmodifiable self contained systems. Modifiable subroutines can be linked into the overall modeling system through a set of interface subroutines, provided there are no problems associated with linking different programming languages. This type of interface is in the following called an 'Internal Interface'. For small modeling systems with a limited number of solvers an internal interface may be an attractive possibility. However, the overall system can become very large and difficult to maintain and it is not possible to include unmodifiable solvers. All practical large scale modeling systems will therefore have to use an 'External Interface'. An external interface is one in which the modeling system writes a model representation to one or more files, calls the solver through a command at the operating system level, waits for it to finish and write the solution to another file, resumes command, and reads the solution back from the file. Further discussions of internal and external interfaces in a general setting can be found in Drud [5].

The setup of external interfaces to subroutine systems and to self contained systems, as implemented in GAMS, are shown in fig. 2 and 3, respectively. From the modeling systems point of view, there is no difference between the two: the modeling system writes a set of files and gives up control by calling an operating system procedure. At the end, this procedure calls the modeling system again and the modeling system reads the solution from another set of files. Provided the files written and read by the modeling system can have the same format there is no real difference. The only apparent difference between the interfaces is the content of the operating system procedure: in one case it consists of a call to one program (fig. 2) and in the other to a sequence of programs (fig. 3). But the modeling system is only concerned with the name of the procedure, not its content.

There is also little difference from the point of view of the solvers. We can use more or less the same read and write routines since the files are the same. The only special programming needed for each subroutine systems is the core allocation and the creation of the algorithm specific data structures, such as sparsity patterns, and there is no way this can be systematized due to the large differences in algorithms. The only special programming needed for self contained systems is the routines that rewrites the input to and rereads the output from this system, and again, little can be systematized here.

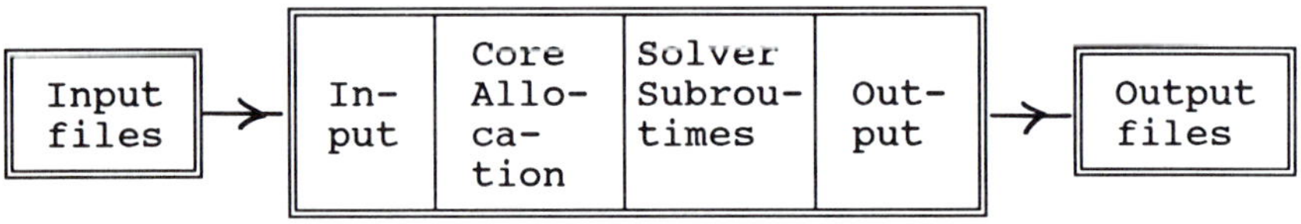

FIGURE 2: An External Interface to a Subroutine System.

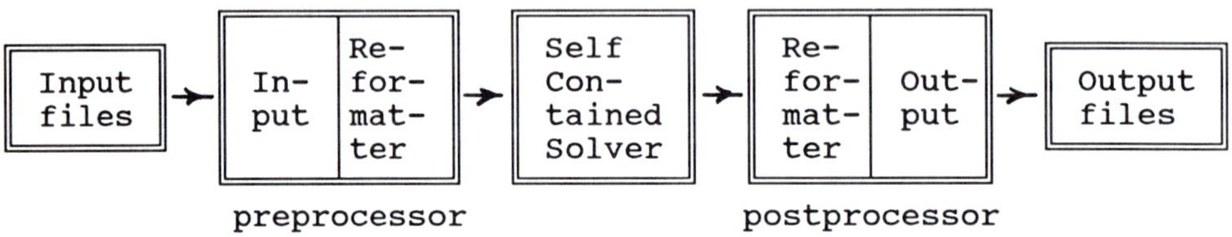

FIGURE 3: An External Interface to a Self Contained Solver.

The key to reusing interface components is a common structure of the interface files. The structure of these files in GAMS are discussed in Bisschop and Brooke [2]: GAMS creates two or three files: a <u>control</u> file, a <u>data</u> file, and possibly a <u>nonlinear instruction</u> file. The control file contains all relevant statistics about the model and about the other file(s): the number of variables (linear and nonlinear), the number of equations (linear and nonlinear), the number of nonzero Jacobian elements (linear and nonlinear), the largest number of Jacobian elements in a column, etc. It is possible from the control file alone to perform all core allocations before the other files are opened. The data file contains bounds, initial values, and types (linear, nonlinear, binary) of all variables and equations, and the sparsity structure, numerical values and types (constant, varying) of the Jacobian elements. The nonlinear instruction file is discussed in section 6.

Note that the description of the control and data files covers general nonlinear models. GAMS, however, uses the same files for linear models; certain fields will just have a fixed value for linear models, and an interface routine for LP can ignore these fields. The fields that are only used for more general model classes are placed at the end of each record so simpler model classes can limit their reading to the first part of each record.

It is important to use an interface mechanism that allows addition of new solvers without having to change the modeling system or the interfaces to old solvers. In GAMS, information about algorithms are provided in a capability table that is read in at initialization time. The capability table contains, in addition to the information in Table 2 above, the calling sequence for the operating system procedure that invokes the algorithm. A new algorithm is therefore from GAMS' point of view added by adding one record to the capability table. The interface files are rather general and they will usually contain the necessary information also for new solvers, and the modeling system can stay intact. The only programming work is in the solver specific components of fig. 2 or 3.

The information in the control and data files are in rare cases insufficient when a new algorithm is added. An example was the addition to GAMS of XMP/ZOOM, see Marsten [14]. The core allocation in ZOOM needs information on the largest number of nonzeros in a column, and this information was not available. It was, however, easy to fix: a few lines of code were added to GAMS to keep track of the largest number of nonzeros in a column, and the information was added at the end of one of the existing records in the control file for use by the interface to ZOOM. All existing interfaces were intact since they simply skipped the new information.

6. NONLINEAR FUNCTIONS.

All nonlinear solvers require a representation of the nonlinearities. Most solvers use a black-box representation through a subroutine: the solver calls the subroutine with a vector of variable values as input, and the subroutine returns values of the nonlinear functions. Any deeper structure of the nonlinearities is ignored. The way the black-box subroutine is created and its inner working is irrelevant for the solver. The modeling system can therefore create it in any convenient way. The most efficient way is usually assumed to be to write a FORTRAN subroutine with the nonlinear functions, compile it into efficient machine code with a good compiler, and link it to the solver routines.

GAMS uses a quite different approach. The nonlinear functions are written to the nonlinear instructions file using a GAMS specific instruction set, and the black-box subroutine is an interpreter that interprets these instructions. The approach was originally chosen because it was fast to implement and rather easy to move between machines, but it was expected that a FORTRAN approach had to be used later to get reasonable execution efficiency. It turned out, however, that the loss in execution efficiency is minimal and in many cases GAMS actually gains overall efficiency. The time spend in the interpreter is seldom more that 15-25% of the overall time in the solver, so faster function evaluations cannot save much. On the other hand, the interpreter approach saves both compile and link time since the solvers can be prelinked into absolute programs with the fixed, model independent interpreter. This saving is on an IBM-PC similar to the time it takes to solve small models of up to 30-40 equations.

7. SOLVER OUTPUT.

When a modeling system resumes control after a solver has executed it must first determine what happened. For this purpose GAMS classifies both what happened to the model, the Model Status, and what happened to the solver, the Solver Status. The possible values of the Model and Solver Status are shown in Table 3 and 4, respectively.

TABLE 3: Model Status as recognized by GAMS

No.	Message text
1	OPTIMAL
2	LOCALLY OPTIMAL
3	UNBOUNDED
4	INFEASIBLE
5	LOCALLY INFEASIBLE
6	INTERMEDIATE INFEASIBLE
7	INTERMEDIATE NONOPTIMAL
8	INTEGER SOLUTION
9	INTERMEDIATE NON-INTEGER
10	INTEGER INFEASIBLE
12	ERROR UNKNOWN
13	ERROR NO SOLUTION

Some of the solver status values need a little explanation. Solver status 4 indicates, that the solver found a problem with the model, issued a message to this effect, and terminated. An example could be that a derivative becomes too large, and the message will identify the row and column of the Jacobian element.

TABLE 4: Solver Status as recognized by GAMS

No.	Message text	Sysout
1	NORMAL COMPLETION	No
2	ITERATION INTERRUPT	No
3	RESOURCE INTERRUPT	No
4	TERMINATED BY SOLVER	Yes
5	EVALUATION ERROR LIMIT	No
6	UNKNOWN	Yes
8	ERROR PREPROCESSOR ERROR(S)	No
9	ERROR SETUP FAILURE	No
10	ERROR SOLVER FAILURE	Yes
11	ERROR INTERNAL SOLVER ERROR	Yes
12	ERROR POSTPROCESSOR ERROR(S)	No
13	ERROR SYSTEMS FAILURE	Yes

The basic principle in error reporting should be, that all error messages should pinpoint the problem as closely as possible using the modelers notation. In the example with the large Jacobian element above, the element should be referred to by the modelers name of the variable and equation. But the solver does not know these names, so the modeling system must merge a message text from the solver with identification information from the modeling system. We have for use with GAMS modified the formats of error messages in the subroutine based solvers to include output processing directives that guide this merge process.

This basic error reporting principle can be difficult to follow with self contained solvers because the error messages, that come as part of a larger systems output file, cannot be modified. The whole systems output file is therefore printed in case of errors over which GAMS has no control. This is indicated by a 'Yes' in the column Sysout in Table 4.

Solver status 5 means, that some of the nonlinear functions defining the model were called outside their domain of definition, e.g. log of a negative number or division by zero. All the nonlinear functions are evaluated in the interpreter mentioned above. It is therefore under full control of the modeling system and it is easy to identify the error exactly and issue an informative error message.

8. CONCLUSIONS AND FUTURE RESEARCH.

The paper has discussed some of the general principles that should be considered when creating a set of interfaces between a modeling system and a set of solvers, and it has indicated how some of the problems have been solved in case of the GAMS modeling system. The key issues are to systematize the interfaces so common software components can be used to build them even though the solvers are very different in structure, and to build the interfaces so that addition of a new solver does not invalidate the old interfaces.

Most of the future research will probably be on the side of the modeling systems. Reformulation will become important. Currently, GAMS requires the modeler to define the class of the model and to select the solver. Automatic detection of model class and selection of the most appropriate solver based on model characteristics will be very important and is still a topic of research.

REFERENCES:

1. Ahlfeld, D., R. Dembo, J.M. Mulvey, and S.A. Zenios: Nonlinear Programming on Generalizes Networks, report EES-85-7, Department of Civil Engineering, Princeton University, Princeton, 1985.

2. Bisschop, J. and A. Brooke: How to place some of your own linear solvers in GAMS using the PC, mimeo, Development Research Department, 1987.

3. Bisschop, J. and A. Meeraus: On the Development of a General Algebraic Modeling System in a Strategic Planning Environment, Mathematical Programming Study, vol. 20, p. 1-29, 1982.

4. Brooke, A., A. Drud, and A. Meeraus: High Level Modeling Systems and Nonlinear Programming, in Nonlinear Optimization 1984, P.T. Boggs, R.H. Byrd, and R. E. Schnabell (eds.), p. 178-198, SIAM, Philadelphia, 1985.

5. Drud, A.: Interfacing new Solution Algorithms with Existing Modeling Systems, Journal of Economic Dynamics and Control, vol. 5, p. 131-149, 1983.

6. Drud, A.: Alternative Model Formulations in Nonlinear Programming - Some Disastrous Results, Operations Research, vol 33, p. 218-222, 1985.

7. Drud, A.: CONOPT - A GRG Code for Large Sparse Dynamic Nonlinear Optimization Problems, Mathematical Programming, vol 31, p. 153-191, 1985.

8. Fourer, R.: Modeling Languages Versus Matrix Generators for Linear Programming, ACM Transactions on Mathematical Software, vol. 9, p. 143-183, 1983.

9. Fourer, R., D.M. Gay, and B.W. Kernighan: AMPL: A Mathematical Programming Language, AT&T Bell Labs Working Paper, 1986.

10. Geoffrion, A.: An Introduction to Structured Modeling, Working Paper no 338, Western Management Sciences Institute, UCLA, Los Angeles, 1986.

11. Gill, E.P., W. Murray, M.A. Saunders, and M.H. Wright: User's Guide for SOL/NPSOL: a FORTRAN Package for Nonlinear Programming, Department of Operations Research, Stanford University, 1984.

12. Kendrick, D. and A. Meeraus: GAMS - An Introduction, mimeo, Development Research Department, World Bank, 1987.

13. Lasdon, L.S., A.D. Waren, A. Jain, and M. Ratner: Design and Testing of a Generalized Reduced Gradient Code for Nonlinear Programming, ACM Transactions on Mathematical Software, vol. 4, p. 34-50, 1978.

14. Marsten, R.E.: The Design of the XMP Linear Programming Library, ACM Transactions on Mathematical Software, vol 7, p. 481-497, 1981.

15. Murtagh, B.A. and M.A. Saunders: A Projected Lagrangian Algorithm and its Implementation for Sparse Nonlinear Constraints", Mathematical Programming Study, vol 16, p. 84-117, 1982.

16. APEX IV Reference Manual, CDC Manual 76070000.

17. Mathematical Programming System - Extended (MPSX) and Generalized Upper Bounding (GUB) Program Description, IBM manual SH20-0968.

18. Sciconic, Product of Scicon Ltd, UK.

MATHEMATICAL PROGRAMMING SOLUTIONS FOR FISHERY MANAGEMENT

João Lauro D. Facó
Institute of Mathematics
Computer Science Department
Universidade Federal do Rio de Janeiro
and
INRIA - Rocquencourt

1. INTRODUCTION

In ecosystems analysis we are mainly concerned with modelling and management of ecological systems. The development of a mathematical model generally involves two phases : determining the structure of the model and finding its coefficients. Once a model has been established it is tested in terms of its predictive capabilities. A model that works may be used to evaluate alternative management programs .Optimization techniques play an important role in this analysis.

Here we shall concentrate our interest, following a previous paper [14], on ecosystems representing interacting multispecies fish populations submitted to increasing fishery pression : Regulation and limitation of the quantities captured are most important in order to achieve a maximum sustainable yield.

Optimal Control Theory has been applied to build model structure and to parameter estimation [5, 11, 12, 15] , but the increase in model complexity as nonlinearities, time lags, inequality constraints on the state and control variables imply critical numerical difficulties. The flexibility and efficient solution procedures of Mathematical Programming methods offer significant advantages in dealing with a general class of these problems. Atkinson (1980) has shown how this approach can be used to treat a broad range of problems and to deal directly with some parameters uncertainty that can be defined as variables by including all explicit and implicit constraints relating their values to the model formulation.

The model consists of a set of coupled discrete time nonlinear difference equations :

$$P(t+1) = F_t \left[P(t), p(t) \right] ,$$

where, $P(t)$ = vector of population concentrations,
$p(t)$ = vector of model parameters,
F_t = differentiable real fonction.

The components of $p(t)$ correspond to competitor and predator interaction coefficients, to growth and death rates, and to other ecological factors that quantify the relationships between populations and/or their environment. These parameters actually represent variables in the context of the optimization formulation for their uncertainty.

NATO ASI Series, Vol. F48
Mathematical Models for Decision Support
Edited by G. Mitra

The system during a given time period is affected by different types of ecological processes:

(1) Natural population mortalities including those resulting from inter-group and intra-group interactions (predation and competition);

(2) Spatial redistribution of the populations among the ocean regions resulting from migration and fishery pression;

(3) Birth and aging within population groups.

The basic model can be stated by a system of difference equations representing the change in population concentration during the time t to t+1:

$$P_i\ (t+1) = S_i\ (t)\ e^{-\alpha P(t)}\ e^{-\beta P(t)}\ [1-R_i\ (t)\ e^{-\gamma P(t)}]\ P_i\ (t),$$

$S_i(t)$ and $R_i(t)$ represent maximal survival/growth and starvation mortality effects; the coefficients α β γ relate to competitor,predator, and prey effects.

A difference equation model has advantages over a differencial equation representation for our purposes. From a biological point-of-view, certain features of fish population dynamics such as migration and spawning occur over a relatively short time period and can be more effectively described as discrete processes. From a practical point-of-view, the discrete set of ecosystem equations have less computational requirements relative to coupled differential equations integration routines. Discrete time models are also compatible with the sample data sets to be used in the model formulation and subsequent analysis.

2. MODELLING OF TUNAS ECOSYSTEM IN SOUTHEASTERN BRAZIL

2.1. Introduction

The tunas fisheries are realised along most of the brazilian coast, by traditional means in the north and northeast, and by industrial processes in the southeast and south. Since 1979 we have noted a great increase in this economical activity. Among the different species we selected the three which show the best economic rates in the 1979-1983 period following Thomaz, Gomes and Facó (1985) and Thomaz (1986) : Katsuwonus pelamis, thunnus albacares and thunnus obesus.

We formulate a dynamic ecosystem to determine the optimal catch rate by species and area in the southeastern coast in Brazil. The model is a modified version of the Lokta-Volterra multispecies interaction and a bioeconomic objective function of net returns to be maximized through time.Some parameters are identified by optimal spatial distribution generated by cluster analysis and production stock model (Fox, 1975) to obtain the biomass and catchability coefficients in each ocean cluster.

The model discussed here will consider the competitivity aspect only. There is no information about predators for tunas in that region and about the classes of preys for these species in Brazil.

2.2. Spatial distribution and parameter identification

Using data from SUDEPE (Fishery Development Agency of Brazil) for the period 1979-1983 about harvest and effort for tuna species in each ocean block of one degree side, we have the CPUE (catch per unit effort) index for the 3 species considered. To obtain an optimal spatial distibution we performed a cluster analysis using the k-means algorithm (Hartigan and Wong, 1974) minimizing the variance within clusters. This way we got 4 clusters shown in figure 1.

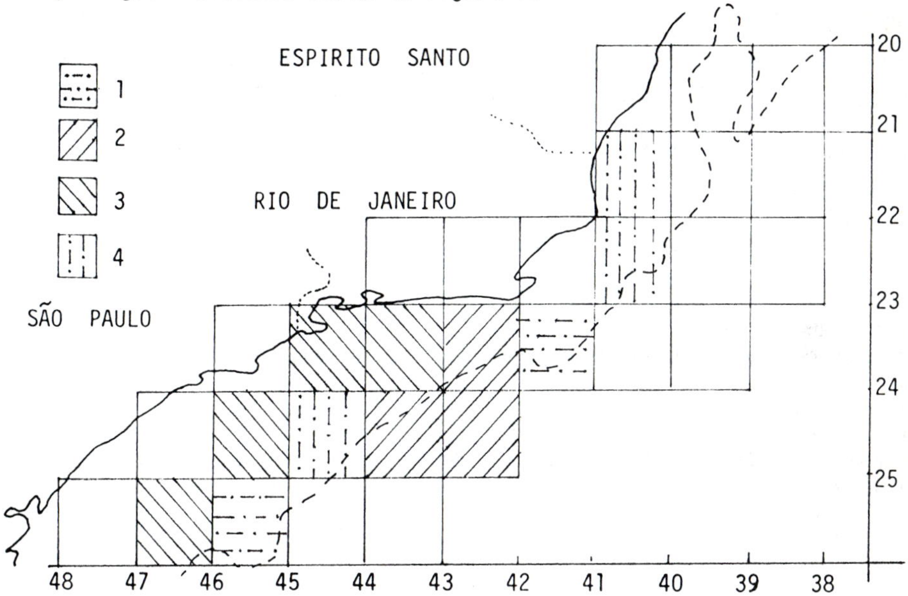

Fig.1. Optimal spatial distribution.

Generalized stock production analysis (Fox,1975) was applied fitting by a least-square method each population in each block. The MSY (maximum sustainable yield), VPS (virgin population size) and capturability indexes are thus computed (tables 1 and 2).

		CLUSTER 1	CLUSTER 2	CLUSTER 3	CLUSTER 4	TOTAL
Katsuwonus	MYS	1079.1	3948.3	9469.2	5773.5	20270
pelamis	VPS	11099.1	7701.3	14433.3	7259.9	40492
Thunnus	MSY	82.2	969.3	72.9	261.9	1386
Albacares	VPS	5002.8	1282.5	179.1	836.4	7301
Thunnus	MSY	1256.1	43.5	181.5	33.3	1514
Obesus	VPS	2988.9	129.9	463.8	1651.2	5233

Table 1. Population sizes (metric tons)

	CLUSTER 1	CLUSTER 2	CLUSTER 3	CLUSTER 4
Katswonus Pelamis	0.0047	0.0033	0.0014	0.0018
Thunnus Albacares	0.020	0.0074	0.0118	0.0190
Thunnus Obesus	0.00013	0.0064	0.00430	0.0079

Table 2. Catchability indexes

We can represent the dynamic ecosystem by coupled difference equations :

$$x_i(t+1) - x_i(t) = [\ r_i - a_{i1}x_1(t) - a_{i2}x_2(t) - a_{i3}x_3(t)\ ]\ \ x_i(t),$$

where, $x_i(t)$ = biomass of population i at time t,

r_i = net growth rate of population i,

a_{ij} = inhibitor effect of the popul. i on the population j,

for i = 1,2,3, and t = 0,1,2,..., T.

The inhibitor effects a_{ij} are estimated taking into account the s clusters generated by the optimal spatial distribution,

$$a_{ij} = \frac{r_i}{K_i}\ c_{ij}$$

$$\text{where,}\quad c_{ij} = \frac{\sum_{h=i}^{s} Pih\ \ Pjh}{\sum_{h=i}^{s} P_{in}^{2}}\ ,\quad i,j = 1,2,\ldots,n,$$

and :

P_{ih} = percentage of the population i in the cluster h,

K_i = carrying capacity of the environment for the pop. i in absence of other competing species (saturation level).

2.3. The Optimal Control formulation for fishery management

The introduction of fishery is considered as a perturbation factor in the dynamic ecosystem. The model must consider the economical interests in exploring this activity constrained by ecological factors in order to avoid the drainage of some of the species harvested.

Let us consider the optimal control model :

$$\text{Max} \quad J = \sum_{t=o}^{T} e^{-\delta t} \sum_{i=1}^{3} d_i u_i(t),$$

so that,

$$x_i(t+1)-x_i(t) = \left[r_i - \sum_{j=1}^{3} a_{ij}x_j(t) \right] x_i(t) - u_i(t),$$

$$\underline{u}_i(t) \leq u_i(t) \leq \overline{u}_i(t),$$

$$a_i \leq x_i(t) \leq b_i, \quad i=1,2,3, \text{ and } \quad t=0,1,2,\ldots,T,$$

where,

$u_i(t)$ = harvesting rate of population i,

d_i = unitary profit of harvesting population i,

T = planning horizon,

$\underline{u}_i$, $\overline{u}_i$, a_i and b_i bounds on x_i and u_i ,

$x_i(o)$ known, and δ = medium discount rate on $[0,T]$.

3. MATHEMATICAL PROGRAMMING APPROACH

The mathematical models formulated can be considered as examples of a standard discrete time Bounded State Nonlinear Optimal Control Problem :

$$\text{Max } L\,(x_o,x_1, \ldots x_T \,;\, u_o, u_1, \ldots, u_{T-1}) \quad \text{so that,}$$

$$x_{t+1} = f_t(x_t\,,\, u_t) \quad , \quad t = 0,1,\ldots, T-1$$

$$\alpha_t \leq u_t \leq \beta_t \quad , \quad t = 0,1,\ldots, T-1$$

$$a_t \leq x_t \leq b_t \quad , \quad t = 1,2,\ldots, T$$

where for all t,

$x_t \in \mathbb{R}^m$ is the vector of state variables,

$u_t \in \mathbb{R}^n$ is the vector of control variables,

L , f_t are continuously differentiable nonlinear functions,

and T is a cardinal number representing the total time periods.

The objective function L is usually of the form :

$$\sum_{t=o}^{T-1} L_t (x_t,u_t) + L_T (x_T)$$

The difficulties in this problem are due firstly to its high dimension unless m,n and T are very small, which makes the use of Dynamic Programming problematic for the excessive combinatorics involved, and secondly to the bounds on the state variables that added to the nonlinearities make the use of Pontryagin's maximum principle based methods very inefficient for the need to solve two-point boundary-value problems.

An approach somewhat different from the previous ones is presented here. This approach uses a Nonlinear Programming Method called Generalized Reduced Gradient (GRG)due to Abadie and Carpentier (1969). An algorithm named GRECO-Gradient réduit pour la commande optimale- by Facó (1977) solves this problem as a specialization of the GRG to optimal control problems exploiting its particular staircase structure.

Atkinson (1980) has already applied Lasdon's code GRG2 [10] with good numerical results.

Let us consider the standard discrete optimal control problem stated before, and see how it can be solved by the GRG method.

Following a suggestion of Abadie [1], the basis is kept in a factored representation taking advantage of the block triangularity of the jacobian. Abadie [2] showed the interest in using some state variables as independent variables in the presence of inequality constraints along some parts of the trajectory of the dynamic system.

We use the Gaussian elimination (LU decomposition) of each diagonal block introducing some criteria for the choice of the set of basic variables at each re-inversion and for searching the independent variable to enter the basis each time we change basis (when a basic variable reaches a bound). The updating of the basis matrix is done as in linear programming by adding a new factor to the representation. Thus we can save storage and use numerically stable techniques which give greater accuracy and less growth of nonzeros in the basis representation.

Algorithm GRECO :

Step 1. For each $t \in \{1,2,\dots,T\}$ obtain the subsets B and N of basic and independent variables by the application of the principles (P1), (P2),(P3),(P4); the factorization of the real basis is established :

$\mathbb{B} = S \; E_1 \dots E_k$, where : S = working basis
$\mathbb{B}$ = real basis, and
E_i = eta-vector, $i=1,2,\dots,k$;

Step 2. Compute the improving direction d_N of the independent variables:

(i) compute the Lagrange multipliers by the procedure BACKW (x,u):

$\psi B = b$, where $b = -c_B$, basic components of the gradient vector;

(ii) compute the reduced gradient $g^N = (\omega^N, \chi^N)$:

$$\omega^t = \frac{\partial L_t}{\partial x_t} - \psi^{t-1} + \psi^t \frac{\partial f_t}{\partial x_t}, \quad t = 1,\dots,T-1$$

$$\omega^T = \frac{dL_T}{dx_T} - \psi^{T-1}$$

$$\chi^t = \frac{\partial L_t}{\partial u_t} + \psi^t \frac{\partial f_t}{\partial u_t}, \quad t = 0,1,\dots, T-1;$$

(iii) compute the projected reduced gradient P_N as in GRG; if $P_N = 0$, stop; apply the conjugate gradients method to obtain the direction d_N;

Step 3. Compute the improving direction d_B of the basic variables by the procedure FORW (x,u) : $\mathbb{B}\, d_B = b$,

where $b = -A^N d_N$;

Step 4. Compute an improved feasible solution :

(i) Linear search on the direction $d = (d_B, d_N)$

new point (x^θ, u^θ) that usually satisfies the bound constraints but not the nonlinear equations.

(ii) by the modification of the basic variables solve the system of nonlinear equations by the procedure FORW (x_N^θ, u_N^θ), and adjusting θ , find a new feasible point so that :

$L(x^\theta, u^\theta) > L(x,u)$.

4. NUMERICAL EXPERIMENTS

Using data from the Working Group on Juvenile Tunas (ICCAT,1982) for the r_i and the parameters computed before, we could obtain all the coefficients and bounds of the stock control model stated above.

Numerical experiments have been performed in a mainframe Burroughs 6700 applying the code GRECO for different planning horizons T. Many degeneracy problems have happened and we had sometimes to employ another version of the code (Facó, 1985). Now we are trying to disaggregate the model in order to be able to manage the stock control in each cluster block.

5. CONCLUSION

The use of Mathematical Programming methods adapted to dynamic ecosystems problems has substancial advantages in terms of the mathematical representation of complex characteristics of the model.

Discrete-time difference equations present significant computational advantages over the usual differential equations forms. It is also more compatible both for describing certain biological phenomenous such as spawning and migration and for use with sampled data sets.

The problems can be solved using available state-of-the-art NLP packages with encouraging results. The large scale capabilities of GRECO makes possible the construction of models with improving complexity and higher disaggregation level.

The general conclusion on the application that we have solved is that multispecies fishery greatly increases the yield from the ecosystem. An optimal fishing strategy can even work as a positive ecological control in the ecosystem,dynamically indicating which species should be fished at each period, contributing this way to equilibrate the competitors and predators populations along the planning horizon. A consistent fishery politics is a real necessity mostly in a developing country like Brazil and the modelling and optimization techniques discussed can be used to make it possible.

REFERENCES

1. J.Abadie.(1970) Optimization problems with coupled blocks Economic Cybernetics Studies and Research 4,5-26.

2. J.Abadie.(1970) Application of the GRG algorithm to optimal control problems. Abadie (Ed.) Integer and Nonlinear Programming, North Holland, Amsterdam.

3. J.Abadie and J.Carpentier.(1969) Generalization of the reduced gradient method to the case of nonlinear constraints. Fletcher (Ed.) Optimization, Academic P., London.

4. C.A. Atkinson.(1980) Analysis of perturbed dynamic systems under parameter uncertainty - a nonlinear programming approach with applications to marine ecosystems. Ph.D thesis, University of California,LA.

5. T.T. Agnew.(1979) Optimal exploitation of a fishery employing a nonlinear harvesting fonction. Ecological Modeling 6, 47-57.

6. J.L.D. Facó.(1977) Commande optimale des systèmes dynamiques non linéaires à retards avec contraintes d'inégalité: une spécialisation de la méthode du GRG. Dr.Ing thesis, Université Pierre et Marie CURIE (Paris VI).

7. J.L.D. Facó.(1985) On the solution of some degeneracy questions in the GRECO algorithm for solving Nonlinear Optimal Control problems 12 th Int. Symp. on Math. Progr., Cambridge, MA.

8. W.W. Fox Jr. (1975) Fitting the generalized stock model by least-squares and equilibrium approximation. Fishery Bulletin 37 (1).

9. I.A.Hartigan and M.A.Wong. (1974) A k-means clustering algorithm. Applied Statistics 28 (1).

10. L.S. Lasdon and A.D. Waren. (1978) Generalized reduced gradient software for linearly and nonlinearly constrained problems. Greenberg (Ed.) Design and Implementation of Optimization Sofltware, Sijthoff and Noordhoff, Netherlands.

11. D. Ludwig. (1979) Optimal harvesting of randomly fluctuating resource I : application of pertubed methods. SIAM J. Appl. Math. 37 (1),166-183.

12. W.J. Palm. (1975) Fishery regulation via Optimal Control Theory. Fishery Bulletin 73 (4); 830-837.

13. A.C.F. Thomaz. (1986) Otimizaçao de Sistemas dinamicos nao-lineares com aplicaçao a politicas de pesca. D.Sc. Thesis, Universidade Federal do Rio de Janeiro.

14. A.C.F. Thomaz, F.J.N. Gomes and J.L.D. Facó. (1984) Dynamic ecosystem with optimal strategy for catch of tunas and tuna-like fishes in southeastern coast of Brazil. IFORS-84 Washington D.C..

15. T.L. Vicent, C.S. Lee, H.R. Pulliam and L.G. Everett (1975) Applications of optimal control the modeling and management of ecosystems. Simulation 24 (3), 65-72.

A General Network Generator

by M. Forster
The Free University of Berlin

1. INTRODUCTION

Many planning problems can be formulated as linear or mixed integer programs and solved using mathematical optimization systems such as MPSX-MIP, APEX and others. For realistic applications, however, model generation and data input tend to become critical bottlenecks. A number of general purpose modelling systems, such as GAMS [3], MAGIC [21], XML [9] etc. produce input data in MPS format, but require trained experts to model all but the most simple planning problems. Special purpose matrix generators are widely used but lack flexibility in the model formulation and alteration stage.

On the other hand, network models are considered fundamental planning tools for the following reasons:

(i) A large number of planning problems can be formulated as network models.

(ii) Highly efficient algorithms are available which can solve such problems orders of magnitude faster than would be possible using standard LP software [17].

(iii) The graphical model representation allows managers, with no mathematical skills or extensive modelling experience, to visualize the model and to actively participate in the modelling process.

Applications to a variety of real-world problems are discussed in [2,5,8,10,11,12,13,14,15]. Universal network modelling techniques are considered in [4,6,12,13,14,20,21].

Network model generators are available for generating certain test problems or a number of special planning problems (e.g. NETGEN [1,16] and [18]). NETGENII [7] is capable of processing statements of a modelling language, but is not designed to handle input data arising in real applications. There seems to be, however, a lack of user friendly network generators for arbitrary network structures.

NATO ASI Series, Vol. F48
Mathematical Models for Decision Support
Edited by G. Mitra

In this paper the general network generator GNGEN will be described. It is based on a generator language, which allows the modeller to specify arbitrary network structures in a simple and concise way. Data are strictly separated from the abstract model.

2. THE MODELLING LANGUAGE

A network is a directed graph G(N,A) consisting of a set of nodes N and a set of arcs A together with one or more integer valued functions defined on A and N. In the following, these functions will be represented by labels assigned to arcs and/or nodes (see [20]). All network optimizers use a representation of the network which consists of a list of all arcs with assigned arc labels and of a list of all nodes with assigned node labels. By contrast, the model specification using GNGEN employs simple set algebraic definitions of sets of nodes and of arcs between certain subsets of nodes. The network generator language GNGEN/L is entirely declarative. Valid data types are INTEGER, SET (or LIST), and ARRAY (see appendix for more information).

The following simple example will be used to demonstrate a network model formulation in GNGEN format: Consider the problem of producing three different goods in two plants and shipping them to three distribution centers. Factory 1 produces only goods 1 and 2. Factory 2 produces only goods 1 and 3. All goods use the same production facility. The demand of each commodity in time period t at each center must be filled. Excess production in period t can be stored at the factory. The 3rd center can only be supplied from factory 2. A graphical representation of this problem is given in figure 1, for periods t and t+1. Upper and lower bounds as well as arc costs have been omitted in order not to clutter the presentation. The corresponding GNGEN formulation is presented in figure 2. It starts with the reserved word NETWORK followed by the problem title. The subsequent section NODESETS defines 3 sets of nodes: Supply, Production, and Distribution (1). These subsets of nodes define the node set N. They are assumed to be pairwise disjoint. Each node of Supply carries the attributes Factory and Time. The attributes Factory, Commodity, and Time are assigned to the nodes of the Production stage. Nodes of the Distribution stage are identified by attributes Center, Commodity, and Time. The attribute Commodity is indexed by Factory (Center respectively), which means that for each Factory (Center) the goods produced (delivered) must be specified in a data file.

Supply	Production	Distribution
Factory, Time	Factory, Commodity, Time	Center, Commodity, Time

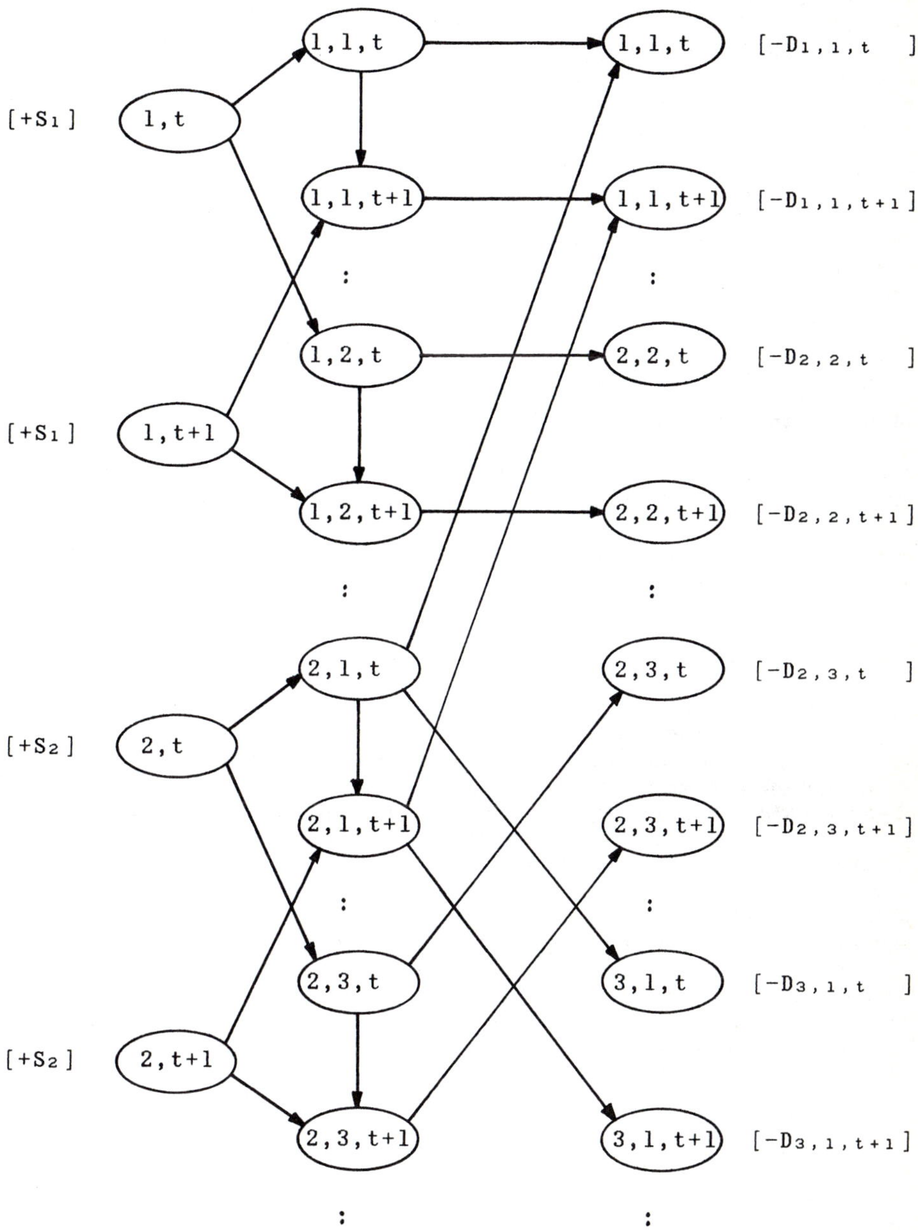

Fig. 1. Network (time periods t and t+1).

The ARCS section (2) generates arcs from all nodes of the node set Supply to members of node set Production provided that both attributes Factory and Time of the start node and the end node are equal. The value of attribute Factory of node s is denoted by s.Factory. Accordingly, p.Factory refers to the factory associated with node p. This ARCS section assigns 3 arc labels: The costs of production of each factory from an array CoP, the lower bound 0, and the upper bound INFINITE. In this example label 1 is the cost coefficient for each arc. Labels 2 and 3 are lower and upper bounds of the arc flow.

```
NETWORK Production_&_Distribution;

NODESETS                                                         /* (1) */
  Supply       = ( Factory, Time ),
  Production   = ( Factory, Commodity [ Factory ], Time ),
  Distribution = ( Center , Commodity [ Center  ], Time );

ARCS FROM s ∈ Supply TO p ∈ Production :                         /* (2) */
          s.Factory   = p.Factory           AND
          s.Time      = p.Time
LABEL     CoP [ p.Factory ], 0, INFINITE;

ARCS FROM p ∈ Production TO p' ∈ Production :                    /* (3) */
          p.Factory   = p'.Factory          AND
          p.Commodity = p'.Commodity        AND
          p.Time + 1  = p'.Time             AND
LABEL     0, 0, INFINITE;

ARCS FROM p ∈ Production TO d ∈ Distribution :                   /* (4) */
          d.Center    ∈ C [ p.Factory ] AND
          p.Commodity = d.Commodity         AND
          p.Time      = d.Time
LABEL     f * Dist [ p.Factory , d.Center ], 0, INFINITE;

NODES     s ∈ Supply  LABEL S [ s.Factory ]                      /* (5) */

NODES     d ∈ Distribution                                       /* (6) */
LABEL   - D [ d.Center , d.Commodity , d.Time ];

ENDNET /* Production_&_Distribution */;
```

Fig. 2. Formulation of the problem.

The ARCS section (3) generates the arcs which model the possibility of storing excess production for one or more time periods: One arc from period t to period t+1 for each factory and each commodity. The arc costs are 0 and the flow in each arc must be positive, which implies labels 0, 0, and INFINITE.

The next ARCS section defines the set of arcs associated with the transshipment of goods from factories to distribution centers. The identifier C is an array of sets. From factory i goods can be delivered to centers in the set C[i] (i=1,2). Furthermore, time attributes must be the same for start and end nodes. The costs of transport are computed from a distance array Dist (multiplied by a constant f). Flows must be positive. The NODES section (5) adds a supply value S[i] to each of the nodes of node set Supply. Finally, NODES section (6) assigns demand values to distribution nodes. Demands D

```
  :
Time := 1..4; Factory   := 1,2; Center := 1..3;

Commodity [ Factory ]   := 1,2; 1,3;
Commodity [ Center  ]   := 1;   2,3; 1;

CoP [ Factory ]         := 150; 200;
C   [ Factory ]         := 1,2; 1,2,3;

Dist [ Factory, Center ] := /*  1        2        3   */
   /*  1    */              1200     1100      900
   /*  2    */               850     1050      520
  :
```

Fig. 3. Part of an input file.

depend on the attibutes Center, Commodity, and Time. The reserved word ENDNET indicates the end of the GNGEN model formulation. Comments must be enclosed in /* */. All the parameters and index sets are hidden data. The identifiers in the formulation of figure 2 implicitly assert that there is some facility which provides the corresponding values (e.g. from an input file or a data base). The generator is capable of evaluating arbitrary arithmetic expressions of input data. Parameters are calculated from data supplied in a separate file (distance matrices, cost vectors etc.). The input processor assigns the values of integer arithmetic expressions, of sets, and of arrays to the data variables of the model, which allows the user to specify attribute sets and parameters in free format. Figure 3 lists some statements of an input file for the problem described above. The input format permits the same arithmetic expressions as the modelling language (including sums). Random parameters can be produced by calling the RANDOM function. The RANDOM function permits test of algorithms on real-world problem structures with random data.

Note the difference between the model form (figure 2) and the data input file:

(i) The model is formulated in declarative style. The order of the file sections tells nothing about the enumeration of the nodes or the sequence of the arcs.

(ii) The input consists of a list of assignments. Whenever an identifer is referenced, its value must be defined.

3. SOME ASPECTS OF THE IMPLEMENTATION

The generator is being implemented using PASCAL on an IBM PC. Attention is paid to both portability and readability of the source code. The program works as follows: It reads two input files, the model file (of Fig. 2) and the data file (of Fig. 3), and writes four output files containing the arc list, the node list, the model listing, and messages (screen by default). First the model is compiled into a list structure, which internally represents the model file (phase 1). When no errors occured during compilation, the input processor is called (phase 2). The input processor reads the data file. Network codes usually need some arrays of length equal to the number of arcs (nodes) of the network. GNGEN keeps the parameter values of the model in internal memory. Inverted lists provide the information which is necessary for the processing of the logical conditions of the ARCS specifications. There is no array of size equal to the number of arcs of the network. This is achieved by generating the set of all successors of a node (forward star) at once and writing it to the output file. Thus, requirements of primary storage are independent of the number of arcs.

The output format is compatible with the SHARE format [1]. One record is written for each arc. Each record contains the number of the initial node, the number of the end node, and the node labels (in the order of the LABEL list of the model). The SHARE format is the form of input required by many network optimizers (like PNET or GENNET). Any other file formats can easily be obtained by replacing the GNGEN output module.

APPENDIX

Data Types

INTEGER : single values and components of structured types
ARRAY : n-dimensional field indexed by attributes
LIST, SET : set of integers
BOOLEAN : integer $\neq$ 0 evaluates to TRUE,
0 evaluates to FALSE

Note: Variable types are never declared in an explicit section, but recognized from the context.

Special Values

INF[INITE] : greater than any integer (or largest value)
RANDOM(*l*, *u*) : generates uniformly distributed random numbers in the range *l*, ... , *u* (*l* = 0 and *u* = largest value by default)

Semantics

NODESETS $S1$ = ($Attributes_1$), ... , Sm = ($Attributes_m$);
defines a number of subsets Si of N (set of all nodes). The sets defined in this way are assumed to partition N. $Attributes_i$ are associated with nodes of Si.

ARCS FROM $f \in S1$: $C1$ TO $t \in S2$: $C2$ LABELS $E1$, ... , En;
defines a subset of A (set of all arcs). $S1$ and $S2$ are sets of nodes (as previously defined). $C1$ and $C2$ are conditions for arcs (f, t). Ej is an arithmetic expression. The value of Ej becomes the jth label of arc (f, t). (The symbol $\in$ may be replaced by reserved word IN.)

NODES $k \in S$: C LABELS $E1$, ... , En;
defines labels $E1$, ... , En for all nodes k of set S, which satisfy condition C.

Besides arithmetic operators known from high level languages (+ , unary and binary - , * , / , MOD , SQUARE), GNGEN/L provides the SUM operator (or Σ):

Σ ($E(j)$: $j \in S$)
evaluates the sum of arithmetic expressions $E(j)$ for all members j of S.

Σ ($E(j)$: $j \in S$: C)
evaluates the sum of arithmetic expressions $E(j)$ for all members j of S, which satisfy condition C. Note: LP modelling languages often use the summation to specify constraints. In GNGEN/L, problems are described columnwise. Hence, the Σ-operator is reserved for calculation of sums.

< , <= or ≤ , =, ≠ or <> , >= or ≥ , >
are the relational operators.
3 < 4 is valid and evaluates to 1 (≡ TRUE),
5 ≥ 1 evaluates to 0 (≡ FALSE).

AND , OR , NOT
are the boolean operators.

REFERENCES

[1] R.Barr, F.Glover, D.Klingman, J.Stutz, Technical Documentation NETGEN, March 1973.

[2] R.Barr, J.S.Turner, "Microdata File Merging Through Large-Scale Network Technology," Math. Prog. Study 15, 1981, pp. 1-22.

[3] J.Bisschop and A.Meeraus, "On The Development of A General Algebraic Modeling system in A Strategic Planning Environment," Math. Prog. Study 20, 1982, pp. 1-29.

[4] R.E.Bixby and W.H.Cunningham, "Converting Linear Programs to Network Problems," Math. of Ops. Res. 5 (3), 1980, pp. 321-357.

[5] R.L.Crum and D.J.Nye, "A Network Model of Insurance Company Cash Flow Management," Math. Prog. Study 15, 1981, pp. 86-101.

[6] W.H.Cunningham, "A Class of Linear Programs Convertible to Network Problems," Ops. Res. 31 (2), 1983, pp. 387-391.

[7] J.J.Elam and D.Klingman, "NETGEN-II: A System for Generating Structured Network-Based Mathematical Programming Test Problems," Lecture Notes in Economics and Mathematical Systems (ed. by J.M.Mulvey), 1982, pp. 16-23.

[8] A.Federgruen and H.Groenevelt, "Optimal Flows in Networks with Multiple Sources and Sinks, with Applications to Oil and Gas Lease Investment Programs," Ops. Res. 34 (2), 1978, pp. 218-225.

[9] R.Fourer, "Modelling Languages Versus Matrix Generators for Linear Programming," ACM Transactions on Math. Software 9 (2), 1983, pp. 143-183.

[10] F.Glover, J.Hultz, D.Klingman and J.Stutz, "A New Computer-Based Planning Tool," Research Report CCS 289, Center for Cybernetic Studies, University of Texas at Austin, 1976.

[11] F.Glover and D.Klingman, "Network Application in Industry and Government," AIIE Transactions 9, 1977, pp. 363-376.

[12] F.Glover, C.McMillan and D.Klingman, "The NETFORM Concept: A More Effective Model Form and Solution Procedure for Large Scale Nonlinear Problems," Proc. of ACM 77 (annual conference), Seattle, October 1977, pp. 283-289.

[13] F.Glover, J.Hultz, D.Klingman, "Improved Computer-Based Planning Techniques," Interfaces 8 (4), 1978, pp. 16-25 (part I), Interfaces 9 (4), 1979, pp. 12-20 (part II).

[14] F.Glover, J.Hultz, D.Klingman and J.Stutz, "Generalized Networks: A Fundamental Computer-Based Planning Tool," Mgmt. Sci. 24 (12), 1978, pp. 1209-1220.

[15] F.Glover, G.Jones, D.Karney, D.Klingman and J.Mote, "An Integrated Production, Distribution, and Inventory Planning System," Interfaces 9 (5), 1979, pp. 21-35.

[16] D.Klingman, A.Napier and J.Stutz, "NETGEN: A Program for Generating Large Scale Capacitated Assignment, Transportation, and Minimum Cost Flow Network Problems," Mgmt. Sci. 20 (5), 1974, pp. 814-821.

[17] R.R.Meyer, "Network Optimization," in [19].

[18] C.M.Murphy and M.S.Hung, "Network Generation using The Prufer Code," Comp. and Ops. Res. 13 (6), 1986, pp. 693-705.

[19] K.Schittkowski (Ed.), Computational Mathematical Programming, NATO ASI Series, Vol.F15, Springer, Berlin, 1985.

[20] R.T.Rockafellar, Network Flows and Monotropic Optimization, John Wiley & Sons, New York, 1984.

[21] H.P.Williams, "Model Building in Linear and Integer Programming," in [19].

A CASE STUDY IN THE USE OF MATHEMATICAL MODELS FOR DECISION SUPPORT IN PRODUCTION PLANNING

Manfred Grauer
University of Dortmund
Faculty of Computer Science
Postbox 50 05 00
D-4600 Dortmund

1. INTRODUCTION

Economic as well as technological considerations have dominated the evolution of industrial structures. These factors have been treated mostly separately by engineers and economists in the past. However, another major factor which has begun to have a decisive influence on the performance of industrial processes is technological risk as well as public and environmental health considerations, in particular those related to toxic and hazardous substances used in industrial production processes.
The issues of controlling process risk, waste streams, and potential environmental consequences of accidental or routine release of hazardous substances are rapidly gaining in importance as a non-negligible part in production planning and its management. To characterize the order of magnitude of those waste streams from a technological and economic point of view it seems worth to mention that they are estimated in World Resources (1987) for the year 1986 by 330 million metric tons. These developments and the availability of advanced information processing tools have forced to take into account all these criteria (e.g. technological, economical, ecological) and to integrate the stages of the engineering design of production processes, its control and the corresponding management problems.
The paper tries to approach some of the problems under the mentioned multiple criteria and to indicate the role of decision support for computer-aided integrated management. This will be done analyzing a production process from chemical industry under normal and exeptional circumstances (emergency situations).

2. THE PROBLEM

The experiences in developing and using optimization-based decision support (see e.g. Grauer, 1983) were the basis to concentrate on integrated production planning under the prospect of hazardous byproducts. On the other hand an

NATO ASI Series, Vol. F48
Mathematical Models for Decision Support
Edited by G. Mitra

ongoing project at the International Institute for Applied Systems Analysis(IIASA) in Laxenburg/Austria was the initial point to choose the chemical process of direct chlorination of phenol as a case (see Fedra, 1985 and Grauer, 1987). This process raised attention in connection with the "Seveso"-accident in Italy in 1978. A simplified technological schema of that process is given in Figure 1.

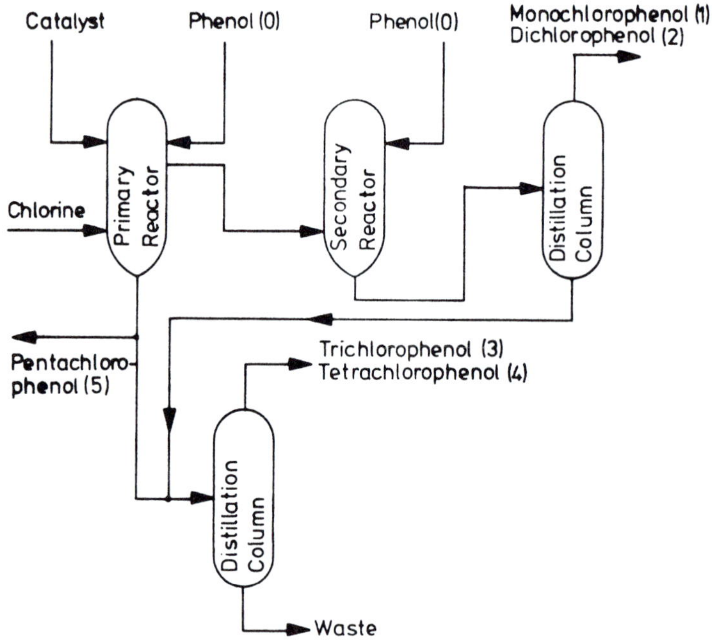

Figure 1. Simplified technological schema of the chemical plant (direct chlorination of phenol)

The extremly toxic 2,3,7,8-tetrachlorodibenzo-p-dioxin and 2,3,4,7-pentachlorodibenzofuran are byproducts of that process. The process representation as well as the process risk description is based on Goldfarb (1981) and Grauer (1986). Thereby it is assumed that the chlorination of phenol(0) proceeds stepwise so that five chlorophenols of commercial value are obtained: monochlorophenol(1), dichlorophenol(2), trichlorophenol(3), tetrachlorophenol(4) and pentachlorophenol(5). These chlorophenols are used as herbicides, bactericides, fungicides and chemical intermediates.

The subprocesses and substances involved in that manufacturing are summarized below in some more detail:

phenol(0)+chlorine -> monochlorophenol(1)+HCL

monochlorophenol(1)+chlorine -> 2,4-dichlorophenol(2)+HCL

2,4-dichlorophenol(2)+chlorine+(ALCL3)->

-> 2,4,6-trichlorophenol(3)+HCL

2,4,6-trichlorophenol(3)+chlorine+(ALCL3)->

-> 2,3,4,6-tetrachlorophenol(4)+HCL

2,3,4,6-tetrachlorophenol(4)+chlorine+(ALCL3)->

-> pentachlorophenol(5)+HCL

pentachlorophenol(5)+chlorine+(ALCL3) -> dioxin(6).

The numbers in parenthesis are used as abbreviations of the substances for the future use in the paper, and ALCL3 indicates a catalyst (anhydrous aluminium chloride) which is added to the reactor when the chlorination has proceeded to the dichlorophenol stage (see Fig.1).
The reaction starts at a temperature of about 70°C and is increased up to 180°C to maintain a differential temperature of 10°C over the product melting point. The process is running batchwise with a total period of chlorination of generally 8 to 10 hours. As shown in Figure 1, phenol is added to the primary reactor and to the secondary reactor. The reactors are heated and by that controlling the production process. The process starts with the introduction of chlorine into the first reactor. The offgases from the first reactor are passed into the secondary one. Separation units, mainly consisting of distillation columns, allow the extraction of the desired products and the hazardous byproduct, here for simplicity assumed to be only dioxin.
The problem of control and management of this chemical plant consists of meeting the demand of the five products (pentachlorophenol is the main product, but mono-, di-, tri- and tetrachlorophenol are also products) and/or maximizing the target products in a time-minimal production period. Here the interdependencies between the different outputs of the process have to be taken into account. That means for instance that the amount of pentachlorophenol is a result of all steps of the reaction and any intermediate product would reduce its throughput. This requests to understand the production profil as a compromise of all target products which meets best the current demand profil.
Moreover to these production criteria the amount of toxic substances (e.g. dioxin) has to be minimized or at least to keep below certain upper bounds. This leads in the normal production mode as well as in non-normal cases (e.g. runaway reaction, operator error, equipment failure, fire, explosion etc.) to the necessity to deal with a dynamic multiple-criteria decision problem. The use of mathematical models as support in such a decision situation is the subject of the further discussion.

On the other hand these mathematical models have to be used already in the design stage when the decision about the principal process chemistry is made and the engineering design of the layout of the plant is done. Of course the decision variables are then different from those in the case of production planning for a given plant. But as well known, in the design stage about 80% of the economic efficiency is determined and also the possibilities to meet ecological and safety requirements. This calls for an integration of decision support for computer-aided management in all these stages.

3. THE MATHEMATICAL MODEL OF THE PRODUCTION PROCESS

The composition and physical properties of reacting materials influence stability, efficiency and quality when manufacturing chemicals. In large-scale operations as indicated above the main reaction is often influenced by other reactions and/or perturbed by less understood secondary reactions. An analytical model (a deep model) can only be an approximation of the production process under analysis and has to be supported by other information and knowledge (shallow model).

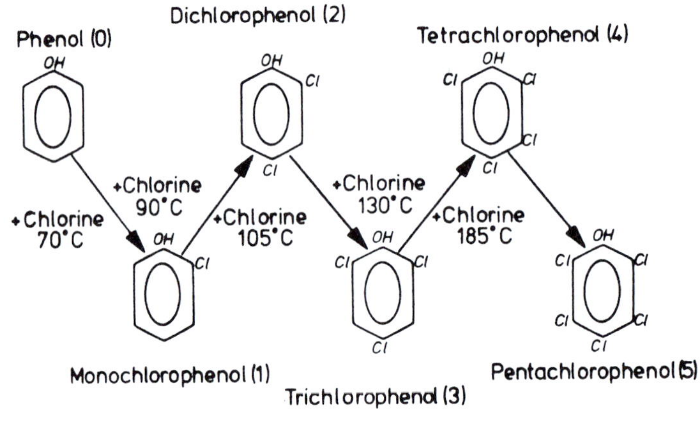

Figure 2. Direct chlorination of phenol (simplified process chemistry)

For the chlorination process the theoretically and experimentally verified conceptual model (deep) is that of a consecutive reaction from phenol(0) over pentachlorophenol(5) to dioxion(6) of the following type:

(0) -> (1) -> (2) -> (3) -> (4) -> (5) -> (6) .

This concept implies ideal mixture conditions in the reactor. The chemistry underlying this concept is presented in Figure 2 in a simplified manner.
The mathematical formulation of this concept is a system of ten differential equations(DE) consisting of:

7 DE for the mass-balances of all substances 0 through 6,
1 DE for the mass-balance of chlorine in the liquid phase,
1 DE for the mass-balance of chlorine-consumption and
1 DE for the energy-balance in the reactor.

In addition to the system of differential equations a set of highly nonlinear algebraic equations represents the interdependencies of densities, reaction coefficients, heat transfer coefficients, etc. from time, temperature, pressure and material composition, e.g.: concentration.
Systems of differential equations of the above described type are usually "stiff", e.g. their solutions contain parts with rapidly decaying components. They are important in numerical analysis because they frequently arise in practical problems (see Smith, 1987) and because they are difficult to solve by traditional numerical methods. For the above system the method of implicit backward differentiation formulas is used (see e.g. Smith, 1987).
The mathematical description of the process is presented here in such detail to give an understanding of the constraints for the finally to solve control/optimization task as part of a decision problem.

4. FORMULATION OF THE PRODUCTION CONTROL PROBLEM

The mathematical model to describe the dynamic behavior of such continuous or semicontinuous(batch-wise) production processes as given above is usually a system of differential equations as follows:

$$\frac{dx(t)}{dt} = F[x(t),u(t),t] \quad , \quad x(t) \in R^m \ , \ u(t) \in R^n \qquad (1)$$

with the given initial state of the production system at the time $t=t_0$:

$$x(t_0) = x_0 \qquad t \in [t_0, t_f] \qquad (2)$$

where x is the state and u the control variable and $[t_0, t_f]$ indicate the time horizon.
Usually the state- and the control-variables are subject to further constraints:

$$g[x(t),u(t),t] \leq 0 \quad , \qquad (3)$$

and

$$h[x(t),u(t),t] = 0 \quad . \qquad (4)$$

It is assumed that the performance measure has the form of the following scalar-valued functional:

$$\min \left\{ \int_{t_o}^{t_f} f[x(t),u(t),t]dt + \Phi[x(t_f)] \right\} . \tag{5}$$

The functional (5) represents the time-dependence of the criteria for the decision processes like economic ones or safety considerations. Under normal production conditions this can be an overall cost-function. For decision problems connected with abnormal situations the integral can represent the amount of toxic substances for which the danger exists to be accidentical released and which has to be minimized.
The most common approach to solve this class of problems is to convert such an optimal control problem (1)-(5) into a static nonlinear programming problem. This can be done by approximating the continuous time-function u(t), i.e. the control-trajectory(or policy) by a discrete time-function. The new decision trajectory or decision policy is derived by choosing an appropriate structure with finitely many free parameters and to consider the state variables x(t) as functions of the control variables through the differential equations (1). Hereby the problem is solved in the reduced space of controls, and the state variables are obtained by the solution of an initial value problem.
Following this approach the interval $[t_o, t_f]$ is partitioned into a (not necessarily equidistant) time-grid:

$$t_o = t_1 < t_2 < \ldots < t_j < \ldots < t_k = t_f , \tag{6}$$

and on this grid the finite set of control variables is defined:

$$\mathbf{u}(t) = [u_1(t_1), \ldots , u_n(t_1), u_1(t_2), \ldots , u_n(t_{k-1})]. \tag{7}$$

The infinite control or decision problem (1)-(5) can then restated in the following way:

$$\frac{dx(t)}{dt} = F[x(t),u_i(t_j),t] , \quad i=1,\ldots,n ; \quad j=1,\ldots,k-1 \tag{8}$$

with

$$x(t_o) = x_o \qquad t \in [t_o, t_f] \tag{9}$$

$$g[x(t),u_i(t_j),t] \leq 0 , \quad i=1,\ldots,n ; \quad j=1,\ldots,k-1 \tag{10}$$

$$h[x(t),u_i(t_j),t] = 0 , \quad i=1,\ldots,n ; \quad j=1,\ldots,k-1 \tag{11}$$

and

$$\min \left\{ \int_{t_o}^{t_f} f[x(t),\mathbf{u}(t),t]dt + \Phi [x(t_f)] \right\} . \tag{12}$$

The nonlinear single-criterion programming problem then is to find the piecewise-constant control strategy (7) which minimizes (12) under the constraints (8)-(11). This is a nonlinear programming problem with an iterative procedure in the constraints and in the objective function. To solve this problem in a reliable manner and sufficiently fast only the direct search (derivative free) Polytop-method was able. This algorithm is from a library of standard programming methods (Grauer, 1987a)
Next is given a brief description of the approach for the actually to solve multiple criteria production planning problem.

5. THE MULTIPLE-CRITERIA APPROACH

Production planning problems as stated earlier are multiple-criteria ones. An approach is needed which transforms the originally multiple-criteria problem into a scalar-valued one to analyse it. Such a transformation has to have two main features. First it has to represent in some way the preference structure of the user to allow to support the decision making process and secondly it must be numerically efficient.
For this transformation the idea of satisficing behavior and its mathematical formalization for decision support is used as developed by Wierzbicki (1982). To give a brief understanding of this approach for the purposes of the current analysis it is assumed that, the decision space $E_u = R^n$ and the set of admissible decisions $U_0 \in R^n$ is compact. Let there be p criteria or objectives of interest to the decision maker, $E_q = R^p$, and let the outcome mapping $f: U_0 \rightarrow R^p$ be continuous, hence the set of attainable outcomes $Q_0 = f(U_0)$ be also compact. Under the assumption that the decision maker wants to maximize all outcomes, the partial ordering of the outcome space is implied by the positive cone $D = R^p_+$. In Wierzbicki (1982) is stated if the cone D is closed and the set Q_0 is compact, then there exist D-efficient or D-optimal elements of Q_0. These are such elements $\hat{q} \in Q_0$ that

$$Q_0 \cap (\hat{q} + \tilde{D}) = \phi$$

where $\tilde{D}$ is the cone D except its origin and $\hat{q} + \tilde{D}$ denotes the set $\tilde{D}$ shifted by $\hat{q}$. The corresponding decisions $\hat{u} \in U_0$ such that $\hat{q} = f(\hat{u})$ are D-efficient as well. The set of all D-efficient outcomes is then:

$$\hat{Q}_0 = \{ \hat{q} \in Q_0 : Q_0 \cap (\hat{q} + \tilde{D}) = \phi \} \quad .$$

For applications in decision support systems (see e.g. Grauer, 1983) a substitute scalarizing function is introduced. The so-called achievement function is a transformation from the p-dimensional objective space into the one-dimensional space: $s: R^p \rightarrow R^1$. This function is guided by reference levels or aspirations of the decision maker about target values or trajectories for the criteria ($\bar{q}_i$) and its maximization leads to D-efficient decisions. In the multiple-criteria dynamic case as discussed here this function can be written as:

$$s(q,\bar{q}) = \min_{t_i \le t \le t_k} \; \min_{1 \le i \le p} \; \mu_i \, [q_i(t) - \bar{q}_i(t)] + \ldots$$

$$\ldots + \delta \sum_{t=t_o}^{t_f} \; \sum_{i=1}^{p} \mu_i \, [q_i(t) - \bar{q}_i(t)], \qquad (13)$$

where $\delta > 1$, $\mu_i \ge 0$ and $\sum_{i=1}^{p} \mu_i = 1$.

The solution of the multiple-criteria problem consists now in finding those decisions (7) which maximize (13) for given reference levels $\bar{q}_i$ under the constraints (8)-(11). This is in principal the same numerical problem as stated in the previous section, i.e. a nonlinear programming problem with an iterative procedure (the solution of the system of differential equations) in the constraints and in the objective function. For the numerical solution the same statements as in section 4 are valid.

6. A CONCEPT FOR THE USE OF THE MODEL IN DECISION SUPPORT

The current prototype module of the mathematical model could support a single user in analysing production planning problems under multiple criteria in an off-line manner. Also in the case of a non-normal situation of the plant the user can run the problem with the objectives either to meet the production goals and/or to satisfy the safety requirements.
A decision support system(DSS) of this off-line type is described in Fedra (1986) and Grauer (1987b). There the interface to the DSS for this dialog is problem-oriented and the whole system is userdriven. Setting certain target levels for the production, for the prodution period (t_f) and/or for the minimization of certain hazardous substances, the user will be answered by the system with the corresponding efficient control strategy and the state trajectory of the chemical plant. The Figure 3 shows a presentation of the process dynamics for one specified efficient decision case.
One production planning run for a result as specified in Figure 3 takes on an IBM-PC XT/AT with an APU-8087 about 40 to 50 minutes. This are then about 20 to 30 function evaluations for the underlying nonlinear programming problem. The same problem is solved on a VAX 11/780 in less than 10 minutes and on a SUN 3/260 in less than 30 seconds.
The software for modeling and optimization is implemented in Fortran-77 and the interface in C. A test to realize both the interface and the numerical part in the language C to improve the portability of the software system is currently underway.

7. ABOUT SOME CONCLUSIONS

The concept of this prototyp module of the mathematical model in that stage is not only usable for the specific process under discussion here, but in a broader range of integrated production planning and the management of emergency cases.

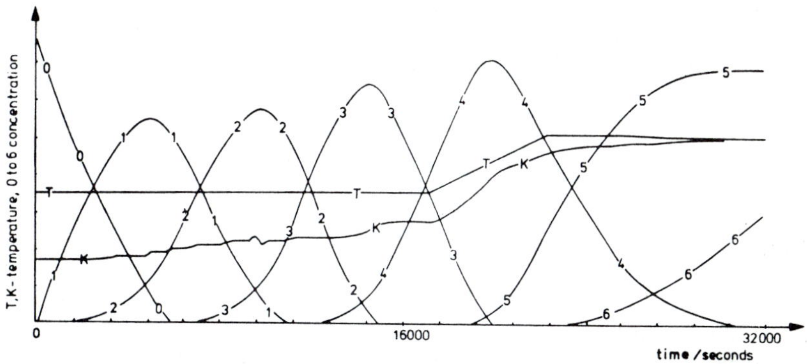

Figure 3. Process dynamics of a chemical plant for the direct chlorination of phenol (T, K - temperature in the reactor and of the coolant in °C and (0), (1), (2), (3), (4), (5), (6)- concentration in kmol/m³ of phenol, mono-, di-, tri-, tetra-, pentachlorophenol, dioxin) after optimization (efficient decision case).

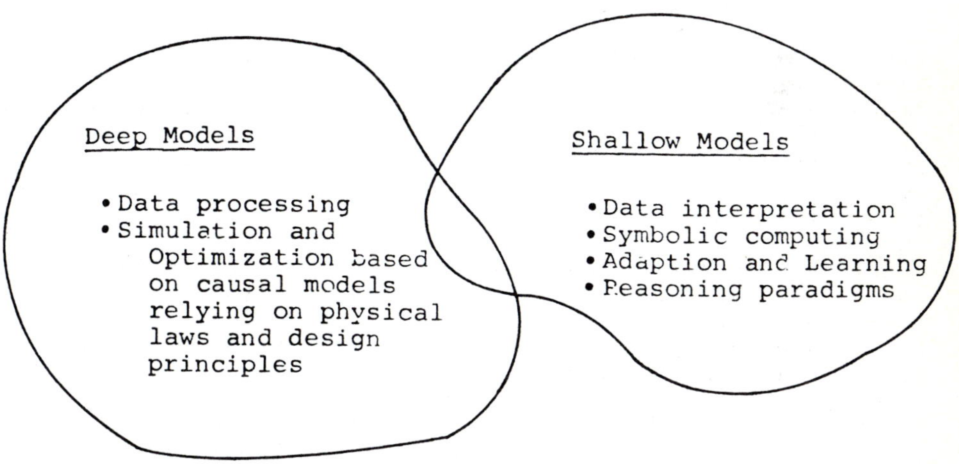

Figure 4. The integration of "deep" and "shallow" models for on-line knowledge-based decision support

The use of mathematical models for decision support in emergency situations is already known for high-order corporate crisis management (see e.g. Andriole, 1986) and in industry for the management of nuclear power plants (see e.g. Embry, 1985). For the application as decision aid in on-line production management the step has to be done from "deep" to "shallow" mathematical models which is indicated in Figure 4. This means the integration of knowledge processing and on-line information from process measurements into DSS. The development of information and communication technology and sensor technology supports this step already and research in this direction is underway (see Galanti, 1986).

REFERENCES

Andriole, St.(1986):Microcomputer-based decision support for high-order corporate crisis managment, in Andriole, St.(Ed.): Microcomputer decision support systems: design, implementation and evaluation, North Holland, 1986.

D'Ambrosio, B.(1987), Fehling,M.R., Forrest, St., Raulefs, P. Wilber, B.M.: Real-time process managment for materials composition in chemical manufacturing, IEEE Expert, Summer 1987, pp.80-93

Embry, D.(1985) and P. Humphreys: Support for decision making and problem solving in abnormal conditions in nuclear power plants, in :Knowledge representation for decision support systems, Methlie, L.B. and Sprague, R.H. (Eds), Elsevier, North Holland, 1985

Fedra, K. (1985): Advanced decision-oriented software for the managment of hazardous substances. part I: structure and design. CP-85-18, International Institute for Applied Systems Analysis, Laxenburg/Austria.

Fedra,K. (1986): Advanced decision-oriented software for the managment of hazardous substances. part II: a demonstration prototyp system. CP-86-10, International Institute for Applied Systems Analysis, Laxenburg/Austria.

Gallanti,M.(1986), Guida,G.:Intelligent decision aids for process environments: an expert system approach, in NATO ASI Series, Vol.F21, Intelligent decision support in process environments, Edited by E. Hollnagel et al., Springer-Verlag, Berlin, Heidelberg 1986

Goldfarb,A.S.(1981), G.R. Goldgraben, E.C. Herrick, R.P. Quellette, P.N. Cheremisinoff:Organic Chemicals Manu-acturing Hazards, Ann Arbor Science, Ann Arbor. 1981

Grauer,M.(1983): A Dynamic Interactive Decision Analysis and Support System (DIDASS) - User's Guide. WP-83-60, International Institute for Applied Systems Analysis, Laxenburg/Austria.

Grauer,M. et al.(1986):Modeling and Optimization of the Process of Chlorination of Phenol, Internal Report of the International Institute for Applied Systems Analysis, Laxenburg/Austria

Grauer,M.(1987a):DSS-toolbox (optimization methods), release 2.d

Grauer,M.(1987b) and K.Fedra: Intelligent decision support for technology assessment: the chemical process industry, in: Toward interactive and intelligent decision support systems, Vol.2, Edited by Y. Sawaragi, K. Inoue and H. Nakayama, Springer-Verlag, 1987

Smith,J.M.(1987): Mathematical modelling and digital simulation for engineers and scientists, Wiley Intersciences, 1987

Wierzbicki,A.(1982):A mathematical basis for satisficing decision making. Mathematical Modelling, Nr.3, pp.391-405

World Ressources 1987(1987), a report by The International Institute for Environment and Development and The World Ressources Institute, Basic Books Inc., New York, 1987

ANALYZE Rulebase

by

Harvey J. Greenberg
Mathematics Department, Campus Box 170
University of Colorado at Denver
1100 Fourteenth Street
Denver, CO 80202 USA

1. Overview of ANALYZE

Function. This is an interactive system to aid the analysis of linear programming models and, optionally, their solution. It is an enhancement of the earlier ANALYZE described in [1], featuring natural language explanations of the model, as described in [2], plus enriched analysis aids.

Explicit query includes tabular or pictorial output, simple and flexible delineation of any portion of the matrix, and blocking. Analysis aids include path tracing, model reduction, infeasibility diagnosis and rates of substitution. The micro-computer version can typically support 1,000 rows, 2,000 columns and 15,000 nonzeroes. Mainframe versions can support any size that will fit in core memory (using supersparse data structure).

Computing environment. This is written in FORTRAN/77 and tested on both mainframes and IBM/XT compatibles.

Getting started. Once entering ANALYZE, online help is provided for an overall introduction and for each command. This can be routed to a file to serve as a hardcopy reference manual. The following section annotates a sample session, showing how to use some of the commands for analysis of an optimal, infeasible or unbounded solution. One focus is to examine the rulebase facility.

2. Sample Session

Figure 1 shows the beginning of an ANALYZE session. The text just after PLEASE LOCK CAPS is from a "PROFILE," which is a user-defined file of ANALYZE commands that is executed before the interactive session begins. In this case the PROFILE just contains remarks for the student. For industrial applications the PROFILE is used to set local string variables, screen parameters or other characteristics for the particular environment. After

NATO ASI Series, Vol. F48
Mathematical Models for Decision Support
Edited by G. Mitra

the ANALYZE prompt, I entered H as an abbreviation of HELP, to see the commands. We shall illustrate uses of only some of these commands.

```
ANALYZE...Version 2.0
by
Harvey J. Greenberg

: Enter ? for introduction       :
: Enter HELP to see commands     :
:................................:

PLEASE LOCK CAPS

Welcome to ANALYZE. I have prepared some exercises for you to become
familiar with Computer-Assisted Analysis of LP models and solutions.
Later you can make your own exercises, using MINOS, FORTLP or XMP to
solve your LP and, perhaps, GAMS or your own program in BASIC, PASCAL
or FORTRAN to generate an LP model.

You should begin your session with ? to get an introduction, and use
HELP to look at commands. A dictionary of exercises may be seen by:
PRINT DICTNARY.PRT
RETURN...back to terminal
ANALYZE ...H
   ANALYZE has 29 commands
   10 Session control commands:
EXECUTE   HELP      OUTPUT    PRINT  QUIT  RETURN   SCREEN
STRING    SWITCH    RECAP
   19 ANALYZE commands:
READIN    SUMMARY   WRITEOUT  SUBMAT    ADDRIM   DISPLAY
COUNT     LIST      PICTURE   SHOWCOL   TALLY    TRACE
EXPLAIN   BLOCK     SYNTAX    REDUCE    RATEOF   SOLUTION
INTERPRT

Enter HELP * to get help for each command
```

Figure 1. Beginning ANALYZE

In Figure 2 I follow the original suggestion to PRINT DICTNARY.PRT, whereupon five exercises are listed. We shall examine only the first with EXEC WOODNET.EXCA. The first command in this EXECUTE read an LP file into memory. The command, itself, is READIN PACKED WOODNET, which could have been echoed, but is hidden. This was originally read in as a matrix file in standard MPS format, followed by reading a MINOS solution file with the command, SOLUTION MINOS WOODNET. Such setups would be done in batch for large models, as in industrial applications. Then, the complete LP file was written to a packed (unformatted) file now read into memory. The second command in this EXECUTE file read in a syntax file, which supports the natural language explanation of rows and columns to be illustrated shortly. Finally, remarks are printed, asking the students to explain the marginal prices of supply and demand rows.

```
ANALYZE ...PRINT DICTNARY.PRT
Here is a dictionary of exercises:
        WOODNET.....a network model (good place to start)
        WOODINFE....an infeasible version of WOODNET
        WOODUNBD....an unbounded version of WOODNET
        TANGINFE....an infeasible product mix problem
        PRSUB.......a simplified energy market model
        FOREST......a forestry model
To analyze one of these, you enter:            EXEC name.EXA
where name is one of the exercise names.
For example, to analyze WOODNET:               EXEC WOODNET.EXA

You may EXEC OVERVIEW.EXA to obtain an overview (also, PRINT OVERVIEW.EXA
to see the commands for this).
RETURN
ANALYZE ...EXEC WOODNET.EXA
 Packed LP file read in
 Syntax file read in
 WOODNET.....an optimal network model.
 Analyze the properties, beginning with model attributes.
 Then, try using the TRACE and RATEOF commands. Try to explain what
 you learn about the model, using the EXPLAIN and SYNTAX commands to
 put your explanation in English. In particular, explain the marginal
 prices of the supply and demand rows.
 RETURN...back to terminal
```

Figure 2. Choosing a problem to analyze (WOODNET)

A reasonable place to become familiar with a model is to look at statistics, which is obtained from the SUMMARY command in Figure 3. Then, since we eventually want to explain marginal prices in English, the SYNTAX command is used to show row classes (Supply and Demand for this example).

```
ANALYZE ...SUMMARY
Problem WOODNET  is to MINIMIZE COST
RHS = HOMOGEN  RANGE = (none)  BOUND = BNDSET

Source file: WOODNET.PCK                    Syntax: WOODNET.SYN

Solution source: MINOS          ...Status = OPTIMAL

LP Statistics:
  36 rows (  1 free) and   93 columns (  0 fixed)
 221 nonzeroes (  23 distinct...  148 ones)
   Density=  6.60%, Entropy=  10.41%, Unity=  66.97%

Row    SPIDE    has the most nonzeroes =    6
Column TMOSECH  has the most nonzeroes =    3
ANALYZE ...SYNTAX ROWS

Row syntax has  2 class(es)...
A row that begins with S balances supply of some material in some location.
A row that begins with D balances demand of some material in some location.
```

Figure 3. Expert query to get familiar with WOODNET

As a first illustration of the experimental rulebase consider using the INTERPRT command, as in figure 4, to get an overview of the model. The response was obtained from instantiating MODEL.RUL, which is part of the rulebase that supports the INTERPRT command. The rule file contains free style text that is printed to the user's screen (or file). When LP information is needed, a keyword or command is referenced. The idea is to capture what an LP expert would do using ANALYZE, then make it accessible (i.e., in the knowledgebase) for the nonexpert.

ANALYZE... I MODEL

Here is an interpretation of WOODNET. There are 36 rows and 93 columns and 221 nonzeroes. The resident solution is OPTIMAL with COST = 25135.

There are 2 entities that determine the row and column syntax as follows.

A row that begins with S balances supply of some material in some location.
A row that begins with D balances demand of some material in some location.

A column that begins with S supplies some material in some location.
A column that begins with D demands some material in some location.
A column that begins with T transports some material from some location to some location.

The entities (that is, the basic dimensions) are:
 material
 location

WOODNET is a network model with 18 production 20 consumption, and 55 transfer activities.

Figure 4. Executing the model interpretation rule

Note that the last information given tells the user that WOODNET is a network model. This was obtained by an ANALYZE command that finds a maximal embedded network, then the rule file tests if all rows and columns are in the network. In this case they were, and the text reflects the expert's construction of MODEL.RUL.

Pursuing the demand side, I next asked for a display of all demand rows, shown in figure 5, with the abbreviated form: D R D. (One of the design philosophies in ANALYZE is to require a minimal number of keystrokes, so all commands and keyworded parameters use telescopic abbreviations[1[. In particular, D abbreviates DISPLAY, R abbreviates ROW, and D is a sufficient mask to delineate names that begin with D.) We arbitrarily begin with the first demand row, namely DMOCH, and we want to explain its marginal price of 73.

ANALYZE ...D R D

20 ROWS ARE IN SUBMATRIX

Name	Stat	Level	Lower bound	Upper bound	Price
DMOCH	L	0	0	0	73.000
DMODE	L	0	0	0	75.000
DMOLA	L	0	0	0	68.000
DMOSE	L	0	0	0	71.000
DMOSF	L	0	0	0	65.000
DOKCH	L	0	0	0	60.000
DOKDE	L	0	0	0	69.000
DOKLA	L	0	0	0	62.000
DOKSE	L	0	0	0	65.000
DOKSF	L	0	0	0	60.000
DPICH	L	0	0	0	22.000
DPIDE	L	0	0	0	22.000
DPILA	L	0	0	0	17.000
DPISE	L	0	0	0	20.000
DPISF	L	0	0	0	24.000
DWACH	L	0	0	0	78.000
DWADE	L	0	0	0	68.000
DWALA	L	0	0	0	75.000
DWASE	L	0	0	0	78.000
DWASF	L	0	0	0	70.000

Figure 5. Display of WOODNET Demand Rows

As an expert, I could begin to trace the flows to arrive at a submatrix that would explain the marginal price of row DMOCH. Instead, I shall let ANALYZE do this for me with the TRACE command, resulting in the 2x3 submatrix shown in Figure 6. The purpose of this is to enable flow descriptions that account for the "delivered price" of 73. The SUBMAT command level is entered only to add the COST row to the submatrix. At the end of figure 6 I have a causal substructure, which in this case is the 2x3 submatrix found by TRACE plus the COST row.

```
ANALYZE ...PICTURE DMOCH,* S=B
                        Picture of submatrix
          T
          M
          O
          S
          E
          C
          H
DMOCH     + = 0
ANALYZE ...TRACE
 TRACE complete...submatrix is set
ANALYZE ...PI
                        Picture of submatrix
          D    S    T
          M    M    M
          O    O    O
          C    S    S
          H    E    E
          1    1    C
          H
DMOCH     -         +      = 0
SMOSE          +    -      = 0
ANALYZE ...SUBMAT

 Submatrix has        2 row(s) and          3 column(s)
 SUBMAT (enter ? for menu)...A R COST

 SUBMAT (enter ? for menu)...
```

Figure 6. LP Expert's use of TRACE to obtain causal submatrix

The subsequent LIST and EXPLAIN commends, shown in figure 7, give the nonzeroes and translations, respectively. For reinforcement (and sometimes for added insight, especially when the submatrix is complex) I used the RATEOF command to see the rates of substitutions with respect to the demand column (DMOCH1). At this point we are in a position to complete the exercise for this demand row; however, let us use the INTERPRT command, as in figure 8.

```
ANALYZE ...LIST
Submatrix has     6 nonzeroes...
  DMOCH      DMOCH1            - 1.00000
  SMOSE      SMOSE1              1.00000
  COST       SMOSE1             55.0000
  COST       TMOSECH            18.0000
  SMOSE      TMOSECH           - 1.00000
  DMOCH      TMOSECH             1.00000
ANALYZE ...*This is a comment to myself...
ANALYZE ...*I now know the 73 is from 55 supply cost + 18 transportation cost
ANALYZE ...EXPLAIN ROWS
 Row COST is the objective row (MINIMIZE).
 Row DMOCH balances demand of mahogany in Chicago.
 Row SMOSE balances supply of mahogany in Seattle.
ANALYZE ...EXPLAIN COLUMNS
 Column DMOCH1 demands  mahogany in Chicago.
 Column SMOSE1 supplies mahogany in Seattle.
 Column TMOSECH transports mahogany from Seattle to Chicago.
ANALYZE ...*I now have the English explanation, but let me check the columns
ANALYZE ...D C
  3 COLUMNS ARE IN SUBMATRIX
Name        Stat   Level      Lower bound      Upper bound      Price
-----------------------------------------------------------------------
DMOCH1      L      25.000       25.000         25.000          73.000
SMOSE1      B      75.000         0               *               0
TMOSECH     B      25.000         0               *               0
ANALYZE ...*Demand column DMOCH is just a slack for row DMOCH...
ANALYZE ...*Look at its rates of substitution wrt basics
ANALYZE ...RATE COL
Rates of substitution for COL DMOCH1  Level = 25.0000  (STAT=L)
Basic var.   Level        COST       Rate       L-BLOCK     U-BLOCK
-----------------------------------------------------------------------
COST         25135.000    - 1.0      73.000     - *           *
TMOSECH      25.000       18.000      1.0       - 25.000      *
SMOSE1       75.000       55.000      1.0       - 75.000      *
-----------------------------------------------------------------------
Least level of DMOCH1        =    0    (TMOSECH)
Greatest level of DMOCH1     =    *    (no block)
```

Figure 7. Expert's final analysis to explain marginal price of row DMOCH

ANALYZE ...SUB R DMOCH

ANALYZE ...I P

Row DMOCH balances demand of mahogany in Chicago. I shall now interpret its price of 73. DMOCH is satisfied by the following activities.

Column DMOCH1 demands mahogany in Chicago with COST = 0.

Column SMOSE1 supplies mahogany in Seattle with COST = 55.

Column TMOSECH transports mahogany from Seattle to Chicago with COST = 18.

Thus, marginal price = delivered cost = 73.

Figure 8. Executing the price interpretation rule

After setting row DMOCH into the submatrix, the user asks for its price interpretation (abbreviated I P). This instantiates PRICE.RUL in the rulebase, which goes through the same reasoning as the LP expert (c.f., figures 6 and 7).

3. Further analysis

Other examples were analyzed, starting with some variations on WOODNET, such as when the marginal price is not equal to the delivered cost. Related scenarios that were infeasible in one case and unbounded in another case were also available. Space does not permit a complete report here, but a separate paper on the details of ANALYZE and its rulebase to support interpretation for non-experts of LP is in preparation.

In conclusion, the current rulebase for ANALYZE is experimental, and it is part of a larger project to develop an *Intelligent Mathematical Programming System* (IMPS)[6]. This is sponsored by a consortium of industries: Amoco Oil Company, General Research Corporation and Ketron management Science, Inc. Their support is not only financial, but also they have provided useful advice and encouragement during the past year.

4. References

[1] H.J. Greenberg, "A Functional Description of ANALYZE: A Computer-Assisted Analysis System for Linear Programming Models," ACM Transactions On Mathematical Software 9 (1983), pp. 18-56.

[2] H.J. Greenberg, "A Natural Language Discourse Model to Explain Linear Programming Models and Solutions," to appear in Decision Support Systems.

[3] H.J. Greenberg, "Computer-Assisted Analysis for Diagnosing Infeasibility in Linear Programming Models," Mathematical Programming Studies 31 (1987) PP. 79-97.

[4] H.J. Greenberg, "Diagnosing Infeasibility in Min-Cost Network Flow Models: Part I: Dual Infeasibility," to appear in IMA Journal of Mathematics in Management.

[5] H.J. Greenberg, "Diagnosing Infeasibility in Min-Cost Network Flow Models: Part II: Primal Infeasibility," to appear in IMA Journal of Mathematics in Management.

[6] H.J. Greenberg, "The Development of an Intelligent Mathematical Programming System," Technical Report, University of Colorado at Denver, Denver, CO, 1987 (also to appear in WORMSC Proceedings, Washington, DC, November, 1987).

Interfacing Optimizers With Planning Languages and Process Simulators

L.S. Lasdon, Dept. of Management Science and Information Systems School of Business Administration University of Texas Austin, Texas 78712

A.D. Waren, Dept. of Computer Science Cleveland State University Cleveland, Ohio 44115

S. Sarkar Execucom Systems Corporation P.O. Box 9758 Austin, Texas 78766

1. Introduction

The use of optimization models in decision support systems is increasing rapidly. Successful applications span the entire planning-scheduling-control hierarchy. Some outstanding examples are the mixed integer linear programming system described by Geoffrion [1974] for distribution system design (strategic planning), a network-based DSS for marketing and distribution of refined petroleum products developed by Klingman et. al. [1985] (short term tactical planning), a vehicle routing and scheduling system [Fisher, et. al. [1982]], and many instances of real time optimization in the process industries (control).

In such systems, the optimization model and its data are sometimes integrated with the optimization algorithm or "solver". This is certainly true when a special purpose algorithm must be designed to exploit model structure, as with the large integer programming models of Fisher and Geoffrion referred to earlier. However, with increasing frequency, the system model is a separate entity, often coded in a modeling language oriented to a specific problem class. Examples of such modeling systems of particular interest include financial planning languages and spreadsheets, e.g. IFPS and LOTUS 1-2-3, and process simulation languages like FLOWTRAN and MASSBAL [SACDA 1987]. These systems were all designed to support first and foremost the fundamental operations of data management, model evaluation or simulation, reporting, model and case management, and graphics. In the last 5 years there has been a strong movement to include optimization capabilities and, more recently, artificial intelligence and expert system features.

Such integrated modeling systems offer many advantages to the user, most of these falling under the categories of flexibility and ease of use. One can peruse and modify data, solve and validate models, and in so doing set the stage for optimization. All this is done in a language designed to fit the class of problems being solved. If the optimization capability is well designed and integrated, the user need not be

NATO ASI Series, Vol. F48
Mathematical Models for Decision Support
Edited by G. Mitra

concerned with transforming the model into a form demanded by a particular solver, or with details of the optimization solution process.

A key issue in such integrated systems is the interface between the optimizer and the modeling language or simulator. This interface must (a) process the model to exclude portions not relevant to the solver and portions which, if excluded, simplify the solution process, (b) determine the nature of the problem (LP, NLP, MIP, network, etc.), (c) provide information needed by the solver during the solution process, e.g. function and gradient values, and (d) report on the solution process (if desired). This paper focuses on the design of such interfaces for two important classes of modeling systems: (1) planning languages and spreadsheets and (2) chemical process simulators. For the former class of systems, our discussion uses IFPS/OPTIMUM as a vehicle. IFPS/OPTIMUM, marketed by Execucom Systems Corporation and described in [Roy, Lasdon, and Lordeman 1986], is the first such system to include an optimization capability. We also briefly discuss 2 related systems, VINO and WHAT'S BEST, which combine with LOTUS 1-2-3. For process applications, we describe three forms in which the problem can be posed to the optimizer. Since these are usually continuous variable nonlinear programs, we also discuss the relative merits of some widely used NLP algorithms in solving process optimization problems, and describe some computational experience.

2. Optimization and Planning Languages

2.1 Planning Language Features

Almost all planning languages are based on a matrix format, analogous to the layout of an accounting ledger page or "spreadsheet." The columns often represent time periods, but can also correspond to products, locations, etc. Each row of the matrix is used to specify a variable, and for each cell (i,j) of this matrix, the planning language permits specification of a rule for computing the value of the variable in that cell. Figure 1 shows a product mix model created using **IFPS**. Lines 1 through 15 are comment lines, describing the problem. Line 16 defines 2 columns representing products and a special column for totals. Lines 17 through 28 define values for variables in each of the first two columns, while line 29 defines values for the special column **TOTAL.** All lines containing a single expression or value (e.g., lines 19 and 22) define the variable in all columns except **TOTAL.** Upon issuing the **SOLVE** command and requesting **ALL** variables, a default report is printed.

IFPS and some other planning languages are nonprocedural, i.e., the statements may be entered in any order. For example, in Figure 1, lines 17 and 18 could have followed line 19. **IFPS** determines a sequence for computation.

The model of Figure 1 is triangular, i.e., the variables can be evaluated sequentially. However, if simultaneous equations are present, **IFPS** detects and solves them as part of the solution process, using a Gauss-Seidel algorithm.

Spreadsheet languages for microcomputers, like 1-2-3 or Multiplan, differ in some respects from planning languages like **IFPS.** Initially, spreadsheet languages referred to variables only by spreadsheet cell location, e.g., a typical variable name was C3, with C indicating the column and 3 the row. However, current versions permit variables to have English-like names. Spreadsheet languages also have a more limited ability to handle models which contain simultaneous equations. However, in the issues considered here, the similarities between spreadsheet and planning languages are more important than these differences. Both are used to specify models composed of systems of equations. Each equation has a single variable on its left-hand side, while the right-hand side expression can have a very general form. In the following sections, only these features are used.

Note that each equation in Figure 1 defines a vector of variables, e.g., line 25 defines **LABOR REQUIRED** in each of the first 2 columns. In the remainder of this paper. The term "variable" refers to a quantity in a particular row and column of the spreadsheet. Hence, **LABOR REQUIRED** in column **GIZMOS** is a different variable than **LABOR REQUIRED** in column **WIDGETS.**

```
MODEL PRODMIX VERSION OF 12/01/82 10:36
1  *THE PATTERSON PRODUCTION COMPANY MAKES TWO PRODUCTS, GIZMOS AND
1  *WIDGETS, MR. PATTERSON IS TRYING TO DETERMINE HOW MANY UNITS OF
3  *EACH PRODUCT HE SHOULD MAKE NEXT MONTH IN ORDER TO MAXIMIZE COMPANY
4  *PROFITS.
5  *
6  *THE GIZMO, BEING A SUPERIOR QUALITY PRODUCT, HAS A PRICE OF
    $5.00/UNIT,
7  *WHILE A WIDGET HAS A PRICE OF $3.00/UNIT.  HOWEVER, EACH GIZMO
    REQUIRES
8  *4 UNITS OF MATERIAL AND 7 UNITS OF LABOR, WHILE A WIDGET REQUIRES
9  *ONLY 2 UNITS OF MATERIAL AND 4 UNITS OF LABOR, A UNIT OF MATERIAL
10 *COSTS $0.60, AND ONLY 28 UNITS ARE AVAILABLE.  A UNIT OF LABOR COSTS
11 *$0.30, AND 50 UNITS ARE AVAILABLE.
12 *
13 *HOW WOULD YOU ADVISE MR. PATTERSON?
14 *
15 *
16  COLUMNS GIZMOS, WIDGETS, TOTAL
    TRAIL VALUES FOR DECISION VARIABLES
17  UNITS PRODUCED=4,4
18  PRICE=5,3
19  REVENUE=UNITS PRODUCED*PRICE
20  MATERIAL PER UNIT=4,2
21  MATERIAL REQUIRED=UNITS PRODUCED*MATERIAL PER UNIT
22  UNIT MATERIAL COST=0.6
23  TOTAL MATERIAL COST=UNIT MATERIAL COST*MATERIAL REQUIRED
24  LABOR PER UNIT=7,4
25  LABOR REQUIRED=UNITS PRODUCED*LABOR PER UNIT
26  UNIT LABOR COST=0.3
27  TOTAL LABOR COST=UNIT LABOR COST*LABOR REQUIRED
```

```
28  PRETAX INCOME=REVENUE-TOTAL MATERIAL COST-TOTAL LABOR COST
29  COLUMN TOTAL FOR L17,L19,L21,L23,L25,L28=COLUMN 1 + COLUMN 2
END OF MODEL
```

Figure 1. Product Mix Model in IFPS

2.2 The User Interface

Once a planning model has been created, an optimization problem is specified by identifying the decision variables, the constraint variables, and the objective variable. The decision variables are the unknowns in the optimization problem, i.e., the "x" vector of a conventional mathematical program. Decision variables can be bounded.

	GIZMOS	WIDGETS	TOTAL
UNITS PRODUCED	4	4	8
PRICE	5	3	
REVENUE	20	12	32
MATERIAL PER UNIT	4	2	
MATERIAL REQUIRED	16	8	24
UNIT MATERIAL COST	0.6000	0.6000	
TOTAL MATERIAL COST	9.600	4.800	14.40
LABOR PER UNIT	7	4	
LABOR REQUIRED	28	16	44
UNIT LABOR COST	0.3000	0.3000	
TOTAL LABOR COST	8.400	4.800	13.20
PRETAX INCOME	2	2.400	4.400

Figure 2. Report Showing Decisions, Constraints, Objective

Specifying a variable as a decision variable overrides the model equation that otherwise defines it. The constraint variables are variables with bounds, and the objective variable has the standard mathematical programming meaning. Given a report in "spreadsheet" format (as shown in Figure 2), these variables can be readily identified. In the figure, the decision variables have been enclosed in triangles, the constraint variables in circles, and the objective variable in a rectangle. This method for formulating optimization problems is easily grasped by persons who have no familiarity with optimization.

```
1 MAXIMIZE PRETAX INCOME(TOTAL)
2 DECISIONS
3 UNITS PRODUCED(GIZMOS, WIDGETS).GE.0
4 CONSTRAINTS
5 MATERIAL REQUIRED(TOTAL).LE.28
6 LABOR REQUIRED(TOTAL).LE.28
? SOLVE
IFPS MODEL SOLUTION-LINEAR
ENTER SOLVE OPTIONS
```

```
? NONE
OPTIMAL SOLUTION
ENTER SOLVE OPTIONS
? ALL
```

	GIZMOS	WIDGETS	TOTAL
UNITS PRODUCED	0	12.50	12.50
PRICE	5	3	
REVENUE	0	37.50	37.50
MATERIAL PER UNIT	4	2	
MATERIAL REQUIRED	0	25	25
UNIT MATERIAL COST	0.6000	0.6000	
TOTAL MATERIAL COST	0	15	15
LABOR PER UNIT	7	4	
LABOR REQUIRED	0	50	50
UNIT LABOR COST	0.3000	0.3000	
TOTAL LABOR COST	0	15	15
PRETAX INCOME	0	7.500	7.500

Figure 3. IFPS/OPTIMUM Dialogue and Solution

Figure 3 shows the **IFPS/OPTIMUM** dialogue for specifying this problem, solving it, and reporting the solution. Line 1 specifies the objective as **PRETAX INCOME** in column **TOTAL.** Lines 2 and 3 identify the decision variables, constrained to be nonnegative. The constraint section in lines 4 through 6 specifies bounds on the variables total material and total labor.

The **SOLVE** command initiates the diagnosis and solution of the problem. The problem is classified as linear, and the user is given the opportunity to review the model solution using the initial values of the decisions. A linear programming code is then invoked to solve the problem. Finally, the values of **ALL** variables in the optimal solution are displayed. Comparison of the solution report with others previously examined facilitates understanding and acceptance of the optimization results. Such comparisons are easy and natural in systems which both simulate and optimize, but are difficult or impossible with conventional mathematical programming systems.

2.3 The Optimizer/Planning Language Interface-Overview

Note that, in Figure 1, the objective and constraints (henceforth called problem functions) are not specified as explicit functions of the decision variables. There are several intermediate quantities (e.g., **REVENUE** and **MATERIAL REQUIRED**) whose values must be computed prior to calculating some problem function. In addition, there are 5 exogenous variables, which are determined by data in lines 18, 20, 22, 24, and 26. The presence of many intermediate and exogenous variables is an important feature of optimization models specified in planning languages. One problem from a large oil company was based on a planning model with over 1000 variables, yet many were exogenous, and there were only 2 decisions and 2 constraints. The intermediate variables make the model much easier to build and understand. However, they create several problems which the optimizer/language interface must resolve. First, if the problem functions are to be computed several times for different values of the decisions, the exogenous variables need to be computed only once. Second, in the above example, it is very desirable to solve an optimization problem involving 2 variables and 2 constraints rather than 1000 of each. Hence, the derivatives of the problem functions with respect to the decision variables must be computed, incorporating the implicit dependence of these functions on the decisions. Finally, the nature of these implicit functions, e.g., linear or nonlinear, must be determined automatically. The modeler may not even know what a linear functions is. In any case, determining linearity by inspection in a large model may be virtually impossible. the presence of some nonlinear expressions in the model does not imply that the problem functions are nonlinear in the decision variables-the variables specified by the nonlinear expressions may not affect any problem function. Summarizing, the optimizer/planning language interface must perform tasks not required in conventional mathematical programming systems. Its functions are:

1. Classify problem variables as exogenous or endogenous.

2. Determine whether each problem function is linear in the decision variables or not, and hence classify the problem as linear or nonlinear. (Further classification, e.g., GUB, Network, etc., may be desirable.)

3. For nonlinear problems, transmit new values of the decision variables from the solver to the planning model, solve the model for the corresponding values of the problem functions, and communicate these back to the solver.

4. compute first partial derivatives of all problem functions with respect to the decision variables, and transmit these to the appropriate solver. This need be done only once for linear problems, and several times for nonlinear ones.

The input information available to perform these tasks depends on the specific language used. The information used by **IFPS/OPTIMUM** is:

1. A list of the variables which occur on the right-hand side of each model equation, and the ability to evaluate any equation for any values of these variables. For example, in line 19 of Figure 1, we have the information that **REVENUE** in each column depends on **UNITS PRODUCED** and **PRICE** in that same column, and we can evaluate the expression **UNITS PRODUCED*PRICE** for any values of these variables.

2. The sequence in which the model variables are to be evaluated, and which variables are involved in each set of simultaneous equations.

3. The ability to solve the model for the values of the problem functions, given a set of values of the decision variables.

4. Which model variables are the objective, decisions, and constraints, and what the bounds are for the latter two.

The last item is provided through the user interface, as discussed in section 2.2 All other information is provided by an analysis of the planning model.

Note that, as implied by item 1 above, each individual model equation is treated as a "black box." Its functional form is never examined. First partial derivatives of model equations are approximated by differencing, and linearity is inferred during a setup phase by testing if all derivatives, evaluated at several points, are constant.

2.4 Variable Classification and Model Reduction

Figure 4 below illustrates the classification of problem variables.

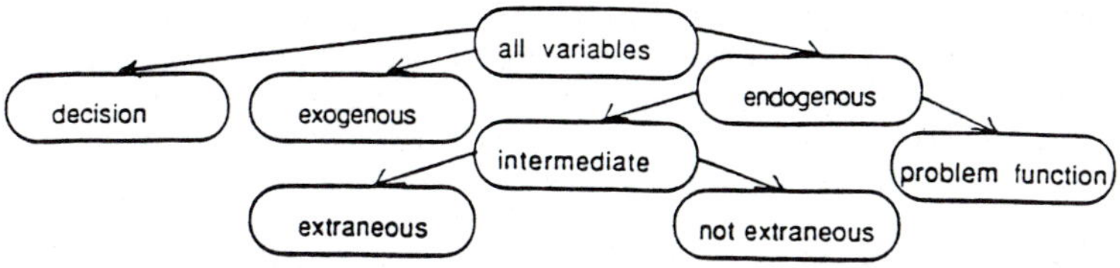

Figure 4-Classification of Variables

Figure 4 illustrates the classification of problem variables. The exogenous variables are those whose values are determined, directly or indirectly, by given data. The endogenous variables are those which depend on the decisions. Some of these are problem functions (i.e., the objective or a constraint), and the rest are intermediate endogenous. Of these, those whose values do not affect any problem function (again, directly or indirectly) are called extraneous.

The user identifies the decisions and problem functions. Classification of the remainder is done by a one-pass, column-by-column procedure, using the computational sequence determined by the language processor. Variables are exogenous if their defining expressions involve only other exogenous variables or data. A simultaneous set is exogenous if its expressions involve only variables within the set, other exogenous variables, or data. Endogenous variables have at least one decision or other endogenous variable in their defining expressions, and a simultaneous set is endogenous if any of its expressions involve at least one endogenous variable. Note that, since a variable may be defined by a different expression in different columns, it may be endogenous in some columns and exogenous in others.

In nonlinear optimization problems, the model must be solved more than once for different values of the decision variables. Significant time savings are possible if exogenous quantities are computed only once. Examination of seven **IFPS** models, ranging from 14 to 103 variables, showed that from 35% to 70% of the variables were exogenous. Evaluating only the endogenous quantities yielded time savings from 4% to 43% of the full model solution time, with the average savings approximately 25%. Further savings are possible by computing extraneous endogenous variables only once, after the optimization is finished (this is not yet done in **IFPS/OPTIMUM**). A backwards pass through the solution sequence can identify these. All endogenous variables which are problem functions are initially marked "used," and all other endogenous variables are initially "unused." During the pass, if a variable is used, all variables on which it depends are also marked used. At termination, all unused endogenous variables are extraneous.

2.5 Partial Derivative Computation

The simplest procedure for obtaining derivatives of the problem functions with respect to the decision variables is to perturb each decision variable, re-solve the model to evaluate the perturbed functions, and approximate the derivatives by difference quotients. In many cases, however, an alternative analytically based approach is both quicker and more accurate. For simplicity, we consider "column invariant" models, where the form of the equations and the classification of variables (endogenous, exogenous, decision) does not change from column to column. In addition, assume that the **"FUTURE"** qualifier does not appear.[1] Let u(t) and y(t) be the vectors of decision and nonextraneous endogenous variables in column t, respectively, of dimensions n and m. Then, suppressing the exogenous variables, the model equations may be written as:

$$g(y(t),\ldots,y(t-s),u(t),\ldots,u(t-c))=0, \qquad t=1,\ldots,T \qquad (2.1)$$

[1]X=Future r Y yields X in column i as the value of Y in column i + r.

where g is an m-vector of functions, assumed differentiable, and s and c are the maximum lags in the endogenous and decision variables, respectively. For most planning languages, g has the form $g = -y(t)+h(y(t),\ldots,y(t-s),u(t),\ldots,u(t-c))$, since every variable appears on the left-hand side of exactly one equation. For models with no simultaneous equations, the Jacobian matrix $\partial g/\partial y(t)$ is triangular, and the components of y(t) may be evaluated sequentially.

Note that (2.1) is a system of difference equations, which is the model form assumed in discrete-time optimal control problems. Planning languages are systems for constructing and solving such equations, and optimization problems formulated in planning languages are constrained optimal control problems. Hence the adjoint equation approach of optimal control (see, for example, Mantell and Lasdon 1978) may be used to compute the needed derivatives as follows. Let $y=(y(1),\ldots,y(T))$, $u=(u(1),\ldots,u(T))$, and let g(t) be shorthand notation for the left-hand side of (1). Define

$$G(y,u)=(g(1),\ldots,g(T))=0 \qquad (2.2)$$

i.e., (2.2) represents the set of all endogenous model equations in all columns. We assume that (2.2) can be solved for y given any u of interest, and that the endogenous jacobian matrix $\partial G/\partial y$ is nonsingular for all y and u. Then, by the implicit function theorem, y is a differentiable function of u, say y(u).

Let f(y,u) be the expression defining a problem function. The reduced problem function corresponding to f is

$$F(u)=f(y(u),u) \qquad (2.3)$$

and the reduced gradient $\partial F/\partial u$ is required by the optimization routines. It may be computed as follows (Lasdon and Waren 1978):

(1) Solve the linear equations

$$\pi(\partial G/\partial y)=\partial f/\partial y \qquad (2.4)$$

for the Lagrange multiplier (row) vector, π.

(2) Evaluate $\partial F/\partial u$ by

$$\partial F/\partial u=\partial f/\partial u-\pi(\partial G/\partial u). \tag{2.5}$$

In (2.4) and (2.5), all elements of $\partial G/\partial y$ and $\partial G/\partial u$ are evaluated at some model solution $(\bar{y}\ \bar{u})$ and (2.5) yields $\partial F/\partial u$ evaluated at $\bar{u}$. Of course, π has its usual "shadow price" interpretation,

$$\pi_i=-\partial f/\partial b_i \tag{2.6}$$

where b_i is the right-hand side of the ith equation in (2.2). Since perturbing this right-hand side is equivalent to perturbing y_i

$$\pi_i=-\partial f/\partial y_i \tag{2.7}$$

i.e., if y_i is viewed as independent, π_i gives the sensitivity of f with respect to y_i.

Since the model equations have the sequential form (2.1), $\partial G/\partial y$ is block lower triangular with square nonsingular blocks. Hence, the large linear system (2.4) decomposes into T smaller sequential systems, which are solved backwards in time. Let $\pi=(\pi(1),\ldots,\pi(T))$ where $\pi(t)$ is the multiplier vector corresponding to the tth set of equations in (2.1). Then the difference equations for the multipliers are

$$\pi(T)B_T=\partial f/\partial y(T), \tag{2.8a}$$

$$\pi(t)B_t=\partial f/\partial y(t)-\sum_{\tau=t+1}^{b}\pi_\tau B_{\tau,t} \quad t=T-1,T-2,\ldots,1, \text{ where} \tag{2.8b}$$

$$b=\min(t+s,T), \text{ and} \tag{2.9}$$

$$B_{\tau,t}=\partial g(\tau)/\partial y(t), \tag{2.10}$$

$$B_t=\partial g(t)/\partial y(t). \tag{2.11}$$

Note that $\partial G/\partial y$ is nonsingular if and only if all matrices B_t are nonsingular. The components of $\partial F/\partial u$ are then evaluated by

$$\partial F/\partial u(t)=\partial f/\partial u(t)-\sum_{\tau=t}^{a} \pi_\tau C_{\tau,t} \quad \text{where} \tag{2.12}$$

$$a=\min(t-c,T) \text{ and} \tag{2.13}$$

$$C_{\tau,t}=\partial g(\tau)/\partial u(t). \tag{2.14}$$

If the model has no simultaneous equations, each B_t is triangular, so (2.8) can be solved quickly. Otherwise, B_t is usually mostly triangular with some small simultaneous blocks. These blocks are solved by a dense matrix LU factorization routine. Each B_t is usually sparse, and the matrices $B_{\tau,t}$ and $C_{\tau,t}$ are very sparse.

In **IFPS/OPTIMUM**, linear programs are solved by the sparsity oriented primal simplex code XMP (Marsten 1981), nonlinear problems by the **GRG2** optimization system (Lasdon and Waren 1978), and mixed integer linear programs by Marsten's ZOOM branch and bound software (Marsten 1987), which uses XMP to solve its LP relaxations. It is interesting to note that, since the primal simplex and **GRG** optimizers are both reduced gradient methods, a "double reduction" of the optimization problem occurs. These optimizers solve a reduced problem in which only the decision variables appear, utilizing reduced gradients as data. This problem is further reduced by the optimizers, by classifying some of these decision variables as dependent.

2.6. Detection of Linear Problem Functions

If the multiplier-based procedures of section 2.5 are used, reduced gradients of each problem function are computed separately. It is important to know if a particular reduced problem function F(u) is linear, since then its reduced gradient can be computed only once. If all problem functions are linear, the problem is routed to the LP solution routine.

An endogenous variable is linear if its defining expression is linear once all exogenous arguments have been fixed at their assigned values- otherwise it is nonlinear. Once this information is known, one can determine linearity or nonlinearity of all reduced problem functions by a single, column by column, forward pass through the solution sequence. All variables are initially unlabeled. During the pass, variables are labeled if their defining equations are nonlinear, or if they depend on other variables which are labeled. At termination, all labeled variables which are also problem functions are judged to be nonlinear. This ignores the possibility that all nonlinear terms may cancel, but that possibility is remote, and is too difficult to detect.

2.7 Computer Implementation

The IFPS/OPTIMUM system is a modular system is a modular system composed of over 60 Fortran subroutines which perform the following major steps:

1. Read the users' specification of which model variables are decisions, constraints, and the objective;
2. Classify the remaining model variables as endogenous or exogenous in both regular and special columns;
3. Compute the nonzero elements of the endogenous and control Jacobian matrices $\partial G/\partial y$ and $\partial G/\partial u$, flagging elements which depend on y or u;
4. Determine if the optimization problem is linear or nonlinear;
5. Compute the reduced gradient $\partial F/\partial u$ for each objective or constraint function F (once for linear problems, when needed for nonlinear problems);
6. Transmit the reduced gradients and other problem data to the appropriate optimizer and, in the case of a nonlinear model, communicate with it during the solution process;
7. Retrieve and report the results of the optimization.

All the above functions are performed by the optimization portion of IFPS/OPTIMUM. The IFPS simulator provides only the simulation capability, the model solution sequence, values of individual model equations, etc.

Steps 1 through 5 are performed as described in the previous sections. In Step 3, $\partial G/\partial y$ and $\partial G/\partial u$ are computed and stored in row order, by differencing each endogenous model equation. For $\partial G/\partial y$, nonzero partial derivatives and their row and column indices are stored in separate, parallel arrays. In solving equation (4) for π, $\partial G/\partial y$ is required by columns in the back substitution process, last column first. Hence, a linked list data structure is used to permit access by columns.

The data structures used for $\partial G/\partial u$ are different, since $\partial G/\partial u$ is usually much sparser than $\partial G/\partial y$, and need only be premultiplied by π in equation (2.4). The product $\pi\partial G/\partial u$ can be computed accessing $\partial G/\partial u$ by rows, so no link arrays are needed. The matrix elements and their column indices are stored in parallel arrays, by rows. Two smaller parallel pointer arrays store the position in these arrays of the start of each nonzero row and the index of that row.

2.8 Spreadsheet Based Optimizers

Recently, two closely related systems have been developed which couple linear optimizers with LOTUS 1-2-3, VINO [Cunningham and Schrage 1985] and WHAT'S BEST [Savage, 1986]. In a typical LP model, some cells of the spreadsheet contain data, others contain values for decision variables, while constraint functions and the objective are specified by formulas in a third set of cells. The principal functional differences between these systems and IFPS/OPTIMUM are:

(1) Formulas which define intermediate variables, but are not themselves constrained (or the objective) are not allowed

(2) All constraint functions are required to be nonnegative (WHAT'S BEST has facilities which permit easy translation of other types of constraints into this format).
(3) Only linear programs can be solved thus far.
Item (1) above means that the methods of sections 2.3 through 2.5 for dealing with implicit functions are not needed. The software is thus greatly simplified, but the user is required to state all constraints and the objective without the use of intermediate formulas.

Of course, the modeling style of a PC system like VINO/WHAT'S BEST is quite different from that of a mainframe system like IFPS/OPTIMUM. Results are immediately displayed in the spreadsheet, which usually combines the input data, model, and report. The effect is much more visual and immediate. Systems like this have the potential to create millions of new users of optimization. Future improvements in these systems and in microcomputer hardware are needed to bring this dream closer to realty.

3. Process Unit Optimization

3.1 Steady State Process Models

A process is a collection of units which transform input streams into output streams, together with pipes which interconnect the units and storage tanks for raw materials, and intermediate and final products. In the example of figure 5, the vector y_i contains the flow rate and quality variables associated with the ith stream. These qualities include compositions, temperature, and other properties such as octane number or

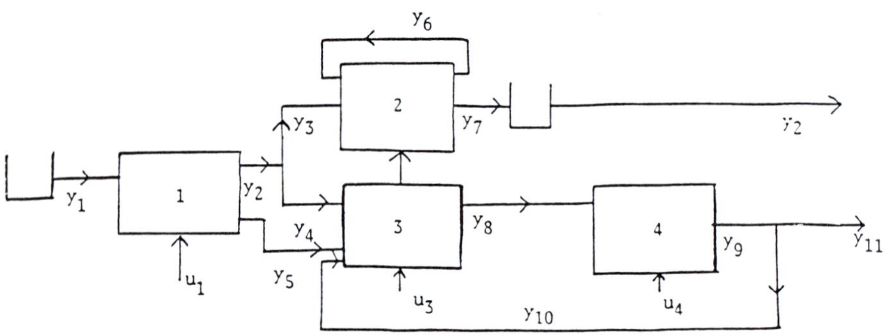

Figure 5 - Process flow diagram

viscosity. The vectors u_i are the control variables, which are independent. The stream splits, e.g. y_2 splitting into y_3 and y_4, and the inputs and outputs to each tank provide additional degrees of freedom.

Let I_j be a vector containing all the inputs to unit j. For example, in figure 5 $I_1 = (y_1, u_1)$, $I_3 = (y_4, y_5, y_{10}, u_3)$. Each unit may then be described by transformations, t_i, which give its outputs as functions of its inputs, e.g. $y_2 = t_2(I_1)$, $y_7 = t_7(I_2)$.

In refinery LP models, typically used for medium term planning, the functions t_i are linear, determined by yield vectors which give the number of units of each output produced by one unit of a particular input. However, real process units are highly nonlinear, and the yield vectors are just approximations to the true nonlinear relationships. In process models for real time optimization, it is important that unit models accurately represent the true behavior of the units, since the model solution is to be used to determine day to day process operating conditions. In fact, many oil and chemical companies are introducing nonlinear yields, qualities, and blending relationships into their planning models. The resulting large sparse, nonlinear models promise to significantly reduce the gaps which now exist between planning, scheduling, and control. Model solutions will be more realistic and accurate, and hence can be converted to actual operating schedules more readily. A more complete description of the need to integrate planning, scheduling, and control in the process industries, as well as the tools and other actions that are needed to do this, is found in [Baker, 1984].

If storage tanks are included in a process model, time dependence is introduced. Most models now used for planning and control are single period, with constraints on some key stocks at the end of the period. If we collect together all such inventory limits, stream splits, and unit transformations, the resulting system of simultaneous nonlinear equations may be written as

$$G(y,u) = 0 \tag{3.1}$$

where y and u are vectors containing all stream and control variables respectively. This system can be solved for the dependent variables y for any permissable values of the controls u.

Solving (3.1) for y given u is the main task of a process simulator. A problem feature which complicates this task is the presence of recycle streams, such as streams 6 and 10 in figure 5. If these recycles were not present, it would be possible to move sequentially from unit one to unit four, computing each ones' outputs once its inputs are known. The system (3.1) would be block triangular. The recycle streams destroy this triangularity and require that some iterative algorithm be used to solve (3.1). If the equation/variable incidence matrix for figure 5 were permuted into block lower triangular form, the columns corresponding to y_6 and y_{10} would be 'spike" columns, containing nonzero entries above the diagonal.

If the values of such spike columns were known, the system equations could be solved sequentially. This can be represented physically by thinking of each recycle stream as being "torn". For example, in figure 6 below recycle stream 6 is torn, so that

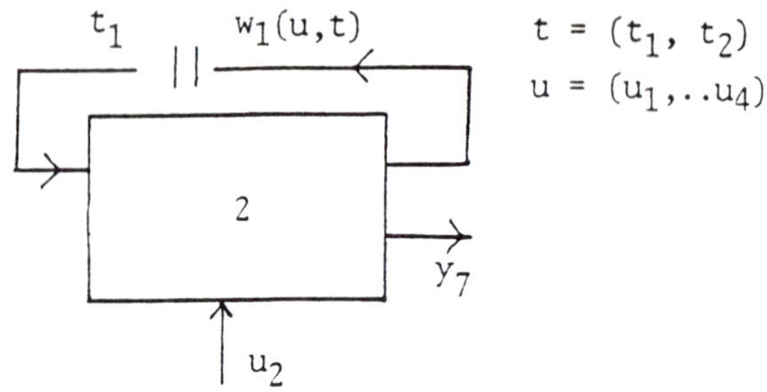

Figure 6 - Tear Stream

its value on the input side of the tear, t_1, is (temporarily) not equal to the value on the output side, w_1. This value depends, in general, on all tear variables t, and on all controls u, and is denoted by $w_1(u,t)$. Any solution to (3.1) must reconnect the tears, i.e. must satisfy the system

$$t - w(t,u) = 0 \tag{3.2}$$

This implicitly defined system is an equivalent, condensed version of the (usually) large sparse system (3.1). Of course, to evaluate w, one must make a pass through all process units, computing their outputs sequentially.

It is interesting to compare process simulators and planning languages/spreadsheets. Both are software systems for building, managing, solving, and reporting the solutions of systems of simultaneous equations. Process models, however, are almost always more highly nonlinear and more implicit than models generally coded in planning languages or spreadsheets. Hence, the equation solvers in process simulators need to be far more sophisticated, often including algorithms for locating a nearly minimal set of tear streams, plus robust implementations of Newton's and the Gauss-Seidel method. In contrast, LOTUS 1-2-3 has minimal facilities for solving simultaneous systems.

3.2 The Process Control Environment

As shown in figure 7, the lowest level of control is concerned with regulation, i.e. insuring that the values of certain dependent process variables remain as close as possible to specified values (called setpoints), despite unpredictable plant disturbances, by adjusting manipulated variables. In a simple regulatory feedback loop, the manipulated variable could be a valve position and the dependent variable a flow rate. In higher level loops, manipulated variables could be flow rates and dependent variables, temperatures or compositions. In the past, regulation was done by analogue measuring, control, and actuator equipment, but it is now commonly performed by digital computers, often powerful minicomputers. These control computers also smooth and store process data, perform monitoring and alarming functions, and can also house any steady state optimization capabilities. The advent of digital control permits sophisticated multivariable regulation algorithms to be

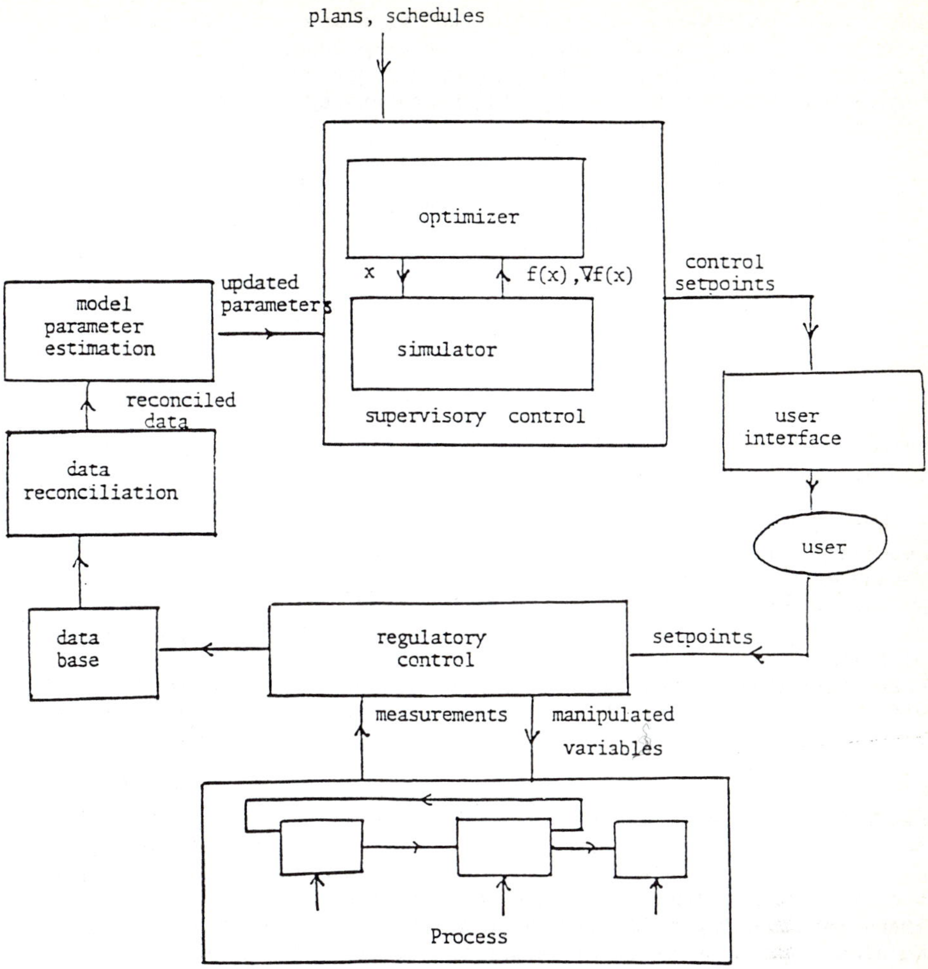

Figure 7 - Supervisory and Regulatory Control

used, in which several manipulated variables are used to regulate several dependent variables simultaneously. In some instances, discrete or continuous time optimal control algorithms may be used to perform the regulation, minimizing the squared error between desired and actual dependent variable values.

Regulatory control effectively interchanges one set of independent variables - the manipulated variables - for another, those being regulated to their setpoint values. This second set is more naturally included in an optimization model that has an economically meaningful objective, e.g. cost, profit, or product quality, and constraints expressing equipment capacities, safety limits, product demands and quality specifications, and raw material availabilities. This problem is solved by a supervisory control level, comprised of a steady state process model and an optimizer. The process model is a set of simultaneous algebraic equations like (3.1) or (3.2), and the optimal values of the control variables u become the setpoints for the regulator loops, usually after scrutiny by process operators.

In such a system, it is important that the process model accurately represent current process behavior. To achieve this, process measurements are used to periodically re-estimate model parameters, such as catalyst activity or heat transfer rates. Of course, these measurements may be noisy, and measuring instruments can malfunction or "drift". The data reconciliation block adjusts process measurements so that they satisfy material and energy balances while minimizing the weighted sum of squared deviations between measured and reconciled values. The optimizer in the supervisory control block may be used to solve this problem.

Real time optimization models may contain only a few variables and constraints, as when a single plant subunit is being optimized. Models dealing with a significant portion of a plant, such as product blending, a distillation column, or a catalytic cracker, are now fairly common. There is a growing tendency toward plantwide models, which may contain hundreds or thousands of variables and equations. For multiunit or complex single unit models, there are three main forms in which the optimization problem can be posed to the optimizer. This is the topic of the next section.

3.3 Coupling Optimizers with Process Simulators

A general process optimization problem may be formulated as:

$$\text{minimize} \quad f(y,u) \tag{3.3}$$

subject to the process model equations:

$$G(y,u) = 0 \tag{3.4}$$

and constraints on the dependent and independent variables:

$$\underline{h} \leq h(y,u) \leq \overline{h} \tag{3.5}$$

These latter constraints often consist of simple bounds on the control and some dependent variables. We consider problems where the process model is large and sparse, and is solved by a process simulator. The conceptually simplest approach is to have the optimizer solve (3.3) - (3.5) directly. Unfortunately, there are few NLP codes capable of solving such large sparse problems. Some which are applicable are successive linear programming [Zhang 1985], MINOS [Murtagh and Saunders 1982], and a version of successive quadratic programming (SQP) specially designed to deal with the large system of equalities (3.4) [Locke 1982]. All 3 algorithms are currently being applied to real problems.

This large sparse NLP approach can be termed complete integration, since all simulator equations and variables (except for those which are exogenous or extraneous, as defined in section 2.4) are included in the set of constraints seen by the optimizer. This may be desirable when the simulator is equation oriented, i.e. has access to all process model equations, and interprets these equations rather than generating and executing compiled code. Interpretive systems provide for easy modification and rerunning of models, since no compile and link steps are required, but they are much slower (up to a factor of ten) than compiled code. In such cases, complete integration offers the possibility of increased speed, by exploiting both the sparsity and partial linearity of (3.4) when evaluating derivatives. Derivatives of linear terms in (3.4) need be computed only once. For nonconstant derivatives, assume that partials of all functions in (3.4) with respect to a specific variable, say y_j, are to be approximated by finite differencing. Then, after y_j is perturbed to $y_j + \Delta y_j$, only those functions which depend nonlinearly on y_j need be evaluated. There are usually less than ten such functions, even in models with thousands of equations. Alternatively, one can compute derivatives symbolically. The symbolic processor must then take advantage of common terms between the functions and their derivatives.

A second approach, partial integration, includes only the tear stream equalities (3.2) in the optimizer constraints, i.e. the NLP solved is

$$\text{minimize } r(t,u) \tag{3.6}$$

subject to the tear stream equalities

$$t - w(t,u) = 0 \tag{3.7}$$

and the inequality constraints

$$\underline{g} \leq g\,(t,u) \leq \bar{g} \tag{3.8}$$

In order to evaluate the implicit functions r and g for given t and u, one inputs (t,u) to the simulator, computes all other model variables y, and then evaluates the objective and constraint functions in (3.3) and (3.5).

This approach is termed partial integration because only a small subset of the model equations, the tear stream equalities, are seen by the optimizer. As in linear programming, almost all large sparse models turn out to be nearly triangular, having at most a few hundred "spike" or tear variables. Hence this optimization problem is much smaller than the completely integrated version (3.3) - (3.5), but is highly implicit, much denser than (3.3) - (3.5), and more highly nonlinear.

NLP's of this type are usually solved by an algorithm that satisfies the tear stream equalities only at optimality. Such an approach is termed infeasible path, and is discussed in [Biegler 1985a] and [Biegler 1985b]. The most popular algorithm for such applications is successive quadratic programming, since it tends to require fewer evaluations of the (expensive) objective and constraint functions than other methods.

Advantages of this approach are reduced problem size, and the fact that the tear stream equations need not be satisfied at each step of the solution process. A disadvantage is that a physically meaningful solution, (i.e. one satisfying the tear stream equalities) is usually not obtained until late in the iterative solution process. If the optimizer fails without producing a feasible solution in a real time optimization application, the process operator must create set point values with little support from his DSS. For this reason, many users find a third approach, the feasible path method, preferable.

This approach requires that the simulator be converged each time the objective and constraints are evaluated, so that each iterate represents a physically meaningful process state. Hence the tear stream equalities are satisfied at each iteration:

$$t - w(t,u) = 0 \tag{3.9}$$

Let t(u) be the vector t which satisfies (3.9). Then the optimization problem solved by a feasible path method is obtained by substituting t(u) into the objective (3.6) and constraints (3.8). Define the reduced objective function

$$R(u) = r(t(u), u) \tag{3.10}$$

and the vector of reduced constraint functions

$$G(u) = g(t(u), u) \tag{3.11}$$

Then the problem to be solved is

$$\text{minimize } R(u) \tag{3.12}$$

subject to

$$\underline{g} \leq G(u) \leq \overline{g} \qquad (3.13)$$

This is just the reduced version of the infeasible path problem (3.6) - (3.9), It involves only the control variables u, and the inequality constraints (3.13) (these may be equalities if $\underline{g}_i = \overline{g}_i$), and is usually much smaller than either of the 2 preceeding formulations. While the large sparse version (3.3) - (3.5) may have thousands of variables and constraints, and the infeasible path problem (3.6) - (3.8) hundreds, there are usually 10 to 20 controls u, and a comparable number of constraints G. However, to evaluate the reduced functions R and G, all the equations of the sparse model must be evaluated several times, once for each iteration as the process simulator is converged.

This feasible path formulation is the one most commonly used in the past, and is often used today for small to medium sized problems. The problem (3.12) - (3.13) is small enough to be attacked by almost all available NLP codes. As before, much of the solution effort is spent in evaluating first partial deviatives of the reduced functions R and G_i. Using R as an example, there are 2 ways to compute $\partial R/\partial u$, numerical and via reduced gradient formulas. Numerically, if e_j is the jth unit vector and Δ_j is the change in u_j, we evaluate

$$\partial R/\partial u_j = (R(u + \Delta_j e_j) - R(u))/\Delta_j \qquad (3.14)$$

This is by far the simplest approach, and is widely used. It allows the simulator to be completely independent of the optimizer, accepting controls and passing back objective and constraint values. However, if the simulator includes any simultaneous equations (tear stream or other) which must be solved iteratively, then the reduced functions R and G are evaluated to significantly less than full machine precision. If these functions have h significant digits then, if Δ_j is of order 10**(-h/2), $\partial R/\partial uj$ has only h/2 significant digits. If $h \leq 6$, this can cause serious problems for any optimizer, and the use of reduced gradent formulas is an attractive alternative.

Reduced gradient formulas are used in IFPS/OPTIMUM, discussed in section (2.5). Define the tear variable differences as

$$a(t,u) = t - w(t,u) \qquad (3.15)$$

Then the reduced gradient of any problem function, say $R(u) = r(t(u),u)$, can be found by first solving the following linear system for the Lagrange multipliers π:

$$\pi\,[\partial a/\partial t] = \partial r/\partial t \qquad (3.16)$$

and then using π in the formula

$$\partial R/\partial u_i = \partial r/\partial u_i - \pi[\partial a/\partial u_i] \tag{3.17}$$

Of course, to use (3.16) - (3.17), the Jacobian matrices $[\partial a/\partial t]$ and $[\partial a/\partial u]$ must be computed. Since $w(t,u)$ is not available in closed form, this is done by differencing, i.e.

$$\partial w/\partial t_i = (w(t + \Delta_i e_i) - w(t))/\Delta_i \tag{3.18}$$

To evaluate $w(t+\Delta_i e_i)$, one perturbs the input side of the ith tear stream and evaluates all values on the output side, which comprise w. In doing this, the tear stream equalities are not re-solved, so $w(t + \Delta_i e_i)$ is generally computed to high accuracy.

3.4 Computational Results

Recently a team including the authors compared 3 of these approaches: (1) infeasible path (IP), (2) feasible path with finite difference derivitives (FP.FD) and (3) feasible path with reduced gradient derivatives (FP.RG), on a realistic plantwide process model. Three NLP codes were tested, (1) the reduced gradient code GRG2 [Lasdon and Waren 1978] (2) a successive linear programming code SLP [Zhang et al 1985] and (3) a successive quadratic programming code SQP [Fan 1985]. Since GRG2 maintains feasibility once it is obtained, it cannot be used in an infeasible path approach. Hence there are 8 possible formulation/solver combinations. For each such combination, 3 problems were solved. These were generated from the plantwide model as follows: (1) one portion of the plant (2) the rest of the plant and (3) both portions together. Computations were done on an IBM 4341, a powerful minicomputer, using an all Fortran sequential modular simulator.

All 8 approach/solver combinations yielded identical final solutions for all 3 problems, but with a wide difference in solution time. The infeasible path approach was fastest, but the feasible path with reduced gradient derivatives was close. The SQP code was fastest, with SLP close behind. GRG2 was much slower, because it required many more function evaluations, which are expensive. The best combination was (SQP,IP), followed closely by (SQP,FP.RG).

3.5 Other Real Time Optimization Applications

In addition to the large models discussed previously, there are many applications which do not require or do not use a process simulator. The model is simply coded in a Fortran subroutine, which may or may not contain internal convergence loops. An important example in which all functions are available in closed form is gasoline blending. This is a very important unit operation in all refineries, and was one of the first applications of linear programming. However, when refinery margins narrow, the nonlinear aspects of product blending become more important. In particular, product octane and volatility are nonlinear functions of the corresponding qualities and quantities of the input stocks.

The paper "Nonlinear Programming Applications at Texaco" [DeWitt, Lasdon, and Waren 1987] describes an interactive nonlinear blending system developed by Texaco and now routinely used by operators in all domestic and 2 foreign refineries. The system is interactive and menu driven, and interfaces to a data base which is updated in real time. This data base includes availabilities and qualities of input stocks, and blend specifications and demands for each product. The user can easily select the stocks and products to be included in a blend, view and modify the relevant data, submit the problem to the optimizer (GRG2 is used), and examine the results. One of several objectives (maximum profit per barrel, maximum profit, minimum deviation of actual octane from its specified lower limit, or a linear combination of the latter 2) may be selected. The system is viewed as being highly effective

4. Applications to Water Resources and Hydrocarbon Resevoir Problems

Several important problems in water resources and in oil and gas field development have been solved by combining optimizers and simulators. In [Wanakule and Mays 1986] a methodology is developed for determining optimal pumping and recharge of artesian and/or nonartesian aquifers, by coupling the GRG2 optimizer with a groundwater simulation model. The particular simulator used solves the two dimensional partial differential equation governing nonsteady state flow in a saturated medium, using a finite difference method in both spatial and time dimensions. This discretization leads to a large sparse system of difference equations which the simulator solves to determine the hydraulic head (or water elevation) in the aquifer given initial and boundary conditions and well pumpage or recharge over time. Since this system is so large, we choose to solve a reduced problem involving only pumpage and recharge variables (these are the decisions). As in previous sections, the reduced gradients of all optimization problem functions are determined using the formulas (2.4) - (2.5). This is a discrete time optimal control problem, so the difference equations for the Lagrange multipliers have the form of (2.8)

A related application to a single phase gas reservoir is described in [Lasdon et al 1986]. There the reservoir simulator solves the partial differential diffusivity equation for the real gas potential given initial and boundary conditions and well flows. Again, a reduced version of the problem is solved, and reduced gradients are computed using multipliers as above. The test problems solved determine well flows in each period to maximize the rate at which gas can be delivered at the end of the planning horizon, while meeting specified demands in each time period. The test problem reservoir consists of 2 coupled portions with low and high deliverabilities, and optimal solutions adapt to this structure in an interesting way.

A third application to a distributed system is described in (Unver, 1987). The problem here is to determine an optimal policy for floodgate opening in a series of dams to minimize damage during projected flood conditions. The simulation model solves a coupled system of partial differential equations expressing conservation of mass and momentum, computing values of flow and water elevation at various points along a string of lakes, dams, and rivers. The simulation model, together with an interactive user interface and a network of data acquisition equipment measuring rainfall and stream flows, is used as a DSS by the Texas Lower Colorado River Authority during flood alerts. The optimization model has been tested on prototype problems, and is now being readied for operational use.

5. Summary and Conclusions

It is clear that optimization models will find increasing use in a DSS environment, and that these environments will become more integrated, offering database, simulation, and optimization capabilities. The methodology described here is important in enabling the optimizer and simulator to work smoothly and efficiently together. A key problem is how to best compute derivatives of those simulator outputs which are used by the optimizer. Reduced gradient formulas using Lagrange multipliers are useful for this purpose. An important related problem is the degree of integration between optimizer and simulator, i.e. which of the simulator equations are included as optimizer constraints. This depends heavily on the situation at hand.

As NLP codes capable of solving large sparse problems become more widely used, the option of including all model constraints in the optimization problem (complete integration) becomes more important. Research is needed to compare this option with partial integration and independence, when both compiled and interpretive simulators are used. We hope to describe such experiments in a future paper.

This research was partially supported by ONR Contract N00014-87-K-0190, the IC^2 Institute, and the Shell Development Company.

References

1. Baker, T., "The Integration of Planning, Scheduling, and Control", Chesapeake Decision Sciences Inc., P.O. Box 65, Berkeley Hts, NJ 07922 (1984)

1a. Biegler, L.T., "Improved Infeasible Path Optimization for Sequential Modular Simulators-I: the Interface", Computers and Chemical Engineering, 9(1985a), 245-256

2. Biegler, L.T., "Improved Infeasible Path Optimization for Sequential Modular Simulators-II: the Optimization Algorithm", Computers and Chemical Engineering, 9(1985b), 257-267

3. Biegler, L.T. and R.R. Hughes, "Feasible Path Simulation With Sequential Modular Simulators", Computers and Chemical Engineering 9(1985), 379-394

4. Cunningham, C. and L. Schrage, "Optimization in Spreadsheets with VINO," Scientific Press, Palo Alto, CA 1985

5. DeWitt, C.W., L. Lasdon and A. Waren, "Nonlinear Programming Applications at Texaco", technical report, Computer and Information Systems Department, Texaco Inc., P.O. Box 37327, Houston, TX 77237

6. Fan, Y. S. Sarkar and L. Lasdon, "Experiments with Successive Quadratic Programming Algorithms" working paper no. 84/85-3-7, MSIS Department, School of Business Administration, University of Texas, Austin, TX 78712 (1985). To appear in Journal of Optimization Theory and Applications

7. Fisher, M.L., A.J. Greenfield, R. Jaikumar and J.T. Lester, "A Computerized Vehicle Routing Application", Interfaces, 12 (1982), 42-52

8. Geoffrion, A.M. and G.W. Graves, "Multicommodity Distribution System Design by Benders Decomposition", Management Science, 20 (1974), 822-844.

9. Klingman, D.W., et. al., "An Optimization Based Integrated Short-Term Refined Petroleum Product Planning System", Report CBDA 123, Center for Business Decision Analysis, University of Texas, Austin, TX 78712, October 1985. To appear in Management Science.

10. Lasdon, L., P.E. Coffman et. al., "Optimal Hydrocarbon Reservoir Production Policies" Operations Research, 4(1986), 40-55

11. Lasdon, L. and A.D. Waren, "Generalized Reduced Gradient Software for Linearly and Nonlinearly Constrained Problems," in Design and Implementation of Optimization Software, H.J. Greenberg (Ed.), Sijthoff and Noordhoff, Winchester, MA, 1978, 363-397

12. Locke, M., R. Edahl and A. Westerberg, "An Improved Successive Quadratic Programming Optimization Algorithm for Engineering Design

Problems", working paper, Department of Chemical Engineering, Carnegie-Mellon University (1982)

13. Mantell, J. and L.S. Lasdon, "A GRG Algorithm for Econometric Control Problems," Annals of Economic and Social Measurement, 6(1978), 581-597

14. Marsten, R.E., "The Design of the XMP Linear Programming Library", ACM Transactions on Mathematical Software, 7(1981)

15. Marsten, R.E., "User's Manual for ZOOM/XMP" Internal Report, Department of Management Information Systems, University of Arizona, Tucson, AZ 85721 (1984)

16. Murtagh, B.A. and M. Saunders (1982), "A Projected Lagrangian Algorithm and Its Implementation for Sparse Nonlinear Constraints", Mathematical Programming Study 16(1982), 84-117

17. Roy, A., L. Lasdon and J. Lordeman, "Extending Planning Languages to Include Optimization Capabilities", Management Science, 32 (1986), 360-374.

18. SACDA, "Massbal MKII", available from SACDA, Engineering Science Building, University of Western Ontario, London, Ontario NGA 5B9, Canada (1987)

19. Savage, S., "The ABC's of Optimization Using What's Best", General Optimization Inc., 225, North Geneva Terrace, Chicago, Illinois 60614 (1986)

20. Unver, Olcay, "Simulation and Optimization of Real-Time Operations of Multireservoir Systems Under Flooding Conditions", Doctoral Dissertation, Department of Civil Engineering, University of Texas, Austin, TX 78712, July 1987

21. Wanakule, N., L. Mays and L. Lasdon, "Optimal Management of Large-Scale Aquifers: Methodology and Applications", Water Resources Research, 22(1986), 447-465

22. Zhang, J., N. Kim and L. Lasdon, "An Improved Successive Linear Programming Algorithm", Management Science, 31(1985), 1312-1331

A MULTICRITERIA DECISION PROBLEM WITHIN THE SIMPLEX ALGORITHM

Istvan Maros

Computer and Automation Institute,
Hungarian Academy of Sciences,
Victor Hugo Str. 18-22
H-1132 Budapest
Hungary

1. INTRODUCTION

The simplex algorithm [1] is not a uniquely defined procedure. The finiteness of the algorithm can be proved under several different strategies for selection of the incoming and the outgoing variables. From theoretical point of view these variations of the simplex method are equivalent in the sense that they all guarantee an optimal solution (if one exists). However, from practical point of view they may be very different in the sense of the computational effort (number of operations, computer time) needed to solve a problem. At present there is a growing need for stable, fast, and flexible LP codes which also show some kind of user friendliness, especially when used on professional personal computers (PC's).

One possible way to reduce the overall computational effort is to try to find a 'good' first feasible solution in Phase-I with the hope that only few iterations will be left for Phase-II. In other words in Phase-I we are faced with a multicriteria decision problem: We want to move towards feasibility and optimality at the same time. However, these two objectives may be conflicting. A 'good' resolution of the problem may require extra work. Therefore the success of this approach depends on the amount of work spent in such a Phase-I procedure.

In this paper we discuss two modifications of the traditional Phase-I procedures which promise some success in this direction. The original version of the first modification appeared in [3]. The implementational details and some computational experiences will also be presented.

NATO ASI Series, Vol. F48
Mathematical Models for Decision Support
Edited by G. Mitra

2. PROBLEM STATEMENT

We consider the LP problem in the following general form:

$$\max z = c'x \tag{1}$$

subject to

$$A x = b \tag{2}$$

$$l \le x \le v, \tag{3}$$

where c, x, l, and v are n-vectors, b is an m-vector, and A is an m by n matrix. A is understood to contain a unit matrix. In this sense constraints in (3) mean bound and range constraints correspondingly.

In Phase-I the sum of infeasibilities is defined in the following way:

$$w = \sum_{i \in M} y(i) - \sum_{i \in P} [y(i)-u(i)] \le 0, \tag{4}$$

where

y(i) is the value of the i-th basic variable,

u(i) is the upper bound of the i-th basic variable,

$M = \{i: y(i) < 0\}$,

$P = \{i: y(i) > u(i)\}$.

The objective in Phase-I is to maximize w. If max(w) = 0 is achieved then a feasible solution is found. If max(w)=0 cannot be reached then the problem has no feasible solution, in other words the problem is infeasible.

The traditional approach of taking into account the true objective function in Phase-I is to form the composite objective function

$$s = w + t*z, \tag{5}$$

where t > 0 is the weight of z, and the objective is to maximize s. This means that in the course of the simplex iterations matrix A of (2) is priced for s. The great advantage of this method lies in its simplicity since it does not require any extra work in pricing. When no column can be selected the solution is s-optimal. If in the s-optimal solution w = 0 then the solution is z-optimal (that is we found an optimal solution to the original problem). If w < 0 then the feasibility of the problem is still to be decided. This can be done by setting t = 0 and pricing A for w which means a pure Phase-I procedure.

Some of the disadvantages of this approach can be summarized as follows:

(i) If the problem is infeasible then the unlucky choice of t and the effort to work for s as long as possible may delay the detection of infeasibility.

(ii) If the problem still turns out to be feasible then the gain in the true objective function may be lost during the pure Phase-I part of the procedure.

(iii) A proper choice of t is problem-dependent and a non-expert or even an average user of an LP system may be puzzeled when trying to decide on t. At the same time a wrong choice can lead to problems (i) and (ii).

Without further analysing the possible other disadvantages of this procedure we simply refer to the fact that in the literature only very limited information is available on the success of this approach though most of the large LP systems are equipped with this composite facility.

3. ADACOMP-1

We obtained quite favourable experiences in a multiple pricing environment with an adaptive composite procedure [3], called ADACOMP-1 in the sequel, which has certain similarities with the traditional method described in the previous section. There are, however, two points in which ADACOMP-1 is essentially different:

(i) In pricing we consider those columns only which show improvement with respect to w,

(ii) We change the t weight factor dynamically in each major iteration.

In ADACOMP-1 the selection of a 'good' entering column is considered as a hierarchical multicriteria decision problem which is resolved in the following way:

First level:

We select columns according to (i). Let J(1) be the index set of candidates with respect to w, i.e.

$$J(1) = \{j: j \text{ nonbasic}, w(j) < 0\},$$

where w(j) denotes the reduced cost of column j with respect to w.

Second level:

From J(1) we select columns for multiple pricing which are the 'best' with respect to s. The index set of these columns is denoted by J(2). Let s(j) be the s-reduced cost of column j

$$s(j) = w(j) + t*z(j),$$

where z(j) is the z-reduced cost of column j. J(2) is defined as

$$J(2) = \{j: j \in J(1),\ s(j) <= s(k) \text{ if } k \in J(2)\}.$$

The cardinality of J(2), denoted by N, is usually limited to a small value like 8.

Third level:

We carry out a suboptimization with the vectors in J(2) using the criterion of largest progress with respect to w.

Going through these three levels we will enter a column into the basis which promises improvement in w and at the same time will cause little harm if any on z.

Adjustment of t

The second important feature of ADACOMP-1 is the dynamic adjustment of parameter t in (5). This is done in every major iteration in the following way:

We use two counters K and L.

K denotes the cardinality of J(1), that is the number of candidates in A with respect to w,

L denotes the number of candidates in J(1) for which s(j)<0, that is the number of such candidates which show improvement for the composite objective function.

If K = 0 then the problem is infeasible (repricing or any further investigations are not necessary).

If K <> 0 then let r = L/K. Clearly 0 <= r <= 1 holds. We divide the [0,1] interval into three disjunct parts denoted by R(1), R(2), and R(3):

```
   R(1)             R(2)                 R(3)
¦---------¦--------------------¦--------------¦
0                                             1
```

The new value of t, denoted by t' is determined as follows:

If r is in R(1), then t' = g1(t) < t

If r is in R(2), then t' = g2(t) == t (identical to t)

If r is in R(3), then t' = g3(t) > t

This can be interpreted so that when most of the candidates with respect to w are also candidates with respect to s (that is r is in R(3)) then in this favourable situation movement in the direction of the true objective function can be given greater weight which is achieved by increasing the value of t at a rate determined by function g3(t).

In the opposite case (when r is in R(1)) optimality becomes less important than feasibility and this is expressed by decreasing t by function g1(t).

When r is in R(2) then we can say that the two components of s are well balanced and there is no need for changing t.

We use the new value of t in the next pricing operation when J(2) is being defined.

It is easy to realize that this procedure creates a great deal of flexibility. The actual choice of parameters (sets R(1), R(2), R(3), functions g1, g3 and the initial value of t) gives the chance to tune the algorithm to every kind of problems.

The advantages of ADACOMP-1 according to [3] are:

(i) usually much better first feasible solution,

(ii) (occasionally considerable) reduction in the overall computational effort (solution time).

Besides the advantages there are also some disadvantages:

(i) extra pricing vector [2] is necessary to obtain w(j) and z(j) separately which requires a multiple BTRAN [4] operation and an extra scalar product for columns in J(1),

(ii) the proper choice of the ADACOMP-1 specific parameters is not a simple matter though 'good' default values are available:

R(1) = [0,1/3), R(2) = [1/3,2/3), R(3) = [2/3,1],

g1(t) = t/2, g3(t) = 2t,

t = 0.5.

Some run statistics with ADACOMP-1 are presented in [3] which are quite promising and seem to justify this approach.

4. ADACOMP-2

The widespread use of PC's has increased the number of non-expert LP users. For them the user friendliness of an LP system is an important issue. Unfortunately, disadvantage (ii) of ADACOMP-1 makes the algorithm and a system based on it a little unfriendly to a user.

By a little modification of ADACOMP-1 we can eliminate most of the disadvantages in (ii) while preserving the favourable features of the procedure. The modified version of ADACOMP-1 is called ADACOMP-2.

The basic idea of ADACOMP-2 is to interpret t as a relative weight of z throughout Phase-I. In other words we define that in the composition of s the contribution of the value of the true objective function and the sum of infeasibilities should be in a prescribed ratio denoted by t. The actual weight of z (denoted by T) is computed at the beginning of each major iteration to maintain this ratio. From

$$\text{abs}(T*z/w) = t$$

we obtain

$$T = \text{abs}(t*w/z), \text{ if } z \neq 0. \tag{6}$$

If z = 0 then the value of T is of no importance and just to make the algorithm working, it is reasonable to set it to 1.0.

With ADACOMP-2 we work in such a way that in the second level of ADACOMP-1 when J(2) is formed then we use T instead of t as the multiplier of z in computing s(j).

At the beginning of Phase-I (when there are usually many candidates with respect to w and when abs(w) is relatively large) this algorithm will give greater weight to z, as it can be seen from (6), so in the first steps real 'good' iterations can be expected. Later, when abs(w) becomes smaller then z will be 'degraded' thus more stress will be put on improving infeasibility.

As to the user friendliness of ADACOMP-2, it is 'easy' to say that the relative weight of the true objective function should be e.g. 0.25 in Phase-I. After this definition all the other disadvantages (ii) of ADACOMP-1 do not appear at all. However, the extra pricing vector is necessary as in ADACOMP-1.

ADACOMP-2 has recently been implemented in MILP linear programming system of the author for IBM PC/XT, AT and compatible computers. It is available in MILP as an optional pricing strategy which can be selected at the beginning of the run. Naturally, in Phase-II MILP automatically stops the extra calculations necessary for ADACOMP-2 in Phase-I.

It is understood that the benefits of applying ADACOMP-2 cannot be predicted. As a matter of fact it may turn out that it does not give any improvement in the total computational effort to solve a problem. Presently it appears so that problems with extensive Phase-I can exploit the advantegeous features of ADACOMP-2 well.

There are two more implementational remarks.

(i) The extra computations of ADACOMP-2 require floating-point arithmetic operations. However, these operations need not be very accurate and therefore the use of single precision arithmetic is sufficient.

(ii) Since the ratio of execution times of floating-point and other types of operations can be very different on different computers (the number 1 decisive factor is the presence or absence of the math coprocessor), therefore the performance of ADACOMP-2 can be better or worse. Hence the decision on applying this algorithm or not should also depend on the parameters of the actual computer used to solve LP problems.

The computational experiences with ADACOMP-2 in MILP are quite favourable. Some of them are summarized in the following tables.

	size row by column		number of nonzeroes	remark
MULTI (min)	62	102	1063	many range constraints
ZG (max)	118	43	621	very degenerate
P19 (min)	285	586	5891	many range constraints
ATLAS464 (min)	318	458	2965	'bad-behaving'
FUELPL (min)	587	810	3724	degenerate

TABLE 1 Problem statistics

	MULTI	ZG	P19	ATLAS464	FUELPL
Optimum	44404	15060	254294	31344	-2071012
z at first feasible solution	502793	9064	1598457	34584	1435180
Total number of iterations	92	87	501	1506	787
Number of iterations in Phase-1	46	71	195	817	609
Total solution time (sec)	17	50	317	4254	2429

TABLE 2 Run statistics without ADACOMP-2

	MULTI	ZG	P19	ATLAS464	FUELPL
Optimum	44404	15060	254294	31344	-2071012
z at first feasible solution	48448	12403	349075	34111	-395331
Total number of iterations	73	75	446	1466	718
Number of iterations in Phase-1	41	63	180	828	581
Total solution time (sec)	13	44	284	3733	2026

TABLE 3 Run statistics with ADACOMP-2 (t = 0.25)

These figures except for FUELPL were obtained on an IBM PC/AT (running at 6 MHz) equipped with a math coprocessor.

FUELPL was solved on an IBM PC/XT (4.77 MHz) with math coprocessor.

References:

[1] Dantzig, G.B., Linear Programming and Extensions, Princeton University Press, 1963.

[2] Greenberg, H.J., "Pivot selection tactics", in H.J. Greenberg (ed.), Design and Implementation of Optimization Software, Sijthoff and Nordhoff, 1978.

[3] Maros, I., "A general Phase-I method in linear programming", European Journal of Operational Research, 23(1986) 64-77,

[4] Orchard-Hays, W., Advanced Linear Programming Computing Techniques, McGraw-Hill, 1968.

INTERACTIVE DISTRIBUTION PLANNING

Oli B.G. Madsen

IMSOR, The Institute of Mathematical Statistics
and Operations Research
The Technical University of Denmark
DK-2800 Lyngby, Denmark

1. INTRODUCTION

In a recent paper by Bocxe and Tilanus (1985) concerning standard software for vehicle scheduling the conclusion was that there is a need for flexible, user-friendly, interactive, and cheap vehicle scheduling software. The author can strongly support this conclusion from experiences in Denmark where almost all software for vehicle scheduling until now have been developed and used on main frames and minicomputers mainly to get reasonable response times and to have the necessary computer memory.

The reasons for interactivity are among other things:

- not all factors in a problem can or are wanted to be quantified
- an interactive system provides the user with more flexibility
- it is possible to combine the speed of a computer, good software, and the experience of a distribution planner
- experience shows that good planners in fact are able to improve heuristic solutions considerably

The reasons for implementation on a personal computer are:

- personal computers are cheap
- it is rather easy to develop fast interactive graphics on a personal computer

The purpose of this paper is to describe an interactive graphics supported system for vehicle scheduling. The system was developed at IMSOR by Bo Sørensen under supervision by the author in the period September 1983 to January 1987. The system which is named MIGA - Modular Interactive Graphics

NATO ASI Series, Vol. F48
Mathematical Models for Decision Support
Edited by G. Mitra

Approach - is implemented in Pascal on a personal computer.

2. THE INTERACTIVE SYSTEM

The MIGA system solves by heuristic methods vehicle scheduling problems with one depot, one commodity, a number of trucks with given capacities, a number of customers with given location, demand, service time, and time window for delivery. The objective is to minimize:

- priority 1: the number of vehicles required
- priority 2: the total scheduling time
- priority 3: the total distance travelled

The user may change the solutions by an interactive dialog with the system. The user communicates with the system by the keyboard and mainly by a mouse. The keyboard is used for non-discrete alpha-numeric information. The communication strategy is dialog based.

The screen layout is shown in figure 1. The main menu will always

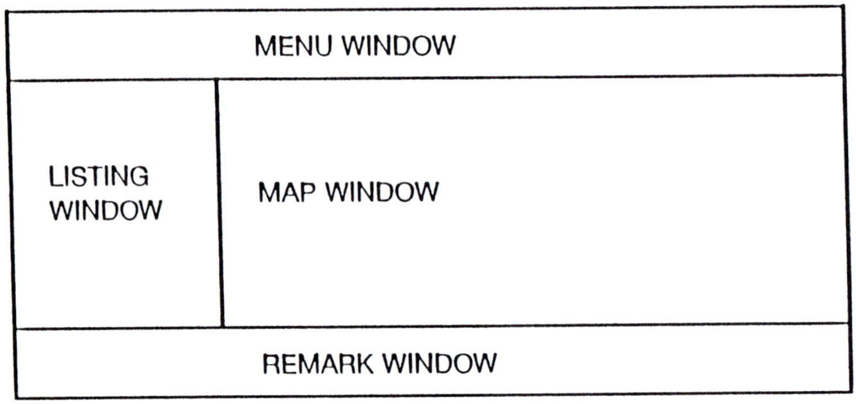

Figure 1 Screen layout

be present in the <u>main menu window</u>. This will give the user an opportunity to <u>select an option</u> from the main menu at any time, even when running a sub-menu; if so the sub-menu will be terminated, and the new option in the main menu will be activated.

When selecting an option from the main menu, move the mouse

cursor (an X on the screen) to the appropriate option and press the button on the mouse, thereby "pulling down" the selected sub-menu. Still with the button pressed, the user points at the appropriate alternative and releases the button. The pull-down menu will disappear again and the selected action will be executed by the system. Figure 2 shows one of the pull-down menus - the SOLVE menu. Using this approach, the main menu is always present and the sub-menus will only appear when called for.

The listing window is used for displaying alpha-numeric listings of e.g. routes and schedules. The listing window is separated from the map window, allowing the user to work sim-

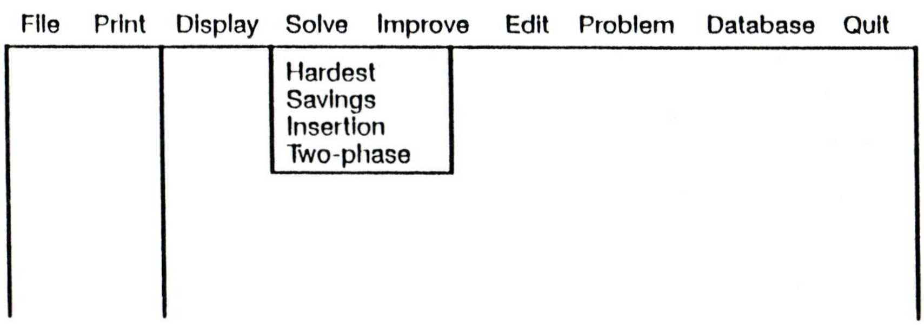

Figure 2 Example of a pull-down menu (the SOLVE menu)

ultaneously with an alpha-numeric and graphic illustrations of the problem.

The map window is primarily used to show the geographic area and the routes associated with the problem currently worked on.

The remark window contains two kinds of information. The far right end of the remark window will show the name associated with the current problem or geographic area. The left part of the window will display different help-information for the user, guiding the user smoothly through the problem-solving process.

In case an input of non-discrete alpha-numeric data is necessary all questions have been standardized to one form thereby avoiding to confront the user with a new kind of question each time an alpha-numeric input is needed.

In case of discrete choices between alternatives these are

incorporated in the menus. Yes/no questions are answered by using the mouse.

When we are considering alpha-numeric display of data, colours serve the purpose of enhancing readability. The colours also serve the purpose of connecting alpha-numeric information with the routes drawn on the map window. This is done by using the colour corresponding to the route in the alpha-numeric display.

Five databases are connected to the MIGA system. A road database holds information of the geographical area in question. A customer database holds information of each customer. A fleet database holds information about the vehicles in the fleet. An order database holds information of the customers to be served within the planning horizon. Finally an internal route and scheduling database holds information on the present planning situation. The road database is not at present implemented in the standard MIGA system but existing road databases may be connected to MIGA. As earlier mentioned the main menu is always present on the screen. If offers the following sub-menus:

- File : Controls all input/output to file
- Print : Controls printing of data from database
- Display : Controls display of data from database
- Solve : Controls use of solution methods
- Improve : Controls use of improvement methods
- Edit : Controls editing of the solution
- Problem : Controls the problem definition
- Database : Controls reading from the database and editing database
- Quit : Controls termination of the program

This display menu makes it possible to control all the output to the listing window and the map window of the screen.

The solution menu allows choice between four heuristic solution methods for problems which are not time constrained and three heuristic solution methods for problems with time window constraints. The four methods are hardest, savings, insertion, and two-phase. A more detailed description of the methods may be found in Sørensen (1986). Numerical experiments seem to show that two-phase usually gives the best results. The three methods for time constrained problems are hardest, savings, and insertion (Sørensen, 1986). The methods bear the same names as the non-time constrained solution methods and as such they are generalizations of these methods. Here experiments shows that insertion usually gives the best results. All methods are especially adapted for use in an interactive environment.

The improvement menu makes it possible to improve solutions from the solution menu or solutions obtained by an interactive dialog between the user and MIGA.

The edit menu gives the user access to a complete route and schedule editor. This implies that the user can edit the planning situation and see the consequences immediately. The user may e.g. move customers, connect customers, prohibit connection between customers, or release special customers or pairs of customers.

3. THE SYSTEM HARDWARE

The system will run on IBM compatible personal computers. The computer should be internally equipped with 640 Kbytes of RAM memory with either two 320 Kbytes disc drives or one 320 Kbytes disc drive and one 10/20 Mbyte hard disc. Furthermore a Microsoft mechanical mouse is needed as pointing device. The screen shall be a colour graphics screen with a spatial resolution of 640 dots vertical and 200 dots horizontal. The standard colour resolution is 16 possible colours for each dot.

4. THE SYSTEM PERFORMANCE

Apart from the solution menu usual operations require less than a second i.e. MIGA works on-line. A 100 point problem without time constraints can be solved by two-phase in 1-2 seconds on an IBM PC/AT. Usually the improvement operation improves the solution by some 5-8% and manual changes may improve the solution by 5%.

A 100 point problem with time constraints can be solved by insertion in 7-15 second on an IBM PC/AT. In addition manual changes may also here improve the solution.

Problems with several hundred customers may easily be solved.

REFERENCES

1. M.A.G. Bocxe and C.B. Tilanus (1985), Testing vehicle sheduling programs for milk collection, European Journal of Operations Research 20, 25-33.

2. B. Sørensen (1986), Interactive distribution planning, PhD thesis from IMSOR, The Institute of Mathematical Statistics and Operations Research, The Technical University of Denmark, DK-2800 Lyngby, Denmark, January 1986.

Mathematical Programming on Microcomputers: Directions in Performance and User Interface

Ramesh Sharda
Oklahoma State University
College of Business Administration
Stillwater, OK 74078 USA

INTRODUCTION

The phenomenal growth of microcomputers in terms of market size and technology has been accompanied by a proliferation of Management Science/ Operations Research software. Recent technical advances in microcomputers include introduction of 80286 or PC/AT type computers, RT/PC, various versions of Macintosh, and most recently, 80386 chip-based computers. In addition, hardware and software has been developed to access several megabytes of memory on a PC. This paper addresses the question of whether the performance of linear programming software has improved at the same pace as the micros.

Sharda and Somarajan (1986) (hereafter referred to as SS) reported the comparative performance of four microcomputer based LP systems. Their results indicated that none of the available LP systems was able to solve all of their test problems. Some problems were even solved to a different (inferior) optimal solution than the one obtained by MPSX. Similar results were reported by Stadtler et al. (1986). The objective of this research was to determine if state of the art of LP software has improved. Thus the paper is, in a way, an update of the tests of SS. Our tests include many more test problems, updated versions of the LP systems tested in SS, and several recently developed advanced LP systems. We also report differences in performance between PCs and 80286 machines. Finally, we offer our observations on areas for further improvement.

What is Available?

Table 1 lists available LP software including publishers, maximum problem size as stated by the publishers, and prices for commercial customers. Some of the packages are also available in smaller capacity versions at substantially lower prices than listed in the table. I have included the largest versions of the respective programs to illustrate the capability of the software on microcomputers.

Table 1 lists 20 LP optimizers. Of these, 15 were introduced within the last three years. As would be expected, this increased availability has

NATO ASI Series, Vol. F48
Mathematical Models for Decision Support
Edited by G. Mitra

been associated with growth in specialized software. For example, many programs are now available to let the OR/MS analyst build the model in a spreadsheet and then perform the optimization. Some other programs have been introduced recently to facilitate the model development process, including specification of the model in quasi-algebraic form. Many programs offer better ease of use and more control of the optimization process than was available earlier. A number of programs include an integer programming option.

Table 2 lists many of the relatively new capabilities of LP software for micros and identifies the packages which include those features.

IMPROVEMENTS IN CAPACITY AND USER INTERFACE

Two major improvements in LP software are increased capacity and user interface. Software is now available with the ability to solve problems as large as with over 32000 non-zero elements in a matrix. The upper limit on number of rows appears to be 2500; the corresponding limit on the columns is 6000. While I have yet to solve a problem that large using these programs, in our tests we have been able to solve a problem with over 14000 non-zero elements in a reasonable time. Availability of computers based on 80286 (e.g., IBM PC-AT) microprocessor also improved speed of the solution process. With the new 80386-based computers, the speed as well as the size of the problems should increase considerably. The increased memory addressing capacity of the 80386 chip should allow us to solve much larger problems than is possible today.

These programs have good user interfaces for preparing LP formulation. Many of the packages accept problem input in MPS format, an industry standard. These packages are identified in Table 2. A number of programs allow input of a problem in expressions format. This is close to the form in which the objective function and constraints would normally be written out in formulating an LP problem. This format allows even a casual user of LP to be able to use the software. LINDO, MPS-PC, Turbo-Simplex, and XA offer this expressions format.

The format accepted by LINDO is quite similar to an actual formulation. A problem is entered by listing the objective function subject to each of the constraints in the usual style. Advanced parsing features of the other three packages offer further flexibility in specification of a problem. For example, these packages allow entering coefficients as percentages or fractions, and nesting of coefficients with parentheses. XA also offers symbolic substitution at run time, allowing the user to specify certain coefficients in a formulation in response to prompts from the program when the problem is solved. MPS-PC and Turbo-Simplex accept constraints with variables on both sides of a constraint. MPS-PC can accept the RHS or objective function as linear combinations of other rows or columns. While none of these features add to the computing power of the LP algorithm, they do make specification of a problem much easier than possible before.

Table 1: General Information on LP Software

Software	Publisher (U.S. except where noted)	Price	Size of Problem	Remarks
DSM	Decision System Support 31871 Via Puntero San Juan Capistrano, CA 92675 (714) 493-3639	$295	m≤80 n≤100 I≤25	Includes other OR/MS models such as EOQ, QP, MIP, etc.
FORTLP	Dr. G. Mitra Department of Mathematics & Statistics Brunel University Uxbridge, Middlesex Great Britain UB8 3PH	*	m≤2,000 n≤3,000 NZ≤20,000	Requires a FORTRAN Compiler.
GAMS/MINOS	Office of Tech. Licensing 105 Encina Hall Stanford University Stanford, CA 94305	$495		Also available from A. Meeraus, World Bank, Washington, DC.
LINDO	LINDO Systems, Inc. P.O. Box 148231 Chicago, IL 60614 (312) 871-2524	$1900	m≤1,999 n≤3,999 NZ≤32,000 I≤200	Smaller versions available for lower prices. Also marketed by The Scientific Press, 540 University Ave., Palo Alto, CA 94301-1985, tel. (415) 322-5221.
LPS-867	Applied Automated Engineering Corp. 65 Main St., Bldg. B Pennington, NJ 08534 (609) 737-6800	$500	m≤2,500 n≤5,000-m NZ≤16,000	Smaller versions available for lower prices.
LP88	Eastern Software Products, Inc. P.O. Box 15328 Alexandria, VA 22309 (703) 549-5469	$99	m≤510 n≤2,510-m I≤45	A mixed integer LP version is available for additional $99.00.
LP/APRIL	Applied Industrial Mathematics Inc. 5143 Lymber Houston, TX 77096 (713) 723-4321	$999	m≤1,000 n≤2,000	
MP	SCI Computing 2640 Parkridge Drive Ann Arbor, MI 48103 (313) 995-5976	$360	m≤400 n≤1,000 I≤50	Also includes many other techniques. The LP module alone costs $80.

MAX	Capital Systems Group, Inc. 1803 Research Blvd., #600 Rockville, MD 20850 (301) 762-1200	$79.95	$m \leq 300$ $n \leq 500$	
MICROLP	Scicon Limited Wavendon Tower Wavendon, Milton Keynes Great Britain MK17 8LX (908)585858	$595	$m \leq 300$ $n \leq 500$	
MILP	Akademiai Kiado Hungarian Academy of Sci. Varoshaz U. 1., H1052 Budapest, Hungary	$2500	$m \leq 800$ $n \leq 2,000$ $NZ \leq 32,000$	
MPS-PC	See MAX above	$395 (8087 ver.)	$m \leq 1500$ $n \leq 2,500$ $NZ \leq 32,767$ $I \leq 126$	
MUSAH-86	Elton Li Department of Agri. Econ. Oklahoma State University Stillwater, OK 74078	*	$m \leq 75$ $n \leq 100$	
Oakland LP	Oakland Group, Inc. 675 Mass. Ave. Cambridge, MA 02139 (617) 491-7311	$500	$8(m+2n) \leq 64,000$	
RAMLP	Miniware Inc. 205 Winchester Rd. Annapolis, MD 21401 (301) 757-5626	$50	$m+n \leq 300$ $mn+3m+4n \leq 13,000$	
Turbo-Simplex	Maximal Software P.O. Box 8612 128 Reykjavik Iceland	$200	$m \leq 500$	
VINO	See LINDO above	$695	$m \leq 2,000$ $n \leq 4,000$ $NZ \leq 32,000$ $I \leq 200$	Smaller version available at a lower price. Also sold by Scientific Press.
What's Best	General Optimization, Inc. 2251 N. Geneva Terrace Chicago, IL 60614 (800) 441-BEST	$995	$m \leq 1,600$ $n \leq 4,000$ $NZ \leq 32,000$ $I \leq 400$	Smaller versions are available at lower prices. Also sold by Holden-Day Inc. 4432 Telegraph Ave., Oakland, CA 94609, (415) 428-9400.

XA	Sunset Software Technology 1613 Chelsea Road, Suite 153 San Marino, CA 91108 (818) 284-4763	\$1,195	$m \leq 1{,}000$ $n \leq 6{,}000-m$ $NZ \leq 32{,}000$	
XPRESS-LP	Dash Associates Blisworth House, Church Lane Blisworth Northants NN7 3BX Great Britain (604)858993	£1,500 £875 without model generator	$m \leq 1000$ $n \leq 2000$	Smaller version available for a lower price.

m = number of rows, n = number of columns, NZ = number of non-zero elements, E, L, G = number of constraints of each type, I = number of integer variables.
*Available for a small (undetermined) fee.

Table 2: Classification of LP Software

Features	Software
1. OR/MS Software including capability to solve medium size LP problems.	DSM, MP
2. "Conventional" LP Software	FORTLP, LINDO, LPS-867, LP88, LP/APRIL, MICROLP, MILP, MP, MPS-PC, Oakland LP, RAMLP, Turbo-Simplex, XA
3. MPS input accepted	FORTLP, GAMS/MINOS, LINDO, LPS-867, LP/APRIL, MICROLP, MILP, MPS-PC, RAMLP, XA, XPRESS-LP
4. Spreadsheet compatible	
a. Only input accepted from a spreadsheet file	MICROLP, MPS-PC, RAMLP
b. Capability to read LP problem from a spreadsheet file and process the LP output in a spreadsheet file	LPS-867, MAX, MUSAH-86, XA
c. Optimization is performed within the spreadsheet program	VINO, WHAT'S BEST, XA
5. Model development systems	GAMS/MINOS, XPRESS-LP
6. Collection of subroutines available for inclusion in a custom program	FORTLP, LINDO, LPS-867, LP/APRIL, Oakland LP
7. Integer Programming	DSM, LINDO, LP88, MAX, MP, MPS-PC, VINO, WHAT'S BEST, XA
8. Macintosh version available	LINDO

Solution Options

Most packages use a bounded variable version of revised simplex method . Some of these also employ the product form of the inverse approach. The sparse matrix techniques allow us to solve large problems on a microcomputer. Some programs permit interaction with the algorithm. For example, LP/APRIL allows the user to set tolerances. Most programs in the 'conventional LP' group let the user interrupt the iteration process, save it and restart from an advanced basis. These options compare well with the ones available for mainframe LP software.

Spreadsheet-based Optimization

There are hardly any microcomputer users who are not familiar with spreadsheet software. A spreadsheet program is an interactive, screen oriented software which converts the memory of a computer to a large matrix. The computer can store the numbers as well as formulae in the cells of this matrix. Once the user develops a set of relationships between variables (cells), it is easy to investigate the effects of various 'what if' scenarios. However, it is natural to extend their use to 'what is best' analysis, a la optimization. Fisher [1986] notes that the models developed using these spreadsheet programs are close to optimization models anyway. One just needs to specify which cells are decision variables, which cells/rows are constraints and which relationship denotes the objective function. An optimization algorithm can then determine the values of decision variables. Fisher also suggests that such an interface for LP input has the potential for expanding the number of people familiar with or using optimization. Bodily [1986] describes many uses of spreadsheets for mathematical analyses.

The convenient data entry/editing features of spreadsheets make it easy to develop the LP matrix. Spreadsheets programs include a copy command which allows a block of numbers as well as relationships to be copied from one worksheet location to another. This can be very useful for developing LP problems having blocks of similar structure, e.g. multiperiod problems or transportation problems.

If the solution output of an LP problem is stored in a spreadsheet matrix, further processing for report generation is extremely easy. This includes calculation of some aggregate variables, presentation of results in graphics form (where appropriate) and development of tables which can be processed by word processors.

There are essentially three ways of performing optimization using spreadsheets. First, some programs simply accept a problem formulation from a spreadsheet file. These programs only allow the LP user to take advantage of the spreadsheet features relevant to problem input. MICROLP, MPS-PC, and RAMLP fall in this group. Other LP packages offer the capability to read the LP problem from a spreadsheet file and also store the optimal solution in such a file. Programs in this category are JANUS, MAX, MUSAH-86, and XA. JANUS, a utility program available with LPS-867, converts a spreadsheet file into the format accepted by LPS-867 and then transforms the problem solution from LPS-867 into a spreadsheet file. The spreadsheet capability of basic XA also falls in this group.

The most comprehensive level of integration with spreadsheets is offered by three packages: VINO, WHAT'S BEST, and XA. These programs reside in the memory with the spreadsheet program. The user creates the spreadsheet, presses one or two keys to draw attention of the optimization algorithm, solves the problem and returns back to the same point in the spreadsheet. This gives the appearance of the spreadsheet program having the optimization capability. All three programs in this category are quite powerful, also offering some integer programming options. With the advent of data services such as Lotus Signal, it is conceivable to receive data from a database (such as stock market), convert these into an LP problem, solve the LP problem, and then prepare the results in a usable form, all in real time. This can open up some financial applications where opportunities may exist to take advantage of timely information.

Overall, the LP software has advanced quite well in this area. With the thousands of users familiar with the idea of modeling through spreadsheets, an opportunity exists for OR/MS analysts to bring at least one aspect of their profession to the casual users of decision making techniques.

Model Development Systems

As Arden [1980] points out, limitations of linear programming do not lie in computational algorithms but rather in the amount of work required to prepare a large problem and use its answers. Greenberg [1983] adds that another bottleneck in using large models is poor documentation of a model in MPS format, which makes it difficult to maintain as well as understand the model. The spreadsheet interface has helped in model development, but its use for large scale LP models is not clear yet.

A recent development is the availability of mathematical modeling languages on the personal computers. Two noteworthy packages are GAMS/MINOS and XPRESS-LP. GAMS/MINOS is a combination of two mainframe programs, GAMS [Bisschop and Meeraus 1982] and MINOS [Murtagh and Saunders 1982]. Both GAMS/MINOS and XPRESS-LP offer powerful algebraic modeling languages. The basic idea is that most LP problems have only a few types of constraints. Using a modeling language, one needs to enter those equations just once. Similar constraints in the LP matrix are automatically generated using only the data defined by the user. GAMS/MINOS as well as XPRESS-LP perform well in this area. Both offer conditional rows and column generation as well as general expressions for coefficients. GAMS/MINOS requires that the data be included in the problem specification whereas XPRESS-LP can read data tables from external files. The latter can also read and write to spreadsheet files. On the other hand, GAMS/MINOS offers linear, quadratic, and general nonlinear programming capability.

There is more to come in this direction. The author is aware of some other attempts to make the model generation process more convenient. These include a menu driven modeling language, a database management system-based model generator and a natural language oriented model development system.

Integer Programming

A number of LP packages offer integer programming. This capability includes support for both zero-one and general integer models. DSM allows a problem with only 25 variables and 25 constraints. LINDO and VINO allow 200 variables to be integer, either 0-1 or general. XA has a complex formula to compute this limit, but its publisher recommends a limit of 40 integral variables. LP88 allows 45 integer variables with the MILP88 option. MAX can solve a problem with 100 integral variables. The limit with the MP7 module of MP is 50. MPS-PC allows 100 integer variables, whereas WHAT'S BEST claims to support up to 400 integer variables. A complete test of these capabilities has not been reported yet. It remains to be seen whether the time taken to solve a problem with 200-400 integer variables is 'reasonable' on a microcomputer.

PERFORMANCE COMPARISONS

Packages Compared

Seven LP systems were tested in this study: Lindo, LPS-867, XA, Oakland LP, Micro-LP, MPS-PC, and Xpress LP. As can be seen, packages of both American and European origin were studied.

The major criteria for package selection was simply that the package must be able to accept MPSX format and that the software was made available to us. While many other LP packages exist, many use their own problem formulation format, such as a Lotus spreadsheet. Their inability to accept MPSX format and the time required to convert each problem into the program's individual format made their inclusion prohibitive.

Test Problems

The packages were evaluated using a test set containing 49 linear programming problems of various size and difficulty. The problems ranged in size from 8 rows, 20 columns, and 56 non-zeros to 1,101 rows, 2,981 columns, and 14,395 non-zeros, including slack variables. All except four of the problems had minimization objective. Table 3 gives the problem name, size in terms of rows, columns, and non-zero elements, density, direction (max or min), and the published optimal value. The test problems were acquired from four major places: Sharda and Somarajan (1986), Gay (1986), Ho (1981), Professor G. Mitra, and the Stanford test set.

Hardware

All packages were tested for performance on both an 8088 machine and an 80286 machine. Both machines were equipped with math coprocessors. The 8088 machine was an IBM XT with 2 floppy drives, one 20MB hard drive, an 8087 math coprocessor, and 640K memory with 1.2M of extended memory. A PC-Designs AT compatible running at 8 MHz with one 1.2M floppy, an internal 20MB hard drive, and 640K available memory was used as the 80286 machine. It also contained an 80287 math coprocessor running at 6 MHz.

Because many packages use swap files to handle large problems, it was important to use the fastest storage device available for these swap files. On the 8088 machine, a RAM memory disk was used when a program could use it. On the 80286 machine, a hard-disk was used. For the purpose of testing, batch jobs were used whenever possible. Several packages are capable of running in a batch format, e.g., Oakland LP and XA. Several other packages were able to be run in a batch mode using DOS 3.1 and its piping feature.

Dependent Variables

Timing was a critical element of these tests. The times given denote the period between the beginning and ending of the iteration process. The time required to read the problem and to print the results was not included. When possible, the software's own internal timing device was used. In all other cases, a stopwatch running in the computer's background memory was used to time the solution process. All packages were allowed to run for, at most, 19 hours. If an optimal solution was not found in that length of time, the iteration process was terminated and the package received a timed-out error for that particular problem.

RESULTS AND ANALYSIS

None of the programs tested were able to solve all of the problems in the test set that were within the program's stated size limits. A number of packages had trouble interpreting some of the problem formats that are acceptable to MPSX. Many packages returned size related errors for large problems that were within the program's size constraints. "Out of memory" and "disk full" errors were common when packages were pushed to their upper size boundaries. The software tested also exhibited some precision problems, claiming a problem was infeasible or unbounded when MPSX had found an optimal solution. The most disturbing problem was a tendency for some packages to return non-optimal solution.

Notwithstanding the above problems, the capability of linear programming software has improved both in the area of speed and size abilities. For example, in SS Lindo solved the problem SCSD1 in 1,348 seconds. The current version of Lindo is now able to solve the same problem in 643 seconds, an increase of 52 percent.

Error handling ability has also changed since the earlier tests. Three of the packages included in this study were also included in the previous comparison. They were Lindo, MPS-PC, and XA, then called LP83. Eleven problems from our test set were also included in the earlier test. Lindo reached an incorrect solution for SCORPION in the first study but solved it correctly here. XA was unable to solve SCORPION, SCSD6, and SCTAP1 in SS due to size limitations but solved these problems correctly in this study. XA solved SCSD1 incorrectly in the earlier study but is now able to solve it to the correct solution. MPS-PC solved the same number of problems from the original test set.

Table 3. Problem Statistics and Time Required To Solve
(In Seconds on an 80286 Machine)

NAME	NUMBER OF ROWS	NUMBER OF COLUMNS	NUMBER OF NON-ZERO	LINDO	LPR867	XA	OAK87	MICROLP	MPS-PC	EXPRESS
25FV47	822	2,393	11,949							
ADLITTLE	57	154	522	55	35	39	65	87	243	34
AFIRO	28	60	116	3	4	1	2	11	14	10
BANDM	306	778	2,965							
BASESETN	48	108	257	5	7	3	29	27	43	
BEACONFD	174	436	3,650	300	72	34	242		518	
BEALE*	171	474	1,073	104	108	72				125
BERGER	65	198	480	11	34		91		137	30
BORE3D	234	549	1,759		228	464	324	570		
BRANDY	221	470	2,371		648	1,021	5,104			
CAPRI	272	625	2,058		558	441			9,327	952
DINAMICO	417	944	4,934		7,159					
E226	226	508	3,264							
ETAMACRO*	401	1,089	2,890	1,568	1,560					
FARM*	8	20	56	1	1	1	1	3	5	4
FFFFF800	525	1,379	6,760	2,316	2,718	784				2,391
FIXMAR	325	777	2,926	1,698	811	508	2,577		6,843	640
FORESTRY	402	1,005	4,196	8,538	1,933	3,616				3,733
FORPLAN	162	583	5,078		245	283				
GFRD-PNC	617	1,092	3,467	687	1,576	1,379				1,174
GROW15	301	946	5,966	10,467		3,895				
GROW22	441	1,387	8,759							
GROW7	141	442	2,774	1,380	2,698	540			10,864	647
HEDGE	93	250	480	35	30	13	65	195	152	80
ISRAEL	175	317	2,533	470	365	325	885		2,513	359
NESM	663	3,586	14,651							
PILOT4	411	1,411	5,556			26,247				
PILOT.JA	941	1,988	14,706							
PROB12B	381	692	3,373	1,220						
PROB31B	384	961	4,668	715	616	637			3,798	2,887
PROB43B	648	1,253	5,368	1,103	1,067	781	3,438		6,226	1,414
RECIPE	92	272	844	11	17	9	198	77		17
REFINE	30	63	185	3	5	1	8	8	22	11
SC205	206	409	758	286	230	246	228	1,836	813	175
SCAGR7	130	270	683	160	129	37	282	133	381	109
SCORPION	389	747	2,097		433	149	1,469			482
SCRS8	491	1,660	4,520	1,726	1,936	2,001				2,058
SCSD1	78	838	3,226	334	169	165	465	314		135
SCSD6	148	1,498	5,814	913	528	830	1,219			1,576
SCTAP1	311	791·	3,683	379	390	347			4,728	1,432
SCTAP2	1,101	2,981	14,395	1,560						4,996
SHARE1B	118	343	1,300	287	228	273	1,438	496	1,385	280
SHELL	537	2,312	5,437	742	997	1,021				1,127
SHIP04S	403	1,861	6,213	283	535	808	2,983			669
STAIR*	357	824	4,214		2,050					
STANDATA	360	1,435	3,398	50	81	308				
STANDMPS	468	1,543	4,154	310	258	434	2,793			
VTP.BASE	199	402	1,113	352	445	154				
WILLETT	185	679	2,532		1,155	1,515				1,293

*All problems are minimized except where noted. Blanks indicate that the problem was either too large for the package or the package did not reach the optimal solution. These results are based on the software vers available to us as of April 2, 1987.

TABLE 4
Speed Ratio of Software Tested

Package	Average Speed Ratio 8088	80286	Times Fastest 8088	80286*
LINDO	2.05	2.05	10	9
LPS867	2.16	1.83	10	12
XA	1.52	1.36	16	21
OAK87	6.95	6.30	0	1
MICROLP	6.86	5.46	1	0
MPS-PC	9.44	11.84	0	0
XPRESS	2.97	2.87	1	3

*Several packages solved a particular problem in the smallest time, this increased the number of times they ranked first.

Efficiency Results

There are two primary ways that efficiency can be measured: by number of iterations required to solve a problem and the time taken to solve a problem. The first is a measure of the efficiency of the algorithms used by the software. There can be a wide variance in iterations required to solve the same problem while taking about the same amount of time. The efficiency measure that the end-user is most likely to be concerned with is the time required to solve problems. Table 3 shows the time taken to solve problems on both machines. While some packages have a tendency to be faster than others, any one program did not always prove to be the fastest.

Table 4 shows a speed ratio for each package. This ratio gives each package a relative rating on the sole basis of speed. This measure is defined as follows:

$$S_j = \sum_{i=1}^{49} (T_{ij}/T_{mini})/A_j$$

Where:

S_j = time ratio for package j
T_{mini} = fastest time a package solved problem i
T_{ij} = time package j took to solve problem i
A_j = number of problems solved correctly by package j

The minimum value of S_j is 1, increasing as the speed of the packages slows.

Table 4 also shows the number of times each package solved a problem the fastest. XA solved the maximum number of problems the fastest on both the XT and AT computers but the number of problems solved fastest varied between computers.

Differences Between Microprocessors

A surprising finding in running the test set on both 8088 and 80286 machines was the discrepancies in the performance. It is, of course, expected that the running time would be less for the AT than for the XT but beyond that, all operations should be identical. This was not the case. In several cases a problem would be declared unbounded or infeasible on one machine but solved correctly on the other. Sometimes the number of iterations would also differ from machine to machine.

It was expected that packages would run faster on an 80286 than on an 8088. This hypothesis appeared to hold true. What was interesting was the fact that the increase in performance difference from package to package. Table 5 gives the average time a package took to solve problems on the AT and XT. The table also shows whether the mean time to solve was significantly different between the 8088 and 80286 machines. As can be seen from this table, the improvement in speed was greater for some packages than for others. This is probably because of the way the algorithm is coded.

TABLE 5
Speed Comparison for the 8088 and 80286 Machines

Package	Mean Time on 8088	Mean Time on 80286	Ratio of XT to AT	Time Statistically Sigficant*
Lindo	1,794	1,138	1.58	No
LPS867	1,914	822	2.33	Yes
XA	3,525	1,335	2.64	No
Oak87	2,503	1,087	2.30	Yes
Micro-LP	473	313	1.51	No
MPS-PC	4,805	2,667	1.80	No
Xpress	2,395	944	2.54	Yes

*Statistically significant at the 95 percent confidence level.

Discussion

These tests pushed the abilities of the tested packages to their limits. None of the packages tested were able to solve all of the problems within the software's stated size limits. LPS-867 was able to solve the most problems within its size ability. It solved 78% of the problems on the 8088 and 80% on the 80286.

Overall, the programs performed better on the 80286 than on the 8088. All program saw an increase in speed from 69 percent for Oakland LP to only 34 percent for Micro LP. Three packages, Lindo, LPS-867, and XA were able to solve more problems on the 80286 than on the 8088. The number solved for the other packages remained the same.

Admittedly, there are some weaknesses of this method of comparison. First, we solved all of our test problems from a null basis. In practice, LP users start from a reasonable basis and then optimize. The latter approach may reduce the solution time considerably. Since the test problems are not our own, we do not have an advanced basis for these problems. Generating a basis using a package and then solving the problem with all of the packages may bias the results. A second problem is with speed ratio. The ratio does not consider the size of the problems solved by a particular package. Our test set had a wide variety of problems which leads us to believe that the ratio is not skewed. We are working on a different performance measure.

The software is also evolving rapidly. Newer versions of the programs claim to reduce the CPU time by a factor of 2 to 3. Our results are based on the versions available to us as of April 2, 1987. Tests with new versions and several other packages will be reported in a later paper.

The purpose of these comparisons is not to endorse one package over the other. Each package has its own strength, especially when user interface is considered. The comparisons tell us as to where the strength of the software is and where there is room for improvement.

FUTURE DIRECTIONS

It is possible to identify many areas where the mathematical programming software should grow. I was surprised by a lack of development in the use of expanded memory to solve larger problems than is possible with the 640K limit of the DOS. While some programs may be able to use the expanded memory as an electronic disk (RAM disk), none of the programs that I reviewed could use the additional memory to solve larger problems. Software publishers are waiting for operating systems software (such as OS/2) to use the extra memory rather than write their own memory management modules. As the new 80386 based machines come into use, the higher speed of the microprocessor and large memory will reduce the solution times, making commercial applications of LP on microcomputers more practical.

There has also been a major growth of Macintosh-type computers which have an architecture better suited for graphics-based applications. However, only one program, LINDO, is available for Macintosh, and it does not make any significant use of the Macintosh interface. The programs can be made more 'user-friendly' using interfaces of this type, also available now on IBM-PC and compatible machines through windowing programs. A related development will be growth of graphics-based tools for model generation, especially in network flow problems.

Recent interest in natural language processing and expert systems could also lead to systems where LP is used in the background as a problem solver, or where the artificial-intelligence techniques are used to develop or interrogate a model. These could also include domain-specific LP systems capable of solving problems of certain types. The major advantage of such systems is that the end user may not know anything about LP and yet the optimization may help them in decision making.

The current state-of-the-art of LP software for micros is good and getting better. The microcomputer technology offers a better vehicle for preparation and delivery of LP models. While the number crunching capability of the microcomputers will probably not match that of the concurrent mainframes, acceptable speed levels and better user interfaces should help in more applications of OR/MS techniques for businesses, large and small.

ACKNOWLEDGEMENT

The author thanks Bryant Bynum for help in performance comparisons. Parts of this paper also appeared in Interfaces.

REFERENCES

[1] Arden, B. W., 1980, What Can be Automated? The Computer Science and Engineering Research Study, MIT Press, Cambridge, MA.

[2] Bisschop, J. and A. Meeraus, 1982, "On the Development of a General Algebraic Modelling System in Strategic Planning Environment," Mathematical Programming Study 20, pp. 1-20.

[3] Bodily, S. E., 1986, "Spreadsheet Modeling as a Stepping Stone," Interfaces, Vol. 16, No. 5, pp. 34-52.

[4] Fisher, M. L., 1986, "Interactive Optimization," Annals of Operations Research, Vol. 5, pp. 541.

[5] Gay, D. M. Electronic mail distribution of linear programming test problems. COAL Newsletter, 1985, December (13), 10-12.

[6] Greenberg, H. J., 1983, "A Functional Description of ANALYZE: A Computer-Assisted Analysis System for Linear Programming Models," ACM Transactions on Mathematical Software, Vol. 9, No. 1, pp. 18-56.

[7] Ho, J. K., & Loute, I. A set of staircase linear programming test problems. Mathematical Programming, 1981, 20, 245-250.

[8] Mitra, G. Personal communication, 1986.

[9] Murtagh, B. A., and M. A. Saunders, 1982, "A Projected Lagrangean Algorithm and Its Implementation for Sparse Nonlinear Constraints," Mathematical Programming Study 16, pp. 84-117.

[10] Sharda, R. & Somarajan, C. Comparative performance of advanced microcomputer LP systems. Computers and Operations Research, 1986, 13(2/3), 131-147.

[11] Stadtler, H., Gronweld, M., & Hermannsen, H. A comparison of LP-software on personal computers for industrial applications. Working paper, Universitat Hamburg, 1986.

AGGREGATION MODELS IN MATHEMATICAL PROGRAMMING

Brigitte M. Werners, RWTH Aachen, 5100 Aachen (F.R.G.)

1. Mathematical Programming Models for Decision Support

A conventional mathematical programming problem can be described as a maximization of a well-defined objective function subject to well-defined constraints on a set of possible alternatives. Standard software tools (for example MPSX, APEX, etc.) can be used to calculate the optimal solution of the model, if the objective function and the constraints are linear functions and the possible alternatives are vectors of real or integer values. This is a very important advantage, but the possibility of application of mathematical programming is limited by the strict structure of the model. The underlying restricting assumptions are as follows:

- The considerations focus on a single objective function.
- The set of constraints differentiates exactly between feasible solutions and infeasible ones even if these violate a constraint only to a very small degree.
- Constraints are aggregated by intersection. This corresponds to the logical "and".
- The set of feasible solutions is independent of the objective function.
- The objective function depends hierarchically on the constraints.

The optimal solution of such a mathematical programming model is feasible, and the value of the objective function of this solution is higher than that of the other feasible solutions.

One possibility to enlarge the model is to simultaneously consider multiple objectives instead of a single one. Here, a variety of solution methods have been developed. They all concentrate on the set of efficient solutions which are not domi-

NATO ASI Series, Vol. F48
Mathematical Models for Decision Support
Edited by G. Mitra

nated. Those methods which determine a single alternative, to be chosen by the decision maker, either aggregate the multiple objectives into one objective function or they use aspiration levels to transform certain objectives into constraints. In both cases a compromise model is formulated with the structure of a conventional mathematical programming problem. Todays approaches (see for instance Sawaragi et al. 1987) integrate the decision maker interactively into the model building process. The aggregation of objectives or their transformation into constraints need not be done in advance but gradually, after additional information about possible solutions is given to the decision maker.

Another extension of conventional mathematical programming problems is to drop the assumption of crisply defined constraints. This is done in fuzzy mathematical programming where degrees of feasibility of solutions are described by membership functions (for an overview see Zimmermann 1986). The optimization procedure takes into account different degrees of feasibility.

An approach to consider multiple objectives and non-crisp constraints simultaneously has been developed (see Werners 1984) and integrated into a decision support system (see the preceding presentation of Zimmermann). Here, objectives and flexible constraints are both modeled by membership functions. Those membership functions describing objectives are determined by the system dependent on the constraints (for details see Werners 1987b). After formulating the basic model the decison maker is supported by additional informations about efficient solutions and their membership degrees. In a subsequent interactive phase the decision maker has the opportunity to change the membership functions. An optimal solution now is one with maximal degrees of membership of objectives and constraints. Using the classical operator for an and-aggregation, the minimum, a crisp compromise model can be formulated which has the structure of a conventional mathematical programming problem. If all membership functions are linear the optimal solution can be determined by using efficient LP codes.

Empirical investigations show that neither the "and" represented by operators which map between zero and the minimum degree of membership, nor the "or" represented by operators which map between the maximum degree of membership and 1, are appropriate to model the aggregation of fuzzy sets representing managerial decisions (see Zimmermann, Zysno 1983). Thus the above mentioned minimum operator does not sufficiently describe all dependencies which exist between fuzzy sets. New additional operators will have to be defined which imply some degree of compensation.

2. Aggregation operators

Bellman and Zadeh (1970) suggested to aggregate the fuzzy sets describing objective functions and constraints by the logical "and" which corresponds to the set-theoretic intersection. Generalizations of the logical connectives "$\wedge$" and "$\vee$" are the operators minimum and maximum or the product and the algebraic sum. They are special kinds of t-norms or t-conorms and such they have the following properties: they are commutative, associative, and non-decreasing in each argument.

Empirical investigations (see Zimmermann, Zysno 1983) lead to the conclusion that those operators are not always appropriate to model decision making. Often people use averaging operators resulting in membership values between the minimum and the maximum, and the aggregation operator depends on the respective context such that for each decision situation another aggregator might be necessary. This implies a lot of difficulties especially for practical applications. One way to bypass these difficulties is to generalize the classical concept of connectives by combining an and-operator and an or-operator using a parameter $\gamma \in [0,1]$. This is why Zimmermann, Zysno (1983) suggest the γ-operator, a combination of the product and the algebraic sum. These connectives cannot easily be used when dealing with mathematical programming problems because of their nonlinear structure.

Easier to handle with respect to mathematical programming is a convex-combination of the minimum and the maximum. This operator models certain compensatory effects, but non-extreme values are not taken into consideration. Thus the aggregation of multiple objectives does not guarantee the selection of an efficient alternative. This is shown in the following example:

	μ_1	μ_2	μ_3
x_1	0.1	0.7	0.7
x_2	0.1	0.2	0.7
x_3	0.3	0.3	0.5

Although x_1 strictly dominates x_2 the aggregation

$$\gamma \min \mu_i(x_j) + (1-\gamma) \max \mu_i(x_j)$$

gives the same result for both alternatives and so they both are elements of the set of optimal solutions. This fact is the consequence of the minimum and the maximum not being strictly monotonic and neither is their convex combination.

To avoid this effect and to allow giving higher weight to middle values new operators are suggested (Werners 1984). The idea is to differentiate between the terms "and" and "or", to allow compensation and to get the minimum when expressing the logical "and" and maximum when intending the logical "or":

$$\mu_{\widetilde{and}} = \gamma \min_{i=1}^{m} \mu_i + (1-\gamma) \frac{1}{m} \sum_{i=1}^{m} \mu_i \qquad \gamma \in [0,1]$$

$$\mu_{\widetilde{or}} = \gamma \max_{i=1}^{m} \mu_i + (1-\gamma) \frac{1}{m} \sum_{i=1}^{m} \mu_i \qquad \gamma \in [0,1]$$

Here γ is the degree of approximating the logical meaning of "and" and "or", respectively. The arithmetic mean gives a compensatory effect. $\gamma = 1$ yields $\mu_{\widetilde{and}} = \min$ and $\mu_{\widetilde{or}} = \max$. The combination of these two operators leads to very good results with respect to the empirical data of Zimmermann, Zysno (1983) which is shown in (Werners 1984). The mathematical structure is rather easy and efficiently to be handled. Both operators are commutative, idempotent, monotonic, continuous, compensatory and generalisations of the logical "and" and "or", respectively (Werners 1984). These operators can be integrated into mathematical programming problems as is shown in the following chapter.

3. Introducing Operators into Mathematical Programs

By introducing the two operators $\tilde{and}$ and $\tilde{or}$ into mathematical programming a wide variety of dependencies between objective functions and constraints can be modeled. In the following considerations we will start from a multiple objective programming model with flexible constraints. This approach contains multiple objective programming or fuzzy models as special cases.

$$\begin{aligned} \text{"}\tilde{\max}\text{"} \quad & G(x) \\ \text{s.t.} \quad & C(x) \tilde{\leq} b \\ & x \in X \end{aligned} \tag{1}$$

with $X \subset R^n$, $G : R^n \to R^1$, $C : R^n \to R^k$, $b \in R^k$.

We assume that the decision maker is able to determine the membership functions of the constraints in advance. We also make the assumption that the decision support system suggests membership functions which are strictly monotonic transformations of the objective functions on a relevant domain (for further details see Werners (1987b). Thus the problem can be interpreted as one which maximizes the degrees of membership of the objectives and the constraints, μ_i, i = 1, ..., m.

The following reflections focus on linear membership functions. In a first stage objectives and constraints are treated equally and just one aggregation operator is admitted. We formulate the resulting models and discuss the solution algorithms and the efficiency of the optimal solutions. In a second stage this approach is extended. Here multiple operators are used simultaneously to model interrelationships between objectives and constraints.

3.1 Using the $\tilde{and}$-operator.

Choosing the $\tilde{and}$-operator for aggregating the membership functions gives

$$\mu_{\tilde{and}}(x) = \gamma \min_i \mu_i(x) + (1-\gamma) \frac{1}{m} \sum_i \mu_i(x)$$

If no compensation exists between objectives and constraints, γ = 1 is required. This, for example, is assumed in conventional single objective programming. The resulting programming model here is:

$$\begin{array}{ll} \max & \alpha \\ \text{s.t.} & \alpha \le \mu_i(x) \quad i = 1, \ldots, m \\ & x \in X \\ & 0 \le \alpha \le 1 \end{array} \tag{2}$$

Provided all μ_i are linear functions then this model can be solved using standard L.P. software. However the optimal solution of (2) is not efficient with respect to problem (1) (see Werners 1987a).
An additional lexmaxmin-algorithm (see e.g. Behringer 1986) determines a particular pareto-optimum from the set of optimal solutions of (2), which is efficient with respect to (1).

If the decision maker wants to model compensatory effects, he should choose $\gamma < 1$ and the following substitution model can be defined:

$$\begin{array}{ll} \max & \alpha + (1-\gamma)\frac{1}{m}\sum_{i=1}^{m}\alpha_i \\ \text{s.t.} & \alpha + \alpha_i \le \mu_i(x) \quad i = 1, \ldots, m \\ & x \in X \\ & \alpha + \alpha_i \le 1 \\ & \alpha, \alpha_i \ge 0 \end{array} \tag{3}$$

This model again is a linear programming model provided all μ_i are linear. If $(\alpha^o, \alpha_1^o, \ldots, \alpha_n^o, x^o)$ is an optimal solution to (3) then x^o is efficient with respect to (1) and $\alpha^o + \alpha_i^o$ are the degrees to which x^o satisfies the objective functions or the constraints, respectively. If standard LP software is used to solve the above problem, no additional computations are required to determine or prove the pareto optimality of the final solution.

3.2 Using the $\tilde{o}$r-operator

The $\tilde{o}$r-operator is a generalization of the concept of disjunction with

$$\mu_{\tilde{o}r}(x) = \gamma \max_i \mu_i(x) + (1-\gamma)\frac{1}{m}\sum_{i=1}^{m}\alpha_i$$

If compensation exists between objectives and constraints then $\gamma < 1$ and the resulting mathematical programming model is:

$$\max \quad \gamma\alpha + (1-\gamma)\frac{1}{m}\sum_{i=1}^{m} \alpha_i$$

$$\text{s.t.} \quad \alpha_i \le \mu_i(x) \quad i = 1, \ldots, m \tag{4}$$

$$\alpha \le \alpha_i \quad \text{for at least one } i = 1, \ldots, m$$

$$x \in X$$

$$0 \le \alpha_i \le 1$$

$$\alpha \ge 0$$

The term

$$\alpha \le \alpha_i \text{ for at least one } i = 1, \ldots, m$$

can be substituted by the following two inequalities using additional 0-1-variables:

$$\begin{aligned} &\alpha \le \alpha_i + y_i && i = 1, \ldots, m \\ &\Sigma\, y_i \le m-1 && y_i \in \{0,1\} \end{aligned} \tag{4b}$$

If $(\alpha^o, \alpha_i^o, x^o, y^o)$ is an optimal solution of (4) then $\alpha^o = \max \mu_i(x^o)$, $\alpha_i^o = \mu_i(x^o)$ and x^o is efficient with respect to (1). Under the condition that all μ_i are linear functions the above model (4) with formulation (4b) is a mixed-integer programming model and can be solved by standard MILP-codes.

If the decision maker chooses the $\tilde{\text{or}}$-operator without compensation, that is $\gamma = 1$, the equivalent substitution model for (1) is a specific disjunctive programming model and can be formulated as follows:

$$\max \quad \alpha$$

$$\text{s.t.} \quad \alpha \le \mu_i(x) + y_i \quad i = 1, \ldots, m \tag{5}$$

$$\Sigma\, y_i = m - 1$$

$$x \in X$$

$$y_i \in \{0,1\} \quad i = 1, \ldots, m$$

$$0 \le \alpha \le 1$$

For the optimal solution (α^o, x^o, y^o) of (5), α^o is equal to $\max \mu_i(x^o)$. However, x^o is in general not efficient with respect to problem (1). Here a lexmaxmax-algorithm can be used which determines a particular efficient solution out of the set of optimal solutions to (5).

3.3 Modelling $\tilde{=}$-constraints

In conventional mathematical programming models an equality-constraint $g(x) = b$ is equivalent to the two inequality-constraints $g(x) \leq b$ and $g(x) \geq b$. Similarly a $\tilde{=}$-constraint $\mu_{\tilde{=}}(x)$ can be formulated by the aggregation of a $\tilde{\leq}$-constraint $\mu_{\tilde{\leq}}(x)$ and a $\tilde{\geq}$-constraint $\mu_{\tilde{\geq}}(x)$. In this case the and-operator without compensation is to be used:

$$\mu_{\tilde{=}}(x) = \min \{\mu_{\tilde{\leq}}(x), \mu_{\tilde{\geq}}(x)\}$$

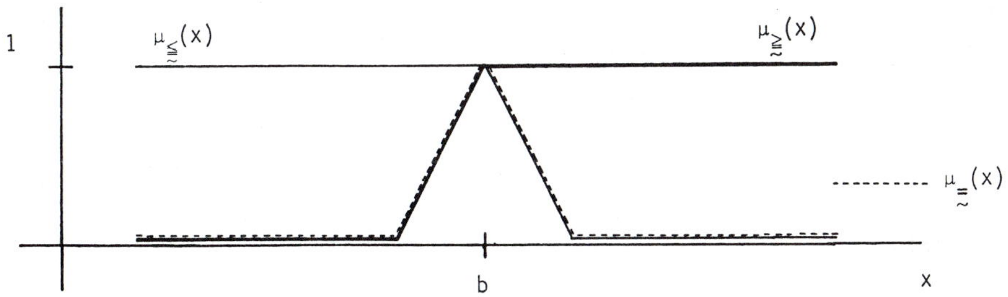

Fig. 1: $\tilde{=}$-constraint

This decomposition of $\mu_{\tilde{=}}$ is necessary because $\mu_{\tilde{=}}$, in general, is not monotonic in x but $\mu_{\tilde{\leq}}$ and $\mu_{\tilde{\geq}}$ are.

If all constraints and objectives of the model under consideration are to be aggregated by the and-operator without any compensation (see model (2)), then the constraint

$$\alpha \leq \mu_{\tilde{=}}$$

can be replaced by the two constraints

$$\alpha \leq \mu_{\tilde{\geq}}$$
$$\alpha \leq \mu_{\tilde{\leq}}$$

and the entire aggregation remains the same.
This is slightly different if a $\tilde{=}$-constraint appears in a model of compensatory aggregation. Here the decomposition of an equality constraint into two inequality constraints has to be done in a previous phase.

The expression "$\alpha_1 \leq \mu_{\tilde{=}}(x) = \min \{\mu_{\tilde{\geq}}(x), \mu_{\tilde{\leq}}(x)\}$" has to be appropriately inserted into the model.

Example:
The first constraint of an aggregation model with the and-operator and compensation is a $\tilde{=}$-constraint. Then the resulting decomposed model is

$$\max \quad \alpha + (1-\gamma)\frac{1}{m}\sum_{i=1}^{m}\alpha_i$$

$$\begin{aligned}
\text{s.t.} \quad & \alpha + \alpha_1 \leq \mu_{1\tilde{\geq}}(x) \\
& \alpha + \alpha_1 \leq \mu_{1\tilde{\leq}}(x) \\
& \alpha + \alpha_i \leq \mu_i(x) && i = 2, \ldots, m \\
& x \in X \\
& \alpha + \alpha_i \leq 1 && i = 1, \ldots, m \\
& \alpha, \alpha_i \geq 0
\end{aligned}$$

Thus the membership function of the $\tilde{=}$-constraint can be understood as a non-compensatory $\tilde{\text{and}}$-aggregation of two membership functions on a hierarchically lower level of the model.

3.4 Hierarchical Aggregation

The aggregations considered so far are rather inflexible because only one operator is used for the entire model. Now it is shown how to aggregate objectives and constraints on different hierarchical levels with different operators. For simplicity we will use the following notations:

- $\vee\gamma(\{\mu_i\}_{i\in I})$ - denotes the $\tilde{\text{or}}$-aggregation of the specified μ_i on the same hierarchical level with a specific γ.
- $\wedge\gamma(\{\mu_i\}_{i\in I})$ - denotes and specifies the $\tilde{\text{and}}$-aggregation.

With this concept a variety of dependencies between objectives as well as between constraints can be modeled. For instance hierarchical dependencies of the type revealed in the empirical investigations about credit worthiness (see Zimmermann, Zysno 1983) can be built into mathematical models. This is exemplarily shown in the following.

<u>Example</u>
In a mathematical programming model six objectives or constraints are described by membership functions $\mu_1, \ldots, \mu_6$ on $x \in X$. The aggregation is to be done as follows:

$$\vee\gamma_1\ (\mu_1, \wedge\gamma_2\ (\mu_2, \mu_3), \ \wedge\gamma_3(\mu_4, \mu_5, \mu_6))$$

Here an $\tilde{\text{or}}$-aggregation with parameter γ_1 of three fuzzy sets with the membership functions μ_1, $\wedge\gamma_2(\mu_2, \mu_3)$, and $\wedge\gamma_3(\mu_4, \mu_5, \mu_6)$ is carried out. The second set of these three fuzzy sets is the result of an $\tilde{\text{and}}$-aggregation of two fuzzy sets, while the third set is formed by an $\tilde{\text{and}}$-aggregation of three fuzzy sets on the same hierarchical level. This is illustrated in fig. 2:

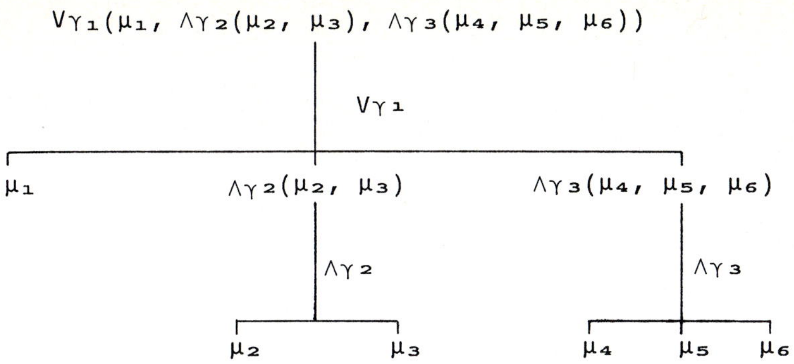

Fig. 2: Hierarchical aggregation

The according mathematical programming model is deduced in a descending order with respect to the hierarchical levels.

First the aggregation $V\gamma_1$ on the highest level is decomposed and according to (4) we have in a first step:

$$\max \quad \gamma_1\alpha^1 + (1-\gamma_1)\,\frac{1}{3}\sum_{i=1}^{3}\alpha_i^1$$

$$\begin{aligned}
\text{s.t.}\quad & \alpha_1^1 \le \mu_1(x)\\
& \alpha_2^1 \le \Lambda\gamma_2(\mu_2,\ \mu_3)\\
& \alpha_3^1 \le \Lambda\gamma_3(\mu_4,\ \mu_5,\ \mu_6)\\
& \alpha^1 \le \alpha_i^1 + y_i \qquad i=1,\ 2,\ 3\\
& \sum_{i=1}^{3} y_i \le 2\\
& x \in X\\
& y_i \in \{0,\ 1\} \qquad i = 1,\ 2,\ 3\\
& 0 \le \alpha_i^1 \le 1 \qquad i = 1,\ 2,\ 3\\
& \alpha^1 \ge 0
\end{aligned}$$

The upper index of α specifies the corresponding aggregation level. In the next step $\Lambda\gamma_2$ and $\Lambda\gamma_3$ have to be decomposed according to (3).

Second step:

$$\max \quad \gamma_1 \alpha^1 + (1-\gamma_1)\ \frac{1}{3} \sum_{i=1}^{3} \alpha_i^1$$

$$\alpha_1^1 \le \mu_1(x)$$

$$\alpha_2^1 \le \alpha_2^2 + (1-\gamma_2)\ \frac{1}{2}\ (\alpha_{21}^2 + \alpha_{22}^2)$$

$$\alpha_2^2 + \alpha_{21}^2 \le \mu_2(x)$$

$$\alpha_2^2 + \alpha_{22}^2 \le \mu_3(x)$$

$$\alpha_3^1 \le \alpha_3^2 + (1-\gamma_3)\ \frac{1}{3}\ (\alpha_{31}^2 + \alpha_{32}^2 + \alpha_{33}^2)$$

$$\alpha_3^2 + \alpha_{31}^2 \le \mu_4(x)$$

$$\alpha_3^2 + \alpha_{32}^2 \le \mu_5(x)$$

$$\alpha_3^2 + \alpha_{33}^2 \le \mu_6(x)$$

$$\alpha^1 \le \alpha_i^1 + y_i \qquad i = 1,\ 2,\ 3$$

$$\sum_{i=1}^{3} y_i \le 2$$

$$x \in X$$

$$y_i \in \{0,1\} \qquad i = 1,\ 2,\ 3$$

$$0 \le \alpha_i^1 \le 1 \qquad i = 1,\ 2,\ 3$$

$$0 \le \alpha_2^2 + \alpha_{2i}^2 \le 1 \qquad i = 1,\ 2$$

$$0 \le \alpha_3^2 + \alpha_{3i}^2 \le 1 \qquad i = 1,\ 2,\ 3$$

Here the decomposition is repeated until all the membership functions are elementary monotonic functions.

4. Operators in the context of the DSS

The previously described aggregation operators are an integral part of the decision support system. They can be used to model a variety of dependencies between objectives and constraints. In practical applications the appropriate operators with their values γ should be determined while the first model is built. In the interactive phase, when additional informations from a decision maker are included into the model, explicit modifications of the aggregation operators are not allowed.

The determination of the appropriate γ can be done in two different ways. The decision maker can describe the structure of dependencies of the objectives and constraints of his problem directly. This can be done simply by using the linguistic terms "and" or "or" as in conventional mathematical programming. Alternatively, the decision maker can evaluate examples with respect to their membership degrees. The underlying aggregation concept is deduced, for example by using statistical methods. In this context it is important to note that the explicit determination of the operators need only be done roughly, for in the subsequent interactive phase, implicit modifications can be done by changing the membership functions.

In the decision support system the global knowledge of the decision maker about a problem is represented in the formulation of the corresponding model which includes the definition of objectives, constraints, and aggregation operators. Further, local information is given by the decision maker during the interactive problem solving process. Thus additional knowledge is requested and is integrated into the solution process of the decision support system.

References

Bellman, R.E., Zadeh, L.A. (1970) Decision-making in a fuzzy environment. Management Science, 17, B-141-B-164.

Behringer, F.A. (1986) Linear multiobjective maxmin optimization and some pareto and lexmaxmin extensions. OR Spektrum, 8, (1), 25-32.

Sawaragi, Y., Inoue, K., Nakayama, H. (eds.) (1987) Toward interactive and intelligent decision support systems. Vol. 1, 2, N.Y., Berlin, Heidelberg.

Werners, B. (1984) Interaktive Entscheidungsunterstützung durch ein flexibles mathematisches Programmierungssystem. München.

Werners, B. (1987a) Interactive multiple objective programming subject to flexible constraints. European Journal of Operational Research, 31, 342-349.

Werners, B. (1987b) An interactive fuzzy programming system. Fuzzy Sets and Systems, 23, 131-147.

Zimmermann, H.-J. (1986) Fuzzy set theory - and its applications. Boston, Dordrecht, Lancaster, 2nd printing.

Zimmermann, H.-J., Zysno, P. (1983) Decisions and evaluations by hierarchical aggregation of informations. Fuzzy Sets and Systems, 10 , 243-266

INTERACTIVE DECISION SUPPORT FOR SEMI-STRUCTURED MATHEMATICAL PROGRAMMING PROBLEMS

H.-J. Zimmermann, RWTH Aachen, 5100 Aachen (F.R.G.)

1. FUZZY MATHEMATICAL PROGRAMMING

1.1 A Basic Possibilistic Model

Let us consider mathematical programming as a specific version of decision making problems. In classical decision theory a decision can be regarded as the action which is feasible (i.e. satisfies the constraints) **and** optimal (i.e. optimizes the objective function). In 1970 Bellman and Zadeh [1970] suggested that in many situations it might be appropriate and even more realistic to model the goal (objective function) as well as the constraints as fuzzy sets. Using the correspondence of the (logical) "and" and the set-theoretic "intersection" they then suggested to consider as the decision the intersection of the fuzzy set representing the goal and the constraint, respectively.

Definition 1:

Let $\mu_{\tilde{C}_i}(x)$, $i=1,\ldots,m, x \in X$, be membership functions of constraints defining the decision space, and $\mu_{\tilde{G}_j}(x), j=1,\ldots,n, x \in X$ the membership functions of objective (utility) functions or goals. A decision is then defined by its membership function

$$\mu_{\tilde{D}}(x) = \mu_{\tilde{C}_i}(x) * \mu_{\tilde{G}_i}(x), \; i=1,\ldots,m, \quad j=1,\ldots,n,$$

NATO ASI Series, Vol. F48
Mathematical Models for Decision Support
Edited by G. Mitra

where * denotes an appropriate, possibly context dependent, "aggregator" (connective).

Let M be the set of points $x \in X$ for which $\mu_{\tilde{D}}(x)$ attains its maximum, if it exists. Then M is called the maximizing decision.

If $\mu_{\tilde{D}}(x)$ has a unique maximum at x_M, then the maximizing decision is a uniquely defined crisp decision which can be interpreted as the action which belongs to all fuzzy sets representing either constraints or goals with the highest possible degree of membership (which might be quite low).

We shall now consider a standard LP in which the decision maker has established an aspiration level, z, as an approximate level of the objective function which he wants to achieve and in which the m constraints are flexible, i.e. they can be violated to certain degrees. This problem can be modelled as

Find x such that

$$\begin{aligned} c^T x &\lesssim z \\ Ax &\lesssim b \\ x &\geq 0. \end{aligned} \qquad (1)$$

Here $\lesssim$ denotes the fuzzified version of $\leq$ and has the linguistic interpretation "essentially smaller than or equal".

We see that (1) is symmetric with respect to objective function and constraints, and we now make that even more obvious by substituting

$$\begin{pmatrix} c \\ A \end{pmatrix} = B \quad \text{and} \quad \begin{pmatrix} z \\ b \end{pmatrix} = d.$$

Then (1) becomes

Find x such that

$$\begin{aligned} Bx &\lesssim d, \\ x &\geq 0. \end{aligned} \qquad (2)$$

Each of the m+1 rows of (2) will now be represented by a fuzzy set, the membership functions of which are $\mu_i(x)$, which can be interpreted as the degree to which x fulfils (satsifies) the fuzzy unequalities $(Bx)_i \leq d_i$, $i=1,\ldots,m+1$, where $(Bx)_i$ denotes the ith row of (2).

If we accept the possibilistic attitude to model the intersection of fuzzy sets by the minimum operator, the membership function of the fuzzy set "decision" is

$$\mu_{\tilde{D}}(x) = \min_{i=1}^{m+1} \mu_i(x) \qquad (3)$$

Assuming that the decision maker is interested not in a fuzzy set but in a crisp "optimal" solution x^o, we could suggest to him the "maximizing solution" to (3) which is the solution to the possibly nonlinear programming problem

$$\max_{x\geq 0} \min_{i=1}^{m+1} \mu_i(x) = \mu_M(x^\circ) \qquad (4)$$

We now have to specify the membership functions $\mu_i(x)$. They should be 0 if the constraints (including objective function) are stronly violated, 1 if they are very well satisfied (i.e. satisfied in the crisp sense); and they should increase monotonically from 0 to 1, i.e.

$$\mu_i(x) \begin{cases} = 1 & \text{if } (Bx)_i \leq d_i \\ \in[0,1] & \text{if } d_i < (Bx)_i \leq d_i+p_i, \quad i=1,\dots,m+1 \\ = \;0 & \text{if } (Bx)_i > d_i+p_i \end{cases} \qquad (5)$$

Using the simplest type of membership function, we assume them to be linearly increasing over the tolerance interval $[d_i,d_i+p_i]$:

$$\mu_i(x) = \begin{cases} 1 & \text{if } (Bx)_i \leq d_i \\ 1 - \dfrac{(Bx)_i-d_i}{p_i} & \text{if } d_i < (Bx)_i \leq d_i+p_i, \quad i=1,\dots,m+1 \\ 0 & \text{if } (Bx)_i > d_i+p_i \end{cases} \qquad (6)$$

The p_i are subjectively chosen constants of admissible violations of the constraints and the objective function Substituting (5) into (3) yields, after some rearrangements

$$\max_{x\geq 0} \min_{i=1}^{m+1} \left(1-\frac{(Bx_i)-d_i}{p_i}\right) \qquad (7)$$

Introducing one new variable, λ, which corresponds essentially to $\mu_D(x)$ in (3), we arrive at

$$\begin{aligned} &\text{Maximize } \lambda \\ &\text{such that } \lambda p_i+(Bx)_i \leq d_i+p_i, \quad i = 1,\dots,m+1, \\ &\qquad\qquad 0 \leq \lambda \leq 1, \\ &\qquad\qquad x \geq 0. \end{aligned} \qquad (8)$$

If the optimal solution to (8) is the vector (λ°,x°), then x° is the maximizing solution (4) to the model (1), assuming membership functions as specified in (6).

Slightly modified versions of the model (6) and (7) result if membership functions are defined as follows:
A variable t_i, $i=1,\dots,m+1$, $0 \leq t_i \leq p_i$, is defined which measures the degree of violation of the ith constraint: The membership function of the ith row is then

$$\mu_i(x) = 1 - \frac{t_i}{p_i}. \qquad (9)$$

The crisp equivalent model is then

$$\begin{aligned} &\text{Maximize } \lambda \\ &\text{such that } \lambda p_i + t_i \le p_i, \quad i = 1,\dots,m+1, \\ &\qquad (Bx)_i - t_i \le d_i, \\ &\qquad t_i \le p_i, \\ &\qquad \lambda, x, t \ge 0. \end{aligned} \tag{10}$$

This model is larger than model (8), even though the set of constraints $t_i \le p_i$ is actually redundant. Model (10) has some advantages, however, in particular when performing sensitivity analysis, which will not be discussed here.

The main advantage of (1) is that the decision maker is not forced into a precise formulation for mathematical reasons, even though he might only be able or willing to describe his problem in fuzzy terms. Linear membership functions are obviously only a very rough approximation. Membership functions which monotonically increase or decrease in the interval $[d_i, d_i+pi]$ can also be handled quite easily, as will be shown later.

So far the objective function as well as all constraints were considered fuzzy. If some of the constraints are crisp, $Dx \le b$, then these constraints can easily be added to the formulation (8) or (10). Thus (8) would, for instance, become

$$\begin{aligned} &\text{Maximize } \lambda \\ &\text{such that } \lambda p_i + (Bx)_i \le d_i + p_i, \quad i = 1,\dots,m+1 \\ &\qquad Dx \le b \\ &\qquad \lambda \le 1 \\ &\qquad x, \lambda \ge 0. \end{aligned} \tag{11}$$

Even though we now have fuzzy and crisp constraints, the model remains symmetric in the sense that objective function(s) and constraints have exactly the same representation. The reason is, of course, that crisp constraints can be regarded as special cases of fuzzy constraints for which the membership functions degenerate to characteristic functions.

1.2 Modifications and extensions

This changes if for the objective function no aspiration level can be established. In this case the notion of a "maximizing set" can be used in order to reestablish the symmetry of the model. In this case the equivalent crisp model becomes [Werners 1985, Zimmermann 1986]:

$$\begin{aligned} &\text{Maximize } \lambda \\ &\text{such that } \lambda(f_o - f_1) - c^T x \le -f_1, \\ &\qquad \lambda p \quad\quad + Ax \le b + p, \\ &\qquad Dx \le b`, \\ &\qquad \lambda \le 1, \\ &\qquad \lambda, x \ge 0, \end{aligned} \tag{12}$$

where f_o and f_1 are the optimal solutions, respectively, of two linear programs, one using the support of the solution space as feasible space and the other the α-cut for $\alpha=1$.

So far we have used the minimum operator to model the intersection and assumed linear membership functions for the fuzzy sets representing objective functions or constraints.

It is quite obvious that linear membership functions will not always be adequate, and it has been shown empirically that the min operator is often not an appropriate model for the "and" used in decision models. We shall first consider the problem of nonlinear membership functions - keeping the min operator as aggregator - and then we shall investigate what happens if other aggregating procedures are used.

The linear membership functions used so far could all be defined by fixing two points: the upper and lower aspiration levels or the two bounds of the tolerance interval.

The most obvious way to handle nonlinear membership functions is probably to approximate them piecewise by linear functions. Some authors have used this approach and shown that the resulting equivalent crisp problem is still a standard linear programming problem. This problem, however, can be considerably larger than the model (10), because in general one constraint will have to be added for each linear piece of the approximation. Quite often S-shaped membership functions have been suggested, particularly if the membership function is interpreted as a kind of utility function (representing the degree of satisfaction, acceptance etc.).

Some authors [Leberling 1981] have shown that nonlinear membership functions can also be acomodated by equivalent linear crisp models. It has even been proven [Werners 1985] that the following holds:

<u>Theorem 1:</u>
Let $\{f_k\}$, $k=1,\ldots,K$, be a finite family of functions $f_k: R^n R^1$, $x^o \in X \, |R^n$, $g: |R^1 |R^1$ strictly monotonically increasing, and λ^k, $\lambda' \in R$. Consider the two mathematical programming problems

$$\begin{aligned} &\text{Maximize } \lambda \\ &\text{such that } \lambda \le f_k(x), \quad k=1,\ldots,K, \\ &\qquad\qquad x \in X \end{aligned} \tag{13}$$

and

$$\begin{aligned} &\text{Maximize } \lambda' \\ &\text{such that } \lambda' \le g(f_k(x)), \quad k=1,\ldots,K, \\ &\qquad\qquad x \in X \end{aligned} \tag{14}$$

If there exists an $\lambda^o \in \mathbb{R}^1$ such that (λ^o, x^o) is the optimal solution of (13), then there exists an $\lambda' \in R^1$ such that (λ'^o, x^o) is optimal solution of (14).

This theorem suggests that quite a number of nonlinear membership functions can be acomodated easily. Unluckily the same optimism is not justified concerning the other aggregation operators.

The computational efficiency of the approach mentioned so far rested to a large extent on the use of the min operator as a model for the logical "and" or for the intersection of fuzzy sets.

As already mentioned in my first contribution, other than the min-operator have been suggested and proven to model human behaviour better in the context of decision- making.

The disadvantage of these operators is, however, that the resulting crisp equivalent models are no longer linear (see, for instance, [Zimmermann , p. 45]), hence reducing the computational efficiency of these approaches considerably or even rendering the equivalent models unsolvable within acceptable time limits.

There are some exceptions to this rule, two of which we want to present in some more detail.
One of the objections against the min operator (see, for instance, [Zimmermann and Zysno, 1980], is the fact that neither the logical "and" nor the min operator is compensatory, in the sense that increases in the degree of membership in the fuzzy sets "intersected" do not influence at all the membership in the resulting fuzzy set (aggregated fuzzy set or intersection). There are two quite natural ways to cure this weakness:
a. Combine the (limitational) min operator as model for the logical "and" with the fully compensatory max operator as a model for the inclusive "or". For the former the product operator might alternatively be used, and for the latter the algebraic sum. This approach departs from distinguishing between "and" and "or" aggregation, being somewhere between the "and" and the "or". (Therefore it is often called "compensatory and").
b. Stick with the distinction between "and" and "or" aggregators and introduce a certain degree of compensation into these connectives.

a. Compensatory "and"

For some applications it seems to be important for the aggregator used to map above the "max operator" and below the "min operator". The γ-operator would be such a connective. For purposes of mathematical programming it has, however, the above mentioned disadvantage of low computational efficiency. An acceptable compromise between empirical fit and computational efficiency seems to be the convex combination of the min operator and the max operator:

$$\mu_c(x) = \gamma \min_{i=1}^{m} \mu_i(x) + (1-\gamma)\max \mu_i(x), \qquad \gamma \in [0,1] \tag{15}$$

For linear membership functions of the goals and the constraints, and denoting the coefficients of the A-matrix and the objective function by d_i, the crisp equivalent model is

$$\max_{x \in X} \left(\min_{i=1}^{m} \gamma\{\mu_i(d_i^T x)\} + (1-\gamma) \max_{i=1}^{m} \{\mu_i(d_i^T x)\} \right). \tag{16}$$

This is equivalent to

$$\begin{aligned} &\text{Maximize } \gamma\lambda_1+(1-\gamma)\lambda_2 \\ &\text{such that } \lambda_1 \le \mu_i(d_i^T x), \quad i=1,\dots,m, \\ &\qquad\qquad \lambda_2 \le \mu_i(d_i^T x) \quad \text{for at least one } i\in[1,\dots,m], \\ &\qquad\qquad x\in X. \end{aligned}$$

or

$$\begin{aligned} &\text{Maximize } \gamma\lambda_1+(1-\gamma)\lambda_2, \\ &\text{such that } \lambda_1 \le \mu_i(d_i^T x), \quad i=1,\dots,m, \\ &\qquad\qquad \lambda_2 \le \mu_i(d_i^T x)+M_{yi}, \quad i=1,\dots,m, \\ &\qquad\qquad \sum_{i\in 1}^{m} y_i \le m-1, \\ &\qquad\qquad y\in\{0,1\}, \\ &\qquad\qquad x\in X, \end{aligned} \tag{17}$$

where M_{yi} are very large real numbers. (17) is a mixed integer linear program which can be solved by available codes (APEX, MPSX, etc.).

b. Fuzzy "and" and fuzzy "or"

Another approach is to distinguish between "and" and "or" and to "soften" these extreme connectives. Details of this approach will be presented by Dr. Werners later on.

1.3 Multi-Criteria-Models

If there exist several objective functions which can directly be represented as fuzzy sets no problems arise: They can easily be added to the model as additional rows without changing the structure of the model.

The approach presented here can, however, also be applied to crisp problems with several objective functions [Zimmermann 1978]. Essentially the notion of a "maximizing set" is used to calibrate the objective functions, using the individual optima and "least justifyable solutions". Thus fuzzy sets are generated which then can be included in the (crisp) model as described above.

2. AN INTERACTIVE SYSTEM FOR DECISION SUPPORT

2.1 Basic Considerations

The basic motivations for the DSS described in the following were to provide an efficient computer based and interactive DSS for mathematical programming type problems which

1. can cope with multiple (fuzzy) objective functions and crisp and fuzzy constraints;
2. uses realistic and empirically tested membership functions,
3. provides adequate connectives which can be chosen by the user context-dependently.

In a DSS which is to be of practical use not only scientific considerations, for instance, of best empirical fit, of membership functions and operators, play a part but also the requirement of efficiency, i.e. computing time, storage space and user orientation. In the following we will have to describe some compromises between empirical fit and efficiency which had to be made in order to keep the overall system practically useful.

Membership Functions

Essentially four types of membership functions were initially considered for the fuzzy sets used in the DSS: Linear and hyperbolic functions, the logistic function and spline functions. Theorem 1 showed how hyperbolic functions can be transformed into equivalent linear membership functions. It can also be shown that hyperbolic membership functions and logistic membership functions are isomorphic mathematical models. By choosing appropriate parameters the resulting membership functions are equal. Determining a cubic spline function, however, requires the determination of quite a number of parameters, which might not be feasable at all for a decision maker. The DSS was, therefore, restricted to accomodate the first three types of membership functions.

Operators

The computational efficiency of the DSS depends primarily on the type of resulting "equivalent model" such as (10), (11) etc. This, however, does not only depend on the membership function chosen or the operator used for aggregation, but the combination of both. We shall show this for 2 operators and different membership functions.

Let us first consider a linear combination of min and max and linear membership functions of the type $\mu_i(c_i^T x)$ as used before:

The resulting models are shown in (16) and (17), respectively.

This is a mixed integer linear program (MILP) which can be solved with available efficient software such as APEX, MPSX etc. This is not true if we use the logistic function as a membership function:

Then the model becomes

$$\max\ [\gamma(1+e^{-\lambda_1}) + (1-\gamma)(1+e^{-\lambda_2})^{-1}] \tag{18}$$

$$\text{s.th. } \lambda_1 \le a_i(d_i^T x-b_i),\ i=1,\dots,m$$

$$\lambda_2 \le a_i(d_i^T x-b_i) \quad \text{for at least one } i\in\{1,\dots,m\}.$$
$$x\in X$$

Similar results can be obtained for the "fuzzy and" operator. The following table summarizes some operator-membership function combinations and their resulting equivalent models.

Membership Function	Operator	Model
Linear	Min	LP
Logistic	Min	LP
Hyperbolic	Min	LP
Linear	min+(1-γ)max	MILP
Linear/Nonlinear	Product	nonconvex NLP
Linear/Nonlinear	γ-operator	nonconvex NLP
Linear	$\widetilde{\text{and}}$	LP
Linear	$\widetilde{\text{or}}$	MILP
Logistic	$\widetilde{\text{and}}$	NLP with lin. cons.

with: $\widetilde{\text{and}} = \gamma \min(x,y) + (1-\gamma)\frac{1}{2}(x+y)$

$\widetilde{\text{or}} = \gamma \max(x,y)+(1-\gamma)\frac{1}{2}(x+y)$

Table 1: Resulting equivalent models

For the DSS only combinations were included that lead to linear equivalent models. They are mentioned again in the following table:

Operator / M.-Function	Min	Min/Max	Alg. Mean	and
Linear	LP	MILP	LP	LP
Logistic	LP			

Table 2: M.-F. Operator Combinations inlcuded in DSS

2.2 EDP-Implementation

The system "DSS" supports a decision maker solving multicriteria problems with crisp and flexible restrictions.

The system consists of three components:

a) Man-Machine Communication
This part has the following tasks:
- to guide the decision maker through the system directed by a menu,
- to present the processed data to the decision maker and
- to facilitate the change of the data and of the decision variables by the decision maker.

b) Data Management
This section contains the activities
- data processing and
- data update.

c) System/Machine Communication
This part is the interface to other software systems, which are used by "DSS". In detail this section
- generates the interface files
- supervises and controls the execution of the software system in use.

The following figure shows the 9 modules of DSS.

Figure 1: Modules of the DSS (see next page)

2.3 Working with the DSS

Using the decision support system first the decision maker has to give his goals and constraints for a fuzzy programming model. Goals and constraints are not treated equally as in the fuzzy decision model of Zadeh mentiond earlier. Instead we consider as the main difference between a fuzzy goal and a fuzzy constraint that the decision maker is able to give more information about a constraint than about a goal. Similar to crisp programming models where he only distinguishes between 0 and 1 degree of membership for satisfying a constraint the decision maker a priori gives a membership function for each constraint. The membership function of a fuzzy maximization goal cannot be given in advance but depends on what is possible when satisfying the constraints. So additional information has to be attained about the dependencies of the model. This can be done by the system. Here extremal solutions are determined optimizing one goal over each of two crisp feasable regions: One which contains all solutions with a degree of membership equal to 1 and another which contains all solutions with nonzero degrees of membership. The results are used to determine membership functions of the goals.
To solve crisp vector maximum problems it was suggested [Zimmermann 1987] to derive a fuzzy set representing the goals from the pessimistic and the ideal solution of the vector-maximum problem. The concept used in the DSS is a generalization which is necessary to handle fuzzy goals under crisp and fuzzy constraints. Aggregating all membership functions i.e. of goals and constraints, a compromise solution is determined. Interactively the decision maker can now change the proposed membership functions until he is satisfied with the compromise solution.
The interactive fuzzy programming system supports a decision maker, especially in two different ways:
- first, it determines extremal solutions and proposes membership functions describing the goals.
- second, it evaluates efficient compromise solutions with additional local informations.

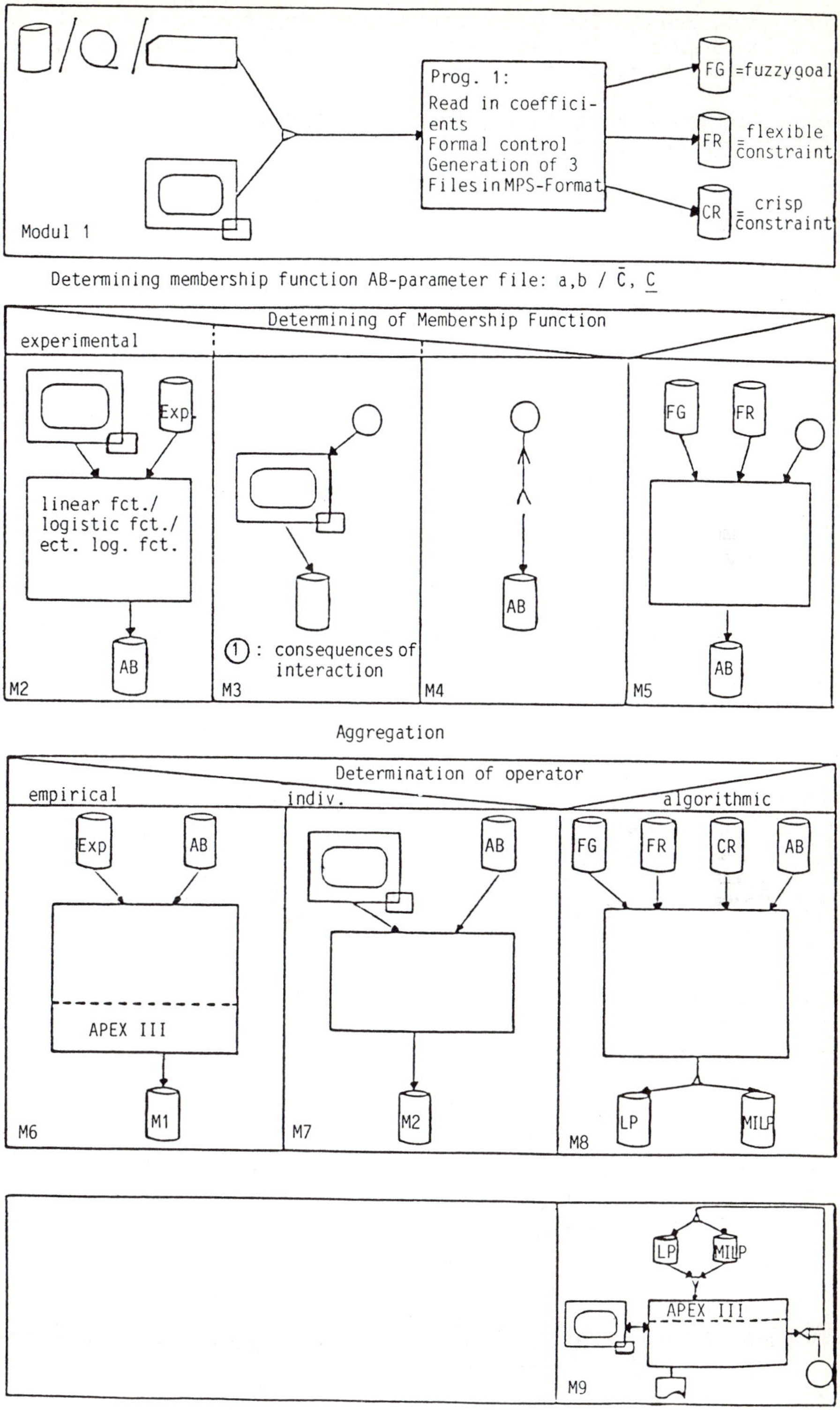
Prog. 1:
Read in coefficients
Formal control
Generation of 3 Files in MPS-Format
FG =fuzzygoal
FR = flexible constraint
CR = crisp constraint
Modul 1
Determining membership function AB-parameter file: a,b / C̄, C
Determining of Membership Function
experimental
Exp.
linear fct./
logistic fct./
ect. log. fct.
AB
M2
1 : consequences of interaction
M3
AB
M4
FG
FR
AB
M5
Aggregation
Determination of operator
empirical
indiv.
algorithmic
Exp
AB
APEX III
M1
M6
AB
M2
M7
FG
FR
CR
AB
LP
MILP
M8
LP
MILP
APEX III
M9

After each presented compromise the decision-maker gets more and more insight into the model and can articulate further preference information:

- local, by modifying membership functions,
- global, by modifying the model.

The following rough flow chart sketches how the DSS works:

Figure 2: Rough flowchart of DSS-operations (see next page)

The system "DSS" is a menu-oriented dialog system for solving multi-criteria problems with crisp and fuzzy restrictions. A static description of the structure shall be omitted, because the structure of the system is highly dependent on the wishes of the decision maker.

For further details the reader is referred to [Zimmermann et al. 1984].

<u>References</u>:

Bellman, R.E., Zadeh, L.A.: Decision making in a fuzzy environment, in: Mgt. Sc. 17(1970), p. B141-164.

Leberling, H.: On finding compromise solutions in multicriteria problems using the fuzzy min-operator, in: Fuzzy Sets and Systems 6 (1981), pp. 105-118.

Werners, B.: Interaktive Entscheidungsunterstützung durch ein flexibles mathematisches Programmierungssystem, München 1984

Zimmermann, H.-J.: Description and optimization of fuzzy systems, in: Int. Journ. of General Systems 2 (1976), pp. 209-215.

Zimmermann, H.-J.: Fuzzy programming and linear programming with several objective functions, in: Fuzzy Sets and Systems 1 (1978), pp. 45-55.

Zimmermann, H.-J., Zysno, P.: Latent connectives in human decision making, in: Fuzzy Sets and Systems 4 (1980), pp. 37-51.

Zimmermann, H.-J. (Principal Investigator), Hillekamp, R., Hintz, G.W., Werners, B., Zysno, P.: Efficient Algorithm for Fuzzy Linear Programming with Multiple Objectives, Final Technical Report, Aachen 1984

Zimmermann, H.-J.: Fuzzy Sets Theory - And Its Applications, Boston, Dordrecht, Lancaster 1985.

Zimmermann, H.-J.: Fuzzy Sets, Decision Making and Expert Systems, Boston, Dordrecht, Lancaster 1987.

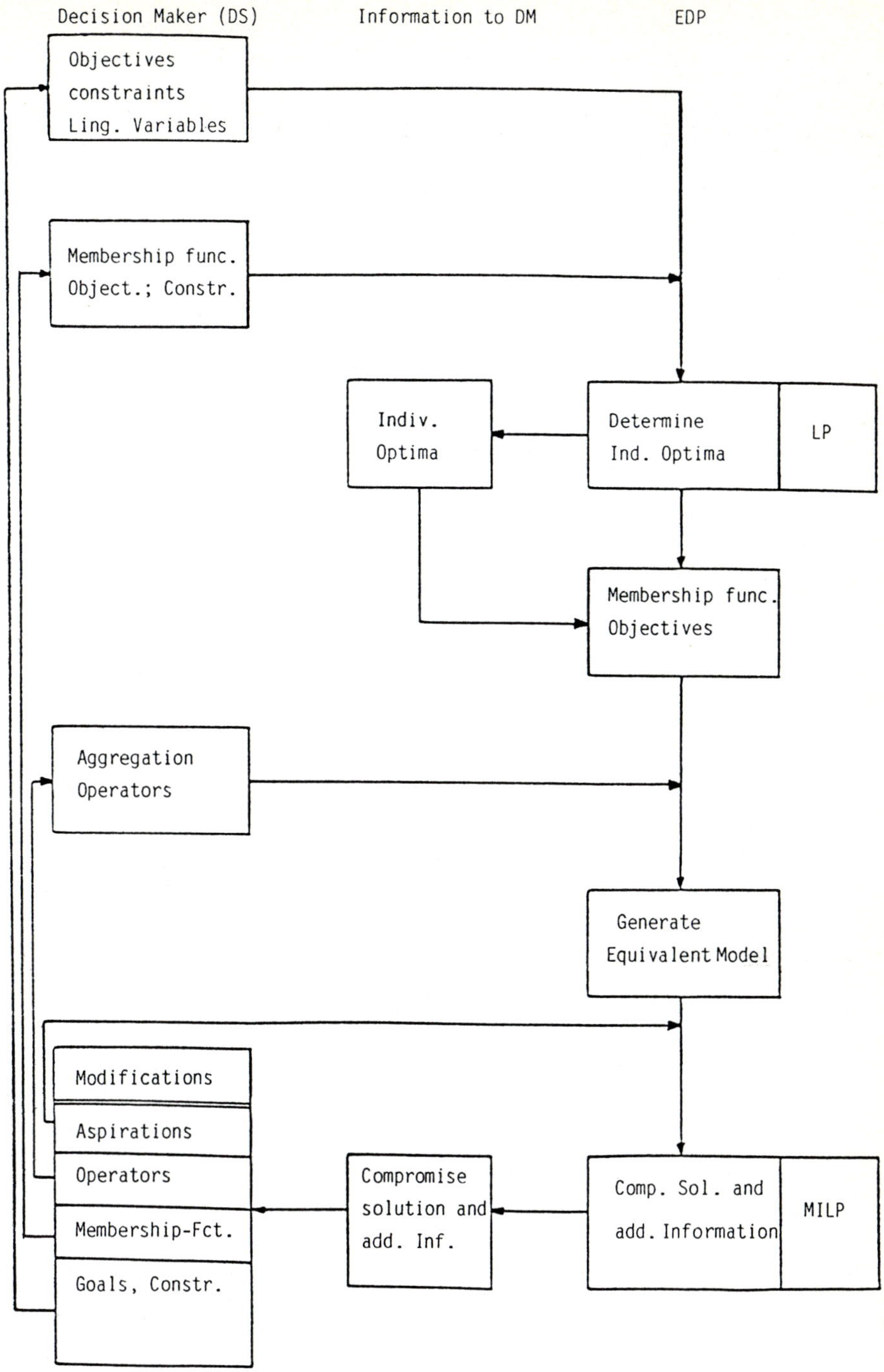
Decision Maker (DS)
Information to DM
EDP
Objectives
constraints
Ling. Variables
Membership func.
Object.; Constr.
Indiv.
Optima
Determine
Ind. Optima
LP
Membership func.
Objectives
Aggregation
Operators
Generate
Equivalent Model
Modifications
Aspirations
Operators
Membership-Fct.
Goals, Constr.
Compromise
solution and
add. Inf.
Comp. Sol. and
add. Information
MILP

Figure 2

SECTION 5:

ROLE OF INFORMATION SYSTEMS IN DECISION MAKING: DATABASE AND MODEL MANAGEMENT ISSUES

RELATIONAL DATA MANAGEMENT AND MODELING SYSTEMS: A TUTORIAL

Daniel R. Dolk
Dept. of Administrative Sciences
Naval Postgraduate School
Monterey, CA 93943
USA

1. INTRODUCTION

The purpose of this tutorial is to offer an overview of the relational model and relational database management systems (RDBMS) with particular emphasis on how they can be used in a management science/operations research (MS/OR) context. There are two underlying themes to the presentation which is intended as a companion piece to another paper included in this volume [11]:

1. RDBMS provide significantly better data analysis tools than are currently available in most MS/OR modeling systems, and

2. RDBMS are vehicles for assimilating modeling resources into an organization's information resource environment; the forces and principles which have resulted in the data management philosophy are equally valid for modeling as well.

The thrust of the discussion is therefore pragmatic rather than theoretical focusing on MIS as opposed to computer science issues. The motivation for data management is examined and the critical requirement of logical and physical independence identified. The hierarchical and network data models are presented as historical counterpoints to the relational model which enforces logical and physical independence via its nonprocedural data manipulation language, SQL. Many of SQL's data manipulation features are demonstrated using the basic transportation model as an example. The essential functions of RDBMS are outlined and ways in which RDBMS can facilitate MS/OR modeling are suggested. Finally, limitations of the relational model and current extensions to RDBMS technology are summarized.

NATO ASI Series, Vol. F48
Mathematical Models for Decision Support
Edited by G. Mitra

2. MOTIVATION FOR DATA MANAGEMENT

Data management has evolved largely in response to the many ills fostered in file-oriented environments which unfortunately still characterize much of MS/OR modeling system practice today. Characteristics of file-oriented environments include:

1. one program-one file: data in a file are usually tailored to one particular application and cannot be used easily by other programs;

2. limited access to data: file environments artificially reduce the information one can derive from data because files are not easily shared or integrated;

3. redundant data: the one program-one file approach results in data being replicated over many files which eventually leads to inconsistent versions of the "same" data.

The underlying philosophy of the data management approach is based on two fundamental principles:

1. data as a shared resource with centralized control, and

2. data independence.

The notion of data as a shared resource presumes that there is some economy of scale with respect to data, i.e. in general there will be multiple sources of demand for any particular instance of data. Rather than replicate the data and distribute it to each of the sources, it makes more sense to provide a single copy of the data along with a standardized way of accessing it. This obviates the problems associated with data redundancy and the tendency for multiple copies of data to fall out of synchronization. Further it provides a centralized source of data which facilitates the establishment and maintenance of data integrity essential to management control of this resource.

Data independence implies that data are stored in a way which is independent of any application program. By providing a uniform means of accessing data via a data manipulation language, all applications are assured of having access to the data they need. This is in direct contrast to the file-oriented environment where data are generally formatted in a way which is especially convenient and efficient for a particular application.

The software system which facilitates the data management approach is a database management system (DBMS) and can be thought of as an operating system for handling data. The DBMS provides a uniform means for defining, storing, and retrieving shared data resources and usually supports one of the logical data models described below.

3. LOGICAL DATA MODELS

Perhaps the most significant characteristic of the data management approach is data independence which is closely allied to the notion of logical and physical independence. Data independence, in the large, refers to the notion that data are viewed, or conceptualized, without consideration of the various application program(s) which may eventually access the data. Consider, as a counterexample, an MPSX [14] file containing data for a linear programming (LP) model, represented in matrix form for eventual solution by a simplex algorithm. The data in this situation have a specific, procedural format which is virtually inaccessible to other programs.

A corollary of data independence is logical and physical independence which means that users should be able to view data without being concerned how data are stored on physical devices such as disk drives ("what" versus "how"). For example, in the relational model, users can view data as tables without being concerned whether the data are stored sequentially, in an ISAM file, or in direct access mode. Logical and physical independence leads naturally to the concept of logical data models, i.e. ways of viewing data which concentrate on the semantics of data (what data means, how data are related, etc.). The details of physical storage of data are left to the DBMS and should be transparent to the user.

There have been a multitude of data models developed but historically, three primary data models have served as the bases for DBMS: hierarchy, network, and relational. A brief overview of the hierarchy and network models is presented as a prelude to the relational model.

3.1 Hierarchy Model

The material presented here is necessarily brief and incomplete. For a more thorough treatment of the hierarchy model, see [9,21].

The hierarchy data model consists of the following:

1. A set of record types;
2. A set of relationships between record types;
3. No more than one relationship between any two record types;
4. Relationships form a tree;
5. All relationships are 1:N (one-to-many).

It should be mentioned here that all DBMS are fundamentally systems for integrating separate files. The hierarchy model simply represents this integration in the form of a tree. Figure 1 provides an example of a 3-level hierarchy consisting of COMPANY/DIVISION/EMPLOYEE. Each level would have been a separate file in the old file processing environment. The files are integrated in the hierarchy model by physically connecting each record at one level with all those records at the next lower level to which there is a logical relationship. Thus, the COMPANY record IBM is connected to the three DIVISION records Marketing, Federal, and R and D. Each of the DIVISION records would in turn be connected to the appropriate EMPLOYEE records to reflect which employees worked for which division. Note that no record may be connected to more than one record above it in the hierarchy, thus we say that the logical relationship is 1:N (one-to-many) down the hierarchy and 1:1 (one-to-one) up the hierarchy.

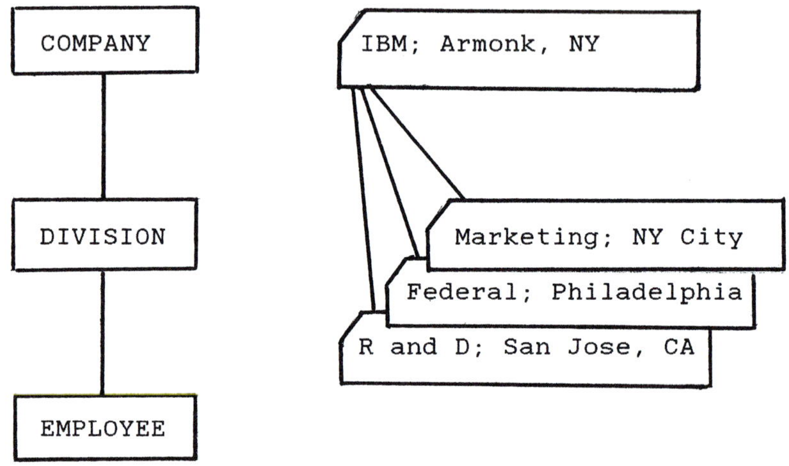

Figure 1: Example of a Hierarchy Data Model

The hierarchy model is a familiar one and relatively easy to implement. Indeed, hierarchical data systems were the forerunners of contemporary DBMS, the most notable example being IBM's Information Management System [17]. The major disadvantage of the hierarchy model is its inability to represent M:N (many-to-many) logical situations. As a result, hierarchical representations facilitate certain kinds of queries at the expense of others and are thus geared towards particular applications. In other words, there is a very limited degree of logical and physical independence.

To demonstrate this phenomenon, consider the transportation model where there are plants shipping a commodity to customers as shown in Figure 2. Assume we tried to model this as a 2-level hierarchy of PLANT/CUST. This structure allows us to answer the query "which customers does the Dallas plant ship to?" easily by simply accessing the Dallas record and seeing which CUST records it's connected to. However, the query "which plants ship to the Chicago customer" is considerably more difficult to answer since it requires accessing each PLANT record and checking which ones are connected to the Chicago CUST. Further, note the redundancy of the Chicago record which must be updated multiple times should there be a change to one of its fields (e.g.: address). This asymmetry is one of the fundamental shortcomings of the hierarchy model.

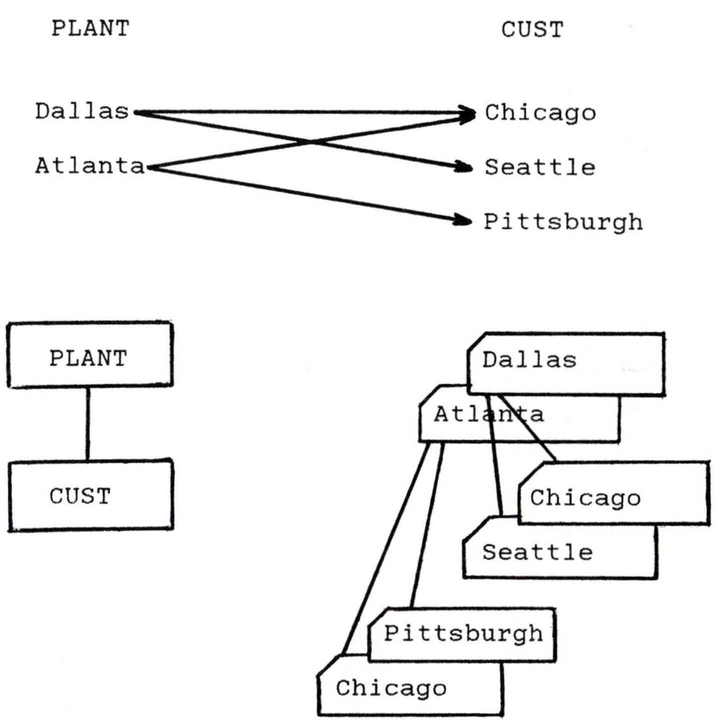

Figure 2: A Hierarchy Representation of the Transportation Model

3.2 Network (CODASYL) Model

The network model overcomes this limitation by allowing confluent hierarchies which meet at a common node [20]. Thus in the network world, we would model the transportation problem by creating a 3rd record type LINK which would be part of two distinct hierarchies having PLANT and CUST as parent nodes respectively (Figure 3). Thus the underlying structure becomes a network instead of a hierarchy.

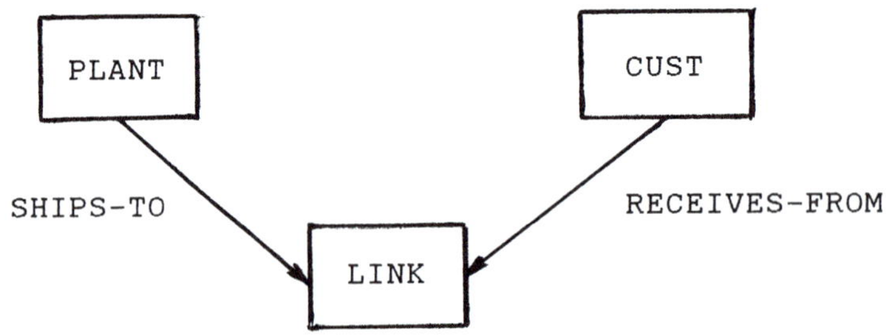

Figure 3: A Network Representation of the Transportation Model

This simple extension to the hierarchy notion was formalized by the CODASYL Data Base Task Group (DBTG) in 1971 [6] and a new terminology introduced. Nodes are **record-types** (e.g., PLANT,CUST,LINK) and relationships between nodes are **sets** (SHIPS-TO and RECEIVES-FROM). The parent node in a set is called the **owner-record** and the sibling node the **member-record**. Logical descriptions of the networks, called **schemas** (Figure 4), consist of a description of all record-types and **items** (fields) within that record-type as well as all sets.

The DBTG specifications also allow different access techniques (called location modes) to be specified for particular sets. For example, the SHIPS-TO set might be sorted by customer-id whereas the RECEIVES-FROM set might be ordered as last-in-first-out (LIFO). This allows the schema to be tailored to particular applications.

Network DBMS became prevalent during the 70's. The M:N logical modeling capability provided significant advantages over straight 1:N hierarchical representations. This, coupled with the "standards" specified by the DBTG committee, resulted in commercially available systems which were able to exhibit reasonably efficient performance.

(Relational systems were still largely experimental during this period [3, 19] partly because of efficiency problems.)

```
SCHEMA NAME IS TRANSPORTATION_MODEL

  RECORD NAME IS PLANT
    DUPLICATES ARE NOT ALLOWED FOR PLANT_ID
      PLANT_ID  TYPE IS CHARACTER 10
      CAPACITY  TYPE IS FIXED     10  2
      NARRATIVE TYPE IS CHARACTER 60

  RECORD NAME IS CUST
    DUPLICATES ARE NOT ALLOWED FOR CUST_ID
      CUST_ID   TYPE IS CHARACTER 10
      DEMAND    TYPE IS FIXED     10  2
      NARRATIVE TYPE IS CHARACTER 60

  RECORD NAME IS LINK
    DUPLICATES ARE NOT ALLOWED FOR PLANT_ID, CUST_ID
      PLANT_ID  TYPE IS CHARACTER 10
      CUST_ID   TYPE IS CHARACTER 10
      COST      TYPE IS FIXED     10  2
      FLOW      TYPE IS FIXED     10  2

  SET NAME IS SHIPS_TO
    OWNER IS PLANT
    ORDER IS SORTED BY DEFINED KEYS
    MEMBER IS LINK
    KEY IS ASCENDING CUST_ID

  SET NAME IS RECEIVES_FROM
    OWNER IS CUST
    ORDER IS LAST
    MEMBER IS LINK
    SET SELECTION IS BY VALUE OF CUST_ID
```

Figure 4: Network Schema for the Transportation Model

The network model fosters the notion of "user as navigator", i.e. the user must find the appropriate path through the network to access the data required. Unfortunately, this can become quite procedural. As a result, networks are often a relatively awkward way for people to view and access their data, especially when networks become complex. Another disadvantage of the network model is that the location mode feature which facilitates reasonable efficiency seriously compromises the notion of logical and physical independence. Specifically, changing a network schema once it has been specified and the database built is quite difficult. This places a high premium on getting the database design right the first time which is an unrealistic expectation in a dynamic data environment.

3.3 Relational Model

Although network DBMS thrived during the 70's, there was intense competition and comparison with the relational model [18]. Codd's introduction of the relational model [7] revolutionized the database world although the market ramifications were not to be felt until about 15 years later.

The relational model provides a seductive blend of a "natural" way of interacting with data bolstered by firm theoretical underpinnings. Specifically, data are viewed simply as 2-dimensional tables. Relationships between data are not hard-wired a priori but can be generated dynamically according to user needs and based on data values. Users may fashion particular views (sometimes called virtual tables) from existing tables which can be then treated like any other tables. Tables can be further manipulated using simple algebraic operators.

Codd's original realtional terminology, though still embraced by academia, has given way to a more pragmatic rendition fostered by the multitude of commercial systems now available. In lay terms (accompanied by the formal terminology in parentheses), the relational model consists of **tables** (relations) comprising **rows** (tuples) and **columns** (attributes). Each column has a **domain** from which subsequent values may be drawn. Each table has a **key** which consists of one or more columns, the values for which will uniquely identify each row in the table. Rows and columns are order-independent and no two rows may be identical.

Figure 5 provides a relational rendition of the transportation model discussed earlier. There are three tables: PLANT, CUST, and LINK. The table PLANT has three columns, **plant_id**, **capacity**, and **narrative**, with the key being **plant_id**. The domain for the capacity column is R+, the positive real numbers. A row of the table corresponds to the collection of values where each column is assigned a value from its domain ("Null" is a special value meaning no value is known; keys cannot be "Null"). A key may be include more than one column as in the table LINK where **plant_id** and **cust_id** are required to determine unique rows.

The relational model is based on set theory and has been fertile grounds for computer science research since its inception. Codd devised both a relational algebra and a relational calculus as a means of manipulating relations which has eventually developed into the SQL data manipulation language described in the next section. Codd also presented design criteria, called **normal forms**, which guide the formation of relations to avoid updating irregularities. Although many normal forms have been identified, the first three normal forms are widely accepted and say, in essence:

1. A relation shall have no repeating groups;

2. Every non-key attribute (column) of a table is a function of the key, the whole key, and nothing but the key [15].

The relations in Figure 5 are in 3rd normal form which means they satisfy these criteria. The LINK table, for instance, is in 1st normal form because it has no repeating groups. If we had tried to model it as LINK(plant_id,{cust_id}) where the curly brackets refer to multiple values of **cust_id**, this would have resulted in records of variable length since different plants would have different numbers of customers. Relational theory insists on fixed length **flat files** as shown in Figure 5.

```
PLANT(plant_id,capacity,narrative)

     'Atlanta',15000,'Atlanta plant'
     'Dallas ',20000,'Dallas plant'


CUST(cust_id,demand,narrative)

     'Chicago    ',7500,'Chicago customer'
     'Seattle    ',4500,'Seattle customer'
     'Pittsburgh',5000,'Pittsburgh customer'


LINK(plant_id,cust_id,cost,flow)

     'Dallas ','Chicago    ',150,2500
     'Dallas ','Seattle    ',175,4500
     'Atlanta','Pittsburgh',210,5000
     'Atlanta','Chicago    ',150,5000
```

Figure 5: Relational Representation of Transportation Model

2nd and 3rd normal forms are based on the concept of **functional dependency** wherein one attribute is depicted as a function of one or more other attributes. For example, we can say that an employee's age is functionally dependent on employee name, since the name uniquely determines the value of age (i.e. if name is 'Fred Smith' then we know Fred's age is 33, say). Functional dependency is an integral part of relational theory but beyond the scope of this tutorial. An extensive literature exists on functional dependency and normalization which the interested reader may consult [15, 22].

Returning to the example, LINK is in 2nd normal form becuase the non-key attributes, **cost** and **flow**, both depend on the composite key, **plant_id** and **cust_id**. If we had included a non-key attribute **cust_address**, this would violate 2nd normal form since **cust_address** depends only on the **cust_id** part of the key. LINK is in 3rd normal form because neither **cost** nor **flow** is a function of each other. If we had included an attribute called **cost_surtax** which was some percentage of **cost**, then this would depend on **cost** and violate 3rd normal form. The details of normalization need not concern us further but it is important to realize that they provide criteria for designing tables which satisfy certain desirable update capabilities.

The relational model will be examined further in the next section. Advantages of the relational approach include the "natural" view of data as tables, the strong underlying theory, the high degree of logical and physical independence, and the apparent acceptance of RDBMS in the marketplace. Although commercial RDBMS have only been available since 1980 in the US, the trend seems to be distinctly towards the relational approach.

Disadvantages of the relational model include a lack of standards concerning what consititutes a relational system. Codd has been very explicit, bordering on dogmatic, concerning the properties of a "pure" relational system. His criteria are severe and have been greeted with skepticism by relational vendors who claim his requirements are unrealistic. Standards have been developed, however, for the SQL data manipulation language [1]. The relational approach has suffered in the past from performance inefficiencies resulting from query optimization [23], i.e. the strategy for accessing the physical representation of the data to answer queries. In particular, queries which require the integration of several different tables can become quite time-consuming. It is not surprising that a system which enforces a high degree of logical and physical independence and which is not oriented towards a particular application will suffer peformance penalties. File-oriented systems will ordinarily outperform DBMS for any particular application but at the cost of limited use of data. Finally, the relational model has limited semantic capabilities, for example it has difficulty representing time [2], mathematical models [4], and various artificial intelligence constructs such as inheritance and rules.

4. RELATIONAL DATA MANIPULATION: SQL

A key to any DBMS is the language which allows users to store, retrieve, and manipulate data. In the relational universe, this is facilitated by SQL which is about to become a standard [1]. Before delving into SQL, a brief background on relational algebra and relational calculus is required.

4.1 Relational Algebra and Relational Calculus

Codd's original paper developed both an algebra and a calculus for manipulating relations (tables). The underlying notion in the algebra approach is that relations are sets and therefore subject to the standard kinds of operations which can be performed on sets. The closure property is critical here, i.e. any algebraic operation on one or more sets must always yield a set as its result.

The various algebraic operations which pertain are (note: the terms "table" and "relation" are used interchangeably):

1. Union, Intersection, Difference: Only if two relations have exactly the same attributes (columns) can these standard set operations be applied.

2. Product: The Cartesian product of two relations is a new relation resulting from the concatenation of every row in the 1st relation with every row in the 2nd relation.

3. Projection: Projection allows selection of a subset of columns in a relation. The relation PLINK(plant_id,cust_id, cost) is a projection of LINK.

4. Selection: Selection allows selection of a subset of rows in a table. Selecting only those rows in LINK where COST > 150 is an example.

   Note that projection and selection allow one to retrieve subtables from within a table.

5. Join: A combination of product, selection, and optionally projection operations. Join is a central concept in the relational model which allows separate tables to be integrated via attributes which the tables have in common. For example, if we want to create a table PROD_LINK(plant_id,cust_id,capacity,demand), we first do a product of PLANT x LINK x CUST, then a selection of rows where PLANT.plant_id = LINK.plant_id and LINK.cust_id = CUST.cust_id and finally a projection of the four columns.

Relational algebra is too procedural to do directly but it provides a conceptual basis for what's taking place when using a nonprocedural language like SQL.

Relational calculus is a different approach to data manipulation which treats relations as predicates in a first order logic. Details of the relational calculus will not discussed here; the interested reader is referred to [22].

4.2 SQL

SQL is the query language by which the user performs data description, manipulation, and control. It is an offshoot of the SEQUEL language developed for IBM's System R experimental RDBMS [5]. SQL is based loosely on relational calculus but can easily be understood in terms of the relational algebra sketched above. It may used as a stand-alone query language or in embedded mode within a high level programming language such as Pascal or Fortran. In its simplest form, it can be used by people with little previous exposure to computer languages but it also has sufficiently sophisticated features that very elaborate and complex queries can be specified by expert users.

The rest of this section provides various examples based on the transportation model relations in Figure 5. The primary intent is to show how SQL can perform elementary data manipulation and analysis for MS/OR modeling applications. Note, for example, that the **flow** attribute in the LINK table is the decision variable in the transportation model and that values for **flow** would be derived from an appropriate optimization algorithm. Thus, many of the features of SQL discussed below can be viewed as post-optimization information filters.

4.2.1 Data description

Data description refers to the definition of the various tables (known as the relational schema) which are to be contained in the database. The assumption is that one has done some form of normalization in generating the structure for these tables. CREATE TABLE is the SQL command for defining a table's structure. The CREATE TABLE command for the PLANT table in Figure 5 is shown below:

```
CREATE TABLE PLANT
(PLANT_ID  CHAR(10)  NOT NULL,
 CAPACITY  NUMBER(10,2),
 NARRATIVE CHAR(60))
```

Since **plant_id** is the key for PLANT, it must be specified as NOT NULL in the schema.

Another important aspect of data description is the ability to create views, or virtual tables, out of existing tables.

The view capability allows users to see only that part of the database in which they are interested. Examples of the view command are presented below in the subsection on data manipulation.

4.2.2 Data entry and modification

SQL's data entry facilities are quite limited. For example, to enter the first row in the PLANT table, one would use the INSERT INTO table command as follows:

```
INSERT INTO PLANT VALUES
('Atlanta',15000,'Atl. plant')
```

This command would have to be repeated for every row to be input which is obviously a tedious process. Most RDBMS provide screen and forms utilities which significantly facilitate the data entry process.

The UPDATE command is used to change values in a particular row. For example, to change the capacity for the Dallas plant from 15000 to 17000:

```
UPDATE PLANT SET CAPACITY = 17000
WHERE  PLANT_ID='Dallas'
```

The DELETE command deletes rows. To reflect the discontinuation of the Dallas-Seattle link, for example:

```
DELETE FROM LINK
WHERE  PLANT_ID='Dallas' AND
       CUST_ID='Seattle'
```

4.2.3 Data manipulation

The full SQL manipulation syntax becomes quite complicated but the basic structure is predicated upon performing projections and/or selections to isolate rows and columns easily, and performing joins to link two or more tables:

```
SELECT attribute(s)
FROM   table(s)
WHERE  boolean_condition(s)
```

The SELECT part of the clause actually specifies the projection whereas the WHERE clause specifies the selection. Joins are also specified in the WHERE clause as we shall see below. The following three SQL commands demonstrate how projection and selection work (Note: for notational convenience, SQL terms are shown in upper case, attribute and table names in lower case, and responses to each query in boldface):

1. "List all information about plants."

```
SELECT *
FROM   plant
```

('*' means list all columns; SQL would list the entire PLANT table as shown in Figure 5.)

2. "List plant_id and capacity for all plants." (Projection)

```
SELECT plant_id,capacity
FROM   plant
```

Atlanta 15000
Dallas 20000

3. "List plant_id and capacity for all plants with capacity greater than 17500." (Selection and projection)

```
SELECT plant_id,capacity
FROM   plant
WHERE  capacity > 17500
```

Dallas 20000

Join is the mechanism by which two or more tables are linked together. Joins can be accomplished only when two tables have attributes in common. For example, tables PLANT and LINK can be joined in the transportation model as can tables CUST and LINK since they have attributes in common. In general, attributes need not have the same name to be joined, but they must have the same domain. Further there must be a logical basis for the join. Thus one would not attempt to join PLANT and CUST on their respective attributes capacity and demand even though those attributes have the same domain. In practice the join could be done but the result would be meaningless. The following example performs a simple join:

"List plant_id & capacity of all plants which ship to Chicago."

```
SELECT plant_id,capacity
FROM   plant,link
WHERE  link.cust_id = 'Chicago' AND
       plant.plant_id = link.plant_id
```

Atlanta 15000
Dallas 20000

Note that two tables must be specified in the FROM clause and that the join is specified in the WHERE clause by the boolean condition plant.plant_id = link.plant_id. SQL provides the table.attribute notation to differentiate between two attributes with the same name in different tables.

One of the most powerful features of the relational model is the ability to define views from underlying tables:

"Create a view for the Dallas production manager which shows his own production capacity, who he ships to, and how much."

```
CREATE VIEW DALLAS_PROD AS
(SELECT plant.capacity,link.cust_id,link.flow
 FROM   plant,link
 WHERE  plant.plant_id = 'Dallas' AND
        plant.plant_id = link.plant_id)
```

This would create the following "virtual" table:

```
20000,'Chicago',150
20000,'Seattle',175
```

which the user can then access like any other table. This exemplifies the concept of logical and physical independence emphasized earlier, for there may well be no physical table as such corresponding to DALLAS_PROD. Views also allow the database (and/or model) administrator to design information filters for various users which gives them exactly the information they need and nothing else.

SQL provides a host of advanced features for more elaborate queries and report generation. Two such features are built-in functions and grouping:

"For the distribution manager, show the total shipping amounts and average cost for each customer."

```
SELECT cust_id,SUM(flow),AVG(cost)
FROM   link
GROUP BY cust_id
```

```
Chicago     7500   162.5
Seattle     4500   175
Pittsburgh  5000   210
```

The GROUP BY clause segments the LINK table into as many groups as there are different cust_id's. Then for each group, flows are summed and costs are averaged.

The SQL subquery allows arbitrarily deep nesting of clauses to facilitate complex queries. The join above can be rendered alternatively as a subquery, for example:

```
SELECT plant_id,capacity
FROM   plant
WHERE  plant_id IN
```

```
        (SELECT plant_id
         FROM   link
         WHERE  cust_id = 'Chicago')
```

Subqueries are evaluated from the bottom up so, in this case, the SELECT clause in parentheses would be evaluated first to yield the set **Dallas** and **Atlanta**. The main clause would then be evaluated to yield the same result as in the join.

Another very useful feature is the macro. Macros allow SQL commands to be saved and invoked with a single command. For example, assume we generate and save the following SQL command as a macro:

"List all low volume (< 1000 units) shipments."

```
SELECT plant_id,cust_id,flow
FROM   link
WHERE  flow < 1000

SAVE LOW_FLOW
```

A user can now invoke this SQL command by simply typing **GET LOW_FLOW**. Macros can also be made parameter-dependent, thus if people have a different concept of what constitutes a low flow, we could parameterize the value as follows:

```
SELECT plant_id,cust_id,flow
FROM   link
WHERE  flow < &low_flow

SAVE LOW_FLOW
```

The "&" indicates to SQL that the user must be queried for the value thus when the user types **GET LOW_FLOW**, SQL will ask for the low_flow value. Alternatively, one could specify **GET LOW_FLOW 1000** and 1000 would be substituted in the query.

The obvious advantage of macros is that they allow the casual user to access the database without having to learn SQL syntax. For familiar, well-structured models like the transportation model, a set of macros can be devised by a model administrator to generate the necessary queries and reports for the user community.

4.2.4 Embedded SQL

The above examples show SQL usage in stand-alone mode. SQL can also be embedded in host programming languages like Pascal, C, or Fortran. In this mode, SQL commands are issued as statements in the program. The program is then precompiled to generate the correct code corresponding to the SQL-specific commands and finally compiled by the regular host language compiler. At execution time, data are retrieved from the RDBMS and stored in program variables using the notion of cursors. Cursors make programming with SQL somewhat tricky but the embedded feature opens the possibility of writing solution algorithms which directly access an RDBMS (see Section 5).

4.2.5 SQL summary

SQL is a nonprocedural language for data description, manipulation, and control in an RDBMS. It is suitable for ad hoc queries by users with little computing sophistication as well as for complex queries and applications requiring programming expertise. Its utility for modeling applications has been demonstrated above. A distinct advantage of SQL is that it is becoming a standard in the relational industry. Not only is it being adopted as a Federal standard [1] but every major relational vendor now offers some version of SQL. This should provide a significant degree of portability across different RDBMS.

The major weaknesses of SQL stem primarily from its lack of robust programming constructs. When SQL was developed about 15 years ago, it was conceived primarily in the context of a data retrieval tool. Current trends in the database world are towards providing an overall application programming environment within the DBMS. To accomplish this, a data manipulation language must facilitate not only retrieval, but also the familiar programming structures like IF-THEN-ELSE, iteration, and recursion. A language with these features would be particularly useful in implementing knowledge-based applications for example, an area in which SQL is not well-suited. It would also be valuable as a model manipulation language around which to develop solution algorithms as discussed below.

5. RDBMS AND MODELING SYSTEMS

A DBMS is the software system which facilitates the storage, access and manipulation of shared data. It can be viewed as an operating system for data resources. A relational DBMS is one which supports the relational data model. There has been a great deal of controversy, much of it generated by Codd himself, concerning the criteria which define a "truly" relational DBMS. Most people agree, however, that all DBMS's, regardless of which data model they support, should provide the general functional capabilities described below [16].

5.1 Functions of a DBMS

A DBMS is a complicated piece of system software because, like an operating system, it must provide multiple users access to multiple data resources. Further, in the general case, a DBMS must be able to facilitate multiple access to the same data resource at the same time. The primary functions of a DBMS are:

1. Data storage, retrieval, and modification. Provide data description and manipulation so that users can define, store, retrieve, and modify data.

2. Data integrity. Since data is community property, the integrity of the data is critical. A DBMS should provide mechanisms for establishing and enforcing data integrity constraints, e.g. automatically flagging data input values which fall outside a predefined range of acceptable values. (Note: DBMS's currently do a poor job of enforcing this kind of data integrity.)

3. Information resource dictionary (IRD). The IRD should contain a description of the data resources available in the DBMS (metadata) and relationships between these resources. It should also catalog data integrity constraints as described above.

4. Concurrent processing. As with operating systems, several users may want to access the same data resource at the same time. Mechanisms to coordinate access in these situations are vital to avoid improper results from multiple concurrent updates and to prevent deadly embrace where two users simultaneously want the data resource which the other has appropriated. Usually some form of resource locking or timestamping is used to resolve potential conflicts.

5. Logical transactions. DBMS's need to support the notion of a transaction where multiple changes to a database must take place before the transaction can be considered logically complete (e.g., updating a payroll file). In this situation either all the changes or none of the changes must be posted to the database in order to maintain data integrity.

6. Recovery from failure. Failure may occur as a result of hardware (disk or CPU crash) or software (transaction aborts while running) malfunctions. Failure may leave the database in a partially modified state which the DBMS must be able to rectify. Transaction logs are commonly used to keep a journal of all database modifications and to be able to back out of partially executed transactions when failure occurs.

7. Security. In general, it is not desirable to allow all users access to all data. The ideal is to provide users access only to those resources for which they have need, and to deny access to the complement of that set. DBMS's provide security mechanisms which restrict user access as specified by a database administrator.

8. Provide utility services. DBMS's provide various utilities which make the particular system easier to use. Examples of these utilities may include report generators, database restructuring/reloading, and interfaces to other DBMS's or file systems.

5.2 Modeling Systems Applications

One of the objectives of this tutorial is to show how the versatile data management capabilities which RDBMS provide can be used advantageously in modeling applications. When comparing RDBMS with matrix generators, for example, the RDBMS are clearly superior in that they provide more flexible data manipulation (e.g.: information filters) as well as offering a high degree of data sharing. Thus, in an RDBMS environment, optimization results are available to anyone who can use basic SQL as opposed to having to learn the laborious procedural syntax of matrix generation systems. In general, it is safe to say that RDBMS provide significantly greater data manipulation capabilties than can be found in most stand-alone modeling systems.

Given the power of RDBMS, the issue arises of how best to interface modeling systems with RDBMS. At least four possible scenarios present themselves:

1. RDBMS as stand-alone;

2. Embedded SQL in solution algorithms;

3. Extended SQL as a programming language;

4. Model management system.

The most obvious scenario is to use RDBMS as a stand-alone repository of modeling data and to build links between the RDBMS and appropriate solution algorithms and/or matrix generators. These links would be programs which transform the data as tables in the RDBMS to the required format of a solution algorithm, and vice versa. For example, a particularly fruitful link would be to connect RDBMS with MPSX. This would provide the best of both worlds for linear programming applications by combining the data manipulation power of a relational system with the solution capabilities of a proven matrix generation system. [10] investigates the RDBMS stand-alone scenario in detail and shows SQL commands which can be used to transform a relational representation of a model into matrix form.

The disadvantage of the stand-alone approach is that a separate link program must be written for each solution algorithm which is to be integrated with the RDBMS. This could result in a significant programming effort if many solution algorithms are to be available in the modeling environment.

Another approach (Scenario 2) is to write solution algorithms which access the RDBMS directly. This would require the use of embedded SQL to perform the necessary input/output in whatever language was being used to develop the algorithm. The obvious advantage is there's only one input/output structure, namely the relational representation. One hopes that algorithm developers would adopt this approach in future applications but there is a serious disadvantage here as well. Although SQL is becoming a standard, this does not carry over to the RDBMS level, thus a program written to access the ORACLE RDBMS will most likely not work if it has to access the INGRES DBMS instead. Thus, solution algorithms would become RDBMS-dependent and lose a large degree of portability. This will remain a problem until there is a resolution to the issue of RDBMS standardization.

Scenarios 1 and 2 are primarily implementation issues and can be realized using existing relational tools. Scenarios 3 and 4 are more conceptual in nature and give rise to a number of research issues. Scenario 3 envisions all data manipulation and algorithm development being done completely within an RDBMS. Thus, there is no longer a concept of an external solution algorithm; rather algorithms are developed entirely in SQL or a suitable substitute. This raises the research question of whether SQL can be extended to provide the necessary programming features for robust algorithm development and, if so, whether it will be efficient enough to solve industrial strength problems in a reasonable amount of time. Current RDBMS performance would argue against this hypothesis but [13] have shown that a recursive form of SQL does surprisingly well in solving certain problems compared with external algorithms. Also, it is reasonable to expect that RDBMS technology will continue to show improvements in performance; recall that commercial RDBMS have only been available since 1980.

The primary advantage of this approach, if realizable, is that, were extended SQL to remain a standard, portability would no longer remain an issue. Thus data and algorithms could be transferred from RDBMS to RDBMS without modification. Further, this approach would facilitate an object-oriented approach to modeling in that algorithms could easily be bound to model instances thus promoting more proper usage of mathematical models. The major disadvantage of this approach concerns the large body of efficient solution algorithms which currently exists for a wide range of models. These algorithms would have to be rewritten in extended SQL if they were to become part of the system and this clearly is a gargantuan task. Even if this scenario turns out to be feasible, it is likely that there will still be a need for interfacing with external algorithms.

The final scenario is an all-encompassing approach which argues for the notion of models as a shared, centralized resource supported by a model management system (MMS). This, of course, is a direct parallel to the data management philosophy wherein the MMS would be to models what the DBMS is to data. This raises a host of research issues with regard to development of the MMS:

1. Model representation: a formal representation for models is required which is equivalent in power to the relational data model [12];

2. Model manipulation: a powerful language is required which performs not only retrieval but facilitates solution and analysis, model integration, and algorithm development as well;

3. Model sharing: control mechanisms (concurrency, security, recovery/backup, integrity) must be established for sharing modeling resources.

This final scenario is considered in more detail in the companion piece in this collection [11]. Suffice it to say here that, in our opinion, the MS/OR community can benefit immensely from adopting a broader approach to modeling which coordinates with existing organizational information resource technology and practice.

6. SUMMARY

The relational data model is based on the view of "data as tables" which is supported by a formalism grounded in set theory. A set of design principles based on functional dependency guide the formation of "normalized" relations. Manipulation of tables can be characterized in the form of a relational algebra or a first order logic. The relational model achieves a very high degree of logical and physical independence which allows users a more "natural" view of data. The tradeoff is in the area of performance but it appears that, despite the relative inefficiency of RDBMS compared to other systems, the relational approach is carrying the day in the database world.

This tutorial has tried to demonstrate the benefits of using RDBMS with modeling applications and has discussed ways in which modeling systems and RDBMS can interact. The major advantages of using RDBMS for modeling purposes can be summarized as:

1. significantly more effective data manipulation;

2. increased data and model sharing under centralized control;

3. access to more organizational information resources;

4. bringing modeling under the organization's information resource umbrella.

Finally, it should be noted that relational technology has been around over 15 years which makes it ancient by computing standards. The relational model, though elegant, has limited semantic range [8]. It is difficult, for example, to represent time, knowledge-based structures, and inheritance properties within the relational framework. There is a particularly strong demand for linking RDBMS with expert system tools such as Prolog. There is also much work currently going on in the area of object-oriented database (and model) management which attempts to extend the range and utility of the relational approach. Although we can certainly expect to see the relational model undergo substantial transformations in the coming years, its utility as a data management tool nevertheless argues strongly for it being an indispensable element in contemporary modeling systems.

7. REFERENCES

1. American National Standards Institute. [Draft proposed] American National Standards database language SQL. ANSI X3H2, American National Standards Institute, New York 1984.

2. Ariav, G. A temporally oriented data model. **ACM Transactions on Database Systems**, 11,4 (December 1986), 499-527.

3. Astrahan, M.M. et al. System R: Relational approach to database management. **ACM Transactions on Database Systems**, 1,2 (June 1976), 97-137.

4. Blanning, R.H. A relational theory of model management. Working Paper No. 85-106, Owen Graduate School of Management, Vanderbilt University, Nashville, TN, 1985.

5. Chamberlin, D.D. SEQUEL 2: A unified approach to data definition, manipulation, and control. **IBM Journal of Research and Development**, 20,6 (1976), 560-575.

6. CODASYL DBTG Report. Conference on data systems languages, ACM New York, 1971.

7. Codd, E.F. A relational model of data for large shared data banks. **Communications of the ACM**, 13,6 (June 1970).

8. Codd, E.F. Extending the database relational model to capture more meaning. **ACM Transactions on Databaase Systems**, 4,4 (Dec. 1979), 397-434.

9. Date, C.J. **An Introduction to Database Systems: Volume 1.** Addison-Wesley: 3rd edition (1981).

10. Dolk, D.R. Model management and structured modeling: The role of an information resource dictionary system. Naval Postgraduate School Working Paper 87-12, Monterey, CA 93943, June 1987 (to appear in **Communications of the ACM**).

11. Dolk, D.R. Model management systems for operations research: A prospectus. NATO ASI Conference on Mathematical Models for Decision Support, 1987.

12. Geoffrion, A.M. An introduction to structured modeling. **Management Science**, 33,5 (May 1987), 547-588.

13. Ho, L., Nygard, K. and Shapiro, L. Data base management systems as solvers in model management systems. Computer Science/Operations Research Dept., North Dakota State University, Fargo ND, 1987.

14. IBM World Trade Corporation. IBM Mathematical Programming System Extended/370 (MPSX/370) Program Reference Manual, 2nd ed. No. SH19-1095-1, New York and Paris, 1976.

15. Kent, W. A simple guide to five normal forms in relational database theory. **Communications of the ACM**, 26,2 (February 1983), 120-125.

16. Kroenke, D.K. **Database Processing, 2nd edition.** Science Research Associates, 1983.

17. McGee, W.C. The IMS/VS system. **IBM Systems Journal**, 16,2 (June 1977).

18. Michaels, A.S., Mittman, B. and Carlson, C.R. A comparison of relational and CODASYL approaches to data-base management, **ACM Computing Surveys**, 8,1 (March 1976), 125-151.

19. Stonebraker, M.R. et al. The design and implementation of INGRES. **ACM Transactions on Database Systems**, 1,3 (1976), 189-222.

20. Taylor, R.W. and Frank, R.L. CODASYL data-base management systems. **ACM Computing Surveys**, 8,1 (March 1976), 67-104.

21. Tsichritzis, D.C. and Lochovsky, F.H. Hierarchical data-base management: A survey. **ACM Computing Surveys**, 8,1 (March 1976), 105-123.

22. Ullman, J. **Principles of Database Systems**. Computer Science Press, Woodland Hills, CA (1980).

23. Wong, E. and Youssefi, K. Decomposition - A strategy for query processing. **ACM Transactions on Database Systems**, 1,3 (1976), 223-241.

MODEL MANAGEMENT SYSTEMS FOR OPERATIONS RESEARCH: A PROSPECTUS

Daniel R. Dolk
Naval Postgraduate School
Dept. of Administrative Sciences
Monterey, CA 93943

1. INTRODUCTION

As modeling becomes more important in our business and decision-making activities, the need for versatile modeling systems becomes more intense. The prevailing paradigm of DSS views model management as one of the three main components of a DSS [20]. The notion of a model management system (MMS) to support this function has been around for 10 years or so [21], yet the development of MMS's has occurred largely on an ad hoc basis. No MMS on a scale equivalent to existing database management systems (DBMS) currently exists.

The purpose of this paper is to give substance to the notion of an MMS and to suggest that, by the confluence of technology from OR and computer science (Figure 1-1), an MMS equivalent in generality and scope to relational DBMS's is now within reach. The discussion will be directed towards operations research (OR) applications, although an MMS should have wide applicability to modeling disciplines lying outside OR (e.g.: programming and database design) as well.

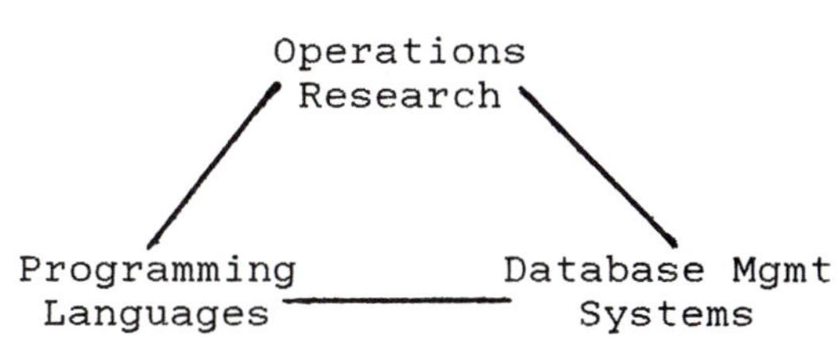

Figure 1-1: Integration of Modeling Traditions from Operations Research and Computer Science

NATO ASI Series, Vol. F48
Mathematical Models for Decision Support
Edited by G. Mitra

The paper is structured as follows. The next section develops the concept of an MMS in terms of its objectives and functional requirements. Section 3 suggests three underlying paradigms from the modeling traditions of OR, programming languages, and database management which can be used to satisfy these functional requirements: structured modeling, object-oriented programming, and relational database management. A production-and-inventory optimization problem is presented and used throughout the succeeding sections to demonstrate the various aspects of an MMS. Sections 4, 5, and 6 describe in more detail how structured modeling, object-oriented programming, and relational DBMS facilitate model description, manipulation, and control respectively. Section 7 summarizes the outlook for an MMS based on the fusion of these paradigms.

2. FUNCTIONAL REQUIREMENTS OF AN MMS

Functional requirements for an information system are often derived in a top-down fashion via iterative refinement [22]. The first step in this process is defining the overall organizational goals and then working down to finer levels of detail.

The overall organizational objective with respect to model management is the recognition of models as a sharable resource requiring systematic management and control [7]. The notion of sharing is critical since the modeling process involves many different participants. Builders, administrators, and end-user clients require access to models at different stages of the modeling life cycle.

The need for managing models requires an information system which we call an MMS, which supports all aspects of the modeling life cycle. In general, an MMS must facilitate the description, manipulation, and administrative control of models in a shared environment. Requirements for each of these dimensions have been developed in previous works [4,8,13].

2.1 Model Description

Critical to the development of model management is an underlying formalism equivalent in power to the relational theory which prevails in the database world. A modeling formalism must prescribe a uniform and consistent means for representing models. Additionally this formalism must be sufficiently robust to capture diverse classes of models since an MMS is intended to be a general tool for supporting "modeling in the large". Without such a theoretical foundation, separate MMS's will, of necessity, have to be built for specific applications.

A modeling formalism must also support the notion of multiple views of a model in the same way relational theory facilitates views of data. The ability to look at different levels of abstraction of a model is essential to support the user community of builders, administrators, and clients. Builders may want a mathematical view, administrators a natural language view, and clients a graphical view of the same model, for example.

A less obvious requirement for model description is that the model structure and its underlying data be relatively independent. In particular, it's important to allow data values to be added, changed, or deleted without having to change the associated model structure. The best example of this occurs in optimization models where the model structure is represented in matrix form. Adding two new destinations to a transportation problem causes new rows and/or columns to be added to the matrix. If the model structure were a full, indexed mathematical description, however, no change would be required to this representation to accommodate new sources or destinations. Model and data independence increases the flexibility of specifying and analyzing model instances.

Another important parameter of model description is model integrity. A formalism must also designate what constitutes a well-specified model in terms of its consistency and completeness.

2.2 Model Manipulation

Model manipulation involves the application of various operators to model descriptions. A modeling formalism must also accommodate model manipulation as well as description. Recall that the relational theory specifies both a relational algebra and a relational calculus as data manipulation operators.

Model manipulation requires more than the operations available in the relational algebra or calculus, however. Specific high level operations relevant to OR models, for example, include evaluation (in the sense that spreadsheets support), satisfaction (feasibility), optimization, and sensitivity analysis. These operators are all composed of sequences of lower level operators, the nature of which varies depending on the model being operated upon. Evaluation of a discrete event simulation model requires significantly different operators from that of an economic forecasting model. What is required, therefore, is an underlying methodology for defining operations on models and then associating these operations with the appropriate model instances to which they apply.

A central concept with respect to model manipulation is the independence of model descriptions from the operators which perform on them. In particular, one view of operators may be simply as a set of algorithms which can be applied to various model instances. Application of one of these algorithms should not require the model description to be changed explicitly by the user. For example, applying a simplex algorithm to optimize a model represented in mathematical form should not require the user to transform the mathematical representation into the appropriate matrix input. This should be done transparently by the MMS.

One ramification of model/operator independence is the need for an extensive library of operator algorithms plus the corresponding transformation procedures for converting model descriptions into the appropriate data structures which these algorithms can manipulate. Model manipulation must also include integrity enforcement operators to ensure the model and data integrity.

2.3 Model Control

An MMS assumes that a single user may access multiple models and, conversely, that a single model may be accessed, possibly concurrently, by many users. Model control is concerned with the coordination of this shared access to model resources. In particular, model control requires an underlying environment which facilitates concurrent access to models and data, supports the independence of data from applications which use that data, enforces security and privacy, provides failure recovery mechanisms, and defines transaction boundaries. In short, this is tantamount to saying that an MMS must provide functional counterparts for models that DBMS's do for data.

2.4 Summary

Figure 2-1 summarizes the major functional requirements of an MMS. There are many similarities to DBMS's but this is not surprising since an MMS must be able to handle the underlying data associated with model structures as well as the structures themselves. An MMS on the scale defined by Figure 2-1 exceeds the capabilities of any existing modeling system (although many systems exhibit a subset of these features; see [14] for a more detailed comparison). However, the theory and technology are now available to realize a system of this generality. The next section presents paradigms from the fields of OR, programming languages, and database management which respectively satisfy the requirements of model description, manipulation, and control.

MODELS AS A SHARED ORGANIZATIONAL RESOURCE

DESCRIPTION	MANIPULATION	CONTROL
Model representation formalism	Manipulation defn methodology	Shared environment
Multiple models/views	Library of operators	Concurrent access
Model/data independence	Model/solver independence	Data/applic. independence
Model integrity	Integrity enforcement operators	Security and privacy, failure recovery
Model integration	Integration operators	Communication protocols

Figure 2-1: Functional Requirements of an MMS

3. PARADIGMS FOR MMS

Building blocks are now available for constructing an MMS which satisfies the functional requirements of Figure 2-1. These building blocks constitute a confluence of technology from the areas of OR, programming languages, and database management. In particular, we propose Geoffrion's structured modeling as the formalism for model description, object-oriented programming as the methodology for model manipulation, and relational DBMS as the environment for model control (Figure 3-1).

In order to show how each of these disciplines satisfies the requisite requirements, we present here a model which will be used as an ongoing example throughout the succeeding sections. The model is a multiperiod production and inventory problem used by [12] to demonstrate various linear programming modeling systems. The problem is to determine the optimal mix of products to manufacture from raw materials on hand. The objective is to maximize profit adjusted by storage costs and the remaining inventory of raw materials. A mathematical representation is displayed in Figure 3-2 and associated data values presented in Figure 3-3.

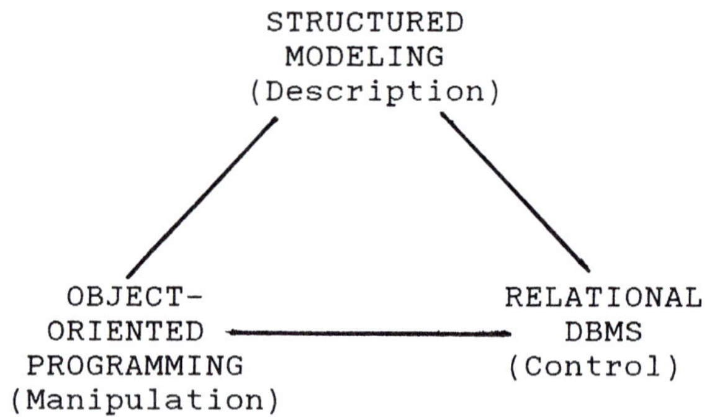

Figure 3-1: An MMS Based on Paradigms from Operations Research and Computer Science

4. MODEL DESCRIPTION: STRUCTURED MODELING FORMALISM

There have been three basic approaches to developing a formalism for model representation:

1. First order logic: representing models as a set of well-formed formulae in the first order predicate calculus (e.g.: [3,6,10]);

2. Relational theory of model management: extending the relational data model to represent mathematical models as well [2];

3. Structured modeling: the use of graphs and hierarchies [13].

The logic approaches, although appealing because of their obvious relevance to artificial intelligence applications, do not provide any semantic support for mathematical modeling beyond the well-known laws of first-order logic. The relational approach suffers from a similar problem in that the relational theory does not seem to offer sufficient semantic robustness to accommodate the complexity of mathematical models. Structured modeling, however, provides a formalism more comprehensive than either of the previous approaches and, because of its direct orientation to OR/MS mathematical modeling, seems ideally suited to serve as the basis of an MMS.

Variable	Description
Xjt	Units of product j manufactured in period t (UNITS_MADE)
Sit	Stock of raw material i at start of period t (STOCK)
Cjt	Estimated profit per unit of product j in period t (PROFIT)
Di	Storage cost per period per unit of raw material i (STORAGE_COST)
Aij	Units of raw material i needed to manufacture one unit of product j (RAWM_REQD)
Bi	Maximum initial stock of raw material i (INIT_STOCK)
Fi	Estimated remaining value per unit of raw material i (EST_UNIT_VALUE)
M	Maximum total unit production per period (TOTAL_PROD)
T	No. of production periods (PERIOD)
P	No. of products (PRODUCT)
R	No. of raw materials (RAW_MATERIAL)

(Maximize profit adjusted for storage cost and value of remaining inventory)

$$\max\left[\sum_{t=1}^{T}\left(\sum_{j=1}^{P} CjtXjt - \sum_{i=1}^{R} DiSit\right) + \sum_{i=1}^{R} FiSiT{+}1\right]$$

subject to:

(Total unit production per period must not exceed max.)

$$\sum_{j=1}^{P} Xjt <= M \qquad \text{for } t=1,\ldots,T$$

(Stock for 1st period must not exceed maximum)

$$Si1 <= Bi \qquad \text{for } i=1,\ldots,R$$

(Stock for next period is stock for present period less raw materials used in present period's production)

$$Sit{+}1 = Sit - \sum_{j=1}^{P} AijXjt \qquad \text{for } i=1,\ldots,R;\ t=1,\ldots,T$$

Figure 3-2: Mathematical Description of Production and Inventory Model

i: Raw materials	j: Products	t: Periods
SCRAP	LOW	87Q1
NEW	MED	87Q2
	HIGH	87Q3

Cjt:		87Q1	87Q2	87Q3
	LOW	25	20	10
	MED	50	50	50
	HIGH	75	80	100

Di :	SCRAP	0.5
	NEW	2.0

Aij:		LOW	MED	HIGH
	SCRAP	5	3	1
	NEW	1	2	3

Bi :	SCRAP	400
	NEW	275

Fi :	SCRAP	15
	NEW	25

M :		40

Figure 3-3: Data Values for Production and Inventory Model

We provide here only those details of structured modeling which are relevant to the model description requirements of an MMS. Figure 4-1 summarizes the basic components of structured modeling. Figures 4-2 and 4-3 show a generic and modular structure for the production and inventory model while Figures 4-4 and 4-5 provide an outline of the genus paragraph syntax and the production and inventory model schema respectively. A more complete description of structured modeling can be found in [13].

Structured modeling satisfies the functional requirements for model description in Figure 2-1. Structured modeling provides an underlying formalism based on acyclic,

Component	Description
Elemental Structure	A finite, acyclic set of elements
Element Types	Each element is one, and only one, of 5 possible types
Entities	Types are either entities ("real world" things) or attributes
Primitive	Existential element undefined mathematically
Compound	Tuple of primitive and/or compound entities
Attributes	Properties of "real world" things
Attribute	Tuple of entity elements + unique value
Variable Attribute	Attribute whose value is determined by later evaluation process
Function	Tuple of elements + a rule for associating unique value to this tuple
Test	Boolean function
Calling Sequence	Tuple portion of an element; those elements which are directly referenced by the element in question
Generic Structure	Elements are partitioned into classes called genera
Similarity	Every element in a genus has the same calling sequence
Genus Graph	A directed graph with a node for every genus and an arc from every genus in that genus' calling sequence
Modular Structure	Rooted tree whose leaves are genera and whose nonleaf nodes are modules
Modular Outline	Indented list representation corresponding to preorder traversal of modular structure
Monotone Ordering	No genus in the modular outline has in its calling sequence a genus appearing further down the outline
Model Schema	A modular outline where each entry is expanded according to a specific syntax

Figure 4-1: Basic Components of Structured Modeling

attributed graphs to represent cross-references among elements of a model, and hierarchies to represent levels of abstraction. All models are defined in terms of elements which may be partitioned into genera (pl. of "genus") and further aggregated into modules. Each element and corresponding genus must be one, and only one, of five possible types. This results in a uniform representation for models encapsulated in the model schema.

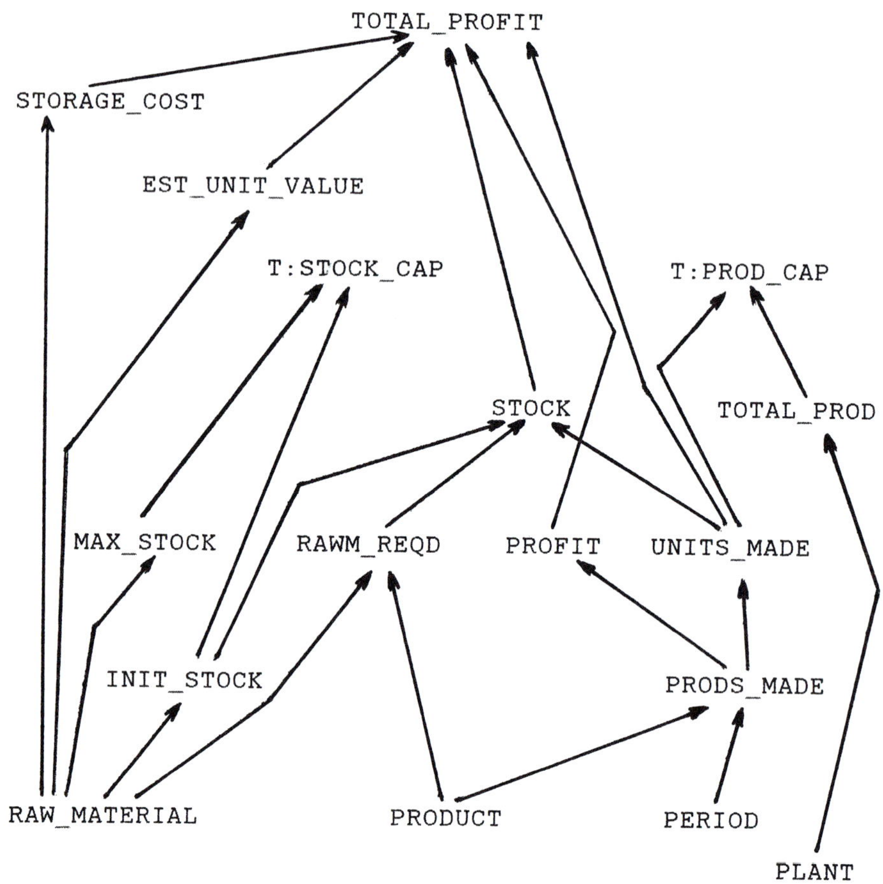

Figure 4-2: Genus Graph for Production and Inventory Model

The model schema representation accommodates many different classes of OR/MS models including optimization, network flow, queuing, and discrete event simulation. Further, a formal notion of view is defined via the modular structure and many views can be imposed on a single model instance. Also, views can be tailored for technical or nontechnical audiences by emphasizing or suppressing mathematical details.

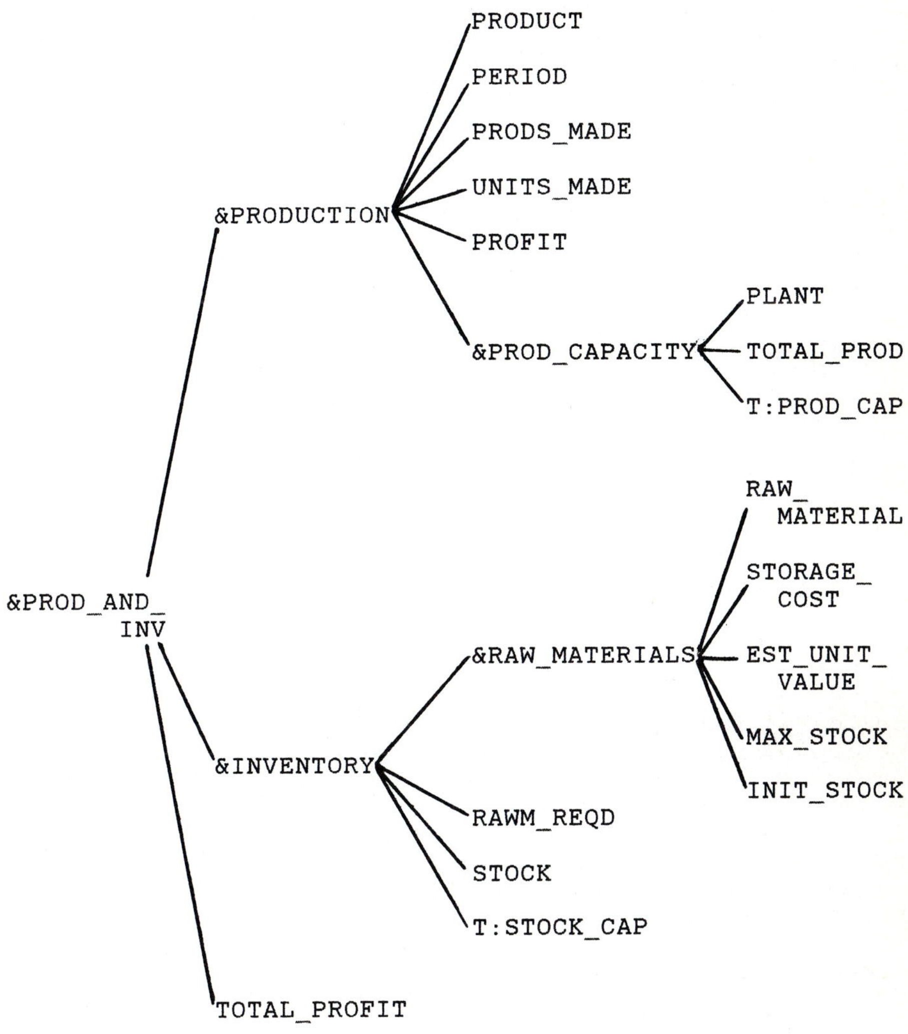

Figure 4-3: Modular Structure for Production and Inventory Model

PARA_NAMEindex(calling_sequence) /element_type/ index_set_statement :range ;generic_rule interpretation

PARA_NAME	Paragraph name (preceded by "&" if paragraph is a module).
index	Single lower case letter if genus introduces an index.
calling_sequence	Generic calling sequence.
element_type	'pe', 'ce', 'a', 'va', 't' (test), or 'f' (function)
index_set_statement	Statement defining element population of genus.
:range	Domain of 'a' or 'va' genus.
generic_rule	Specifies calculation of 't' or 'f' genus.
interpretation	Narrative description of paragraph.

Figure 4-4: Brief Outline of a Genus Paragraph

Model/data independence is also supported in the sense described in Section 2. Every generic structure can be transformed into a set of relational tables which captures the associated elemental detail (underlying data) of the model [11]. Figure 4-6 shows one such set of tables for the generic structure in Figure 4-2. The data in these tables can be modified without altering the model schema. For example, one could add new products to the PRODUCT relation without changing anything in the schema. Note that the converse is not true, however. Adding or deleting new genera or changing calling sequences may result in a different set of tables.

Model integrity is supported as well because there is a precise definition of a structured model. For example calling sequences must be acyclic, certain calling sequences are forbidden (e.g.: attributes can't have attributes in their calling sequence), and monotone ordering must prevail within the modular structure (e.g.: no genus can have more than one parent in the hierarchy). These integrity constraints can be checked easily by an MMS.

```
&PROD_AND_INV  Production and inventory model.

 &PRODUCTION  Production module.
  PRODUCTj/pe/ There is a list of products manufactured.
  PERIODt/pe/ There is a list of production periods.
  PRODS_MADE(PRODUCTj,PERIODt)/ce/ {PRODUCT}x{PERIOD}
   There is a matrix of products made during periods.
  UNITS_MADE(PRODS_MADEjt)/va/ {PRODS_MADE}: R+ Units of
   product j made in period t.
  PROFIT(PRODS_MADEjt)/a/ {PRODS_MADE}: R  Estimated
   profit per unit of product j in period t.
  &PROD_CAPACITY  Production capacity module.
   PLANT/pe/ There is a plant where production occurs.
   TOTAL_PROD(PLANT)/a/ {PLANT}: R+  The plant has a pro-
      duction capacity.
   T:PROD_CAP(UNITS_MADEjt,TOTAL_PROD)/t/ {PERIOD} ;
     SUMj(UNITS_MADEjt) <= TOTAL_PROD  Have the total
     units made exceeded the production capacity?

 &INVENTORY  Inventory module.
  &RAW_MATERIALS  Raw materials module.
   RAW_MATERIALi/pe/ There is a list of raw materials.
   STORAGE_COST(RAW_MATERIALi)/a/ {RAW_MATERIAL}: R+
     Every raw material has a unit storage cost.
   EST_UNIT_VALUE(RAW_MATERIALi)/a/ {RAW_MATERIAL}: R+
     Every raw material has an est. unit salvage value.
   MAX_STOCK(RAW_MATERIALi)/a/ {RAW_MATERIAL}: R+  Every
     raw material has a maximum initial stock.
   INIT_STOCK(RAW_MATERIALi)/a/ {RAW_MATERIAL}: R+  Every
     raw material has an initial stock.
  RAWM_REQD(RAW_MATERIALi,PRODUCTj)/a/ {RAW_MATERIAL} x
   {PRODUCT}: R+ The amt of raw material i req'd to
    manufacture a unit of product j.
  STOCK(INIT_STOCKi,RAWM_REQDij,UNITS_MADEjt)/f/
   {RAW_MATERIAL}x{PERIOD}
   INIT_STOCKi  if t=1;
   STOCKit-1 - SUMj(RAWM_REQDij*UNITS_MADEjt-1)  if t>1;
    There is a stock of raw material i on hand at begin-
    ing of period t.
  T:STOCK_CAP(MAX_STOCKi,INIT_STOCKi)/t/ {RAW_MATERIAL}
   INIT_STOCKi <= MAX_STOCKi ; Does amount of raw-mat.
    in stock at start of 1st period exceed the maximum?

 TOTAL_PROFIT(STORAGE_COSTi,EST_UNIT_VALUEi,PROFITjt,
              STOCKit,UNITS_MADEjt)/f/ 1 ;
  SUMt(SUMj(PROFITjt*UNITS_MADEjt) - SUMi(STORAGE_COSTi*
    STOCKit)) + SUMi(EST_UNIT_VALUEi*STOCKiT+1)  Total
   profit adjusted for storage cost and ending inventory.
```

Figure 4-5: Model Schema for Production and Inventory Model

```
RAW_MATERIAL(rawm_id,storage_cost,est_unit_value,
    max_stock,init_stock,t:stock_cap,interpretation)
 'scrap',0.5,15.,400.,250.,True,'Scrap raw material'
 'new  ',2.0,25.,275.,200.,True,'New raw material'

PRODUCT(prod_id,interpretation)
 'low ', 'Low quality product'
 'med ', 'Medium quality product'
 'high', 'High quality product'

PERIOD(per_id,t:prod_cap,interpretation)
 '8701',Null,'1st production period'
 '8702',Null,'2nd production period'
 '8703',Null,'3rd production period'

PLANT(plant_id,total_prod,interpretation)
 'Birmingham',40.,'Production capacity in tons'

PRODS_MADE_IN_PER(prod_id,per_id,units_made,
     profit_per_unit,interpretation)
 'low ','8701',Null,25.,'Low quality prod. in 1st per.'
 'low ','8702',Null,20.,'Low quality prod. in 2nd per.'
 'low ','8703',Null,10.,'Low quality prod. in 3rd per.'
 'med ','8701',Null,50.,'Med quality prod. in 1st per.'
 'med ','8702',Null,50.,'Med quality prod. in 2nd per.'
 'med ','8703',Null,50.,'Med quality prod. in 3rd per.'
 'high','8701',Null,75.,'High quality prod. in 1st per.'
 'high','8702',Null,80.,'High quality prod. in 2nd per.'
 'high','8703',Null,100,'High quality prod. in 3rd per.'

RAWM_USED_IN_PROD(rawm_id,prod_id,rawm_reqd,interpret.)
 'scrap','low ',5.,'Amt of scrap to produce unit of low'
 'scrap','med ',3.,'Amt of scrap to produce unit of med'
 'scrap','high',1.,'Amt of scrap to produce unit of hgh'
 'new  ','low ',1.,'Amt of new to produce unit of low'
 'new  ','med ',2.,'Amt of new to produce unit of med'
 'new  ','high',3.,'Amt of new to produce unit of high'

STOCK_PERIOD(rawm_id,per_id,stock,interpretation)
 'scrap','8701',Null,'Stock of scrap--start of 1st per'
 'scrap','8702',Null,'Stock of scrap--start of 2nd per'
 'scrap','8703',Null,'Stock of scrap--start of 3rd per'
 'new  ','8701',Null,'Stock of new--start of 1st per'
 'new  ','8702',Null,'Stock of new--start of 2nd per'
 'new  ','8703',Null,'Stock of new--start of 3rd per'

TOTAL_PROFIT(total_profit,interpretation)
 Null,'Profit adjusted for inventory and usage'
```

Figure 4-6: Elemental Detail Tables for Production and Inventory Model

5. MODEL MANIPULATION: OBJECT-ORIENTED PROGRAMMING METHODOLOGY

In the previous section, we have shown how structured modeling can be used to describe models. In this section we consider how to define and apply manipulation operators to models.

Model manipulation refers to all those things that one may conceivably do to a model instance, for example, build, modify, solve, document. In general, one cannot predict what model operations will be appropriate for OR models. Although Geoffrion has identified four basic operations (retrieval, evaluation, satisfaction, and optimization), not all of these operations are appropriate for all model instances. For example, it may not make sense to optimize certain discrete event simulation models or to find a feasible solution for a multiple regression. Further, the specific details of these basic operations may vary from model to model. The optimization algorithm for a mixed integer programming model is quite different from that for a simple linear programming model, for example. A desirable feature of an MMS is that it allow only valid operations to be performed on any model instance. This requires that model instances must somehow be paired with the "proper" operators.

Of particular interest in this scenario is forging a link between the model-builder and the end-user, or client. Once a model has been built, it ideally will be made available to the client for use in supporting decision-making. It is reasonable to expect that these decision-makers will not have the same level of technical expertise as the model builders. Some safeguarding mechanism is required to insure that the community of end-users accesses and manipulates the model in a fashion consistent with what the builders intended. For example, an MMS should prevent a situation where a user tries to solve a nonlinear optimization model using a simplex algorithm. On the other hand, an MMS should identify situations where data for a specific LP model transforms it into an instance of a network model which is therefore solvable by a more efficient algorithm than simplex.

5.1 Model Manipulation Language

Towards this objective we introduce a model manipulation language (MML) as a vital component of an MMS through which the user specifies, either procedurally or nonprocedurally, what operations are to be performed on which model instances. An MML must provide the following fundamental capabilities to satisfy the basic model operations:

(1) Ad hoc, nonprocedural retrievals of model schemas and associated data; this can be supported using existing database languages like SQL;

(2) Association of model-specific operations (such as OPTIMIZE, SATISFY, or EVALUATE) with model instances; this characteristic is known as **encapsulation** and involves, among other things, forging links with existing algorithms to solve and evaluate models;

(3) A procedural programming language for defining, and then applying, operations dynamically within the MMS environment.

These three steps define a migration path from existing database language capabilities to a fully functional model manipulation environment. A logical first approximation to an MML is to simply adopt a data language like SQL. Indeed, SQL can be used to satisfy the first requirement above straightforwardly (see [9] for a detailed description of one way this can be accomplished). The primary objection against relying on SQL alone as an MML is that it lacks model-specific operators which not only retrieve data but transform it according to pre-specified procedures. For example, the SOLVE operation for a regression model requires application of an ordinary least squares algorithm to the retrieved data. No such capability exists in SQL which performs primarily the SELECT .. FROM .. WHERE data retrieval operation.

An MML must provide a bridge from the model representations based on structured modeling to the rich body of solution and evaluation algorithms which the OR community has devoted so much effort in developing. Embodied in this transition is the notion that not all algorithms can be applied to all model representations. It is therefore necessary to associate which operations are valid for which models in such a way that model users cannot apply incorrect operations. The concept of encapsulation introduced in object-oriented programming supports this second objective.

In the most general situation, there may not be existing algorithms on which to draw in order to properly manipulate a model. Algorithms may have to be developed specifically for a model instance. This seems particularly true for discrete event simulation where the notion of solving a model is often equivalent to writing a program in a suitable language. A logical environment for developing these algorithms is the MMS itself so that the algorithms, like the model representations, could reside in the MMS. This requires an MML equivalent in power to high level languages such as Pascal but tied directly to a DBMS. In the OR world, this would eventually result in algorithm developers writing new code (or converting old code) in the equivalent of an extended database language. Although this may seem like heresy to a community deeply concerned with computing efficiency, it would have the advantages of eliminating artificial interfaces to external environments as well as providing a uniform treatment of models and their data. Further, the loss of efficiency may not be as severe as imagined [16].

5.2 Object-Oriented Programming

The need for pairing models with appropriate operators suggests a current paradigm from the programming language field known as object-oriented programming (OOP). OOP is currently in vogue because of the success of languages like SmallTalk [15] but appropriately one of the first examples of OOP occurred in OR applications with the development of the Simula 67 language [5] for discrete event modeling.

The object-oriented universe, like Simula 67, is comprised of objects which are data structures coupled with the procedures which can act on those objects. These procedures are invoked by messages sent from one object to another via an established communication protocol. There are three main concepts associated with OOP: **class inheritance**, **encapsulation**, and **communication protocols**.

The notion of class and inheritance are central to the object-oriented paradigm. Instances of similar objects (e.g.: linear optimization models) are referred to as a class. All members of a class share the same messages, i.e. have the same set of procedures which act upon them (for example, simplex optimization). Objects which differ slightly can be specified as subclasses which inherit some or all of the attributes and messages of the superclass. For example, an integer programming model could be specified as a subset of the linear optimization class, and inherit the messages of that class except for the SOLVE, or OPTIMIZE, message. This would be specified as some appropriate branch-and-bound algorithm for this particular subclass of models.

Encapsulation refers to identifying objects and those procedures which can be applied to those objects. Although inheritance provides powerful programming language features, encapsulation is equally important for the MMS case because it facilitates the proper access and manipulation of models by people who were not involved in the building of these models. This provides a critical bridge between the technical model builder and the nontechnical decision maker.

Communication protocols govern the sending and receiving of messages and the resultant evocation of procedures involved in responding to messages. Initially, at least, most message sending in an MMS environment would occur between users and models as a result of user-specified commands in a model manipulation language (MML). If the user specifies

SOLVE for an optimization model, for example, this may result in a message being sent to the model (object) to evoke a particular solution algorithm (XMP, say).

Message-sending between models might occur in the case of integration where two models must be linked to form a composite model. If it were desired to link an inventory and a transportation model, for example, the former might send a message LINK to the latter which would react by scanning the transmitting model to see whether a link was possible, and if so, how to accomplish it. This is a very complex situation, however, which requires further research to implement. Initially, we will assume that the MML defines the communication protocol in an MMS.

The application of object-oriented principles to model management has been considered before. The basic premise is to regard model elements (e.g.: structured modeling components) and models themselves as objects which have encapsulated with them the appropriate procedures, or messages. The MML is the vehicle for sending messages. [6] introduced the model abstraction as a structure for model objects which could accommodate knowledge-based reasoning as well. [18] discussed implementation of structured modeling within a SmallTalk-like environment. [1, 11] have also presented possible MMLs relevant for OR applications.

5.3 Production and Inventory Example

How would an object-oriented MMS be administered and how would it look to the end-user, or decision-maker? We describe one scenario below, although by no means the only possible or desirable one. During the development and testing phases, only model builders would have access to a model. Once the model was deemed available for "public" release, a model administrator in concert with the builders would define the appropriate operations allowed for the intended end-user community.

In particular let's assume the 4 basic operations suggested earlier (with the associated MML command in parentheses): retrieval (SELECT), evaluation (EVAL), satisfaction (SATISFY), and optimization (SOLVE). Further assume a slight extension to the SQL database language:

```
SELECT data_item(s)                 <operator> data_item(s)
FROM   relation(s)          ===>    FROM       relation(s)
WHERE  boolean conditionals         WHERE      boolean conditions
```

where <operator> may be any of the 4 MML commands. Encapsulation requires that, somewhere in the database, model instances be associated with procedures which will be invoked in response to MML commands (Figure 5-1).

In the simple example in Figure 5-1, we are assuming the MMS has access to the XMP optimization library. The SELECT command can be implemented using the standard features of SQL. Figure 5-2 shows a relational representation of the production and inventory model schema which would be stored in the database along with the associated data in Figure 4-6. These representations can be easily queried using SQL (see [9] for examples).

Sample commands for each of the model operations are shown in Figure 5-3. The EVAL operation is equivalent to a spreadsheet evaluation where all test and function elements are evaluated from the available attribute values (note that variable attributes corresponding to decision variables in optimization models may not have any values until SOLVE is performed). The SATISFY and SOLVE operations access the appropriate XMP routines as shown. Note that the EQNMTX routine converts the model representation to a sparse matrix representation for manipulation by XMP. The sequence number is used to establish an order in which the routines are to be applied.

Notice that as a result of encapsulation, the same MML command specified for different model instances may invoke entirely different procedures. Whereas SOLVE specified for the production and inventory model invokes XMP routines, SOLVE specified for a regression model may invoke an ordinary least squares subroutine from a statistical library. SATISFY specified for the production and inventory model invokes the feasibility subset of the routines required for SOLVE whereas SATISFY for a regression may be deemed not applicable.

The connection between the operations encapsulated within a model and the procedures which implement them is clearly critical in an MMS. Procedures may appear in two different forms which we shall call **external** and **internal**. External procedures are algorithms which have been developed independently of the MMS and are made available through some library of operations accessible by the MMS. The XMP library of optimization routines [19] and the IMSL library of mathematical subroutines are examples of libraries which could form the basis of OR model manipulation operators. Use of external procedures requires the MMS to transform model representations into the appropriate data structures which those procedures require. After the procedure has been executed, the MMS must then also transform the results into a form compatible with the model representation. This frees the user from having to worry about unnecessary, intermediate procedural representations but at the cost of a high degree of overhead for the MMS.

Internal procedures, on the other hand, are those which are developed, and subsequently invoked, entirely within the MMS environment (in particular, this means within a relational

DBMS environment; see next section on model control). Most RDBMS's facilitate the formation and subsequent saving of complex queries as **macros**. Once formed, these macros can then be invoked by a single word command. [9] has shown how structured models can be represented in an RDBMS and macros developed to enforce structured model integrity.

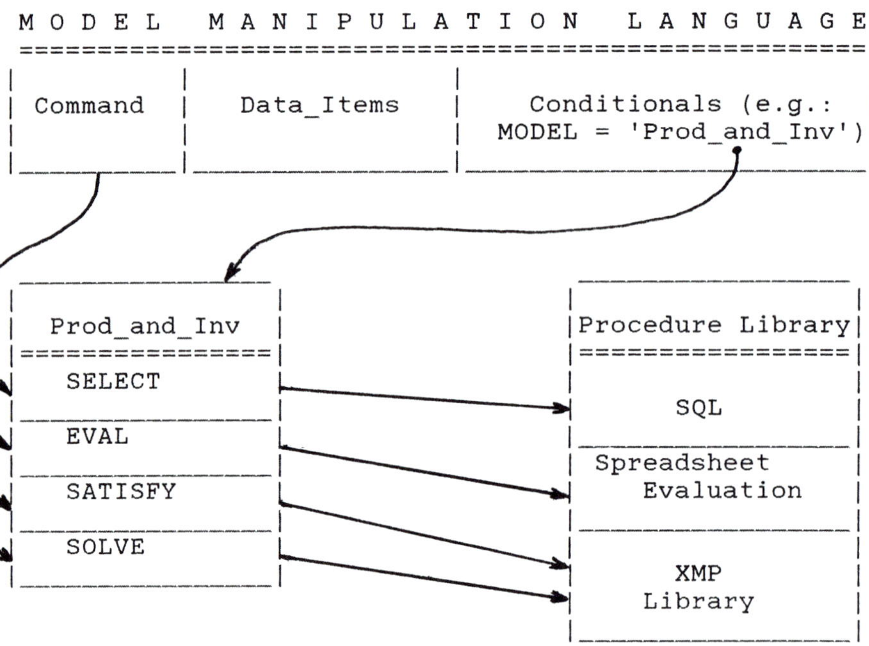


```
ENCAPS(model,verb,seq_no,procedure)

'prod_and_inv','select ',1,'sql'
'prod_and_inv','eval    ',1,'spreadsheet'
'prod_and_inv','satisfy',1,'xmp.xfeas'
'prod_and_inv','solve   ',1,'xmp.xmaps'
'prod_and_inv','solve   ',2,'eqnmtx'
'prod_and_inv','solve   ',3,'xmp.xslack'
'prod_and_inv','solve   ',4,'xmp.xpriml'
```

Figure 5-1: MML and Encapsulation

Model Elements

```
MODEL('&PROD_AND_INV','Production & inventory model',..)
MODULE('&PRODUCTION','Production module',..)
MODULE('&INVENTORY','Inventory module',..)
MODULE('&PROD_CAPACITY','Production capacity module',..)
MODULE('&RAW_MATERIALS','Raw materials module',..)
PE('PLANT','Mfg_Plant',..)
PE('PRODUCT','Products',..)
PE('RAW_MATERIAL','Raw materials',..)
PE('PERIOD','Production periods',..)
CE('PRODS_MADE','Products made in production period',..)
ATT_TYPE('STORAGE_COST','Unit storage cost / period',..)
  :
VA('UNITS_MADE','Units of product made in period',..)
TEST('T:PROD_CAP','SUMj(UNITS_MADEjt) <= TOTAL_PROD',..)
TEST('T:STOCK_CAP','STOCKi1 <= MAX_STOCKi',..)
FCN('STOCK','STOCKi1 = INIT_STOCKi ; ...',..)
FCN('TOTAL_PROFIT','SUMt(SUMj(PROFITjt*UNITS_MADEjt)..')
```

Generic Structure

```
CALLS('RAWM_REQD ', 'ATT ', 'RAW_MATERIAL', 'PE ')
CALLS('RAWM_REQD ', 'ATT ', 'PRODUCT     ', 'PE ')
CALLS('PRODS_MADE', 'CE  ', 'PRODUCT     ', 'PE ')
CALLS('PRODS_MADE', 'CE  ', 'PERIOD      ', 'PE ')
CALLS('STOCK     ', 'FCN ', 'INIT_STOCK  ', 'ATT')
CALLS('STOCK     ', 'FCN ', 'RAWM_REQD   ', 'ATT')
CALLS('STOCK     ', 'FCN ', 'UNITS_MADE  ', 'ATT')
CALLS('T:PROD_CAP', 'TEST', 'TOTAL_PROD  ', 'ATT')
CALLS('T:PROD_CAP', 'TEST', 'UNITS_MADE  ', 'ATT')
  :
```

Modular Structure

```
CONTAINS('&PROD_AND_INV','MODEL','&PRODUCTION','MODULE')
CONTAINS('&PROD_AND_INV','MODEL','&INVENTORY','MODULE')
CONTAINS('&PROD_AND_INV','MODEL','TOTAL_PROFIT','FCN')
CONTAINS('&PRODUCTION','MODULE','PRODUCT','PE')
  :
CONTAINS('&PRODUCTION','MODULE','&PROD_CAPACITY','MODULE')
CONTAINS('&INVENTORY','MODULE','&RAW_MATERIALS','MODULE')
  :
CONTAINS('&INVENTORY','MODULE','T:STOCK_CAP','TEST')
CONTAINS('&PROD_CAPACITY','MODULE','PLANT','PE')
  :
CONTAINS('&RAW_MATERIALS','MODULE','RAW_MATERIAL','PE')
  :
```

Figure 5-2: Relational Representation of Model Schema for Production and Inventory Model

Selection

```
SELECT rawm_id                   SELECT e2name, e2type
FROM   raw_material              FROM   call
WHERE  t:stock_cap='False'       WHERE  e1name='TOTAL_PROFIT
                                    and model='PROD_AND_INV'
```

Evaluation

```
EVAL   t:stock_cap,t:prod_cap,stock
FROM   raw_material,period,stock
WHERE  model = 'PROD_AND_INV'
```

Satisfaction

```
SATISFY t:stock_cap, t:prod_cap
FROM    raw_material,period
WHERE   model = 'PROD_AND_INV'
```

Optimization

```
SOLVE  max(total_profit)
FROM   raw_material, ... , profit
WHERE  model = 'PROD_AND_INV'
```

Figure 5-3: Sample Queries for Model Operations

A natural extension to internal procedures would be to develop all model manipulation operators, including SOLVE, as macros. In this way, all procedures could be invoked from within the RDBMS thus eliminating the costly interfacing with external algorithms. [16] have demonstrated the feasibility of this approach by developing solution algorithms in database languages for several simple OR models with surprisingly efficient results. Although it is premature to claim that database languages have sufficiently powerful constructs to support complex OR algorithm development, the trend in DBMS products is towards providing a high level programming environment as an integral part of the DBMS. It is reasonable to expect therefore that capabilities for internal procedures will evolve with this trend thus strengthening support for the object-oriented paradigm and its application to model management.

5.4 Summary

The application of object-oriented principles to an MMS satisfies the following MMS requirements:

1. Underlying methodology: the notion of models as objects consisting of model schemas, data, and messages provides a convenient conceptual framework consistent with current accepted programming principles;

2. Proper usage of models: encapsulating operators with their respective models enhances the probability that models will be used as their builders intended;

3. Model/solver independence: model representations and the procedures which act upon them are distinct entities within the MMS; the MMS automatically transforms model representations into the data structures required by a library of external procedures or else facilitates development of internal procedures;

4. Potential model integration: development of appropriate communication protocols between models (e.g.: communicating sequential processes [17]) may be a promising vehicle for facilitating linkages between models.

6. MODEL CONTROL: RELATIONAL DBMS

Model control refers to the ability to provide shared access to multiple models while still maintaining centralized control. The underlying assumption in an MMS environment is that any single user may access multiple models while, simultaneously any single model may be accessed by multiple users. Notice the fundamental difference between this situation and the proliferation of single-user spreadsheets which prevails in many organizations today. The latter is strictly a single user-single model situation where sharing is minimal.

Building an environment which supports shared access of modeling resources demands a complex array of features for maintaining the integrity of those resources:

(1) Concurrency mechanisms are required to insure that two or more people may access the same model or data simultaneously without destroying model or data integrity.

(2) Security mechanisms are necessary to control which people may legitimately access modeling resources.

(3) Backup and recovery procedures are also needed to sustain the integrity of underlying databases in the case of system failure.

Implementing these sharing mechanisms introduces a great deal of complexity into any underlying MMS. Indeed, the bulk and commensurate expense of any commercial DBMS is devoted to supporting these features as opposed to the basic data storage and retrieval operations. The availability of these control features in existing commercial DBMS's and particularly relational DBMS's (RDBMS's) is a strong a priori argument for adopting RDBMS as the underlying environment for implementing an MMS.

Although RDBMS's facilitate extensive control and sharing, they do not fully satisfy the requirements shown in Figure 2-1. The MMS counterparts of concurrency, security, and backup/recovery present unique problems which are discussed below. Nevertheless, it makes more sense to build from the available features provided by existing RDBMS's than to develop the requisite MMS sharing mechanisms from scratch.

One of the ramifications of supporting model control is the need to provide concurrent access to a model instance, i.e. the ability to allow two or more users access to the same model simultaneously. This requirement has many potential manifestations in the modeling world:

(1) A model-builder may change a model schema while an end-user is solving the model; for example, consider someone changing the production and inventory schema to include multiple plants while another user is solving the single plant version; An MMS should be able to support both activities concurrently;

(2) One user may be changing a model's data, for example adding raw materials to the production and inventory model, while another user is solving the model;

(3) Two users may be changing the same data;

(4) Two users may be solving the same model with the same or different data.

The above is not an exhaustive list of possible concurrencies in an MMS but it does demonstrate some of the knottier problems that may be encountered. Notice that RDBMS concurrency mechanisms currently only handle the third situation.

Another aspect of shared modeling resources is the need for security protection schemes in order to control who has access to what information. Security mechanisms are familiar features of current DBMS's but an MMS again presents unique problems. Consider the potential for reverse engineering a model to uncover either sensitive data values or underlying equations. For example, if the input data (the attribute values in structured modeling terms) for the production and inventory model are classified but the equations (function and test elements) and output data (variable attribute values) are not, it will likely be quite possible to reverse engineer the model by evaluating it and then determining what the attribute values are. In such a case, it may be necessary to additionally protect some or all of the function and test elements to insure that access to the attribute values remains uncompromised.

The notion of shared information resources also demands backup and recovery facilities for maintaining the integrity of model descriptions in the event of hardware or software failure. If two users are solving the production and inventory model using different data when the computer suffers a power failure, how does the MMS recover from this situation so that both users still retain the integrity of their original input data and the model schema?

An MMS requires extensions to existing RDBMS control and sharing capabilities to handle the complexities of modeling environments. These should provide interesting research opportunities in the development of MMS technology.

Control and sharing features are an important reason for adopting RDBMS as the foundation for MMS but there are other reasons as well. In particular, we suggested in previous sections that the relational environment is well-suited to support the model description and manipulation aspects of an MMS in addition to model control. Relational view mechanisms facilitate the representation of structured modeling as a set of relations. Relational data languages such as SQL and QUEL and their derivatives provide a foundation from which to build an MML along the lines suggested in section 5.3. As relational technology matures and user acceptance increases, it will become increasingly attractive to implement MMS's in a relational environment.

7. CONCLUSIONS

We have established an association between each of the major dimensions of model management and paradigms from the fields of OR, programming languages, and database management. Structured modeling has been suggested as a foundation for model description, object-oriented programming for model manipulation, and relational DBMS for model control. The confluence of these three areas of technology indicate that we currently have the available tools for building an MMS which is far more general and versatile than preceding modeling systems.

Efforts are currently underway to build an MMS based on the principles outlined herein. The system will use the ORACLE RDBMS as a foundation and structured modeling as the model representation paradigm. ORACLE has been chosen because it supports "standard" SQL and also because it provides spreadsheet capabilities directly tied to its databases. Initially, operations in support of econometric forecasting and optimization models will be provided.

The actual implementation details of an MMS are beyond the scope of this paper but the author is aware of three other independent projects which are also directed towards development of such a system. It would appear that a critical threshold has been reached and that we will soon begin to see the emergence of prototype MMS's. This is an exciting prospect for there are many research issues to which this work will give rise. The evolution of MMS technology promises an expanded recognition of the art of modeling and the role that it plays in organizational decision making.

8. REFERENCES

1. Blanning, R.W. Conversing with management information systems in natural language. **Communications of the ACM**, 27, 3 (March 1984), 201-207.

2. Blanning, R.H. A relational theory of model management. Working Paper No. 85-106, Owen Graduate School of Management, Vanderbilt University, Nashville, TN, 1985.

3. Bonczek, R.H., Holsapple, C.W. and Whinston, A.B. A generalized decision support system using predicate calculus and network data base management. **Operations Research** 29,2 (1981), 263-281.

4. Bonczek, R.H., Holsapple, C.W. and Whinston, A.B. **Foundations of Decision Support Systems**. Academic Press, Orlando, FL., 1981.

5. Dahl, O.J., Myhrhaug, B. and Nygaard, K. Simul 67--Common base language. Norsk Regnesentral, Oslo, Norway, May 1968.

6. Dolk, D.R. and Konsynski, B.R. Knowledge representation for model management. **IEEE Transactions on Software Engineering** SE-10,6 (Nov. 1984), 619-627.

7. Dolk, D.R. and Konsynski, B.R. Model management in organizations. **Information and Management** 9, 1 (August 1985), 35-47.

8. Dolk, D.R. A generalized model management system for mathematical programming. **ACM Transactions on Mathematical Software** 12,2 (June 1986), 92-125.

9. Dolk, D.R. **Model management and structured modeling: The role of an information resource dictionary system**. Presented at Mini-Conference on Structured Modeling, UCLA, August 20-22, 1986.

10. Dutta, A. and Basu, A. An artificial intelligence approach to model management in decision support systems. **Computer** 17,9 (Sept. 1984), 89-97.

11. Farn, C.K. An integrated information system architecture based on structured modeling. Ph.D. Thesis, Graduate School of Management, UCLA, 1985.

12. Fourer, R. Modeling languages versus matrix generators for linear programming. **ACM Transactions on Mathematical Software**, 9,2 (June 1983), 143-183.

13. Geoffrion, A.M. An introduction to structured modeling. **Management Science**, 33, 5 (May 1987), 547-588.

14. Geoffrion, A.M. Modeling approaches and systems related to structured modeling. Working Paper No. 339, Graduate School of Management, UCLA, February 1987.

15. Goldberg, A. and Robson, D. **SmallTalk 80: The Language and Its Implementation**, Addison-Wesley, Reading, MA, 1983.

16. Ho, L., Nygard, K. and Shapiro, L. Data base management systems as solvers in model management systems. Computer Science/Operations Research Dept., North Dakota State University, Fargo, ND, 1987.

17. Hoare, C.A.R. Communicating sequential processes. **Communications of the ACM**, 21, 8 (August 1978), 666-677.

18. Lenard, M. An object-oriented approach to model management. **Proceedings of the 20th Hawaii International Conference on System Sciences**, January 1987.

19. Marsten, R.E. The design of the XMP linear programming library. **ACM Transactions on Mathematical Software**, 7,4 (1981), 481-497.

20. Sprague, R.H. and Carlson, E.D. **Building Effective Decision Support Systems**. Prentice-Hall, 1982.

21. Will, H.J. Model management systems. In **Information Systems and Organization Structure**. E. Grochla and N. Syzperski, Eds. Walter deGruyter, Berlin, 1975, 467-482.

22. Yourdon, E. and Constantine, L.L. **Structured Design**, Prentice-Hall, Englewood Cliffs, NJ, 1979.

STRUCTURED MODEL MANAGEMENT

Melanie L. Lenard
School of Management
Boston University
Boston, Massachusetts 02215
U. S. A.

1 INTRODUCTION

Decision Support Systems (DSS) are usually considered to have three major components--namely, sub-systems for data, dialog, and model management. Most of today's database management systems (DBMS) provide decision support by means of extensive data management capabilities combined with a variety of dialog facilities (commands, menus, graphical displays, etc.) for invoking and controlling operations on the database. Some systems--for example, fourth generation languages like NOMAD2 (Trademark, D&B Computing Services, Inc.)--also provide a modeling capability. However, it is clear that the model management component of such systems is at a primitive stage of development compared to the data and dialog components.

Improving the technology for model management must begin with careful consideration of a basic question, namely: "What is a model?" or more precisely, "How should a model be represented?" Traditionally, when someone of the management science/operations research (MS/OR) persuasion has said "Here is my model," he or she has been referring to a collection of statements in some modeling language (perhaps even the language of mathematics) or perhaps to a collection of subroutines in some general purpose programming language. However, for the purposes of model management, what is needed is a representation of models that in some sense makes all models "look alike". Moreover, if this representation is an organized collection of data (i.e. a database), this opens up the intriguing possibility of using a database management system as the integrating mechanism for a DSS.

Structured modeling [5], which was discussed in depth in a previous lecture [9], makes possible just such a representation. In what follows, we propose a design for a model management system based on structured modeling. We begin by describing a conceptual foundation for the proposed system derived from the object-oriented programming paradigm. Next, we discuss a plan to implement the system by representing structured models as a relational database and then using data management functions to accomplish most model management functions. We will report on our progress to date in building a prototype of a "structured model management system" (SMMS) and suggest directions for future work.

NATO ASI Series, Vol. F48
Mathematical Models for Decision Support
Edited by G. Mitra

2 AN OBJECT-ORIENTED VIEW OF MODELS

We have found it useful [8] to approach the problem of designing a SMMS using some concepts taken from object-oriented programming [11]. Object-oriented programming languages are ideal for applications, such as simulations, where it is necessary to represent collections of things that interact in unexpected ways. The first interactive display-based implementation was the SMALLTALK language [6]. Over the past few years, object-oriented programming languages have become popular in the artificial intelligence community, often as add-ons to LISP, for example, the language LOOPS [1].

The common element in object-oriented programming is the "object". Objects are entities that combine the properties of procedures and data, in contrast with conventional programming languages where procedures and data are handled separately. All of the action in object-oriented programming comes from sending "messages" between objects. Instead of invoking a procedure to perform an operation on an object, one sends the object a message. Objects respond to messages using their own procedures or methods. Groups of similar objects are referred to as a Class. Messages are usually designed in standardized sets of related messages called protocols.

```
Magnitude
     Character
     Number
          Float
          Integer
     Look-upKey
          Association (A Key-Value Pair)

Collection
     SequenceableCollection
          ArrayedCollection
               Array
               String (An Array of Characters)
          OrderedCollection
               SortedCollection
     Bag
     Set
          Dictionary (A Set of Associations)
```

Fig. 1. Some SMALLTALK Objects

In addition to message-sending, the second major idea in object-oriented programming is specialization, or class inheritance. Objects that are almost like other objects can be specified as sub-classes which inherit the properties (in particular, the procedures) of their super-class and also have some special properties of their own. In most object languages, objects are divided into two major categories, classes and instances. The instances of a class are objects which are so similar that they share the same set of messages. In an object language, "integer" would be one sub-class of class "number", while "3" and "4" would be instances of class "integer". Figure 1 shows some of the classes and sub-classes of Objects provided in SMALLTALK.

2.1 Structured Models as Objects

In order to apply the object-oriented paradigm, we must first organize the structured modeling framework into a hierarchy of object classes. Figure 2 enumerates the classes of objects in a structured model using the conventions of SMALLTALK.

The basic Objects of a structured model are Elements, of which there are three types: Entities, Attributes, and Functions. The class Entity has two subclasses, PrimitiveEntity and CompoundEntity, indicating that both primitive entities and compound entities can have special properties, in addition to those they have in common. Function is shown as a subclass of Attribute because it inherits some properties, such as having a "value", while having special properties, such as having a "rule" for determining its value. In turn, Test is shown as a subclass of Function, indicating that it inherits all the properties of Function but that it has a special one (its value is always a logical "True" or "False").

Each Element in a structured model, other than a PrimitiveEntity, has a calling sequence, that is, an ordered list of elements on which it is definitionally dependent. The ElementalDependencies are a subclass of Associations (an Association is a Key-Value pair). ElementalDependency has three subclasses:

(1) Every CompoundEntity is a "CompoundOf" other Entities.
(2) Every Attribute is an "AttributeOf" some Entity.
(3) Every Function is a "FunctionOf" some Attributes.

(The inverse of the Associations "CompoundOf", "AttributeOf", and "FunctionOf" are "ComponentOf", "IndexOf", and "ArgumentOf", respectively.)

For example, if LINK_AB is a CompoundEntity representing a (directed) transportation link from PLANT_A to CUST_B, then among the instances of the class "CompoundOf" there will be the following two Associations: (LINK_AB, 1: PLANT_A) and (LINK_AB,2: CUST_B), where ":" separates the Key from the Value of the Association.

In SMALLTALK terms, the Set of all ElementalDependence Associations in the model constitutes a Dictionary. Since this Dictionary corresponds to the elemental structure of a structured model, we show ElementalStructure as a subclass of Dictionary.

In a structured model, Elements of the same type can be grouped into a Genus if they satisfy the property of "generic similarity". Thus, there is a class Genus with three subclasses, each of which is a Set of Elements of the corresponding type.

Correspondingly, there is a subclass of Association, GenericDependence, itself having three subclasses, as shown in the Figure. For our example, the genus LINK is dependent on the PLANT and CUST genera, in that order; so, among the instances of the class "GenericCompoundOf" there will be the two Associations: (LINK,1: PLANT) and (LINK,2: CUST). The Set of all GenericDependence Associations constitutes a SMALLTALK Dictionary, which is called GenericStructure, because it corresponds to the generic structure of a structured model.

At the highest level of aggregation, a Module in a structured model corresponds to an Array of one or more related Genera. (It is an Array rather then a Set because its elements must be at least partially ordered, that is, the ith Genus may call on the jth Genus in the Module only if i is less than j.) A CompoundModule is an Array whose elements may include other Modules as well as Genera. This gives rise to a class of Associations between Modules, namely ModularDependence, and a Dictionary of these Associations, namely ModularStructure.

Finally, there is an object shown as a sub-class of Composite-Object, termed Structured-Model. A Composite-Object contains a prescribed list of Objects from other Classes. In this case, a Structured-Model is a collection of one or more Elements, Genera, and Modules, together with their Dictionaries, which satisfy the conditions of elemental acyclicity, generic similarity, and monotone ordering.

- Element
  - Entity
    - PrimitiveEntity
    - CompoundEntity
  - Attribute
    - FixedAttribute
    - VariableAttribute
    - Function
      - Test

- Genus (A Set of Elements)
  - EntityGenus
    - PrimitiveEntityGenus
    - CompoundEntityGenus
  - AttributeGenus
    - FixedAttributeGenus
    - VariableAttributeGenus
    - FunctionGenus
      - TestGenus

- Module (An Array of Genera)
  - CompoundModule

- Association
  - ElementalDependence
    - CompoundOf
    - AttributeOf
    - FunctionOf
  - GenericDependence
    - GenericCompoundOf
    - GenericAttributeOf
    - GenericFunctionOf
  - ModularDependence
    - ModularCompoundOf

- Dictionary
  - ElementalStructure
  - GenericStructure
  - ModularStructure

- Composite-Object
  - StructuredModel

Fig. 2. Structured Modeling Objects

2.2 Model Manipulations as Messages

In object-oriented programming, an Object has, in addition to its class and instance variables, a set of Methods for responding to Messages it may receive. Given an interpretation of a structured model as a collection of Objects, the next step is to interpret model manipulations as Messages.

Often, Messages can be arranged in standardized groups known as Protocols. For example, every Class must have a Protocol for creating, updating, or deleting its instances, its place in the hierarchy, and its MethodDictionary. In addition, every Set must have a Protocol for adding and deleting its elements.

Figure 3 shows a number of the Protocols for the class Dictionary in the SMALLTALK language. In addition to Protocols for Creating/Updating/ Deleting, there are various Protocols for Accessing or Testing which, in database terminology, are queries. At a minimum, then, the objects constituting a structured model should be able to respond to any or all of the messages to which its superclass (be it a Set, an Array, or a Dictionary) can respond.

Class Protocols

Creating/Updating/Deleting	ClassVariable
	ClassDescription
Accessing (NamesOf?, ValuesOf? NumberOf?)	MethodDictionary
	SubClass, SuperClass
Testing (IsIt[...]?,. Includes[...]?, Accesses[...]?)	Instance
	Instance Variable

Set Protocols

Adding/Deleting an Element

Testing (NumberOf: Elements?)

Dictionary Protocols

Adding/Deleting an Association (Key-ValuePair)

Accessing (ValueAt: [aKey]?)

Testing (Includes: [aValue]?)

Fig. 3. Some SMALLTALK Protocols

For example, the class of structured modeling objects, AttributeGenus, being a subclass of Set, should respond to Messages for Creating/Updating/ Deleting instances and instance variables, for Adding/Removing elements from its instances, and for Accessing/Testing the number or names of instances and their elements. Thus, many model manipulations such as "Change the Data_Type of the Attribute SUPPLY_AT_PLANT to Integer" or "Delete PLANT 101 from the list of Plants" can be accomplished by implementing the equivalent of the SMALLTALK Class and Set Protocols.

However, there are other higher-level model manipulations, such as restructuring by integration or aggregation, which have no immediate analog in the SMALLTALK protocols. Therefore, it will be necessary to include among the Methods known to the StructuredModel a Method that would be invoked in response to a Message such as "IntegrateWith: [a Model] by a

Join over :[aGenusName]". The Method would include the sending of a variety of Messages (e.g. Test, Access, Create, Update, Delete) to the components of the Models being integrated.

Another category of high-level model manipulations comprises those which assign values to VariableAttributes and Functions by "evaluating", "solving", or "optimizing" the model. (These correspond to applying what are popularly known as "what if?", "what works?", and "what's best?" methodologies, respectively). We will call model manipulations of this kind "value assignments". For example, "optimizing" a model means assigning values to all the VariableAttributes so that the value of every Test is "True" and some Function is maximized or minimized. This is usually accomplished by invoking a numerical procedure such as the Simplex algorithm for linear programming. Therefore, the Model should have a Method for responding to a Message such as "Minimize: [a Function]". The Method will normally include preparing input to and processing output from an optimization software package.

An alternate way to implement value assignment manipulations would be to create a new Class of Composite-Objects. For example, an LPModel would be a Composite of Rows, Columns, Coefficients, Right-Hand Sides, and Bounds. Then, an instance of the class Module would respond to a Message "AsLPModel" by transforming itself to an instance of LPModel, if possible, while only the class LPModel would respond to a Message such as "Minimize: [aRow]".

A subclass of LPModel could be SolvedLPModel differing from its superclass in that values have been assigned to Rows and Columns (namely the primal and dual activity levels resulting from the solution of the linear program). In turn, there would be a subclass of Structured Model, called OptimizedModel, again differing from the super-class only in that values have been assigned to Functions and Attributes. To complete the process, then, SolvedLPModel should respond to a Message "AsOptimizedModel" by transforming from its "Rows, Columns" representation to its "Modular, Generic" representation as "OptimizedModel".

3 MODELS AS DATA

Given the interpretation of a structured model in object-oriented terms set forth in the previous section, one could consider building a model management system using an object-oriented language such as LOOPS (this is the approach being taken by Oldford and Peters [10]). An alternative is to represent the Objects in a structured model as data, so that the Methods can be written in one or more of the languages of a DBMS, while relying on the object-oriented paradigm to suggest the form and functional structure of the model management system. The latter approach has the obvious and important advantage of making the integration of Model Management and Data Management straightforward.

Although there have been some proposals for an object-oriented DBMS [2], they are not widely available. Instead we propose to use a DBMS based on the relational data model [4] as the vehicle for implementing a SMMS. A relational DBMS (RDBMS) provides "objects" such as relations, attributes, domains, keys, and tuples having as defined operations (methods) all of the capabilities of the Query Language (e.g. SELECT or PROJECT), the Data Definition Language, (e.g. CREATE and DELETE relations, DEFINE attributes) and the Data Manipulation Language (INSERT, UPDATE, DELETE tuples).

Additionally, most RDBMS provide access to more primitive classes of objects such as Numbers and Characters, along with operations such as elementary mathematical and string manipulation functions.

Modular Relations

MODULE (Mod_Name: Interp)

CONTENT (Mod_Name, SeqNo: Contains)

Generic Relations

E_GENUS (E_Name: Etype, Interp)
A_GENUS (A_Name: Atype, Attr_of, Datatype, Interp)

CMPND_OF (CE_Name: Calls1, Calls2)
FNCTN_OF (F_Name: F_or_T, Rule, Calls1, Calls2)

Elemental Relations

E (E_Name, Index: El_Name)
AREAL (A_Name, Index: Value)
AINT (A_Name, Index: Value)
ACHAR (A_Name, Index: Value)

CE (CE_Name, Index, Calls: C_Index)

Fig. 4 Structured Modeling Relations

3.1 Structured Models as Relations

The first step toward building a SMMS using a RDBMS is designing a relational database representation of the Objects in a structured model. The database shown in Figure 4 is a somewhat revised version of an earlier proposal [7]. There are three groups of relations, namely Modular, Generic, and Elemental Relations, corresponding to the three levels of structure in a structured model. (Dolk [3] has developed a similar proposal in the context of a model dictionary system.) The tuples in the CONTENT, CMPND_OF, FNCTN_OF, and CE relations of Figure 4 correspond to instances of four of the subclasses of Association (namely, ModularDependence, GenericCompoundOf, GenericFunctionOf, and ElementalDependence) shown in Figure 2. Selecting the attributes A_Name and Attr_of from the A_GENUS relation would yield a relation whose tuples correspond to instances of the GenericAttributeOf subclass of Association.

All instances of the class Module are enumerated in the MODULE Relation. All instances of the Entity and Attribute sub-classes of Genus are enumerated in the corresponding (E_GENUS and A_GENUS) Generic Relation. All instances of the Entity subclass of Element are enumerated in the E relation. All instances of the Attribute subclass of Element (having real, integer, or character values), are enumerated in the AREAL, AINT, and ACHAR relations, respectively. The other attributes of these relations are, in object-oriented terminology, instance variables. For example, in A_GENUS, the tuple:

(sup: FA, plant, real, "Plant supply capacities (tons)")

conveys the information that one instance of the class AttributeGenus has the name SUP, belongs to the subclass ("Type") FixedAttribute, is an AttributeOf the PLANT genus, takes on values in the domain ("Datatype") of real numbers, and has as its Interpretation ("Interp") the string "Plant supply capacities (tons)".

3.2 Model Management as Data Management

Given this model representation, the next step is to find a way to implement the various model management functions in terms of operations on the structured model database. It is of particular interest to determine to what extent the functions of "structured model management" can be accomplished using the existing dialog and data management facilities of a database management system.

Relying on the object-oriented view for guidance, we note first that a create/update/delete protocol for the CompositeObject StructuredModel translates into create/update/delete protocols of the component parts, namely the instances of Element, Genus, and Module classes (and sub-classes), and their Associations. Thus, in database terms, creating updating, and deleting a model is a matter of creating, updating, and deleting the relations shown in Figure 4, and can be implemented with the Data Definition Language of the DBMS.

At a finer level, a create/update/delete protocol for instances of a Class such as AttributeGenus is equivalent to creating, updating, and deleting a tuple in the corresponding relation, in this case, the A_GENUS relation. To maintain the integrity of the database, deleting an AttributeGenus requires at some point updating any FunctionOf Associations in which it was the argument, as well as deleting the tuples in the Elemental Relation which assigned values to the members of the deleted Genus.

Higher level model manipulations for restructuring (e.g. integration of models) or value assignment (e.g. optimizing) will require more complex "methods" taking the form of programs in the Data Manipulation or Query Language of the host DBMS. "Value Assignment" protocols will also require going outside of the DBMS to access mathematical software capable of performing the required computations.

In the next section, we will discuss how some of these model management functions are being implemented in a prototype SMMS.

4 A PROTOTYPE MMS

A prototype of a Structured MMS is being developed for a desktop computer, in particular, an IBM PC/XT. The primary software product we are using is KnowledgeMan (Trademark, Micro Data Base Systems, Inc.). KnowledgeMan is basically a relational DBMS augmented by a procedural programming language and a spreadsheet capability. We are also using LP83 (Trademark, Sunset Software) to solve the linear programming models.

4.1 Restrictions

In order to simplify implementation of the prototype, we have imposed the following restrictions on the models:

No modules are used.

No indexing variables (e.g. i, j, k) are used.

Every entity genus has its own index set.

Every function, test and attribute genus must be indexed by a single entity genus.

All function and test rules are specified at the generic level. (There are no elemental rules.)

The entity elements comprising each compound entity element must be specified at the elemental level. (There are no generic index set statements.)

All attributes are assumed to be real-valued.

Initially, this prototype is intended to handle only linear programming (LP) models. Accordingly, we have limited the allowed function rules to just two (SUM, for sums within a single genus; and DOT, for dot products of two genera) and the test rules to three (GE, LE, EQ). For the "DOT" function and the "GE", " LE", and "EQ" rules, at least one of the two arguments must be a fixed attribute genus. Also, both arguments must have the same index set.

As an illustration, consider the structured modeling treatment of the classic transportation model discussed in detail in the previous lecture [9]. Figure 5 is the summary of the model, which is repeated here because it has been changed slightly (by the addition of a compound entity genus, NETWORK, and two function genera, INFLOW and OUTFLOW) to accommodate the above restrictions. The relational database representation of the transportation model is shown in Figure 6. (Note that although indexing variables and modules are shown in the summary, they are not represented in the database.)

&SDATA SOURCE DATA

PLANTi There is a list of PLANTS.

SUPi Every PLANT has a SUPPLY CAPACITY (tons).

&CDATA CUSTOMER DATA

CUSTj There is a list of CUSTOMERS.

DEMj Every CUSTOMER has a nonnegative DEMAND (tons).

&TDATA TRANSPORTATION DATA

LINKk There are some transportation LINKS from PLANTS to CUSTOMERS. There is at least one LINK incident to each PLANT, and at least one LINK incident to each CUSTOMER.

NETWORKn There is a TRANSPORTATION NETWORK which is a collection of transportation LINKS.

FLOWk There can be a nonnegative transportation FLOW (tons) over each LINK.

COSTk Every LINK has a TRANSPORTATION COST RATE ($/ton).

&RESULTS

OUTFLOWi There is a total OUTGOING FLOW at each PLANT.

INFLOWj There is a total INCOMING FLOW for each CUSTOMER.

$TOTALn There is a TOTAL COST associated with the FLOWS over all LINKS in the NETWORK.

T:SUPi For each PLANT, is the OUTGOING FLOW less than or equal to its SUPPLY CAPACITY? This is called the SUPPLY TEST.

T:DEMj For each CUSTOMER, is the INCOMING FLOW exactly equal to its DEMAND? This is called the DEMAND TEST.

Fig. 5. Summary of Transportation Model

E_GENUS

ENAME	ETYPE	INTERP
cust	pe	A list of customers
plant	pe	A list of plants
link	ce	Some transportation links
network	ce	The transportation network

CMPND_OF

CENAME	CALLS1	CALLS2
link	plant	cust
network	link	-

A_GENUS

ANAME	ATYPE	ATTR_OF	INTERP
dem	FA	cust	Customer demands (tons)
sup	FA	plant	Plant supply capacities (tons)
cost	FA	link	Unit costs of transportation
flow	VA	link	Amounts shipped
outflow	F	plant	Shipments out
inflow	F	cust	Shipments in
T:dem	F	cust	Meeting demands
T:sup	F	plant	Not exceeding supplies
$total	F	network	Total cost

FNCTN_OF

FNAME	F_OR_T	RULE	CALLS1	CALLS2
outflow	F	SUM	flow	-
inflow	F	SUM	flow	-
T:dem	T	EQ	inflow	dem
T:sup	T	LE	outflow	sup
$total	F	DOT	cost	flow

Fig. 6a. Generic Relations for Transportation Model

E

ENAME	INDEX	EL_NAME
cust	1	pitts
cust	2	atl
cust	3	clev
plant	1	dal
plant	2	chi
link	1	dal-pitts
link	2	dal-atl
link	3	dal-clev
link	4	chic-pitts
link	5	chic-clev
network	1	the network

AREAL

ANAME	IND	VALUE
sup	1	20000.00000
sup	2	42000.00000
dem	1	25000.00000
dem	2	15000.00000
dem	3	22000.00000
cost	1	23.50000
cost	2	17.75000
cost	3	32.45000
cost	4	7.60000
cost	5	25.75000

CE

CENAME	IND	CALLS	C_IND
link	1	plant	1
link	1	cust	1
link	2	plant	1
link	2	cust	2
link	3	plant	1
link	3	cust	3
link	4	plant	2
link	4	cust	1
link	5	plant	2
link	5	cust	3
network	1	link	1
network	1	link	2
network	1	link	3
network	1	link	4
network	1	link	5

Fig. 6b Elemental Relations for Transportation Model

4.2 Protocols

In designing the protocols for the prototype, we have taken as given the database objects (relations, attributes, tuples, etc.) and the associated protocols for creating, updating, deleting, testing and accessing those objects. Constructing a SMMS then is equivalent to defining the Object Class "StructuredModel", in particular, its instance variables and methods. An instance of this class is equivalent to an instance of the relational database in Figure 4. Although there are many methods which might be appropriate for this class, we have selected just two protocols for immediate implementation. They are "create/update/ delete" and "optimize".

Create/update/delete protocol. To implement this protocol, we have written three KnowledgeMan procedures: CRMODEL, UPDMODEL, and DELMODEL.

To create a structured model of the transportation problem under the model name "trans", for example, the user types (in KnowledgeMan):

```
crmodel using "trans"
```

The procedure creates appropriately named instances of all the relations in a structured model and then offers the user the opportunity to create tuples in each of them, in effect, creating instances of the Objects which are parts of the StructuredModel CompositeObject.

The DELMODEL procedure is invoked in a similar way. It deletes appropriately named instances of the structured modeling relations.

The UPDMODEL procedure operates at the relational level, and allows three different kind of updates (create, update, delete) to be performed on the tuples in each relation. So, the user must specify the desired operation and the relation, as well as name of the model. For example, typing

```
updmodel using "del", "a_genus", "trans"
```

enables the user to delete any or all instances of the class AttributeGenus (equivalently, tuples in the A_GENUS relation) of the transportation model.

ROWS

RNAME	BTYPE
$total1	e
inflow1	e
inflow2	e
inflow3	e
outflow1	e
outflow2	e

RHS

RNAME	VALUE
$total1	0.0000
inflow1	0.0000
inflow2	0.0000
inflow3	0.0000
outflow1	0.0000
outflow2	0.0000

BOUNDS

CNAME	VALUE	RTYPE
inflow1	25000.0000	FX
inflow2	15000.0000	FX
inflow3	22000.0000	FX
outflow1	20000.0000	UP
outflow2	42000.0000	UP

COLUMNS

CNAME	RNAME	VALUE
flow1	$total1	23.5000
flow2	$total1	17.7500
flow3	$total1	32.4500
flow4	$total1	7.6000
flow5	$total1	25.7500
flow1	inflow1	1.0000
flow4	inflow1	1.0000
flow2	inflow2	1.0000
flow3	inflow3	1.0000
flow5	inflow3	1.0000
flow1	outflow1	1.0000
flow2	outflow1	1.0000
flow3	outflow1	1.0000
flow4	outflow2	1.0000
flow5	outflow2	1.0000
$total1	$total1	-1.0000
inflow1	inflow1	-1.0000
inflow2	inflow2	-1.0000
inflow3	inflow3	-1.0000
outflow1	outflow1	-1.0000
outflow2	outflow2	-1.0000

Fig. 7 MPS Relations for a Transportation Model

Optimize Protocol. Since the prototype is supposed to manage linear programming models, the second essential protocol for a StructuredModel is "Optimize". Its purpose is to find optimal value assignments for all the Attributes in a given model which optimize (maximize or minimize) some specified function element subject to the condition that all test elements evaluate to "true".

We have chosen to implement the response to the message "Optimize" in two steps. The first step is to convert the Structured Model to a different relational representation (see Figure 7) which mirrors the "rows, columns, bounds" sections of a file representing an LP in "MPS format" (for better or worse, the industry standard). The second step is creating an MPS formatted file and submitting it to an LP solver to obtain the optimal values.

In converting to the "rows, columns, bounds" representation of an LP model, we have adopted the following conventions. There is a column in the LP matrix corresponding to each variable attribute and each function element in the model. Thus, the LP solution will provide values for all elements whose values are not specified in advance. There is a row in the LP matrix corresponding to each function element. The row constitutes a defining equation for the function element. Therefore, it is an equality constraint with a right-hand-side of zero and a coefficient of "-1" in the column corresponding to the function element being defined. Each test element (LE, GE, EQ) in the model is converted to the corresponding bound (upper,lower, or fixed, in MPS terminology) on the appropriate column. The objective function row consists of a single entry, a "+1" in the column corresponding to the function element specified as the objective by the user. (See Figure 7 for the MPS form of the Transportation Model.)

The interface from the DBMS to the LP "solver" takes the form of an ASCII file containing the matrix description in MPS format. The interface from the LP solver to the DBMS is an ASCII file containing all the column names and their optimal values.

Unfortunately, KnowledgeMan does not have a DOS window permitting access to other programs; so, the solution process is invoked by executing a batch procedure file under DOS. It has the following three steps:

(1) invoke a KnowledgeMan procedure which

(a) prompts the user for model name and objective,

(b) performs integrity checks on the model,

(c) converts the structured model relations to the corresponding MPS relations, and

(d) outputs an ASCII file containing the problem description in MPS format;

(2) invoke LP83 to input the problem description file, solve the LP problem, and output an ASCII file containing the solution;

(3) invoke a KnowledgeMan procedure which converts the solution file to a KnowledgeMan relation containing optimal value assignments for all function and variable attribute elements.

Figure 8 shows the optimal value assignments obtained by solving the transportation model represented in Figures 6 and 7.

It is worth noting that the procedure which converts the structured modeling relations to MPS relations is written entirely in (the KnowledgeMan equivalent of) relational algebra.

ANAME	IND	VALUE
$total	1	1056250.00000
flow	1	0.00000
flow	2	15000.00000
flow	3	5000.00000
flow	4	25000.00000
flow	5	17000.00000
inflow	1	25000.00000
inflow	2	15000.00000
inflow	3	22000.00000
outflow	1	20000.00000
outflow	2	42000.00000

Fig. 8 Optimal Value Assignments for a Transportation Model

5 DIRECTIONS FOR FUTURE WORK

It is clear that much needs to be done before we have a useful structured model management system. Future work will be directed along two major lines of investigation.

First, we need to extend the range of models which can be represented as structured models. In order to handle more complex linear programming models, we will need to add to the allowed set of function rules. A further extension to nonlinear programming models is possible by using factorable functions [7] to represent nonlinear functions in the model base.

As we extend the range of models, we will also need to extend the range of solvers available to assign values. Obviously, nonlinear models will require nonlinear optimizers. However, we will also need to interface with network optimizers and other LP codes. Besides optimization, of course, we will need to provide for evaluation or simulation and equation solving.

Second, we need to extend the range of operations that can be performed on the models. Accessing/Testing will be the next protocol implemented using the database query language. Integration of models, a matter of merging two structured model databases, is essential to building larger and more complex structured models and will be a priority.

Finally, we anticipate that using the SMMS in its current form requires considerable expertise on the part of the user for performing such tasks as formulating the model, choosing a solver, diagnosing errors, and explaining results. An "expert system shell" may provide the technology for codifying that expertise.

6 CONCLUDING REMARKS

If the promise of DSS is to be fulfilled, the technology for model management must be advanced to the level of the technology for data management. This is a difficult problem whose solution will likely require a multi-disciplinary approach, drawing on expertise in database management, artificial intelligence, and programming languages, as well as MS/OR.

The work described here is a first step in this direction. We propose to use the structured modeling meta-model as a basis for a model management system. Concepts borrowed from object-oriented programming help to delineate the objects constituting a "structured model" and the operations or "methods" which must be provided to manage those objects. A DBMS based on the relational data model provides most of the building blocks for the proposed system and the integrating mechanism with data and dialog components of a DSS. A prototype system is being constructed with a restricted set of function rules and a limited range of operations to show the feasibility of using structured model management to manage at least linear programming models.

Planned future developments will extend the range of models that can be represented and the range of operations that can be performed on them. We anticipate that much "expert knowledge" about building and using models will also be incorporated.

At this point in the development of model management technology, there are far more questions than answers. There is an opportunity--indeed, a need--for creative and original thinking about the nature of mathematical modeling and how its potential contribution to decision support may be more fully realized.

REFERENCES

1. Bobrow, D. G., and Stefik, M. (1981), The Loops Manual, Tech. Rep. KB-VSLI-81-13, Knowledge Systems Area, Xerox Palo Alto Research Center.

2. Copeland, G. and Maier, D. (1984), Making Smalltalk a database system, ACM SIGMOD, June, 316-325.

3. Dolk, D. R. (1986), Model management and structured modeling: The role of an information resource dictionary system, Dept. of Administrative Sciences, Naval Postgraduate School, Monterey, CA, August.

4. Dolk, D. R. (1987), Relational data models and relational data base systems: A tutorial, Proceedings, NATO Advanced Study Institute, Mathematical Models for Decision Support, July-August.

5. Geoffrion, A. M. (1987), An introduction to structured modeling, Management Science 33:5 (May), 547-588.

6. Goldberg, A., and Robson, D. (1983) Smalltalk-80, Addison-Wesley, Reading, MA.

7. Lenard, M. L. (1986), Representing models as data, Journal of Management Information Systems, 2:4, pp. 36-48.

8. Lenard, M. L. (1987a), An object-oriented approach to model management, Proceedings, Twentieth Hawaii International Conference on System Sciences, Volume I, 509-515, January.

9. Lenard, M. L. (1987b), Fundamentals of structured modeling, Proceedings, NATO Advanced Study Institute, Mathematical Models for Decision Support, July-August.

10. Oldford, R. W., and Peters, S. C. (1985) DINDE: Toward more statistically sophisticated software, Technical Report No. 55, MIT Center for Computer Research in Economics and Management Science, Cambridge, MA.

11. Stefik, M., and Bobrow, D. G. (1986), Object-oriented programming: Themes and variations, The AI Magazine, 5, pp. 40-62.

ACKNOWLEDGMENTS

The author wishes to thank Deniz Devrim and Ata Koseoglu, both of whom contributed time, talent, and dedication to the work of implementation.

This research was supported in part by National Science Foundation Grants No. RII-8310337 and No. SES-8520260.

Choice Theory and Data Base

James C. Moore, William B. Richmond and Andrew B. Whinston
Krannert Graduate School of Management
Purdue University
West Lafayette, IN 47907, U.S.A.

1. INTRODUCTION

The choice problem, choosing an alternative to maximize some index (e.g. utility), constitutes the majority of decision problems encountered. The decision maker's payoff depends upon the state of the world and the choice made. To solve the choice problem, the decision maker gathers information to determine the true state of the world, and then selects the best available alternative. In choosing a durable good, such as a VCR, the possible states of the world consist of the possible VCRs. The decision maker gathers information on the VCRs by reading *Consumer Reports*, talking to salesclerks, reading the trade magazines, etc. By gathering information, the decision maker reduces his/her uncertainty about which alternative is best; therefore allowing him/her to make a better choice.

Different choice models are applicable in different choice situations. We classify the choice scenarios into four groups based on their generality and on the number of decision makers:

1. Single decision maker, single choice situation.
2. Single decision maker, multiple choice situations.
3. Multiple decision maker, single choice situation
   A. Each decision maker solves his or her choice problem individually, but they all use a common choice process.
   B. The decision makers work as a team to solve a common choice problem.
4. Multiple decision maker, multiple choice situations
   A. Each decision maker solves his or her choice problem individually, but they all use a common choice process.
   B. The decision makers work as a team to solve a common choice problem.

An expert system is a typical example of a Group 1 choice model. In Mycin, for example, there is a single decision maker, the doctor; a single choice situation, selecting the proper treatment; and multiple problem instantiations, the patients (or more precisely, the patient visits). The doctor gathers information on the patient's disease by running tests, and he/she submits the test results to Mycin, which analyzes the data, identifies the disease and chooses a treatment for the patient.

NATO ASI Series, Vol. F48
Mathematical Models for Decision Support
Edited by G. Mitra

Group 2 models are the most common. The Hierarchical Elimination Method (HEM) [21], Elimination by Aspect (EBA) [20], Lancaster's consumer choice model [9], Luce's choice model [10], AHP [17], etc. all fit into Group 2. Each model was designed to apply to an individual decision maker in a variety of choice situations. In EBA, for example, the decision maker successively eliminates alternatives by selecting desired attributes and eliminating the alternatives that lack the chosen attributes. This model is applicable to choosing VCRs, wines, cars and anything else where the choice depends on the alternatives' attributes.

Group 3B corresponds to distributed expert systems and group decision support systems designed for a single application, such as a group DSS for plant location. Group 4B contains a plethora of group decision support models based on such techniques as aspiration levels, the Delphi technique, and group utility functions. Examples of group decision models include NEGO [6], GDS1 [7], economic social choice functions [11], and a revised Delphi approach [19].

Group 3A corresponds to the optimal file search, or the common index problem [14]. In this scenario each user is a decision maker and choosing the best record is the problem. All of the users must use a common choice process, the search algorithm, for selecting a record in the file. Group 4A corresponds to data base queries. Each user can pose many types of queries or choice problems, depending on the structure and contents of the data base, but the system forces each user to use a particular choice process - the one supported by the query system.

We view data base retrieval as a choice problem because in most decision situations, the decision maker wants to know what the best available alternative is, not if there are alternatives with properties (A and B and C) or (D and E and F). Data base systems are designed to support all or nothing retrievals where either the requested record exists and is returned or nothing is returned. To find the best available record in a traditional data base system, the decision maker must design his/her own search algorithm. He/she must:

1. determine a characterization of the best available alternative
2. formulate a query that determines if the characterization exists or not
3. if the characterization does not exist or if it matches too many records, the decision maker must repeat steps 1 and 2 until a suitable solution is found.

Both the efficacy and efficiency of this method depend on the user's knowledge of the contents of the data base, and on the user's willingness to spend his/her mental resources. By treating queries as choice problems, the data base system becomes responsible for evaluating the information and presenting a manageable set of information that is relevant to the choice problem.

2. CHOICE MODELS

Since we view queries as choice problems, we need to determine a choice model appropriate for expressing and executing the queries. We start with a brief survey of some choice models developed in different disciplines, and evaluate their applicability to data base systems. We then introduce a normative decision model that includes the information-acquisition process and discuss the data base model resulting from the decision model.

Due to its importance, psychologists, management scientists and economists continue to investigate facets of the choice problem. Psychologists probe the human choice process to discover the heuristics people use and the biases people employ when making choices [20,21,22]. Management science searches for sensible methods and techniques that overcome people's foibles and lead to good choices [5,7,17]. Economics investigates the choice problem's structure to determine the properties of optimal choices [9,11,12].

Economic theory treats the choice problem as a maximization problem and tends to ignore the choice process. One economic formulation of the choice problem is:

$$\begin{gathered}\text{Maximize } \; U(z) \\ \text{subject to } \; p\cdot x \le k \\ \text{with: } \; z = By;\; x = Ay;\; x,y,z \ge 0\end{gathered}$$

where: $U(\cdot)$ is a utility function; z is a collection of attributes; x is a set of objects; y is a collection of activities; k is the budget (initial endowment); and A and B are transformation matrices [9]. Determining a consumer's optimal commodity bundle is an intractable nonlinear program, but because economic theory assumes a closed, convex set of alternatives, this formulation of the choice problem can still be used to study the properties of an optimal choice (e.g., the marginal utility of different attributes or commodities).

In real-life choice problems and in data base queries, the decision maker faces a finite set of alternatives and requires a process for making choices. A common normative method for solving the choice problem is to sequentially search through the alternatives, calculating each alternative's utility and selecting the alternative that maximizes utility. Two difficulties arise with this approach. First, people find it difficult to specify their utility function. Second, even with a fully specified utility function or an ideal alternative (which need be neither available nor possible), the cost of evaluating and selecting the best alternative may outweigh any benefits gained over a random or otherwise non-utility maximizing choice.

Psychologists assert that people develop heuristics to reduce the amount of mental resources they must use. These heuristics impose a structure on the choice problem and reduce the quantity of information to be processed. Tversky and Sattath [21], for example, claim that people choose a solution by successively eliminating alternatives that lack a desired characteristic until only a single alternative remains. Although this could be implemented as a data base query system by having the user rate the attributes, the process may lead to poor choices. Since the data base system can process certain types of information less expensively than a human, a choice method used by people may be inappropriate for a data base system. To arrive at an appropriate algorithm, we must determine the trade-off between the value of improved information and the cost of processing.

Management scientists operationalize the economic choice model with mathematical programming; they proscribe heuristic choice processes (e.g., outranking and aspiration levels) that result in "good" choices and they elicit and assess individual and group utility functions for use in the choice models. The mathematical programming models work for choice problems that fit the economic assumptions, but are inappropriate for data base models. The heuristics operationalize some of the human techniques studied by the psychologists. Although the heuristic processes may work in a data base environment, we want to use a normative model that explicitly accounts for the tradeoff between the increased cost of more information and the increase in the value of the decision: a model that describes the choice process of a rational individual; an individual who includes the cost of making the choice in determining which alternative to select.

We take a normative decision theoretic view of the individual choice problem (queries) and we design choice algorithms with respect to this view. In taking a normative decision theoretic view, we include the cost of the choice process in determining the "best" available alternative, so a readily accessible, good alternative may be preferable to an excellent, but inaccessible alternative. Since we include the cost of the search in determining the goal of the search, choice algorithms differ from algorithms developed in computer science. In computer algorithm theory, algorithms are designed to minimize some time measure (e.g., worst case time) while obtaining a fixed result or partition; whereas choice algorithms are designed to determine the best final partition of the state space for making a choice or decision. The partition results from computations, comparisons and other experiments that provide information about the true state of the world. Each experiment divides the state space into subsets that are mutually exclusive and exhaustive. For example, if the state space is the set of all VCRs, then the experiment "Type of VCR" partitions the state space into three mutually exclusive and exhaustive subsets: VHS VCRs, Beta VCRs and 8mm VCRs.

Another example may clarify some of these points. In the computer file search problem, a person requests a specific record from the file. The computer searches the file and if the requested record is in the file, the computer displays it. If the record is not in the file, the computer tells the person that the requested record does not exist. In algorithm theory [1] the file search algorithms always obtain the finest partition - they distinguish between each record in the file. The file search algorithms are then evaluated on the time required to reach the finest partition.

Moore and Whinston [16] use a decision theory framework to solve the file search problem, and they show that reaching the finest partition is optimal only when the payoff and cost functions meet certain criteria. In general, decision algorithms will not necessarily obtain full information (partition the state space into unique elements). Distinguishing between alternatives or states of the world must be economically justifiable. If for each element in a set of alternatives, the utility of choosing any alternative from the set is the same, then distinguishing between these alternatives is suboptimal. If the cost of distinguishing between alternatives outweighs the benefits of doing so, then distinguishing between the alternatives is suboptimal.

2.1. Example

We present an example that we will use throughout this paper to illustrate our points. Suppose you want to choose a wine for dinner tonight, and the restaurant stocks a large assortment of wines produced since 1945. There are over 10,000 wines produced in France, 6,000 in the U.S., 5,000 in Germany, 5,000 in Italy, and 2,000 in Portugal and Spain, not to mention the wines produced in the rest of the world - and that is for just one year. Since the restaurant caters to a high-tech crowd, and since a traditional wine list would weigh 30 pounds, the restaurant computerized its wine list. In addition to the vintner, the estate, and the vintage, the wine data base includes data on where the grapes were grown, the wine's characteristic with respect to its smell, color, taste and aftertaste, as well as wine experts' comments and ratings (Table 1 contains a partial data base listing).

A customer's goal is to search the data base (or have the system search the data base) to find the wine that will best complement the meal. The diner must make a tradeoff between the amount of time spent searching the data base and the appropriateness of the wine - the more time spent in search, the better the wine.

3. DECISION MODEL

We model the choice process using a decision model first presented by Moore and Whinston [15]. In this model, a choice or decision is a function of eight variables:

$$\mathbf{D} = \langle X, \phi, \omega, D, A, \{M_a \mid a \in A\}, c, r \rangle$$

where:

- X is the state space.
- D is the set of possible final decisions or choices.
- ϕ is a probability distribution over the set of alternatives, X.
- $\phi(x)$ represents the probability that x is the best available alternative, so for the wine example, $\phi(x)$ is the frequency of a wine x being the best available wine.
- ω is a function of the true best alternative, x, and the decision or choice d. $\omega(x,d)$ represents the gross payoff of choosing d when x is the best available alternative.
- A is the set of information gathering actions. It represents the computations and comparisons available to the data base system.

Table 1. Wine Data Base

Attributes	Attribute Values
Type	Red, White
Region	Bordeaux, Burgundy, Napa, Sonoma Douro, Vinho Verde
Year	1945 - 1985
Color	Brick, Garnet, Ruby, Purple Straw, Gold, Green tint
Smell	Truffles, Earth, Cherry, Chocolate, Plum Spicy, Herbal, Citric, Pear
Taste	Rich, Full, Cherry, Oak, Plum, Spicy, Citric, Honey, Pear, Fig, Earth
Aftertaste	Long finish, Moderate finish, Clean, Lemony

	Wine	Region	Year	Type	Color	Smell	Taste	Aftertaste
1.	Cos d' estournel	Bordeaux	1966	Red	Brick	Truffles	Rich	Long
2.	Cos d' estournel	Bordeaux	1961	Red	Brick	Earth	Rich	Moderate
3.	Echezeaux	Burgundy	1984	Red	Garnet	Cherry	Spicy	Long
4.	Moillard Beaune	Burgundy	1984	Red	Garnet	Citric	Cherry	Moderate
5.	Heitz Martha's V.	Napa	1982	Red	Garnet	Choc'lte	Full	Long
6.	Caymus	Napa	1978	Red	Ruby	Choc'lte	Oak	Long
7.	Kenwood	Sonoma	1978	Red	Garnet	Plum	Cherry	Moderate
8.	Kenwood	Sonoma	1983	Red	Ruby	Plum	Cherry	Long
9.	Barca Velha	Douro	1982	Red	Purple	Earth	Full	Moderate
10.	Taylor Vintage Port	Douro	1983	Red	Purple	Spicy	Plum	Long
11.	Ch. Carbonnieux	Bordeaux	1985	White	Straw	Citric	Earth	Clean
12.	Ch. Oliver	Bordeaux	1984	White	Straw	Herbal	Citric	Clean
13.	Le Montrechet	Burgundy	1966	White	Gold	Truffles	Honey	Lemony
14.	Domaine Lapierre	Burgundy	1985	White	Straw	Earth	Pear	Lemony
15.	Geyser Peak	Sonoma	1985	White	Straw	Pear	Pear	Lemony
16.	William Wheeler	Sonoma	1985	White	Straw	Herbal	Fig	Clean
17.	Silverado	Napa	1985	White	Straw	Herbal	Citric	Lemony
18.	Sequoia Grove	Napa	1984	White	Gold	Citric	Pear	Clean
19.	Palacio da Brejoeria	Vinho Verde	1984	White	Straw	Earth	Earth	Clean
20.	Tormes Baiao	Vinho Verde	1984	White	Green tint	Earth	Earth	Clean

$\{M_a \mid a \in A\}$ is the partition of the state space resulting from action a. So if X is a set of wines and if a is: "Type of wine" then $\{M_a\} = \{\{M_{a1}\},\{M_{a2}\}\} = \{\{x_1,\ldots,x_m\}, \{x_{m+1},\ldots,x_n\}\}$ where $x_1,\ldots,x_m$ are red wines and $x_{m+1},\ldots,x_n$ are white wines.

c is a function of the information actions, where c(a) is the cost of executing action a.

r is the maximum number of experiments allowed.

The goal is to determine an information and decision strategy, σ, that maximizes $\Omega(\sigma)$ - $G(\sigma)$, where:

σ defines a sequence of actions that partition the state space.
At each element of a partition a (possibly different) action is specified. For each element of the final partition, σ determines the decision (choice) to be made.

Ω is the expected value of the strategy σ.

$\Omega = \sum P(B)\cdot\omega(x,d)$, where d is the decision taken when the information-gathering strategy ends in partition element B, and $\Pi(B)$ is the probability of reaching partition element B.

Γ is the expected cost of the strategy σ.

$\Gamma = \sum \Pi(B)\cdot C(B)$, where C(B) is the cost of executing the experiments that result in partition element B.

4. DATA BASE MODEL

Implicit within the decision model lies a data base model. A data base model specifies a method for describing and obtaining information about objects and the relationships among the objects. In the decision model, the objects of interest are represented by elements of the state space. The relationships among and within objects are represented by experiments, and the query algorithms are represented by information and decision strategies.

The specification of the state space depends upon how we formalize the choice problem and includes all of the objects of interest. In choosing records from an ordered file, the gaps between the records must be specified as well as the records. In choosing a best element from a file or data base, the state space could consist of classes of utility functions, and the goal would be to match the user's utility function with one class of functions in the state space. The utility function would then point to the record in the data base that maximizes the chosen utility function. In the most natural specification of the state space, the elements of the state space are records in the data base. We use this interpretation in the remainder of this paper.

Executing an experiment, $a \in A$, partitions the state space, $\mathbf{X}$: $\mathbf{M}_a = \{M_{a1},M_{a2},\ldots,M_{an(a)}\}$, where $M_{ay} = \{x \in \mathbf{X} \mid a(x) = y\}$, $y = 1,\ldots,n(a)$ [n(a) is the number of possible outcomes for experiment a]. Equating the experiments with the objects' attributes, each experiment partitions the objects into classes with identical attribute values. In the wine example, the Taste attribute (experiment) partitions the wine into 11 classes.

Letting **X** = Wines = $\{x_1, x_2, \ldots, x_{20}\}$ then experiment a = Taste results in:

$$\mathbf{M}_{Taste} = \{M_{Rich}, M_{Full}, \ldots M_{Cherry}, M_{Earth}\},$$

where, for example M_{Cherry} = the wines that taste of cherries = {4,7,8}. Executing a series of experiments refines the partition of **X**. So executing the Taste experiment and then the Type experiment partitions the record into sets of wines of the same type and taste (e.g., red wines that taste of cherries). Executing every experiment a ∈ A results in the finest partition of the state space that is achievable with the experiment set A. We denote the finest partition B^A. B^A does not necessarily partition the state space into unique elements. If the experiments consist solely of partial hash functions, then B^A represents the hash buckets. (A hash function calculates a record's location in storage based on the record's key. In general, the location calculated is the location of a group (bucket) of records. To find the desired record, the bucket is searched sequentially. A partial hash function provides the location of a group of buckets, which must then be searched sequentially.)

The set of subsets of X that can be obtained by a sequence of experiments will be denoted A(X). We can define a partial order, ≤, over A(X) such that for B and B' ∈ A(X), B ≤ B' iff B is a subset of B'. (A(X),≤) forms a lattice (see Figure 1). Each element, B, of A(X) is fully defined by the set of experiment-signals used to obtain B. For B = {7,8} in the wine data base, B is defined by Taste = Cherry and Smell = Plum. We define B(A) to be the set of experiment-signals used to arrive at B. A set B' = {1,4} is not an element of A(X) since there does not exist a set of experiment-signals, B'(A), that results in B'. Using the sets of experiment-signals, we define the meet, +, and the join, ×.

The meet of B and B' = $\{x \in X \mid \forall y \in B(A) \cap B'(A) : a(x) = y\}$
The join of B and B' = $\{x \in X \mid \forall y \in B(A) \cup B'(A) : a(x) = y\}$

For example, if B = {1,2} and B' = {13}, then B + B' = {1,2,3,...20} = X. To see this, first note that B(A) = {Color = Brick} and B'(A) = {Taste = Honey}. B(A) ∩ B'(A) = ∅, so $\{x \in X \mid \forall y \in \emptyset : a(x) = y\}$ = X (none of the y values are specified for any attribute, so all x ∈ X satisfy the criteria). As an example of the join, if B = {2,9,14,19,20} and B' = {1,2,3,4,5,6,7,8,9,10}, then B × B' = {2,9}. Here, B(A) = {Smell = Earth} and B'(A) = {Type = Red}, so B(A) ∪ B'(A) = {Smell = Earth, Type = Red}; thus $\{x \in X \mid \forall y \in B(A) \cup B'(A) : a(x) = y\}$ is the set of all wines that are red and smell of earth, which is {2,9}. Under these two definitions for the meet and the join, the greatest element of the lattice is X, the state space, and the least element is ∅, the empty set.

The interpretation of the join is fairly straightforward. The join of B and B' is the set of alternatives that is common to both B and B'. To explain the meet, we look at an information strategy. Assume the information strategy for a particular individual is as shown in Figure 2.

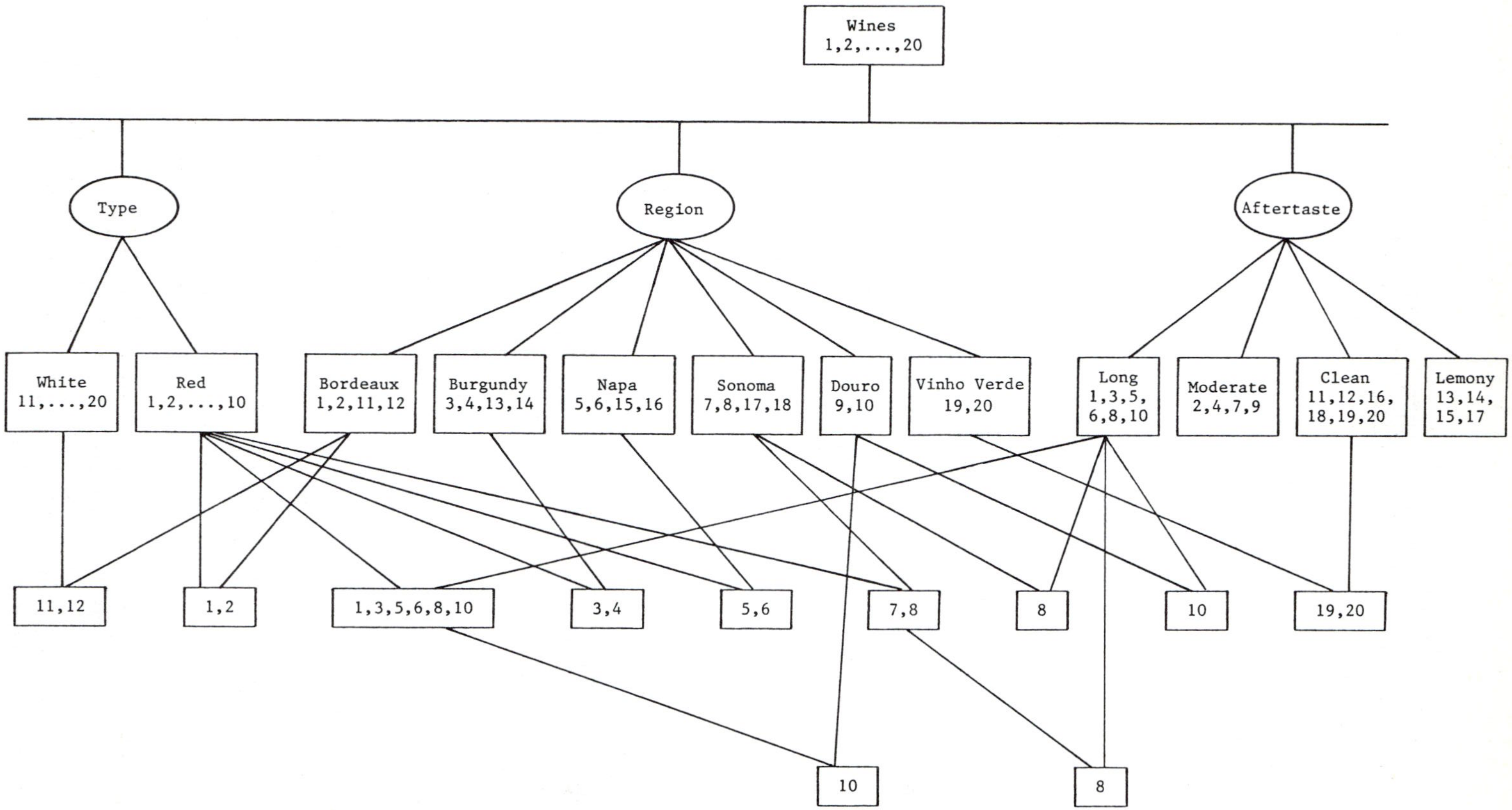

Figure 1. Partial Diagram of the Wine Lattice Resulting from Attribute Experiments

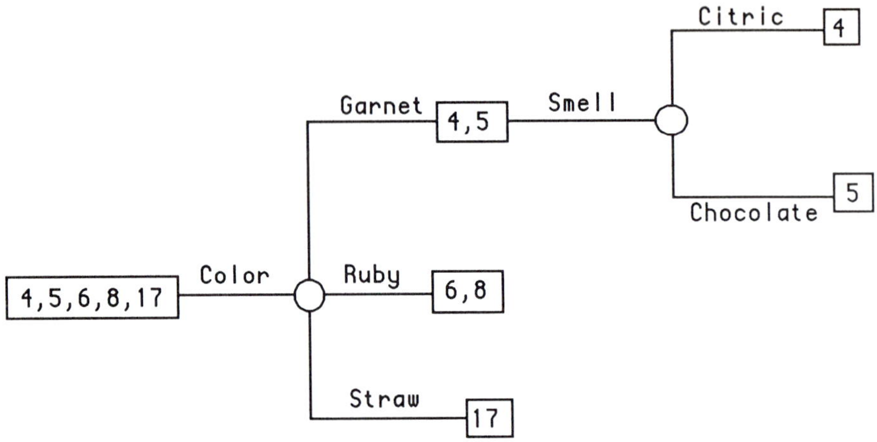

Figure 2. Information Strategy

The meet of any two elements, B_1 and B_2, is represented by the node where the paths from B_1 and B_2 to the root intersect. The meet defines a common starting point from which both elements of the lattice are derived. A set of elements (e.g., {9,10}) can occur several times within the lattice. Each occurrence is the result of a different sequence of experiments. Specifically, each alternative occurs as an individual set, $\{x_i\}$, up to k! times (where k is the number of attributes.)

The lattice is a structure that is being proposed as a data base model [8,18] and as an object-oriented programming language model. The partition data base model [18] is similar to the model presented above. The partition data base model is based on the concept of a partitioning. A data base consists of a set of objects, e, drawn from a universal set w. Each of the objects' attributes induces a partitioning on the set of objects e. A partitioning is defined as a family of mutually disjoint subsets of e. (The definition of a partitioning does not exclude the empty set; whereas the definition of a partition does. Neither the definition of a partition, nor the definition of a partitioning require the family of subsets to be exhaustive).

The data base's essential information is carried by the partitionings. The data base begins with a universe, U, of atomic partitionings about which information is stored. More detailed information is derived using the sum, +, and the product, ×, operators. Given two partitionings Q and R, Q+R is the least upper bound or meet of Q and R and Q×R is the greatest lower bound or join of Q and R. The product and sum operators satisfy the lattice postulates (indempotence, commutativity, associativity, and absorption), so the set of all partitionings forms a lattice. The join is equivalent to the join for the decision model. The meet differs from the one described above because the meet of two elements of the lattice need not be in the lattice. For example, if B = {1,2} and B' = {13}, then B + B' = {1,2,13} instead of {1,2,3,...,20}. To date, search algorithms over a lattice have not been developed. Spyratos [18] suggests that a deduction process will be applicable, but he does not develop the idea.

The lattice of partitions that results from a set of experiments, A, represents all possible strategies that do not include the null experiment. Strategies that do not result in complete information are represented by a path that does not go to the lowest (indvidual element) level. A lattice structure induced by the experiments exists regardless of the set of experiments used. The set of experiments, $A = \{a_1, \ldots, a_n\}$, where a_i partitions the set of alternatives into $\{\{x_i\}, \{X \backslash x_i\}\}$ also forms a lattice. Since choice models, both normative and empirical, induce a lattice on subsets of the alternatives, it seems natural that the elements of a data base model should form a lattice, and that retrieval algorithms correspond to choice processes that trace a path through the lattice. When we define a common group process (algorithm) for choosing records in the data base, we restrict the focus to a small portion of the lattice. This portion of the full lattice corresponds to the type lattice used in object-oriented models [2]. When studying either individual choice strategies, or a common group strategy, using the full lattice structure is excessive. However, when we look at group choice problems (Groups 3A and 4A), the complete lattice becomes more relevant. Each individual has his/her own choice process, which can be defined over the lattice. Using the concept of the meet, we can determine the common starting point where the individuals agree on the choice strategy and on the set of acceptable alternatives. Additionally, if the individual strategies do not obtain complete information, then the concept of the join can be used to combine the individuals' knowledge.

The set of experiments and the resulting lattice determine the types of queries that the system can efficiently process. Data base theory's fascination with attribute and is-a based lattices stems from the assumption that the system will be used for processing traditional information retrieval. The relationship between the type of experiments and the type of queries leads us to discuss the relationship between data base and choice theory in two sections: one on exact match queries, which uses attribute experiments, and another on best match queries, which require a different set of experiments. We start with exact match retrieval, and since we approach a data base retrieval as a choice problem, we look at how a rational individual chooses an alternative from a set. The choice process corresponds to the data base retrieval process that would be ideal for the individual. We assume that a decision maker begins with no information about the alternatives. He/she performs a series of information gathering actions, and each action partitions the set of alternatives and reduces the number of alternatives under consideration. The action chosen at each step depends on the results of all of the previous actions. The goal is to determine a sequence of actions that will result in an optimal partition of the set of alternatives.

The choice process depends on what we assume about the decision maker and what the decision maker knows about the offered set. Initially, we assume that the person knows the form of his/her ideal alternative, but does not know its identifier, and that he/she has a spoiled brat payoff (utility) function. The spoiled brat payoff function is:

$$w(x) = \begin{cases} \varpi & \text{if the desired alternative is returned} \\ 0 & \text{if any other alternative is returned} \end{cases}$$

The decision maker wants what he has asked for or nothing. (This is a standard assumption in data base search. The system assumes the user knows the record he/she wants, and if the desired record is not in the data base then the system returns a null response). The optimal information acquisition strategy depends on what other information the decision maker has. If the decision maker knows the characterization of all of the other alternatives, he/she can determine an optimal strategy. For example, if the decision maker knows the records in the wine data base are characterized by the tuple (Region, Color, Smell) and the available alternatives are:

4. (Burgundy, Garnet, Citric),
5. (Napa, Garnet, Chocolate),
6. (Napa, Ruby, Chocolate),
8. (Sonoma, Ruby, Plum),
17. (Napa, Straw, Herbal),

and the best available alternative is (Napa, Garnet, Chocolate), then the optimal strategy is to partition the alternatives based on Color and then Smell (or vice versa) (see Figure 2). If the decision maker faces a choice from a randomly drawn set of k alternatives, where k is fixed and known, then we can calculate a strategy that minimizes the expected number of experiments (cost) over all subsets of alternatives of size k. If the decision maker faces a choice from a randomly drawn subset of alternatives, where the cardinality of the subset is unknown, then the optimal choice strategy minimizes the expected cost over all possible subsets of alternatives. This is the choice scenario usually faced by an individual. For example, assume the set of all possible alternatives is:

Type		Region		Price	
Red	White	Bordeaux	Burgundy	$100/bottle	$10/bottle
1	0	1	0	1	0
1	0	1	0	0	1
1	0	0	1	1	0
1	0	0	1	0	1
0	1	1	0	1	0
0	1	1	0	0	1
0	1	0	1	1	0
0	1	0	1	0	1

At any given time only some subset, which is initially unknown to the decision maker, is available. An optimal strategy, when the decision maker knows only the ideal point and when each subset of the alternatives is equally likely, is to test each attribute in succession Type, Region and then Price. (Due to the assumption that all possible subsets are equally likely, the order of the experiments is immaterial). Depending on the actual set of available alternatives, the desired alternative may be selected or shown not to exist without executing every experiment. [Note that in each case we assume that the person gets the requested best available alternative. This assumption lets the strategy depend only on the best, requested alternative.]

So far, we have been describing an individual choice process. The data base problem differs from the individual choice problem, since instead of a fixed user searching a random set of alternatives, we have a random user searching a fixed alternative set. Since there are multiple users of the data base, each with his/her own utility function and best available record, an optimal choice process would be different for each user. The data base system could provide each user with his/her own optimal algorithm; however, we generally expect the data base system to provide a common choice process -- a common sequence of information gathering actions (computations) and the resulting final partition, which is in some sense good for all of the users. We can determine a search strategy for a particular data base instantiation and user population if we know the optimal search strategy for each class of users (a class of users has the same choice alternative) and know the distribution of the requests.

To create the group strategy, take the experiment that occurs most frequently in the optimal individual strategies. This experiment will partition the set of alternatives. For each set in the partition, determine the relevant optimal individual strategies and take the most frequent experiment as the next experiment in the group strategy. Continue this process until the choice tree is determined. [Note: In some cases, there will be more than one optimal individual strategy. All optimal individual strategies must be included in deciding which experiment to use in the group strategy.]

The group strategy may or may not be optimal (the least expected cost) for the group. We present this method of constructing a group strategy to show how the individual strategies relate to the group strategy. We can use dynamic programming to determine optimal strategies for both individuals and the group. To obtain a solution using dynamic programming is infeasible, except for small sets of alternatives. We look at alternative methods of constructing choice strategies after discussing more choice scenarios and their relationship to data base retrieval.

We have assumed that the individual always gets the ideal alternative when it is available, and we have not included the cost of gathering the information in determining the choice. The cost of the choice process frequently affects which alternative a human chooses, but it is ignored in the data base literature. For electronic shopping, information retrieval (e.g., article indexes) and other data base systems that charge for using the system, the incremental cost of using the system must be justified by improved choices.

We again begin by looking at the individual choice process. We assume that the ideal (requested) alternative is available and that the gross payoff function for the choice process is:

$$-[u(x^{*}) - u(x_d)\cdot]$$

where

x^{*} is the ideal alternative

x_d is the chosen alternative

$u(\cdot)$ is a linear utility function.

The net payoff function is $-[u(x^{*}) - u(x_d)] - C(B)$ where $C(B)$ is the cost of gathering information that results in partition element B (from which the final choice is made). We assume that if the number of alternatives in B is greater than 1, then the choice from the alternatives in B is random. The optimal strategy depends on more than just the ideal alternative.

For example, if we want to select a wine and the attributes available are:

Type, Color, Smell, Taste and Aftertaste

and the ideal alternative is

19. (White, Straw, Earth, Earth, Clean)

then the optimal strategy (ignoring the cost of gathering information) consists of executing: Color = Straw, Smell = Earth, and either Taste = Earth or Aftertaste = Clean. The only alternative remaining in the partition is the desired alternative (see Figure 3).

When we include the cost of gathering information in making a decision, the strategy depends more intimately on the payoff (utility) function. Assume $u(\cdot)$ is defined as:

$$u(x) = 100 \text{ White} + 100 \text{ Straw} + 100 \text{ Earth} + 100 \text{ Earth} + 100 \text{ Clean},$$

and any other attribute value adds 0 to the payoff. Let the cost per experiment be 100. The optimal strategy is to take a single experiment, Taste = Earth (see Figure 4). The resulting partition element is B = {11,19,20}. A random choice from this set has an expected value of 433, so the expected net payoff is -[500 - 433] -100 = -167. A completely random choice has an expected net value of -[500 - 155] - 0 = -345, so it pays to take the experiment. Taking two experiments could lead to a payoff of at most -200, which is not justifiable.

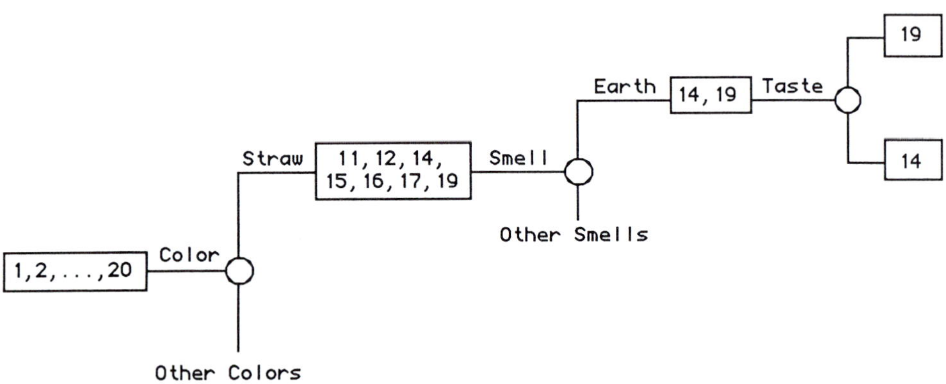

Figure 3. Costless Information Gathering Strategy

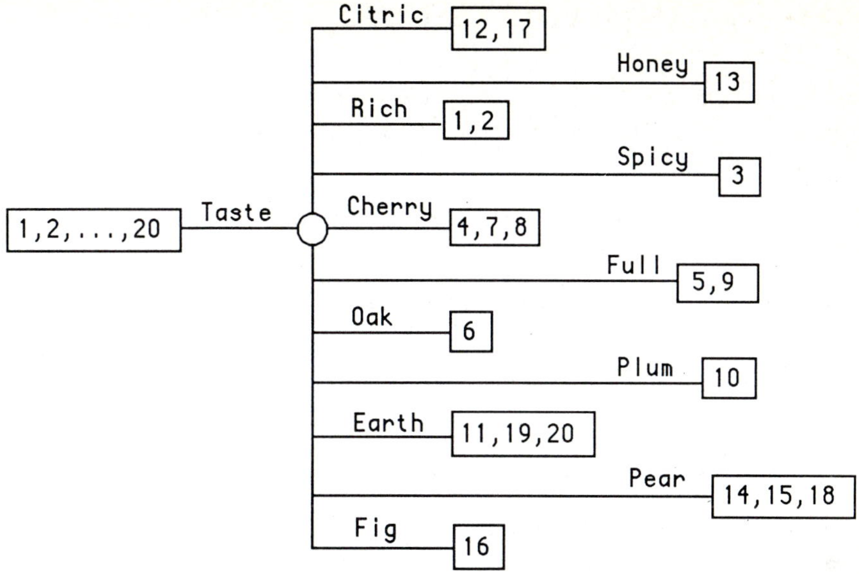

Figure 4. Information Gathering Strategy That Includes Cost of Information

To change the optimal strategy, all we have to do is change the utility function. If

$$u(x) = 100 \text{ White} + 100 \text{ Straw} + 100 \text{ Earth} + 100 \text{ Earth} + 100 \text{ Clean} + 99 \text{ Green tint},$$

(so the ideal alternative remains #19), then the optimal strategy is to take the Color experiment and to choose wine #20 (Figure 5). This strategy has a net payoff of -[500-499] - 100 = -101 versus -[500 - 466] - 100 = -134 for the original strategy. In this case it is optimal to take a wine known not to be the best available, rather than continue the choice process.

As an aside, note that in this example, only the Color attribute carried information relevant to the choice. Mendelson and Saharia [13] use an economic model to determine on which attributes data should be collected and stored. Including the cost of the choice process plays a similar role. If the choice of the alternative is the final goal, then only information relevant to the choice process needs to be kept in the data base.

Again, we can use dynamic programming to determine an optimal strategy that accounts for the cost of experimentation, but it is infeasible except for small sets of alternatives. We can try to use the individual strategies to create the common group strategy, but this is more problematic than before. As an example, consider trying to derive a common choice process for the two individuals with the linear utility functions defined above. For each person, only a single experiment is

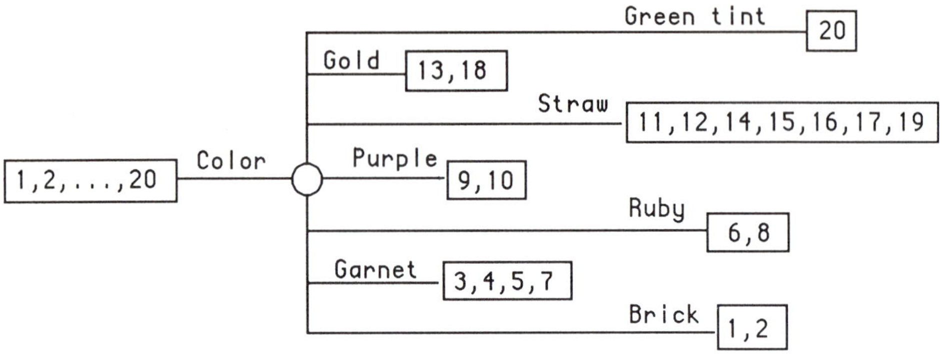

Figure 5. Information Gathering Strategy for Revised Utility Function

justifiable, but the experiments that each wants to take is different. To determine the optimal strategy requires an interpersonal comparison of utility, and deciding which of the two individuals should be better off. These issues are discussed in the economic social choice literature and bargaining literature, but are largely ignored in data base theory.

We are more interested in finding the best available alternative than in a requested alternative. There are two approaches to solving this type of query. Each approach is characterized by the type of input to the query. In one approach, the input is a characterization of the ideal choice. A distance function or similarity measure is used to find the record in the data base closest to the ideal point. This approach is discussed in the computational geometry literature [4] and [3]. The major drawback for this type of approach is that the same similarity measure is used for all queries. So if the same ideal point is used in two queries, then the same response will be returned. From a choice standpoint, this is not desirable. Consider two choice scenarios with the same ideal point -- a bottle of 1961, Red Bordeaux from Chateau Margaux. Both utility functions are functions of Year, Type, Region and Estate. The first person is a wine snob, whose utility is primarily a function of Estate. The second person is a neophyte oenophile whose utility is based on vintage charts. Assuming that the ideal bottle is not carried by the restaurant, then the best available wine will be different for each person. The first person wants any bottle of Chateau Margaux; whereas the second person wants any bottle of 1961, Red Bordeaux. In the second approach, the user enters a utility function which is used to calculate the ideal point. The problem with this approach is that it can require evaluating each alternative.

Before looking for a common algorithm for a group of users, we look at solving the problem of how an individual would find his/her best alternative, and then use the solution as a stepping stone to deriving a choice process for the group of users. If we assume that the individual begins with no knowledge about the alternatives, and that the experiments partition the alternatives based on attribute values, then under what conditions can he/she find the best alternative?

We look at how an individual chooses a bottle of wine. If the individual has never had wine and knows nothing about wine, then a list of wines and their attributes is meaningless. To describe the choice process we would have to include experiments such as: read wine guides, talk to salesclerks, and attend wine tastings. We assume, therefore, that the person using the data base knows something about wine; that he/she knows what the attributes mean (such as big means full-bodied, strong, robust, and assertive, and earthy means tasting of the soil in which the grapes were grown).

So given this knowledgeable and economically rational oenophile, how does he/she go about selecting a wine? If we assume that the alternatives' attributes form a tree structure whose terminal nodes represent alternatives; that the decision maker knows the attributes form a tree (as assumed in HEM), and that the decision maker knows his/her preferences over the abstract formulation of the alternatives, then to select the best alternative requires a single experiment. Since the alternatives' attributes form a tree, each alternative is identified by a single attribute. Since the decision maker knows his/her preferences, he/she knows which characteristic attribute is associated with his/her most preferred alternative. So the only experiment required is to determine which alternative has the associated characteristic attribute.

These are heroic and unreasonable assumptions. Instead, let's continue to assume that the decision maker knows his/her utility function, but now the attributes do not necessarily form a tree. In addition, assume that the utility function is of the form:

$$u(x) = \sum b_i \cdot a_i$$

where b_i is the weight assigned to attribute value a_i. As an example we look at the reduced data base:

Color {Straw, Garnet, Ruby} = $\{C_1, C_2, C_3\}$

Type {Red, White} = $\{T_1, T_2\}$

Taste {Pear, Earth, Cherry, Spicy} = $\{t_1, t_2, t_3, t_4\}$

$X = \{3,4,7,8,11,14,15,19\}$

Let's now assume that the person's utility function is:

$$u(x) = 10C_1 + 20C_2 + 20C_3 + 10T_1 + 20T_2 + 5t_1 + 10t_2 + 15t_3 + 20t_4.$$

To choose the best wine, the decision maker does not need to test either the type or the color of the wine. The utility associated with each wine's color-type combination is the same (30). The only attribute that distinguishes between the wines' utility is taste. A choice algorithm over a changing data base for this particular individual reduces to a search of the taste attribute for the highest-valued attribute value, and the actual order of the experiments would depend on the probability of each attribute being in the data base.

Finally, let us assume that the decision maker's utility function is:

$$u(x) = 100C_1 + 90C_2 + 80C_3 + 50T_1 + 40T_2 + 5t_1 + 4t_2 + 3t_3 + 2t_4.$$

To choose the best wine, the decision maker uses an EBA type strategy, eliminating all of the wines that do not maximize the Color attribute, and with the wines still under consideration, eliminating all wines that do not maximize the Type attribute, etc., so it is only in very specific circumstances, such as having a lexicographic preference ordering, that an individual can select the best available alternative (wine) by partitioning the alternatives based on their attributes.

In a more general case, where any linear utility function is allowed, finding the best available alternative can not be guaranteed using only attribute experiments. For an individual trying to select the best available alternative from an unknown set of alternatives, the approach taken in the computational geometry literature of finding the alternative closest to the ideal alternative, will work. The experiments partition the alternatives based on their similarity to an ideal point. The optimal strategy depends on the probability of the data base corresponding to each subset, and corresponds to a strategy that an individual might use when trying to find the best alternative using a traditional data base retrieval system. In an individual choice scenario, however, it is unlikely that experiments that partition the alternative based on the distance to an ideal point exist.

When we try to generalize each of the best alternative strategies to create a common choice for a group of users we run into problems. When each user's preferences fit one of the special cases, but the discriminating attribute differs or the lexicographic ordering differs, then to use attribute partitionings we have to first discriminate between the individuals, which is as hard or harder than the original problem. In the more general case where the decision makers can have any linear utility function, a common similarity or dissimilarity measure does not exist. These problems have long been recognized, and have been avoided by using a common (dis)similarity measure. What has not been addressed is the effect of the (dis)similarity measure on the outcome of the choice. Different measures result in different choices for the same ideal point. The issue of the appropriate measure is exacerbated when the cost of the choice process is included in determining the choice.

5. CONCLUSION

Data base queries are a type of choice problem. When decision makers use a data base system, they are interested in the best alternative, not whether a certain class of alternatives are available. A data base system should, therefore, support query algorithms based on the choice process. Different choice situations correspond to different types of retrieval processes, e.g., traditional information retrieval corresponds to assuming the user has a spoiled brat utility function. For different types of choice scenarios, different types of experiments and computations are required, but at present are not available. We need to investigate retrieval processes other than those based on attributes.

6. REFERENCES

[1] A.V. Aho, J.E. Hopcroft and J.D. Ullman, *The Design and Analysis of Computer Algorithms*, Addison-Wesley Publishing Co., Reading, Mass., pp. 115-119.

[2] H. Ait-Kaci and R. Nasr, "Login: A Logic Programming Language with Built-in Inheritance," *Journal of Logic Programming*, Vol.3, 1986, pp. 185-215.

[3] W.A. Burkhard and R.M. Keller, "Some Approaches to Best-Match File Searching," *Communications of the ACM*, Vol. II, No. 2, pp. 159-185.

[4] J.H. Friedman, J.L. Bently and R.A. Finkel,"An Algorithm for Finding Best Matches in Logarithmic Expected Time," *ACM Transactions on Mathematical Software*, Vol.3, No.3, Sept. 1977, pp. 209-226.

[5] R.L. Keeney and H. Raiffa, *Decisions with Multiple Objectives: Preferences and Value Tradeoffs*. Wiley, New York, 1976.

[6] G.E. Kersten, "NEGO - Group Decision Support System," *Information and Management*, Vol. 8, No. 5, 1985, pp. (237-246).

[7] G.E. Kersten, "A Procedure for Negotiating Efficient and Non-Efficient Compromises," forthcoming in *Decision Support Systems*, 1987.

[8] M.A. Ketabachi, V. Berzins and K. Maly, "Generalization Per Category: Theory and Application," *Proceedings of the 8th Annual International Conference on Information Systems*, 1986.

[9] K.J. Lancaster, "A New Approach to Consumer Theory," *Journal of Political Economy*, Vol. 74, No. 2, 1966, pp. 132-157.

[10] D. Luce, *Individual Choice Behavior*, John Wiley & Sons, Inc., New York, 1959.

[11] D. Luce and H. Raiffa, *Games and Decisions: Introduction and Critical Survey*, John Wiley & Sons, Inc. New York, 1957.

[12] J. Marschak and R. Radner, *Economic Theory of Teams*, Cowles Foundation, 1972.

[13] H. Mendelson and A.N. Suharia, "Incomplete Information Costs and Database Design," *ACM Transactions on Data Base Systems*, Vol. II, No. 2, 1986, pp. 159-185.

[14] J.C. Moore, W.B. Richmond and A.B. Whinston, "A Decision Theoretic Approach to File Search," forthcoming in *Computer System in Economics and Management*, 1988.

[15] J.C. Moore and A.B. Whinston, "A Model for Decision-Making with Sequential Information-Acquisition - Part 1," *Decision Support Systems*, Vol. 2, No. 4, 1986, pp. 285-307.

[16] J.C. Moore and A.B. Whinston, "A Model for Decision-Making with Sequential Information-Acquisition - Part 2," *Decision Support Systems*, Vol. 3, No. 1, 1987, pp. 47-72.

[17] T.L. Satty, "Concepts, Theory and Techniques, Rank Generalization, Preservation and Reversal in the Analytic Hierarchy Decision Process," *Decision Sciences*. Vol. 18, No.2, 1987, pp. 157-177.

[18] N. Spyratos, "The Partition Model: A Deductive Database Model," *ACM Transactions on Database Systems*, Vol. 12, No. 1, 1987, pp. 1-37.

[19] B. Tell, "An Approach to Solving Multi-Person Multiple-Criteria Decision-Making Problems," in *Multiple Criteria Problem Solving*, S. Zionts, ed., Springer-Verlag, Berlin, 1977, pp. 462-481.

[20] A. Tversky, "Elimination by Aspects: A Theory of Choice," *Psychological Review*, Vol. 79, 1977, pp. 281-299.

[21] A. Tversky and S. Sattath, "Preference Trees," *Psychological Review*, Vol. 86, No. 6, 1979, pp. 542-573.

[22] A. Tversky, P. Slovic and D. Kannaman, *Judgement Under Uncertainty: Heuristics and Biases*, Cambridge University Press, New York, 1982.

SECTION 6:

METHODS OF ARTIFICIAL INTELLIGENCE IN DECISION MAKING: INTELLIGENT KNOWLEDGE BASED SYSTEM

A FINANCIAL EXPERT DECISION SUPPORT SYSTEM

M.A.H. Dempster* and A.M. Ireland
Dalhousie University
***and Balliol College, Oxford**

1 INTRODUCTION

Corporate management decisions require domain knowledge, analytical skills and expert judgment for decision making in an uncertain environment. These decisions are often made with the help of decision support systems, which provide automated computation and data analysis but rely on knowledgeable users or consultants to direct the system operations and interpret results. Expert systems technology, by modelling the knowledge and reasoning of human experts, offers the opportunity to incorporate model management and interpretation knowledge within decision support systems. Such systems can make complex modelling techniques directly accessible to non-expert users.

This paper presents the conceptual design for MIDAS (Manager's Intelligent Debt Advisory System), a debt management decision support system which supports model-based, hierarchical strategic financial planning for a Canadian Crown-owned public utility. The system provides selected models appropriate to the decision process; configures and solves the models on user request; explains, interprets and refines their results interactively and assists the user in evaluating alternative borrowing plans. In the following sections, we present descriptions of the problem motivation and domain, §2, overall system architecture, §3, and the major system components, §§4–6. We concentrate here on the modelling components, as our research to date has focused on them; however, we also outline the direction of our expert systems efforts in §§7,8. Section 9 contains a summary and conclusions.

2 BACKGROUND

2.1 The Problem Domain

The corporate debt manager's task is to minimize the *costs* and *risks* of borrowing to meet debt financing *requirements*, which are determined by the firm's investment decisions. Major borrowing decisions include selection of borrowing *sources* (domestic and foreign) and *types* of debt used, *timing* of borrowing and debt calls, *term mix*, bond issue *features* (call options, sinking funds, etc.) as well as the use of interest rate or currency *hedges* and *swap contracts*. Debt costs include *issue costs* (underwriting

NATO ASI Series, Vol. F48
Mathematical Models for Decision Support
Edited by G. Mitra

commissions, legal and administrative costs), *interest costs* over the term of the debt and *discounts* or *premiums* that arise on issue and early redemption of debt. If borrowing is done in foreign markets, *exchange rate* fluctuations also result in gains or losses. (*Taxes* also effect costs for private sector borrowers; however, we initially ignore taxes in MIDAS because the corporation for which it is designed is non-taxable.) Risk is generally considered either in terms of *cost variation* or the *likelihood* of costs rising *above* a tolerable *level*.

A strategic borrowing plan sets out the borrowing decisions that will effectively meet these cost/risk goals, given future rate forecasts of subjective expectations; such a plan is often developed by describing several likely *rate scenarios* and determining the *cost implications* of decision alternatives for each scenario in either a *deterministic* or *contingency-planning* framework. The strategic plan is used as a guideline for operating decisions, which also consider actual rates and economic conditions at decision time. Often strategic plans are implemented in a planning environment in which the plan is updated in the light of current information at regular (quarterly or annual) intervals over a *rolling horizon* of fixed length.

Debt management has been relatively neglected by finance theorists, although it is a significant area of concern for corporate financial managers. Theorists generally agree that imperfect capital markets offer opportunities for management to increase firm value through debt decisions, e.g., Modigliani and Miller [41], Brennan and Schwartz [15], Boyce and Kalotay [10,11], Brick and Ravid [16]. A few attempts have been made to characterize a firm's optimal combination of debt maturities, Morris [42,43], Agmon, Ofer and Tamir [1], Barnea, Haugen and Senbet [4], but no unified theory exists to guide debt planning.

2.2 Debt Management Modelling

Lack of normative theory has not prevented application of known modelling techniques to debt management. *Linear* and *integer programming* have been applied deterministically to the investment decision with capital rationing, e.g., Lee [38], which corresponds to the borrowing problem with the signs of variables and inequalities reversed. Crane [17], Bradley and Crane [12,13,14], Crane, Knoop and Pettigrew [18], and Lane and Hutchinson [37] have applied *scenario-based stochastic linear programming* to optimizing the debt maturity mix and to managing fixed-income investment portfolios (again analogous to borrowing but with signs reversed). Shapiro [46] applies *scenario-based stochastic mixed integer programming* to the purchase and management at minimal discounted cost of a dedicated fixed-income portfolio including callable bonds. These models optimize for appropriate major strategic decisions but, due to computational complexity, generally exclude some tactical decisions faced by debt managers such as the specific features or covenants to include in particular debt issues. They incorporate uncertainty through branching rate scenarios with associated probabilities (see Figure 5).

Dynamic programming has also been applied to debt management; in particular, to bond refunding by Elton and Gruber [21], Kalymon [31] and Boyce and Kalotay [10,11]. As with stochastic linear programming, uncertainty is handled through probabilistic rate scenarios.

Simulation is recognized as a technique for evaluating complex investment portfolios, e.g., Hertz [29], Bradley and Crane [13]. Howard [30] uses simulation to project costs and risk arising from individual borrowing decisions and strategies. This technique allows detailed calculation of the expected consequences of alternative decisions, but it does not in itself provide decision criteria; alternatives must be eliminated or selected using management's subjective criteria or analytical techniques such as *mean-variance* analysis or *stochastic dominance* (Levy and Sarnat [39]).

These sources describe the use of single models to assist in particular decisions, but the combined use of various model types is generally not reported. However, it is clear that optimization and simulation models offer *complementary* advantages for debt management decision support since one suggests *optimal* decisions with simplifying assumptions while the other allows testing of alternatives in greater *detail.*

3 CONCEPTUAL DESIGN

The MIDAS system is designed to support rolling hierarchical strategic planning for debt management, using optimization and simulation models integrated, assisted and extended by an expert system interface. The two models incorporate uncertainty in a consistent manner, as described below, and are complementary in their contributions to plan development. Expert systems components, operating interactively under user control, assist in formulation and provide detailed guidance in interpretation and refinement of models and plans using a common knowledge base. The system thereby assists untrained users in using sophisticated models directly, rather than with human expert intervention.

MIDAS's task is to produce one or more acceptable strategic (contingency) plans for borrowing by a single corporation over its planning horizon, given corporate borrowing requirements, objectives, constraints and expectations about future significant rate movements. MIDAS supports a three-stage hierarchical decision process (Figure 1) in which *known model structures* are instantiated and used at appropriate stages. First, a *first-pass plan* incorporating major decisions is developed using a stochastic optimization model. Second, the resulting optimal but incomplete plan is *refined heuristically* by adding details not considered in stage 1, which may make the plan no longer optimal but which must be considered in a complete plan. This stage may result in several alternative plans which must be tested further. Third, *simulation* modelling is used to project the future cost and risk behaviour of alternative plans; the plans are then *evaluated* according to corporate objectives and a set of "best" plans selected for discussion and implementation. We can think of this process as a *generate-and-test* exercise in which the optimization model is used to prune the initial search space to a *single* plan before alternatives are generated heuristically.

MIDAS's proposed architecture reflects this decision process, incorporating modelling or heuristic subsystems to carry out each hierarchical planning step (Figure 2). All modules operate under the control of a *menu-driven interface* and access a common *knowledge base* of conceptual knowledge and control rules. An *initialization module* requests corporate *goals*, operating *parameters* and *assumptions* including *future rate scenarios*, guiding the user in their input and commenting on their consistency and

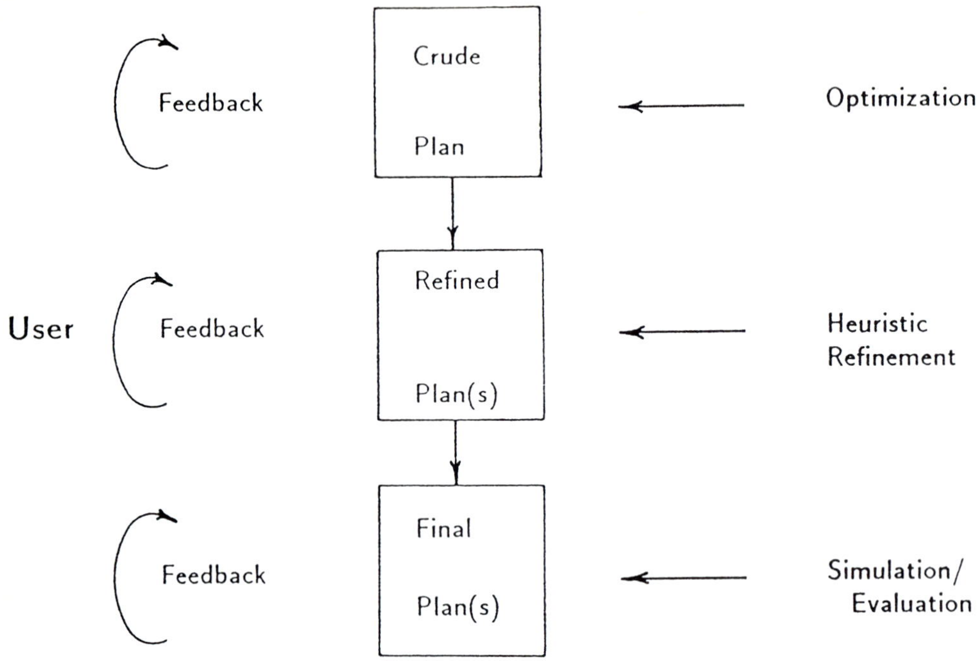

Figure 1. Hierarchical Planning: A "smart" interface helps the planner review, explain, compare and revise results at each stage

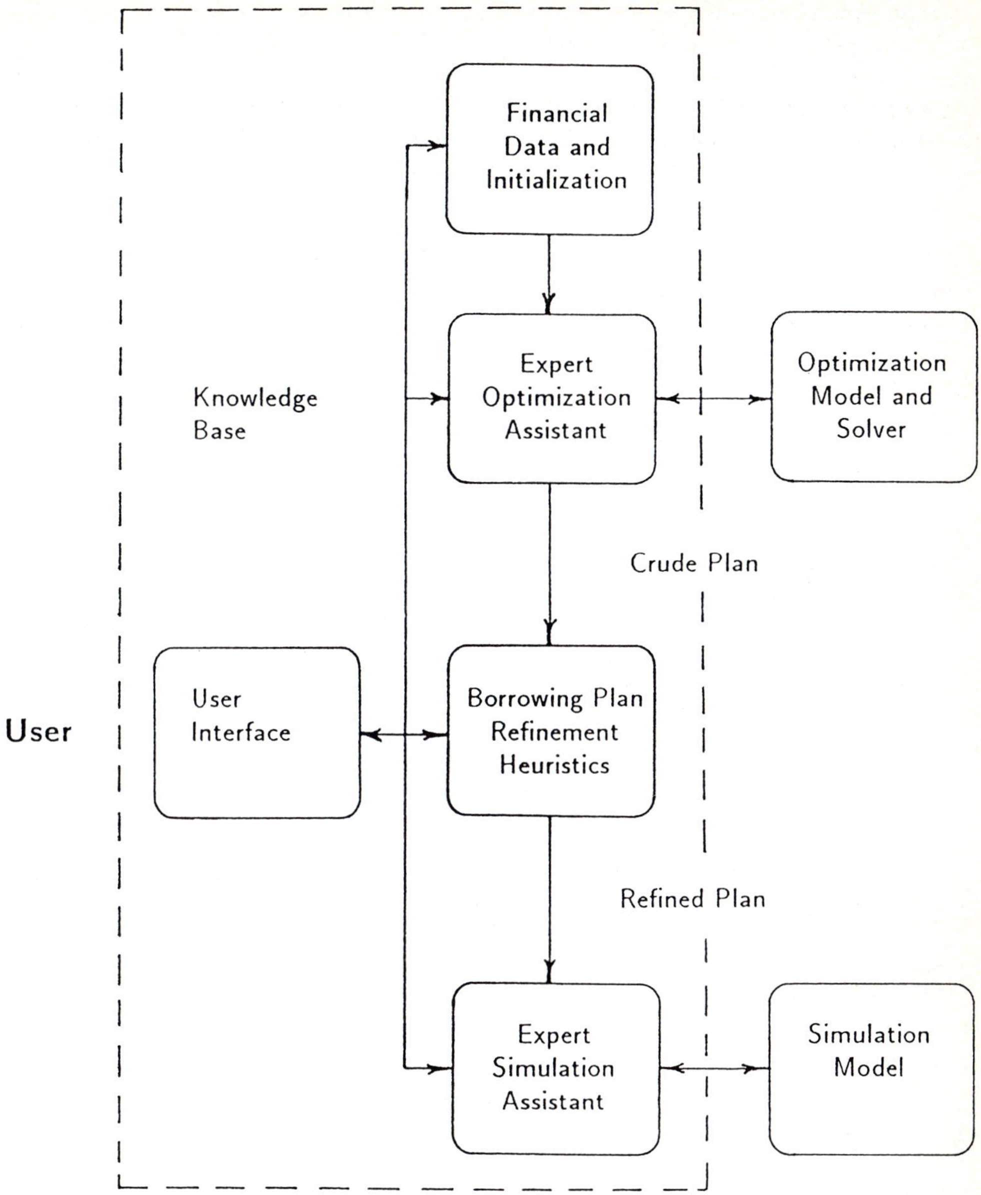

Figure 2. MIDAS Conceptual Design

reasonableness based on modelling and economic knowledge in the knowledge base. The *stochastic programming model* is then *instantiated* with coefficients calculated from the current parameters and *solved* to produce a crude borrowing plan. The *stochastic model expert* reviews model output, responds to user requests for explanations, comments on results, identifies and tests appropriate sensitivities, recommends modifications to the model instantiation and carries out user-suggested or approved changes to the model, including calls to the *solver*.

When stochastic modelling is completed, *rules* incorporating debt management knowledge are used to construct *alternate borrowing contingency plans*. These are then *simulated stochastically* using rates generated randomly from distributions consistent with the scenarios used initially. A *simulation expert* then repeats the *explanation/analysis suggestion/refinement* loop with the simulation model results. The resulting *alternative plans* are evaluated with respect to corporate goals (which have also been considered in developing individual plans) and the *"best" plans* are *retained* for consideration by the debt manager.

An acceptable borrowing *contingency plan* in MIDAS contains a list of *borrowing actions* of the form (rate preconditions, time, market, debt type, amount, debt features) which provide funding as required over the planning horizon leaving minimal debt to the future and within other constraints specified by the borrowing corporation. In addition, the plan includes decision *guidelines* to be followed, such as the conditions under which debt should be *called*. The planning process thus consists of defining and evaluating sets of required borrowing actions and decision guidelines to produce acceptable plans based on the current evaluation criteria. Initially, MIDAS contingent borrowing actions specify the *debt term*, *timing* and *legal features* for *domestic* debt issued over the time period. (Later extensions will include foreign debts, hedging and swaps.) Plans are evaluated, consistent with accepted finance theory, according to their appropriately discounted costs and risks (cost and terminal debt variance) over the planning horizon along with other criteria specified by management.

The system is designed for primary implementation in KEE, NL MENU and common LISP, with the stochastic programming model formulation and solver(s) implemented in FORTRAN and linked to the KEE system via Ethernet communications (alternatively, via a common operating system).

4 STOCHASTIC PROGRAMMING MODEL

Initial strategic planning in MIDAS is done using a stochastic linear programming model similar to those of Bradley and Crane [12,13,14] and Lane and Hutchinson [37]. The model utilizes the deterministic linear programming equivalent to minimize retirement value of terminal debt at the user's planning horizon, given borrowing requirements, operating and marketing constraints and probabilistic scenarios for expected interest rate movements. It produces a borrowing contingency plan consisting of decisions to borrow, hold and retire amounts of each available type of debt in each time period and contingent on prior rate movements as realized in each scenario. The MIDAS model extends previous borrowing models by incorporating:

(a) *callable debt* and

(b) *recourse* via cash surpluses and short-term borrowing.

4.1 Model specification

Model specifications are given in Figure 3. Subscripts s and t refer to *time periods*, quarterly or yearly at the option of the user. Superscript k identifies the major *debt types*, distinguished by *market* of issue, *term* and the presence or absence of a *call option* available to the borrower. The *event sequences* are *scenarios* of significant *rate movements* over time (although in principle any other uncertain parameters of the basic model—such as cash requirements—could also be included); these may be thought of as paths through a tree of possible rates beginning with the rate at time $t = 0$ and branching when significant economic or political events occur (Figure 5). These *anticipated* rate movements and their associated probabilities are *specified* by the user and might incorporate either *expert* rate forecasts or *subjective* assessments of expected future rate movements. In either case, rate scenarios are typically built from a *base*—mean or median—scenario by elaboration of specific alternative events and probabilities.

Notation:

$s, t = 0, \ldots, T$ denote *time periods*

T is the *length* of planning period or *horizon*

$k = 1, \ldots, K$ denotes an available *debt type*

$e_j := e_{j1}, e_{j2}, \ldots, e_{jT}, \quad j = 1, \ldots, J$ denotes a *sequence* of (rate) *events*.

(e_j) indicates that a variable or parameter is *contingent* on the event sequence e_j.

Decision Variables:

$B^k_t(e_j)$	dollar amount at par of debt type k *borrowed* at the beginning of period t.
$O^k_{s,t}(e_j)$	dollar amount at par of debt type k borrowed in period s and *outstanding* at the beginning of period t.
$R^k_{s,t}(e_j)$	dollar amount at par of debt type k borrowed in period s and *retired* at the beginning of period t.
$S_t(e_j)$	dollar value of *surplus* cash held at the beginning of period t.

Parameters:

$r^k_{s,t}(e)$	*interest payment* in period t per dollar outstanding of debt type k issued in period s.
f^k_t	*issue costs* (excluding premium or discount) per dollar borrowed of debt type k issued in period s.

$g^k_{s,t}(e_j)$	*retirement premium* or *discount* per dollar for debt type k issued in period s, if retired in period t. (These parameters are used to define *call options* and to value the debt portfolio at the end of the planning period.)
$i_t(e_j)$	*interest earned* per dollar on surplus cash in period t.
$p(e_j)$	*probability* of event sequence e_j, $j = 1, \ldots, J$. ($\sum_{j=1}^J p(e_j) = 1$.)
C_t	*cash requirement* for period t. If negative, C_t indicates an *operating surplus*.
M_t	*maximum* allowable *cost* of debt service in period t.
Q^k_t	*maximum borrowing* of debt type k in period t.
q^k_t	*minimum borrowing* of debt type k in period t.
$L_t(e_j)$	*minimum* dollar amount of debt (at par) *retired* in period t.
$U_t(e_j)$	*maximum* dollar amount of debt (at par) *retired* in period t.

Objective:

$$\min E(\mathbf{D}_T) = \sum_{j=1}^J p(e_j) \sum_{k=1}^K \sum_{t=1}^T \left(1 + g^k_{t,T}(e_j)\right) \left[O^k_{t,T}(e_j) - R^k_{t,T}(e_j)\right] + (1 - f^k_T) B^k_T(e_j)$$

(expected cost of retiring outstanding debt at end of period T)

Constraints:

Cash Requirements

For $j = 1, \ldots, J$ and $t = 1, \ldots, T$

$$\begin{aligned} C_t = \sum_{k=1}^K \Big\{ & (1 - f^k_t) B^k_t(e_j) && \text{(net new borrowing)} \\ & + i_{t-1}(e_j) S_{t-1}(e_j) && \text{(interest earned on surplus cash)} \\ & + S_{t-1}(e_j) && \text{(surplus cash in previous period)} \\ & - S_t(e_j) && \text{(surplus cash in this period)} \\ & - \sum_{s=0}^{t-1} \Big[r^k_{s,t}(e_j) O_{s,t}(e^j) && \text{(interest on outstanding debt)} \\ & - (1 + g^k_{s,t}(e_j)) R^k_{s,t}(e_j) \Big] \Big\} && \text{(cash outflows on repayment).} \end{aligned}$$

Debt inventory by type

For $j = 1, \ldots, J$, $s = 0, \ldots, t-2$, $t = 1, \ldots, T$ and $k = 1, \ldots, K$

$$O^k_{s,t}(e_j) - O^k_{s,t-1}(e_j) + R^k_{s,t-1}(e_j) = 0$$

$$O^k_{t-1,t}(e_j) - B^k_{t-1}(e_j) - R^k_{t-1,t}(e_j) = 0\,.$$

Maximum cost of debt

For $j = 1, \ldots, J$, $t = 1, \ldots, T$ and $k = 1, \ldots, K$

$$\sum_{s=1}^{t-1} r_{s,t}^k(e_j) O_{s,t}^k(e_j) - i_{t-1}(e_j) S_{t-1}(e_j) \leq M_t \, .$$

Market maximum borrowings

For $j = 1, \ldots, J$, $t = 1, \ldots, T$ and $k = 1, \ldots, K$

$$B_t^k(e_j) \leq Q_t^k \, .$$

Market minimum borrowings

For $j = 1, \ldots, J$, $t = 1, \ldots, T$ and $k = 1, \ldots, K$

$$\textit{either} \;\; B_t^k(e_j) = 0 \;\; \textit{or} \;\; B_t^k(e_j) \geq q_t^k \; (\geq 0) \, .$$

Maturity smoothing

For $j = 1, \ldots, J$ and $t = 1, \ldots, T$

$$L_t(e_j) \leq \sum_{k=1}^{K} \sum_{s=0}^{t-1} R_{s,t}^k(e^j) \leq U_t(e_j) \, .$$

Nonnegativity

For $j = 1, \ldots, J$, $s = 0, \ldots, t-1$, $t = 1, \ldots, T$ and $k = 1, \ldots, K$

$$B_t^k(e_j) \geq 0 \qquad O_{s,t}^k(e_j) \geq 0 \qquad R_{s,t}^k(e_j) \geq 0 \qquad S_t(e_j) \geq 0 \, .$$

Figure 3. MIDAS Stochastic Programming Model

Because current interest (and exchange) rates determine costs for new and retiring debt, the decision variables and many of the parameters of the model are dependent on prior rate movements (which, of course, determine current rates in any time period). *Decision variables* are the *amounts* of each debt type *borrowed, outstanding* and *retired* in each period and the amount of *surplus cash* held in each period; the last variable allows for (simple) *recourse* through overborrowing and holding cash (invested at a current short-term earnings rate) in some periods. Debt types might include short-term bank credit; short-term commercial paper; short-, medium- and long-term bonds issued in domestic or foreign public markets; domestic and foreign private placements and other particular types of debt available to the borrower.

The *objective function* expresses the *retirement cost* of the *total debt* outstanding at the end of the planning period, where *terminal debt* amounts resulting from contingent decisions in each period are weighted by the probability of their event sequences. It is *assumed* that all new long-term debt is issued at *par*, so that the market interest rate equals the coupon rate and there is no premium or discount on issue. Selection of an appropriate corporate *discount rate* for discounted cash flow analysis presents a problem since the borrower's cost of new debt is determined by the solution to the model rather than exogenously. The essential tradeoff between lower costs of debt service and higher terminal debt outstanding can be modelled either by minimizing the *discounted* cost of debt service subject to an upper bound on the retirement cost of terminal debt or by minimizing the latter subject to an upper bound on the cost of debt service in each period. We have opted for the latter in order to obviate the necessity of having to specify a *a priori* a *corporate* discount rate which represents the corporation's (average) *cost of capital.*

The most important constraint in the model is the cash requirements definition, which assumes that cash requirements are *exogenously* determined from operating and capital surpluses or deficits before interest payments. This results in interest payments being financed by debt to the extent that they are not covered by operating surpluses. Coefficients for this constraint include interest rates for each new debt in each period, premium or discount on retirement (including the exercise of call options), issue costs and interest rates for surplus cash. Debt type inventory identities maintain the connection between borrowed, outstanding and retired debt of each type issued in each period. Operating policies specified by the borrower include maximum and minimum amounts to be borrowed from individual sources in any one period, smoothing of debt maturities over time periods and maximum allowable debt service costs over the periods of the plan.

Although they *could* be made to depend on rate scenarios, specifying a maximal cost of debt service M_t in each period $t = 1,\ldots,T$ as $\prod_{s=1}^{t}(1+\rho_s)M$, where ρ_t is an economy-wide (predicted) *inflation rate* in period t, allows a measure of control of debt service *risk* in all contingencies (i.e. across all rate scenarios) by setting the single parameter M in current dollars. (A similar constraint for controlling retirement risk of terminal debt involving a maximum allowable terminal debt $\prod_{s=1}^{T}(1+\rho_s)D$ in terms of an amount D specified in current dollars could also be imposed.) Such constraints incorporate an aversion to "downside" risk which remains computationally tractable, partially compensates for the risk-neutral objective function and appears to correspond to the behaviour of corporate treasurers (Bradley and Crane [13]).

4.2 Problem structure and solution method

The method of strategic debt planning presented in Figure 3 and discussed above is technically a scenario-based *dynamic stochastic recourse* model. For a recent survey of the theoretical aspects of such models based on *general* (as opposed to finite discrete scenario-type) stochastic processes of data evolution, the reader is referred to Dempster [19]. Progress has also recently been made in the provision of efficient computational techniques, here termed *solvers*, for optimizing practically sized scenario-based models of this type, Birge [6], Gassmann [25,26], Dempster [19], Merkovsky [40], Rockafellar and Wets [45], Dempster *et al.* [20], which render the approximation approach of Kusy and Ziemba [36] unnecessary. A *standard input format* has also been specified by Birge *et al.* [7] for their instantiation. MIDAS's stochastic progamming model is implemented to this FORTRAN standard, so that the data defining a model instance is input from the MIDAS knowledge base in this format and a suite of subroutines are employed to translate it to a data structure appropriate to the solver utilized.

The cash requirements, debt inventory and maximum cost of debt constraints of the MIDAS stochastic programming model exhibit the *lower triangular* structure typical of dynamic recourse models. (This pattern generalizes the lower bidiagonal structure of discrete time (stochastic) control models.) All other constraints in a given period are *instantaneous*, i.e. do not depend on past values of data or decision variables. Providing that the net borrowing coefficients $1 - f_t^k$ of new borrowings in the cash requirements constraints are *scenario independent*, all recourse coefficients in a given period are *deterministic*. This requirement is crucial to the efficiency of linear programming decomposition techniques (as used by Bradley and Crane [12,13,14]) in that many subproblems can then be made to differ only in their right hand side vectors at solution time. More recently, efficient implementations of *nested Benders decomposition* for stochastic linear programming have been developed, Birge [6], Gassmann [25], and this approach has been applied by Gassmann [25,26] to a scenario-based dynamic forestry model of practical size with very reasonable computational effort. An appropriate version of this solver is the first to be applied to the MIDAS stochastic programming model.

Ultimately, however, we intend to employ *augmented Lagrangean* techniques based on *nonanticipative constraint relaxations*—which have been applied very effectively to the standard *two* period Ho-Loute test problems, Dempster [19], Merkovsky [40], Dempster *et al.* [20]—appropriate to the multiperiod case. Currently, test problems are being developed on the basis of *eight* periods of a five year plan: four quarters of the first year and the four successive years. Aside from its superior computational efficiency relative to other methods on two period problems, Dempster *et al.* [20], the advantage of this approach is that the dual variables on the relaxed constraints may be interpreted as marginal *expected values of perfect information* (*EVPI*) and used to eliminate inessential scenarios in a given model instance. We expect to use this feature to advantage in the interactive development of strategic debt plans based on significant rate event scenarios.

4.3 Model refinement and parametric analysis

As indicated above, the MIDAS system is designed to aid the interactive development of strategic plans for management of corporate debt by multiple runs of the mathematical models involved. In the case of the stochastic programming model, this process involves multiple calls to the solver either with successively refined instances of the model or parametric variation of key data. Model refinement is primarily for two purposes: to complete the solution of the model produced by the linear programming solver and to simplify the model currently specified. Similarly, parametric analysis has mainly a twofold aim: to investigate the stability of borrowing decisions in an (expected) optimal plan with respect to specified rate data and to evaluate the "downside" risks inherent in it. We mention briefly here an instance of each of these four concerns, but fully expect to investigate further questions with similar techniques as the MIDAS system develops.

The maximum and minimum borrowing constraints as stated in Figure 3 are not fully specified mathematically. They may be correctly handled using standard *mixed integer* linear programming techniques (*cf.* Shapiro [46]), for $j = 1, \ldots, J$, $k = 1, \ldots, K$ and $t = 1, \ldots, T$, as

$$\begin{aligned} B_t^k(e_j) - \delta_t^k(e_j) Q_t^k &\leq 0 \\ B_t^k(e_j) - \delta_t^k(e_j) q_t^k &\geq 0 \,, \end{aligned}$$

where $\delta_t^k(e_j) = 0$ or 1. Relaxing this last requirement to $0 \leq \delta_t^k(e_j) \leq 1$, the resulting constraints are appropriate to a linear programming solver, but then the corresponding variable subsequently must be set to 0 or 1 either for re-solution or for evaluation at the simulation level of the MIDAS system. (The alternative of *heuristic tree search* on these binary variables as utilized by Shapiro [46] is deemed too computationally costly at the present stage of MIDAS development.) The provision of *sinking funds* when sinking fund bonds form a part of the optimal plan can be handled by similar, but more complicated, techniques (due to the necessity for new decision variables).

More sophisticated model refinement and resolution by the augmented Lagrangean solver involves reduction of specified scenarios using the optimal Lagrange (marginal EVPI) multipliers associated with the *nonanticipative* constraints which specify that *current decisions* must depend only on *past data* in each period. If in a given period the value of marginal EVPI associated with a given scenario is relatively low, it is worth considering a refined model in which this scenario and all those that branch from it in subsequent periods are deleted. In principle, the resulting instance may be solved more quickly with little loss of accuracy, but this is a claim which can be investigated explicitly in the present context with the simulation component of the MIDAS system.

Similarly, although the sensitivity of optimal plans to rate changes may in principle be evaluated using *parametric* (large scale) *linear programming* techniques, this may in practice be more efficiently evaluated by simulation. In either case, the aim is to establish the range of key rate changes with which an optimal plan remains (essentially) invariant.

Parametric analysis involving multiple calls to the solver can be extremely useful in evaluating the *risks* inherent in an optimal (model) plan, Bradley and Crane [14], Shapiro [46]. For example, in the MIDAS stochastic programming model the tradeoff between M and the present value of expected optimal retirement cost can be evaluated both *explicitly* and at the *margin* (using the appropriate dual variables). A more direct *risk* versus *mean* (expected) objective function value tradeoff can be obtained by inclusion in the model of the final period constraints for $j = 1, \ldots, J$

$$\textstyle\sum_{k=1}^{K} \sum_{t=1}^{T} \, (1 + g_{t,T}^k(e_j))[O_{t,T}^k(e_j) - R_{t,T}^k(e_j)] + (1 - f_T^k) B_T^k(e_j) \leq \prod_{s=1}^{T} (1 + \rho_s) D \,.$$

Then the D versus $\prod_{s=1}^{T}(1+\rho_s)^{-1} E(\mathbf{D}_T)$ relationship can be investigated parametrically using D as a measure of *dispersion* of the present value of the retirement cost of terminal debt $\mathbf{D}_T$, *cf.* Bradley and Crane [13,14].

5 PLAN REFINEMENT HEURISTICS

The stochastic programming model provides a partial contingent borrowing plan which is optimal but simplified since (a) some less crucial debt features may be ignored for computational simplification, and (b) the decision variable values produced by the model may not be correctly or easily implementable in their initial form. The necessarily binary δ variables discussed in the previous section provide an example of the first situation of (b). An example of the second is provided by the fact that public bond issues are floated in amounts such as \$75, \$150 or \$200 million rather than the \$89.46 million which might be a solution to the linear model. To bring the model's proposed plan closer to a "real world" implementable one, heuristics are thus used which incorporate knowledge of the model's solution and of practical and desirable plan characteristics. The resulting plan (multiple alternatives may be generated at this stage) are passed to the simulation for further analysis and evaluation.

MIDAS's plan refinement rules (extending those in the previous section) are being developed jointly with an experienced corporate treasurer and professional underwriters, working with model results for case studies. They operate by *forward chaining* (applying all if-then statements whose premises are satisfied) until all feasible alternate plans have been created.

6 PLAN SIMULATION

The simulation component of MIDAS is a discrete time interval oriented module which uses parameters and calculations consistent with the optimization model to test a *contingent* borrowing plan over a specified planning horizon. Its main output, consistent with the objective function of the stochastic programming model, is a probability distribution of the net cost of retiring the debt portfolio at the end of the planning period. Other plan performance indicators, such as a distribution for discounted cash flows, are also calculated for later use by the plan evaluation rules. The simulation uses interest rates generated (pseudo-)randomly from distributions consistent with the event sequences assumed in the stochastic programming model, and may be done for quarterly or yearly intervals, as specified by the user.

6.1 Simulation Parameters

A general description of the simulation is given in Figure 4. Inputs to the model include a tree of anticipated future interest rate movements for each market of interest, future cash requirements over the planning horizon and all borrowing decisions making up the borrowing plan to be tested. The borrowing decisions specify the types, dollar amounts and timing for debts to be issued over the planning horizon, contingent on prior rate movements. Debts which refund called or maturing issues may be *explicitly* included in these decisions or generated *automatically* by heuristics within the simulation.

Output:	(a) Distribution for terminal debt portfolio retirement cost net of sinking funds.
	(b) Distributions of other borrowing plan performance indicators, such as present value of cash flows or costs, useful for heuristic evaluation.
Input:	(a) Future interest (or exchange) rate scenarios.
	(b) Cash requirements.
	(c) Borrowing plan.
	(d) Decision rules for calling and refunding.
Calculated cash flows and balances over the planning period:	(a) New borrowing, net of issue costs.
	(b) Principal outstanding.
	(c) Interest payments.
	(d) Principal repayments.
	(e) Premium or discount on principal repayments.
	(f) Sinking fund requirements, earnings and withdrawals.
	(g) Sinking fund balances.
	(h) Surplus cash balances.
	(i) Interest on surplus cash balances.

Figure 4. MIDAS Borrowing Plan Simulation

The first two inputs are, we recall, also inputs to the stochastic programming model. When the two models are used together to generate and test a borrowing plan, the same rate tree and cash requirements are used. The set of borrowing decisions is either specified by the user or, when both models are used, is the output from the optimization model, refined heuristically by MIDAS prior to the simulation as described in §5.

In addition to the above parameters, heuristic decision rules are specified for calling and refunding situations encountered by the simulation. This feature adds flexibility by allowing MIDAS planning rules or the user to vary the calling and refunding strategies in conjunction with particular borrowing plans.

6.2 Rate Scenarios and Simulated Future Interest Rates

Interest costs for the new debts specified in the borrowing plan are determined from randomly-generated *yield curves* (expressing interest cost as a function of term). A *base* yield curve is generated for each financial market for each interval over the planning period. This is done by: (a) randomly generating enough points to determine a curve and (b) connecting the points with a function approximating a yield curve shape. Because historical interest rate data is most readily available for government securities, MIDAS's base yield curves reflect government rates. Yields for specific debt types for the borrower are estimated by adding "spreads" to the rate taken from the base yield curve. Spreads may be estimated from historical averages or generated randomly using historical distributions.

At present MIDAS uses a simple logarithmic curve form based on two points—a long-term rate (15 or 20 years, depending on the availability of historical data on which to base the distributions) and a short-term rate (3 months or 1 year). Following Howard [31], rate changes are assumed to follow a random walk. To maintain consistency with the stochastic programming model, the random generation of future interest rate points uses distributions reflecting the underlying rate tree.

New rates are generated as follows: given an event sequence e_j, the *long-term rate* at time t, denoted by $\mathbf{l}_t(e_j)$, is generated according to

$$\Delta \mathbf{l}_t(e_j) := \mathbf{l}_t(e_j) - l_{t-1}(e_j) = \mathbf{r}_t(e_j)$$

where $r_t(e_j)$ is a random variable with a *normal* distribution (Ayers and Barry [3]) with mean depending on t and e_j and fixed variance based on historical rates in the relevant financial market. The short-term rate $\mathbf{s}_t(e_j)$ at time t, for the event sequence e_j, is given by

$$\Delta \mathbf{s}_t(e_j) := \mathbf{s}_t(e_j) - s_{t-1}(e_j) = w\mathbf{r}_t(e_j) + \mathbf{v}$$

where w is a constant and $\mathbf{v}$ is a normally-distributed random variable with mean 0 and variance based on appropriate historical rates.

The yield curve connecting the short- and long-term rates at time t has the form

$$y = a + b\ln(\tau)$$

where y is the *yield* and τ is the *term* (time to maturity) of the debt. The exact curve is, of course, determined once the two points are generated.

To illustrate this process, suppose that expected interest rates and changes (e_j) are as in Figure 5. At time $t = 0$, the long-term rate $l_0(e_j)$ is 10%. At $t = 1$, $\Delta l_1(e_j)$ is randomly chosen from a normal distribution with mean 1.6% and standard deviation 1%. If $\Delta l_1(e_j) = 1.2\%$, then $l_1(e_j) = 10 + 1.2 = 11.2\%$. If the relationship between long- and short-term rates is given by

$$\Delta s_t(e_j) = 1.1\Delta l_t(e_j) + v$$

and $\mathbf{v}$ is realized as $v = .03$, then

$$\Delta s_t(e_j) = (1.1)(1.2) + .03 = 1.35\% .$$

(a) Long term interest rate event tree with ranges

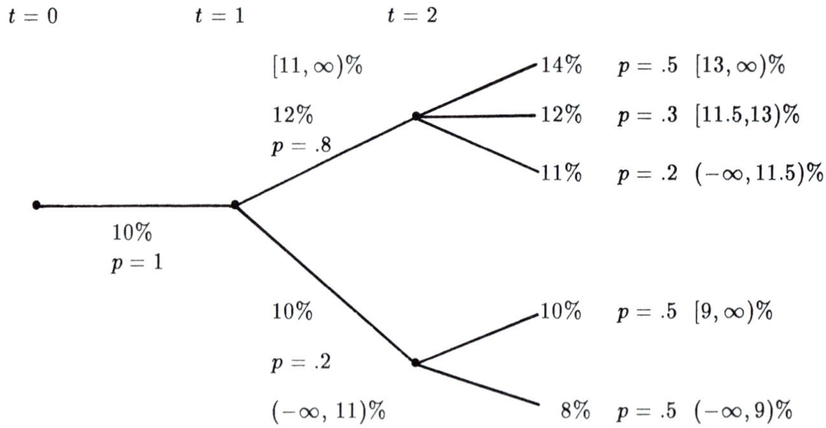

(b) Restatement of tree as sequence of rate changes

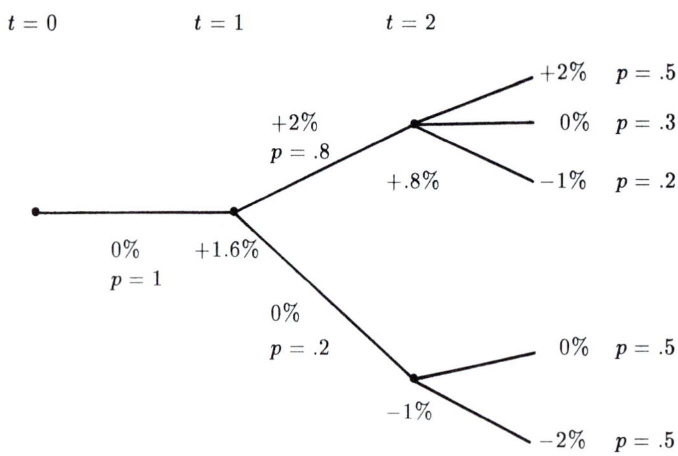

Figure 5. Interest Rate Simulation

If $s_0(e_j) = 8.5\%$, then $s_1(e_j) = 8.5 + 1.35 = 9.85\%$. If long-term debt has a 20-year term and short-term debt a 1-year term, then the yield curve connecting $l_1(e_j)$ and $s_1(e_j)$ is the solution to simultaneous equations $11.2 = a + b \ln 20$ and $9.85 = a + b \ln 1$.

At time $t = 2$, we determine that, since $l_1(e_j) = 11.2\%$ lies in the interval $[11, \infty)$, it is on the higher rate path for $t = 1$, the new distribution mean for rate generation is 2%.

The entire generation process is then repeated, giving new points and a rate curve for $t = 2$.

Although this approximation process is crude in that it ignores the historical forms of rate change distributions contitioned on prior changes, it is simple and theoretically consistent (since normal random variables conditioned on normal random variables remain normal).

The logarithmic curve form used above was chosen as a useful first approximation of yield curve shape. More complex forms, based on three or more points, have been established to give better fits to past data; in particular, see Bradley and Crane [12] and Bierwag [5]. Using a curve in one of these forms is a natural extension to improve the precision of the MIDAS simulation.

6.3 Simulation Calculations and Output

For each *simulation pass*, a sequence of yield curves is generated and cash flows and balances are calculated for the borrowing decisions specified in the borrowing plan for that rate sequence. The corresponding retirement cost of terminal debt is stored as one observation of the simulated empirical terminal debt distribution. Discounted cost and cash flow distributions can similarly be calculated from the basic data of each pass. (The appropriate corporate discount rate for each period can either be supplied by the user or calculated approximately as the average cost of capital in an optimal contingency plan generated by the optimization model.) The simulation is repeated to create distributions of multiple observations.

These distributions of plan characteristics are used to graphically display plan behaviour and to evaluate the plan using analytical criteria. Other statistics on the plan may also be calculated; examples of these include cash surpluses and deficits, weighted average terms, weighted average interest rates for the debt portfolio over time and the average retirement cost of debt at the end of the planning horizon. These statistics and the distributions serve as facts for subsequent rule-based explanation and evaluation of results.

This simulation is more powerful than others we are aware of in the literature in several ways. First, it models a borrowing plan rather than a single borrowing decision. Second, the realization of the plan is contingent (dynamic) rather than predetermined at the outset of the planning period. Third, its implementation allows a great deal of flexibility in its use; for example, rate modelling can be made deterministic (single scenario) rather than stochastic (multiple scenario), plans can be limited to individual decisions, and multiple contingent plans can be modelled and compared.

7 KNOWLEDGE BASE

MIDAS's knowledge base provides a consistent data source and communications vehicle for the mathematical and heuristic subsystems. (In keeping with KEE terminology, we use the term *knowledge base* to refer to both *rules* and to *frames* containing structured conceptual knowledge.)

Frames in MIDAS fall into four main categories: (1) *corporate* knowledge (goals, planning constraints, evaluation criteria), (2) *financial/economic* knowledge (debt sources, types of debt available, market requirements, future rate expectations) (3) *modelling* knowledge (variables and their explanations and relationships, input and output formats, random rate generators, other mathematical functions, prototypical modelling situations), and (4) system and *input/output* objects such as menus, reports and graphs. *Active values* and procedural code (*methods*) activated by *messages* to *objects* handle I/O functions, maintain data consistency and carry out simulations as described above.

Frames, inheritance and methods within frames allow an economical knowledge representation of related objects which applies in a natural way to our financial domain. Objects are defined by their attributes and the procedures which operate on their attribute values; for example, debts are defined as objects which have principal, an interest rate, an issue date, and other attributes as in Figure 6, along with methods to calculate their cash flows. Attributes of all debts are defined once in the "DEBTS" object class (Figure 7). Through inheritance, the BONDS subclass automatically acquire all attributes of DEBTS; attributes and methods specific to BONDS, such as underwriting commissions and their calculation, are defined in that object. An individual bond instance such as B in Figure 7 is represented as a "member" of the BONDS subclass; it inherits its attributes from BONDS and establishes values for those attributes through inherited input methods, active value calculations and modification by rules. Cash flows and balances for a single bond issue are calculated for simulation purposes by methods in the bond instance; cash flows and balances for an entire group of debts can be easily generated by combining those of the individual group members.

Complex bonds are *composite* objects built from *component* objects which carry their own parameters and methods. For example, a callable bond issue is a basic bond linked via a pointer to a call option object, and a bond issue with a sinking fund points to a specific sinking fund object. This representation approach allows modelling of debts as collections of components and can easily be extended to incorporate creation of new types of debt in the knowledge base as composites of principal, payment, interest and other building blocks.

Rules in the knowledge base handle overall control through *backchaining* (i.e. backwards reasoning—*induction*—by recursively searching the network structure of the rule base to find a chain of if-then statements which imply a goal consequence) to organize and achieve major subgoals in the decision process and *forward chaining* (recursive *deduction* as explained in §5) in the planning and model management subsystems.

8 EXPERT SYSTEM MODELLING ASSISTANCE

Although mathematical modelling techniques provide information for debt decisions, they require extensive knowledge and experience to be used effectively. Modelling is therefore limited to situations where managers have advanced training and skilled staff or consultants are readily available. This suggests that *modelling expertise* is a useful application of expert systems, which provide knowledge representation and reasoning ability and serve to make expertise available when it is scarce (Waterman [52]).

DEBTS Slots

member:
CF.ACCRUED.INTEREST (local)
CF.INTEREST (local)
CF.ISSUE.COSTS (local)
CF.PRINCIPAL (local)
CF.PRINCIPAL.OUTSTANDING (local)
CF.RETIREMENT.COSTS (local)
CF.ROLLOVERS (local)
CF.TOTAL (local)
CURRENCY (local)
DEBT.ID (local)
IRR (local)
MARKET (local)
MENUITEMS (local)
MTH.CALC.CFS (local)
MTH.CALC.ENDING.PRICE (local)
MTH.CALC.INTEREST (local)
MTH.CALC.IRR (local)
MTH.CALC.NPV (local)
MTH.CALC.TOTAL.CFS (local)
MTH.DISPLAY.CFS (local)
MTH.INITIALIZE.CFS (local)
MTH.UPDATE.DEBTS (local)
NPV (local)
ORIGINAL.PRINCIPAL (local)
PRINCIPAL (local)
PRINCIPAL.OUTSTANDING (local)
RETIREMENT.SCHEDULE (local)
TERM (local)

BONDS Slots

member:
BORROWER.PRICE (local)
BORROWER.RATE (local)
CALL.OPTION (local)
CF.ACCRUED.INTEREST
CF.INTEREST
CF.ISSUE.COSTS
CF.PRINCIPAL (local)
CF.PRINCIPAL.OUTSTANDING
CF.RETIREMENT.COSTS
CF.ROLLOVERS
CF.TOTAL
COUPON.RATE (local)
CURRENCY
DEALER.PRICE (local)
DEBT.ID (local)
ENDING.PRICE (local)
EXTEND.OPTION (local)

BONDS Slots

INTEREST.PAYMENTS.PER.YEAR (local)
INVESTOR.YIELD (local)
IRR
ISSUE.ADMIN.COSTS (local)
ISSUE.COMMISSION.RATE (local)
ISSUE.DATE (local)
ISSUE.DISCOUNT.OR.PREMIUM (local)
ISSUE.QUARTER (local)
ISSUE.TOTAL.COSTS (local)
ISSUE.YEAR (local)
MARKET
MATURITY.DATE (local)
MATURITY.MONTH (local)
MATURITY.QUARTER (local)
MATURITY.YEAR (local)
MENUITEMS
MTH.ADD.BOND (local)
MTH.BOND.INPUT (local)
MTH.CALC.BOND.CFS.TEST (local)
MTH.CALC.CFS (local)
MTH.CALC.ENDING.PRICE (local)
MTH.CALC.INTEREST (local)
MTH.CALC.IRR
MTH.CALC.NPV
MTH.CALC.TOTAL.CFS (local)
MTH.CHANGE.BOND (local)
MTH.CREATE.REFUNDING.BOND (local
MTH.DELETE.BOND (local)
MTH.DISPLAY.CFS (local)
MTH.INITIALIZE.CFS (local)
MTH.MSG.WINDOW (local)
MTH.PROMPT.WINDOW (local)
MTH.REFINANCE (local)
MTH.RETIRE (local)
MTH.UPDATE.DEBTS (local)
MTH.UPDATE.SPECIAL.FEATURES (loc
NPV
ORIGINAL.PRINCIPAL
PRINCIPAL (local)
PRINCIPAL.OUTSTANDING
PUBLIC.PRICE (local)
QUARTERS.INTEREST.PAID (local)
REDEMPTION.OPTION (local)
RETIREMENT.SCHEDULE
ROLLOVER.BOND (local)
SERIES (local)
SINKING.FUND (local)
TERM (local)

Figure 6. Representative Units in KEE Knowledge Base for MIDAS

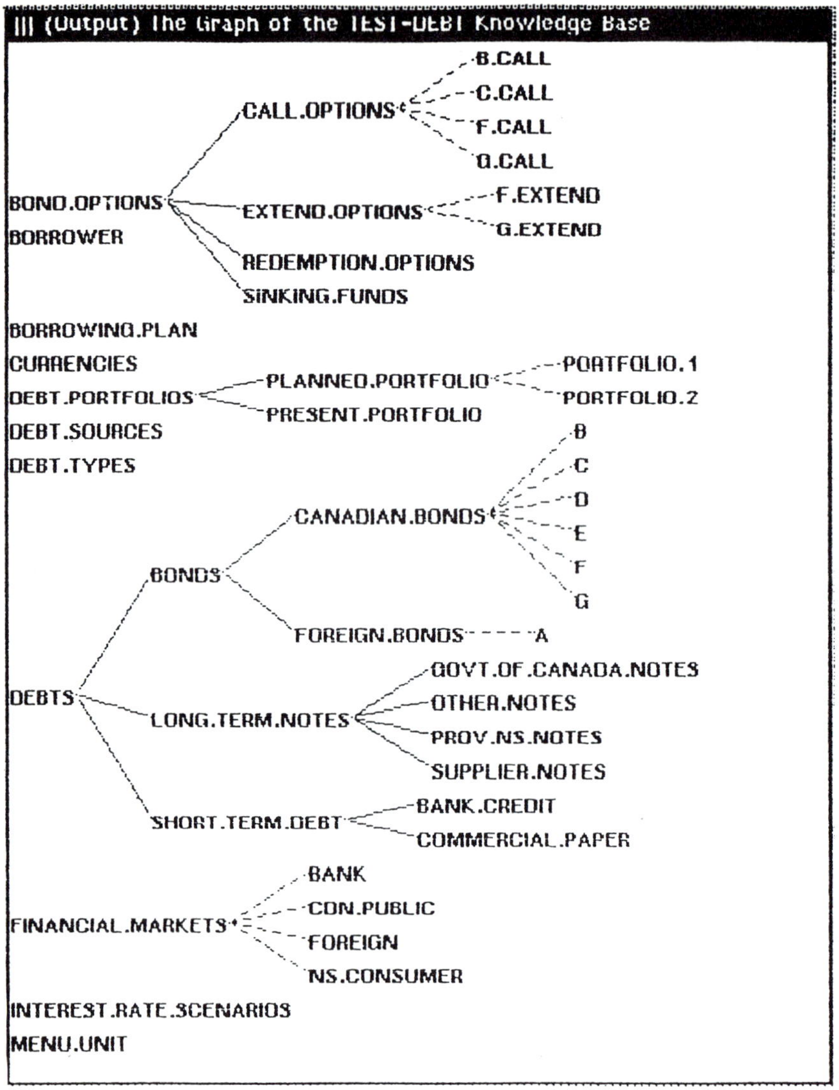

Figure 7. Schematic of Part of KEE Knowledge Base for MIDAS

To effectively use modelling, managers must be able to do the following:-

(a) Clearly state the conceptual problem to be solved.

(b) Identify the type or types of model, if any, appropriate in a given situation.

(c) If a model type is identified, translate the conceptual problem statement into a mathematical representation solvable by the chosen modelling technique.

(d) Identify and obtain or estimate the data necessary to apply the model, including assumptions, known facts and forecasts.

(e) Translate the data into model parameters.

(f) Solve the model's mathematics to produce numerical results.

(g) Understand the means by which the results were produced in order to identify and test sensitivity to significant factors, refine the results and recognize their limitations.

(h) Translate the solution into a conceptual answer to the original problem statement.

The potential for using expert systems to assist in these functions is well recognized, Turban and Watkins [51], Fordyce and Sullivan [24], Blanning [8], Kowalik [35], and several of the functions are targets of extensive research. Examples include Fedorowicz and Williams [22], Murphy and Stohr [44] and Shen [47] for expert systems techniques for representing modelling knowledge and formulating various model types without (*explicit*) specific domain focus, and Sivasankaran and Jarke [49] and Singh and Cook [48] for model identification and formulation within specific domains.

Our research is restricted to a *specific problem domain* using *known model types.* We can therefore use the system to guide tasks (a)–(f) relatively easily, using prespecified generic models, an internal database for existing corporate debt, an extensive menu- and form-driven user interface and a *rules-operating-on-frames* control structure interposed between the interface and the data and models. For *prototypical* parametric and sensitivity analysis and plan refinement the *frames-containing-rules* control structure popularized by Aikens [2] is used. The major role of expert systems techniques in MIDAS is in assistance in model understanding, sensitivity testing and result refinement, which are crucial to the use of our models by untrained managers. To our knowledge, these tasks have not yet been demonstrated for *multiple models* or for models of the *complexity* of those in MIDAS.

Explanation of model relationships and results for *simple* financial models in the form of financial statements is demonstrated by Bouwman [9]. This system reasons qualitatively with verbal descriptions of changes in financial figures over time; its main goal is to develop a causal description for a company's present condition. Its techniques appear useful for analyzing complex causal relationships of the sort found in financial planning models. Kosy and Wise, in ROME [32,33,53] explain resource allocation plans quantitatively, using underlying mathematical equations describing known relationships in the plans; their system successfully develops causal path descriptions for chains of simple calculations. However, neither their system nor Bouwman's *distinguishes* between *simple* and *complex* relationships to tailor explanations. Also, neither system guides *sensitivity analysis* and *multiple run comparison*, although both provide foundations for doing so. We are designing MIDAS's expert simulation modelling assistant to overcome these limitations.

Explanation of simulation modelling requires knowledge of the financial relationships in the debt management domain which are articulated in the models being used, along with knowledge of the distributions used for random variables and the meaning of simple result distributions. Optimization explanation requires, in addition, extensive knowledge of the theory, structure and solution properties of the models used, as discussed briefly in §4. Greenberg [27,28] is investigating explanation of linear programming models for energy management in his ANALYZE system; we are studying the extent to which his and similar work may be combined with simulation explanation to operate effectively in the integrated modelling environment.

9 SUMMARY AND CONCLUSIONS

This paper has described the overall conceptual design for MIDAS, a domain-specific decision support system incorporating expert systems assistance for application, explanation and extension of the results of integrated optimization and simulation models. In the terminology of Kitzmiller and Kowalik [34], MIDAS is a *symbolic-numeric* knowledge-based system *deeply-coupled* using object-oriented programming techniques (Fikes and Kehler [23], Stefik and Bobrow [50]). The four advantages of such systems they mention are all being addressed in the MIDAS design, namely:-

1. Extension and enhancement of the capabilities of existing numerical methods (stochastic linear programming and simulation).
2. Intelligent user interface to extract required knowledge and interpret results of numerical computations.
3. Learning and induction from numerical computations including sensitivity and parametric analysis.
4. Intelligent processing to reduce numerical computational loads.

To these we may add another:-

5. Testing new numerical techniques (augmented Lagrangean methods for stochastic optimization) in a specified domain of practical importance.

We have implemented most of the simulation component, which in itself provides a useful decision tool for our corporate partner in this research. We are now engaged in detailed specification, design and prototyping of an expert subsystem for explaining the simulation in response to menu-based queries, as a first step toward a comprehensive subsystem for simulation application assistance and ultimately an integrated model management system for debt management strategic planning. We are also currently involved in implementing the stochastic programming model and solvers.

In a clearly *specified domain* such as debt management, a specific expert decision support system such as MIDAS appears to have many advantages. Because the *decision process* for major decisions can be *partly anticipated* or structured, the system can be designed to support it in depth through applicable models. Because models are specified according to the decision process, formulation problems are minimized. And because the *economic* and *financial* knowledge and *mathematical relationships* needed for decisions are *limited, relatively stable* and *common* to all models in the system, a knowledge base can support *multiple models* in terms familiar to the manager who is not a modelling expert.

ACKNOWLEDGEMENTS

We wish to acknowledge the contributions of our coworkers on the MIDAS project, E.G. Achorn, S.H. Hinds and S.I. Topiwala. We are also grateful to P.T. Cox, I. Fooladi, H.I. Gassmann and G.S. Roberts for helpful comments and discussions.

This research, and the Dalhousie Courseware Development Project of which it forms a part, is supported by the Bank of Nova Scotia, Digital Equipment Corporation, Unisys Corporation, the Nova Scotia Power Corporation, Northern Telecom, the Natural Sciences and Engineering Research Council of Canada and the Social Sciences and Humanities Research Council of Canada.

REFERENCES

1. Agmon, T., A.R. Ofer and A. Tamir [1981]. Variable rate debt instruments and corporate debt policy. *Journal of Finance* **36**, 113–125.

2. Aikens, J.S. [1983]. Prototypical knowledge for expert systems. *Artificial Intelligence* **20**, 163–210.

3. Ayers, Herbert F. and John Y. Barry [1979]. The equilibrium yield curve for government securities. *Financial Analysts' Journal* (May-June 1979), 31–39.

4. Barnea, Amir, Robert A. Haugen and Lemma W. Senbet [1981]. Market imperfections, agency problems and capital structure: A review. *Financial Management* **10**, 7–22.

5. Bierwag, Gerald O. [1987]. *Duration Analysis: Managing Interest Rate Risk.* Ballinger Publishing Company, 238–245.

6. Birge, J.R. [1985]. Decomposition and partitioning methods for multistage stochastic linear programs. *Operations Research* **33**, 987–1007.

7. Birge, J.R., M.A.H. Dempster, H.I. Gassmann, E.A. Gunn, A.J. King and S.W. Wallace [1987]. A standard input format for multiperiod stochastic linear programs. Working paper WP-87-118, System and Decision Sciences, International

Institute for Applied Systems Analysis. To appear in: *COAL Newsletter*, Mathematical Programming Society.

8. Blanning, Robert W. [1987]. A survey of issues in expert systems for management. In: Barry G. Silverman, ed., *Expert Systems for Business*. Addison-Wesley, Reading, Mass., 24–39.

9. Bouwman, Marinus J. [1983]. Human diagnostic reasoning by computer: An illustration from financial analysis. *Management Science* **29**, 653–672.

10. Boyce, W. M. and A. J. Kalotay [1979a]. Tax differentials and callable bonds. *Journal of Finance* **34**, 825–838.

11. _______ [1979b]. Optimum bond calling and refunding. *Interfaces* **9**, 36–49.

12. Bradley, Stephen P. and Dwight B. Crane [1972]. A dynamic model for bond portfolio management. *Management Science* **19**, 139–151.

13. _______ [1975]. *Management of Bank Portfolios*. John Wiley, New York.

14. _______ [1980]. Managing a bank bond portfolio over time. In: M.A.H. Dempster, ed., *Stochastic Programming*. Academic Press, London.

15. Brennan, Michael and Eduardo Schwartz [1978]. Corporate income taxes, valuation and the problem of optimal capital structure. *Journal of Business* **51**, 103–114.

16. Brick, Ivan E. and S. Abraham Ravid [1985]. On the relevance of debt maturity structure. *Journal of Finance* **40**, 1423–1437.

17. Crane, Dwight B. [1971]. A stochastic programming model for commercial bank bond portfolio management. *Journal of Financial and Quantitative Analysis* **6**, 955–976.

18. Crane, Dwight B., Frederick Knoop and William Pettigrew [1977]. An application of management science to bank borrowing strategies. *Interfaces* **8**, 70–81.

19. Dempster, M.A.H. [1986]. On stochastic programming: II. Dynamic problems under risk. Technical report DAL TR-86-5, Department of Mathematics, Statistics and Computing Science, Dalhousie University. To appear in *Stochastics*.

20. Dempster, M.A.H., H.I. Gassmann, E.A. Gunn and R.R. Merkovsky [1987]. Lagrangean dual decomposition methods for solving stochastic programmes with recourse. (In preparation.)

21. Elton, Edwin J. and Martin J. Gruber [1971]. Dynamic programming applications in finance. *Journal of Finance* **26**, 473–506.

22. Fedorowicz, Jane and Gerald B. Williams [1986]. Representing modelling knowledge in an intelligent decision support system. *Decision Support Systems* **2**, 3–14.

23. Fikes, R. and T. Kehler [1985]. The role of frame-based representation in reasoning. *Communications of the ACM* **28**, 904–920.

24. Fordyce, Kenneth and Gerald A. Sullivan [1986]. Decision simulation (DSIM): One outcome of combining expert systems and decision support systems. In: L.F. Pau, ed., *Artificial Intelligence in Economics and Management.* Elsevier Science Publishers, Amsterdam, 31–40.

25. Gassmann, H.I. [1987a]. Multiperiod stochastic programming. Ph.D. thesis, Faculty of Commerce and Business Administration, University of British Columbia.

26. Gassmann, H.I. [1987b]. Optimal harvest of a forest under uncertainty. Working paper No. 59, School of Business Administration, Dalhousie University.

27. Greenberg, Harvey J. [1987a]. A natural language discourse model to explain linear programming models and solutions. *Decision Support Systems* **3**, 333–342.

28. _______ [1987b]. The development of an intelligent mathematical programming system. Paper presented at the Washington Operations Research/Management Science Chapter (WORMSC) Meeting.

29. Hertz, D. B. [1964]. Risk analysis in capital investment. *Harvard Business Review* **42**, 95–106.

30. Howard, C. Douglas [1986]. Applications of Monte Carlo Simulation to Corporate Financial Liability Management. Paper presented at the Financial Management Association Conference, New York.

31. Kalymon, Basil A. [1971]. Bond refunding with stochastic interest rates. *Management Science* **18**, 563–575.

32. Kosy, Donald W. and Ben P. Wise [1984]. Self-explanatory financial planning models. In: *Proceedings of the National Conference on Artificial Intelligence, Austin, Texas*, 176–181.

33. _______ [1986]. Overview of ROME: A reason-oriented modeling environment. In: L.F. Pau, ed., *Artificial Intelligence in Economics and Management.* Elsevier Science Publishers, Amsterdam, 21–30.

34. Kitzmiller, C.T. and J.S. Kowalik [1987]. Coupling symbolic and numeric computing in knowledge-based systems. *The AI Magazine* **8**, Summer, 85–90.

35. Kowalik, J.S., ed. [1986]. *Coupling Symbolic and Numerical Computing in Expert Systems.* North Holland, Amsterdam.

36. Kusy, M.I. and W.T. Ziemba [1986]. A bank asset and liability model. *Operations Research* **34**, 356–376.

37. Lane, Morton and Peter Hutchinson [1980]. A model for managing a certificate of deposit portfolio under uncertainty. In: M.A.H. Dempster, ed., *Stochastic Programming.* Academic Press, London.

38. Lee, Cheng F. [1985]. *Financial Analysis: Theory and Application.* Addison-Wesley, Reading, Mass.

39. Levy, Haim and Marshall Sarnat [1984]. *Portfolio and Investment Selection: Theory and Practice.* Prentice-Hall International, Englewood Cliffs, New Jersey.

40. Merkovsky, R.R. [1987]. Near-linearly convergent procedures for convex and large scale optimization based on linear programming: Theory and applications. Ph.D. dissertation, Department of Mathematics, Statistics and Computing Science, Dalhousie University.

41. Modigliani, F. and M. Miller [1963]. Corporate income taxes and the cost of capital: A correction. *American Economic Review* **53**, 433–443.

42. Morris, James R. [1976a]. On corporate debt maturity strategies. *Journal of Finance* **31**, 29–37.

43. _______ [1976b]. A model for corporate debt maturity decisions. *Journal of Financial and Quantitative Analysis* **11**, 339–357.

44. Murphy, Frederic H. and Edward A. Stohr [1986]. An intelligent system for formulating linear programs. *Decision Support Systems* **2**, 39–47.

45. Rockafellar, R.T. and R.J-B. Wets [1987]. Scenarios and policy aggregation in optimization under uncertainty. Working paper WP-87-119, System and Decision Sciences, International Institute for Applied Systems Analysis.

46. Shapiro, Jeremy F. [1987]. Stochastic programming models for dedicated portfolio selection. In: *Proceedings of the NATO Advanced Study Institute: Mathematical Models for Decision Support. Val D'Isere, France.*

47. Shen, Sheldon [1987]. Knowledge management in decision support systems. *Decision Support Systems* **3**, 1–11.

48. Singh, Madan G. and Roderick Cook [1985]. A new class of intelligent knowledge-based systems with an optimization-based inference engine. *Decision Support Systems* **1**, 299–312.

49. Sivasankaran, Taracad and Matthias Jarke [1985]. Logic-based formula management strategies in an actuarial consulting system. *Decision Support Systems* **1**, 251–262.

50. Stefik, M. and D.G. Bobrow [1986]. Object-oriented programming: Themes and variations. *The AI Magazine* **6**, Winter, 40–62.

51. Turban, Efraim and Paul R. Watkins [1986]. Integrating expert systems and decision support systems. *MIS Quarterly* **10**, 121–136.

52. Waterman, Donald A. [1986]. *A Guide to Expert Systems.* Addison-Wesley, Reading, Mass.

53. Wise, Ben P. and Donald W. Kosy [1986b]. Model-based evaluation of long-range resource allocation plans. In: L.F. Pau, ed., *Artificial Intelligence in Economics and Management.* Elsevier Science Publishers, Amsterdam, 93–102.

A KNOWLEDGE-BASED SYSTEM FOR PRODUCTION CONTROL OF FLEXIBLE MANUFACTURING SYSTEMS

G.-W. Hintz RWTH Aachen

1. Introduction

Due to the changing market demands and under the heavy pressure of competition, product life cycles have permanently become shorter. Therefore, the production companies have less time to develop new products and to install the needed plants (Bolwijn/Kumpe 1986, p. 41). A lot of effort has been taken to increase the efficiency of the manufacturing process by investing into highly automated production units (for instance NC- and CNC-machines). Now, it has been realized that it is inevitable to integrate these units in order to meet the requirements of flexibility and quality as well as that of efficiency (Mortimer 1985, p. 22). A central element of integration and automation are Flexible Manufacturing Systems (FMS). By an FMS we understand an integrated manufacturing system consisting of work stations linked by a computerized material handling system capable of making it possible for jobs to follow diverse routes through the system. An example of an FMS is given in fig. 1. FMS facilitate small batch sizes, high quality standards and efficiency of the production process at the same time.

NATO ASI Series, Vol. F48
Mathematical Models for Decision Support
Edited by G. Mitra

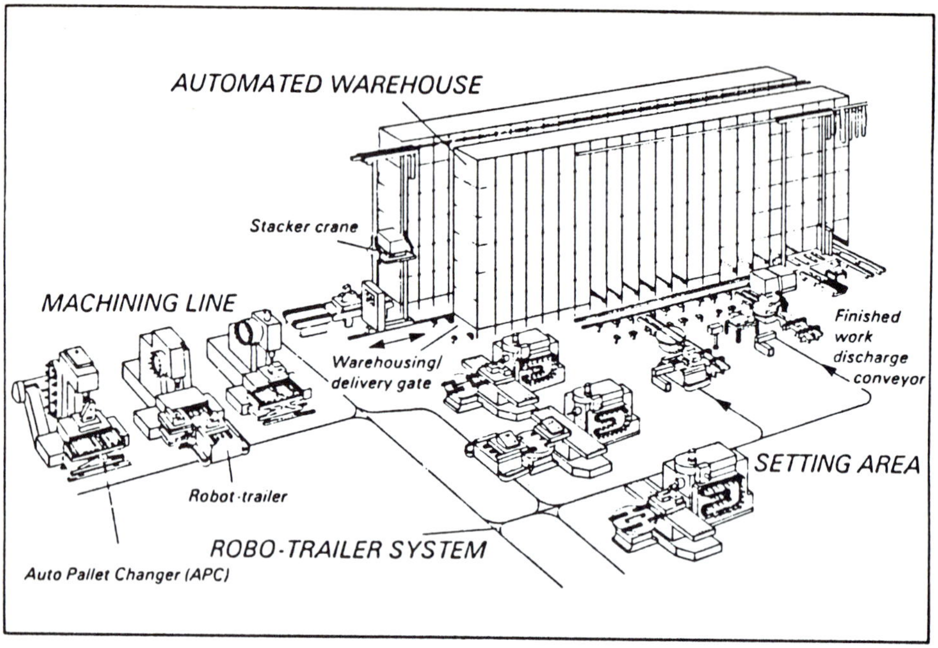

Figure 1: Example for an FMS (Hartley 1984)

In order to be able to use all these potentials, it is necessary to reorganize the manufacturing area and to develop dedicated systems for production planning and control or PPC (Aggarval 1985, p. 8). The starting point for this is an adequate distribution of the tasks between a centralized PPC-system and a decentralized PPC-system for each FMS which takes over the local coordination and optimization.

Thus, the central system can concentrate on the global tasks of optimal production coordination which tend from purchase and construction to manufacturing, assembling and distribution.

This can be done by placing complete orders to the FMS`s. Then the decentralized system is responsible for meeting the due dates and for an internal optimization for the FMS.
The decentralized system has to be dedicated to the special demands of the FMS in order to meet the objectives

- to minimize the flow times,
- to minimize due date deviations and
- to maximize machine utilizations

as well as possible. Generally these objectives are conflicting.
Furthermore, the combinatorial character of this problem makes exact optimization approaches inapplicable. Finally, the problem is rather ill-structured because many interdependencies and uncertainties render the results of specific actions unpredictable. Therefore, a solution procedure has been developed which combines both methods from Operations Research and

Artificial Intelligence and which is able to handle these difficulties (Hintz 1987).

In chapter 2, we will give a short survey of the complete decentralized PPC-system dedicated to an FMS. In chapter 3, the content of the knowledge-based system is described. The most important results from a simulation study for evaluating the knowledge-based system are given in chapter 4.

2. Concept of the developed PPC-System

In the following we will briefly describe the main elements of the developed hierarchical PPC-system dedicated to the special needs of FMS (Hintz 1987). It consists of four steps.

In the first step a simultaneous capacity requirement planning is processed with the objective to meet due dates as well as possible. In contrast to the usual successive methods a simultaneous approach based on Linear Programming has been developed. This was made possible by the special production structure in which nearly the complete manufacturing can be performed within the single but aggregated capacity unit of an FMS. The result is a short-term production program with mostly balanced machine utilization which optimally meets the due dates.

The tooling of the machines will be determined in the second step according to the special short-term production program. The main objective of this step is to increase the flexibility of the FMS by maximizing the overlapping of the tools on the different machines under the restriction of the limited capacity of the tool magazines. This redundancy of tools yields a more flexible and, therefore, more efficient manufacturing process.

The task of the third step is to determine the release schedule of the workpieces, i.e. the order and time when a specific part is loaded into the FMS for processing. For prismatic parts this means that the part has to be fixed on a special pallet and is brought to a well defined point of release where the automatic transportation system can pick it up.

In the fourth and final step the machine schedule will be determined. We suppose that we have n parts to be processed by m machines. For each part we have technological constraints which demand a particular order of the operations. In contrast to the commonly known machine scheduling problem each machine can process different operations and most of the operations can be processed by different machines (depending on the technical specifications and the tooling of the machines).

In the following the determination of the release schedule and the machine schedule for FMS are summarized to the term production control. This will be done by the knowledge-based system which will now be discussed in more detail. The complete four-step PPC-system is shown in fig. 2.

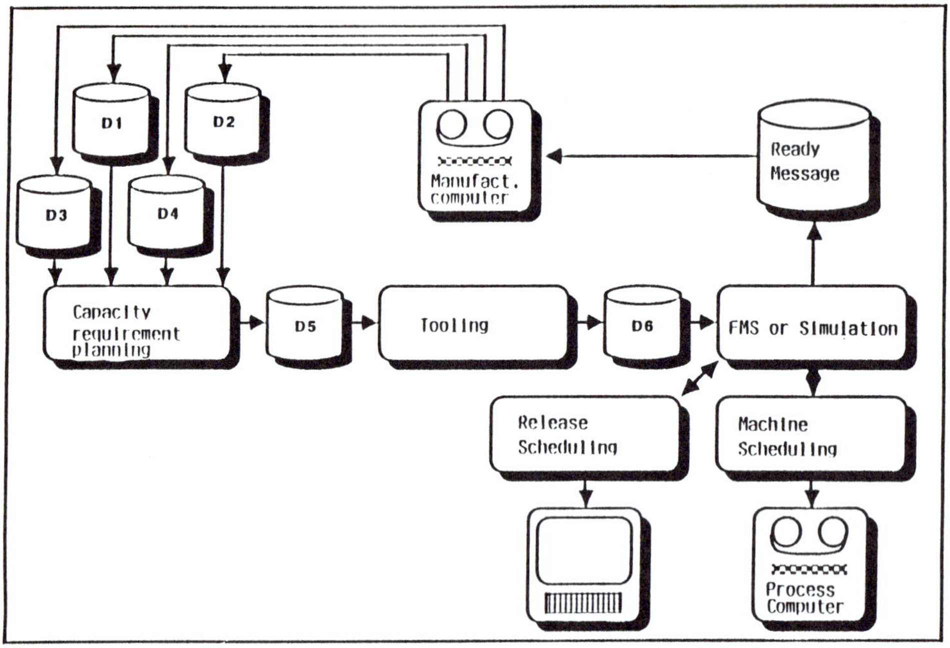

Figure 2: Overview of the complete PPC-system.

In this context, we interpret a knowledge-based system as an expert system which does not include components of knowledge acquisition and explanation. By an expert system we understand a computer program which can deduce solutions for specific problems in a way similar to a human being. In addition to the analysing and evaluating features for production control known from usual PPC-systems in expert systems, we are enabled to store and process the experience and special knowledge of experts who are familiar with the problem and its context. In order to realize that, we need special methods for processing both numerically and linguistically expressed knowledge and to make inferences from the given knowledge. Such methods have been developed in the theory of fuzzy sets from which we have taken the concept of linguistic variables and of approximate reasoning.
The description of the main theoretical results of fuzzy set theory, linguistic variables and approximate reasoning which are used in the system can be found in this book. See f.i. (Zimmermann 1988). More detailed informations of the topics are given in (Zadeh 1973), (Zadeh 1981), (Zimmermann 1986).

3. Production Control of an FMS by a Knowledge-Based System

The main goal of the knowledge-based system for production control of FMS is to deduce "optimal" decisions for the release and the machine scheduling. In the decision process several alternatives are judged according to one or several criteria. Each criterion can consist of several sub-criteria.

Thus the criteria are concretized until they are easily understandable or operationalized. This procedure yields a hierarchy of criteria which already has proved to be useful in several applications (e.g. Zimmermann/Zysno 1982).

Figure 3 shows the hierarchy of criteria used for the release scheduling

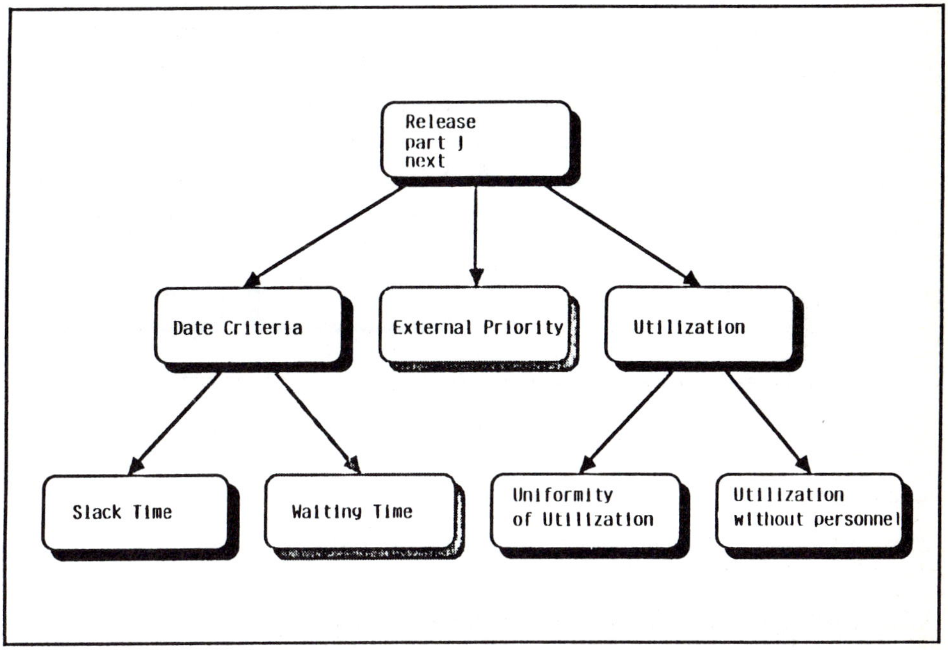

Figure 3: Hierarchy of criteria for release scheduling

The complete rule set and the explanation of the rules are given in (Hintz, 1987).

In figure 4, the hierarchy of criteria for machine scheduling is shown.

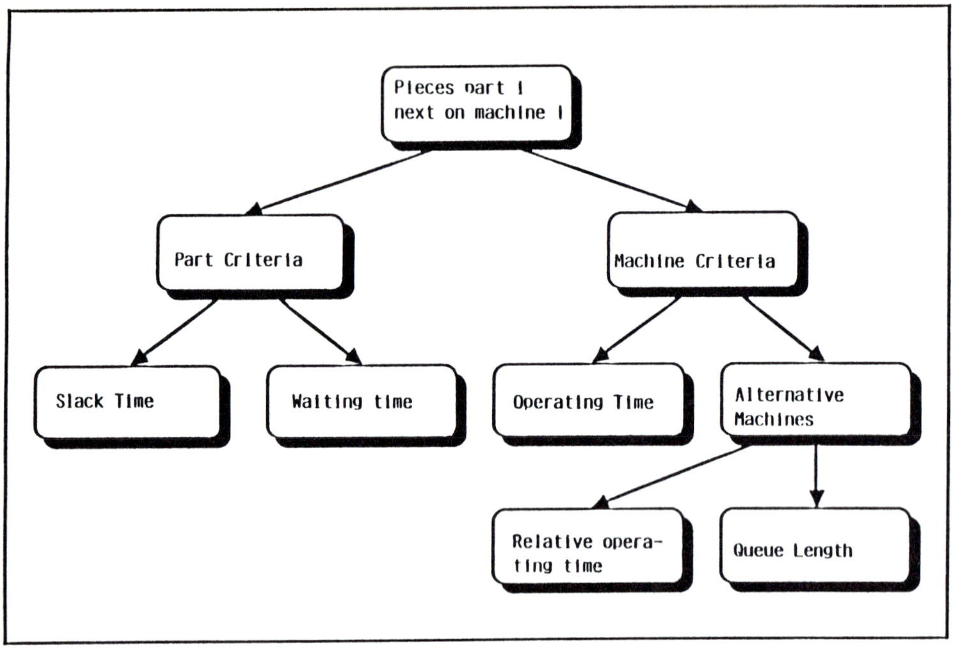

Figure 4: Hierarchy of criteria for machine scheduling

The rule set is also given and explained in (Hintz 1987).

4. Simulation Study for the Knowledge Based System

In order to evaluate the knowledge based system for release and machine scheduling a general simulation program for FMS has been developed (Herling/Hintz 1986). It considers

- machines and other operating stations,
- tooling
- storage capacities,
- transportation facilities,
- paletts and fixing units and
- work pieces.

Thus the simulation program is quite a good model of a real FMS. In order to simulate different FMSs one only has to change the appropriate input data, but not the program itself.

The data for the simulation runs have been generated randomly but according to the structure of typical realized FMS`s. This structure is mainly based on an observation of more than 150 FMSs installed all over the world (Mertins 1985), but also on observations by the author himself (Hintz 1987).

Both the simulation program and the knowledge-based system are written in FORTRAN 77. At present they run on a VAX 11/780 or on an IBM AT. The computing time on the VAX is at about 200

CPU-seconds for 3200 operations. The time for a single decision is at about 2 10^{-2} CPU-seconds on the VAX or 0.7 CPU-seconds on the AT.

The decisions of the knowledge-based system for release scheduling (KBR) have been compared with the following priority rule:

Release the part for which the number of the parts already released divided by the total lot size is minimal (L).

The knowledge-based system for machine scheduling (KBM) is compared with the often tested priority rule COVERT (C) which is an alternative combination of processing and slack time. Other priority rules have also been tested, but the complete series are only taken for the above described priority rules.

This yielded 4 combinations for release and machine scheduling which have been evaluated according to the

- mean in-process waiting time (w)
- part of lots that have met their due dates (D) and
- mean machine utilization (U).

The aggregated results are as follows:

Release	Machine Scheduling	W[min]	D[%]	U[%]
L	C	2923	61	79
L	KBM	2895	48	81
KBR	C	2859	96	77
KBR	KBM	2884	97	80

Comparing KBR/KBM with L/C it results that the knowledge-based system dominates the priority rules i.e. it is better according to each of the three objectives.

We can also see that the combination L/KBM does not yield good results except for the machine utilization. The main strength of the knowledge-based system lies in the fact that the decision criteria can be coordinated very well.

Of similar importance as the quality of the decisions is the possibility to improve the results according to a single objective criterion without heavy (or even any) loss according to the other. This has also been shown in simulation studies (Hintz 1987).

5. Summary

The developed knowledge-based system for production control of FMSs yields significantly better results than conventional priority rules according to all three examined objectives. One main reason for this seems to be that it is able to take all relevant information into consideration and interpret them adequately according to the specific situation. Furthermore, it can very easily be modified according to the specific demands of the management adding or changing linguistic variables and/or rules. Thus the knowledge-based system is very flexible.

The computational effort of the system is so low that it can easily be implemented as a decentralized production control system dedicated to the need of FMSs.

References:

Aggarwal, S.C. (1985): MRP, JIT, OPT, FMS?, in: Harvard Business Review 5 (1985) S.8-16

Bolwijn, P.T.; Kumpe, T. (1986): Toward the Factory of the Future, in: The McKinsey Quarterly Spring (1986) S.40-49

Cohen, B.; Murphy, G.L. (1984): Models of Concepts, in: Cognitive Science Series 8 (1984) S.27-58

Hartley, J.: FMS at Work, Bedford 1984

Herling, Ch.; Hintz, G.W. (1986): Ein Programm zur Simulation von flexiblen Fertigungssystemen, Arbeitsbericht des Instituts für Wirtschaftswissenschaften Nr.86/08, RWTH Aachen, 1986

Hintz, G.W. (1987): Ein wissensbasiertes System zur Produktionsplanung und -steuerung für flexible Fertigungssysteme, Düsseldorf 1987

Mertins, K. (1985): Entwicklungsstand flexibler Fertigungssysteme, - Linien-, Netz- und Zellenstrukturen, in: ZwF 80 (1985) S.249-265

Mortimer, T. (ed.) (1985): Integrated Manufacture, Bedford 1985

Zadeh, L.A. (1973): The Concept of Linguistic Variables and its Application to Approximate Reasoning, Memorandum No. ERL-M411, University of California, Berkeley 1973

Zadeh, L.A. (1977): A Theory of Approximate Reasoning, Memorandum No. UCB/ERL M77/58, University of California, Berkeley 1977

Zimmermann, H.J. (1986): Fuzzy Set Theory - and its Applications, 2. Aufl., Boston, Dordrecht, Lancaster 1986

Zimmermann, H.J.; Zysno, P. (1982): Ein hierarchisches Bewertungssystem für die Kreditwürdigkeitsprüfung im Konsumentenkreditgeschäft, in: DBW 42 (1982) S.403-417

Zysno, P. (1982): The Integration of Concepts within Judgmental and Evaluative Processes, in: Trappe, R.; Klir, G.J.; Pichler, F.R. (eds): Progress in Cybernetics and Systems Research Vol. VIII, 1982, S.509-516

Zimmermann, H.-J.: Fuzzy Set Theory and Inference Mechanism, Springer 1988 (in this book)

A KNOWLEDGEBASE FOR FORMULATING LINEAR PROGRAMS

Frederic H. Murphy

1. INTRODUCTION

Every book on linear programming has at least one chapter on formulating linear programs, illustrating the various uses to which they can be put. Some books such as Gass, [11] or Schrage, [20], spend a substantial amount of time going over different formulations in detail. Typically, a few examples are presented followed by a description of the simplex algorithm. A more formal approach is possible and it can be translated into an intelligent system that aids in the process of formulating a linear program.

Dantzig [7] presents a structured approach to formulating linear programs. Welch [21] has developed a system called PAM that draws on some standard structures, simplifying the process of using Dataform [6] in matrix generation. Breitman and Lucas [4] developed a system called PLANET for using linear programming in various production situations at General Motors where the model is built using simple queries and entering data. Binbasioglu [1] developed concepts for a knowledgebase for representing production-oriented linear programs. Geoffrion [12] describes a structured approach to building general models.

This paper describes the knowledgebase for a system designed to aid in formulating linear programs. See Murphy and Stohr, [17] for a description of the system known as LPFORM. Here, we present the systematic view of semantic relationships in linear programming models.

There are several reasons for building an intelligent system that assists in model building. To begin with, the use of linear programming has been limited to professionals who are knowledgeable in matrix generation software. PAM is the first step away from this, but it is data driven rather than organized around the algebra of linear models.

Experienced practitioners ignore the algebraic statement of the model beyond the initial model description, but this is due as much to having committed it to memory or not having it available as anything else. Yet, during the conceptual design phase it is used constantly. Also, the symbolic statement is integral to good documentation, and, since it is the most compact statement, it is the first step for someone learning an existing model. With current systems the symbolic statement, if it exists, is constructed by hand and is usually out of date. One of our goals is to make the algebraic statement a useful tool in model design, construction, analysis and maintenance.

NATO ASI Series, Vol. F48
Mathematical Models for Decision Support
Edited by G. Mitra

To build an intelligent system one must formalize the procedures used by experts in the field. Although we, as operations researchers, view the process of formulating linear programs as an art, the fact that so many models have similar characteristics shapes our perceptions and provides opportunities for systematizing the process of model building. To begin with, the formulation process involves problem recognition, problem classification, symbolic definition, data collection and model statement generation.

Knowledge about an LP model can be grouped into three categories: data, structure, and meaning. Data contain knowledge beyond their numerical values. That there are data values for an activity implies the existence of the activity. Also, coefficients have units that aid one in piecing together an LP, and one consistency check is to make sure that units match in a constraint. Structure involves using information about indices to piece together the LP from previously defined components through a series of matchings. This form of knowledge was addressed in Murphy, Stohr and Ma [18]. This paper explores meaning as a component of the knowledge base. That is, we are exploring the knowledgebase required for representing meaning when generating a symbolic statement of a linear program.

2. THE NOTION OF TRANSFORMATION

One key to understanding the nature of linear programming models is that they represent physical actions of transforming inputs into outputs. Another way of saying that there is a transformation is to say that there is some sort of flow. There can be a flow of inputs into a product, a flow of items from one location to another, or a flow of inventories through time. This notion of flow is embodied in the activity analysis approach of Dantzig [7] where activities are black boxes that transform inputs into outputs. Pictorially, we have the following representation of a linear programming activity:

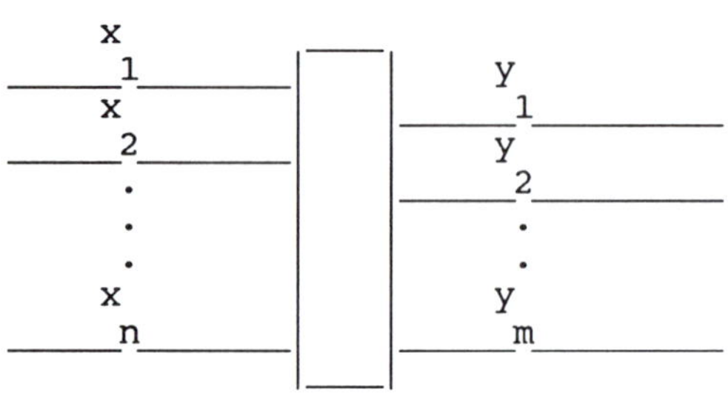

FIG 1 The Inputs and Outputs of an LP Activity

Linear and integer programs are often treated together in discussions on the art of formulation. In fact, many integer programs are simply linear programs with integer restrictions. However, typically there are many variables that represent logical decisions. The set covering problem is an example of such a model. Each variable represents the choice of one schedule versus another. That is, the solution has meaning only when the variables take on the values of 0 or 1; 2 would have no meaning. With linear programs, producing 3.75 chairs in a product mix does have a legitimate meaning. One can say either that we will complete 3 chairs in this period and do the remaining .25 of the work on the fourth chair in the next period or that we will take the production plan from the linear programming solution and juggle the production levels of other products so that we produce 4 chairs. A linear program's fractional solution has a meaning even if one cannot produce, ship or inventory a fraction of an item. Moreover, the absence of logical variables in LP's often simplifies the formulation process. For this reason we confine ourselves to a consideration of linear programs.

In our terms an object is described by three dimensions: what is being measured, where it is and when it exists in that place. As a consequence, each constraint can be defined using indices indicating what, where and when and any other information necessary to uniquely identify a row. The indices need not be ordered and need not be three dimensional when indicating form, time and place in the usual sense. For example, the item may be the ith component of the jth product and it is indicated by the pair (i,j). This pair is, however, the index for form. Also, as long as the names on the index sets are carried along, the order of the indices is unimportant.

A state can be altered by a transformation. A transformation in form converts a collection of indices denoting "whats" into another collection of indices describing "whats" while leaving place and time identical. Place and time transformations make analogous adjustments to other index sets. There are three basic transformations: transformations in place, in time and in form. As shown in Figure 2, each activity can be identified by the same triples for the constraints plus the action taken as follows. A transformation in form has indices corresponding to inputs and outputs, indices for where, when and an added index for how, if there are alternative approaches. Transformations in place are distinguished by having indices on what, when and how, plus from where to where. Transformations in time have indices on what, where and how and from when to when.

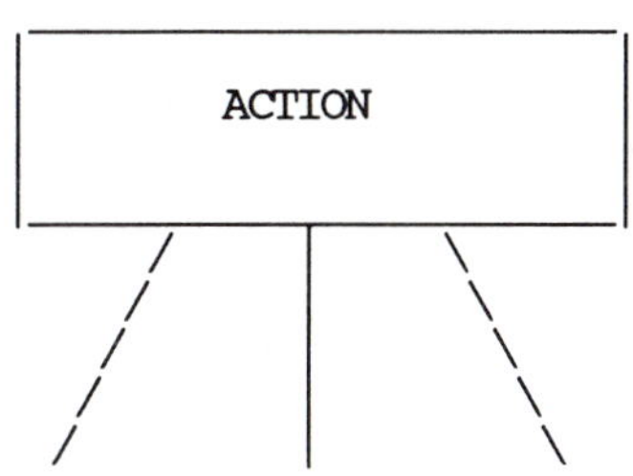

PLACE	FORM	TIME
From where	Where	Where
To where		What
	From what	
	To what	From when
What		To when
When	When	
How	How	How

FIG 2 Index Combinations for Transformations

One can also have compound activities such as a simultaneous transformation of place and time if it takes one period to ship the product so that what is shipped at time t is available at time t+1.

3. TEMPLATE MODELS

From the linear programming modeler's perspective, the logical units of linear programs are the models that represent the three aspects of production described above: transformations in place, time and form. That is, the same categorization of the activities applies to submodels. We recognize the transportation model as a transformation in place, the manpower planning model as a transformation in time and the product mix model as a transformation in form, e.g. raw materials are physically transformed into a final product.

We now present the simple models that form the building blocks for a larger system. We also present some template constraints that have a special structure including one that represents a measure of input or product quality, the blending problem.

Before we describe the common template models, we summarize two forms of knowledge representation that are needed to capture the appropriate information about the templates. These are semantic nets and frames. (See Winston 1984 for a more complete discussion of the subject.) Semantic nets represent a network of relationships among entities. Taking the relationship "is a," and saying that "linear program" is an entity we can say a template that represents a form transformation has an "is a" relationship to "linear program", the same is true for time and place templates. We can also say that a product mix model is a form transformation. By the same token, the transportation and transshipment models are connected to the place transformation category by "is a" relationships. One can see that by having "is a" be an arc in a graph there is a network of linkages among entities. Figure 3 illustrates a semantic net of templates.

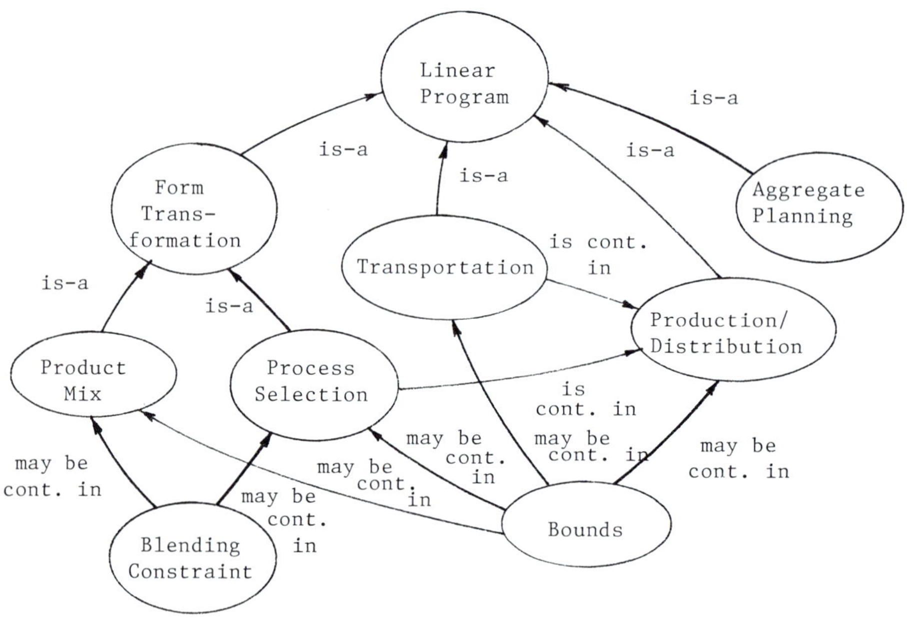

FIG 3 An Example of a Semantic Net of Templates

One can define other relationships among entities in the semantic net. For example, one can define the relationship "may be contained in" to state that, say, a distillation unit or a blending model may be contained in a refinery model. The semantic net is not always a tree as in the examples that have been presented thus far. Expanding the "may be contained in" relationship, one can say that a reactor model and a blending model may be contained in a model of chemical reactions. Thus, the blending model appears as a submodel in two different LP's.

Frames consist of an object (eg. a node) and slots that contain information about the object. We can think of a frame as a list. Thus, a frame about LP's contains slots with information on actions, restrictions and objectives. A slot or slots can be reserved to establish some relationship between the object of interest and some other object. By assuming that the properties of the more general entity carry over to the more specific entity, we can successively refine the definition of a model by working from the general towards a more specific statement of a model. With each refinement of the definition of a submodel more information is known about the characteristics of the submodel. The new information is stored in slots associated with the object that defines the latest refinement. Thus, with the product mix model one has slots noting that the objective is to maximize profit, the activities are production levels of different products and the restrictions are resource limits.

We now present common template models organized as transformations in place, time, and form. By using the "is a" relationship, we can organize the information about templates into a semantic net.

3.1 Transformations in Place

A transformation in place is a production process where entities are physically relocated (e.g. the classical transportation problem). The inputs to the process are the supply of materials and transportation services and the outputs are materials delivered to the appropriate locations. The formulation for the standard transportation model is as follows:

$$(1) \qquad \min \sum_{ij} c_{ij} x_{ij}$$

$$\text{s.t.}$$

$$\sum_{j} x_{ij} \le s_i$$

$$\sum_{i} x_{ij} \ge d_j$$

The well-known features of this model are:

- each activity intersects one supply row and one demand row and there is an activity for every combination of supply and demand rows where flows are allowed.
- supply rows are less-than-or-equal-to constraints and demand rows are greater-than-or-equal-to constraints.
- the nonzero coefficients are all 1's.
- there is one constraint for each input and each output,

where inputs and outputs are defined in terms of the attributes of form, place and time.

In organizing a knowledgebase for transformations in place one first distinguishes between transshipment and transportation models. For transportation models the frame consists of a list of sources, a list of sinks, the forms of supply and demand constraints and objective function coefficients. For the transshipment model the frame also includes a list of the transshipment nodes and the form of a transshipment constraint. The next issue is whether there are gains or losses associated with the movement of the good. Both the transshipment and transportation model frames include a slot for gains or losses. The slot would contain information on whether or not there are gains or losses and, if so, a reference to a database containing the data values. The system would then have a rule that the gain or loss coefficients belong in the demand constraints or on supplying activities in transshipment constraints. Since there are often alternative methods of transporting a good, the frames must contain a slot describing the alternative transportation methods, if any, which we call modes. The slot has a list of modes and database references on limits and utilization rates for each mode and source-destination pair.

3.2 Transformations in Time

There are basically two types of problems having a time dimension. The first is the class of scheduling problems where we want to set up a cyclic schedule. Here, time is not linear in the sense that period T+1 is the same as period 1. In this situation we want the intelligent system to use modulo arithmetic when indexing in time so that, for example, staff who have not completed a work cycle carry over to the first period. The second is the class of multi-period planning problems where T represents the truncation of an infinite horizon. If there are any physical products that are modeled, then there is no cycle unless one wants the ending inventory and labor force to match the beginning inventory and labor force. With these production models the basic structure of the static form and place transformations described above are replicated for each time period and some linking variables and constraints are added.

In the theory of production, capital, labor and materials are used to produce goods. When adding a time dimension, each of these resources should be treated differently in the formulation. Materials differ from capital and labor. We consume materials but we use only the services of capital and labor.

With materials, if storage is possible, we are dealing with inventories and we have intertemporal links that transfer goods from one period to the next. In the tableau, typical inventory activities have a +1 in a period t constraint and a -g in a period t+1 constraint. The constraints that are intersected by the activity are the ones indexed by the material in successive time periods. Here g indicates the gains or losses. That is, the product in period t is the input, along with storage costs, to a process where the output is the additions to the product in period t+1. The inventory constraint fragment for product j in period t+1 looks as follows:

$$(2) \qquad -g_j I_{jt} + I_{jt+1}$$

We use the sign conventions for supply and demand from the general constraint (2).

With capital stock or members of the workforce, once the equipment or facilities come into existence, they remain at a positive availability until retired. There are two alternative formulations, depending on whether we keep track of capital stock by when it is acquired, termed vintaging, or we aggregate all of the capacity together.

If one does not distinguish vintages of equipment or labor, then one can have an inventory structure analogous to the structure for materials. In this situation we assume that equipment of different ages performs the same and either there are no retirements or a fixed percentage is expected to retire each time period. Thus, the only information we have to keep is the total amount of equipment available. The form of the model parallels the structure for inventories. When the capital stocks are inventoried, we keep track of the total amount of equipment of a given type. This is done as follows:

$$(3) \qquad a y_{t-1} + z_t - y_t = 0$$

$$\sum_j m_{tj} x_{tj} - y_t \leq 0$$

The activities z_t represent the process of adding new capacity in period t and the y's tell how much of the added capacity is available in each period. The coefficient a is the fraction of capacity that carries over from one period to the next. In period 1 one can have either y_0 equal to existing capacity or one can eliminate the variable y_0, having a right hand side equal to existing capacity. Since both formulations are correct, we choose to place existing capacity on the right-hand side of the first period constraint. The operational activities, the x's, describe how the capacity is utilized and are part of the representation of some transformation in form.

Note that the distinction between an input and a resource creates the need for a second constraint to account for the amount of capacity. The limit on using capacity reflects the time availability and the material balance is separate because using the capacity does not consume it and it remains available in the next time period.

If we account for a capital resource by vintage, by which we mean the year acquired, there is an activity with an entry for each constraint in which the resource is used. Say the resource addition activity intersects only one row in each period, its availability varies throughout its life and the efficiency of the equipment varies with its vintage and age. Then the model can have the following structure:

$$(4) \qquad \sum_j m_{tj} x_{tj} - v_1 y_t \leq 0$$

$$\cdots\cdots\cdots\cdots\cdots$$

$$\sum_j m_{t+n-1j} x_{t+n-1j} - v_n y_t \leq 0$$

Here, y_t indicates the amount of capacity added in year t, v_1 through v_n indicate the availability of capacity in the periods 1 through n since the equipment was acquired, where n is the life of the equipment. Also, m_{tnj} indexes the amount of capacity required for each unit of x_{t+n-1j}, where x_{tnj} is the level of operation in mode j in the nth period since the capacity was acquired. The time period associated with this constraint is t+n-1.

If one distinguishes vintage but the operating characteristics remain the same, the constraints (4) can be replaced by the following single constraint in each time period:

$$(5) \qquad \sum_j m_{tj}\, x_{tj} - \sum_{k\leq t} v_{t-k+1}\, y_k \leq E_t.$$

where E_t is the amount of currently existing capacity available in period t. The difference between this constraint and the constraints in (4) are that the operating characteristics of available capacity are the same over all vintages. Consequently, one need only have operating variables determined by mode of operation, not by mode and vintage. And rather than having separate capacity constraints for each vintage, only one constraint is required.

In building linear programs when there are alternative formulations, some are often more efficient than others in solution time. A good measure of the efficiency of the formulation is the number of nonzeroes in the constraint matrix. Thus, if the v's are constant over the life of the equipment but the equipment has a shorter life than the planning horizon, there is a more efficient formulation than (5) that will produce the same solution:

$$(6) \qquad y_{t-1} + z_t - z_{t-n} - y_t = 0$$

$$\sum_j m_{tj} x_{tj} - v y_t \leq 0$$

where z_t is the amount purchased in time period t and n is the equipment life. In this formulation we add the resource acquired, z, into a total of the resource and then subtract it out at the end of its life. This structure replaces trapazoidal structures dense with 1's, as in the following figure, with extra constraints having at most 4 nonzeros.

```
1
1 1
1 1 1
1 1 1 1
1 1 1 1 1
  1 1 1 1 1
    1 1 1 1 1
```

FIG 4 Matrix Structure of Activities Representing a Resource with a Fixed Life of Five Years

Thus, when the equipment life exceeds 4 years, there are fewer nonzeros with (6).

Since there may be a representation of the construction of the capital stock, the z's may intersect other constraint rows. If there is no representation of the construction of the capital stock, the only other nonzero coefficient is the cost in the objective function, unless there are free rows that carry accounting information not involved in the optimization.

The frames first distinguish cyclic scheduling models from finite horizon models by incorporating two nodes, "cyclic" and "finite-horizon," linked to the time transformation node by "is-a" relationships. The cyclic LP object has a frame that consists of a list that itemizes or contains procedures for itemizing possible cyclic schedules. The finite horizon object is partitioned into components that relate to materials and resources. The materials object contains a frame that lists the materials that are inventoried, the template constraint (2) and data base references on coefficients for gains and losses during storage (eg. yeast grows and alcohol evaporates). Also, the frame contains information on inventory capacity or capacities, ie. whether there are limits and to what products the limits apply.

With resources the frames become more complicated. The frames must contain the appropriate constraints selected from (3) through (6). The frame includes slots having answers for the following questions:

1. Is the availability constant over the planning horizon or declining exponentially over time?

2. Does the resource have a fixed life shorter than the planning horizon and constant availability over its life?

3. Is the efficiency constant over the life of the equipment?

If the answers are no to 3, then the problem structure is as in (4) where everything is distinguished by when the equipment is bought and how it is used. If the answer is no to 1 and 2 and yes to 3, then the structure is as shown in (5) where the available capacity is combined into a single utilization constraint. When the answer to 1 and 3 is yes and the equipment life is longer than the planning horizon, we have the structure with the single equipment inventory variable in (3). When 1 is false and 2 and 3 are true, the more efficient structure in (6) is appropriate. Also, when the answers are no to any of the questions, the frame has to contain the appropriate information or database references on availabilities and/or efficiencies. Furthermore, the frame has to contain information on whether there are added restrictions on resource additions or utilization.

The implications of the answers to the three questions may be summarized using the following truth table:

	Value			Appropriate Constraints
Question	1	2	3	
	T	T	T	(3)
	-	-	F	(4)
	F	F	T	(5)
	F	T	T	(6)
	T	F	-	not possible

One feature of capital and labor is that it is often possible to expand temporarily the capacity of labor through overtime (at the same time expanding machine capacity) and it is possible to layoff workers. To incorporate overtime, we add an activity, say u_t, that expands capacity in each period and we add the following restriction:

$$(7) \qquad u_t - ay_t \leq 0.$$

This constraint restricts the amount of overtime to some fraction of the regular time available from the workforce. Thus, there have to be slots containing information on overtime or expanded utilization. The slots have to contain information on the cost and restrictions on the availability of overtime. The possible restrictions are a simple upper bound or a relative bound as in (7). There may be others that users would want to add later.

There are other variations in time constraints that could be added to the knowledgebase. One could be limits on growth in resources or inventories:

$$(8) \qquad x_{t+1} - ax_t \leq 0.$$

Another could be keeping track of vintages as with wine or trees.

3.3 Transformation in Form

The place and time portions of the semantic net are relatively simple when compared to the portion of the network for form. Also, the user will rarely have to expand the components of the knowledgebase that have been described for place and time. With transformations in form the number of variations expands dramatically and users will want to add their own tailored templates.

The product mix problem is the simplest representation of a transformation in form. Here inputs are materials, labor and machine capacity. Each activity x_j represents the level of output for product j. The coefficients a_{ij} represent the amount of resource i required to produce a unit of product j. The statement of the general product mix model is the same as the statement of the general linear program:

$$(9) \qquad \max \sum_j p_j x_j \quad \text{s.t.} \quad \sum_j a_{ij} x_j \leq b_i$$

The coefficient p_j is the profit on product j and b_i is the availability of resource i. An aspect of this model deserves mention. There are no equations for the output products. The reason for this is that we presume that all units of a given product can be sold at a fixed price. We may draw the following conclusion:

- the only time we need a constraint associated with an input or an output is when there is no market that can provide an effectively infinite supply or demand at a fixed price.

Upper and lower bound constraints on the activities in (9) can be added without changing the essential interpretation of the problem. However, an alternative transformation in form, which we shall term the process selection model, expresses requirements for meeting a given level of demand for product j, d_j, using alternative production technologies k, incurring costs c_{jk} or earning profits p_{jk}:

$$\text{(10)} \qquad \min \sum_{jk} c_{jk}\, x_{jk} \quad (\text{or } \max \sum p_{jk}\, x_{jk})$$

s.t.

$$\sum_{jk} a_{ijk}\, x_{jk} \leq b_i$$

$$\sum_{k} x_{jk} \geq d_j$$

With this variant of the model, we allow alternative production technologies, indexed by k, for producing enough of a product to meet a minimum demand of product j. This is the formulation of a production function with a limited set of technologies and resource limits. It can be used to approximate the convex, nonlinear production functions used in economics.

The differences between the product mix and process selection linear programs are in the added constraints on demand requirements and (potentially) the objective function. There is also a double index on the variables and coefficients in the process selection model. However, once the demand constraints are dropped that is a cosmetic difference.

If the template is part of a model with more than one stage in the production process and there are stages that follow, the correct template is the process selection model and this information has to be in the knowledgebase. The first reason why the process selection model is appropriate is that there have to be equations that link the outputs of the process to the next stage. The necessary constraint fragments are the demand constraints in the process selection model. Second, as mentioned above, one accounts for revenues at the point of demand; therefore, an objective function fragment consisting of costs is what is appropriate.

The knowledgebase with both the product mix and process selection models has frames for the two model types that describe the contents of each of the models. The frame for product mix has slots for referencing the profit data for for the objective function, the different products and their production technologies, the resource and material limits and activities for acquiring more materials and resources. The process selection frame has almost the same information. The differences are that the objective function coefficients are usually costs and there has to be a slot for a reference to the demands.

Three more templates for form transformations deserve mention. The first one is the Leontief substitution input-output model. In this model there is one output produced from multiple inputs and the outputs are used as inputs to produce other outputs. In the standard input-output model one can trace a circuit or circuits starting with some output that becomes an input, to the output to an input, etc. that returns to the original output. In this model the matrix has 1's on the diagonals and negative coefficients off the diagonal. The model is common in economic planning and can be solved very simply (see Dantzig [7]).

In some production processes there are multiple outputs from a single input. These typically deal with raw materials. Examples include distillation of crude oil into petroleum products and the feed mix model, where for each input the outputs are the constituents of the input. There is no generally accepted name for this category. Probably the best strategy is to add the different models individually to the knowledgebase in some "other model" category.

The third template that should be mentioned is the general activity with multiple inputs and outputs.

4. TEMPLATE ROWS

So far we have described typical templates with the bulk of the focus on blocks of columns and rows or the activities. One can garner added information from looking at the model as a collection of rows. First, there are economic relationships that determine the direction of the inequality for standard constraints. Second, there are special constraints that can be added to a model, such as blending quality restrictions. Third, there is the objective function. Fourth, there are bounds on activities. Some of these rows can be included in the model template frames by using a "may have" relationship as in Binbasioglu. For now we have chosen to treat them as distinct nodes in the semantic net. The rows can be linked to a template using a "may be contained in" relation when building a new template or model.

4.1 Economic Relationships

Central to economics is the notion of supply and demand. A complex production system has processes where inputs are outputs of other processes. That is, the demand for inputs in one production stage requires a supply of outputs from another. And the stage that requires the inputs is limited, in part, by the outputs of the previous stage. Although the sign conventions are awkward in practice, by noting that supply must be greater than or equal to demand, one can unify the different types of constraints into the following single constraint:

$$-sv + uv \leq sc - uc \qquad (11)$$

where

- sv = the sum of the supply variables (scaled by appropriate constants)
- uv = the sum of the use variables (also scaled by the appropriate constants)
- sc = the constant measuring fixed supply
- uc = the constant measuring fixed demand

A resource limit constraint becomes $uv \leq sc$ and the standard material balance becomes $-sv + uv \leq 0$. Note that if one assumes the coefficients in the sums are positive, not all combinations are meaningful and feasible. For example, $-sv \leq sc$ is not meaningful since it will never bind and $uv \leq uc$ is never feasible with a positive uc. This structure allows one to check partially the reasonableness of the solution and establishes the sign conventions in linking constraint fragments.

One can construct constraints that reverse the inequality. An example is a utilization requirements constraint that says a resource must be fully utilized. The demand can be greater than supply in a given period if the the work can be inventoried for future periods, where at some point the cumulative demand will be met.

The section of the semantic net for added constraints that do not come from a predefined template must contain frames describing the variables referencing the coefficients and constants and noting whether the inequality follows the normal economic pattern or not.

4.2 Quality of Inputs or Outputs

In some models there are restrictions that are neither input nor output constraints. These are restrictions on quality and are also known as blending constraints. A blending constraint represents a different dimension to modeling production systems. In all of the other models we have assumed a rigidly defined product and have dealt with transformations that either produce move or store the product. Here we specify bounds on product quality, that is, we define the product in terms of its attributes. To recognize when we have a blending problem, we note that there is at least one attribute of the product that is distinguished from the name of the product and the requirements of this attribute are specified as a minimum or maximum per unit of the product. For example, gasoline is distinguished by attributes such as octane and volatility and different components blended into gasoline have different octanes and volatilities. A blending constraint to ensure that an attribute meets a specified level takes the form:

$$\frac{\sum_j f_{ij} x_j}{\sum_j x_j} \geq b_i \tag{12}$$

which then becomes the following linear constraint:

$$\sum_j (f_{ij} - b_i) x_j \geq 0.$$

Defining input or output quality does not entail the addition of new activities; it consists of adding a constraint on activities already present. The form portion of the knowledgebase has to have an object for attributes that is linked to the product mix and process selection templates. Thus, when there is an attribute restriction, as opposed to a material or resource limit, a blending constraint should be added.

The knowledgebase then contains an object for representing blending with a frame containing slots for data references, the direction of the inequality and the form of a blending constraint. Since this constraint includes activities that are form transformations, we link this object to the form transformation object using "may be contained in" to indicate that this constraint is appended to a set of activities. Also, since the thought process of a user could follow a path including the notion of a special constraint, we include an "is a" link to the special constraint object.

4.3 Objective Function

An objective function totals all revenues, if any, and subtracts all costs, if any. The profit is the sales price net of costs. The costs included are only those costs for resources not accounted for in the constraints as fixed resources. That is, costs or profits include expenditures or revenues that remain constant per unit for a wide range of production or consumption levels or can be considered approximately constant over a narrow range specified by bounds on the activities.

From the perspective of an economic system, either we have (1) fixed supply or demand and solve for a market clearing price, (2) we have a fixed price and determine how much supply or demand there is at that price or (3) we have supply/demand curves.

With an intelligent system, we would know to include a cost for a resource used if there is a cost for the resource specified in a data base and no limit on its availability. If there is both a cost and a limit, the knowledgebase would include a constraint and we as users would have to decide whether or not to use a cost in the objective function. The deciding factor is whether or not the cost is incurred even if the resource is not used. For example, in the case of capital equipment a cost is incurred when the equipment is acquired and, therefore, should be included in the objective only if the activity represents the decision to acquire the equipment. Alternatively, we include costs in the objective when they vary with the level of use. The best place to include the operating costs is in the objective coefficient of the activity that uses the resource. We also include the costs in the objective function when using a step function approximation to a supply curve where each step has a cost of production but there is a limit on the resource availability.

Typically, in large linear programs with embedded networks one uses only costs at source nodes and accounts for prices at nodes that are sinks. That is, costs are built up by accumulating expenses as they are incurred and a profit maximizing objective is constructed by calculating revenue where sales are made and subtracting costs where they are incurred.

If one has specified the templates properly, the knowledgebase has a slot in all frames that define templates noting which objective function fragments are associated with maximization and which are associated with minimization. The objective function is constructed by subtracting minimization components from maximization and then the problem is solved as a maximization model. If there are no maximization components, the objective remains a minimization problem. Tests are then performed to make sure that there are no variables with maximization components in the objective function that have outputs that feed into other outputs. (An output may be sold as an intermediate good, but this must be done by a separate activity from the producing activity.)

Since the objective function pieces are associated with the templates, we do not include an object in the knowledgebase for objective function; instead, we include a set of rules for combining the pieces into the objective function in the portion of the knowledgebase containing the rules for constructing the full LP.

4.4 Bounds

There are two types of bounds that are of interest. The first is the standard upper or lower bound on a single activity. Since LP solvers lump all of these bounds together in a single row, we can do the same. Thus, in the frame for any template we should have the capability to specify the existence and database location of any bounds, we also need the capability to add bounds when ever desired. Consequently, we need an object called bounds that can be linked to any template. This object can be appended to any template through a "may be contained in" link when building a specific model or template.

The second class of bounds of interest are generalized upper and lower bounds. In this type of constraint a class of activities is summed together and have either upper or lower limits. As with regular bounds these constraints can be directly included in a template or retained as a separate object linked to a template through a may be contained in link. The generalized bound object has slots for the activities to be summed and a reference for the numerical values of the right hand side.

5. DEFINING NEW TEMPLATES OR FORMULATING A MODEL

Either defining a new template or formulating a new model requires the same procedures. In effect a complete LP is a template that contains everything we want to represent in a model. We can either construct a new frame containing the requisite information as is done with the templates described above or we can use a "may be contained in" relationship to define the model. For example, we can define a production-distribution model with two "may be contained in" statements. One would define the object of interest as a production-distribution model and say that it contains a process selection model and it contains a transportation model. The composition rules described in Murphy, Stohr and Ma [18] then combine the two templates into the following linear program:

$$\text{(13a)} \qquad \min \sum_{jkm} c_{jkm} x_{jkm} + \sum_{mnj} c_{mnj} t_{mnj}$$

s.t.

$$\text{(13b)} \qquad \sum_{jk} a_{ijkm} x_{jkm} \le b_{im}$$

$$\text{(13c)} \qquad \sum_{k} x_{jkm} - \sum_{n} t_{mnj} = 0$$

$$\text{(13d)} \qquad \sum_{m} t_{mnj} \ge d_{nj}$$

where x_{jkm} is the amount of product j produced using technology k at plant m and t_{mnj} is the amount of product j shipped from plant m to destination n.

The composition rules used are that objective function costs from the templates are added together into a single objective function and that constraints with identical sets of indicies that are not summed are combined into one constraint. The latter rule is applied in (13c) and the indices that form the match are the pair m and j. If there is any potential for ambiguity about where the linking constraints occur, an "is linked to" relationship would allow one to specify the appropriate material balances.

Now, sometimes the same template is contained in the same model more than once. Thus, the "may be contained in" relationship has to recognize that having two different occurences of the same template is possible and be able to distinguish which version of the same template is used where. The example we choose is for electric utility capacity planning.

An important feature of the utility industry is that it produces a good, electricity, that cannot be stored readily until it is needed; therefore, it must be generated at the time of demand. The way the industry represents the fluctuations in demand is with a load duration curve, which is constructed by plotting the hourly demands as a function of time and then sorting the hours from highest to lowest demand. This leads to the monotonically decreasing function shown in Figure 5. One can approximate this curve with the blocks that are also in the figure. The area of each of the blocks represents a demand to be met. The height of each block represents the amount of capacity needed. And the width of each block measures the number of hours that the capacity operates.

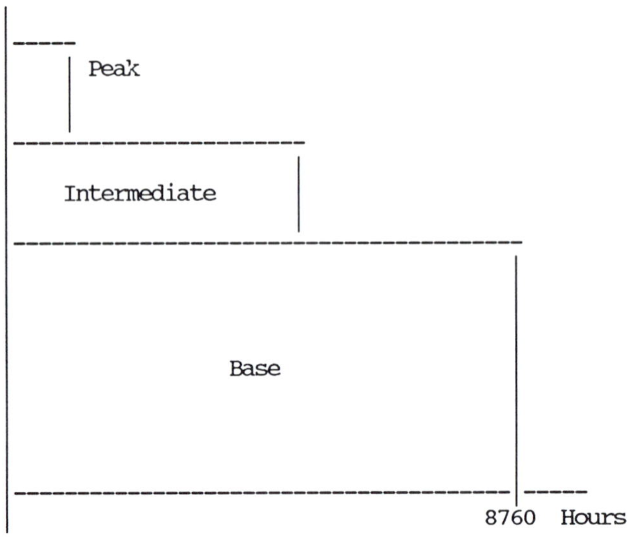

FIG 5 A Load Duration Curve

Electricity can be generated from a variety of plants: coal, gas or oil-fired steam, gas or oil combined-cycle, gas or oil turbines, nuclear, and hydroelectric. The coal and nuclear plants have the lowest operating and fuel costs, with the exception of hydroelectric plants, but they also have the largest capital costs and the longest construction lead times. Given the fluctuations of electricity demand, it is not financially sound to build coal and nuclear plants to meet the peak demands. The optimal choice is a combination of plants, so that the expensive, low-fuel-cost plants can be used almost continuously, and the cheap, but high-fuel-cost (or perhaps old, less efficient) plants may be used as little as a few hours per year.

The constraints of the LP look as follows:

(14a) $a_{iB}x_{iB} + a_{iI}x_{iI} + a_{iP}x_{iP} - w_i \le F_i$

(14b) $x_{iB} + x_{iI} + x_{iP} - z_i \le G_i$

(14c) $\sum_i d_{ij}x_{ij} - f_i y = 0$ for j = B, I, P

(14d) $y \ge E$

where w_i and z_i are supplies of fuel and capacity of type i: x_{iB}, x_{iI}, x_{iP} are the amount of capacity of type i used in base, intermediate and peak; a_{iB}, a_{iI}, and a_{iP} are the amounts of fuel consumed per unit of capacity i operating in base, intermediate and peak; F_i and G_i are the fuel inventories and existing capacities of type i; the d_{ij} are kilowatt hours of output per unit of operation for j = B, I, P; the f_i are the fractions of the demand for a kilowatt that are demands for base, intermediateand peak power and E is the number of kilowatt hours demanded.

This model consists of two process selection models. Constraints (14a and b) are the material and resource constraints for a process selection model consisting of the variables x, w and z. The demand constraints for this process selection model are (14c). The second process selection model consists solely of the variable y, and the inputs are the outputs of the first process selection model while the demands are the single constraint (14d). Note that each time the "may be contained in" relationship is used, it links a version of a template that is presumed unique to the situation. Thus, either the parameters are specified or the system expects parameters to be specified for each occurence of the contains relationship.

A user of the system who is working with electricity planning models would add this template to the system by expanding the knowledgebase using procedures contained in LPFORM. It should be clear that there is a wide variety of templates. Thus, there needs to be a mechanism for learning. This mechanism involves categorization and memorization.

6. BUILDING AN ALGEBRAIC REPRESENTATION OF LARGE MODELS

Experienced practitioners know that LP models can get very large very quickly because of dimensionality. Each new dimension of time or place that is added increases the size of the model multiplicatively. Thus, when working interactively to define a model it may seem that the process of building a model can become bogged down by the size of the model. This is not the case, however, when working with the algebraic statement. In this section we illustrate that the representation stays physically small with two examples.

Using the LPFORM system with this knowledgebase, the modeler will be able to proceed in either a 'top-down' or 'bottom-up' fashion. In the former approach, the submodels and their linkages are described in successive layers of detail. At the lowest level the templates are specified. This approach is outlined in detail in Murphy and Stohr, [17]. In the 'bottom-up' approach the individual templates are each specified. We then link the small models into larger systems using the composition rules described in Murphy, Stohr and Ma [18].

We can illustrate how the templates can be combined to form a larger system by starting with a simple process selection model and adding spatial and time dimensions.

The basic process selection model is (10) repeated:

$$(10) \qquad \min \sum_{jk} c_{jk}\, x_{jk}$$

s.t.

$$\sum_{jk} a_{ijk}\, x_{jk} \le b_i$$

$$\sum_{k} x_{jk} \ge d_j$$

Adding end product inventories to the basic model we get the following:

$$(15) \qquad \min \sum_{jkt} c_{jkt}\, x_{jkt} \sum_{jt} v_{jt}\, I_{jt}$$

s.t.

$$\sum_{jk} a_{ijkt}\, x_{jkt} \le b_{it}$$

$$\sum_{k} x_{jkt} + I_{jt-1} - I_{jt} \ge d_{jt}$$

We see that the effect of adding a time dimension with inventories is to add a time index t to all variables and coefficients and to add the constraint fragments associated with inventory variables.

We now return to the basic model (10) and add a spatial dimension to represent multiple plants and delivery of products to warehouses:

$$(16) \qquad \min \sum_{jkf} c_{jkf}\, x_{jkf} + \sum_{jfs} u_{jfs}\, y_{jfs}$$

s.t.

$$\sum_{jk} a_{ijkf}\, x_{jkf} \le b_{if}$$

$$\sum_{k} x_{jkf} - \sum_{s} y_{jfs} \ge 0$$

$$\sum_{f} y_{jfs} \ge d_{js}$$

To the basic model we add an index f for the factories; add in the transportation objective function equation fragment, where u_{jfs} is the cost of shipping j from f to s and y_{jfs} is the amount shipped; add constraint fragments to the original demand constraints, turning the original demand constraints into material balance constraints, and add demand constraints for each product j at each warehouse s. We could continue the process almost indefinitely, elaborating on the different dimensions that the model could take.

This example illustrates one of the aspects of the approach taken here to model formulation. When working at the algebraic level, models that eventually have thousands of variables and constraints can be expressed in a few equations and inequalities, making the model more comprehensible to the model builder. Also, errors in formulation can be detected sooner.

Acknowledgement: This paper includes work done jointly with Pai-chun Ma and Edward A. Stohr and is part of a project to build an expert system for formulating linear programs. The initial research has been supported by International Business Machines.

REFERENCES

1. M. Binbasioglu (1986), "Knowledge Based Modelling and Support for Linear Programming," Ph. D. Dissertation, New York University.

2. M. Binbasioglu and M. Jarke (1986), "Domain-Specific DSS Tools for Knowledge-based Model Building," Decision Support Systems, 2, June-July.

3. J. Bisschop and A. Meeraus (1982), "On the Development of a General Algebraic Modeling System in a Strategic Planning Environment," Math. Prog. Study 20, 1-29.

4. R. L. Breitman and J. M. Lucas (1987), "PLANET: A Modeling System for Business Planning," Interfaces, 17, no. 1.

5. M. Brodie, J. Mylopoulos and J. Schmidt (1984), On Conceptual Modeling, Springer-Verlag.

6. J. B. Creegan (1985), "Dataform: A Model Management System," Ketron, Inc., Arlington Va.

7. G. B. Dantzig (1963), Linear Programming and Extensions, Princeton University Press, Princeton, NJ.

8. D. R. Dolk (1986), "A Generalized Model Management System for Mathematical Programming," ACM Transactions on Mathematical Software, 12, 2 pp. 92-126.

9. D. Dolk and B. R. Konsynki (1984), "Knowledge Representation for Model Management," IEEE Transactions on Software Engineering, 10.

10. R. Fourer, D. M. Gay and B. W. Kernighan (1987), "AMPL: A Mathematical Programming Language," AT&T Bell Laboratories, Murray Hill, N.J.

11. S. Gass (1985), Linear Programming: Methods and Applications, McGraw-Hill, New York, NY.

12. A. M. Geoffrion (1987), "An Introduction to Structured Modeling," Management Science, 33, 5, pp. 547-588.

13. M. Lenard (1986), "Representing Models as Data," J. Management Information Systems, 2, 4 pp. 36-48.

14. P. Ma, F. H. Murphy and E. A. Stohr (1987), "A Graphics Interface for Linear Programming."

15. P. Ma, F. H. Murphy and E. A. Stohr (1986), "The Science and Art of Formulating Linear Programs," to appear in IMA Journal of Mathematics in Management.

16. P. Ma, F. H. Murphy and E. A. Stohr (1986), "LPSPEC, A Language for Representing Linear Programs."

17. F. H. Murphy and E. A. Stohr (1986), "An Intelligent System for Formulating Linear Programs," Decision Support Systems 3, March.

18. F. H. Murphy, E. A. Stohr and P. Ma (1987), "Composition Rules for Building Linear Programming Models from Component Models," Working Paper.

19. W. Orlikowski and V. Dhar (1986), Imposing Structure on Linear Programming Problems: an Empirical Analysis of Expert and Novice Models," Proceedings on the National Conference on Artificial Intelligence, Philadelphia, Pa.

20. L. Schrage (1987), Linear, Integer and Quadratic Programming with LINDO, Scientific Press, Palo Alto.

21. J. S. Welch (1987), "PAM-A Practitioner's Approach to Modeling," Management Science, 33, 5 pp 610-625.

A Knowledge-Based System for Integrated Solving Cutting Stock Problems and Production Control in the Paper Industry

W. Nickels, RWTH Aachen

1. Introduction

An important problem in the field of production planning and control in the paper industry is the determination of patterns for cutting production rolls into the finished roll and sheet sizes depending on the customers\` demand. This problem is usually called cutting stock problem.
In most of the available publications only the trim loss, i.e. the amount of material in a pattern which can not be used furthermore, is considered as objective function which has to be minimized [Dyckhoff et al. 1984], [Hinxman 1980]. For this special type of problem a wide variety of algorithms were developed which were based on Linear Programming [Gilmore/ Gomory 1961, 1963, 1965], but a great number of heuristics are also available, see f.i.[Dyckhoff et al 1984], [Haessler 1978, 1979].

Unfortunately, it is not satisfying to consider only the minimization of trim loss in the most real cases where cutting stock problems occured because frequently, at least in the paper industry, the material has a low value per unit weight [Haessler 1971]. Other aspects caused much higher costs. Therefore, it is necessary to take the following objective functions into consideration. These may be minimization of pattern changing or numbers of set ups, maximization of employment of capacity and minimization of delay in order to fulfill costomers\` demands.

These facts and the often difficult constraints depending on technical, quality and customers\` requirements, have the result that in most of the practical cases it is not possible to solve the so-called cutting stock problems with methods of linear programming or heuristic algorithms. Therefore, most of the problems have to be solved with especially developed algorithms or planning and control systems [Dyckhoff et al. 1984], [Haessler 1971].

Furthermore, one has to realize that frequently manual procedures are superior to algorithmic solutions because many requirements are considered only by implicitly using expert knowledge which bases on experience and associative knowledge.

NATO ASI Series, Vol. F48
Mathematical Models for Decision Support
Edited by G. Mitra

In this paper a method is developed which tries to use this implicit knowledge to solve a special problem of production planning in the paper industry. This problem occurs in the production process of a paper mill where sheets of different sizes, depending on customers` demands, have to be cut out of production rolls in a two stage production process where the production rolls are produced on a paper machine.

The main goal of the knowledge based planning system is the determination of a solution for the corresponding cutting stock problem also considering machine scheduling and inventory control aspects.

This paper is divided into four chapters. After the introduction in chapter 1, chapter 2 gives a description of the special problem.

The concept of the knowledge based system of determining an integrated solution of the cutting stock problem with regard to machine scheduling and inventory control is described in chapter 3.

Finally, in chapter 4 concluding remarks are given.

2. The Problem

The description of the problem considered in this paper is divided into two parts. The production process and the manufactured goods of the paper mill are described in part 1. Furthermore, customer requirments and quality dependent constraints as well as inventory control aspects of the problem are discussed.

In the second part a detailed analysis and characterization of the problem is given. A classification of the problem is made in part 3 finally.

2.1 The Production Process and the Products

The products which are manufactured in the considered paper mill are rolls and sheets of different sizes and quantities depending on customers` demands. In this paper only the production process of the sheets is treated.

The customers` orders of sheets can be differentiated by

- the size of the sheets
- the quantity of the orders, where this quantitiy can be overrun or underrun by a tolerance of about 10% of the ordered quantitiy,
- the sort of the paper
- the area weight
- the due date
- standard or non-standard size.

The differentiation of standard and non-standard sizes is of interest because the demand of standard sizes may be fulfilled by inventory products.

Here, however, one has to consider also the fact that the main purpose of stock keeping is to use it to fulfill short term demand. Therefore, the stockkeeping of the standard sizes has to be hold on a sufficient level and this fact is to be considered in the planning system also.

The production process of the sheets is a three stage process. On the first stage the paper is manufactured on the paper machine in great lots of production rolls with standard sizes. One lot of the same sort and area weight of paper is produced periodically every 14 days.

These production rolls are to be slit into order dependend master rolls on a machine winder on the second stage. These master rolls will then be cut into sheets on simplex cutters according to the cumstomers` demand. (Figure 1)

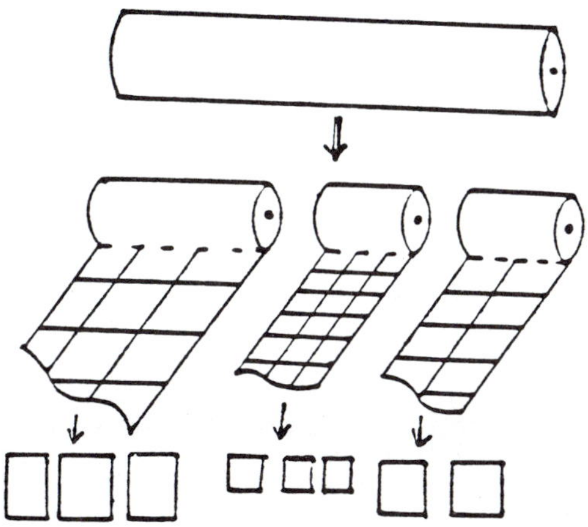

Figure 1: Principle of cutting sheets

The paper machine works on-line with the above mentioned machine winder. Therefore, the machine winder has to keep up with the continuously producing paper machine, where there is only a limited amount of storage space for in-process inventory. A further technical constraint is the limited number of knives.

After this cutting process a number of more or less different simplex cutters are available.

The differences of these machines can be summarized by the following characteristics:

- Number of knives for cutting the widths of the sheets

- Interval of possible length of sheets which are possible to be cut
- Speed of production
- Maximal and minimal size of master rolls
- Maximal and minimal diameter of master rolls
- Amount of time of set ups
- Informations of qualification for cutting special sorts and sizes.

Common characteristics of the simplex cutters are:

- They can only cut one length at the same time
- They have to cut one or more rolls simultaneously because the paper webs have to be slit one upon another in order to get a feasible cutting weight which lies in a given interval
- They can process only a maximum number of master rolls simultaneously
- There is a possibility of in- process inventory before starting the cutting process
- The setups of the simplex cutters cause an amount of time and costs of the material which is lost during the time the machine is adjusted. These costs and amounts of time can not be quantified exactly because they depend on the sequence of orders, the qualification of the operators, the quality of the paper and the exactness of the machine. Only opinions about the desirability of different set ups are available.

2.2 Analysis and Characterization of the problem

In this section we will give a detailed description of the problem and its classification as cutting stock problem.

The problem of building a production planning system for the production process described above can be divided into the following subproblems:

I. The determination of the lot size of one sort of paper in order to fulfill the customers` demand. This can be achieved by the production programme of the machine winder after generating the cutting patterns. In practise usually the lot size is determined after generating the patterns. Here an amount of about 10% is added to the quantity in order to compensate differences which are caused by bad quality paper which is produced on the paper machine and by the amount of material used by set ups of the simplex cutters.

II. Feasible order groups and the corresponding sizes of master rolls have to be determinated. Feasible order groups are the combinations of orders with sheets of the same sizes or at least the same widths, because the size of the master roll can be calculated by putting one or more sheets side by side in the paper web.

   - It may also be necessary to combine orders of "similar" widths in one order group. This can occur if the length of the master roll is too shoort to fulfill the requirements of feasible cutting weight and minimal diameter of input rolls for the simplex cutters. Obviously it is possible to generate differently sized master rolls of one order group in most of the cases. These different sizes can be used alternatively as input data in the pattern generating procedure.

III. The next subproblem is the problem of generating "good" cutting patterns in order to fulfill customers` demand under sufficient consideration of inventory and machine scheduling aspects.

The following decisions have to be made to solve this subproblem:

- Generating of possible patterns by putting the master rolls side by side
- The pattern length has to be calculated. This is the length of the paper web with only one pattern (one combination of master rolls). In most of the cases this is very complicated as the following points have to be taken into consideration:
  a) The quantities of the order groups can be very different and therefore the lengths of the master rolls are different, too.
     By taking into account this fact only patterns of master rolls are possible the lengths of which are "similar" or which can be partitioned in several master rolls of smaller lengths.
  b) Furthermore, the minimal feasible length of a pattern, depending on the minimal cutting weight and minimal diameter constraints has to be taken into account.
- Also informations about the inventory stock of sheets with standard sizes can be considered. This information can be used to decide whether an order with standard sizes or a part of it can be met by inventory products or in the other possible case whether supplementary ininventory orders of standard sizes can be used to fill no desirable patterns.
- Finally aspects of machine scheduling are to be regarded by deciding what size of possible alternative master rolls of one order group is to be produced on the the simplex cutter.
  Smaller sizes are easier usable for pattern generation and give lengths of greater dimension, where it is easier to fulfill the pattern length constraint. But small rolls of greater length are not desirable to manufacture at the simplex cutters because the running time will increase, employment of capacity will decrease.

IV. The machine scheduling problem, e.g. the assignment of orders and machines and the sequencing of the orders will not be discussed in this paper. But the aspects of machine scheduling have to be taken into account in the planning system.

The problem described above has to be solved by considering the following objective functions:

- minimization of trim loss
- minimization of set ups
- maximization of employment of capacity
- minimization of delay and amount of shortage.

The subproblems which have to be considered are being summarized in Table 1:

I.	Determination of lot size
II.	Determination of feasible order groups
III.	Generation of cutting patterns
IV.	Machine scheduling problem

Table 1: Subproblems

2.3 Classification of the Problem

Cutting stock problems are cases concerned with the design of material. The objects which have to be cut are basically threedimensional. But in most of the cases only one or two dmensions are relevant to the problem. Therefore we can differentiate [Dyckhoff et al. 1984]

- one-dimensional
- two-dimensional and
- three-dimensional cutting stock problems.

In addition to this design a subdivision in

1.5 - dimensional or
2.5 - dimensional cutting stock problems

is often made in publications [Dyckhoff et al. 1984],[Haessler 1978].

This occurs if one dimension of the material is not uniquely determined, for example the width of a roll is given, but the number of rolls and their diameters are variable and only the weight of the whole order is given.

In order to this classification, the problem described above can be classified as a 1.5-dimensional problem with a multidimensional objective function and some supplementary constraints.

A number of publications are available which deal with 1.5-dimensional or multi stage cutting stock problems, e.g. [Dyckhoff et al. 1984], [Haessler 1978]. Here, however, they consider either only one objective function or work with two objectives, but do not give the possibility to take into account all the necessary constraints for the actual problem. Furthermore in many cases manual procedures in which these facts are at least implicitly considered are frequently superior to the solutions which are generated by algorithmic procedures. This is caused by the fact that in most of the cases mathematical models are incomplete and insufficient regarding to the complex and badly structured practical problems. This experience is based on examinations the author has made in the paper industry because the persons who solve the problems in practise use implicitly their experience and knowledge which is based on associative knowledge without building an exact model of the problem.

Therefore and because of the complexity and bad structure of the problem the author has decided to develop a knowledge based system and to enquire the underlying knowledge from experts in paper mills. This way of solving badly structured problems and especially cutting stock problems is suggested also in publications, e.g. [Mertens/ Allgeyer 1983], [Negoita 1985].

The concept of this knowledge based system is described in chapter 3. The description of the main theoretical results of fuzzy set theory, linguistic variables and approximate reasoning which are used in the system can be found in this book. See f.i. [Zimmermann 1988]. More informations on these topics are given in [Zadeh 1973], [Zadeh 1971], [Zimmermann 1986].

3. The Knowledge-Based Production Control System

In this chapter we will describe the principal structure of the system in the first part. In the following parts the subprocedures of the system will be described. Input of the systems are data belonging to the orders of paper sheets which are specified by:

- quantity of the order
- sort of the paper
- area weight of the paper
- size of the sheets
- due date of the order.

With these data the system starts.

3.1 Principal Structure of the System

The system is divided into two main parts. In part 1 the orders are first sorted by their sorts and area weights. One of these classes of the same characteristic is called a order-class. The processing of one order-class is described below.
Furthermore the first procedure determinates feasible order groups and corresponding sizes of master rolls.

The second part deals with these order groups and generates at first clusters of master rolls with smaller lengths and then generates cutting patterns. Here also the supply of inventory products and the manufacturing programme of the paper machine and machine winder is determinated. Figure 2 summarizes the structure of the system with its main duties.

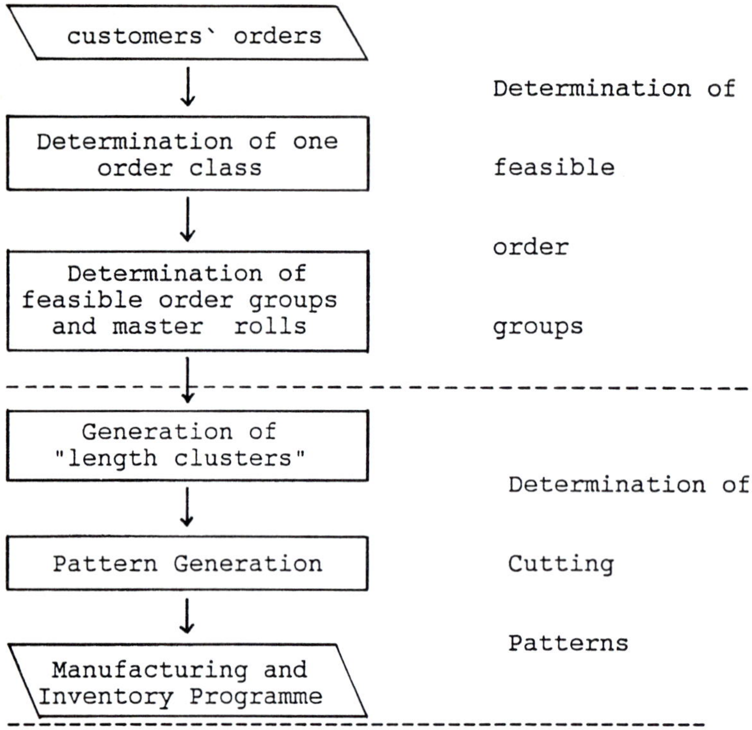

Figure 2: Structure of the system

3.2 Determination of feasible order groups

In this part of the system the feasible order group and the corresponding master rolls are generated. Feasible order groups contain orders of sheets with one of the following criteria:

- equal sizes of sheets
- equal width of sheets
- similar width of sheets
- similar width of master rolls.

Here we have to recognize that it is not desirable to combine orders with only similar width because the sizes of the master rolls depend on the sheets with the greatest width and causes supplementary trim loss. Therefore the system has to decide whether to combine similar widths or not. This decision depends on the minmal possible length of a master roll regarding the cutting weight and minimal diameter constraints of the simplex cutters. How this decision is made will be shown after the description of the procedure which is given below.

Determination of feasible order groups

STEP 1: Combine all orders with the same size or width of sheets to order groups.

STEP 2: Determine all possible sizes of master rolls for each order group.

STEP 3: a) Test if all lengths of the master rolls are greater than the minimal allowed length. Stop.

b) If any length of alternative master rolls of one order group is less than the minimal length, decide whether to combine order groups of similar sizes or not. If yes go to 4 otherwise stop.

STEP 4: Combine the determined order groups of similar sizes, goto 3.

The decision for each order group in STEP 3b) is made by rules which are ordered hierarchically. This method has proved with good results e.g. [Zimmermann, Zysno 1982]. The criteria are linguistic variables (Table 2) and the inference is done with approximate reasoning (Fig. 3).

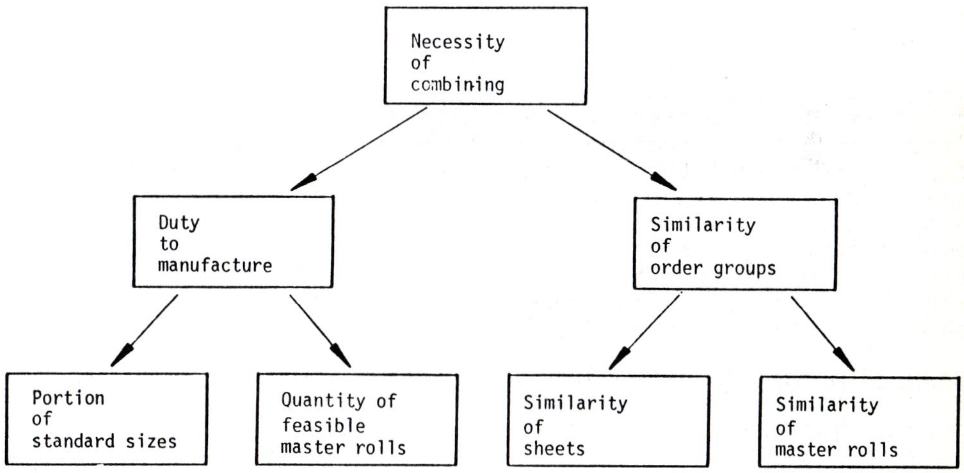

Figure 3: Hierarchy of criteria for combining simlar order groups

The terms of similarity of master rolls are, for example:

high - medium - low,

where the basis variable is the lowest difference of the width of the master rolls corresponding to the order groups.
The terms of necessity of combining are:

high - medium - not any.

An order group has to be combined if the necessitiy of combining is high with a degree of membership greater than a given α-level, $\alpha \in [0,1]$.
After finishing this procedure the determination of cutting patterns starts.

3.3 Determination of Cutting Patterns

In this section we will describe the generation of patterns which determine how the master rolls of the order groups have to be manufactured at the machine winder.
As it is only possible to combine rolls with similar lengths in one pattern the procedure starts by generating fuzzy clusters of rolls with similar lengths. These fuzzy clusters are fuzzy sets and the degree of membership of each master roll to the different clusters is determiated. After this determination pattern generation starts for each cluster where it has to be recognized that the alternative master rolls of the same order groups have a positive degree of membership in different clusters. The pattern generation is run successively until customers` demand is fulfilled as best as possible according to the objective functions. Here inventory stock is taken into consideration also.

The clustering procedure runs in the following way:
At first the centres of the clusters have to be determinated. After this determination the membership values of the master rolls are calculated. Furthermore master rolls the length of which can be divided into different sizes of smaller lengths are ordered to all clusters the lengths of the centre of which are matched by these runs. Their degree of membership is set to one. Let n be the number of master rolls and l_i, $i=1,..,n$ their lengths, let furthermore d be a parameter which has to be set at the beginning $d \in (0,1)$.

Generation of "length clusters"

STEP 1 Initialize $j=1$ $k_j=1$

STEP 2 Determine i_o with
$l_{i_o}(1-d) \le l_{k_j}(1+d) < l_{i_o+1}(1-d)$,
if possible, otherwise set $i_o=n$.

STEP 3 Set the length of the centre

$$Lj = \frac{1}{i_o+1-k_j} \sum_{k=k_j}^{i_o} l_k$$

STEP 4 If $i_o \neq n$ Set $j = j+1$ $k_j = \frac{i_o}{2}$, goto step 2, otherwise goto step 5.

STEP 5 Determination of $f_j(i)$, that is the degree of membership of master roll i to cluster j:

$$f_j(i) = \begin{cases} 1, & \text{if } L_j \in [l_i(1-0.1), l_i(1+0.1)] \text{ or if the length can be divided like described above} \\ 1 - \dfrac{l_i - L_j}{L_j}, & \text{if } L_j \notin [l_i(1-0.1), l_i(1+0.1)] \text{ and } \dfrac{l_i}{2} \leq L_j \leq 2l_i \\ 0 & \text{otherwise.} \end{cases}$$

Here the degree of one is determined because 10% is the allowed tolerance of overrun and underrun of customers` demand.

After this calculation of fuzzy length clusters the pattern generation starts.
This procedure generates successively patterns by starting with one cluster. Here the following decisions have to be made:

- which cluster will be considered next
- which orders have to be combined in each cluster because there are alternative clusters
- what is a sufficiently good pattern with respect to the objective functions.

The procedure of pattern generation will run in the following way:

Pattern Generation:

STEP 0 Initialize M, α, P(see STEP 2)

STEP 1 Select the next cluster to deal with (Fig. 4), if there is no more cluster stop.

STEP 2 Select the order of high necessity of combining ($\geq\alpha$) (Fig. 6) with highest degree of membership and generate M different patterns which have less than p% trim loss. Here the orders with lower necessity of combining are used successively to fill the patterns, also supplementary inventory sizes can be used if necessary.

STEP 3 Choose the best pattern regarding the trim loss and the necessity of combining the other orders in the pattern (Fig. 5).

STEP 4 Actualize the dates, f.i. all corresponding criterions of the orders in the chosen pattern and purge orders with supplied demand.

STEP 5 If there is any order which has to be selected in Step 2 go to Step 2, otherwise go to Step 1

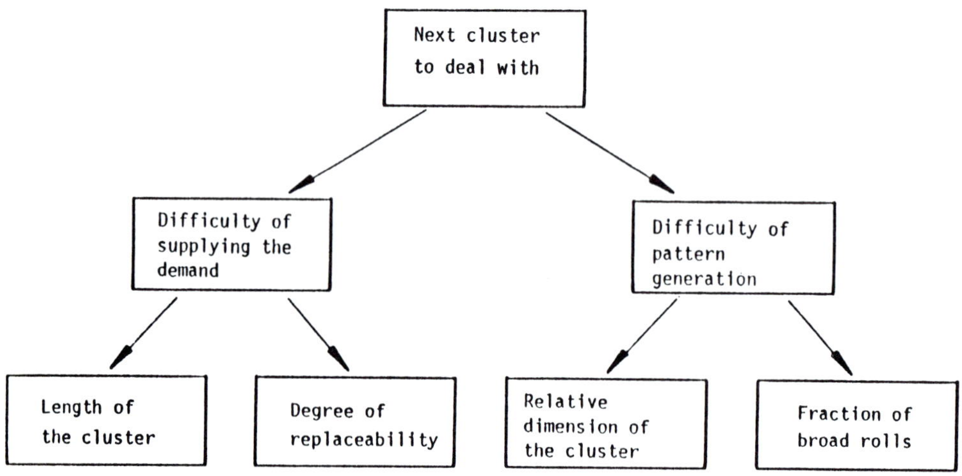

Figure 4: Hierarchy for the choice of the next cluster

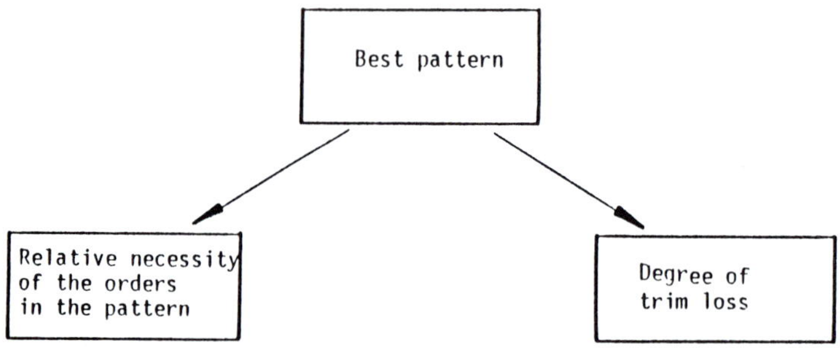

Figure 5: Hierarchy for the choice of the best pattern

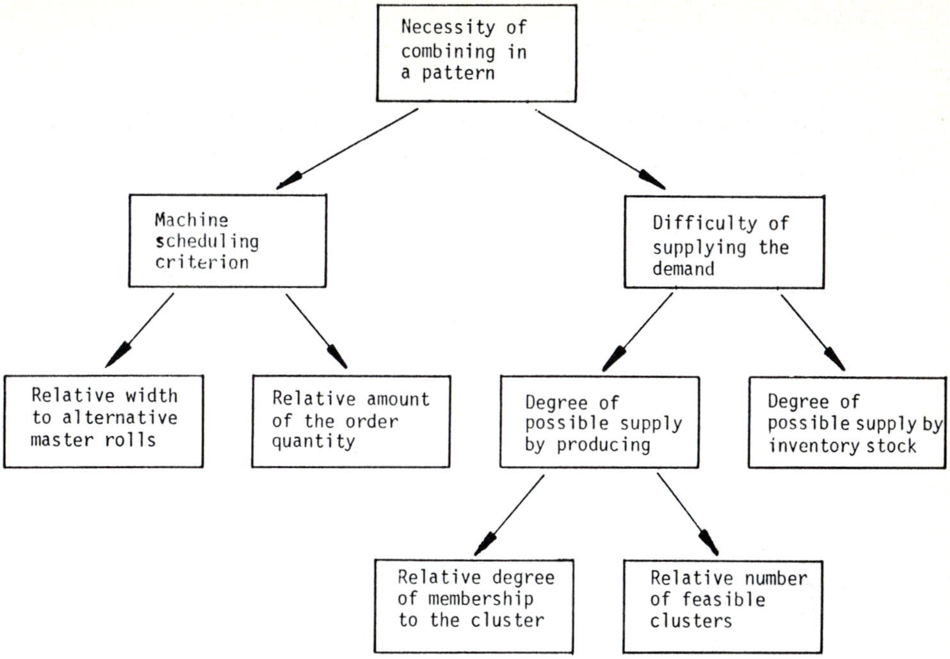

Figure 6: Hierarchy for the necessity of combining

The above described procedure works until no orders are to be combined in patterns regarding the rule set.

After this procedure the lot size of the paper machine, the production programme of the machine winder and the demand and supply of inventory products is determined.

4. Concluding Remarks

In this paper a cutting stock problem and its interdependencies to machine scheduling and inventory control are described. Therefore a multi objective function regarding these problems is considered with the aim of getting an integrated solution to the production control problem. Because the objective functions are conflicting and caused by the fact that the manually generated solutions have been superior to computer programs in most of the application cases, a knowledge based system is developed which tries to deal with the problem in a way a human expert does.

The expert knowledge was enquired with methods of knowledge acquisition from experts of the paper industry. This knowledge is represented by methods of fuzzy set theory. This seems to be a good way to match the way of thinking of a human expert.

References

Dyckhoff, H., Kruse, H.J., Abel, D., Gal, T.: Trim Loss and Related Problems, in: OMEGA, The International Journal of Management Science 13, 1985, pp. 59-72.

Gilmore, P.C., Gomory, R.E.: A Linear Programming Approach to the Cutting Stock Problem, in: Operations Research 9, 1961, pp. 849-859.

Gilmore, P.C., Gomory, R.E.: A Linear Programming Approach to the Cutting Stock Problem, Part II, in: Operations Research 11, 1963, pp. 863-888.

Gilmore, P.C., Gomory, R.E.: Multistage Cutting Stock Problems of Two and More Dimensions, in: Operations Research 13, 1965, pp. 94-120.

Haessler, R.W.: A Heuristic Programming Solution to a Non-Nonlinear Cutting Stock Problem, in: Management Science 1971, pp. B739-B802.

Haessler, R.W.: A Procedure for Solving the 1.5-Dimensional Coil Slitting Problem, in: AIIE Transactions 10, 1978, pp. 70-77.

Haessler, R.W.: Solving the Two-Stage-Cutting-Stock Problem, in: OMEGA, The International Journal of Management Science 17, 1979, pp. 145-151.

Hintz, G.W.: Ein wissensbasiertes System zur Produktionsplanung und -steuerung für flexible Fertigungssysteme, Düsseldorf 1987

Hinxman, A.: The Trim Loss and Assortment Problems, A Survey, in: European Journal of Operational Research 5, 1980, pp. 8-18.

Mertens, P., Allgeyer, K.: Künstliche Intelligenz in der Betriebswirtschaft, in: Zeitschrift für Betriebswirtschaft 53, 1983, pp. 686-709.

Negoita, C.V.: Expert Systems and Fuzzy Systems, London, Amsterdam 1985.

Zadeh, L.A.: The Concept of Linguistic Variables and its Application to Approximate Reasoning, Memorandum No. ERL-M411, University of California, Berkeley 1973.

Zadeh, L.A.: A Theory of Approximate Reasoning, Memorandum No. UCB/ERL M77/58, University of California, Berkeley 1977.

Zimmermann, H.J.: Fuzzy Set Theory - and its Applications, 2nd printing, Boston, Dordrecht, Lancaster 1986.

Zimmermann, H.J., Zysno, P.: Ein hierarchisches Bewertungssystem für die Kreditwürdigkeitsprüfung im Konsumentenkreditgeschäft, in: DBW 42 (1982), pp. 403-417.

Zimmermann, H.J.: Fuzzy Set Theory and Inference Mechanism, Springer, 1988 (same book)

1. EXPERT SYSTEMS: THE STATE OF THE ART

M J Rijckaert, V Debroey, W Bogaerts
Katholieke Universiteit Leuven, Belgium

1.1. What is an expert system ?

"An expert system is a computer program that embodies **expertise** about a particular domain, and can use **symbolic reasoning** techniques to solve problems in this domain; problems that would need the assistance of a human expert in the real world. An expert system should also be able to **explain** its conclusions." This definition embraces the four main characteristics that distinguish an expert system from a "conventional" program (Waterman 1986) :

. Expertise

. Symbolic reasoning

. Depth

. Self-knowledge

1.1.1. Expertise

Expert systems use a large amount of **knowledge** about a particular, well-defined, narrow domain; thus they are essentially knowledge-processing systems whereas conventional programs are data-processing systems. Characteristics of this knowledge is that it is often subjective, ill-formed, possibly incomplete and subject to change.

However, having access to the knowledge alone doesn't make experts. Expertise also means having the **skill** to use this knowledge efficiently, in order to arrive at a solution quickly (e.g. by taking short-cuts instead of performing an exhaustive search). This skill should therefore also be present in an expert system. And expertise is robust: when faced with incorrect or incomplete data, an expert can still use general knowledge ("common sense") and problem-solving methods ("reasoning from first principles") to arrive at a satisfactory conclusion. Such a robustness, however, is not yet present in may today's expert systems (cfr Section 2.3).

1.1.2. Symbolic reasoning

Conventional programs process firm, fixed data; these are useful for algorithmic processing. The knowledge inherent in this processing is therefore "hidden" in the program code, the computer translation of the algorithm. In an expert system, the knowledge is **explicitly** represented in **symbolic** form, in a structure called the **knowledge base** (the issue of knowledge representation is

NATO ASI Series, Vol. F48
Mathematical Models for Decision Support
Edited by G. Mitra

therefore a central one in expert systems). The expert system can manipulate these symbolic structures in the course of solving a problem. This manipulation or **reasoning** is carried out by a so-called **inference** engine using a set of **heuristic rules** (as opposed to an algorithm) appropriate to the given domain.

Human experts also have the ability to convert a problem stated in some manner, into a form that is more suited for efficient solution. This **problem reformulation** capability is not present in most of the present-day expert systems.

1.1.3. Depth

An expert system has **depth**; this means that it operates in a narrow domain, tackling difficult and challenging problems (the kind of problems that call for human experts). This implies that it will have to use complex rules (and usually a large number of those). This complexity brings with it new problems that have to be addressed such as:

How to manage large knowledge bases; can we guarantee their correctness (consistency) when we add new rules?

How to represent the same knowledge in different ways, on different levels of detail; and to guarantee that they are always in agreement with one other.

How to solve problems using multiple, co-operating expert systems (the so-called "blackboard" systems).

1.1.4. Self-knowledge

Another essential requirement for an expert system is the ability to reason about its own processes. An obvious use for this **self-knowledge** is the **explanation** facility: the system should be able to explain how it has arrived at a particular conclusion, or why it is asking for a particular piece of information. In present-day expert systems, this is usually done by tracing the line of inference, and reciting the rules that were used during this inference, sometimes enhanced by "canned texts" that clarify the purpose of the rules (since these rules may be so complex that the average user cannot understand them).

This can hardly be called "real explanation", of course. What is needed is the ability to connect the inference steps with fundamental domain principles as justifications" (Brachman 1983) - an ability that obviously requires the knowledge of these basic principles. Another desirable feature would be the ability to tailor the explanation to the user, i.e. to his level of knowledge in the given domain ("user modeling").

Another aspect of this self-knowledge is the possibility of exploiting **meta-knowledge**, i.e. knowledge about the (domain) knowledge. This higher-level knowledge may be made explicit, in the same way as the domain knowledge, given rise to "meta-rules" that may be used to guide the problem-solving strategy, such as (Waterman 1986):

IF : More than one rule applies to the situation,
THEN: Use rules supplied by experts before rules supplied by novices.

1.2. The components of an expert system

Figure 1 shows a simple representation of a typical expert system. The core of the system consists of the knowledge base and the inference engine.

The knowledge base contains in symbolic form the facts and rules that capture the expertise in the application domain. The inference engine applies these rules, using one or possibly a combination of problem-solving strategies, on the specific data supplied by the user in a particular case. These user-supplied, problem-dependent data, as well as the expert system's intermediate and final results, are stored in a data base (sometimes called "short term memory" or "working memory" because its contents are only retained during the current run. At the start of the run it is empty).

The user interface module conducts the dialog with the user of the expert system in an appropriate manner; usually using some restricted subset of natural language, or perhaps by means of a graphical editor. Its role is to interpret the user's commands, questions and volunteered data, and to present the results of the system, answers to questions and explanations, to him or her. The explanation module of the system is usually seen as part of this user interface. In systems that try to give meaningful explanations, or to tailor their explanations to the skill level of the user, however, this explanation module becomes an important part of the system, containing quite a lot of "intelligence" on its own, namely, knowledge about how to conduct a meaningful dialogue with a user and how to build and maintain a model of the user.

Some expert systems contain additional modules that are only used by the developers of the system, not by the end users. A knowledge acquisition subsystem, for example, might be present to speed up the process of adding new rules to the knowledge base via the means of a specialized rule editor. There may also be facilities for maintaining the consistency of the rules, for the automatic generation of test cases etc.

1.3. How to build an expert system

The development of an expert system comprises roughly two main phases (see Figure 2). In the first phase, the problem is identified and clearly defined, and the key concepts and relations that are needed to characterize the problem are formulated. The second phase then deals with the formulization of the knowledge, the implementation and the testing of an appropriate architecture for the system. Of course there will be a constant refinement of the system, if necessary accompanied by a revision of the representation and/or conceptualization decisions, before the final expert system becomes operational.

1.3.1. identification

Expert systems are not suited for just any kind of problem solving. If the knowledge of the domain is firm, fixed and formalized, and the solution process can be described in an algorithm, then a conventional computer program is obviously the way to go. If on the other hand, the knowledge is subjective, partly judgmental, ill-codified and subject to change, then an expert system with its heuristic approach might be more appropriate (Buchanan 1983). The first step in constructing an expert system is thus one of **identifying** the problem characteristics.

1.3.2. Conceptualization

The main task of the expert system builder: extracting the domain knowledge from the experts and transferring it into an appropriate machine representation, is, except for trivial problems, a difficult one. The process is generally known as **knowledge engineering**, and the person who performs it as **knowledge engineer**.

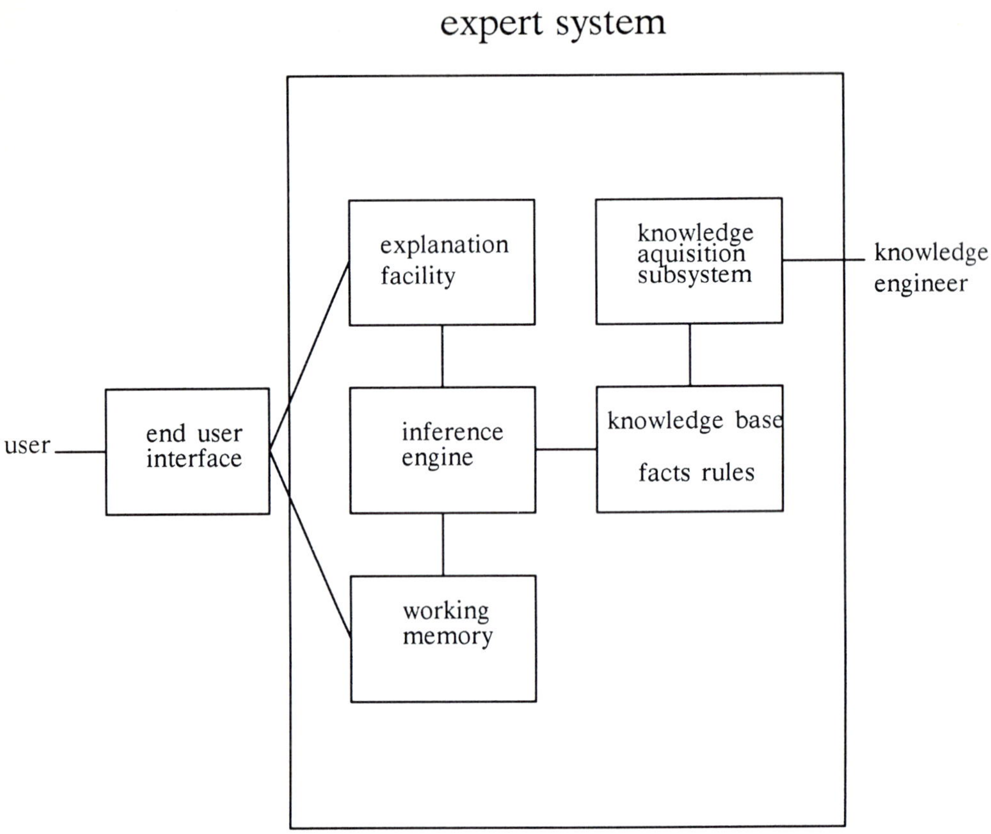

Figure 1 – A simple representation of a typical expert system. The "core" of the system consists of the knowledge base and the inference engine.

A knowledge engineer needs diverse skills to do his work. First of all, he should be familiar with the application domain, although not at "expert" level. The initial task of the knowledge engineer will therefore be, to familiarize himself with the nature of the problem, the jargon, etc. in order to be able to conduct a meaningful dialog with the domain experts.

The actual process of extracting the knowledge from the experts is usually termed the **knowledge acquisition** phase. This is a difficult task, because experts often aren't used to making their knowledge explicit. Much of it is applied subconsciously, using rules of thumb and judgement; and experts seem to find it hard t write down or verbalize these. They may regard things which are important in the problem-solving process as "matter of fact" and simply forget to mention them. It is the job of the knowledge engineerto extract this knowledge, with which the expert system will be built. This is usually done through a series of taped interviews with the expert. Other techniques that are sometimes used are: observing the expert at work (perhaps using video recording equipment), letting him "think aloud" while he is solving a problem, etc.

This is clearly an iterative process, in which the knowledge engineer gradually builds up an overview of the basic concepts, their important characteristics, how they are interrelated, and how they are used by the expert. Sometimes this calls for subtle psychological skills, as some experts might not be very willing to "give away" their private knowledge to be put in computer program.

1.3.3. Formalization

The ultimate aim of the knowledge acquisition phase is, to represent that knowledge in a symbolic form in a computer. This involves mapping the various concepts, heuristics, and processes isolated during knowledge acquisition, into an appropriate form. Here the knowledge engineer needs to know about the various knowledge representations and reasoning techniques, and to select those that most closely match the problem at hand. Factors that influence this choice are, among others:

- are the concepts structured or not?

- do causal relations have to be explicitly represented?

- are the concepts accurate and precise, or inaccurate and unreliable?

- how are data acquired or deduced? What kind of questions can be asked to obtain data?

In most cases, this process will lead to the selection of a software "tool" that supports the knowledge representation and reasoning schemes chosen. Such tools are called "shells", as they are basically an expert system stripped of its domain-dependent knowledge: they provide a framework for representing and manipulating knowledge; the knowledge, however, has to be supplied by the user (i.e. the knowledge engineer).

Some of these shells offer only one particular scheme (e.g. rules with backward chaining); most shells for small (personal) categories fall in this category. Others incorporate different representation and reasoning mechanisms, from which the knowledge engineer can choose the most appropriate; these "toolkits" are therefore applicable to a much wider range of problems. They normally need fast, powerful computers such as the new Lisp machines or Unix-based "supermicros".

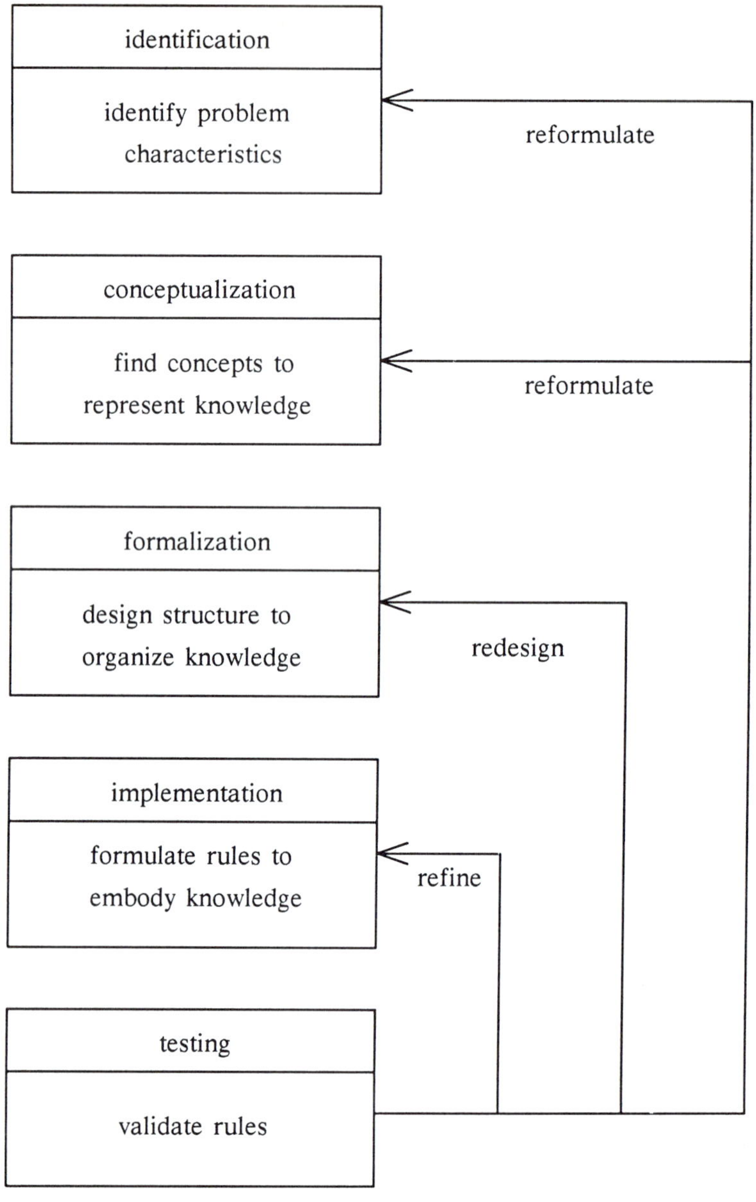

Figure 2 – Stages in the building of an expert system (Buchanan 1983)

1.3.4. Implementation

Having chosen the tool, the next step is to fit the domain knowledge into its representational framework. The endresult of this will be an executable program, the working expert system. Initially, however, a small **prototype system** will usually be built, that contains only a small part of the total knowledge, but that can already be applied to some sample problems. The purpose of this prototype is not only to demonstrate the effectiveness of the chosen tool for

the given problem, but, perhaps more importantly, to be able to quickly identify weak points and inconsistencies in the knowledge base. It can also be used to give the human experts (and the management) a concrete feel of how the final system will look like, early in the development phase.

1.3.5. Testing

Once the prototype system is up and running (albeit with only a handful of rules), it should be tested with a variety of problems to determine weaknesses in the knowledge base and inference structure, such as:

- errors in input/output characteristics (the system asks for the wrong kind of data; or it asks them in an "unnatural" order; the conclusions may be inadequate or incomplete, etc.);

- errors in inference rules (the premise may be incorrect or incomplete; the conclusions may be wrong; there may be cases that are not covered by some rule; rules may contradict or subsume each other; when working with uncertainties, the certainty factors may need adjusting, ...);

- errors in control strategy (the order in which rules are applied may be "unnatural", leading to confusing or unnecessarily complex explanations);

The prototype system can also be used to test the adequacy of the human–computer dialog (menu or commands, "natural" language, graphical interface ...).

1.3.6. revisions

As a result of testing, there will be an almost constant revision of the prototype system. In the first place this means refining the knowledge base, adjusting the rules and the control structures to arrive at the desired behavior, adding new rules to fill gaps in the system's knowledge, and so on. If these revisions do not result in acceptable performance of the system, however, a more drastic redesign of the architecture or knowledge base should be undertaken. And in some cases it may even be necessary to go further back and reformulate (or enlarge) the set of concepts or relations on which the system is based.

1.4. Knowledge representation

There is at present no universally applicable method of representing "knowledge" in a computer program. Therefore an important task of the knowledge engineer is, to choose a representation mechanism that can accomodate the specific characteristics of the problem domain.

The part of the expert system that embodies the domain knowledge is called the **knowledge base.** There are basically two types of knowledge that will need to be represented in the system: **declarative** knowledge and **procedural** knowledge. The declarative part of the knowledge base describes "what" the objects (facts, terms, concepts, ...) are that are used by the expert (and the expert system). It also describes the relationships between these objects. This part of the knowledge base is sometimes referred to as the "data base" or "facts base".

The procedural part of the knowledge base contains information on **how** these objects can be used to infer new conclusions and ultimately arrive at a solution. Since this "how-to" knowledge is usually expressed as (heuristic or other) **rules**, it is generally known as the "rule base".

In the following sections we will look briefly at a few methods used for representing declarative and procedural knowledge (there are of course many more). Most of these methods have their origins in artificial intelligence research, in such diverse areas as mathematical logic, cognitive psychology, human language understanding, automated theorem proving etc.

1.4.1 The facts base

1.4.1.1. Semantic networks

In a semantic network, the nodes represent the concepts (words, objects) the program is dealing with, while the relationships between the concepts are represented by associative links (directed arrows) between them. The idea of semantic networks is generally acknowledged to M. Ross Quillian, who used it as a means of modeling human language behavior (Quillian 1967).

As an example, Fig. 3 shows a simple semantic network representing the following facts (Alty 1984):

"Smith is a manager"
"Smith works in the Production Department located in Building-1"
"Smith is 40 years old"
"Smith has blue eyes"

Actual semantic networks can of course become quite large and complex.

The implementor normally has the freedom (and the responsibility) of ascribing the precise meaning (semantics) to the nodes and relations. This can be regarded as the major drawback of semantic networks: the meaning of the relations is not apparent from the network structure - one has to know their interpretations.

Some types of relations such as the "is-a" link:

Smith —is-a→ manager —is-a→ man

are particularly useful since they express the idea of "specialization". Since "man" is a generalization of "manager", the link from "manager" to "man" may be followed to find more general knowledge about Smith as a man (as opposed to merely a manager).

Note that the two links in the previous example are actually of a different nature and should therefore be given different names: the first one expresses the fact "Smith is a particular manager", while the second one states that "every manager is a man". In other words: "Smith" is an **instance** of the class "managers", while "managers" is a **subclass** of the more general class "man".

instance-of   subclass-of

Smith ——————→ manager ——————→ man

The symbolic structures described in the next two sections can be regarded as special (restricted) kinds of semantic networks.

1.4.1.2. Frames

A frame system is basically a semantic network where the only links allowed are the "instance-of" and the "subclass-of" links. All the other information is encoded within the nodes, here usually called "frames" or "units".

A frame describes all relevant properties of a particular object or fact. Each property is represented as a "slot" in the frame. The contents of that slot can be the **value** (or values) of that property, a pointer to another frame where the value can be found, or instructions on how to obtain the value when it is needed (compute it, read a sensor, ask the user ...). Other information relevant to the slot's property may be stored on "facets" inside the slot: things like the range of legal values for the property, limits on the number of values (cardinality), comments, etc. Figure 4 shows part of a possible frame for manger Smith (Figs. 4 – 5 were produced with KEE (Knowledge Engineering Environment), a software development environment that uses frames as its central representation mechanism (IntelliCorp 1986a)).

Every frame has a special "type" slot, the "is-a" or "ako" (a-kind-of) slot. This slot allows a frame to **inherit** properties from other frames; thus it is the equivalent of the "is-a" link of semantic networks (it is in fact the only semantic link allowed between frames). Here again we have to distinguish between "instance" and "subclass" links. If we represent a frame system as a semantic network using only these links, we get a hierarchical structure like in Figure 5. Each frame inherits the characteristics of the frame(s) above it, and it can add to, change or delete these.

In general, class frames are used to define the characteristics (slots) common to all class members; for instance, the "managers" frame will have slots for "department", "salary", and so on; but it will not put values in these slots. This is done in the member units. Sometimes a class frame may however provide a default value; for example, a "birds" frame could have a default value of "yes" in its "can-fly" slot. Every bird frame would then automatically inherit this value.

This shows that frames can provide for "expectation-driven" reasoning, or "reasoning by default": if we are told that object "X" is a bird, we may reasonably

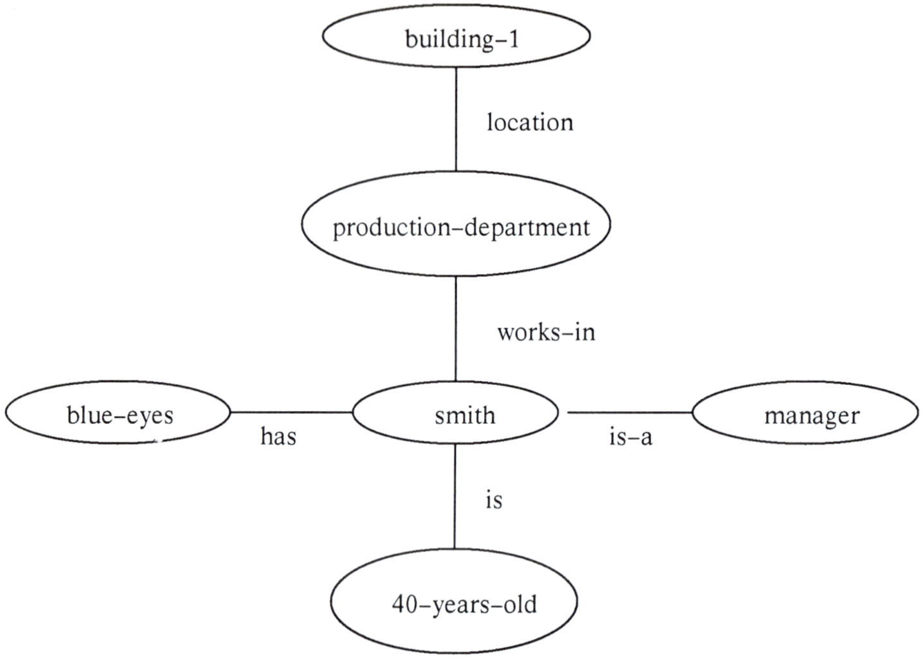

Figure 3 - A simple semantic network (Alty 1984)

expect that it can fly (if later it turns out that X is a penguin, we will of course have to revise this hypothesis).

The idea of frame representation is credited to Marvin Minsky (Minsky 1981), who stressed the possibilities of such a mechanism for dealing with prototypes, defaults, multiple perspectives, etc.

1.4.1.3. Object–Attribute–Value Triplets

A much simpler way of knowledge representation, that has been used in many expert systems especially MYCIN and its following (EMYCIN, M1, ...) (Shortliffe 1976) is the so-called "object–attribute–value" triplet. All the facts are encoded in such triplets, for example

(Smith   age   40)
(Smith   department   production)

Again this representation is only a special case of semantic network representation; there are only two kinds of links: the object–attribute link (roughly a "has–a" link) and the attribute–value link (which can sometimes be thought of as an "is–a"link, as in the second example).

1.4.2. The rule base

As for declarative knowledge, a number of different mechanisms have been developed for representing procedural knowledge; some systems may need to integrate several of these techniques.

1.4.2.1. Logic systems

Since the procedural side of an expert system deals with drawing conclusions from already established facts, it is only natural to use logic for this.

Logic is only concerned with the **validity** or truth of arguments, and the methods for deriving valid conclusions from

given assumed facts. Logic systems use the so-called predicate calculus. The programming language PROLOG was specially developed to work with this formalism (Clocksin 1981).

Individual assertions may be represented in PROLOG as:

works–in(smith, production).
department(production).

and so on. They can be combined using the normal NOT, AND and OR operators.

The primary mechanism for deriving new assertions from existing ones is **modus ponens**: if we know that " if P then Q" and "P" are true, then we can conclude that "Q" is true. Such a "rule" would be expressed in PROLOG as

```
Unit: Smith in knowledge base Corporation
Created by vital on 7-16-87 11:10:33
Modified by vital on 7-16-87 11:21:27
  Member Of: MEN, MANAGERS
```

```
Own slot: AGE from Smith
   Inheritance: OVERRIDE.VALUES
   ValueClass: NUMBER
   Cardinality.Min: 1
   Cardinality.Max: 1
   Values: 40

Own slot: DEPARTMENT from Smith
   Inheritance: OVERRIDE.VALUES
   ValueClass: DEPARTMENTS
   Values: PRODUCTION-DEPT

Own slot: EYE-COLOR from Smith
   Inheritance: OVERRIDE.VALUES
   ValueClass: (ONE.OF BLACK GREEN GREY BLUE BROWN)
   Values: BLUE

Own slot: SALARY from MANAGERS
   Inheritance: OVERRIDE.VALUES
   ValueClass: NUMBER
   Cardinality.Min: 1
   Cardinality.Max: 1
   Values: UNKNOWN

Own slot: WEIGHT from PEOPLE
   Inheritance: OVERRIDE.VALUES
   ValueClass: NUMBER
   Values: UNKNOWN
```

Figure 4 – Part of a "frame" for manager Smith (in KEE, a frame is called a "unit")

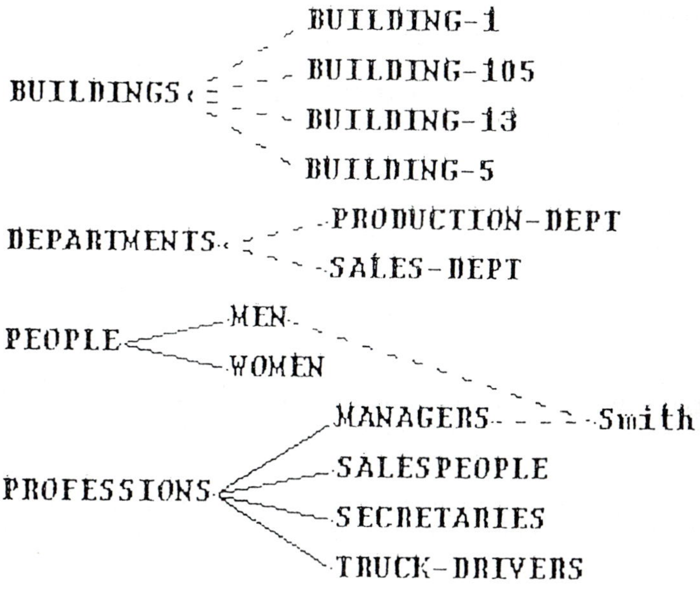

Figure 5 – Example of "inheritance trees" in a frame-based knowledge representation system. The solid lines represent class-subclass links; dotted lines are class memberships

Q :- P.

for example :

will_get_wet :- raining, no_umbrella.

where the comma is the "and" operator.

Another inference rule is the **rule of universal specialization**: if we know that for all things X, P(X) is true, and A is such a thing, then we can conclude that P(A) is true. For example, from

computer(cray).
unreliable(X) :- computer(X).

we can conclude

unreliable(cray).

The "X" in the second clause is an uninstantiated quantifier; PROLOG will try to "prove" this clause by looking for values of X that will make it true. It does this using a built-in searching mechanism, based on backward chaining (see later).

While theoretically sound, logic systems have some drawbacks for use in "real-world" applications: they only work with the values "true" or "false", and cannot deal with uncertain or unknown facts (see e.g. the "support logic programming" of (Baldwin 1987) for extensions to PROLOG for dealing with uncertainty); and they are inherently **monotonic**, i. e. conclusions remain valid and will never have to be revised. This is clearly not applicable to the real world.

1.4.2.2. Rules and Production Systems

The most popular form for representing procedural knowledge in an expert system is in the form of "if - then" rules :

IF premise THEN conclusion

In this form, rules superficially resemble the clauses in logic systems. Here, however, we are not dealing with logic classes but with general, often heuristic statements which in some situations may even be invalid.

We can go a step further, and remove even more limitations on the contents of the premise or conclusion. There may be some calculations in the premise part, for example; or the conclusion may call some external program, display something on the screen or ask a question to the user. A more appropriate form for these kind of rules is then:

IF situation THEN action

They are generally called "production rules" or "productions". (see e.g. Davis 1977; browston 1985). The control part of the program (see section 1.5) will determine if the "situation"-part of the rules is matched by the current state of the facts base; if it is, it will execute the "action"-part, thereby transforming the situation into a new one, hopefully closer to the desired solution. Sometimes this may turn out not to be the case, and the effects of the rule will have to be undone and another rule tried (thus removing the monotonicity constraint of logic systems).

An expert system can have hundreds such rules, and in a given situation many rules can match a given situation. The system therefore need a **control mechanism** to decide which rule to fire (see section 1.5).

1.5. Reasoning mechanisms

The part of the expert system that applies the rules in the rule base to the facts in the data base, is usually called the "inference engine" and may be ambitiously called the "reasoning" part of the system. There are basically two strategies for using the rules: forward-chaining and backward-chaining. Some expert systems tools will only use one of the two, others will provide both and let the knowledge engineer choose the most appropriate one or even switch from one strategy to another and back.

1.5.1. Forward chaining

"Forward chaining" is also known as "antecedent-driven" or "data-driven" reasoning. A forward chaining inference engine will select a rule with premises that match the known facts. If such a rule is found, its "then"-part is executed; as a result, new facts may be added to the facts base. The inference engine will then look for a new candidate rule, execute it, and so on, until there is no rule left that applies. Then the reasoning stops and the system may present its conclusions to the user.

A forward chainer therefore needs some facts to start reasoning; these should be supplied (by the user, by reading some sensors, ...) at the start of the run.

Examples of "shells" based on forward chaining are the OPS5 family of programs (Forgy 1977, Brownston 1985, Moskowitz 1986), and the KAPPA system developed at the authors' laboratory.

The key process in a forward chainer is the selection process. Usually several rules will match the knowledge base; how does it select the next rule to fire? (this process is called conflict resolution). A simple solution could be: scan all the rules starting with the first, and fire the first one that matches. Then start again at the top, and so on. This approach has the disadvantage that the order of the rules becomes important; it is no longer possible to regard each rule as an isolated piece of knowledge, and the process of adding new rules becomes much more difficult. Another approach is, to embed the control structure in the production system itself by using explicit "goals" (that is, elements in working memory representing a desired state). Every rule will only match a particular kind of goal, and will thus only fire when such a goal is present. Special rules will then have to be present that recognize when a particular goal has been achieved, disable it by removing the goal element from working memory, and possibly create a new goal. This kind of control is normally used in OPS5 programs. Ass an example, the following rule from a simple robot planning system says that, if the goal is to hold something, and it's on the floor, then you should first walk over it:

```
(goal  ^status active  ^type holds  ^object <w>)
(object  ^at  <p>  ^on floor)
```

```
-->
(make goal ^status active ^type walk-to ^object <p>)
```

This rule creates a new (sub)goal, and OPS5's control strategy assures that rules matching this goal will now fire first, since rules matching the most recent additions to the working memory are selected first. This strategy also prevents a particular rule instantiation (i. e. with particular values for the placeholders <w> and <p>) from firing more than once, thus preventing the system from getting in a loop.

1.5.2. Backward chaining

A backward chaining mechanism will start with a given hypothesis or goal, and will try to "prove" that goal using the facts and rules in the knowledge base. If the fact confirming the goal is already there, fine; but at the start of the run, there will be no facts so the inference engine will have to call the rule base. It will go and look for a rule that concludes the goal. If it can now establish the validity of that rule's premises, the job is done. Therefore it will select each of these premises in turn as a new "sub-goal", and set out to "prove" them in the same way as with the original goal. This is thus inherently a recursive process.

If it turns out that there is no rule that concludes a certain fact, the inference engine has to turn to the user: it will then ask him if that fact is true or not. Thus it will only ask things which are not in the facts base and which cannot be established by the rules.

Backward chaining also has its control issues. For instance, if, while pursuing a top goal A, the system has to resolve subgoals X, Y, Z, in what order should it achieve them? If several rules can apply in order to achieve a goal, which one should be selected first?

The second question concerns **rule ordering**. Usually the shell or tool that is being used to build the expert system, will have a fixed, hopefully efficient rule ordering algorithm, e. g. select the first matching rule, select the rule with the least number of premises, ... In the KEE backward chaining rule system (IntelliCorp 1986b), the knowledge engineer can choose between different orderings: "least premise complexity first"; "greatest premise complexity first"; "least rule weight first" (using weighting factors assigned by the knowledge engineer to the rules), "greatest weight first", and he can also define his own functions like "weighted least premise complexity" and so on.

The first question concerned **goal selection**. It is essentially a tree traversal problem, where the nodes in the tree are the goals and the branches link antecedents to consequents (fig. 6). Usually, a backward chainer works in a **depth-first** fashion: when a goal calls for the resolution of several subgoals, it will exhaustively generate and search the path corresponding to the first subgoal in a "top-down" fashion before returning to top node and generating and searching the next path. This type of goal selection was the one used in MYCIN (Buchanan 1984) and has been adopted in a great many expert system tools. It is also the built-in goal resolution algorithm in the PROLOG programming language (Clocksin 1981).

In **breadth-first** search, the controller will produce one node for each subgoal below the current goal's node, and test each of them in "left-to-right" order before moving down the tree. In **best-first** search, the controller will also generate all nodes at the next level first, but will then select the node with the shortest goal stack (the least number of subgoals) for expansion. In the KEE system,

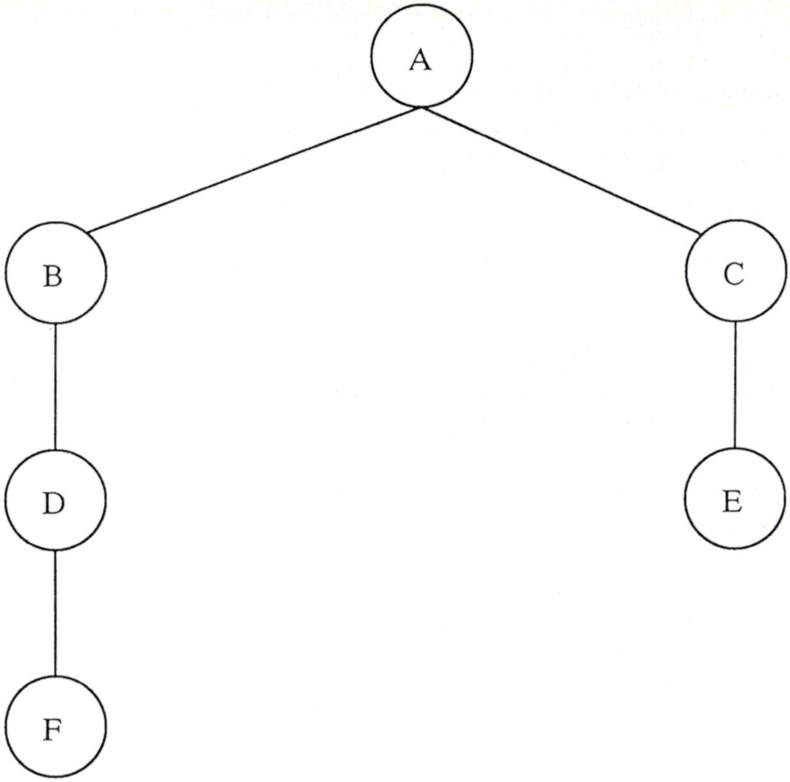

Figure 6 – A schematic representation of a backward chaining tree. The nodes in the tree are the goals and the branches link antecedents to consequents. In "depth–first" search, the tree is traversed in the order ABDFCE; in "breadth–first" search in the order ABCDEF and in "best–first" search in the order ABCEDF

again, the knowledge engineer has the freedom to choose from all these methods or to define his own (IntelliCorp 1986b).

1.5.3 comparison between forward and backward chaining

Forward chaining is particularly suited for design tasks (e.g. the configuration of computer systems (the R1 - later XCON - system (McDermott 1982)) and planning problems. Here the desired goal state is usually described by a number of constraints, but within these constraints the number of solutions may well be infinite (or at least extremely large). In such a case backward chaining, which starts by selecting a particular goal, is less appropriate (though not a priori excluded). Backward chaining on the other hand is better suited to problems of selection or diagnosis, where the number of outcomes is known and limited.

Forward chaining systems in the OPS5 tradition have the advantage, that the control mechanism is, up to a certain point, explicitly present in the rule base, and can be fine-tuned by the knowledge engineer to fit the particular problem. This may make such a system harder to implement then a backward-chaining one, however. Also some people believe that the "knowledge" should be strictly isolated from the "control of the knowledge".

A badly-designed forward chaining system may seem to lack direction, generating all kinds of facts with the hope that they may lead to a solution. A backward-chaining system, especially a depth-first searching one, concentrates on one goal at a time and thus has built-in kind of "focusing" capability. Backward chaining systems can also be very inefficient, however. In pursuing goal C in the rule

if A and B then C

the system might generate a very deep search tree in trying to establish goal A, while the fact "not B" might already be in the working memory! So the order of premises in the rules is not independent from the control strategy (a breadth-first system would not have this deficiency,, but it would not have the "goal-oriented" nature depth-first systems have).

Another difference concerns the nature of the dialog with the user: in backward chaining, the expert system will only ask things when it needs them. This means that the dialog is controlled by the computer, and the user only needs to answer its questions. In forward chaining, the user can volunteer his data to the program, so the control of the dialog shifts more to his side.

Nowadays many expert system tools try to get the best of both worlds by providing for forward chaining as well as backward chaining; thus the user could volunteer his data at the start of the run, and the system could forward chain on these, possibly invoking backward chaining to solve some intermediate goals. Systems such as KEE (IntelliCorp 1986b) allow the knowledge engineer to freely mix forward and backward chaining, limit the search to particular groups of rules, define his own customized control algorithms, to arrive at quite efficient, specialized inference methods.

1.5.4. Explanation

In the current expert systems, "explanation" is usually regarded as a by-product of the inference process. By retracting the goal stack, a backward chaining system can tell "why" it asks a certain item - i.e., what goal is being pursued, what the rule is that may establish that goal, all the way up to the top level goal - or "how" it found a conclusion - by keeping a trace of what rules where used in the derivation of each conclusion. This is clearly more a debugging aid than a real explanation.If the rules are obscure or implementation-specific, the explanation will be also (Browston 1985). It is sometimes enhanced by the addition of "canned texts" to the rules, that explain in more comprehensible terms what the purpose of the rule is, giving perhaps some references to the "knowledge source" of the rule where more details can be found. In forward chaining systems, e.g. built using OPS5, explanation facilities are not provided but have to be put in the knowledge by the expert system builders themselves (by adding "trace elements" to the working memory that keep track of rule invocations) (Brownston 1985).

This is about all the explanation that most "first-generation" expert systems can give. Some variations on this theme may be present; for example, the user could ask the system "Why was "X" not among the conclusions?". However, there are clearly shortcomings: first of all, no real justifications of the inference steps in terms of fundamental domain principles can be given - because the system doesn't know them: all it knows are the heuristic rules which may be the result of lumping together a whole string of cause-and-effect relations. In other words, the system has only "shallow" or "compiled" knowledge and no "deep" or "fundamental" knowledge. This is one of the major research issues in building "second-generation" expert systems: to give them a model of the basic principles underlying the problem domain, and a capability for reasoning from cause to effect (see Part 2).

Another drawback of current explanations is, that the **control mechanism** is not included in the explanation process. It is hidden inside the inference engine, unaccessible to the user of the system. In many cases, the strategy used by the control mechanism will be dictated by efficiency reasons and will have bear little or no relation to the reasoning strategy used by the human experts. It would be desirable that this "control knowledge" could be available for explanation in the same way as the domain knowledge is. One possibility would be, to reformulate it as **meta-knowledge** rules that can be used in the same way as the domain-specific rules. The system can the interpret "why" questions in a new way, namely "why was the system designed like that?" These meta-knowledge rules could then take the following form (Lenat 1983):

IF the search space is moderately small,
Then exhaustive search is feasible.

This is only one way in which "meta-knowledge" can be put to use in an expert system (see section 2.3)

1.5.5. Inexact reasoning

In many cases, the knowledge and facts we wish to represent in an expert system are not 100% certain. Also the conclusions drawn by heuristic rules may not be universally true. People constantly use terms like "probably", "very likely", "sometimes" to qualify their assertions.

Various theories and mechanisms for dealing with uncertainty have been developed. In some cases, it may be possible to assign **probabilities** to the various hypotheses and assertions (both a priori probabilities and conditional probabilities given certain evidence), for example when they are derived from a statistical analysis of a large body of experimental results. In these cases, **Bayes' theorem** may be used in the reasoning process. This mechanism was used in the PROSPECTOR system for assisting geologists in interpreting field data (Duda 1979), and its domain-dependent successor, KAS (Knowledge Acquisition System).

However, most of the time it is not possible to assign probability values to all the rules. In MYCIN, the uncertainty with which a rule's conclusion could be drawn from its premises was not regarded as a statement of probability but as a **measure of belief** (Shortliffe 1975). In MYCIN and its domain-independent cousin EMYCIN ("Empty MYCIN"), the certainty of a given fact (O-A-V triplet) was expressed as a "certainty factor" (cf) ranging from -1 (absolutely certain that it is not true), over 0 (completely unknown) to +1 (absolutely certain that it is true). Such certainty factors were also added to the conclusions of the rules, and expressed the belief in the truth of these conclusions given absolute certainty about the premises. When some premises were not known with 100% certainty, the certainty factor of the conclusion would be reduced accordingly. For ultimately deciding which of its conclusions were true and which were false, a (empirically determined) threshold value of 0.2 was used: if the cf > 0.2, the fact was considered to be true; if it was < -0.2, it was considered to be false. Many expert systems today use certainty factors in one way to another, although the MYCIN team realized that this approach had its shortcomings, and tried to give it a sound theoretical basis using the Dempster-Shafer theory of reasoning with uncertainty (Buchanan 1984, Shafer 1976).

When the expert system uses concepts that are themselves inexact, such as "tall" or "heavy", **fuzzy set theory** may be used. An assertion like "John is tall" is then interpreted as "John belongs - to some degree - to the set of tall people". This set is not a "crisp" set but a fuzzy set, and the degree of membership of a particular person in it will depend on his or her height. This degree is usually expressed as a real number in the interval é0,1ù. Thus a man of 210 cm might have ạ degree of membership 1 ("definitely tall"), while a man of 175 cm might have a degree of membership 0.5. For a clear expose of how fuzzy sets can be combined, and how the fuzzy result of a production rule can be derived, we may refer to (Negoita 1985).

2. ADVANCED ISSUES IN EXPERT SYSTEMS RESEARCH

While the techniques for building expert systems as explained in Part 1 are well established and are being used successfully in building operational systems, they do have a number of limitations, some of which we have already met, such as (Muller 1986):

- Narrow band of knowledge, with lack of knowledge of own limitations, only solving problems generally in one way.

- Little or no cross-checking, unable to cope with many situations.

- Handcrafted slow knowledge acquisition process, with tedious incremental modifications.

- Poor explanation facilities.

To overcome these limitations, many and large research projects are underway throughout the world. These aim a.o.:

- to extend the scope of expert systems (to more complex domains; to new tasks such as monitoring and control of real-time processes; to integration with other technologies like database systems, to other roles such as intelligent tutoring systems, ...);

- to improve their "intelligence" (deep knowledge; quantitative models; causal reasoning);

- to ease the process of building and maintaining them (automated knowledge acquisition; learning systems);

- to improve the quality of the human-computer dialog (natural language; effective explanations; user modeling);

- to develop models for the validation and verification of knowledge based systems, etc.

In the following sections we will take a brief look at the different problems facing these projects.

2.1. Real-time systems

If we want to introduce knowledge-based systems in real-time environments, like in the control room of industrial processes or nuclear power plants, or in autonomous vehicles, we immediately encounter some problems specific to these domains:

- the sheer **amount of data** with which the system may have to work. There may be many hundreds of signals that have to be monitored, perhaps every second. This task in itself can place a heavy burden on the computer.

- the **time-dependent behavior** of the process being monitored or controlled. Not only will the inference made by the expert system have a limited period of validity; we would also like to look ahead and predict how the process will evolve in the future, and perhaps plan some actions to influence this expected evolution. This means that our expert system should have some means of reasoning with time and about time.

– the **pressure of time**: the expert system must be fast enough, or its inferences will not be consistent anymore with the state of the process. Along with this the system will have to conduct a dialog with the human operator, so there should be some scheduling mechanism to coordinate these activities. This is made even more delicate by the fact that the dynamics of the process may vary greatly, between for example normal operating conditions and emergency situations.

Several research projects are underway to tackle some of these problems. To cope with in/out flow, special machine architectures (e.g. Transputer cards) may be necessary (e.g. PICON (ref) uses a separate processor for the data collection, linked to the Lisp machine on which the expert system runs).

To look ahead in time, some form of **possible worlds reasoning** could be used. Here the state of the process at a given instant is called a "world", and the reasoning mechanism can construct the possible worlds or hypothetical situations that the process may be in at a later time, given the knowledge about the past and the present and about the behavior of the process. However such a mechanism will need careful control to avoid a combinatorial explosion of such worlds (Arlabosse 1985).

To cope with the time pressure, it may be necessary to implement special "quick response" expert systems, that only come into action in fast-changing, time-critical situations. For the interface to the human operator, still other "dialog experts" could be used to filter the large amount of information and present it in an appropriate form, perhaps using graphics and multiple windows. Such an approach is the subject of the ESPRIT project GRADIENT (Graphical Dialogue Environment).

2.2 Expert systems in complex domains

The classical, one knowledge base – one inference engine architecture of expert systems, is adequate for many "narrow" application domains such as diagnosis or fault finding, where the knowledge can be expressed in a uniform way and manipulated in an equally uniform way. However, if we try to apply this paradigm to more complex, real-world problems we will encounter difficulties. To solve such problems, we will need to use different kinds of knowledge (e.g. numeric models as well as heuristics), different methods for using this knowledge (quantitative – number crunching – as well as qualitative – knowledge based), and to be able to look at the problem on different levels, from the general overview down to the detailed look at the subsystem or component. Such problems are often tackled using some form of **distributed problem solving approach**. This means that the problem solving activity is viewed as a collaborative effort of several different problem-solving agents or experts, each with its own specialization (Talukdar 1986).

Systems involving different cooperating sources of knowledge are usually termed as **blackboard systems**. The classic example is the HEARSAY-II system for continuous speech understanding. To accomplish this task, different kinds of knowledge need to be used: how to identify phonemes in the incoming speech signal; how to group these in words and sentences; and how to determine the meaning of these words. These subtasks are handled by different expert systems, working in parallel; they communicate with one other by means of a central, structured database called the **blackboard**. Individual experts post their results on the blackboard, and read new messages from it, which may be relevant to their particular subtask.This process is usually **event-driven**, i.e. a change on the blackboard can "trigger" or activate a knowledge source. If there are several knowledge sources that are triggered, a scheduling mechanism will choose one to execute its action. For this, it will use knowledge about knowledge source reliability, expected value of the knowledge source's action, etc. Another approach is to distribute the control task among several separate "management" expert systems whose task is to coordinate the different problem solvers, monitor overall progress, cut off unpromising search efforts, etc.This approach will naturally lead to the establishment of separate domain and control blackboards. Some control problems that arise here are: how to manage access to the data on the blackboard; how to handle conflicting results; what control scheme to use (competitive or cooperating); how to allocate computing resources among the different agents; what to do when goals cannot be met; etc. (Hayes-Roth 1985; Talukdar 1986).

Blackboard architecture is particularly suited to implementation in parallel or distributed systems; for example, the quantitative or number-crunching part of the system (probably written in FORTRAN or C) may be running on a conventional computer, while the rule-based elements are executing on a Lisp machine.

2.3. Deep knowledge and causal knowledge

A major criticism often directed against expert systems using heuristic rules-of-thumb is, that they can handle only a limited range of problems in a narrow domain. They don't know their own limits: when presented with a problem that is just outside their domain of knowledge, they will often fail to recognize this and produce meaningless results. In other words, they do not have the desirable property of "degrading gracefully". And finally, they can hardly be considered to "know" their subject material: when asked for explanations all they can do is resurgirate the rules. They cannot explain them in terms of the underlying principles because they don't know these terms.

The knowledge present in these systems is usually termed **shallow** or **compiled** knowledge. It consists of heuristics and empirical associations (stimulus - response; action - effect). It is often approximate and fragmentary. It is called **shallow** because it doesn't contain the underlying basic concepts like causality, intent, or fundamental physical principles; and **compiled** because an empirical association is in fact a combination or compilation of several basic cause-and-effect relations.

In contrast, the term **deep** systems is used to refer to systems that do possess a causal model, an explicit representation of the structure and behavior of the components making up the physical system being reasoned about, a means of using first physical principles, etc. Deep knowledge is structured, precise and relies on established formal theories. Shallow knowledge mainly comes out of observing a system from the outside, without bothering about what causes the external behavior; while deep knowledge mainly derives from observing the system from inside, trying to discover the first causes of its operation and behavior (Guida 1985).

An expert system with deep knowledge should be able to improve upon the performance of a shallow system. It should be able to handle new or unfamiliar problems for which empirical associations alone are not enough. And it can lead to better explanations.

A typical application of the first issue is in fault diagnosis in physical systems. Much research is currently directed toward diagnostic systems with deep knowledge; see for example (SIGART 1985). Shallow systems can only diagnose those faults that are explicitly mentioned in their heuristic rules. A system with deep knowledge, however will have a representation of the **structure** of the physical system (what are its components; how are they connected; how are they grouped in subsystems); of the behavior of the individual components; and of the causal patterns of behavior and structure (to infer the behavior of a composite component). The behavior of the system as a whole can then be related to its structure and the functionality of the components. By comparing this expected behavior with the actual behavior, it should be possible to find the faulty component and construct an explanation of what went wrong (Bylander 1985, Sembugamoorthy 1985, davis 1984, deKleer 1987). Since deep knowledge is general in nature and not intended for one particular purpose, it can also be used in other problem solving structures apart from the pure diagnostic one, e.g. in "what would happen if ..." situations.

Having deep knowledge will also allow the system to provide better explanation, and thus gain credibility. The user can ask for more and more detailed explanations and he/she will see that the knowledge employed by the expert system is indeed built on sound underlying principles (Chandrasekaran 1984).

Of course, the distinction between "deep" and "shallow" knowledge is not an absolute one. A model is not deep or shallow per se, but only with respect to some other model (Guida 1985). An efficient expert system will not be using solely deep knowledge, but may use several models, each describing the system on a different level of abstraction. The "surface" level will contain compiled knowledge, efficiently structured and tailored for a specific goal. If the problem at hand does not match this goal, or if it is too complex to be handled using only heuristics, the system can fall back on a deeper model, where the knowledge is more general, domain-independent and flexible. This can also be applied in the generation of explanations with different levels of detail. It should be even possible to build "knowledge compilers" that can compile shallow knowledge, intended for a particular problem solving activity, from deep knowledge; this has been mentioned in (Sembugamoorthy 1985).

2.4 Learning and automated knowledge acquisition

A human expert was once a novice; he/she collected his/her expertise by learning - learning from examples, learning by analogy, learning from their own mistakes... . Expert systems however start out as experts : when they become operational, all the available expertise will already be present in their knowledge bases. And unlike a human expert, an expert system normally has no way of adding to this expertise, or to adapt it to the changing world. This has to be done by the knowledge engineer.

Since the process of knowledge acquisition can be long and expensive, a system that can automatically acquire or "learn" new knowledge, evolving as it were from "novice" to "expert", would be welcome. Such a system should be able to (Forsyth 1986):

- cover a wider range of problems

- give more accurate solutions

- obtain answers at lower costs

- simplify stored knowledge

Since experts not only possess more knowledge than novices; they also use it more efficiently. Thus a learning system not only has to acquire new knowledge;

it also has to be able to refine its reasoning process and rearrange its knowledge in more efficient structures. This is a very ambitious program, and a lot of research will have to be done before such systems will become workable. Several models of how experts acquire new knowledge and reasoning skills have been proposed and are being studied in research labs; see (Kolodner 1984) and (Riesbeck 1984).

Some success has already been achieved on less ambitious tasks, such as the automatic construction of knowledge bases by **rule induction** from a series of examples. The ID3(Interactive Dichotomiser) algorithm, for example (Quinlan 1982) builds a **decision tree** for identification problems given a list of outcomes for various combinations of the data. This tree is then traversed by the run-time or consultation module. This algorithm has been applied in commercial programs such as ExpertEase and SuperExpert. Of course, the only "learning" capability of these systems lies in the fact that the resulting tree is better suited to the identification task than the original list; other than that, they contain exactly the same information.

2.5. Advanced user interface

There has been a growing interest recently in the area of user interfaces or man–machine interfaces of computer systems - especially when these systems pretend to have expert knowledge and to be able to make "intelligent" decisions. It is realized that excellent decision making capabilities alone are not enough to guarantee user acceptability; attention also needs to be paid to the interaction between the expert system and the users. People will be more willing to interact with a system that behaves in a friendly and flexible way than with a system with a spartan and unforgiving user interface - even if the latter system is more knowledgeable than the former. However in most of today's expert systems and expert system shells, the user interface is far more of the latter type than of the former. The dialogue is usually restricted to making a selection in a series of menus, giving one– or two–word commands, answering a series of yes/no or multiple choice questions, and so on.

The adequacy of such interactions has been recognized, however, and today much effort is being put into making the user interface friendlier and more "intelligent". Areas being investigated in this respect include dialog control, explanation facilities, user modeling, the use of natural language, and the effects of new technology. An overview of current work in these areas can be found in (Berry 1987). It should be realized that not all of these facilities will be needed in a given expert system; which ones will be most beneficient depends on the application domain, the aims of the system (problem solving, training, ...), the type of users, the capabilities of the computer system etc.

Dialog control is concerned with the way the dialog between the system and the user is managed. Is one side controlling this dialog, with the other side just answering the questions? or is it a mixed–initiative dialog where both partners have equal priorities? Until now, the dialog in most expert systems was controlled by the machine, with the user's role restricted to answering the questions asked. It has been realized, that human consultations are much more cooperative in nature, and that it would be desirable - for some application areas at least - for expert systems to give more initiative to the user. These areas include medical applications and systems operating in real time (Berry 1987).

The need for good **explanation facilities** has been stressed already. They can help the knowledge engineer in the testing and debugging of the system; they can assure the user that the system's knowledge and reasoning is correct; and they can be used to instruct novice users about the knowledge present in the system. These latter roles - rarely present in current systems - will benefit from research in other areas as natural language processing and user modeling (so the system can adapt its explanations to the level of the user).

User modeling then is concerned with giving the expert system the possibilities to tailor its behavior to the needs of the individual user: "know your user". A simple possibility is, to classify the user in one of several categories or "prototypes" (inexperienced, knowledgeable, expert, ...) by asking some questions at the start of the consultation. The system can then choose its terminology, level of explanations and so on in accordance with this category. A more sophisticated system might keep a model for each individual user, and adapt it over time - for example, as a result of using the system, the user will become more knowledgeable and require a different sort of help or explanation. Systems which will benefit most from having this capability are those whose main task is the transfer of knowledge (intelligent tutoring systems, intelligent help systems).

Like that of user modeling, the problem of **natural language processing** is still very much a research issue. Mixed-initiative dialog, cooperative problem solving, and explanation generation are the most obvious areas where a natural language (NL) interface would be useful. Some current systems possess a limited NL interface using a restricted vocabulary and grammar. A full-scale NL capability is still a long way off, however, and it is not clear whether such a capability is really needed. In fact some applications rely less on words than on diagrams or formulas. With the new advances in human-computer communication technology, it becomes possible to give expert systems the "most appropriate" language interface - either text or graphics. High-resolution bit-mapped displays, color, windowing, mouse control or touch-sensitive screens, are all being used to improve the man-machine interaction. While these features were initially only available on specialized "development" machines" they are now becoming more widely available, for example in top-of-the-line personal computers.

2.6. Validation and evaluation

As the use of expert systems spread from the academic and research centers to commercial and "real-world" environments, there has been a growing need for **validation** of the knowledge bases incorporated in these systems. Can we be sure that an expert system for medical diagnosis will never make a mistake? That the rules present in the system can account for all possible combinations of circumstances, and that they don't lead to inconsistency?

The term **validation** has been use in several different meanings with respect to expert systems (St Johanser 1986). The first one is concerned with more or less formal or automated methods to check that the expert system is internally consistent and complete. The ONCOCIN program, for example, checks the completeness and consistency of a set of production rules where all the parameter values can be determined with certainty (Suwa 1984). It detects **conflicts** between rules - i.e. if two rules with the same conditions can fire in a given situation and assign different values to a parameter; **redundancy** in the rule set - i.e. in a given situation at least two rules with the same decision succeed; and **missing rules** - i.e. in a situation where inference is required there is no rule that can produce the desired conclusion. A similar rule-checking method is described in (Puuronen 1987). In (Rousset 1987) a method is suggested to prove the "weak" validity of a knowledge base: that, given an initial fact base which is consistent, the system will never produce an inconsistent result (the expert system consists here of a set of production rules that is applied in forward chaining fashion to an initial set of facts; the facts are expressed as attribute-value pairs). The method will find all consistent initial fact bases such that, after running the rule base on these facts, the resulting rule base is inconsistent. None of the above methods considers uncertain reasoning. In (Paass 1986) a method is proposed for the evaluation of inference nets incorporating probabilistic rules and propositions, where probabilities may be uncertain (only a range for the probabilities is known). While these methods work with small-scale systems, it is not yet clear how they could be applied to large, complex systems without requiring enormous computational resources.

A second use of the term validation, is gaining **acceptance** by the users of the expert system. In principle, this should be carried out in much the same way with other computer systems, through a thorough testing and acceptance phase. In practice however, it turns out that expert systems are rarely subjected to rigorous acceptance tests because of a lack of a detailed specification against which to check the finished product. In expert system acceptance is often taken as acceptance of the expert (he agrees that the system gives the correct answers for a number of test cases), and not of the end-users (who may not be experts; who may employ a different jargon; who may misinterpret the meaning of confidence factors in the conclusions etc.). It is argued that expert systems should be developed along the same lines as other commercial software, i.e. with a detailed specification, an extensive test phase, and thorough evaluation before release to the end-users. Emphasis on the "prototyping" approach to building expert systems, and superficial testing ("it works") - mainly resulting from the evolution of expert systems out of academic artificial intelligence laboratories - from obstacles which may prevent a widespread acceptance of expert system technology in the business world (St Johanser 1986).

Finally, "validation" is often used in context of **evaluation of performance** of an expert system. How does the system perform with respect to the human whose function it is emulating? Here again, this subject has mostly been treated in a informal, causal way by expert system builders - if not neglected altogether. Usually the performance of the system is established by comparing its results on a series of problems with known solutions, to those of the expert(s) who helped design the system; or by asking the human experts how they rate the conclusions of the expert system (Soula 1987). Such a comparison is complicated by the fact that the human experts themselves will often draw different conclusions in a given case.

To be really acceptable, however, an evaluation of performance should be carried out using a sound experimental design set out in advance, and be subject to a detailed statistical analysis of its results. In (St Johanser 1986) a minimum schema for such an evaluation is proposed: compare the system's performance with four categories of humans (unexperienced users - users with some skill and training - qualified users - recognized top experts), in two tests (accuracy of predictions of real world outcomes; similarity of judgment to those of top experts), of two test populations (a random selection of cases, and a set of "difficult cases), and with two quantities (cost and speed). This need to make evaluations more formal and rigorous is echoed in (Berry 1987).

Summary

Expert systems are no wonder drug. They cannot be applied to just any problem, even if we had a suitable problem, we have to be aware of their limitations. Nevertheless, if we make sure that a number of basic requirements are met (a well-defined application domain, non-trivial problem for which the necessary knowledge is available, and - last but not least - a realistic management attitude), then we may expect that investing in expert systems may lead to benefits in such areas as

* better decision making

* increased productivity

* turning knowledge into a capital asset

* training

* customer service

* control of industrial processes (fault detection, operator assistance, ...)

References

J. L. Alty, M. J. Coombs.(1984) *Expert Systems : Concepts and Examples.* NCC Publications.

F. Arlabosse (1985) Reasoning with time and about time: Some aspects of temporal logic. In: *Expert Systems and Optimisation in Process Control,* Unicom Seminars Ltd., 152–157.

J.F. Baldwin. (1987) An uncertainty calculus for expert systems. In: *Approximate reasoning in intelligent systems, decision and control, ed. by E. Sanchez and L. Zadeh,* Pergamon Press, 33–54.

D. C. Berry, D. E. Broadbent. (1987) Expert Systems and the man–machine interface. Part two : the user interface. *Expert Systems,* February 1987. Vol. 4 No. 1 18–27.

R. J. Brachman, S. Amarel, C. Engelman, R. S. Engelmore, E. A. Feigenbaum, D. E. Wilkins. (1983) What are Expert Systems?. *Chapter 2 in (Hayes–Roth 1983).*

R. J. Brachman, H. J. Levesque. (1985) *Readings in Knowledge Representation,* Morgan Kaufmann.

L. Brownston, R. Farell, E. Kant, N. Martin. (1985) *Programming Expert Systems in OPS5,* Addison–Wesley.

B. G. Buchanan, D. Barstow, R. Bechtal, J. Bennett, W. Clancey, C. Kulowski, T. Mitchell, D. A. Waterman. (1983) Constructing an Expert System, *Chapter 5 in (Hayes–Roth 1983).*

B. G. Buchanan, E. H. Shortliffe. (1984) *Rule–Based Expert Systems: the MYCIN Experiments of the Stanford Heuristic Programming Project,* Addison–Wesley

T. Bylander, B. Chandrasekaran. (1985) Qualitative Reasoning about Physical Systems, In (*SIGART 1985*).

B. Chandrasekaran, S. Mittal. (1984) Deep versus compiled knowledge approaches to diagnostic problem–solving, In: *Developments in Expert Systems, ed. M. J. Coombs,* Academic Press, 23–34.

W. E. Clocksin, C. S. Mellish. (1981) *Programming in Prolog,* Springer– Verlag

R. Davis, B. Buchanan, E. Shortliffe. (1977) Production Rules as a Representation for a Knowledge–Based Consultation Program, Artificial Intelligence 8 (1), 15–45.
R. Davis. (1984) Resoning frum first principles, In: *Developments in Expert Systems, ed. M. J. Coombs,* Academic Press.

J. de Kleer, C. Williams. (1987) Diagnosing Multiple Faults, *Artificial Intelligence* 32, 97–130.

R. O. Duda, J. Gaschnig, P. Hart. (1979) Model design in the PROSPECTOR consultant program for mineral exploration, In: *Expert Systems in tyhe Microelectronic Age, ed. D. Mitchie,* Edinburgh University Press.

C. L. Forgy, J. Mc Dermott. (1977) OPS, A Domain– Independent Production

System Language, In: *Proceedings of the 5th International Joint Conference on Artificial Intelligence MIT*, 973–939.

G. Guida. (1985) Reasoning about physical systems: shallow versus deep models, In: *Expert Systems and Optimisation in Process Control,* Unicom Seminars Ltd. 82–106.

F. Hayes-Roth, D. A. Waterman, D. B. Lenat. (1983) *Building Expert Systems*, Addison-Wesley.

F. Hayes-Roth. (1985) A Blackboard Architecture for Control, *Artificial Intelligence 26*, 251–321.

IntelliCorp. (1986a) KEE Software Development System User's Manual, *Intellicorp Document number 3.0-U-1.*

IntelliCorp. (1986b) KEE Software Development Rulesystem3 Reference Manual, *Intellicorp Document number 3.0-RR-1.*

J.L. Kolodner. (1984) Towards an understanding of the role od experience in the evolution from novice to expert, In: *Developments in Expert Systems, ed. M. J. Coombs*, Academic Press, 95–116.

D. Lenat, R. Davis, J. Doyle, M. Genesereth, I. Goldstein, H. Schrobe. (1983) Reasoning about Reasoning, *Chapter 7 in (Hayes-Roth 1983).*

J. McDermott. (1982) R1: A Rule-Based Configurer of Computer Systems, *Artificial Intelligence* 19, 39–88.

M. Minsky. (1985) A Framework for Representing Knowledge, In: *Mind Design, ed. J. Haugeland*, The MIT Press (1981) (*reprinted as Chapter 12 in (Brachman (1985)*).

R. L. Moore, L. B. Hawkinson, C. G. Knickerbocker, L. M. Churchman. (1984) A real-time expert system for process control, *1st Conf. on Artificial Intelligence Applications IEEE,* 569–576.

L Moskowitz. (1986) Rule-Based Programming, *Byte* November, 217–224.

R. C. Muller (1986) New Directions in Expert Systems, In: *Knowledge-Based Systems '86,* Online Publications, 325–333.

C.V. Negoita. (1985) *Expert Systems and Fuzzy Systems,* Benjamin Cummings Publ. Co.

G. Pass. (1986) Consistent Evaluation of Uncertain Reasoning Systems, *6th Int. Workshop on Expert Systems and their Applications, Avignon*, 73–94.

S. Puuronen. (1987) A Tabular Rule-Checking Method, *7th Int. Workshop on Expert Systems and their Applications, Avignon*, 257–268.

M. R. Quillian. (1967) Word Concepts: A Theory and Simulation of some Basic Semantic Capabilities, *Behavioral Science* 12, 410–430 (*reprinted as Chapter 6 in (Brachman (1985)*)).

J. R. Quinlan. (1982) Semi-automous acquisition of pattern-based knowledge, In: *Introductory Readings in Expert Systems, ed D. Mitchie,* Gordon and Breach.

M.-C. Rousset. (1987) Sur la Validite des Bases de Connaissances: le systeme COVADIS, *7th Int. Workshop on Expert Systems and their Applications, Avignon,* 269–282.

V. Sembugamoorthy, B. Chandrasekaran. (1985) Functional Representation of Devices as Deep Models, In: (*SIGART 1985*).

G. Shafer. (1976) *A mathematical theory of evidence*, Princeton University Press.

E. H. Shortliffe. (1976) *Computer-Based Medical Consultations: MYCIN*, American Elsevier.

SIGART (1985) Special Section on Reasoning about structure, Behavior and Function, eds. B. Chandrasekaran, R. Milne, *SIGART Newsletter* July, 4–55.

G.Soula, X. Thirion, J.-M. Guliana, I. Navez, B. Vialettes, J.-L. San Marco, V. Ledoray. (1987) Une Validation Multicentrique du Systeme Expert PROTIS, *7th Int. Workshop on Expert Systems and their Applications, Avignon,* 239–255.

J. T. St Johanser, R. M. Harbidge. (1986) Validating expert systems: problems and solutions in practice, In: *Knowledge-Based Systems '86,* Online Publications, 215–229.

M. Suwa, A. C. Scott, E. H. Shortliffe. (1984) Completeness and Consistency in a Rule-Based System, In: (*Buchanan 1984*), 653–665.

S. N. Talukdar, E. Cardozo, L. Leao, R. Benares, R. Joobbani. (1986) A system for Distributed Problem Solving. In: *Coupling Symbolic and Numerical Computing in Expert Systems, ed. J. S. Kowalik,* Elsevier, 115-122.

D. A. Waterman (1986) *A Guide to Expert Systems,* Addison-Wesley.

AUTOMATED SUPPORT FOR FORMULATING LINEAR PROGRAMS

Edward A. Stohr

Graduate School of Business Administration
New York University

1. Introduction

Linear programming (LP) models have been used to support operational and planning decisions in every major industry - including petroleum, steel, forestry, manufacturing, communications and banking. However, applications have been limited by the difficulties in model formulation, management and interpretation (Johnson [1987]). Rapid advances in computing have made it possible for us to solve far larger models than we can understand. To maximize the benefits from the considerable progress that has been made in the development of efficient computational algorithms, we need to reduce the cost of modeling and improve both the quality of models and the decision processes associated with their use.

An important research goal is to help modelers cope with the complexity of large-scale models so that they can devote a greater proportion of their time to understanding the subject to be modeled and to analysing model results. Since successful models can have a long life and can be used by many different people, we also need to develop procedures to automate the production of documentation during the model building phase and to maintain it during subsequent revisions. Finally, we need to conduct behavioral studies to learn how information contained in models can be made more accessible to users so that they can gain deeper insights and make higher quality decisions.

Research aimed at automating model building and management has begun to generate useful results. New approaches to LP modeling and analysis are described in Balci [1985], Bisschop and Meeraus [1982], Breitman and Lucas [1987], Fourer, Gay and Kernighan [1987], Greenberg, Lucas, and Mitra [1986], Nance and Balci [1983] and Welch [1987]. Greenberg [1983] describes a system for analysing the structure of LPs and diagnosing problems. Geoffrion [1987] has

NATO ASI Series, Vol. F48
Mathematical Models for Decision Support
Edited by G. Mitra

developed a comprehensive framework for model building and management called structured modeling; some extensions appear in Dolk [1987] and Lenard [1986]. Binabsioglu and Jarke [1986] describes the use of knowledge-based techniques to help automate the process of formulating linear programming models.

There are six steps in using any modeling technique: recognition of a problem to be solved, identifying the solution technique to be used, formulating the model, linking the model parameters to data values, solving the model and analysing the results. The research described in this paper is concerned with the formulation phase of the modeling process. The focus is on linear programming formulations because they are an important class of models in and of themselves and because they are rich in structure. Since there has been little work in this area, there are few guidelines as to what functions can and should be automated, and virtually no experience in designing and building an effective man/machine interface. To test our design strategy, we are building a prototype system, LPFORM, which helps automate the formulation process (Ma [1987], Murphy and Stohr [1986]).

This paper describes our approach to designing the man-machine interface and developing the theory needed to support enhanced modeling and analysis. The next section provides an overview of the design principles underlying the system and a brief description of the system itself. Section 3 describes the interface by means of a short example. Section 4 contains an overview of the reasoning process. Finally, Section 5 explains how various kinds of knowledge (about syntax, semantics, physical transformations and previously defined templates) are represented and used to help the formulation process.

2. Overview of System

To improve the modeling process, we must understand how people formulate and build models and how the computer can assist this process. Our goals are to reduce the amount of bookkeeping required formulate a model and to provide enough flexibility to enhance the creative processs of model building. How these goals can be achieved is a research question that can be resolved only empirically. However, we have proposed the following design strategy and are incorporating it in a prototype system. There are three major components:

- Multiple problem representations ranging from a graphical, non-mathematical representation to a more traditional algebraic representation and an annotated data dictionary.

- Support for a number of different problem-solving strategies that reduce the complexity of the formulation process (hierarchical decomposition, reuse of previously defined model components and a non-procedural, piece-meal approach to problem specification).

- Capabilities not available in other software (relational database, consistency checking, model management).

The interface supports several different styles of problem representation. The interplay between these specification modes and their potential for making the user's task less demanding requires further research. Some parts of the model specification may be easier to state in one form and others in another. For example, we suspect that the overall structure of a problem is most easily visualized and stated graphically. This will certainly be true of transportation network structures - up to a certain level of detail. Other requirements may best be stated in terms of previously stored parcels of knowledge in the form of constraint and problem templates e.g. "this problem involves a product-mix and several transportation sub-problems." Many requirements are best stated with an activity orientation - for example "we have buying, selling and inventorying activities at each of our warehouses" (in LPFORM, three activity icons would be placed in the warehouse block). Still other problem requirements, and in particular, policy constraints, are best stated with a row orientation e.g. "the total tons of product produced in each factory has to be less than certain given limits" or "the unions require that the total overtime hours of each kind of labor be distributed equitably". LPFORM supports all of these different classes of input although, in its present form, row-oriented requirements have to be stated algebraically for the most part. A simple extension will allow more English-like expressions of policy requirements.

A major objective of the system is to reduce the complexity of large-scale modeling by providing a number of automated aids and by supporting different formulation strategies. Hierarchical decomposition is supported by allowing the modeler to depict the problem graphically in layers of increasing detail. Properties of objects at higher levels are automatically inherited by lower level objects. This is a top-down approach to modeling. A bottom-up approach is also supported. This involves building and testing component models and then combining them into larger models. LPFORM automates the saving and reuse of models and parts of models and supports interactive queries about models stored previously in the model bank. A final strategy, is to allow uses to define their model requirements as they come to mind rather than to impose any strict order.

Model builders also need support for a number of laborious tasks that must be performed during the modeling process. First, the LPFORM system provides a relational database for data retrieval and manipulation (Stohr [1986]). Second, since the formulation process itself is being supported, there are many opportunities to check the accuracy of the problem statement as it is being produced rather than after the final tableau has been generated (Murphy et al [1987]). Finally, the model management facilities include an on-line model dictionary and query facility and a method for automatically retrieving and combining model components to build larger models (Ma [1987]).

LPFORM translates from an iconic problem representation to an algebraic statement of the model and finally produces the input needed by solvers such as LINDO (Schrage [1987]) or IBM's MPSX (IBM [1975]). Figure 2-1 shows the structure of the prototype system.

```
             Model-builder
                   |
          _________v__________
         | LPFORM Interface   |
         |____________________|
                   |
           LPSPEC Statements
                   |
          _________v__________
         |  LPFORM Analyser   |
         |____________________|
                   |
                   v
      MPS Statements to Optimizer
```

Figure 2-1: The LPFORM System

The LPFORM Interface is being built on an IBM PC/AT class machine using a set of graphics tools written in the C programming language (EVA [1987]). A prototype of the LPFORM Analyser has been implemented in PROLOG (Ma [1987]). The two subsystems are loosely coupled. The Interface sends the results of the user specification to the Analyser in the form of statements in the LPSPEC language (Ma et al [1987]). Each LPSPEC statement captures a single action made by the user in the graphics interface. The next two sections of the paper describe these two subsystems in more detail.

3. Graphical Representation

The graphical specification language uses blocks, links and templates to aid in model formulation. A model is represented by a collection of interconnected blocks. A block is a collection of zero, one or more linear programming activities that are separated in space or time from other activities. Blocks provide a convenient way for a modeler to decompose the real world. For example, one block may be a template representing the production of raw materials, a second may be a template representing the conversion of raw materials into finished products, and a third may represent consumption of finished goods. The links between blocks represent activities involving space or time transformations. A template is an LP submodel that can be simply a collection of constraints or a complete LP. A number of different standard models - transportation, product-mix, blending and so on - are stored in the model base and can be retrieved and combined into larger models.

Hierarchical layers are supported by allowing blocks to represent collections of blocks (or sub-blocks) plus their linkages. For example, a refinery model may be a single block in an initial LP and subsequently decomposed into blocks representing individual refinery units and links representing pipe connections. Finally, blocks can be replicated in either space of time.

The graphics interface is explained in detail in Ma et al [1987]. Figure 3-1 shows a sample screen.

```
 ___________________________________________________________________________________
| PROBLEM: widget_model          VERSION: 1   LAST UPDATE: 10/06/87 | DATA:        |
| LOAD  SAVE  PROB-DATA  DATABASE  DICTIONARY  UP  DOWN  SOLVE  QUIT|              |
|___________________________________________________________________| MODE: DATA   |
| LEVEL: 1  GRAPH: 1          CURRENT OP: LINK_BLOCK                |  REL:   r    |
|        FACTORIES                       MARKETS                    |  TAB:   t    |
|        ______________________          _____                      |  PAR:   p    |
|       |           X          |        |     |                    |  SET: {s}    |
|       |           |          |        |     |                    |______________|
|       |  RAW_MATS |          |        |     |                    | STRUCTURE:   |
|       |  ------->|           |        |     |                    |              |
|       |           |WIDGETS   |   T    |     |                    |  C-B:  []    |
|       |           |--------->|=========>|   |                    |  L-B:  -->   |
|       |  DOLLARS  |          |        |     |                    |L-O-I: :-->   |
|       |  ------->|           |        |     |                    | B-IO: =[]=   |
|       |           |          |        |     |                    |  D-I:  .:.   |
|       |______________________|        |_____|                    |  D-C:  |_|   |
|                                                                   |  D-R:  0=0   |
|                                                                   |  D-T:  ___   |
|                                                                   |  D-A:  =|-   |
|                                                                   |  C-M:  <     |
|___________________________________________________________________|  REP:  ]]]   |
| BACK []  FORWD []  DELETE []  UNDELETE []  SHOW-DET []  ERASE []  |  OPT:  ^/v   |
| LINK TYPE: SPACE[] TIME[]          FLOW VAR: T____                |              |
|___________________________________________________________________|______________|
```

Figure 3-1: Graphic Screen for LPFORM

The screen contains a central work area where graphs can be drawn and three sets of commands. The commands in the top border are used for major operations such as loading and saving the problem statement, accessing the database, moving up and down a hierarchical level in the model, and solving the model to produce the algebraic formulation and then, optionally, the mathematical solution.

The commands in the bottom border, operate on the graphical images in the center of the screen. These allow the user to step backwards and forwards through prior model building steps, to delete and restore model components, to show the detail underlying a part of the problem representation, and to erase the screen.

The commands used for modeling are on the right of the screen. The data commands in the upper part of the right-border allow the user to link the symbolic model to the data either interactively during the terminal session or by specifying links to existing data in a database. A relational database query language, which is part of the interface system, is used to perform queries and to manipulate the data.

The commands for defining model structure are in the lower part of the right-hand border and are associated with icons. To place an object on the screen, users point (with the cursor or another device such as a light-pen) to the command and then to a position on the screen. They are then led through a series of questions associated with the command or asked to fill in an electronic form to supply necessary textual information. The model building commands include Create-Block (C-B), Link-Block (L-B), Def-Activity (D-A) and Call-Model (C-M). The first command creates a block that can be filled with an activity or a template, the second links blocks for which the output of one is an input to another, the third defines a linear programming activity in terms of its inputs and outputs and the fourth places a template (submodel) into a block.

Figure 3-1 also shows the graph that would be constructed to define a production and distribution problem, "Make-and-ship", in which widgets, j, are produced at factories, f, and shipped to markets, m. The modeler places 'block icons' for the factories and markets on the computer screen, links the two blocks to define the transportation activity, and then places an 'activity icon' in the factories block. As these actions are performed, the user is prompted for the names of the blocks, the decision variables (X and T) and the inputs and outputs of the production activity. Given the problem specification shown in Figure 3-1 the following algebraic statement will be produced:

$$\text{Min: } \sum_{j \in Widgets} \sum_{f \in Factories} c_{j,f} X_{j,f} + \sum_{j \in Widgets} \sum_{f \in Factories} \sum_{m \in Markets} w_{j,f,m} T_{j,f,m}$$

$$\text{St: } \sum_{j \in Widgets} a_{i,j,f} X_{j,f} \leq b_{i,f} \qquad \forall i \in RawMats, f \in Factories$$

$$- X_{j,f} + \sum_{m \in Markets} T_{j,f,m} = 0, \qquad \forall j \in Widgets, f \in Factories$$

$$\sum_{f \in Factories} T_{j,f,m} \geq d_{j,m}, \qquad \forall j \in Widgets, m \in Markets$$

The remainder of this section explains this process in more detail. LPFORM processes a succession of problem representations: (1) the graphical screen interfaces presented to the user, (2) the LPSPEC language statements, (3) an internal tableau representation, (4) the algebraic statements output to the Matrix Generator, and finally, (5) the MPS form of the problem statement as input to the solver. Figures 3-3 through 3-6, which illustrate representations (2) and (3), contain computer outputs from a test run. The design of the user interface is discussed more fully in Ma et al [1987]. The model is developed using two alternative approaches. The first uses basic concepts of LPFORM to construct the model from 'first principles'. In other words, the components of the model, blocks, activities, links and so on, are described by the user in detail as in the illustration above. The second approach to model formulation involves the use of pre-existing LP model templates that are "mapped" on to the Make-and-ship problem. The formulations resulting from both approaches are the same.

3.1. First Principles Approach

Figures 3-1 through 3-5 show some of the screens generated by a user defining the Make-and-ship problem from first principles. The user decomposes the problem hierarchically into two layers. The first layer consists of an abstraction - there are only two blocks representing factories and warehouses and a single transportation link between them. The second level contains the representation of all the individual factories and warehouses of the real problem. If it is assumed that all factories can ship to all warehouses (or if infeasible links are given infinite costs in the data) there is no need to draw the second, more detailed, level of the problem. Each actual factory and warehouse will inherit the properties specified for the parent "factories" block; each actual warehouse will inherit the properties of the "Warehouses" block and the system will implicitly assume a completely connected graph. If these conditions are not true, the connected graph is automatically generated and the user can delete edges that do not apply. Alternatively, if the second level graph is complex, as will be the case in many real world applications, the user can specify an external table that specifies the arcs.

The first step is to define the highest level of blocks (for Factories and Warehouses) using the *CREATE-BLOCKS (C-B)* command and to link them using the *LINK-BLOCKS (L-B)* command. Figure 3-1 shows the screen at the end of this step.

Next, the user specifies the production activities in the Factories blocks using the *DEF-ACTIVITIES (D-A)* command. The screen in Figure 3-2 is obtained by pointing to the D-A command on the right of the screen and then to the Factories block. D-A is modeled after the activity modeling approach in Dantzig [1963], in which an activity set is defined by its inputs, outputs, activity coefficients, and objective coefficients (profits or costs). After the detailed specification of the activity has been completed, the network representation is restored, but the specified block is highlighted to indicate that it is not a simple demand, supply or transshipment point.

In the next step, the user specifies the members of the sets represented by Factories, Warehouses, Widgets and Rawmats using the *SET* command. The members of the set can be entered interactively (e.g. "W1, W2, W3."), or by a relational database query (e.g. "SELECT Warehouse_name FROM Warehouse WHERE Region = USA."). Here, Warehouses is an external relational database table containing Warehouse_name and Region fields (amongst others).

The final step in defining the problem is to specify the direction of optimization using the *OPT* command in the lower right corner of the screen. After this interaction, the user saves the problem (using the SAVE command in the top of the screen) and then selects the SOLVE command to generate the LPSPEC statements.

```
 ___________________________________________
| ACTIVITY SET: widgets___                  |
| ACTIVITY VAR: x___                        |
| INPUTS:                                   |
| raw_mats  ______                          |
| OUTPUTS:                                  |
| widgets ______________                    |
| OBJ. COEFFT : cst______                   |
| OBJ. TYPE   : cost______________          |
| ACT. COEFFTS: a__________                 |
| UPPER BOUNDS: #________________           |
| LOWER BOUNDS: #________________           |
| UNITS       : #________________           |
| MATH PROP   : linear____________          |
| ACT. TYPE   : product_mix_______          |
|                                           |
|___________________________________________|
```

Figure 3-2: Define Production Activity

Each of the commands in the graphic interface has a corresponding LPSPEC statement that captures the information provided by the user. The LPSPEC statements from the above interaction are listed in Figure 3-3 in the order in which they were generated by the user. The LPSPEC command processor can check for missing or ambiguous information and request clarification from the user.

After compilation of the LPSPEC statements, the inferencing rules are invoked and the algebraic terms of the model are created and assembled into their proper positions in the algebraic statement by the LPFORM Analyser System. Finally, the model is cross-referenced to its data and to entries in the data dictionary.

The internal tableau representation (Figure 3-4) and model data dictionary (Figure 3-5) are the final result of the reasoning process in LPFORM.

The internal tableau can be used to check the formulation. It has been designed to display simultaneously both the algebraic and the tableau (block) structure of an LP problem. If the problem is large, the display is spread across several screens.

In Figure 3-4, there are columns for each decision variable and rows for the objective and each constraint. The columns and rows are labeled by the decision variables and RHS constants together with their indices. Summations are identified by an 'S' followed by the list of indices over which the summation is to be performed enclosed by braces. Note that the balance equation for widgets has been correctly generated by the system.

```
>>>>>> Compiling LPSPEC File: mkship.fst <<<<<<

Statement No: 1
create_block(make_and_ship,[factories,warehouses])

Statement No: 2
link_block(space,explicit,[factories,warehouses],t)

Statement No: 3
def_transport(widgets,[factories,warehouses],1,#)

Statement No: 4
def_activity(factories,[widgets],x,[rawmats],[a],[widgets],cst,
cost,#,#,#,linear,product_mix)

Statement No: 5
def_set(factories,[north,south,west])

Statement No: 6
def_set(warehouses,[nwh,swh,wwh])

Statement No: 7
def_set(widgets,[w1,w2,w3])

Statement No: 8
def_set(rawmats,[r1,r2,r3])

Statement No: 9
optimize(min,make_and_ship,cost,symbolic)
```

Figure 3-3: LPSPEC for First Principles Approach

```
PROBLEM/MODEL/FRAGMENT = make_and_ship.

ROW\COL        X(f,i)              T(f,w,i)               RHS
OBJ=           +S{f;i}cst[f;i]     +S{f;w;i}tr[f;w;i]     MIN
Use[f;r]       +S{i}a[f;r;i]                              < +b[f;r]
Use[f;i]       +1[f;i]             -S{w}1[f;w;i]          > +0[f;i]
Supply[w;i]                        +S{f}1[f;w;i]          > +d[w;i]
```

Figure 3-4: Internal Tableau for Make-and-ship Model

The data dictionary for the Make-and-ship model is shown in Figure 3-5. The symbols on the left appear in the algebraic statement. The roles of some of the constraints have been inferred by the system. For example, LPFORM has recognized Factories as a "From-Block" and d as the right-hand-side of a "demand" constraint.

This is the basic representation from which problem statements for different matrix generators can be constructed in a straight-forward fashion. Note, however, that the problem representation above is purely symbolic and contains no information on data values. This information must be included in the

```
* Symbol convention of make_and_ship *

Set Reference:
SYMBOL:      SET NAME:
-----------------------------------------------------------------
f          : Factories
             Meaning: block, from_block.
r          : Rawmats
             Meaning: input.
w          : Warehouses
             Meaning: to_block.
i          : Widgets
             Meaning: output, commodity.

Activity Reference:
SYMBOL:      ACTIVITY (VARIABLE):
-----------------------------------------------------------------
X(f,i)     : X(Factories,Widgets)
T(f,w,i)   : T(Factories,Warehouses,Widgets)

Coefficient Reference:
SYMBOL:      COEFFICIENT (DATA):
-----------------------------------------------------------------
cst[f;i]   : Cst[Factories,Widgets]
a[f;r;i]   : A[Factories,Rawmats,Widgets]
1[f;w;i]   : 1[Factories,Warehouses,Widgets]
1[f;i]     : 1[Factories,Widgets]
O[f;i]     : O[Factories,Widgets]
b[f;r]     : Rhs?*^factories^rawmats[Factories,Rawmats]
d[w;i]     : Rhs?*^demand^warehouses^widgets[Warehouses,Widgets]
tr[f;w;i]  : Obj?*^factories^warehouses^widgets[Factories,
             Warehouses,Widgets]
```

Figure 3-5: Data Dictionary for Make and Ship Model

problem statements sent to the matrix generator. Basically, any data values input interactively by the user, for example, the elements of the sets in the above example, or the retrieval and data manipulation commands input by the user or inferred by the system, are output verbatim to the next phase of the model generation process. More details are given in Ma et al [1987].

3.2. Model Mapping Approach

A major goal of LPFORM is to allow model elements developed in one project to be reused in others. This facilitates a bottom-up approach to model building in which submodels are tested and then combined into larger models. LPFORM, contains a number of standard templates (for Transportation, Blending, Product-mix, Process-selection, etc.). Alternatively, users can build their own models using the first principles approach and store them in the model bank for later use.

Referring to Figure 3-1, it is intuitively obvious that the Make-and-ship model consists of a product-mix problem and a transportation problem. This approach is implemented in LPFORM using the *CALL-MODEL* (C-M) command. Figure 3-6 shows the formulation of the same problem using the model mapping approach.

```
>>>>>> Compiling LPSPEC File: mkship.map <<<<<<

Statement No: 1
create_block(make_ship,[factories,warehouses])

Statement No: 2
def_set(factories,[north,south,west])

Statement No: 3
def_set(warehouses,[nwh,swh,wwh])

Statement No: 4
def_set(widgets,[w1,w2,w3])

Statement No: 5
def_set(rawmats,[r1,r2,r3])

Statement No: 6
call_model(transportation,make_ship,
     [from_block,to_block,commodity],[factories,warehouses,widgets]
     [flow],[t],
     [gain_or_loss],[1])

Statement No: 7
call_model(product_mix,make_ship,
     [block,input,output],[factories,rawmats,widgets],
     [volume],[x],
     [tech_coef,available_input],[a,b])

Statement No: 8
optimize(min,make_ship,cost,symbolic)
```

Figure 3-6: LPSPEC Statements for Model-Mapping Approach

The C-M command "maps" the names of indices, variables and data coefficients in the stored template into those that will be used in the new model. Thus, in this example, "from-block", "to-block", and "commodity" become, respectively, "factories", "warehouses" and "widgets". The standard templates are defined to be as general as possible. If the new model has no need for some of the indices in the stored template, they can be dropped. Conversely, the user can add indices to a model by using the Replicate command (see Ma et al [1987]).

4. Inference Process for Generating LP Models

This section of the paper explains how statements such as those shown in Figures 3-3 and 3-6 are converted into an algebraic problem statement. To ensure a robust and widely applicable approach, LPFORM focuses on properties that are valid across all LP's and brings in more subject-specific information only as needed. The properties of LPs can be divided into syntactic, semantic and domain-specific categories. Syntactic information consists of symbols and the rules that combine the symbols into a model. Semantic information incorporates knowledge about the physical entities being represented. In order to provide the maximum generality, we concentrate on the physical principles that underlie all linear programs. These include the properties of resources, commodities and networks, and ideas from the field of dimensional analysis (Kurth [1972]). Domain-specific information provides individual instances of the general concepts and information on special requirements associated with these instances. For example, in a job shop application, a lathe belongs to the class "machines", which is a subclass of "resources" at the most general level. Associated with the class of machines may be policies and constraints that can be automatically incorporated in the model by the system. Thus, domain-specific knowledge enhances the power of the system in aiding the formulation process. Our research to date concentrates on syntactic and semantic information, developing general principles applicable to all model building areas. The use of domain related knowledge in formulating LPs is described in Binbasioglu and Jarke [1986].

4.1. The Reasoning Process

The reasoning process has the following steps:

1. The user specifies the problem using the graphic interface; LPSPEC statements are generated.

2. The LPFORM Analyser parses the internal representation and performs some consistency checks.

3. The network structure of the problem is analysed; if the problem is a pure network, the appropriate model template is invoked.

4. If there are non-network components (e.g. production activities associated with one or more blocks), the appropriate constraint fragments and templates are invoked to generate the "model pieces".

5. The model pieces are assembled into their positions in the algebraic representation; consistency checks are performed, redundant pieces are discarded and missing pieces are added.

6. The internal representation of the algebraic statement and the model data dictionary are generated.

7. The data coefficients in the problem statement are associated with values stored in external tables and relational databases.

8. The input to the tableau generator is generated.

9. The output of the tableau generator is fed to the solver and the problem is solved.

10. A report-writer and analysis system is invoked to process the results of the LP run.

4.2. Generation of the Model Components

Section 3 described the various modes of input available to the user. Much of the expertese embodied in the system consists of rules for translating from inputs given in these different forms into the algebraic components of the model. The basic components in the internal representation of LP constraints are "model pieces" which are algebraic terms with their associated summations. Larger model components such as constraints, subproblems and complete LP problems are simply collections of model pieces. This approach allows great flexibility in generating LPs and in combining templates of previously stored models into larger models.

The various objects in the user specification each generate one or more model pieces from more fundamental templates stored in the system's model base. Thus, an inventory icon results in a set of pieces embodying the standard inventory relationships, while a link between blocks contributes pieces corresponding to a transportation problem and so on. The model pieces comprising the standard component types are stored in a general form so that they can be tailored to fit the particular problem; thus, indices can be added or dropped as needed.

For example, in the graphical representation in Figure 3-1, "Warehouses" is an "exogenous demand" block (a block that has inputs but no outputs or internal activities). In the first principles approach, the following constraint fragment is automatically generated: $\geq d_{w,i}$. This consists of one "piece" (the inequality and the coefficient). Similarly, the Def-activity command in Figure 3-3 will generate a constraint fragment with two pieces:

$$\sum_{j \in Widgets} a_{i,j,f} X_{j,f} \leq b_{i,f}, \qquad \forall i \in RawMats, f \in Factories$$

A major area for research involves the discovery of appropriate standard components and the rules by which they can be generated from the user's input and synthesized into the complete LP.

4.3. Problem Synthesis Using Syntactic Information

We are developing rules for combining model pieces into a complete LP using syntactic information consisting primarily of index and variable names Murphy et al [1987]). This is analogous to solving a jigsaw puzzle, and we call the mechanism in Step 5 above, the "Puzzler".

We define an index set to be a collection of symbols denoting the indices (subscripts) associated with a variable or data coefficient. Each individual index identifies a 'dimension' of the data or variable and takes on values within some well-defined domain. For a given constraint and variable with coefficients in that constraint, let:

$V = \{\text{indices on the variable}\}$
$C = \{\text{indices on the coefficient of the variable}\}$
$S = \{\text{indices that are summed over their whole domain}\}$
$P = \{\text{indices that are summed over a subset of their domain}\}$
$Q = \{\text{indices of subsets over which partial sums are taken}\}$
$R = \{\text{indices that identify the individual constraints}\}$

To illustrate these definitions, consider the following example:

$$\sum_{i} \sum_{j \in J(i)} a_{i,j,k} X_{i,j,k} \leq b_k, \quad \forall k$$

then V = {i,j,k}, C = {i,j,k}, S = {i}, P = {j}, Q = {i}, R = {k}.

In a properly specified LP where all indices are explicit:

(1) $\quad R = (V \cup C \cup Q) - (S \cup P).$

This relationship helps LPFORM: (1) infer the complete problem from its component parts, (2) adjust the model when a part of the model is replicated in some dimension such as place or time, and (3) check the correctness of the final formulation.

Each model piece has row and column "labels". The row label for a piece includes its row index set (computed from the right-hand side of (1)) plus semantic information on the meaning of the indices and the physical units associated with the activity. The column label for a left-hand side piece consists of the variable name, the variable index set, V, and semantic information as for the row label. The output from Steps 3 and 4, above, is a set of model pieces. In Step 5 the Puzzler searches through these pieces to determine the unique row and column labels. This establishes the overall dimensions of the tableau. Next, the pieces are assigned to the tableau based on their row and column labels. Redundant pieces are discarded and, where possible, missing pieces are automatically generated as described below. Finally, the Puzzler performs some consistency checks - for example, the body of the tableau must have at least one piece assigned to every row and column. The Puzzler can also warn the user if the model contains disjoint subproblems.

To illustrate the process for the Make-and-ship problem, consider the tableau representation in Figure 4-1.

Row Label:	Column Label: [X,j,f]	[T,f,m]	RHS
OBJ:	$\sum_j \sum_f c_{j,f} X_{j,f}$ +	$\sum_j \sum_f \sum_m w_{j,f,m} T_{j,f,m}$	
[i,f]	$\sum_j a_{i,j,f} X_{j,f}$		$\leq b_{i,f}$
[j,f]	$-X_{j,f}$ +	$\sum_m T_{j,f,m}$	$= 0$
[j,m]		$\sum_f T_{j,f,m}$	$\geq d_{j,m}$

Figure 4-1: Illustration of Jigsaw Puzzle Reasoning

The first constraint is generated by the product-mix sub-problem and the third by the transportation sub-problem. In the second constraint, which represents the balance equation for widgets, the second term comes from the Transportation sub-problem. The first term in this constraint is supplied automatically by LPFORM. The rule used to do this is to search for matching column and row index sets and to supply a diagonal sub-matrix if no term is present in the corresponding position in the tableau. In this case, -1's are placed in the tableau.

The success of this process depends on the ability to distinguish all the rows and columns of the tableau. The column and row labels contain information in addition to the index sets because the latter do not necessarily contain enough information to ensure uniqueness. Some initial theoretical results concerning what can and cannot be done with index information are given in Murphy et al [1987].

5. Knowledge Representation

Knowledge representation affects both efficiency and functionality. Functionally, the system should: (1) provide a source of knowledge about the models in the model base and their structure. (2) provide guidance to users in the selection and composition of components of larger models, (3) facilitate the acquisition of domain specific knowledge as outlined below.

The basic entities of linear programs (activities, constraints, resources, commodities) and other organizational entities (blocks, links, and submodels) are represented by a network of frames. A frame is a stereotyped representation of some situation which is adjusted to a current situation by changing certain details (Winston [1984]). As a data structure, a frame consists of "slots" containing the descriptive attributes of the object, default values and or procedures that should be invoked if needed, and relationships to other objects. Thus, a frame for a complete LP contains slots with information on the objective, activities and constraints (a product-mix model, has slots noting that the objective is to maximize profit, the activities are production levels of different products, and the constraints are resource limits). In our context, another slot points to the model pieces associated with the template.

As discussed above, part of the knowledge contained in LPFORM is in the form of rules to generate the model pieces and to combine them into a problem statement. Other types of knowledge can be used, not only to help translate from the user input to the final algebraic statement, but also to provide more intelligent support to the model builder. Three important sources of knowledge are the types of physical transformation associated with activities, template models and domain-specific information.

Knowledge Concerning Transformations

Linear programming models involve three basic transformations: transformations in place, in time and in form. A transformation in form converts input "whats" into output "whats" while leaving place and time identical. Place and time transformations make analogous adjustments to "where" and "when". As shown in Figure 5-1, a transformation in form has indices corresponding to inputs and outputs, indices for "where" and "when" and an added index for "how" if there are alternative approaches. Transformations in place are distinguished by having indices on "what", "when" and "how", plus "from where" and "to where". Transformations in time have indices on "what", "where" and "how" and "from when" and "to when". In many cases, these indices are implicit rather than explicit - for example, production activities are usually indexed by their associated outputs i.e. only on the "to what" dimension. Compound transformations involving more than one of the fundamental transformations are possible.

The data structure used to represent the index set for each variable and coefficient has slots for each of the roles in Figure 5-1. Information on the meaning of indices allows LPFORM to improve on the syntactic rules for composing LPs and to detect missing model pieces in some circumstances.

Knowledge in Templates

Each template has an associated frame with slots recording its usage in dif-

PLACE	FORM	TIME
From where To where	Where	Where
What	From what To what	What
When	When	From when To when
How	How	How

Figure 5-1: Index Roles in Transformations

ferent models and pointing to its component model pieces. As discussed above, users can add to the model base at any time. A query facility allows users to browse through the the model base. It is possible, for example, to retrieve all models using a given resource or all with a common activity. A procedure to generate a precedence map of all models having common inputs and outputs, is being implemented. We are currently studying the appropriate set of standard templates to be included in the model base.

Domain-Specific Knowledge

Domain-specific knowledge can be used to make the system more powerful in particular applications. First, the data dictionary of general concepts (activities, resources, etc.) can be extended to include more terms thereby allowing users to state their problems in more familiar language. Thus, labor can be related to the general concept of resource by an "is-a" relationship and specific classes of labor to the more generic category, labor, and so on.

Second, the different classes of entitities can be associated with information that either must, or might, be applicable to particular models. Thus, with labor, any union restrictions must be embodied in constraints in the model, while various optional work force smoothing relationships might be incorporated at the user's discretion. This will allow the system to operate as an expert assistant suggesting possibilities for consideration by the modeler.

Finally, local terms can be related to an organization's data base. For example, each category of labor could be linked to tables containing current wage rates, standard piece rates and so on. This would allow the system to automatically generate database retrieval statements to link the symbolic statement of the problem to current data values.

6. Conclusion

Our strategy has been to develop a general approach to model formulation that is applicable to all LPs. We have done this by concentrating on syntactic and semantic properties. More powerful systems, suitable for non-expert users as well as expert users, will probably require the acquisition and use of domain-specific knowledge.

The prototype system is now operational and is able to solve a range of problems. There are a number of interesting questions concerning the approach that can only be resolved through usage. The most important of these is whether the approach outlined in this paper will, in fact, improve productivity and lead to higher quality models. Other questions concern the effectiveness of the graphic interface in reducing the cognitive load on the modeler and improving the quality of the models produced.

In the near future, we intend to test the LPFORM system and to improve its capability in the linear programming domain. After that, we will investigate the possibility of applying a similar approach to other modeling situations.

References

1. O. Balci (1985), "Requirements for Model Development Environments," Technical Report CS83022-R, Department of Computer Science, VPI&SU, Blacksburg, VA.

2. M. Binbasioglu (1986), "Knowledge Based Modelling and Support for Linear Programming," Ph. D. Dissertation, New York University.

3. M. Binbasioglu and M. Jarke (1986), "Domain-Specific DSS Tools for Knowledge-based Model Building," *Decision Support Systems*, vol 2, June-July.

4. J. Bisschop and A. Meeraus (1982), "On the Development of a General Algebraic Modeling System in a Strategic Planning Environment," *Math. Prog. Study 20*, 1-29.

5. R. L. Breitman and J. M. Lucas (1987), "PLANET: A Modeling System for Business Planning", *Interfaces*, Vol 17, No 1, Jan-Feb, 1987.

6. G. B. Dantzig (1963), *Linear Programming and Extensions*, Princeton University Press, Princeton, NJ.

7. D. Dolk (1987), "Model Management Systems: A Perspective," presented at NATO/ASI Conference "Mathematical Models for Decision Support", Val D'Isere, France.

8. EVA UIMS/GDB (1987), User Manual, Expert Vision Associates, Cupertino, California.

9. R. Fourer, D. M. Gay and B. W. Kernighan (1987), "AMPL: A Mathematical Programming Language," AT&T Bell Laboratories, Murray Hill, N.J.

10. A. M. Geoffrion (1987), "An Introduction to Structured Modeling," *Management Science*, vol 33, no. 5, pp. 547-588.

11. H. J. Greenberg (1983), "A Functional Description of ANALYZE: A Computer-Assisted Analysis System for Linear Programming Models." *ACM TOMS 9*, 18-56.

12. IBM Mathematical Programming Extended/370(MPSX/370). Program Reference Manual, SH19-1095. IBM Corporation, Paris France, 1975.

13. E. Johnson (1987), "Directions for Mathematical Programming Software and Integer Programming Reformulations," presented at NATO/ASI Conference "Mathematical Models for Decision Support", Val D'Isere, France.

14. R. Kurth (1972), *Dimensional Analysis and Group Theory in Astrophysics*, Pergamon.

15. M. Lenard (1986), "Representing Models as Data," *Journal of Management Information Systems*, vol 2, no 4 pp. 36-48.

16. P. Ma (1987), "An Intelligent Approach to Formulating Linear Programs", Ph.D. Dissertation, New York University.

17. P. Ma, F. H. Murphy and E. A. Stohr (1986), "The Science and Art of Formulating Linear Programs," *IMA Journal of Mathematics in Management*, (to appear).

18. P. Ma, F. H. Murphy and E. A. Stohr (1987), "Design of a Graphics Interface for Linear Programming Models," Working Paper, Center for Research in Information Systems, Graduate School of Business Administration, New York University.

19. F. H. Murphy and E. A. Stohr (1986), "An Intelligent System for Formulating Linear Programs," *Decision Support Systems*, Vol 2, No 1, Jan-Feb, 1986.

20. F. H. Murphy, E. A. Stohr and P. Ma (1987), "Composition Rules for Building Linear Programming Models from Component Models,"

Working Paper, Center for Research in Information Systems, Graduate School of Business Administration, New York University.

21. R. E. Nance and O. Balci (1983), "The Objectives and Requirements of Model Management," Technical Report CS83024-R, VPI&SU, Blacksburg, VA.

22. L. Schrage (1987), *Linear, Integer and Quadratic Programming with LINDO*, Scientific Press, Palo Alto.

23. E. A. Stohr (1985), "A Mathematical Programming Generator System" Working Paper, Center for Research in Information Systems, Graduate School of Business Administration, New York University.

24. J. S. Welch (1987), "PAM-A Practitioner's Approach to Modeling," *Management Science*, vol 33, no 5 pp 610-625.

25. P. H. Winston (1984), *Artificial Intelligence*, Addison-Wesley, Boston, MA.

THE ENVIRONMENT APPROACH TO DECISION SUPPORT

Clyde W. Holsapple and Andrew B. Whinston
Management Information Research Center
Krannert Graduate School of Management
Purdue University
West Lafayette, IN 47907

INTRODUCTION

Decision support depends on the effective management of several types of knowledge [2]. Beyond the descriptive knowledge (i.e., data, information) with which management information systems are concerned, decision support systems are also able to manage procedural knowledge. A procedure, also called a model, specifies an algorithm that tells how to derive new knowledge in the sense of facts, expectations, or beliefs. Thus a decision support system (DSS) normally has a knowledge system capable of holding both data and models. The DSS's software is a problem processing system that can manipulate the knowledge system contents in response to user requests. These requests must be valid statements in the DSS's language system which defines the syntax, grammar, and semantics of a language that the problem processor can understand. The generic DSS structure is illustrated in Figure 1.

If a DSS has a customizable interface, its knowledge system also holds linguistic knowledge (e.g., a vocabulary, macros, other language system specifications) and/or presentation knowledge (e.g., forms, menus, templates). Because the problem processor uses these two kinds of knowledge in interacting with a user, they are sometimes collectively called "dialogue" knowledge. In recent years, reasoning knowledge has increasingly come to be regarded as an important candidate for inclusion in a DSS's knowledge system [2,6]. This is knowledge that specifies what conclusions are valid when certain situations exist. As such it can serve as a kind of meta knowledge, specifying what the problem processor can reasonably do with other knowledge system contents in light of current circumstances. For instance, reasoning knowledge can give the problem processor domain-specific intelligence that allows it to know when to invoke a model, what data are to be analyzed by the model, what presentation mode is appropriate for displaying the results, and so forth.

NATO ASI Series, Vol. F48
Mathematical Models for Decision Support
Edited by G. Mitra

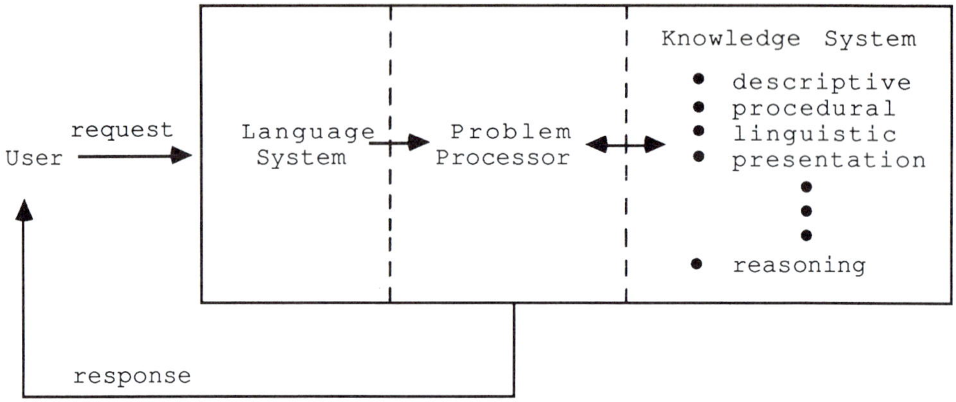

Figure 1. Generic DSS

We are today faced with numerous software tools that can aid in the construction of a DSS. However, it is generally true that none is adept at dealing with all kinds of knowledge pertinent to decision support. Each typically embodies one main technique of knowledge management (e.g., data base management, spreadsheet analysis, programming, rule management). But no single technique is adequate for handling a DSS's diverse knowledge representation and processing needs. Traditional software tools have not been designed to serve as the generalized problem processor [2] with diverse knowledge management capabilities. In fact, some DSS research takes a reductionist view of decision support software, referring to separate components such as a data manager, a dialogue manager, and a model manager.

In contrast, we adhere to the view of a generalized problem processor as a _single_ piece of software, possessing the knowledge management capabilities traditionally found in separate software tools. Here, we further formalize the notion of generalized problem processors by treating them as environments for knowledge management. First, there is a brief discussion of knowledge worker productivity as the motivation for research into the notion of a knowledge management environment (KME). Both users and builders of decision support systems are knowledge workers. We then examine the landscape of a KME, pointing out its parallels with a physical environment. This is followed by a description of the levels at which different kinds of users (system developers, application developers, and end users) would interact with a KME. It is clear that the environment notion as outlined here suggests a large area of research that has yet to be explored. We close by identifying several relevant research topics that deserve investigation.

KNOWLEDGE WORKER PRODUCTIVITY

While computers are important problem solving aids in areas such as engineering, education, and science, their widest impact and usage is in the business world. This includes the administration of both private (e.g., corporate) and public (i.e., government) organizations. Since the advent of computer usage, a major issue has been the productivity of persons who use computers. There has been significant progress in the direction of increasing the productivity of both computer professionals and do-it-yourself computer users. The primary impetus for this progress has been rooted in the ongoing evolution of software toward greater convenience, power, and flexibility.

Each species of software tool has progressed incrementally in response to user needs. Successive generations inherit the proven traits of their forebearers, while adapting to sensed needs by offering new traits. The progression of tools within a species can be seen as an unfolding of the potential of particular knowledge management techniques. For instance, spreadsheet analysis is a computer-based technique for managing (i.e., representing and processing) knowledge. The potential of this technique has continued to unfold from its first emergence in the late seventies through the VisiCalc and 1-2-3 eras. Other techniques such as programming, data management, and text management have undergone their own unfoldments.

But each technique or software species has tended to evolve in its own world with little regard for the others. The present state of, say, relational data management owes little to, say, text management and vice versa. Could the future evolution of either benefit from the other? This, we believe, is a question that is both interesting and important with respect to all pairs of knowledge management techniques currently used for business computing. It is also germane for relatively new techniques such as rule management and demon management, which have yet to be widely employed for business computing.

Going a step further, to what extent can many traditionally separate techniques be used in group formation? While each technique retains its identity, there is the larger and more potent identity of the group as a whole. It is able to accomplish far more than any one or collection of the individual techniques that participate in it, provided the techniques are blended into a coordinated and harmonious team. The development of such a group tool depends on avoiding a separative, strictly compartmentalized perspective with respect to knowledge management techniques. Rather than a software zoo of separately caged tools, we are interested in a natural environment that serves as a single tool. On entering this environment, a user is able to interact with it to exercise any of its innate techniques individually or in tandem for decision support purposes.

Continuing improvements in existing knowledge management techniques and the invention of new techniques will help the cause of increasing user productivity. But we believe the greatest increase will come from the fusion of these techniques into a single tool that serves as a rich environment for managing diverse kinds of knowledge. A couple of analogies are suggestive of the potential value. First, consider a collection of individually talented persons each with skills in a different area versus the effects that can be achieved when these persons can function effectively as a group. Second, consider a person whose skills can only be individually exercised (e.g., in sequence or even in parallel) versus the effects that can be achieved when those skills can be freely fused at will. In each analogy, the second alternative is clearly superior and corresponds to the environment notion that we propose to investigate.

In simplest terms, knowledge management is an essential activity of workers in modern organizations, business computing is concerned with various useful techniques for managing knowledge, no single technique is best (or even applicable) to all problems faced by a worker, and there is a need for increased knowledge worker productivity. An important research direction aims to help meet this need by exploring, formulating, and analyzing an environment approach to business computing. Such an approach will generally reflect the nature of business organizations, exhibit much of the flexibility inherent in a person's mental knowledge management facility, avoid relying on such crudities as switching among separate software tools and "integrate" them via cut-paste or extraction file mechanisms, accommodate a wide (possibly growing) assortment of techniques in such a way that none dominates or constrains the others, and eliminate conventional barriers among these techniques.

In short, we intend to take a fresh theoretical look at business computing by constructing a unified framework that embraces the major techniques used for business computing and allows for intimate interplay among them. The framework will not only serve as a blueprint for implementing knowledge management environments (i.e., generalized problem processors). It will also serve as a conceptual basis for the comparative study of seemingly diverse techniques, for identifying directions in which they may evolve, for stimulating and facilitating the invention of new techniques, for understanding how techniques can be fused or blended, and for furthering research concerned with the infrastructure of knowledge-based organizations [8].

Conceivably, different kinds of users could enter the knowledge management environment (KME) and use its language. It could be used by a tool builder to devise a new knowledge management tool (e.g., a KME for business computing rather than engineering). It could be used by an application developer to devise an application system (e.g., for accounting, marketing, strategic planning). The products of either of these classes of computer professionals could be used by non-professionals, end users.

At its raw level, the KME is unconcerned with the representation and processing of data bases, spreadsheets, programs, and so forth. It is concerned with knowledge at a very elemental and largely unstructured level, yet has the facilities for augmenting itself by defining more complex kinds of knowledge. For instance, a KME for business computing would typically have facilities for managing the likes of data bases, spreadsheets, and programs in a highly integrated fashion. That is, the raw environment becomes furnished with various knowledge management techniques that are of relevance to its users.

Our strategy in developing the knowledge management environment is to build on the principle of software synergy [5] while incorporating ideas from the area of object-oriented languages. There is a growing body of work that is concerned with adapting object-oriented and functional programming notions to data base management [1,3]. This paper embodies a similar spirit, but is not restricted to the narrow domain of data base management. Furthermore, it is consistent with the structuring of roles in an organization [2].

A WALK THROUGH THE ENVIRONMENT

Our vision of a knowledge management environment uses the everyday notion of physical environments as a paradigm. Physical environments are designed to serve some purposes of persons who enter them. Physical environments may be relatively undeveloped and unfurnished. Alternatively, they may be highly developed, furnished to effectively meet specialized purposes. The person who enters a raw environment typically works at altering it to develop its potential along certain lines, so it can more readily serve some specialized purpose. The person who enters a more furnished environment typically expects to make immediate use of it, with little or no development work.

Concepts

Here, we are concerned with a conceptual environment rather than a physical environment. That is, it is populated by concepts rather than physical objects [2]. In keeping with the tradition of object-oriented languages, a concept could be regarded as a conceptual object. For instance, a KME may contain the concept of a customer (i.e., knowledge about a customer) but does not contain the customer itself, as a physical environment could. A KME can hold not only conceptual representations of physical objects, but of abstract objects as well. An account or a skill is an example of a concept that could be encountered in a KME, but which has no concrete counterpart. In summary, when a person enters a KME to become its user, he or she encounters a variety of concepts. The environment may be furnished with only a small number of generic or primitive concepts. Alternatively, it may have a wealth of ready-made concepts. For instance, a KME for business computing would already be furnished with such concepts as data base, spreadsheet, text, form, program, and so forth. An even more specialized KME might be one designed to serve the purposes of personnel managers. It would be furnished with more specialized concepts such as employee, department, job, skill, biography, budget, and so on.

Properties

Like a physical object, a concept normally has one or more properties. Properties are attributes that characterize a concept (qualitatively and/or quantitatively). Properties provide the basis for differentiating, comparing, contrasting, identifying, and understanding concepts. Of course a property may itself be viewed as a concept having properties of its own. For instance, SALARY might be a property of the EMPLOYEE concept. That is, an employee's salary is a way of characterizing that employee. However, SALARY itself can be treated as a concept having properties such as TYPE (e.g., fixed point number), SIZE (e.g., seven digits, two of which are decimal), PICTURE (e.g., leading dollar sign with comma insertion), DEFAULT (e.g., 0), and so forth.

Messages and Methods

In a physical environment, one object can act upon other objects, causing them to behave in certain ways. Of course, the kinds of actions that can be taken on a particular object depend on the intrinsic nature of that object. An action that is commonplace with respect to one object may well be infeasible for another object. The person who enters the physical environment can also take actions with respect to the environment's objects. In some cases, those objects may even be able to act upon the person. In effect, upon entering an environment, the person (with all of his or her properties) becomes an active object in that world.

By analogy, a KME concept can act upon other concepts. One concept acts on another by sending a message. The message identifies what behavior is desired on the part of the receiving concept. This suggests that a concept can have a repertoire of behaviors. In effect, a message selects one of the receiving concept's possible behaviors and causes the actions inherent in that behavior to manifest. In keeping with object-oriented terminology, the possible behaviors of a concept are called methods.

As an example, an EMPLOYEE table and a BUDGET spreadsheet may be two concepts in the environment. Suppose the spreadsheet is in the midst of reevaluating its cell values in response to a message it has received. In so doing, it may send a message to EMPLOYEE requesting that the table calculate the salary average. When the table responds with the average, the spreadsheet resumes its method making use of the average in determining cell values. This, by the way, is an illustration of what was meant by the previously noted idea of knowledge fusion. Conversely, a table could send a message to a spreadsheet. In either event, two traditionally separate techniques of managing knowledge are fused in such a way that each can contribute to the processing of the other. The message passing mechanism allows multiple techniques to work as a group without user intervention, switching, cut-paste, etc.

Again by analogy, it should be clear that once a user enters a KME he or she becomes a concept in the environment. Like other concepts, the user has certain properties (e.g., name, security clearance), can send messages to other concepts, can receive messages from other concepts, and has methods for carrying out various behaviors on request. For example, it might have been the user who sent a message to BUDGET, requesting a reevaluation of cell values. Conversely, BUDGET may send a message to the user (as well as to EMPLOYEE) in the course of the reevaluation method. This could be a request for some subjective assessment of partial reevaluation results. The user employs a method (e.g., a mental method) to generate the assessment and responds so it can be factored into the remainder of the reevaluation.

Classes Versus Entities

In a KME we distinguish between two kinds of concepts: classes and entities. When entering a physical environment, the principle of classification is extremely helpful in getting one's bearings. Even though classification is a simple notion and perhaps taken for granted, it is nevertheless an important key to understanding the environment. For instance, it is useful to know the difference between animate and inanimate objects. The class of animate objects could be better understood by realizing that it has subclasses such as animal and person. Further, customer and employee are subclasses of the person class. The ability to assess what class a particular object belongs to generally helps one understand what kinds of actions can reasonably be taken on that object.

Similarly, in a KME a class is a structural, organizing concept. Its properties have no values. A class can have members, each of which inherits the class' properties and methods. These members are instances of the class. Their common characteristics are defined by the class to which they belong. It is possible for a concept to be the member of multiple classes, inheriting the properties and methods of each. Each member can have properties and methods in addition to those inherited.

In contrast, an entity is a concept having values for its properties and having no members. It does not define the characteristics of any other concept. As an example, consider the concept of a relational data table. A table has certain properties (e.g., its name, creation date, security codes) and methods (e.g., the algebraic select and project operations). The table concept is a class whose members are specific tables such as those for employee data, department data, skill data, and so on. Each of these specific tables is itself a concept that inherits the properties and methods of the table class. Each is an example of an entity. For instance, the employee table has values (e.g., EMPLOYEE, 5/14/87, abc) for each of its properties and there is no notion of instances of the employee table concept.

For purposes of this discussion, we define an end user as a user who is able to work on (e.g., create, alter, delete) entities, but not classes. The end user may be aware of classes and their associations, but cannot work on them. For an end user, these are givens. From an end user's perspective, all classes are prefabricated. In contrast, we define a developer as one who is involved with defining classes and their associations. From a developer's viewpoint, the environment may include some prefabricated classes.

Definitional Relationships

The relationship between a class and its members is definitional [2] and is often referred to as an "isa" relationship in the literature of semantic nets and object-oriented languages [11]. The members of a class need not be entities, but may themselves be classes with their own members. As a result, we can consider an environment's concepts to be organized into a lattice structure by way of their definitional, "isa" relationships. Visually, this would be a directed acyclic graph whose nodes are concepts and whose arcs denote class membership. Thus a class structure organizes entities into groups based on common properties. The entities in a class can be ordered (e.g., lifo, fifo, sorted by a property value) and normally differ in terms of their values for the common properties. For efficiency we adopt the convention that an entity may not be the member of multiple classes [1].

Associative Relationships

By themselves, definitional relationships are normally quite inadequate for representing the relationships that can exist among concepts. Concepts can also be related in an associative manner [2]. Just as objects in a physical environment can be associated with each other in various ways, associative relationships can exist among concepts belonging to different classes (or even the same class). In an association, at least one concept serves as the agent and at least one concept serves as the object of the relationship. For instance, DEPARTMENT CONTAINS EMPLOYEE, JOB FILLEDBY EMPLOYEE, JOB NEEDS SKILL, and EMPLOYEE POSSESSES SKILL are four associations. The DEPARTMENT concept is the agent of the CONTAINS relationship and EMPLOYEE is its object. EMPLOYEE is also the object of FILLEDBY, but is the agent of POSSESSES. JOB is the agent in both the FILLEDBY and NEEDS associations. The SKILL concept happens to be the object of both NEEDS and POSSESSES.

An association between classes can be either one-to-one, one-to-many (e.g., CONTAINS, FILLEDBY), or many-to-many (e.g., NEEDS, POSSESSES) with respect to the classes' members. That is, associations are inherited. Just as an ordering may be specified for entities that are members of the same class, so too may agent and object orderings be specified for an association. Associations lead to the notion of entity composites. A composite is a collection of associated entities from one or more classes.

Presentation Modes

A person in a physical environment is able to look at an object from different angles or perspectives. Similarly, it should be possible to view a KME's entities in various ways. For instance, a program might be viewed textually, as a flowchart, a module interconnection diagram, etc. [9]. This suggests that there may be multiple presentation modes affiliated with a class and that they are inherited by the class members. A presentation mode can be conceived as being a method that causes an image to be displayed on an I/O device. Because the user may want to send messages to (i.e., manipulate) the image, the image itself may be considered to be a concept having properties and methods of its own.

Actual Versus Virtual Entities

Departing momentarily from the physical paradigm (unless one admits the reality of apparitions), we make a distinction between actual entities and virtual entities. An actual entity is one whose property values exist somewhere in the environment's knowledge system. In contrast, a virtual entity is one whose property values do not actually exist. The values can nevertheless be conjured up on demand as if they actually do exist. However, the values of a virtual entity are not subject to change. As an example, regression is a concept whose properties might be characterized as independent coefficients, dependent coefficients, predictors, and correlation coefficients. Conceivably, the regression class can have an infinite number of members (i.e., entities whose values define particular regressions).

Just as a concept (e.g., end user) should be able to examine an employee entity by supplying its ID number in a message, it should also be able to examine a regression entity by supplying its independent and dependent coefficients in a message. Classes with virtual entities give a practical means for effectively capturing large or infinite numbers of entities in a knowledge system. Like other classes they are still susceptible to inheritance and message passing, which can be significant for applications concerned with model management.

Laws of Nature

Returning to the physical environment, certain laws of nature will be operative. The interactions and behaviors of objects in the environment are inescapably subject to these laws. A law enforces the manifestation of some behavior within the environment in response to the occurrence of an event. For instance, when an attempt is made to move some object, that attempted action is subject to the laws that govern object movement. The result of the attempt may be a successful execution of the object's movement method, the rejection of that method (e.g., because of a law that prohibits movement to an occupied position), or side effects such as the movement of other objects (e.g., to allow the target object to be moved). Effects of a law may or may not be apparent or surprising to the object requesting the action.

In a KME, it may also be useful to permit laws governing the interplay of concepts. Some such laws are implicit in the definitional and associative relationships that exist among concepts, as well as in the properties and methods specified for the environment's concepts. But these may be insufficient. For example, when a message is sent to change the values of an entity, the environment should permit the changes only if they are correct and should perhaps see to it that additional changes are made to other objects. That is, it can be useful to identify constraints (i.e., laws) on the generic change method that differ with respect to different classes of concepts.

As a result, we propose that an environment should be vigilant. It should watch for the occurrences of events and ensure that appropriate processes are undertaken automatically when a particular event happens. There should be a mechanism that allows a developer to specify what process to carry out when a certain event happens. It is then up to the environment to enforce this law or constraint. Such event triggered processing suggests that a demon management facility should be inherent in the KME [4]. A demon (i.e., event triggered process) consists of a sequence of messages and perhaps some control logic. Unlike a method, a demon can spring into action without being explicitly requested in a message. If demons are bound to concepts, then they can be thought of as defining the concepts' self-activating behaviors as opposed to the requested behaviors embodied in methods.

Security

When a person enters a physical environment, various objects may be hidden or inaccessible. Others may be partially accessible. Another person entering the same environment may have different access privileges. The same situation can arise for users of a knowledge management environment. There should be a built-in mechanism that allows the developer to specify the extent of access for each concept. That is, a concept has security properties that characterize its accessibility to users. When a user sends a message, the environment checks to ensure that the receiving concept is authorized to carry out the requested method for that user.

Language Features

Message passing is accomplished via a language which forms the medium for communication among concepts in an environment. At its simplest, this is a command language that is understood by all concepts. Because a user functions as a concept, it is very important that the language be English-like (e.g., avoiding unnecessary formalisms and notation). The KME's language system is composed of all possible messages (i.e., commands). In understanding the language, a concept is able to send any message to any other concept subject to the methods that can be handled by the receiving concept and subject to the observance of access privileges. From a developer's point of view, the language should be expandable, allowing the introduction of new messages that correspond to newly developed methods. The language should also be customizable, even to the point of allowing end users to work with natural language or menu-oriented message sending.

From a developer's standpoint, what must a KME provide? Its language must allow the developer to examine existing classes, define new classes, specify class properties and methods, associate classes, create entities, and establish inter-entity associations. If the commands to accomplish such tasks are messages, then the environment must already contain at least one concept (i.e., class) to receive the messages. This pre-existing concept(s) must correspondingly have the methods to execute the commands. The further one proceeds from a raw KME, the more pre-existing concepts there will be.

USERS' ACTIVITIES

Figure 2 portrays classes that might reasonably exist in a KME to be used for developing KMEs for business computing. Notice that PROPERTY, ASSOCIATION, and PROCESS can themselves be regarded as classes (i.e., subclasses of CLASS) at an abstract level. Various developers would augment these to yield environments for constructing application systems, each of which may itself be regarded as a KME. The augmentations would occur primarily in the area of adding subclasses to the CLASS concept. Their properties would be entities that are members of the PROPERTY subclasses (e.g., floating properties). Their methods would be members of the METHOD class.

In Figure 2, classes are denoted by rectangles enclosing respective class properties. Definitional relationships are depicted as dashed lines that point toward class members. For instance, PROPERTY is an innate class whose properties are DEFAULT_VAL, DEFINITION, FEASIBLE_VALS, and the properties inherited from CLASS (including those that CLASS inherits from CONCEPT). In turn, PROPERTY defines the common properties of its five member concepts. One of these members is the class of numeric properties, which has two properties (PICTURE and LABEL) in addition to those of the more generic PROPERTY concept. While the diagram acknowledges the METHOD concept as a member of the PROCESS class which is a member of CONCEPT, it does not identify specific methods pertaining to specific classes. Specific methods are entities belonging to the METHOD class. Similarly specific users, specific signed integer properties, and specific demons are all entities. As such, they are not explicit in the class diagram of Figure 2.

However, the ENTITY_SET concept does provide a mechanism for dealing with entities. Consider, for instance, the SIGNED class. Its members will consist of the set of all signed integer properties that a developer creates in the environment. These properties can be used in defining new classes. A KME with the initial structure of Figure 2 treats the set of all signed integer properties as one member of the ENTITY_SET class. Similarly, other members of this class would include the set of user entities, the set of text character properties, the set of methods, and the set of demons. Clearly, the ENTITY_SET methods would include basic processes for working on ordered and unordered sets (e.g., finding the next entity in a set, finding an entity based on certain value criteria).

Suppose a developer has a KME with the class structure of Figure 2 as its initial knowledge system contents. The properties of these classes do not exist as entities in the knowledge system, but are directly understood by the KME's problem processor

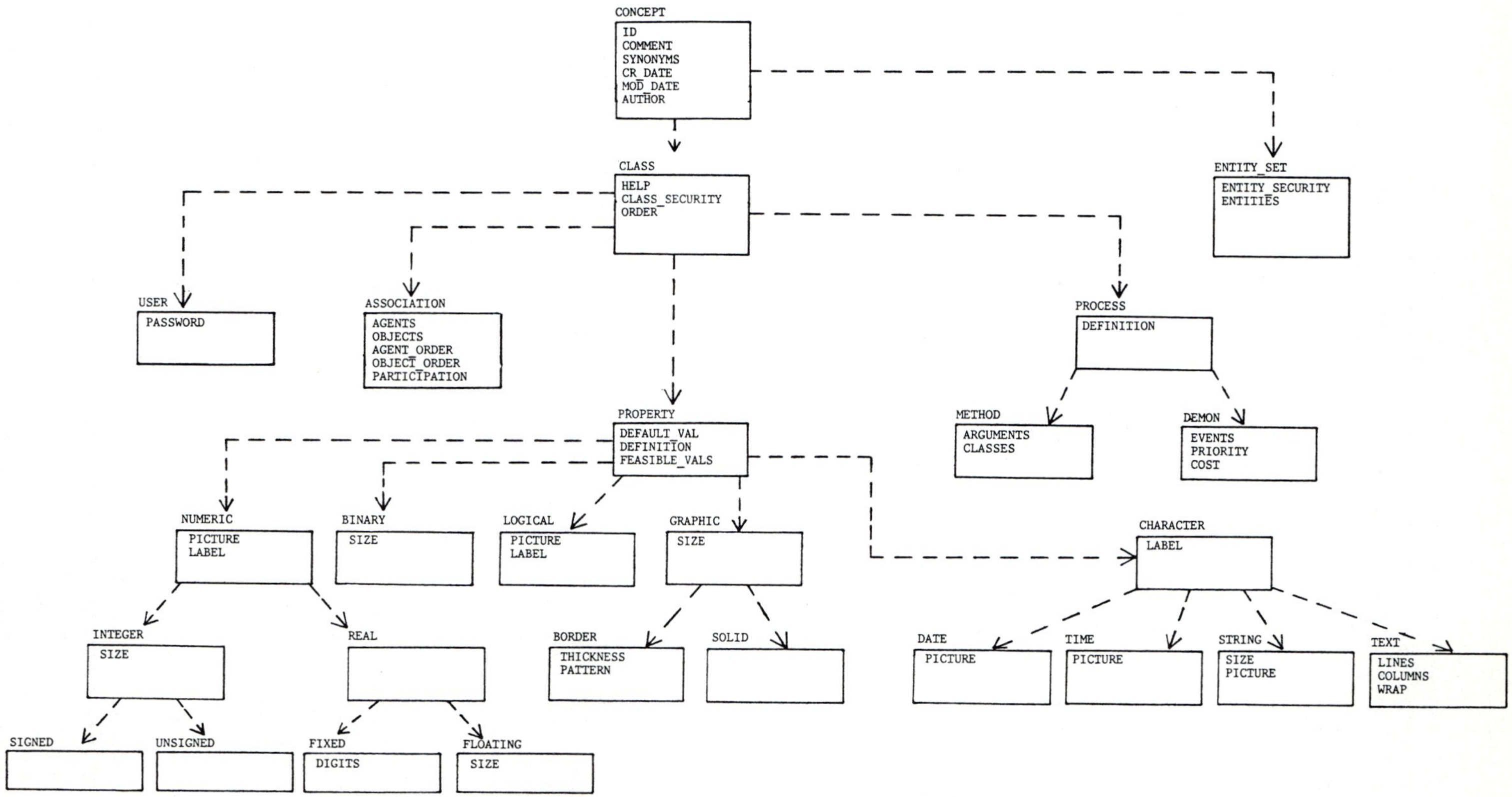

Figure 2. An Innate Class Structure

software. For example, CR_DATE (a property of CONCEPT) does not exist in the entity set for the character data property. In fact, all entity sets implied by the initial class structure are initially empty. The initial methods for these classes are indigenous to the problem processor software. In other words, the initial definitional structure of classes, the properties of these classes, and their methods are not subject to revision by the developer. They are innate aspects of the environment. They are the prefabricated concepts with which a developer can work.

The developer may want to augment the environment to give it an ordinary tabular data management capability. This involves the new concepts of table and record. A message is sent to CLASS to use its DEFINE method to define a new subclass named TABLE. In addition to inheriting usual CLASS properties, TABLE might have additional properties such as KEY. The KEY property would be created as a member of the entity set for STRING. Similarly, the RECORD class would be defined with a property such as MARK (a member of the entity set for LOGICAL) for allowing a record to have a marked or unmarked status. The definitions of these two new classes implicitly result in two new members of the ENTITY_SET concept, both of which are null sets.

Because tables and records are associated concepts in the sense that a table holds records, a one-to-many HOLDS relationship would be created with TABLE as the agent and RECORD as the object. As a result, the entity set for ASSOCIATION would include an entity whose ID value is HOLDS, whose AGENT value is TABLE, whose object value is RECORD, whose PARTICIPATION value is 1:N (i.e., one-to-many), and so forth. By inheritance, the HOLDS association will make it possible to assign records to tables and to later determine which records are held in which tables. Notice that if it were desired to allow a record to be held in multiple tables, the PARTICIPATION value would be M:N (i.e., many-to-many).

In addition to augmenting the KME with new classes and associations, a developer may also want to create new methods for the new classes. Of course all methods that initially exist for CLASS are inherited by TABLE and RECORD. These include such abilities as defining new subclasses, deleting subclasses, examining class properties, and altering class properties. In addition, innate ENTITY_SET methods allow for creating entities in a class' entity set, deleting entities, altering the values of entity properties, finding entities in a set, assigning object entities to agent entities with respect to associations, removing such assignments, finding objects associated with an agent and vice versa, viewing entity values, and so forth. Creating a new method consists of creating a new entity in METHOD's entity set. For instance, the developer might create a method for the RECORD entity set that produces a sorted list of these records held in a table, if such a method does not already exist for the general CLASS concept.

Once a data management technique has been built into a KME, the environment might then be used for application development purposes. As Figure 3 suggests, subclasses of RECORD such as EMP and DEPT might be defined. Their properties such as ENAM, EADDR, DNO, and DNAM would be created as entities in the entity sets for various PROPERTY subclasses. The associations such as CONTAIN and MGR would be created as new entities in the ASSOCIATION entity set. Similarly, EMP and DEPT entities would be added to the TABLE entity set.

With the foregoing additions to the KME, it becomes an environment for an end user who can use the ENTITY_SET methods to manipulate (e.g., create, delete, alter, associate, view) instances of the EMP and DEPT classes. In practice, an end user may not directly send messages to entity sets. Instead, messages may be sent to a program which, in turn, handles message sending to the entity sets. Such a program would itself be an entity in the knowledge system, belonging to the PROGRAM class (which likely would be a subclass of PROCESS).

RESEARCH DIRECTIONS

As these simple examples indicate, a KME can be adapted to the needs of a continuum of users ranging from systems developers to application developers to end users. The examples are obviously skeletal in nature, but they are suggestive of a viable environment approach to knowledge management. The environment can be augmented to offer numerous knowledge management techniques such as the management of spreadsheets, rules, forms, and program models. The examples are also useful in identifying numerous research areas that deserve investigation.

1. The characteristics of a minimal KME. What are the minimal classes, properties, and methods needed by systems developers?
2. Extensions and refinements to the KME suggested by Figure 2. What else is needed to allow it to serve as an environment for implementing all the traditional knowledge management techniques of business computing, such that each can send messages to the others? Are additional innate classes or properties needed? Precisely what innate methods should exist?
3. The mechanics and language of method and demon building. As new classes are invented, what facilities exist for defining their methods? That is, what values are valid for the DEFINITION property of PROCESS? How can both message sending and conventional control structures be accommodated in the definition of a process?
4. Developer support features of the KME's problem processor. What innate features should the environment have to

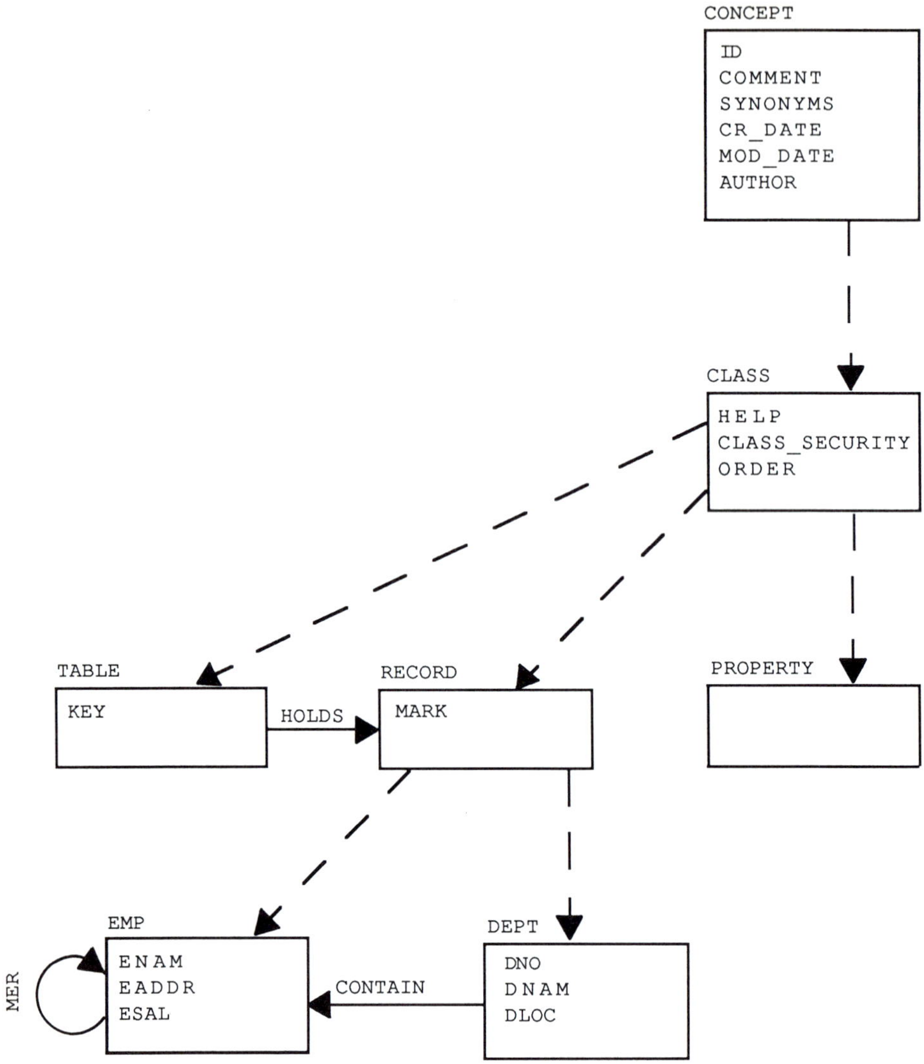

Figure 3. Introducing New Classes and Associations

facilitate the analysis, design, testing, and optimization of developer additions to a KME's knowledge system?

5. User interface facilities. How can linguistic and presentation knowledge be captured in the knowledge system and serve as a customized user interface to the environment?
6. Examination of the correspondences between a KME and an organization. To what extent can a KME emulate and enhance knowledge management in an organization, including such activities as the coordination of roles (e.g., of active concepts), learning, and group decision-making?
7. Implementation considerations. How might a class' properties, methods, demons, and entity sets be implemented? What storage structures are appropriate?
8. Applicability of a basic KME as a framework for understanding and contrasting diverse knowledge management techniques.

A key element in exploring these research avenues will be the creation of a language that defines what messages a person can send upon entering the KME. It also determines the messages that concepts can send to each other. Clearly, the language must take the innate classes, properties, and methods into account (see [7] for examples). The language should also be extensible, in the sense of allowing messages that correspond to new methods introduced by developers. Initial work on such a language is discussed in [10].

CONCLUSION

A generalized problem processor for building decision support systems is a single software tool, not a collection of tools. In the interest of promoting knowledge worker productivity, we submit that both a DSS and the tool (i.e., problem processor) used to build a DSS be viewed as an environment for managing diverse types of knowledge. For instance, model management should not occur in a vacuum or as an isolated phenomenon, but in concert with other knowledge management techniques. The environment approach to decision support views models as one type of concept in a knowledge management landscape. Many other types of concepts (e.g., tables, records, rules) can exist in the same environment.

Traditionally distinct types of concepts can interact with each other inside of an environment by way of associations and messages. Thus a model (i.e., an object) can send a message to another object (e.g., records, rules) in the course of its execution. Conversely, other objects can send execution messages to models because the models are concepts in their own right. Thus a synergistic effect is achieved among diverse types of concepts. This notion of an environment, allowing a coordinated interplay among diverse and related concepts, is potentially an important one in terms of the flexibility, power, and convenience of decision support systems. The actualization of this potential is dependent on subsequent research that this paper endeavors to stimulate.

REFERENCES

[1] J. Banerjee, et al., "Data Model Issues for Object-Oriented Applications," *ACM Transactions on Office Information Systems,* vol. 5, no. 1, 1987.

[2] R.H. Bonczek, C.W. Holsapple and A.B. Whinston, *Foundations of Decision Support Systems,* Academic Press, New York, 1981.

[3] O. De Troyer, J. Kenstermans and R. Meersman, "How Helpful Is an Object-Oriented Language for an Object-Oriented Database Model?," *Proceedings of International Workshop on Object-Oriented Database Systems,* Pacific Grove, CA, 1986.

[4] C.W. Holsapple, "Adapting Demons to a Knowledge Management Environment," working paper, School of Management, Purdue University, 1986.

[5] C.W. Holsapple and A.B. Whinston, "Aspects of Integrated Software," *Proceedings of the National Computer Science,* Las Vegas, 1984. Reprinted in 1986 *NCC Proceedings.*

[6] C.W. Holsapple and A.B. Whinston, *Business Expert Systems,* Richard D. Irwin, Homewood, IL, 1986.

[7] C.W. Holsapple and A.B. Whinston, "Knowledge Representation and Processing in Economics and Management," *Conference on Integrated Modeling Systems,* Austin, 1986.

[8] C.W. Holsapple and A.B. Whinston, "Knowledge-Based Organizations," *Information Society,* vol. 5, no. 2, 1987.

[9] S.P. Reiss, "PECAN: Program Development Systems that Support Multiple Views," *IEEE Transactions on Software Engineering,* vol. 11, no. 3, 1985.

[10] R. Stansifer, P. Bhasker and A. Whinston, "Combining Deduction with Objects and Functions," working paper, Computer Science Department, Purdue University, 1986.

[11] W.A. Woods, "What's in a Link: Foundations for Semantic Networks" in *Representation and Understanding* (eds., D.B. Bobrow and A. Collins), Academic Press, New York, 1975.

SECTION 7:

REPRESENTATION OF UNCERTAINTY IN MATHEMATICAL MODELS AND KNOWLEDGE BASED SYSTEMS

EXPERT SYSTEMS' FRONT END: EXPERT OPINION

Roger M. Cooke
Department of Mathematics and Informatics
Delft University of Technology

Introduction

Whereas computers have traditionally excelled in deductive reasoning, most areas of science, engineering, medicine and policy analysis are dominated by inductive, or inexact reasoning. Uncertain conclusions are drawn from uncertain evidence via uncertain rules of inference. The ability to reason with uncertainty is sometimes considered the hallmark of human rationality. With the advent of expert systems, computer science has applied itself to the task of representing and implementing inexact reasoning in computer programs.

Recent years have witnessed an explosion of methodologies for representing and propagating uncertainty in expert systems. Probabilistic or quasi-probabilistic methods include confirmation theory, the theory of belief functions, interval inference and Bayesian updating. Non-probabilistic methods include non-monotonic (default) reasoning and fuzzy logic. Current research in expert systems is concerned with debating the relative merits of these methodologies and developing alternatives.

The present paper will not contribute directly to this debate. Its purpose is rather to draw attention to another set of problems which (in the author's opinion) should be of major concern to designers of expert systems, but which at present is not.

All expert systems have a "front end", namely human experts. Ultimately, the applicability of expert systems will be limited, not by problems in representing and propagating uncertainty, but by the quality of expert opinion which is fed in at the beginning. Considered as a source of data, expert opinion has many advantages; it is cheap, readily accessible and inexhaustible. It has one grievous disadvantage, however, it is extremely noisy. The central problem at the front end is reducing the noise, or put differently, determining what (and who) an expert is.

The purpose of this paper is to describe techniques for expert resolution, that is, for evaluating and combining expert opinion, These techniques have been developed within the Bayesian framework, as Bayesian or subjective probability provides a strong normative basis for representing uncertainty. The axioms of probability and in particular the relation between (subjective) probability and limiting relative frequency provide the principle tools for reducing the noise in expert opinion. This is not to say that other methods for representing uncertainty could not perform equally well or better. Indeed, it is hoped that proponents of other methodologies will be

NATO ASI Series, Vol. F48
Mathematical Models for Decision Support
Edited by G. Mitra

inspired by the Bayesian techniques to develop their own "front ends".

This paper is organized as follows. **Section 1** presents some illustrative examples of expert opinion in practice. **Section 2** discusses the basic notions of expert resolution, calibration and entropy. **Section 3** takes up the notion of proper scoring rules and shows how the latter concepts emerge naturally from proper scoring rules. Section 4 presents theory of weights for combining expert opinion on the basis of generalized proper scoring rules. The discussion in the first two sections is informal, the latter two sections are more technical.

Section 1: Expert opinion in practice

Risk analysis was probably the first "hard science" to make extensive use of quantified expert opinion in the form of subjective probabilities. It is therefore appropriate to rehearse a few examples from this field.

The first large scale risk analysis was the Reactor Safety Study (1975) which endeavored to calculate the risks of nuclear power plants for the general public. In order to calculate this risk the probability of a core meltdown per reactor year had to be calculated. It is interesting to remark that the erstwhile contractor for this type of work, the Brookhaven National Laboratory, had steadfastly refused to perform this calculation, claiming that only a "fringe member of the statistical community" could propose such a thing (Fuller (1975) p. 148).

The Reactor Safety Study required a large number of failure probabilities which could not be reliably estimated from available data. Thirty experts (agencies or consulting firms involved with nuclear energy) were asked to estimate failure probabilities for 60 components. Not every expert estimated each component, but the total matrix gives a good impression of the divergence of expert opinion. The results for one component, the failure probability of high quality steel pipe of diameter at least three inches, per section hour, are given in **Table 1**. The thirteen responses range from 5E-6 to E-10. The Reactor Safety Study used for its calculations the value E-10, with 90% confidence bounds of 3E-9 to 3E-12.

source	value
1. LMEC	5×10^{-6}
2. Holmes	1×10^{-6}
3. G.E.	7×10^{-8}
4. Shopsky	1×10^{-8}
5. IEEE, a	1×10^{-8}
6. IEE,b	1×10^{-8}
7. NRTS Idaho	1×10^{-8}
8. Otway	6×10^{-9}
9. Davies	3×10^{-9}
10. SRS	2×10^{-9}
11. IKWS Germany	2×10^{-10}
12. Collins	1×10^{-10}
13. React. Incd.	1×10^{-10}
RSS estimate	1×10^{-10}
90% confidence bounds	$3 \times 10^{-9} - 3 \times 10^{-12}$

Table 1
Estimates of failure probability per section-hour of high quality steel pipe (Reactor Safety Study (1975), p. III-7).

Calling the spread of expert opinion for a given component the ratio of the largest to the smallest estimate, the average spread over the 60 components was 167,820. If one outlier (with a spread of E7) is eliminated, then the average spread for the remaining components was 1173. (By comparison, the average ratio between the upper and lower 90% confidence bounds used by the Reactor Safety Study for the 60 components was 126).

Expert opinion remains an essential data source for risk analysis in the nuclear sector. In the recent Reactor Risk Reference Document (1987) the regulator is told that he must learn to live with the attendant uncertainties:

...a best-estimate or mean value of risk would imply far more precise, statistically based information than is actually possessed. In situations where the reasonable range within which the value of the risk might lie varies over three orders of magnitude, it is very important that the regulator understand the assumptions and considerations driving the analyses...Therefore, the risk results discussed here do not contain any best estimates of mean values - they are presented in the form of a range within which the true value is reasonably expected to lie. (Reactor Risk Reference Document (1987), p. I-4).

Nuclear energy is not the only area in which experts disagree dramatically. Shooman and Sinkar (1977) conducted a study into the risks associated with grounded type electric lawn mowers. They collected opinions from 12 experts regarding the probabilities for events which might contribute to an electric shock accident, with the intention of combining these probabilities to derive the probability for a shock accident. A description of the events estimated together with the results are reproduced as **Table 2**.

Definition of Hazard events

E_g The event that a person is grounded or has a low resistance while operating the lawn mower. (Low resistance is that resistance which is sufficiently small to cause an electric shock for the specifioed operating voltage.)

E_0 The event that the wire-plug of the mower is in while the mower is being repaired or adjusted.

E_1 The event that a person touches a "live" part of the lawn mower. The live part considered here is a part which is normally live when a mower is connected to the supply, and not a part that has become live due to a fault.

E_2 The event that a person touches cut (E_3) or damaged (E_4) cord when the mower is connected to the supply.

E_3 The event that the cord is cut due to some sharp object either while the mower is in operation or stored.

E_4 The event insulation of the cord does not work. (Damage due to environment, prolonged and/or abusive use, etc.).

E_5 The event that a person touches the conductive part of the body (includes handle, blade, etc.) when the mower is connected to the supply.

E_6 Consumer does not have a grounded outlet box.

E_7 Ground wire is either broken or disconnected at the grounding terminal.

E_8 High impedance gounding circuit exists.

ESTIMATED PROBABILITY OF THE EVENT
First Round Grounded Type

Expert / Event	1	2	3	4	5	6	7	8	9	10	11	12
E_g	0.5	0.5	0.75	0.5	0.5	0.005	1.0	0.9	0.005	0.005	0.3	0.1
E_0	0.25	0.1	0.1	0.01	0.0001	0.00028	0.66	0.8	0.0001	0.0045	0.0225	0.878
E_1	0.05	0.01	0.001	0.001	0.5	0.	0.1	0.2	0.0001	0.0001	0.00028	0.001
E_2	1.0	1.0	0.9	0.8	0.001	0.007	1.0	1.0	0.005	0.0055	0.01	0.2
E_3	0.1	0.05	0.01	0.01	0.05	0.0007	0.1	0.7	0.0001	0.0001	0.0125	0.0078
E_4	0.05	0.1	0.005	0.05	0.002	0.00007	0.05	0.05	0.0001	0.00015	0.01	0.01
E_5	1.0	0.7	0.8	1.0	0.001	0.007	1.0	1.0	0.005	0.006	1.0	0.022
E_6	0.35	0.2	0.2	0.2	0.65	0.0035	0.6	0.75	0.005	0.0015	0.425	0.6
E_7	0.05	0.005	0.001	0.1	0.00002	0.000003	0.05	0.05	0.0001	0.000002	0.002	0.001
E_8	0.05	0.001	0.01	0.05	0.001	0.000003	0.02	0.05	0.0001	0.000002	0.002	0.00035

Table 2
Definitions and estimates of hazard events for electric lawn mowers (Shooman and Sinkar (1977)).

The above serve to illustrate the extreme spread typical of probabilistic expert opinion. Similar examples of probabilistic expert opinion from diverse fields could be produced to reinforce the conclusion emerging from the above discussion: Any responsible use of expert opinion must incorporate some mechanism for filtering expert opinion so as to reduce the spread whenever possible.

Section 2: Basic concepts of expert resolution; calibration and entropy

A wide variety of techniques for reaching, deriving, or imposing consensus has been proposed in the literature. Even a cursory review of this literature lies far beyond the scope of the paper. However, we should mention that the popular Delphi-type techniques and various so-called "social interaction" techniques for reaching a consensus have been seriously examined by psychometricians in the 1970's, using some of the techniques discussed in the sequel, and been found ineffective, and sometimes counter-effective (see. e.g. Sackman, (1975), Seaver (1977) and Fischer (1981)). In this section we illustrate two concepts via psychometric tests which can be implemented in a rigorous probabilistic context. In the following section we shall see how these concepts emerge naturally from the theory of proper scoring rules.

Calibration

Roughly speaking, calibration is intended as a measure of the degree to which probabilistic assessments "correspond to reality". The basic idea is best introduced by means of an example. The example simultaneously illustrates the so-called discrete method for encoding subjective probabilities.

Suppose an expert states his probability that it rains tomorrow. Tomorrow we will know whether it rains, but this knowledge will not help us evaluate this single assessment. However, if we have a large number of assessments from this expert for the probability of "rain the next day", then we can group together those days for which the assessments were the same, and compare these assessments with the observed relative frequency of rain.

Murphy and Winkler (1977) performed such a comparison involving 24,859 precipitation forecasts for the Chicago area. **Figure 1** plots the resulting subjective probabilities against the observed relative frequencies. If the probability forecasts were *perfectly calibrated*, then the data points would lie on the line through the origin with unit slope. The Chicago weathermen exhibit excellent calibration. More recent studies (Murphy and Daan (1982), (1984)) confirm these findings and demonstrate that calibration improves as weathermen are confronted with their own performance. These are among the most encouraging examples of the use of expert opinion.

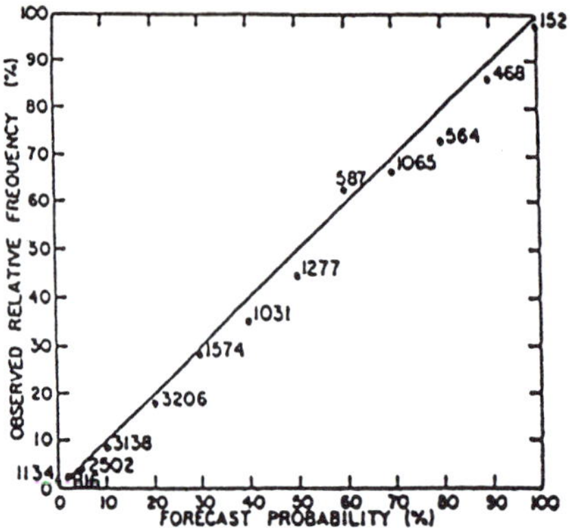

Figure 1

Calibration data for precipitation forecases. The number of forecasts is shown for each point (Murphy and Winkler (1977)).

Expert calibration is not always so good. **Figure** 2 shows calibration for Army physicians' diagnoses of pneumonia. In this study the actual incidence of pneumonia was later determined radiographically.

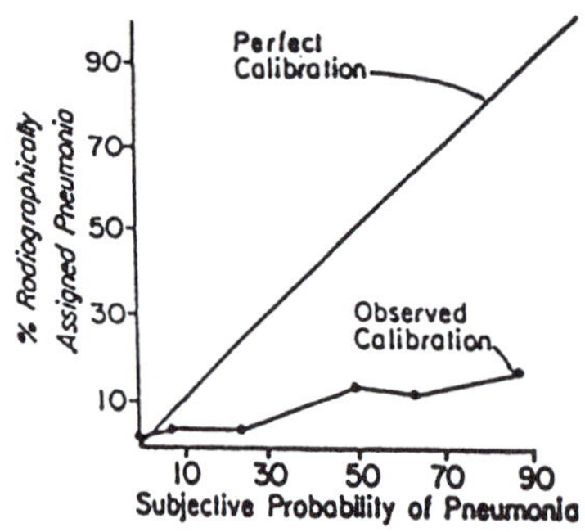

Figure 2

Calibration of physicians' diagnoses of pneumonia (Christensen-Szalanski and Bushyhead (1981))

We should mention that some calibration tests of the above type have been criticised for methodological flaws (Cooke et al. (1988).

Entropy

Entropy is a measure of the lack of information in a probability distribution. A definition will be given in the next section, but it is convenient to introduce the notion here by means of an example. This example also illustrates a different method for encoding probabilities, the so-called quantile (or fractile) method.

Suppose an expert is called upon to estimate the value of an uncertain quantity with a continous range. An example taken from the experiment described below, is "the maximal efficiency of the Tyne RM1A gas turbine". Instead of asking for a point estimate, suppose we elicit various quantiles from his subjective probability distribution. A good picture of his state of knowledge can be obtained by eliciting the 1%, 25%, 50%, 75% and 99% quantiles from his distribution. A block function can be fitted to the elicited quantiles so as to approximate the expert's subjective probability density function. (Once the endpoints of the range are fixed, such a block function is the "minimum information fit" for the given quantiles.) An example is pictured in **Figure 3**.

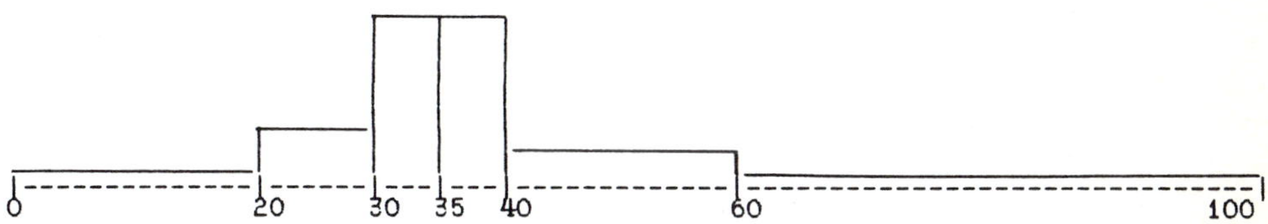

Figure 3

A minimum information block function fit for the 1% (20), 25% (30), 50% (35) 75% (40) and 99% (60) quantiles from a subjective distribution for the quantity "maximal efficiency of the Tyne RM1A gas turbine". The range for this quantity is 0% - 100%.

Entropy is a measure of the degree to which the probability function is "spread out". If the expert is quite certain about the maximal efficiency of the Tyne RM1A gas turbine, then his quantiles will lie close together and his distribution will have a low entropy. On the other hand, if he is quite uncertain about this quantity, his quantiles will be farther apart and the entropy in his distribution will be greater.

(Of course, entropy can also be defined for discrete probability assessments. Referring to **figure 1**, assessments with low entropy would assign probabilities for rain close to 0 or 1.)

If we elicit the *same* quantiles for a large number of uncertain quantities with a practically) continuous range, then we can also calibrate the probability assessments by recording the percentage of true values falling between the various quantiles. For example, if the expert were perfectly calibrated, then we should expect 24% of the true values to fall between the 1% and 25% quantiles, etc.

From the substantial psychometric literature on this subject we know that experts typically display extreme "overconfidence" on probabilistic assessments. On quantile tests for calibration of the above type 40 - 60% of the true values typically fall outside the 1% and 99% quantiles (see Lichtenstein et al. (1982) for a review).

The importance of calibration and entropy in connection with combining expert opinion emerges from a psychometric experiment recently conducted in Delft (Cooke et al. (1988)) in which the following results were found. On items relating to their field of expertise, experienced operators of sophisticated technical systems are significantly better as a group than inexperienced operators with respect to both calibration and entropy (i.e. calibration is better and entropy is lower). On general knowledge items no significant difference was found. This strongly suggests that good calibration and low entropy both correspond to features which we associate with "expertise". However, within each group there was a significant negative correlation between good calibration and low entropy, and the correlation was generally dramatic at the extremes. A "truly good expert" should be good with respect to both calibration and entropy. There was one such expert for the technical items (from a group of 34) and no such expert for the general knowledge items. **Table 3** shows the subjects' ranks with respect to calibration and "negentropy" (negative entropy, also called "information") so that a good expert should be ranked high (i.e. close to 1) with respect to calibration and negentropy.

	General Knowledge		Technical Knowledge	
Rank	Calibration Rank	Negentropy Rank	Calibration Rank	Negentropy Rank
1	i	e	e	e
2	i	i	e	e
3	e	i	e	e
4	i	i	e	e
5	i	e	i	e
6	i	e	e	i
7	e	i	e	e
8	e	i	i	i
9	i	i	i	i
10	i	i	i	e
11	e	e	e	i
12	e	i	i	i
13	i	e	i	i
14	i	i	i	i
15	i	e	e	i
16	i	i	i	e
17	e	i	i	i
18	e	e	i	i
19	i	i	i	i
20	e	i	e	i
21	i	e	i	i
22	e	e	e	i
23	e	i	i	e
24	i	o	i	e
25	e	i	e	i
26	e	e	i	i
27	e	e	i	i
28	i	e	i	i
29	e	i	i	i
30	i	i	i	i
31	e	e	e	i
32	i	i	i	i
33	i	i	i	e
34	i	i	i	i
35	i	i		
36	i	e		
37	i	i		

i denotes inexperienced operator; e denotes experienced operator

Table 3
Correlations between calibration and negentropy for experienced and inexperienced operators on general knowledge and technical items (Cooke et al. (1988)).

Section 3: Proper scoring rules

A scoring rule is a real-valued function of an assessed probability distribution and an observed value (by "probability distribution" we shall mean either a probability mass function or a probability density function, according to whether the variable in question is discrete or continuous; these should not be confused with a cummulative distribution function, which is called a distribution function in the case of continuous variables). Consider an uncertain quantity with possible outcomes $i = 1,\ldots n$. Let $p = p_1,\ldots p_n$ be a probability distribution over the possible outcomes with p_i the probability for outcome i, and let $R(i,p)$ be the score for assessment p on observing i. Let E_p denote expectation with respect to p. The negatively (positively) sensed scoring rule R is *strictly proper* if for every distribution p

$$\min_{p'} (\max) E_pR(i,p') = E_pR(i,q) \text{ if and only if } q = p.$$

If assessors are rewarded for their assessments according to an improper scoring rule, then they are being encouraged to state a probability assessment at variance with their true opinion. The best known strictly proper scoring rules are (Winkler and Murphy (1968)):

$$R(i,p) = 2p_i - \sum_{j=1}^{n} p_j^2 \quad \text{(quadratic scoring rule)}$$

$$R(i,p) = p_i/(\sum_{j=1}^{n} p_j^2)^{1/2} \quad \text{(spherical scoring rule)}$$

$$R(i,p) = \ln(p_i) \quad \text{(logarithmic scoring rule).}$$

Savage (1971) provides a characterization of the class of strictly proper scoring rules. Under the quadratic and spherical scoring rules the scores depend on the assessments of outcomes which did not in fact occur (for $n > 2$). A scoring rule is called *relevant* if the scores depend only on the assessments of the observed outcomes. Following Winkler (1969), relevance is felt to be an important property for scoring rules in the context of combining expert opinion. Shuford et al. (1965) proved the surprising result that the logarithmic score (plus a constant) is the only strictly proper scoring rule which is relevant.

De Groot and Fienberg (1986) give an additive decomposition of proper scoring rules into a "calibration term" and a "refinement term". This generalizes an earlier result of Murphy (1973). Consider N uncertain quantities with identical, finite ranges. An expert classifies each quantity into one of B "probability bins" and associates with each bin a distributions r_i, $i = 1,\ldots B$. Let n_i denote the number of items placed in the i-th bin, and let s_i denote the sample distribution of the observed outcomes for the items in the i-th bin, $i = 1,\ldots B$. Let R be a strictly proper scoring rule, and let $R(r,n,s)$ denote the total score gotten by summing the scores for all uncertain items, and let $E_p(R(r)) = \Sigma p_j R(j,r)$. De Groot and Fienberg's decomposition can then be expressed as:

$$R(r,n,s) = \sum_{i=1}^{B} n_i E_{s_i} (R(r_i) - R(s_i)) + \sum_{i=1}^{B} n_i E_{s_i} R(s_i).$$

Note that the right hand side is a random variable, as the sample distributions with respect to which the expectations are taken, are random variables.

The first term is the "calibration term". Since R is proper, it equals zero if and only if the expert is perfectly calibrated. If R is negatively sensed (so that lower scores are better), then this term is non-positive. The second term is the "refinement term". Note that the choice of R completely determines the calibration and the refinement terms. Note also that *the calibration term by itself is not a proper scoring rule.*

Recall that the logarithmic scoring rule was the only strictly proper scoring rule which was relevant. Substituting the logarithmic rule for R in the De Groot Fienberg decomposition, we obtain:

3.1 $$R(r,n,s) = -\sum_{i=1}^{B} n_i I(s_i, r_i) - \sum_{i=1}^{B} n_i H(s_i)$$

where, letting A denote the range of possible outcomes (the same for each uncertain item) and $r_i(a)$ the probability assigned to $a \in A$ by distribution r_i:

3.2 $$H(s_i) = -\sum_{a \in A} s_i(a)\ln(s_i(a)),$$

3.3 $$I(s_i, r_i) = \sum_{a \in A} s_i(a)\ln[s_i(a)/r_i(a)].$$

$H(s_i)$ is termed the *entropy* or negative information in the distribution s_i. $I(s_i,r_i)$ is called the *relative* or *discriminal information* of the distribution s_i with respect to the distribution r_i. This latter quantity is always non-negative, and is zero if and only if $s_i = r_i$. The quantity $\Sigma n_i H(s_i)$ is simply the entropy in the joint sample distribution over all uncertain items when the items are independent. The entropy in the expert's joint *assessments*, assuming independence, is $\Sigma n_i H(r_i)$.

The following facts are also important in interpreting (3.1). Let p be any probability distribution over the outcomes $i = 1,\ldots K$. Let s be a sample distribution over these outcomes generated by drawing a large number N of independent samples from the distribution p. Then the quantity $2NI(s,p)$ is asymptotically chi square distributed with K-1 degrees of freedom (Hoel (1971), p.227). Further, the sum of independent chi square variables is itself chi square, and the degrees of freedom add. Under the assumption of independence, this means, referring to (3.1), that the quantity $\Sigma 2n_i I(s_i,r_i)$ has a known asymptotic distribution. If u denotes the uniform distribution over $1,\ldots K$, then the entropy of s can be written as:

3.4 $H(s) = \ln(K) - I(s,u)$.

Hence, again assuming independence, the quantity $2n_i H(s_i)$ has an asymptotic chi square distribution. These facts will prove useful in the next section. Of course, the calibration and refinement terms in (3.1) are not independent, so the distribution of R(S) cannot be derived by elementary means.

Section 4: Combining expert opinion

Production rule expert systems with a probabilistic "inference engine" require expert assessments of conditional probabilities. Once the extreme spread of expert probabilistic assessments is acknowledged, the designer of such an expert system faces the question, how should the assessments of experts be combined?

The literature on combining probabilistic assessments is vast. A classic reference is Winkler (1968), and an excellent recent survey of the mathematical literature can be found in Genest and Zidek (1986). If there is a decision maker with a well defined prior distribution over the quantity in question and prior conditional distributions for the joint assessments of experts given values of the quantity in question, then one of various Bayesian schemes could be suggested (see e.g. Morris (1977), Lindley amd Singpurwalla (1986), Martz and Bryson (1983), Mosleh and Apostolakis (1986)). These schemes place formidible assessment burdens on the decision maker and invoke severe symplifying and modeling assumptions. For this reason the prospects for an implementation in expert systems in the near future appear dim.

More promising are techniques of weighted or convex combination, also known as linear opinion pooling. The main reason for studying convex combinations in this context derives from the following fact. Let P be the set of probability distributions over a σ-field F of events, and let $T(P_1,...P_n)$ be an arbitrary function from P^n into P. If for some function $F: [0,1]^n \rightarrow [0,1]$

$$T(P_1,...P_n)(A) = F(P_1(A),...P_n(A))$$

for every $A \in F$, then T can be written as:

$$4.1 \quad T(P_1,...P_n) = \sum_{i=1}^{n} w_i P_i$$

for some non-negative weights w_i such that $\Sigma w_i = 1$ (McConway (1981), Wagner (1982)).

The question is, how should the weights w_i be determined? The obstacle to be overcome in developing a theory of weights for expert resolution was first signalled by Winkler (1969). If the theory of weights is known to the experts, they will experience their weights as scores, and will try to be as "heavy" as possible. Hence, weights should be proper scoring rules. Winkler showed that the earliest and perhaps most natural method for defining weights (Roberts, (1965)), namely choosing weights proportional to the assessed probabilities of previously observed outcomes, is grossly improper.

Several authors have proposed using proper scoring rules for "evaluating" expert probability assessments, though until recently no concrete proposal for defining a system of weights had been made.

The problem with using a scoring rule like R(r,n,s) in (3.1) for defining a weight is the following. R(r,n,s), being a function of observed outcomes, is a random variable and its values cannot be meaningfully interpreted without knowing (or assuming) something about its distribution. For example, suppose we consider the logarithmic scoring rule in (3.1). This score is negatively sensed and its maximal value, 0, is obtained when the expert assigns probability one to all values which in fact occur. Clearly, the meaning of the score 0 will strongly depend on the number N of quantities which are assessed. Further, the maximal value of the entropy term in (3.1) will obviously depend on the total sample distribution of the N uncertain quantities.

For these reasons, it is clear that scores for different experts can only be compared if the experts have assessed the same quantities; and even then a difference in scores cannot be interpreted without knowing something about the distributions of the scores.

These problems can be overcome by appealing to a more general notion of scoring rule. For precise definitions and proofs the reader must be referred to (Cooke (1987)). Only the principle results can be given here.

For convenience, we focus on discrete tests involving uncertain events (i.e. indicator variables with possible values 0, and 1). An expert sorts these events into B probability bins. We assume that the true values will eventually become known, and that an expert probability assessor receives a weight determined by his assessments and the observed values. The weight zero is possible. Expert assessments for unobserved events will be combined according to (4.1) by normalizing their respective weights to unity (assuming not all weights are zero).

Scores of the type (3.1) score each assessment plus outcome individually, and add these scores to determine a total score for the set of uncertain quantities. A *scoring rule for average probabilities* assigns a score R(r,n,s) for the set of quantities as a function of the assessed bin probabilities r, the numbers of items in each probability bin, and the sample distributions.

A negatively (positively) sensed scoring rule for average probabilities is *P-strictly proper* for a set *P* of (joint) distributions for the uncertain events if for all P $\in$ *P*:

the minimum (maximum) over r of the expected score with respect to P *is attained when and only when each bin probability is equal to the expected number of occurrences with respect to* P *in that bin divided by the number of events in that bin.*

In the following discussion we take *P* to be the set of product distributions where the variables in the same bin are identically distributed. We shall call a rule *strictly proper* if it is strictly proper for all distributions. Unless otherwise stated we shall be referring to scoring rules for average probabilities. The reference to "average probabilities" is explained by the following fact of elementary probability theory: the average of the probabilities for a finite set of events is equal to the expected number of occurrences, divided by the number of events.

The following results are proved in (Cooke (1987)):

Referring to the notation of **section 3**, let $n = (n_1, \ldots n_B)$, $s = (s_1, \ldots s_B)$, $r = (r_1 \ldots r_B)$, then

4.2 $$R(n, s, r) := \sum_{i=1}^{B} 2n_i I(s_i, r_i) \text{ is strictly proper.}$$

(4.2) is noteworthy in light of the fact that the calibration term in (3.1) was not a proper scoring scoring rule in the sense defined in **section 3**. Under the assumption that the events are independent (implied by the restriction to $\mathcal{P}$), R(r,n,s) is asymptotically chi square distributed with B degrees of freedom. Of course, the value of R(r,n,s) depends on the number of items being assessed. This feature can be avoided by using the distribution of R. Let F denote the cummulative chi square distribution function with B degrees of freedom. Define:

4.3 $$w_\alpha(r, n, s) = \begin{cases} 1 \text{ if } 1 - F(R) > \alpha \\ 0 \text{ if } 1 - F(R) \le \alpha \end{cases} \quad ; \alpha \in (0, 1).$$

4.4 $$W_\alpha(r, n, s) = (1 - F(R)) * w_\alpha(r, n, s).$$

(4.3) corresponds to a Fisher type significance test at the level α. Scoring with respect to (4.3) is equivalent to rejecting an expert if the (asymptotic) probability of observing a score at least as large as R, under the hypothesis that the events are independent and the events in the i-th bin have probability r_i, $i = 1,\ldots B$. Otherwise the expert is accepted. (4.4) corresponds to degrees of acceptance according to the probability of observing a score larger than R. By "asymptotically strictly proper" we mean the following: for any assessment vector r' not equal to the limiting average probabilities π, there is $N_{r'}$ such that for all $n > N_{r'}$, $E_P R(\pi,n,s) > E_P R(r',n,s)$.

4.5 $w_\alpha(r,n,s)$ and $W_\alpha(r,n,s)$ are asymptotically $\mathcal{P}$ strictly proper.

(4.5) enables us to treat expert probability assessors as classical statistical hypotheses and score them via classical significance tests. The proofs depend on the fact that $\alpha > 0$. The above scores are sensitive to calibration, but not to entropy. The following result enables us to take entropy into account.

Let G(n,s) be any (measurable) function of the sample distribution s, and n, then

4.6 If R(r, n, s) is $\mathcal{P}$ strictly proper, then so is R(r, n, s) + G(n, s).

We could for example choose $G(n,s) = \Sigma(n_i/N)H(s_i)$. However, for this choice, the maximal possible value for G would depend on the number of events which actually occur (the "base rate"). A better choice utilizes the distribution of:

4.7 $$G(n, s) := \sum_{i=1}^{B} 2n_i I(s_i, S)$$

where S is the total sample distribution for all events. Large values of G correspond to a "high resolution of the base rate S" which would be unlikely to result from mere statistical fluctuations under the distribution S. If the subject assigned variables to bins randomly, then G(n,s) would have a chi square distribution F with B degrees of freedom. 1 - F(G) may be interpreted as the significance level at which the random-assignment-hypothesis could be rejected. Large values of F(G) therefore correspond to high resolution of the base rate, regardless what the base rate is. From (4.6) it follows that

4.8 $\beta w_\alpha(r, n, s) + (1 - \beta)F(G)$ and $\beta W_\alpha(r, n, s) + (1 - \beta)F(G))$ are asymptotically *P* strictly proper for any $\beta \in (0, 1)$.

(4.8) describes a family of weights which are sensitive to both calibration and entropy.

The weights in (4.8) are still subject to two criticisms. First, an expert can receive zero weight (i.e. be rejected) only if F(G) = 0. This severely compromises the notion of significance testing. Second, the sample distributions s_i need bear little resemblance to the assessed distributions r_i, even though the expert significantly resolves the base rate S.

Both problems can be met by focusing on the entropy in the assessed distributions, rather than that of the sample distributions. Define:

4.9 $$H(n, r) = \sum_{i=1}^{B} (n_i/N)H(r_i).$$

Propriety for a score using H(n,r) cannot be demostrated using (4.6). In fact, no non-trivial functional combination of H(n,r) with a proper scoring rule will yield a proper scoring rule. However, combinations can be given which are asymptotically strictly proper.

4.10 $w_\alpha(r, n, s)/\alpha H(n, r)^\beta$ and $W_\alpha(r, n, s)/\alpha H(n, r)^\beta$ are asymptotically strictly proper for all positive α, β.

(4.10) yields weights which have asymptotic propriety, which reward good calibration and low entropy, and which take the value zero whenever w (resp. W) is zero. It should be noted that the weights given in (4.8) and (4.10) allow different trade-offs of the relative contributions of the calibration and entropy terms. This contrasts with the situation in (3.1) where the trade-off between calibration and refinement is not flexible. Note finally that the weights in (4.6) and (4.10) depend on the distributions of the calibration and entropy terms, and in this sense are independent of the specific test variables from which they are derived. In other words, we can meaningfully compare scores for different experts gotten from different test variables.

Conclusion

Experience with expert probabilistic opinion indicates that expert assessments are generally characterized by extremely wide spreads.

Consulting *one* expert and feeding his probabilistic assessments into an expert system is simply foolhardy. Moreover, psychometric studies have demonstrated convincingly that probabilistic assessors are sometimes quite good, and sometimes quite poor with respect to calibration. Further, there is evidence that group behavior with respect to calibration and negentropy improves with experience. Any responsible expert system design should therefore incorporate a mechanism for filtering and combining expert input.

It was suggested that convex combinations of probabilistic assessments is a natural tool in the context of expert systems. The central problem is to determine a theory of weights for combining expert assessments.

Scoring rules based on summing scores for individual variables did not provide a suitable basis for such a theory. On the other hand, scoring rules for average probabilities generate a number of asymptotically proper weights which reward good calibration and low entropy, and whose numerical values are meaningful independent of the particular test variables on which they are based.

References

Christensen-Szalanski, J. and Bushyhead, J. "Physicians' use of probabilistic information in a real clinical setting" Journal of Experimental Psychology: Human Perception and Performance. 7, 928-935, 1981.

Cooke, R. Mendel, M. and Thijs, W. Calibration and Information in expert resolution Automatica, Januari 1988.

Cooke, R. "A theory of weights for combining expert opinion" Delft University of Technology, Report 87-25, 1987.

Fisher, G.W. "When oracles fail - a comparison of four procedures for aggregating subjective probability forecasts" Organizational Behavior and Human Performance, 28 69-110, 1981.

Fuller, J. We Almost Lost Detroit Ballantine Books, New York, 1975.

Genest,C. and Zidek, J. Combining probability distributions: a critique and annotated bibliography, Statistical Science, vol. 1 nr. 1, 114-148, 1986.

De Groot, M. and Fienberg, S. Comparing probability forecasters: basic binary concepts and multivariate extensions. In Bayesian Inference and Decision Techniques, P. Goel and A. Zellner (eds), Elsevier, 1986.

Lichtenstein, S. Fischhoff, B. and Phillips, D. Calibration of probabilities: the state of the art to 1980, In D. Kahneman, P. Slovic, and A. Tversky (eds) Judgment under uncertainty: heuristics and biases. Cambridge, Cambridge University Press 306-335, 1982.

Lindley, D. and Singpurwalla, N. "Reliability and fault tree analysis using expert opinion" J. Amer. Stat. Assoc. 81/393 87-90, 1986.

Martz, H. and Bryson, M. "On combining data for estimating the frequency of low probability events..."Nuclear Science and Engineering 83, 267-280, 1983.

McConway, K. Marginalization and linear opinion pools "J. Amer. Statis.Assoc. 76, 410-411, 1981.

Morris, P. Combining expert judgments: A Bayesian approach, Management Science vol 23, nr. 7, 679-693, 1977.

Mosleh A. and Apostolakis, G. "Models for the use of expert opinion" Low Probability High Consequence Risk Analysis (ed. Waller & Covello) Plenum Press, New York, 107-124, 1984.

Murphy, A. A new vector partition of the probability score, J. of Applied Meteorology, 12 595-600, 1973.

Murphy, A. and Daan, H. "Subjective probability forecasting in the Netherlands, some operational and experimental results" Meteorolog. Rundschau 34/5 99-112, 1982.

Murphy, A. and Daan, H. "Impacts of feedback and experience on the quality of subjective probability forecasts: comparison of results from first and second years of the Zierikzee experiment" Mon. Weather Rev. 112/3 413-423, 1984.

Reactor Safety Study WASH 1400, NUREG-75/014, 1975.

Reactor Risk Reference Document NUREG/1150, 1987.

Roberts, H. Probabilistic prediction, J. Amer. Statist. Assoc. 60, 50-62, 1965.

Sackman, H. Delphi Critique, Expert Opinion, Forecasting and Group Processes. Lexington Books, 1975.

Savage, L. Elicitation of personal probabilities and expectations, J. Amer. Statis. Assoc. vol. 66, nr. 336, 783-801, 1971

Seaver, D. "How groups can assess uncertainty: human interaction versus mathematical models" Proc. int. conf. cybernetics and soc. Washington DC, 19-21 sept. 1977.

Shooman and Sinkar, "Generation of reliability and safety data by analysis of expert opinion" Proceedings 1977 Annual Reliability and Maintainability Symposium. p. 186-191.

Shuford, E. Albert, A. and Massengill, H. Admissible probability measurement procedures, Psychometrika, vol 31, nr. 2 125-145, 1966.

Wagner, C. "Allocation, Lehrer Models and the consensus of probabilities" Theory and Decision. 14, 207-220, 1982.

Winkler, R. and Murphy, A. "Reliability of subjective probability forecasts of precipitation and temperature" Appl. Stat 26/1 41-47 1977.

Winkler, R. and Murphy, A. "Good probability assessors, J. of Applied Meteorology. vol. 7. 751-758, 1968.

Winkler, R. The consensus of subjective probability distributions, Management Science, vol. 15 nr. 2, 861-875, 1968.

Winkler, R. Scoring rules and the evaluation of probability assessors, J. Amer. Statist. Ass. 64, 1073-1078, 1969.

Winkler, R. On "good probability appraisers". In Bayesian Inference and Decision Techniques, P. Goel and A. Zellner (eds) Elsevier 1986.

Fuzzy Set Theoretic Approaches to Natural Language in Decision Support Systems*

Weldon A. Lodwick
Department of Mathematics, Campus Box 170
University of Colorado at Denver
1100 Fourteenth Street
Denver, CO 80202 USA

I. INTRODUCTION

The problem that is addressed in this paper is depicted in Figure 1. In particular, the following questions are addressed here: To what extent can fuzzy set theory be applied as an interface to (ambiguous) natural language descriptions of problems for which a computer resident DSS was designed to handle? Can both precise and ambiguous natural language descriptions be handled by fuzzy set theory in a robust way?

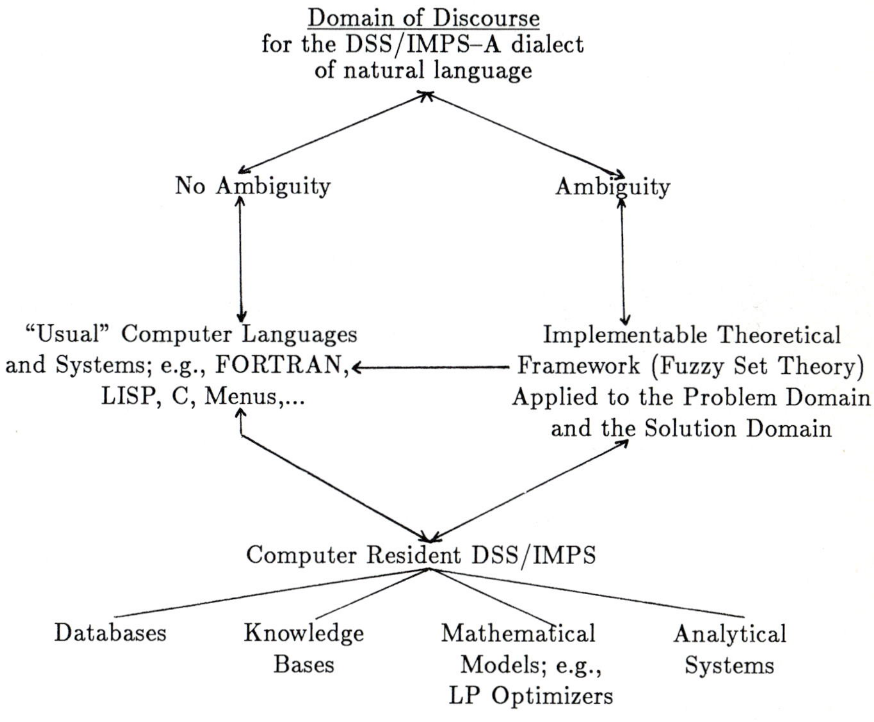

Figure 1. Natural language process.

*This work was partially supported by the Industrial Consortium to Develop an *Intelligent Mathematical Programming System*.

NATO ASI Series, Vol. F48
Mathematical Models for Decision Support
Edited by G. Mitra

Of concern to this exposition is to explore the ability of fuzzy set theory to handle some levels of complex natural language expressions. This study considers two types of ambiguity for which the applicability of fuzzy set theory is explored. They are:

1. Linguistic—ambiguous expressions such as "high," "low," and "much" along with modifiers of these terms such as "very" or "slightly" which arise in the context of a DSS.
2. Incompleteness
   a. Model specification—incomplete knowledge of the system or problem relevant to a DSS.
   b. Information—incomplete data associated with a DSS.
   c. Knowledge—incomplete specification of rules and/or equations governing the system or problem should a knowledge base be part of the DSS.

The decision support system (DSS) which will serve as a prototype for this exposition is the Intelligent Mathematical Programming System (IMPS) being developed by Professor Greenberg [2,3]. It is assumed that the DSS in question has the following attributes:

1. Accessible database(s) and knowledge base(s) consisting of:
   a. Existing facilities (plants), location and distances of these plants to supply and distribution centers,
   b. Relevant input and operational costs, constraints, requirements, linkages, etc.,
   c. Rules governing the dynamics of acquisition, production and distribution,
   d. A "dictionary shell" containing: (i) relevant key words with "slots" for aliases/synonyms; i.e., the key words are a node/cluster about which the system can attach aliases as these are uncovered through interaction with the user, (ii) pointers from the nodes to the relevant areas in the database(s),
2. A linear programming model library consisting of prototypical model shells with pointers to the database(s) and knowledge base(s).

The numeric or "quantitative" data are of four types: real numbers, real interval numbers, probabilities, and fuzzy sets.

Example: Assume that a petrochemical company person in charge of deciding the production levels for various types of pretroleum products to be offered over the next five months for region X has described the problem to the IMPS. The computer system upon searching the database finds that the projected demands for gasohol, regular leaded, regular unleaded, and premium unleaded gasolines are missing for region X. The manager uses her/his expert knowledge to estimate these values in terms of the words "high," "medium," and "low" demands together with modifiers. For the purposes of this example, assume that the fuzzy sets describing high, medium, and low demands for the above gasoline products are given by Figure 2 below and are in the database. It is noted that the fuzzy set depicted in Figure 2 is subjective and in *context*; that is, they refer to their respective petroleum product's demand in the region in question. Other fuzzy sets would need to be developed for "low supply" of a specified type of crude oil from Saudi Arabia, for example.

The following is the dialogue between the computer and the manager:

> Input the projected demand for gasohol (over the next five months)
> EXTREMELY LOW
> Input the projected demand for leaded regular gasoline (over the next five months)
> LOW TO MEDIUM
> Input the projected demand for regular unleaded gasoline (over the next five months)

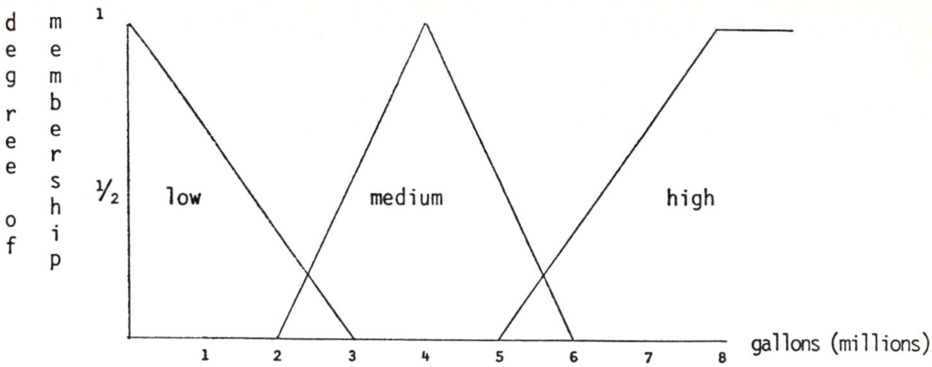

Figure 2. Five-month projected demand for petroleum fuzzy sets.

> VERY HIGH
> Input the projected demand for premium unleaded gasoline (over the next five months)
> SORT OF MEDIUM

The component parts of the above dialogue are as follows. The terms HIGH, MEDIUM, and LOW for which fuzzy sets are available are called *primary terms*. The primary terms are referential; that is, they refer to the various types of gasoline, and of course the projected demands for these products over the next five months in region X. Thus, hidden in the above responses are the linkages to which the responses apply. These linkages we call the *context* of the natural language discourse. The terms EXTREMELY, VERY, and SORT OF are called *hedges*. Lastly, the term TO is called a *range*. Both hedges and ranges transform the shapes of the fuzzy sets modified by these terms; that is, they "fine tune" fuzzy sets. Thus, from primary terms, it is possible to obtain a variety of expressions suitable for computer processing. The result of the above dialogue might have the (graphical) translations depicted in Figure 3.

From Figure 3, the IMPS takes the input into a linear programming model as sets of ranges on the right hand side. The output from the linear programming model would be a fuzzy production schelule. Ideally, the system would send back two types of output, the graphical representation of the fuzzy production schedule and the natural language representation of these graphs which could be mixed such as that depicted in Figure 3. Certainly the former output type is possible to implement while the latter is a harder problem as we shall see.

This example illustrates the potential of fuzzy set theory as a framework for natural language discourse from the user to the computer. The theory can be viewed as a bridge between the precise milieu which the computer requires and the ambiguous world in which most problems exist. Gupta [4] states: "Fuzzy set theory is an attempt to remove 'linguistic' barriers between humans, who think in fuzzy terms and machines that accept only precise instructions." On the other hand, Sowa [9, p. 40] observes that, "The reason language has fuzzy terms is not that human thought is fuzzy, but that the world is fuzzy."

It is assumed that the reader has some familiarity with fuzzy set theory, fuzzy numbers, and the operations on these. The definitions, operations and notation are found elsewhere in these Proceedings (see Zimmermann [14]). The exceptions are given next.

The degree of membership characterizing all elements of U with respect to A is called the *membership function* and denoted by the corresponding lower case letter $a(x)$,

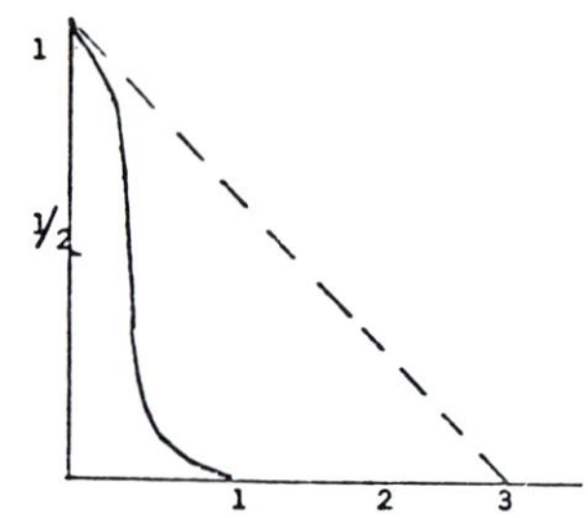

Figure 3a. EXTREMELY LOW demand for gasohol.

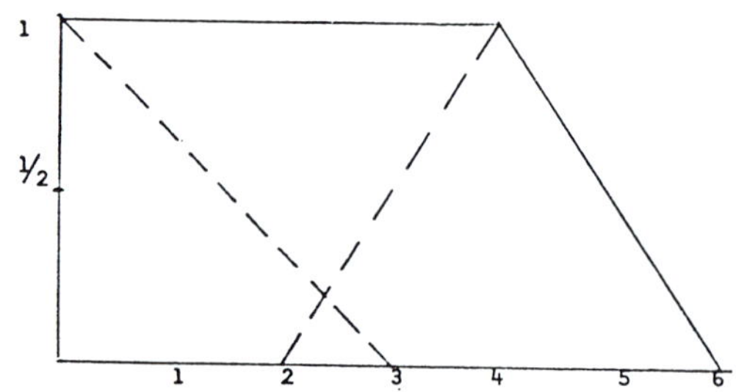

Figure 3b. LOW TO MEDIUM demand for regular leaded.

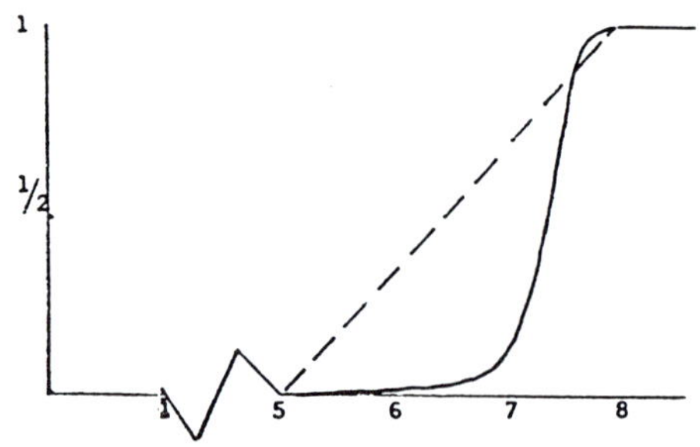

Figure 3c. VERY HIGH demand for regular unleaded.

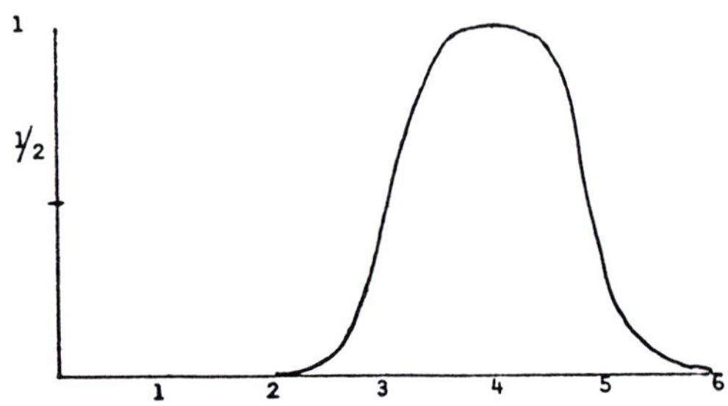

Figure 3d. SORT OF MEDIUM demand for premium unleaded.

for x in U. For this exposition, the capital letters $A, B, \ldots, K$ denote fuzzy sets and $a(x), b(x), \ldots, k(x)$ denote the corresponding membership functions, respectively.

$$\text{Fuzzification: } \text{FUZ}(A) = \cup\{a(x) * (K(x)\backslash x, \quad \text{for all } x \text{ in } U\},$$

where $\cup$ is the fuzzy union, $K(x)$ maps U into a fuzzy subset B of U for each x in U, and $*$ is the multiplication of the real number $a(x)$ and $k(x)$ for each x in U.

The operation of fuzzification "spreads out" the elements of A with nonzero degree of membership according to $K(x)$. $K(x)$ acts like a filter in reverse; it takes clear signals and "fuzzifies" them. The support of the membership function of A is $\{x : a(x) > 0\}$ which is set in the classical sense. The result of fuzzification is dependent on K and acts on the support of A. Thus, the notation $\text{SF}(A; K)$, read "support fuzzification of A with respect to K," is used here instead of the notation $\text{FUZ}(A)$.

II. NATURAL LANGUAGE COMPUTATIONS

Several steps must precede the stage at which the DSS is able to process natural language. In particular, the DSS must parse the input. Secondly, it must recognize, from the parsed input and its own databases and knowledge bases, when it has sufficient information to be able to compute. Once the DSS has gone through these two steps, the natural language input is ready to be processed. Thus, we have three steps: (1) parsing, (2) recognizing, and (3) linguistic processing. The problems of parsing natural language input and recognition are by no means trivial tasks. However, these problems are set aside to focus upon linguistic processing (see Figure 4 below).

Parsing—
Decomposition, syntax

Recognition—
Semantics

Linguistic Processors—
Composition into entities that
can be handled by the DSS

Figure 4. Stages of natural language processing.

Parsing—A decomposition into component parts as used by the linguistic processors.

Recognition—The determination by the DSS of when it has sufficient information, from the natural language input, to start up the linguistic processors.

Linguistic Processors—The fitting of the natural language input into the component parts and a composition into entities suitable for processing by the DSS.

We begin the study of natural language processing by defining *linguistic variable*.

> A linguistic variable is a variable whose values are natural language expressions referring to some quantity of interest. These natural language expressions are then, in turn, names of fuzzy sets composed of the possible numerical values that the quantity of interest can assume [7, p. 21].

The formal definition of linguistic variable is due to Zadeh [11]. However, the above working definition will suffice for now. Equipped with this concept, the component parts of natural language (Schmucker [7]) can be classified in the following way:

PRIMARY_term—Linguistic variables for which we have associated fuzzy sets.

HEDGE—Modifiers of primary terms.

FUZZIFIER—Fuzzification of primary terms.

RANGE—Two phrases separated by the key word TO.

RELATION HEDGE—Modifiers of relations.

RELATIONAL—Two phrases separated by the key word THAN.

RELATION—These are words such as "higher." A list for particular applications would have to be created.

NUMBERS—Fuzzy numbers or the fuzzification of real numbers.

Hedges, relations, relational hedges, and relationals are "simply" algorithms which transform a fuzzy set input into a fuzzy set output much as in FORTRAN, the symbols SIN(x) or EXP(x) transform x according to an algorithm.

3.1 Linguistic Processing. The function of the linguistic processors is to determine from the parsed input what type of process is required. Two such linguistic processes are *phrases* and *sentences*. Secondly, the linguistic processors compute the (fuzzy) value of the parsed linguistic expressions. Schmucker [7] modifies Hoffman's and Neitze's [5] use of the Backus-Naur Form (BNF) which is illustrated next by an example in the context of the IMPS.

Example (The petroleum example revisited)

The Component Parts

PRIMARY_term
primary := high|medium|low|confident

HEDGE
not, very, extremely, fairly, ..., sort of

FUZZIFIER
about, barely, reasonably, ..., null

RELATION
higher, lower, more, ..., less

RELATION HEDGE
much, ..., slightly

NUMBER
one, two, ..., ten, ..., 1, 2, ..., 10, ...

The linguistic processors, phrase and sentence, are created as follows.

LINGUISTIC PHRASE

<phrase> := (<hedge primary> | <range phrase>) - <confidence>

<confidence> := SF(CONFIDENT;<fuzzifier>)

<range phrase> := <hedge primary> TO <hedge primary>

<hedge primary> := <hedge(primary)> | <primary> | <fuzzy number>

<primary> := <primary_term>

<fuzzy number> := SF(NUMBER;<fuzzifier>)

LINGUISTIC SENTENCE

<sentence> := <compound phrase> | <simple phrase>

<compound phrase> := <conjunctive phrase> | <range phrase>

<simple phrase> := <relational phrase> | <hedge primary>

<conjunctive phrase> := <relational phrase> AND|OR <relational phrase>

<range phrase> := <hedge primary> TO <hedge primary>

<relational phrase> := <composite relation> THAN <hedge primary>

<composite relation> := <relational hedge><relation> | <relation>

<hedge primary> := <hedge(primary)> | <primary> | <fuzzy number>

<primary> := <primary_term>

<fuzzy number> := SF(NUMBER;<fuzzifier>)

An implementation of the above requires the development of the methods to obtain fuzzy sets from the hedges and relational phrases. We have already seen how fuzzification works. In the above, the function notation hedge(primary) means that the "hedge" is a rule which works on "primary." It suffices to show how to obtain a few linguistic computations since all are essentially done in the same way. The ones presented are found in Zimmermann [12,13]. It should be emphasized that the (fuzzy) operations that are used to compute are *subjectively* determined though considerable thought and empirical research has preceded their formulation.

MORE OR LESS primary_term := SF(primary_term;K)

NOT primary_term := complement of primary_term

PRETTY primary_term := NORM((INT(primary_term) AND INT(CON(primary_term))))

RATHER primary_term := NORM(INT(CON(primary_term)) AND CON(primary_term)))

SLIGHTLY primary_term := NORM(primary_term AND NOT VERY primary_term)

SORT OF primary_term := NORM((INT(DIL(primary_term)) AND INT(CON(primary_term))))

VERY primary_term := CON(primary_term)

For range expressions, we have the following:

$$A \text{ TO } B := \text{convex hull } \{A \cup B\},$$

where the union is the fuzzy union of fuzzy sets A and B. (See Figure 5.)

The keyword "THAN," as applied to the construction <composite relation> THAN <hedge primary> given above, denotes an action (shifts, intensifications, negations, complementations, or normalizations, for example) to be performed on <hedge primary>. The appropriate action, along with its direction and magnitude, is obtained from <composite relation>. For example, the phrase "more than medium" would shift the fuzzy set "medium" to the right a number of units determined by "more."

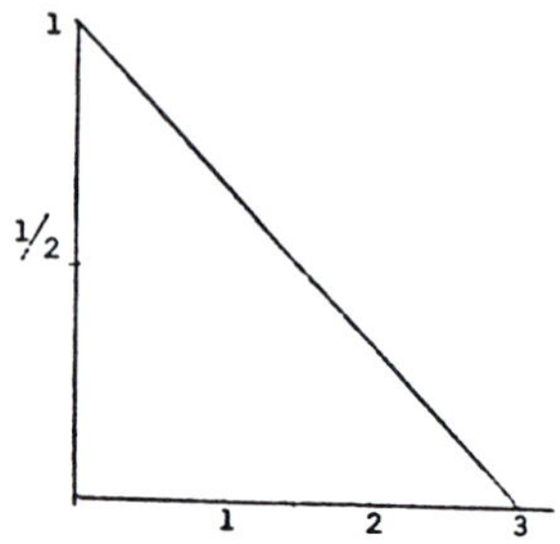

Figure 5.a. LOW.

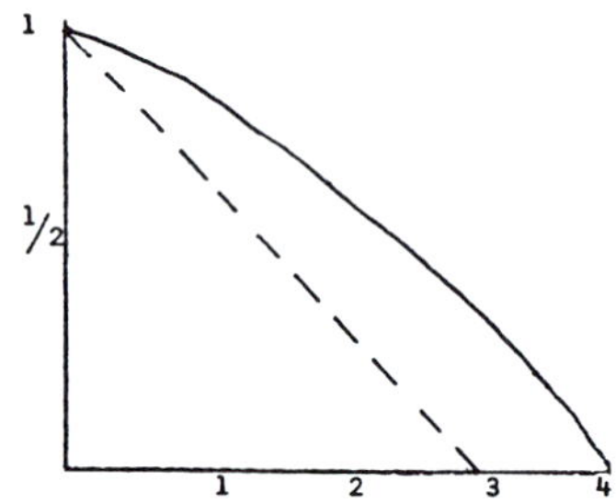

Figure 5.b. MORE OR LESS LOW.

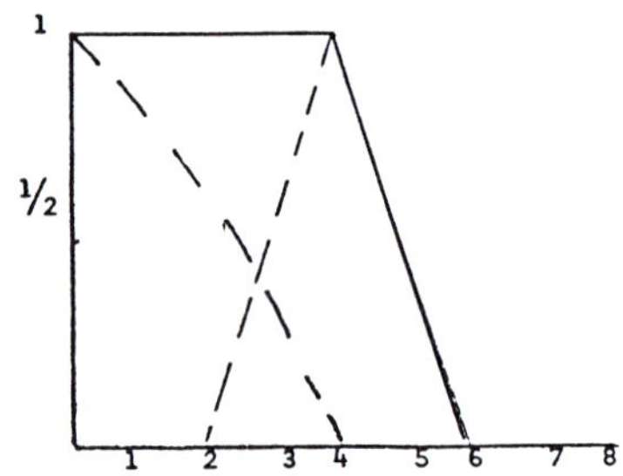

Figure 5.c. MORE OR LESS LOW TO MEDIUM.

III. THE TRANSLATION FROM FUZZY SETS TO NATURAL LANGUAGE

This section makes very brief mention of the inverse problem to the one which has been the main focus of the discussion so far. Zimmermann [12, p. 135] calls this process *linguistic approximation*, and in Zimmermann [14], 19 different *measures of similarity* are given. Suppose A is a fuzzy set for which a natural language expression is being sought. Schmucker [7, p. 33] proposes the following process though he does not describe it in the terms used below. This method is *not* recommended as will be discussed below but serves to illustrate the complexity of the inverse problem. Let the set of all fuzzy sets for which there are natural language expressions be

$$\begin{aligned} B = \{B_i : B_i & \text{ corresponds to a natural language expression,} \\ & \text{for } i = 1, \ldots, n, \text{ where } n \text{ is the number} \\ & \text{of all possible natural language expressions} \\ & \text{that are available to the DSS}\}. \end{aligned}$$

Then take the $L_2[0,1]$ norm (the Hilbert norm) of the difference of the corresponding membership function $(a(x) - b_i(x))$; that is, let the distance between fuzzy set A and B_i be defined as

$$d(A, B_i) = \left(\int_U [a(x) - b_i(x)]^2 \, dx\right)^{\frac{1}{2}}.$$

The natural language expression which corresponds to A is the expression corresponding to the B_i whose distance $d(a, B_i)$ is closest to zero.

The application of the above approach to complex DSS in general and the IMPS in particular should be avoided since there will usually be a combinatorially explosive number of possible fuzzy sets B_i. The number of possible B_i corresponds to the number of all possible phrase and sentence constructions from the component parts, many if not most of which will make no sense to human beings. Thus, the probability that a nonsense expression will be closest to the fuzzy set in question is quite high. Another problem arises when two B_i's have the same minimum distance to the fuzzy set A. These two sets could have entirely different natural language interpretations. These issues are discussed again in the context of the next section.

IV. ISSUES, LIMITATIONS, AND SPECULATIONS

The fuzzy set implementation of hedges and linguistic variables as presented herein has *not* been empirically tested to the extent that it has gained wide acceptance by the fuzzy set community. Fuzzy set theory can provide a useful framework *if* the empirical evidence eventually supports the fuzzy set interpretations of hedges and linguistic variables.

Moreover, the ultimate usefulness of fuzzy set theory for natural language processing in the context of DSS hinges on its ability to handle more complex structures than those presented here. To be sure, Schmucker [7, Chap. 5] uses fuzzy set theory to develop what can be considered a DSS called "The Fuzzy Risk Analyzer," using the structure presented in the previous section. It seems clear that for Schmucker's risk analyzer, fuzzy set theory is a useful framework. However, for a DSS such as the IMPS, the context of the natural language input is critical. For example, in the petrochemical discourse, the linguistic processor must know that the input "EXTREMELY LOW" refers to "demand for gasohol over the next 5 months in region X." Looking back at the formulation as presented in the previous section, for "EXTREMELY LOW" to also be a valid input for the supply of petroleum of various grades, new linguistic processors would have to be created. Clearly, the linguistic processors need to be made more flexible if this approach is to be utilized for more complex DSS such as the IMPS. This is not as critical an issue for the "Fuzzy Risk Analyzer" since its context is the same, risks to which a computer system may be subjected. Let us look at some approaches to the above issues.

Consider the simplest concatenation that can occur, a <phrase><phrase>. The simplest structure in this case is <hedge><hedge><primary_term>; for example, "SLIGHTLY VERY HIGH" or "VERY SLIGHTLY HIGH." There are at least three ways to compute such a concatenation: (1) as a composition, (2) as a certainty measure, or (3) as a fuzzy weighted mean.

The composition approach would allow for the component parts to act on component parts so that "SLIGHTLY VERY HIGH" is interpreted as SLIGHTLY acting in accordance to its definition on the fuzzy set VERY HIGH. This is a very computationally appealing approach but requires the modification of the linguistic processors so that they can act on themselves much as recursive calls of a subroutine in PASCAL or C. The definition that would be added to the linguistic processor is

$$< \text{hedge1} >< \text{hedge2(primary\_term)} >:= \text{hedge1(hedge2(primary\_term))}.$$

Is this computationally appealing method semantically correct? Are there rules that could be put into a knowledge base describing when it makes sense to concatenate with composition and when to use some other approach?

The certainty measure approach would consider "SLIGHTLY VERY HIGH" as a measure of belief or disbelief in the sense that Shortliffe and Buchanan [8] developed. According to this approach, evidence 1 would be "SLIGHTLY," evidence 2 would be "VERY," and the hypothesis (using this term rather loosely) would be "HIGH." Using Shortliffe's and Buchanan's measure of belief, we would get:

$$\begin{aligned} < \text{hedge1} > < \text{hedge2(primary\_term)} >:= &\ \text{hedge1(primary\_term)} \\ &+ \text{hedge2(primary\_term)}[1 - \text{hedge2(primary\_term)}]. \end{aligned}$$

The fuzzy weighted mean approach is as follows for the above:

$$\begin{aligned} < \text{hedge1} > < \text{hedge2(primary\_term)} >:= &\ (w1[\text{hedge(primary\_term)}] \\ &+ w2[\text{hedge2(primary\_term)}])\,/(w1 + w2), \end{aligned}$$

where $w1$ and $w2$ are fuzzy weights (fuzzified numbers or fuzzy numbers).

The arithmetic operations in the fuzzy weighted mean are all fuzzy arithmetic operations. This approach is the one used by Schmucker [7, pp. 44–56]. However, one problem with the fuzzy weighted mean (besides how to choose the fuzzy weights) is that to perform the requisite fuzzy arithmetic, all the terms must be fuzzy numbers. This cannot be guaranteed given the operations which describe hedges and relations. For example, the membership function for "MEDIUM" is undoubtedly a bell-shaped curve. Any operation involving "NOT" will transform the characteristic function of "MEDIUM" into a fuzzy set which is not a fuzzy number according to the definition (see [6]). Clearly, any computer implementation of the fuzzy weighted mean as a way to concatenate phrases must take care to insure that the entities it uses in the arithmetic operations above are fuzzy numbers.

The issue of more flexible linguistic processors has at least two aspects, (1) the incorporation of the context of the discourse into the linguistic processors and (2) the use of phrases and sentences as "building blocks" to allow for the concatenation of these structures. The problem of contexts could be handled by creating another component part called "context," for example. The primary terms could then be identified not only by name but by context in much the same way as an array or "case of" identifies several variables with the same name. When in a natural language discourse, the context would be known and passed to the linguistic processors.

The linguistic processors could themselves be building blocks by adding a higher level metalinguistic processor which defines how phrases and sentences can be put together. This would allow for the rules of the concatenation to be defined such as in <phrase><phrase> mentioned above.

Lastly, the problem of mapping a fuzzy set to natural language is a very challenging one. Fuzzy clustering techniques seem to be an unproductive approach unless the context of the discourse can sufficiently narrow the possible natural language expressions from which the association is to be made. Even so, the question of the appropriateness of the natural language expression closest in the $L_2[0,1]$ norm is an open question. A "linguistic filter" to eliminate nonsense phrases and sentences is essential. Should such a filter be rule-based or a numerical algorithm? Can the filtering process be made to reflect the context of the discourse?

Minimum distance, fuzzy clustering, or pattern recognition algorithms would seem to be a useful approach if the comparison space were the set of the sensible natural language expression germane to the context of discourse. How would one construct such a comparison space? Is there a special "linguistic metric" appropriate to the context of the discourse that could be devised?

Another approach that could be explored is to construct linguistic *output* processors where these would work in a reverse fashion from the phrase and sentence processors developed in the previous sections. That is, a linguistic output processor would take fuzzy sets as "primary_term" inputs and produce linguistic variables along with modifiers as outputs. Within its structure could be fuzzy clustering algorithms in context of the discourse.

BIBLIOGRAPHY AND REFERENCES

1. I. R. Goodman and H. T. Nguyen, 1985. *Uncertainty Models for Knowledge Based Systems*, North-Holland.
2. H. J. Greenberg, 1987a. "Pursuits," *IMPS Consortium Report No. 2*, University of Colorado at Denver.
3. H. J. Greenberg, 1987b. "Where Are We Going with the Development of an Intelligent Mathematical Programming System?" *IMPS Discussion Paper*, University of Colorado at Denver.
4. M. M. Gupta, 1977. "Fuzzy-ism—The First Decade," in *Fuzzy Automata and Decision Processes*, M. M. Gupta, G. N. Saridi, and B. R. Gaines (eds.), Elsevier.
5. L. J. Hoffman and L. A. Neitzel, 1980. "Inexact Risk Analysis," *Proceeding of the IEEE 1980 International Conference on Cybernetics and Society*, Boston, Massachusetts.
6. A. Kaufmann and M. M. Gupta, 1985. *Introduction to Fuzzy Arithmetic*, Van Nostrand Reinhold.
7. K. Schmucker, 1984. *Fuzzy Sets, Natural Language Computations, and Risk Analysis*, Computer Science Press.
8. E. H. Shortliffe and B. G. Buchanan, 1975. "A Model of Inexact Reasoning in Medicine," *Mathematical Bioscience*, Vol. 23, 351–379.
9. J. F. Sowa, 1984. *Conceptual Structures: Information Processing in Mind and Machine*, Addison-Wesley.
10. L. A. Zadeh, 1972. "A Fuzzy-Set-Theoretic Interpretation of Linguistic Hedges," *Journal of Cybernetic*, Vol. 2, 4–34.
11. L. Zadeh, 1975. "The Concept of a Linguistic Variable and Its Application to Approximate Reasoning," *Information Science*, Vol. 8 (pp. 199–249, 301–357), Vol. 9 (pp. 43– 80).
12. H. J. Zimmermann, 1985. *Fuzzy Set Theory—and Its Applications*, Kluwer Nijhoff.
13. H. J. Zimmermann, 1987a. *Fuzzy Sets, Decision Making and Expert Systems*, Kluwer Nijhoff.
14. H. J. Zimmermann, 1987b. (These Proceedings.)

STOCHASTIC PROGRAMMING MODELS

FOR DEDICATED PORTFOLIO SELECTION

by Jeremy F. Shapiro
Massachusetts Institute of Technology
and
Resource Management Systems

INTRODUCTION

Dedicated bond portfolios, even when they are conservatively assembled and managed, are still subject to major uncertainties and risks. Uncertainties associated with interest rates, and their effect on bond prices, have received the greatest attention from financial planners and theorists. Other uncertainties include the cash requirements or liabilities of the dedicated portfolio, the possibility of bond re-calls or defaults due to bankruptcy, to name just a few. Joehnck[1] has a lengthier discussion of these and other risks associated with dedicated and other fixed income portfolio selection problems.

Many articles have appeared in recent years proposing immunization approaches that the fixed income portfolio manager can follow to control risk in the face of interest rate uncertainties. These approaches, often linked to duration measures (Fisher and Weil[2], Biermag et al[3]), are meant to guarantee that the portfolio's value does not fall below some target value at the end of a pre-specified horizon. Although duration was originally a theoretical development based on restrictive assumptions (MacCauley[4]), some authors suggest that it possesses reasonable empirical properties even when these assumptions do not hold (Christensen, et al[5]).

A development that parallels research on immunization is the recent introduction of optimization, or mathematical programming, models for fixed income portfolio selection. These are data driven models that allow financial managers to explicitly minimize the cost of assembling or re-assembling a portfolio to meet future requirements or liabilities, subject to constraints on the bonds' attributes. Duration might be included as an attribute to be constrained.

NATO ASI Series, Vol. F48
Mathematical Models for Decision Support
Edited by G. Mitra

Most large investment houses in the United States are using some type of mathematical programming model for fixed income portfolio selection. To date, these have been exclusively deterministic models that assume all data pertaining to the future, including interest rates, are known with certainty. Uncertainties are examined indirectly by sensitivity analyses, or by performing scenario tests on key parameters, such as interest rates, to see how the optimal solutions vary. While these approaches have their value, the analysis is incomplete because each model optimization assumes there is only one scenario of the future, and moreover that it will occur with certainty.

In this paper, we demonstrate how mathematical programming models for fixed income portfolio selection can be extended to explicitly treat uncertainties and risk. Specifically, we will develop stochastic programming with recourse models that allow a dedicated portfolio manager to consider simultaneously multiple scenarios of an uncertain future. The models calculate optimal contingency plans for each scenario which in turn are explicitly considered in the calculation of an optimal here-and-now purchasing (and/or selling) strategy for the portfolio. In effect, the here-and-now strategy is an optimal hedge against future uncertainties, taking into account the contingency plans that have been predetermined for each scenario.

Stochastic programming allows a direct and intuitive modeling of uncertainties. The results these models produce are not dependent upon assumptions about parallel shifts in the yield curve, or any other restrictive assumption on the underlying probability generating structures. Moreover, uncertainties are not limited to interest rates. Any combination of factors is allowed. All that is required is an objective or subjective forecast or judgment of the scenarios to be considered and their associated probabilities.

The modeling approach for dedicated portfolio selection that we propose here appears new. Bradley and Crane[6] report on a stochastic programming model for managing bank bond portfolios that is similar in spirit to ours, but which predates recent research developments in fixed income and dedicated portfolio research. Moreover, our models are in part an outgrowth of large scale deterministic models for dedicated portfolio selection that are currently in active use by brokerage houses.

In the following section, we review deterministic mathematical programming models for dedicated portfolio selection. In the section after that, we extend the deterministic models to stochastic ones. We then illustrate the stochastic programming approach with a numerical dedicated portfolio selection problem. The paper concludes with remarks about future research.

DETERMINISTIC MATHEMATICAL PROGRAMMING MODELS

In this section, we review deterministic mathematical programming models for fixed income portfolio selection. The basic model we present determines a minimal cost purchasing strategy for bonds whose income streams are used to meet forecasted cash requirements or liabilities. After that, we discuss briefly extensions of the basic model. At the end of this section, we discuss practical implementations of these models. In the following section, the models are extended to stochastic models that explicitly treat uncertainties.

Indices:

j bonds ($j = 1,\ldots, N$)

t time periods ($t = 0, 1,\ldots, T$)

Parameters:

c_j = current market price for bond j (measured in dollars; par = \$100)

f_{jt} = cash flow produced by bond j at the end of period t (from coupons and principal re-payment; measured in dollars)

L_t = cash requirement or liability to be paid at the end of period t (measured in millions of dollars)

q_j = conditional minimum purchase quantity of bond j (minimal quantity that must be purchased if any of bond j is purchased at all; measured in thousands of bonds)

Q_j = maximum allowable purchase of bond j (measured in millions of dollars)

a_t = re-investment rate for period t (return at the end of period t of \$1 invested at the end of period t-1)

Decision Variables:

x_j = quantity of bond j to be purchased here and now (measured in thousands of bonds)

s_t = cash surplus to be accumulated at the end of period t (measured in millions of dollars)

$$d_j = \begin{cases} 1 \text{ if bond } j \text{ selected for the portfolio} \\ 0 \text{ otherwise} \end{cases}$$

The basic (deterministic) mathematical programming model for fixed income portfolio selection is the mixed integer program

Minimize

$$\sum_{j=1}^{N} c_j x_j + s_0 \tag{1a}$$

subject to

$$\sum_{j=1}^{N} f_{jt} x_j + a_t s_{t-1} - s_t = L_t \quad \text{for } t = 1, \ldots, T \tag{1b}$$

$$\left.\begin{aligned} x_j - q_j d_j &\geq 0 \\ x_j - Q_j d_j &\leq 0 \end{aligned}\right\} \text{ for } j = 1, \ldots, N \tag{1c}$$

$$x_j \geq 0, \quad s_t \geq 0, \quad d_j = 0 \text{ or } 1 \tag{1d}$$

The objective function (1a) in this model is the sum of bond purchases plus an initial cash investment s0 that is guaranteed to return $a_0 s_0$ at the end of the first period in the planning horizon. Initial cash investments are typically required to cover cash requirements or liabilities in early periods (usually months) before coupons or principal re-payments are realized in sufficient quantities.

The constraints (1b) are cash balance equations stating that cash from coupons and principal re-payment, plus re-investments of the cash surplus from the previous period, must at least equal the forecasted requirements or liabilities for the period. Any cash left over becomes the cash surplus that is re-invested for the current period. For conservative portfolio selection, a_t is sometimes taken to be small or even zero.

The constraints (1c) impose the logical condition that either $x_j = 0$ (when $d_j = 0$) or $q_j < x_j < Q_j$ (when $d_j = 1$). The imposition of these constraints in important to ensure that the model produces realistic, implementable answers since a fixed income portfolio manager will usually insist on a fairly large threshold q_j for the purchase of each bond j.

Extensions

The basic model just described can be extended in a number of directions. First, we can easily add constraints on attributes; for example, average S&P rating, average maturity, no more than 20% in utility bonds, etc. Such constraints can be expressed as linear inequalities of the form

$$\sum_{j=1}^{N} t_{ij}x_j \begin{cases} \leq & b_i \\ = & b_i \\ \geq & b_i \end{cases}$$

where t_{ij} is the value of the attribute associated with bond j, and b_i is its target value. Attribute constraints may include one or more duration constraint.

Similar constraints can be added limiting the proportion of the portfolio invested in a specified industry to no more than or no less than a specified percentage. Zero-one constraints on the d_j can limit the number of individual bonds in the entire portfolio, or limit the number of bonds from a specified subset of the universe of bonds. The basic model can also be easily modified to impose the condition that the bond quantities be bought in integer lots between the limits q_j and Q_j.

Finally, the objective function in the model can be replaced by other objective functions. These might include maximizing yield, maximizing rating, and so on. In principle, any attribute can be designed as the objective function to be maximized or minimized. Multi-objective optimization of the portfolio can be carried out by optimizing a weighted average of the different objective functions, or by the imposition of goal or target constraints on them.

The basic model and the extensions just described pertain to the single fund fixed income selection problem. The same constructs can be used to model multiple funds. For these problems, however, we must add constraints on flows between funds reflecting legal and management policies. We may also wish to employ a different objective function; for example, in the case of multiple construction funds, an objective function that maximizes the number of time periods whose requirements are covered by the fund.

Current Technology

The discussion above has focused on features of deterministic mathematical programming models currently employed by large brokerage houses to analyze dedicated portfolio selection problems. Before leaving this discussion, it is worthwhile discussing briefly the technology available for implementing efficient and effective planning systems embodying these models.

Specialized optimization routines are desirable for large dedicated portfolio selection problems involving liabilities in the hundreds of millions or even billions of dollars, several hundred periods, and 200 or more bonds. We have developed LP approximations to reduce the number of bonds that must be considered, and layered branch-and-bound searched based on decision variable priorities that greatly speed up model optimization. Even the largest models can be optimized in less than 20 CPU minutes, usually in less than 10 CPU minutes, on a mainframe computer.

By contrast, many smaller companies and financial institutions wish to solve smaller dedicated portfolio selection problems arising in pension planning, municipal construction project financing, and so on. Developments over the past five years make it possible to completely model and optimize these problems on microcomputers (Resource Management Systems[8]). A hybrid technology in which the micro is connected to a mainframe containing bond price information, and which can perform large scale model optimization if he need arises, is an attractive configuration.

STOCHASTIC PROGRAMMING MODELS

The models discussed in the previous section assume that all data pertaining to future fixed income portfolio planning is known with certainty. In other words, the model considers a single, deterministic scenario of the future. We relax this assumption by explicitly modeling multiple scenarios of the future, each with an associated probability of occurrence. Although only one of these scenarios will actually occur, our analysis proceeds by computing optimal contingency plans for all of them. This information is then used to compute a here-and-now bond selection strategy that optimally hedges against these contingency plans.

The type of model just described is called stochastic programming with recourse (see Wagner[9], Bienstock and Shapiro[10]). Stochastic programming has been extensively studied as a theoretical construct in the operations research literature, but infrequently applied up until this time. However, computer technologies, such as those discussed at the end of the previous section, have progressed to the point that the approach is viable for practical real-world problems.

In the discussion that follows, we present three related examples of stochastic programming models for fixed income portfolio selection. These examples are small, but not trivial, and were chosen to illustrate the types of questions that can be asked and answered by the models. The examples are merely selections from a large family of possible models for analyzing fixed income problems. A numerical example of our models is discussed in the following section.

EXTENSIONS TO THE BASIC MODEL

We begin with a discussion of the new indices, parameters and variables that need to be added to the deterministic model of the previous section.

New Indices:

k scenarios of the uncertain future ($k = 1, 2, \ldots, K$)

t^* last time period when all parameters known with certainty

New Parameters:

L_{kt} = cash liability to be met in period t under scenario k

a_{kt} = re-investment rate for period t

p_k = probability that scenario k will occur

v_{kt} = discount factor for cash flows in period t under scenario k

New Decision Variables:

M_{kt} = additional cash required in period t under scenario k

With this background, we can state our basic stochastic programming model

minimize

$$\sum_{j=1}^{N} c_j x_j + \sum_{k=1}^{N} \sum_{t=t^*+1}^{T} p_k v_{kt} M_{kt} + s_0 \tag{2a}$$

subject to

$$\sum_{j=1}^{N} f_{jt} x_j + a_t s_{t-1} - s_t = L_t \tag{2b}$$

for $t = 1, 2, \ldots, t^*$

For $k = 1, 2, \ldots, K$

$$\sum_{j=1}^{N} f_{jt} x_j + a_{kt} s_{k,t-1} - s_{kt} + M_{kt} = L_{kt} \tag{2c}$$

for $t = t^*+1, \ldots, T$

$$\left.\begin{aligned} x_j - q_j d_j &\geq 0 \\ x_j - Q_j d_j &\leq 0 \end{aligned}\right\} \text{ for } j = 1, \ldots, N \tag{2d}$$

$$x_j \geq 0,\ s_{jt} \geq 0,\ s_{kt} \geq 0,\ M_{kt} \geq 0,\ d_j = 0 \text{ or } 1 \tag{2e}$$

The objective function (2a) includes the here-and-now costs

$$\sum_{j=1}^{N} c_j x_j + s_0$$

as before. To these we add the expected discounted costs

$$\sum_{k=1}^{K} \sum_{t=t^*+1} p_k a_{kt} M_{kt}$$

of the additional cash M_{kt} that will be needed in later periods to meet liabilities. The liability constraints (2b) have precisely the same form as the liability constraints (1b) in the deterministic model. This is because we assume that liabilities and interest rates for the first t^* periods are known with certainty.

For each scenario k, the constraints (2c) for $t = t^*$, $t^*+1, \ldots, T$, are the probabilistic liability constraints to be satisfied. Unlike the deterministic case, we cannot be sure that the liabilities L_{kt} can be met by cash flows from bond investments and re-investment of cash surpluses. For this reason, we have included the recourse variables M_{kt} representing cash that must be added in period t to meet the liabilities under scenario k.

The reader should note that re-investments of cash surpluses in each period are now dependent on the scenario rate of return a_{kt}. This number should be directly derived from the risk free rate of interest i_{kt} for that period by the relation $a_{kt} = 1 + i_{kt}$. Moreover, we compute the discount factor

$$v_{kt} = 1/(\prod_{t=1}^{T} (1+i_{kt}))$$

Note also that, unlike the deterministic model where the analyst may feel obliged to assume conservatively low re-investment rates, in our stochastic programming model, the forecasted rates a_{kt} in each scenario.

<u>Incorporating Call Options</u>

A major concern of financial planners in times of high interest rates is the possibility that bonds with call options will in fact be called when interest rates decline sufficiently. Thus, if a low cost scenario actually comes to pass, the planner may suddenly be faced with large amounts of surplus cash that need to be re-invested, but at lower rates than would have been received from the coupons of the called bond.

The basic model described above can be readily extended to incorporate the uncertainties associated with call options. The analysis permits the planner to decide here and now whether the risk associated with a call option inhibits him from purchasing the bond.

For expositional simplicity, we assume that only one bond, say bond $j = j^1$, has a call option. Moreover, we assume that the call option will be realistically exercised only under one scenario, say scenario K which we can assume to be the low cost scenario. Again for expositional simplicity, we assume that bond j1 will be called during this scenario in period $t^{**} \geq t^* + 1$ if it is ever to be called. We let r_{j1}, t^{**} denote the premium rate at which the bond is called in this period.

Finally, we let p_{K0}, p_{K1} and denote the probabilities associated with the new scenarios, K0 corresponds to "the bond is never called"; K1 corresponds to "the bond is called in period t**". Since these scenarios are a refinement of scenario K in the basic model, we have

$$p_{K0} + p_{K1} + p_{K2} = p_K$$

Extending the basic model to incorporate the possibility of a call on bond j_1 in period t** is relatively straightforward. The objective function (2a) is the same except the summation involving k is extended include the two new scenarios replacing scenario K.

The constraints of our model remain unchanged except constraints (2c) pertaining to scenario k which must be split into two new scenarios starting in period t**. In particular, we have for k = 0

$$\sum_{j=1}^{N} f_{jt}x_j + a_{Kt}s_{k0,t-1} - s_{K0t} + M_{K0t} = L_{Kt}$$

for t = t**,...T

and for k = K1

$$\sum_{\substack{j=1 \\ \text{and } j \neq j1}}^{N} f_{jt^{**}}x_j + r_{j1,t^{**}}x_{j1}$$

$$+ a_{Kt}s_{K1,t^{**}-1} - s_{K1,t^{**}} + M_{K1,t^{**}} = L_{Kt^{**}}$$

and

$$\sum_{j=1}^{N} f_{jt}x_j + a_{Kt}s_{K1,t-1} - s_{K1t} + M_{K1t} = L_{Kt}$$

for t=t** + 1,...,T

where

$$s_{K0,t^{**}-1} = s_{K1,t^{**}-1} = s_{K,t^{**}-1}$$

Note that the linkage from scenario K to the two new scenarios K0 and K1 is via the cash surplus term $s_{K,t^{**}-1}$.

Cost vs. Risk Tradeoff

The pension manager or financial officer responsible for the dedicated portfolio is at risk in the face of the uncertainties because he may be asked at some future time to put more money into the portfolio to cover its liabilities. The manager can control this risk by placing a constraint of the form

$$\sum_{t=t^*+1,}^{T} M_{kt} \leq R \tag{4}$$

on all the scenarios. Thus, under any eventuality (scenario), the maximal amount of additional money that he may be required to put into the portfolio is R.

If R is very large, the additional amount paid in under all scenarios will be less than R. Even if R is relatively small, R may not be reached exactly due to the lumpiness inherent in our bond selection. For certain values of R, the constraints (2d) may lead to an optimal portfolio in which constraint (4) is not satisfied exactly, although it does affect the portfolio's selection. At the extreme, with R = 0, the manager takes no risk and selects here-and-now a portfolio that guarantees that no additional money will be required to meet liabilities.

In a specific application, the manager may have a choice of R, based on political or other considerations. In other circumstances, this choice may be less clear. In such an instance, we can optimize the model parametrically to obtain a cost vs. risk curve analogous to the return vs. risk curve of classical equity portfolio theory (e.g., Alexander & Francis[11]). The manager must then use his judgment in deciding where on the curve he would like to be in structuring his fixed income portfolio. An example of a cost vs. risk curve is provided in the following section where we present a numerical example of the models.

Stochastic Programming Methodologies

We complete this section with three comments about stochastic programming models and methods for optimizing them as they relate to the dedicated portfolio selection models just discussed. First, the reader may have noticed that the uncertainties about interest rates were abruptly resolved at the start of period t*+1, after which we knew with certainty which of the three scenarios obtained for the remainder of our planning horizon. This was clearly a gross oversimplification of the way in which forecasts about interest rates are determined and evolve. The simplification can be justified, at least in part, by the fact that we are mainly concerned with an optimal here-and-now portfolio selection. Thus, we may be willing to accept the simplification because it nevertheless provides us with useful information about future contingency plans upon which we base our here-and-now hedging against the uncertainties.

On the other hand, if we decide that the simplification is overdrawn, we can choose to extend the stochastic programming model to one with more stages during which the interest rates evolve in a probabilistic manner. Figure 1 contains a tree depicting such a multi-stage evolution of interest rates.

In any event, whether or not we are willing to accept the implication inherent in the model described above, that model can be viewed mathematically as an approximation to more complex models in which the scenarios are played out in more detail. The interest rate scenarios that we know with certainty starting in period t^*+1 in the above model are the mathematical expectations of probabilistic interest rate forecasts stretching out until the end of our planning horizon. In short, the model developed above is but one in a series of stochastic programming approximations that we could develop for analyzing the effect of interest rate uncertainties on dedicated portfolio selection strategies. More research is required to understand the nature of these approximations and how best to apply them to dedicated portfolio selection problems.

Secondly, we have not addressed in our model development how one proceeds from a descriptive forecasting model of interest rates and liabilities to scenarios in a stochastic programming model. Space does not allow us to discuss these techniques, although they are obviously important to our model construction. It suffices to say that effective techniques for extracting scenarios from forecasting models do exist and could be readily implemented in a planning system embodying the stochastic programming models. The reader is referred to Hiller[12] for details.

Finally, we mention that stochastic programming with recourse models are well structured for the application

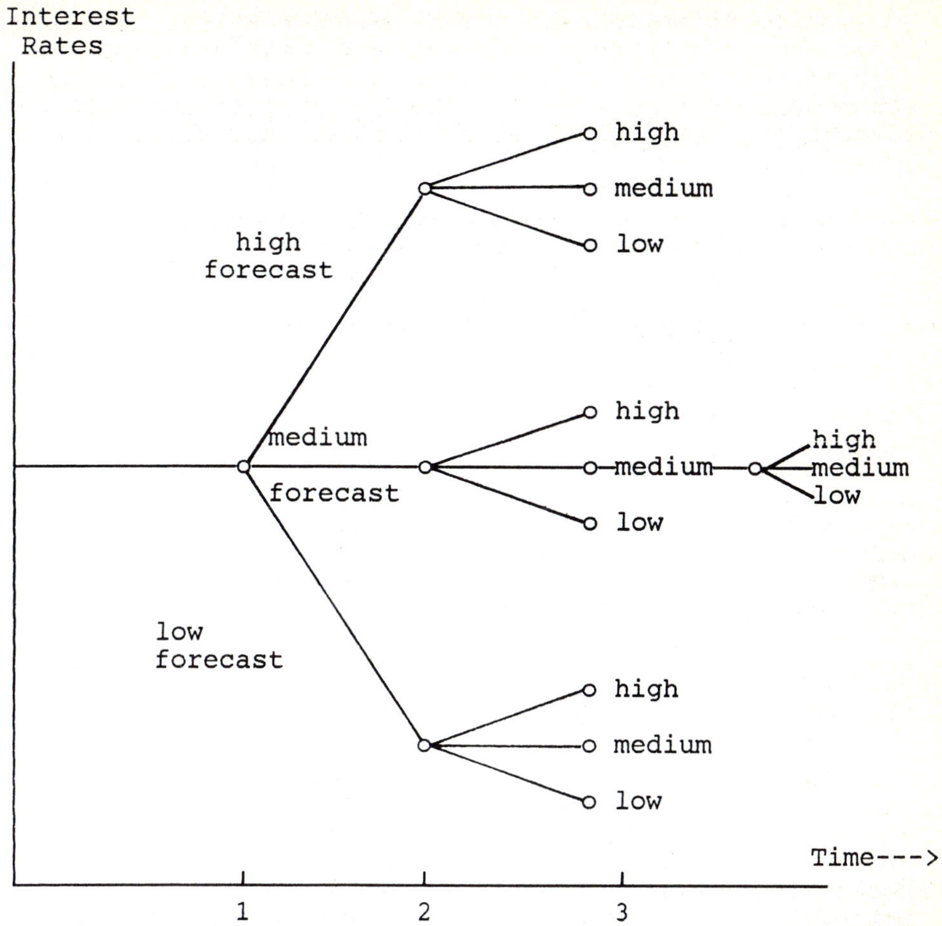

FIGURE 1: Multi-stage Interest Rate Forecasting

of decomposition methods. This means that very large models could be broken down into manageable sub-models that in turn could be systematically reassembled. The sub-models in this case are the linear programs for determining contingency plans for each scenario, plus a master mixed integer programming sub-model for determining the here-and-now bond selection strategy. A decomposition approach based on this methodology was successfully implemented by Bienstock and Shapiro[10].

ILLUSTRATIVE EXAMPLE

We illustrate the stochastic programming models discussed in the previous section with a numerical example. The example involves the 8 bonds displayed in Table 1 and the liability stream displayed in Table 2. For simplicity, we have assumed the liabilities are known with certainty and that it is uncertainty about interest rates that drives the analysis. Notice that bond 8 has a call option starting in year 4. A premium of 3.2 points will be given if the bond is called at the end of year 4; the premium declines linearly until the maturity date at the end of year 12.

Interest rate uncertainties and the possibility that bond 8 will be called are the two stochastic elements that we wish to explicitly model. Table 3 lists the three interest rate scenarios that we will consider. For expositional simplicity, we assume that the only scenario under which bond 8 will be called is scenario 3. Moreover, the only period in which it may be called is period 7; we assess a probability of .5 that it will be called in that period.

Given this description of the uncertainties, our 15 year planning horizon is broken into three stages: the first stage consisting of the first three years during which all data is known with certainty; the second stage consisting of years 4, 5, 6 during which we know which interest scenario has occurred but do not know whether or not bond 8 will be called; the third stage consisting of years 7 through 15 during which all the uncertainties have been revealed (interest rates and bond calls). Contingency actions of putting more money into the portfolio are allowed in both the second and the third stages. The different scenarios are depicted graphically in Figure 2. Note that the example actually involves four scenarios: high interest rate, medium interest rate, low interest rate/bond 8 called, low interest rate/bond 8 not called.

BOND DATA

TABLE 1

BOND NUMBER	PRICE	COUPON	MATURITY (years)
1	095.375	.085	5
2	100.125	.09	12
3	103.50	.0925	15
4	099.00	.105	3
5	091.00	.075	6
6	089.00	.07	8
7	088.00	.0675	11
8*	119.50	.12	12

NOTES:

All bonds have maximum purchase quantity equal to 50,000, conditional minimum purchase quantity equal to 10,000.

* Bond callable starting in year 4.

STOCHASTIC PROGRAMMING EXAMPLE

LIABILITY STREAM

TABLE 2

YEAR	LIABILITY ($ x 10^6)
0	10
1	11
2	12
3	14
4	15
5	17
6	19
7	20
8	22
9	24
10	26
11	29
12	31
13	33
14	36
15	40

STOCHASTIC PROGRAMMING EXAMPLE

INTEREST RATE SCENARIOS

TABLE 3

YEAR	SCENARIO 1	SCENARIO 2	SCENARIO 3
1	.08	.08	.08
2	.08	.08	.08
3	.08	.08	.080
4	.085	.08	.075
5	.09	.08	.07
6	.095	.08	.065
7	.10	.08	.06
8	.105	.08	.06
9	.11	.08	.06
10	.11	.08	.06
11	.11	.08	.06
12	.11	.08	.06
13	.11	.08	.06
14	.11	.08	.06
15	.11	.08	.06
PROBABILITY OF OCCURRENCE	0.20	0.50	0.30

STOCHASTIC PROGRAMMING EXAMPLE

SCENARIO DESCRIPTIONS

FIGURE 2

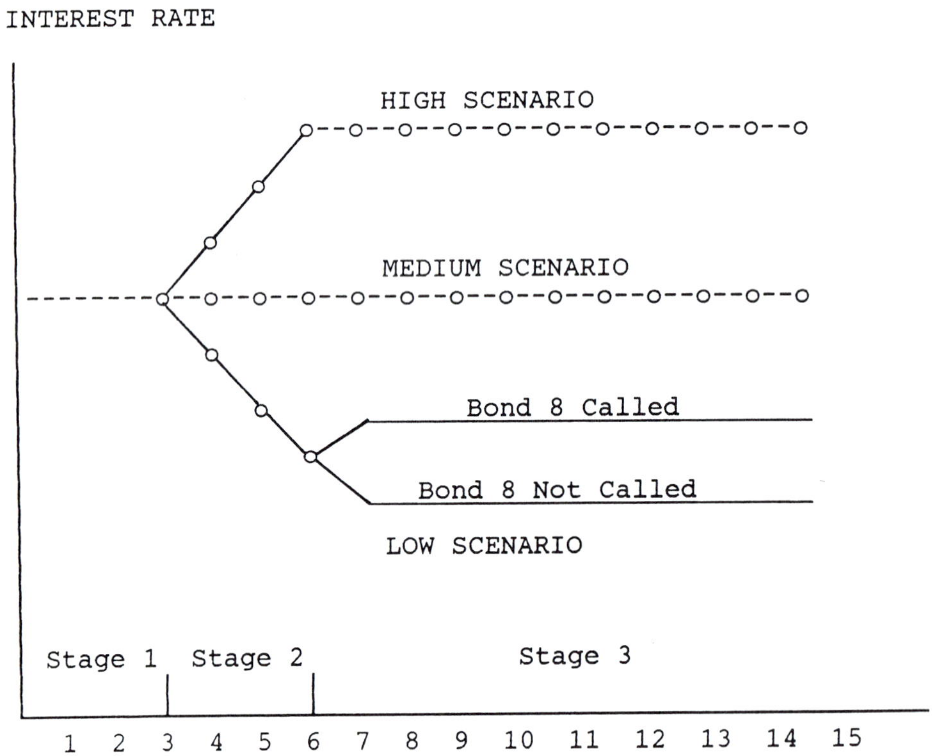

FIGURE 2: **Stochastic Programming Example Scenario Descriptions**

We made a number of runs with our stochastic programming model varying the risk permitted during the second and third stages. Recall that risk is measured by the amount of additional money that must be put into the dedicated portfolio to cover shortfalls in income. The results are listed in Table 4.

At zero risk, that is, when a portfolio must be selected here-and-now that guarantees an income stream covering all scenarios, a spread of bonds not including the callable bond is optimal. At relatively small levels of risk, the callable bond becomes somewhat attractive as a alternative to the lower yielding bonds 6 and 7.

With risk unconstrained, the optimal choice is to eschew bond 8 and select instead the higher yield bond 4, despite the fact that it matures early. The optimal contingency plan under the low interest scenario is then to pump a total of $97.85M into the portfolio towards the end of the planning horizon.

Bond 5 appears attractive at all levels of risk because it matures at the end of year 6 when the added cash can be used to meet rising liability payments, and when there is a likelihood that it can be profitably re-invested. A summary of the risk binding scenarios is given in Table 5.

Figure 3 is a plot of expected cost versus risk. Since this plot has a "knee" at approximately $20M risk, we can conclude that the financial manager has three distinct qualitative choices available to him in the face of uncertainties. He can be very risk averse and choose the conservative portfolio associated with zero risk. Second, he can be moderately conservative (moderately risky) and include the high yielding but callable bond 8, but not include the high yield, early maturing bond 4. He must then be prepared to pump more money into the portfolio in later years, especially under the low interest rate scenario. Third, he can be less conservative (more risky), and choose bond 4 over bond 8, and be prepared in the low interest rate scenario to pump a relatively large amount of additional cash into the portfolio in years 12, 13, and 14.

Finally, Table 6 lists the results of portfolio optimization when we replaced the stochastic model by two version of its expected value model. In version one, we replaced all of the cash flows by their average or expected cash flows. Specifically, the cash flow from bond 8 was taken to be its average over the four scenarios; the reinvestment rates after period 3 were taken to be the average of the three interest rate scenario reinvestment rates. In version two, we chose

STOCHASTIC PROGRAMMING EXAMPLE

OPTIMAL BOND SELECTION STRATEGIES

TABLE 4

RISK	0	5	10	20	40	500 (97.85)
BOND						
1	0	0	0	0	0	0
2	50.0	50.0	50.0	50.0	50.0	50.0
3	36.6	36.6	36.6	36.6	23.9	0
4	0	0	0	0	10.0	38.7
5	10.0	42.4	50.0	50.0	50.0	50.0
6	32.5	42.3	0	0	0	0
7	46.4	0	0	0	0	0
8	0	0	24.8	22.2	21.0	0
Here-and-Now Cost	176.80	167.00	163.28	160.17	155.29	133.88
Future Expected Cost	0	8.19	11.28	13.78	18.60	39.92
TOTAL COST	176.80	175.19	174.53	173.95	173.89	173.76

STOCHASTIC PROGRAMMING EXAMPLE

BINDING SCENARIOS

TABLE 5

Risk ≤ 5	Low Interest Scenario
	\$5M added in Period 4
Risk ≤ 10	Low Interest/Bond Called Scenario
	\$4.24M added in Period 4 \$5.76M added in Period 7
Risk ≤ 20	Low Interest/Bond Called Scenario*
	\$12.33M added in Period 9 \$ 7.67M added in Period 14
Risk ≤ 40	Low Interest/Bond Called Scenario
	\$40M added in Period 14
Risk Unbounded	Low Interest Scenario
	\$16.0M added in Period 12 \$ 8.9M added in Period 13 \$73.7M added in Period 14

* Low Interest/Bond Not Called Scenario

\$8.87M added in Period 11
\$5.83M added in Period 14

Medium Interest Rate Scenario

\$4.69M added in Period 11
\$3.89M added in Period 14

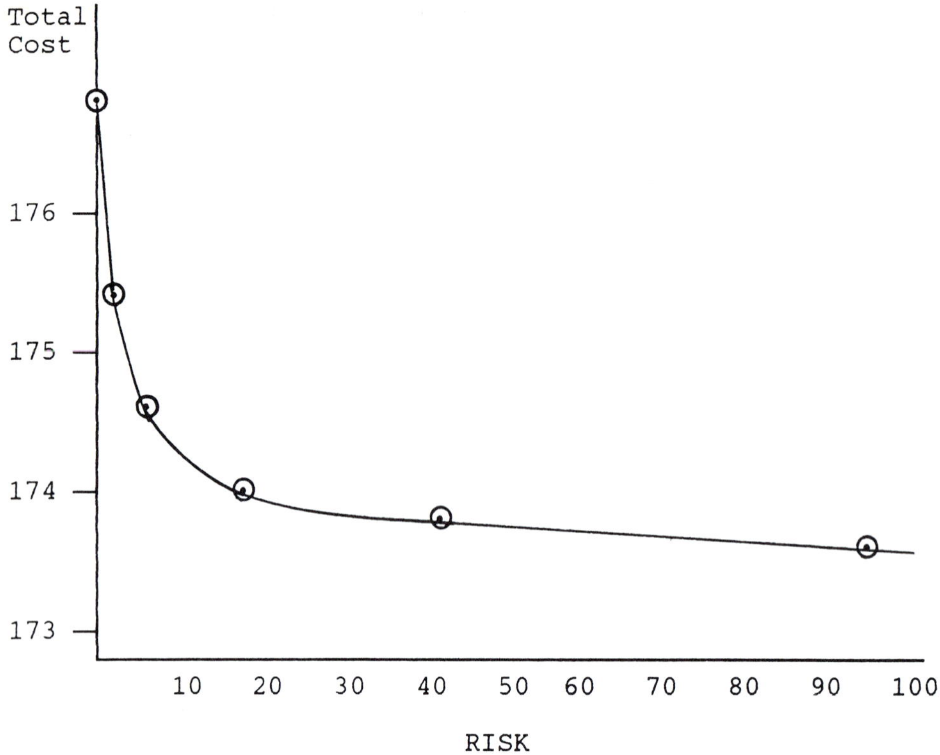

FIGURE 3: Total Expected Cost vs. Risk Stochastic Programming Model

STOCHASTIC PROGRAMMING EXAMPLE

AVERAGE CASES

OPTIMAL BOND SELECTION STRATEGIES

TABLE 6

BOND	AVERAGE REINVESTMENT RATE	CONSERVATIVE REINVESTMENT RATE
1	0	0
2	50.0	33.9
3	0	36.6
4	10.0	0
5	47.9	0
6	0	21.7
7	0	16.4
8	50.0	50.0
TOTAL COST	173.09	175.35

the least favorable scenario (that is, the low interest rate scenario) as the one on which to base reinvestments. As the reader can see, the expected value models produced significantly different results than the stochastic models - for example, the callable bond 8 looks much more attractive in the deterministic, expected value models than it does in the stochastic models.

CONCLUSIONS AND AREAS OF FUTURE RESEARCH

The stochastic programming with recourse models that we have presented in this paper offer the portfolio manager new perspectives on selecting bonds for the portfolio. By explicitly describing all relevant scenarios of the future, and analyzing them from a global perspective, the manager can avoid unduly biasing the decision in favor of one scenario over another. The extremely conservative approach taken by some managers that reinvestments of cash surpluses will not yield any interest income can clearly be avoided. In any event, the manager can use the stochastic programming models to explicitly evaluate the tradeoff between money invested here-and-now and expectations about additional money that will be needed to meet future liabilities.

Many straightforward extensions of the basic models are possible. Uncertainties about future liabilities, bond defaults, or mortgage backed securities, for example, could be included in our models. We are currently developing a stochastic programming model related to the ones described above for fixed income problems, such as bond selection, for mutual funds, where the goal is to maximize capital gains rather than to minimize the costs of meeting liabilities. We expect to complete a companion paper about that model in the near future.

At the technical modeling level, basic and applied research needs to be performed to evaluate the varied stochastic program ming model approximations possible for dedicated and fixed income portfolio selection. As we pointed out, our main interest in modeling future uncertainties is to determine an optimal, or demonstrably good, here-and-now bond selection strategy. The impact of more or less detail about future uncertainties on the here-and-now strategy is not yet well understood. As the numerical examples illustrated, however, even the coarsest descriptions of future uncertainties allow a much richer analysis of the portfolio planning problems than purely deterministic models.

Finally, we look forward to a practical test of our new modeling ideas. Plans are underway to implement a large-scale version of the basic model. We hope to report on the results of this experiment in the near future.

REFERENCES

1 M. D. Joehnk (1983), An Introduction to Fixed Income Securities, Chapter 1 in _The Handbook of Fixed Income Securities_, edited by F. J. Fabozzi and I. M. Pollack, Dow Jones-Irwin.

2 L. Fisher and R. Weil (1971), Coping with the Risk of Interest Rate Fluctuations; Returns to Bondholders from Naive and Optional STrategies, _Journal of Business_, 44, pp. 408-431.

3 G. O. Biermag, G. G. Kaufman and A. Toevs (1983), Duration: Its Development and Use in Bond Portfolio Management, _Financial Analysts Journal_, 39, pp. 15-35.

4 F. R. MacCauley (1938), _Some Theoretical Problems Suggested by the Movement of Interest Rates, Bonds, Yields and Stock Prices in the United States Since 1865_, Columbia U. Press.

5 P. E. Christensen, S. G. Feldstein, F. J. Fabozzi, (1983), Dealing with High Corporate, State and Municipal Pension Costs by "Dedicating" a Bond Portfolio, Chapter 37 in _The Handbook of Fixed Income Securities_, edited by F. J. Fabozzi and I. M. Pollack, Dow Jones-Irwin.

6 S. P. Bradley and D. B. Crane (1972), A Dynamic Model for Bond Portfolio Management, _Man. Sci_., 19, 139-151.

7 R. W. Brown, W. D. Northup and J. F. Shapiro, LOGS: A Modeling and Optimization System for Business Planning, _Computer Assisted Decision Making_, edited by G. Mitra, North-Holland, 1985.

8 rms (1987), _FIDO User's Manual_, Resource Management SYstems, Cambridge, Massachusetts, USA.

9 H. M. Wagner, (1969), _Principles of Operations Research_, Prentice-Hall.

10 D. Bienstock and J. F. Shapiro (1987), Optimizing Resource Acquisition Decisions by Stochastic Programming, to appear in _Management Science_.

11 G. J. Alexander and J. S. Francis (1986), _Portfolio Analysis_, Prentice-Hall.

12 R. S. Hiller (1986), Stochastic Programming Approximation Methods with Application to Multistage Production Planning, Ph.D. Thesis, Operations Research Center, MIT, Cambridge, MA.

PROBABILISTIC AND NON-PROBABILISTIC REPRESENTATION OF UNCERTAINTIES IN EXPERT SYSTEMS

H.-J. Zimmermann, RWTH Aachen, 5100 Aachen (F.R.G.)

CONTENTS:

1. Introduction

The definitions of "expert systems" vary considerably. Rather than specifying here which of the numerous definitions we accept, or introducing an additional definition, we shall just mention a number of features of expert systems, which might be accepted by most designers and users of expert systems and which seem to be of relevance with respect to fuzzy sets:

a. The intended area of application is restricted as to its scope, ill-structured and uncertain. Therefore, no well-defined algorithms are available or are efficient enough to solve the problem.

b. The system is - at least partly - based on expert knowledge which is either embodied in the system or which can be obtained from an expert and be analysed, stored and used by the system.

c. The system has some inference capability suitable to use the knowledge - in whatever way it is stored - to draw conclusions.

d. The interfaces to the user on one side and the expert on the other side should be such that the expert system can be used directly and that no "human interpreter" is needed between the system and the user or expert.

e. Since heuristic elements are contained in an expert system, no optimality or correctness guarantee is provided. Therefore and in order to increase the acceptance by the

NATO ASI Series, Vol. F48
Mathematical Models for Decision Support
Edited by G. Mitra

user, it is considered to be at least desirable that the system contains a "justification" or "explaining" module.

It is obvious that expert systems are aimed at ill-structured problems. Ill-structured normally indicates uncertainty with respect to the prevailing structure. We shall consider the term "uncertainty" as the label of a generic category which includes non-dichotomous structures, i.e. structures of the more-or-less type rather than of the yes-or-no type. Before discussing ways to model uncertainty we shall briefly discuss sources, appearances and types of uncertainties in expert systems.

2. Types of Uncertainty in Expert Systems

In order to appreciate different types of uncertainty it might be helpful to consider an expert sytem the knowledge base of which uses rules to represent the knowledge and the inference engine employs some type of logical deduction rules, such as predicate calculus, dual logic or similar. The knowledge base would, for instance, contain the rule "If A then B". From observing the problem situation we would judge "A is true" (the fact), and then conclude "Then B is true" (conclusion).

Usually the following assumptions are being made:

a. A and B are deterministic statements.

b. The phenomina contained in A and B are crisply defined, i.e. it is clearly defined what belongs to A and what not.

c. The A observed in reality is identical to the A contained in the rule.

d. The rule is correct (true), not contradictory to a similar rule contained in the knowledge base, and only contains two quantifiers (the universal and the existence quantifier).

Particularly in ill-structured situations, however, these are rather unrealistic assumptions. If the assumptions were valid we would generally not need expert systems, i.e. the expertise of human experts, but the problem solution could be found algorithmically.

Let us consider statements which are not of the assumed type:

"The probability of hitting the target is .6".

This is certainly a probabilistic statement with quantitative probability given. It could properly be modelled using classical probability theory of the Kolmogoroff-type.
But how about "**The chances of winning are good**"? Here quantitative probabilities are missing, and it is already more difficult to apply probability theory. In "**It is likely that we will make a good profit**" not only quantitative probabilities are missing, but in addition the term "good profit" is not uniquely defined. If we finally consider a statement of the

type **"The experiences of expert A suggests convincingly that B will happen, but expert C does not believe that B will occur"** it becomes obvious that probability theory will not longer be adequate to model these relationships.

The above mentioned examples concerned more or less the character of the statements contained in the antecedents and conclusions of the inference.

Another type of uncertainty, **dissimilarity**, occurs whenever the objects of the observed facts are not identical with the components in the rules. Strictly speaking, at least in classical logic, we could not arrive at a conclusion at all. In many real situations, however, a similarity of the observed facts with the components of the rules might still allow a certain conclusion. This similarity is certainly not a dichotomous feature, but rather a matter of degree, which has to be modelled accordingly.

Eventually the inference process itself may contain uncertainties: The degree to which an observation is true, reliable or supported is normally called **material truth**. This obviously has some influence on the truth of the conclusion. In addition, however, the rules themselves may not be completely reliable or deterministic. This degree which also has to enter the computation of the degree of truth of the conclusion, may be called "**formal truth**". Closely related is the question of evidence enforcement: How should the reliability of positive independent or dependent evidences be taken into account and combined with that of negative evidences with respect to the reliability or truth of the final conclusion?

3. PROBLEMS OF MODELLING UNCERTAINTIES IN EXPERT SYSTEMS

Which particular problem in modelling uncertainty occur will depend

1. on the type of application (context),

2. on the kind of available input,

3. on the type of interface input - knowledge base,

4. on the inference mechanism used, and

5. on the character of the desired output.

Context:
The context wil certainly determine the kinds of uncertainty which have to be taken into account. It will also influence the constraints (time etc.) under which the knowledge and information processing has to occur. Partly it will also determine the input which is available.

Input/Output:
Input to an Expert System is knowledge (rules, for instance) and information (facts, observations etc.). Both can be avai-

lable in numerical, quantitative, crisp or in qualitative, linguistic form. Both types of information might be connected with various kinds of uncertainty (probability, truth, possibility etc.) which again can be expressed either numerically or linguistically. Similar holds for the output: It might be necessary that a crisp conclusion (decision) is required - possibly connected with certain measures of uncertainty, or it can be preferable to obtain the output linguistically, facilitating the communications with human users.

Essentially two types of problems arise:

If the input or the desired output is in another form than the information processed in the inference engine a transformation from linguistic into numerical (crisp) information (**defuzzification**) or vice versa (**fuzzification**) has to be performed.
If the input/output is linguistic and the inference engine processes also linguistic information (for instance linguistic variables) then some kind of **matching** or **linguistic approximation** has to be performed whenever the input or output granules are not identical to the granules defined or obtained in the inference engine.

Inference Mechanism
Reasoning under conditions of uncertainty normally creates two major types of problems:
Each type of uncertainty of the antecedents has to be properly carried along to the conclusions. If different types of uncertainty exist, one might want to combine (aggregate) different measures of uncertainty into one measure of overall uncertainty.

Both problems are obviously considerably simplified if one holds the view that there is only one common calculus for uncertainty. We do not share this view, however, because in this case it would not be necessary or meaningful to distinguish between different theories of uncertainty such as probability theories, possibility theory etc. Empirical evidence also does not support this view.

4. TOOLS TO MODEL UNCERTAINTY IN EXPERT SYSTEMS

4.1 Probability Theory

4.1.1 Bayes Approach

Let us consider the rule

If A then C
A is true (Antecedent)
Then C is true (Conclusion).

In the most frequently applied Baysian approach the Baysian inversion theorem is used:

$$PR(C|A) = \frac{Pr(C)}{P(A)} Pr(A|C) \quad \text{or} \quad Pr(C) = \frac{Pr(C|A)}{Pr(A|C)} Pr(A).$$

Here Pr(C|A) is the probability of C given A etc.

Objections against this approach are, first of all, that aspects of uncertainty may be included which are non-probabilistic in nature. Computationally this approach becomes prohibitive if the events are considered fuzzy and are represented as fuzzy sets.
A second criticism is the need to identify point values for the probabilities of events which may by far be overstatements of our actual knowledge of the likelihood of occurrence of that particular event, even if it can be modelled crisply.

One should also realize that the inclusion of negative evidence is difficult and that there is no rule which specifies uniquely, which piece of evidence is used to determine the conditional part of the formula and which for the probability part [Shafer 1986].

4.1.2 Dempster-Shafer`s Theory of Evidence

Dempster and Shafer assume that probabilities can only be assigned to subsets of the universe and not to atomic elements.

Example 1:
Let us assume that in a data base we have the following information about the number of children of employees:

Empl. Name	No. of children	Between 3 and 5 children?
1	1,2	impossible
2	1	impossible
3	4,5	certain
4	5,6	possible
5	6	impossible

Let us now ask the query: "What portion of the employees has between 3 and 5 children?" (with the interpretation "What is the probability of an employee having between 3 and 5 children"). This is certain for employee 3, possible for employee 4 and impossible for employees 1, 2 and 5.
Dempster and Shafer compute the **lower probability** as the portion of subsets (focal elements) for which the query is certainly true and the **upper probability** as the portion of focal elements for which the query is possibly true, i.e. 1 - minus the portion for which the statement cannot be true. In our example these probabilities are 1/5 and 2/5, respectively.
The lower probability is also called **measure of belief**, Bel(A), and the upper probability **measure of plausibility**, PL(A). While Bel(A) considers evidence supporting A, PL(A) considers evidence supporting the contrary. The following relationships hold:

$$\begin{array}{ll} PL(A) & = Bel(A) = 1 \\ PL(A) & = Bel(A) = 0 \\ PL(A) & = 1- Bel(\neg A) \\ PL(A \cap B) & \leq PL(A) + PL(B) - PL(A \cup B) \\ Bel(A \cap B) & \geq Bel(A) + Bel(B) - Bel(A \cup B) \end{array}$$

In the meantime this theory has been extended to include not only crisp, but also fuzzy events.

4.1.3 Possibility Theory

We now define the

$$\begin{array}{l} Pos(A \cap B) = \min \{Pos\ A,\ Pos\ B\} \\ Pos(A \cup B) = \max \{Pos\ A,\ Pos\ B\}. \end{array}$$

In analogy to plausibility and belief we can now define a

Possibility measure $\pi(A \cup B) = \max \{\pi(A), \pi(B)\}$

and a

Necessity Measure $N(A \cap B) = \min \{N(A), N(B))\}$; $N(A) =$
$= 1 - Bel(\neg A))$
with the following properties:

$$\begin{array}{lll} \min & (N(A), N(\neg A)) & = 0 \\ \max & (\pi(A), \pi(\neg A)) & = 1 \\ \pi(A) < 1 & N(A) & = 0 \\ N(A) > 0 & \pi(A) & = 1. \end{array}$$

Example 2:
We know possibility distributions of the number of children:

Empl. Name	Number of children	
1	(1,.8),(2,1)	impossible
2	(1,1)	impossible
3	(4,.6),(5,1)	possible
4	(5,.8),(6,1)	impossible
5	(6,1)	impossible

Let us now ask the question "How possible is it than an employee has 3 or 4 children"?

Let us call the query Q and denote by f the "focal elements".

Then

$$\pi(Q) = \max_{Q \cap f \neq 0} \{\pi_i\} = .6 \text{ and}$$

$$N(Q) = \min_{Q \cap f = \emptyset} (1-\pi_i) = \min \{.2,0,0,0,.2,0,0\} = 0$$

and the answer would be:

"The possibility of an employee having 3 or 4 children is .6 and the necessity is 0".

4.3 Fuzzy Set Theory

4.3.1 Aggregation Operators

Numerous operators have been suggested in fuzzy sets. They can be classified according to their interpretation (whether they are supposed to model the "and", the "or" etc.) or with respect to their mathematical properties. Three major groups can be distinguished:

1. Conjunction Operators
2. Disjunction Operators
3. General Operators

Conjunction operators correspond to an "and"-aggregation of fuzzy sets. From a mathematical point of view Dubois and Prade [1984] defined binary conjunction operators, C, as follows:

$\forall x_1,\ x_2 \in [0,1],\ C(x_1,x_2) \leq \min(x_1,x_2).$

From the point of view of interpretation the "fuzzy and" [Werners 1984] would also belong to the "conjunction-operators". Mathematically, however, they would be called "averaging operators". In order to avoid any kind of confusion we will here stick to a classification according to the mathematical properties and not the semantic interpretation of the operators.

Binary **disjunction** operators, D, are defined accordingly as

$\forall x_1,x_2 \in [0,1],\ D(x_1,x_2) \geq \max\ (x_1,x_2).$

General operators do either not distinguish between "and" and "or", or they "soften" the notions of "and" and "or", respectively. Two subclasses can be distinguished: "Averaging" operators which map between conjunction and disjunction operators and "Inclusive" operators, which map between 0 and 1 (for instance the "γ-operator" [Zimmermann, Zysno 1980].

Two of the most discussed families of disjunction and conjunction operators are the so-called triangular norms and triangular conorms, which are monotonic, commutative and associative. (Averaging operators are generally symmetric, and idempotent, but not associative.) For suitable negation operators, N(x), such as N(x)=1-x, T-norms, T, and T-conorms, S, are duals in the sense of the following generalization of De Morgan`s law:

$$S(a,b) = N(T(N(a),N(b)))$$
$$T(a,b) = N(S(N(a),N(b))).$$

For some averaging operators which are linear combinations of dual pairs of t- and s-norms the associativity can be maintained. Bonissone and Decker [1986] mention 6 of these pairs. They also show, that when applied to varying degrees of granularity of linguistic variables which represent input and output, between three and six indifference classes of these pairs can be determined. This facilitates considerably the appropriate choice of context dependent associative averaging operators in expert systems.

4.3.2 Fuzzy Matching and Linguistic Approximation

It was already mentioned that "classical" expert systems generally assume that observed facts are identical to the components of knowledge stored in the rules. Obviously complete identity and complete mismatch are only extremes. In general observed facts will match the components of the rules more or less. A number of methods have been suggested to measure and express the degree to which facts, i.e. observed patterns, match the components predefined in the knowledge base. Cayrol [Cayrol, Farreny and Prade 1982] suggest, for instance, to use the concept of possibility and necessity to express the simlarity between observations and defined pattern which are both modelled as fuzzy sets. This min-max approach is certainly not the only way to measure the degree of similarity of patterns. Bonnissone [Bonnissone, Decker 1986; Bonnissone 1982] sugest the power of a fuzzy set (its cardinality), the entropy , the first moment of the membership function and its skewness as characteristic features of fuzzy sets. A quadratic weighted distance in the feature space is then used to evaluate the similarity between two fuzzy sets.
Zwick, Carlstein and Budescu [1986] consider nineteen measures to express the similarity of fuzzy sets.

A special type of pattern matching is what Bonnissone calls "linguistic aproximation": Let us assume that we have defined a linguistic variable "Probability" to express the probability of the output of an expert system. Let the term set of this linguistic variable contain 5 terms. The linguistic probabilities of conclusions emerging from the inference process are characterizd by their membership functions. These membership functions will presumably not match any of the terms defined to express the probability of the outputs linguistic approximation now tries to find the term of the predefined output term set which is most similar to the computed fuzzy set which is the result of the inference process. The computational efforts of this matching process obviously depends to a large extent on the power of the term set, the restrictions imposed on the shapes of membership functions, and on the simlarity measures used in the matching process!

4.3.3 Fuzzy Logic, Approximate Reasonng, Plausible Reasoning

The above mentioned three notions are used with different interpretations. We shall, therefore, define them here in order to avoid confusion when using them in the context of expert systems.

In dual logic and all derived systems of reasoning connectives (and, or, negation) are defined by truth tables, only allowing the values "true" or "false" (0 or 1). The reasoning is normally performed by using tautologies such as modus ponens, modus tollens etc.

In **fuzzy logic** statements are still crisp, but the truth values are expressed as linguistic variables, hence allowing for degrees of truth or truth qualification rather than only the use of either true or false.

Approximate Reasoning can handle fuzzy sets in the antecedents and normally yields also fuzzy sets in the conclusion. Main tools are the generalized modus ponens and the compositional rule of inference.

Definition:
Let $\tilde{R}(x)$, $\tilde{R}(x,y)$ and $\tilde{R}(y)$, $x \in X$, $y \in Y$ be the fuzzy relations in X, X Y and Y, respectively, which act as fuzzy restrictions on x, (x,y) and y, respectively. Let $\tilde{A}$ and $\tilde{B}$ denote particular fuzzy sets in X and X Y. Then the **compositional rule of inference** asserts, that the solution of the relational assignment equations $\tilde{R}(x) = \tilde{A}$ and $\tilde{R}(x,y) = \tilde{B}$ is given by
$\tilde{R}(y) = \tilde{A} \circ \tilde{B}$, where $\tilde{A} \circ \tilde{B}$ is the composition of $\tilde{A}$ and $\tilde{B}$.

A further generalization is allowed in **plausible reasoning.** Here the "facts" contained in the antecedents do no longer have to be identical, but can differ from each other slightly. If $\tilde{A}$, $\tilde{A}`$, $\tilde{B}$ and $\tilde{B}`$ are fuzzy statements then the generalized modus ponens would, for instance, read:

$$
\begin{array}{ll}
x \text{ is } \tilde{A}`, & \text{(Premise)} \\
\text{If } x \text{ is } \tilde{A} \text{ then } y \text{ is } \tilde{B} & \text{(Implication)} \\
\hline
y \text{ is } B` & \text{(Conclusion)}
\end{array}
$$

Naturally some more qualifications of the relationship between $\tilde{A}$ and $\tilde{A}`$, $\tilde{B}$ and $\tilde{B}`$ are needed in this case.

The following graph summarizes possible uncertainties and their modelling in expert systems.

Figure 1: Uncertainties in Expert Systems (see next page)

5. THE PRESENTATION OF UNCERTAINTY

One important aspect of uncertainty modelling is certainly the method to process uncertain information. When feeding this information into other information systems or into machines (process control) it might even be rather unimportant in which way the information about uncertainty is presented. If, however, information about uncertainty is obtained from human experts and/or if it is intended to be used by human decision makers, the formal type of representation becomes very impor-

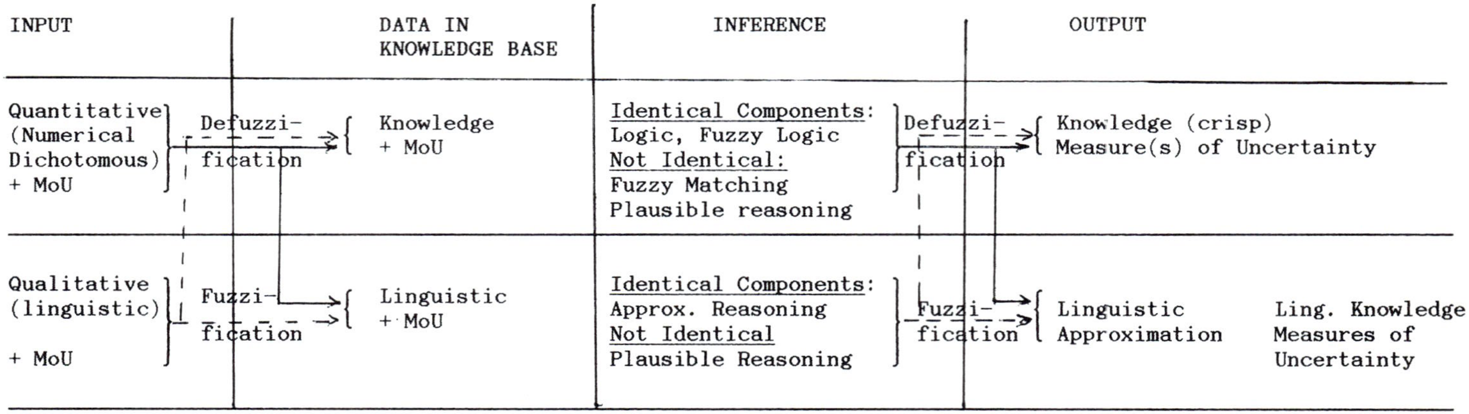

Measures of Uncertainty: Probability, Possibility, Evidence, Truth, Fuzziness, Belief

Figure 1: Uncertainties in Expert Systems

enatotab.hz

tant. Due to our limited capability to perceive and process large amounts of information simultaneously, the synchronisation of the granularity with the human capabilities of perceiving information becomes extremely relevant.
The two poles between which we have to find a compromise when deciding about the type of presentation are simplicity (often closely related to acceptance by the user) and perfection or completeness of the types of uncertainty we want to present.

So far there exist only very few empirical results which indicate the influence of the type of presentation of uncertainty on the ease and performance of use by human users [see, f.i., Zwick, Carlstein, Budescu 1987]. We shall, therefore, only indicate possible ways of presenting uncertainty to users. We shall exemplarily assume that one accepts four kinds of uncertainty: Stochastic uncertainty (probability), degree of similarity between facts and components of rules, linguistic (lexical) uncertainty and the degree of (formal) truth.
First of all these uncertainties can be represented separately or aggregated as one "over-all-degree" of uncertainty. The former presentation (f.i. as "certainty factors") has probably more appeal for a practitioner, but it has two major disadvantages:

1. The aggregation of different uncertainties presupposes an appropriate, possibly context-dependent aggregation procedure.
2. The user can no longer recognize the "uncertainty mix" which leads to a specific uncertainty factor.

The disaggregated way of presentation, on the other hand, provides more information, but it leaves the user with the problem of aggregation and it might not be very appealing to people not too well trained in uncertainty modelling.
Apart from the degree of aggregation uncertainty can be expressed as scalar, interval, distribution or linguistically. Considering probability we can state a probability as a real number between 0 and 1, as lower and upper probability, as a fuzzy number (possibility distribution) or in terms of the linguistic variable probability, such as "highly probable", "not likely" etc.

The following table exhibits exemplarily representations of uncertainties:

	Aggregated	Dis-Aggregated
Scalars	Uncertainty Factor UF = .4	{Prob=.4;Poss=.8,Sim=.8 Truth=.7}
Intervals	Uncertainty = [.4,.8]	Prob=[.4;.8] Poss/Nec=(.4,.6) Sim[.6,.8] Truth[.4,.8]
Distri-butions	Uncertainty = appr. .5	Prob./Poss/Sim/Truth= {.4,.6,.7,.7} (fuzzy numbers)
Linguistic Terms	Uncertainly is moderately high	The truth of A being highly probably is low. The similarity of A and A` is high.

Most results have so far been presented for the combination of (linguistic) fuzziness and (stochastic) probability, focussing on fuzzy random variables, the probability of fuzzy events etc. [see Zwick, Wollstein 1987]. They seem to indicate that this combination can be achieved reasonably well. If one interpretes on the other hand, the degree of truth as the degree of consistency (of positive and negative evidence) then a dual measure representing these three fuzzy dimensions seems to be meaningful. The formulation could certainly be linguistic, possibly with underlying numerical scales [see Wallstein et al. 1986].

For the output of an expert system one could obviously also use further alternatives such as simultaneous supply of all dis-aggregated measures, subsequent or optional presentation or any combination.

6. AVAILABLE TOOLS AND FUTURE PERSPECTIVES

6.1 Expert Systems, Tools and Languages

In the recent past quite a number of expert sytems and -tools have been developed on the basis of fuzzy set theory. As usual some of them have been obtained by emptying expert systems of the context dependent knowledge base (for instance, REVEAL). Others have been designed from the very beginning as inference engine. The following table surveys these tools. This table does not include the older area of fuzzy control, the systems of which in a sense coul also be considered as expert systems. The last system mentioned in the table - VLSI - is not a software tool, but a fuzzy inference engine on a chip which performs 80000 FLIPS (Fuzzy Logixc Inference Per Second).

(Table: See following pages)

The table is by far not exhaustive.

6.2 Future Perspectives

Advances, improvements and new developments can be expected in 4 directions:

1. So far expert systems and -tools have primarily been developed in Artificial Intelligence, Decision Support Systems in Operations Research and efficient systems for databank management in other areas, such as management, CAD etc. There has not been a cross fertilization between these areas which could have helped to improve some of the weaknesses of all of these systems. In the future I expect hybrid systems, taking advantage of the tool kits of all these areas and thus improving the overall performance of the system.

2. The user-orientation of these systems will improve. While nowadays a major part of the developments are still tools - far apart from the real user of an expert system - the fraction of expert systems will have to increase if there is to be a future for that line of investment.
   The effort to gain more user acceptance by a higher degree of user orientation might lead to a more frequent use of linguistic variables and similar tools.

3. Uncertainty will certainly be treated more carefully in the future and the use of nonprobabilistic modelling will increase.

4. The use of fuzzy set theory increases the volume of data to be stored and processed. Therefore, inference engines using fuzzy logic or approximate reasoning will still have to become more efficient than they are today.

References:

1. Adamo, J.M.: Fuzzy decision trees, in: Fuzzy Sets and Systems 4 (1980), pp. 207-219.

2. Adlassnig, K.-P., Kolarz, G., Scheithauer, W.: Present state of the medical expert systems CADIAC-2, in: Med. Inform. 24 (1985), pp. 13-20.

3. Alexeyev, A.V.: Fuzzy algorithms execution software: The FAGOL-System, in: Kacprzyk, J., Yager, R. (edts.), 1985, pp. 289-300.

4. Appelbaum, L., Ruspini, E.H.: ARIES: An approximate reasoning inference enquire, in: Gupta et al. (edts.), 1985, pp. 745-755.

Name	Application Area	Knowledge Representation Inference	Uncertainty	Reference
ARIES	Tool	Rules, nets	Multiple truth qualification	[Appelbaum, Ruspini 1985]
CADIAC-2	Medical Diagnosis	Rules	Degrees of confidence	[Adlassnig et al. 1985]
FAGOL	Tool	Fuzzy algorithms	Fuzzy probabilities	[Alexeyev 1985]
fINDex	Forecasting	Rules, Ling. Variables	Ling. Variables	[Whalen, Schott 1985]
FLIP	Tool	Fuzzy Logic	Degrees of Belief, Weights	[Giles 1980]
FLOPS	Mgmt. of imprec. Databases	Rules Weakly nonmonotonic	Truth qualific. Ling. Variables	[Buckley et al. 1986]
FRDB	Tool	Fuzzy relations	Qualific. Ling. Var.	[Zemankova, Kandel 1985]
FRIL	Tool	Fuzzy relations	Truth qualific.	[Baldwin 1985, 1979]
Fuzzy Planner	Tool	Fuzzy logic	Truth qualific.	[Kling 1973]
METABOL	Tool	PROLOG-clauses Relations	Plausibility Credibility	[Ernst 1985]
PROSPECTOR 2	Mineral Exploration	Semantic+Inference Networks	Bayes Fuzzy Logic	[Benson 1986]
PRUF	Tool	Poss. Theory App. Reasoning; Rules	Truth, prob. Poss. Qualific.	[Zadeh 1981]
REVEAL	Tool (Mgmt., Planning)	Rules	Poss. Qual.	[Jones 1985]

Name	Application Area	Knowledge Representation Inference	Uncertainty	Reference
SLOP	Tool	Support Logic Programming	"Support Pairs"	[Baldwin 1986]
SPERIL-II	Damage assessment	Rules	Dempster, Shafer	[Ogawa et al. 1985]
SPHINX	Medical Diagnosis	Trees, Rules	Similarity Index, Uncertainty Inter-val	[Fieschi et al. 1982]
SPII-1	Tool	Rules	Necessity, Poss.	[Martin-Clouaire, Prade 1986]
TAIGER	Tool	Rules	Necessity, Poss.	[Farreny et al. 1986]
VLSI	Hardware Tool	Fuzzy Logic, Rules	Certainty factors	[Togai, Watanabe 1986]

Table 1: Expert systems and - tools using fuzzy set theory

5. Baldwin, J.F.: Support logic programming, in: Int. Journal of Int. Systems 1 (1986), pp. 73-104.

6. Baldwin, J.G., Guild, N.C.F.: Comparison of fuzzy sets on the same decision space, in: Fuzzy Sets and Systems 2 (1979), pp. 213-232.

7. Benson, I.: PROSPECTOR: An expert system for mineral exploration, in: Mitra, G. (ed.), 1986, pp. 17-26.

8. Bonissone, P.P.: The problem of linguistic aproximation in systems analysis, Ph.D. Thesis, DEECS, Berkeley 1979.

9. Bonissone, P.B.: A fuzzy set based linguistic approach: Theory and applications, in: Gupta, M.M. and Sanchez, E. (edts.): Approximate Reasoning in Decision Analysis, Amsterdam 1982, pp. 329-339.

10. Bonissone, P.P. and Decker, K.S.: Selecting uncertainty calculi and granularity, in: Kanal and Lemmer (edts.), 1986, pp. 217-247.

11. Buchanan, B., Shortliffe, E. (edts.): Rule-based expert systems (Sec. Pr.), Reading, Mass. 1985.

12. Buckley, J.J., Silver, W., Tucker, D.: A fuzzy expert system, in: Fuzzy Sets and Systems 21 (1986)

13. Cayrol, M., Farreny, H., Prade, H.: Fuzzy pattern matching. Kybernetes 11 (1982), pp. 103-116.

14. Dubois, D., Prade, H.: Criteria aggregation and ranking of alternatives in the framework of fuzzy set theory, in: Zimmermann, Zadeh, Gaines (edts.): Fuzzy Sets and Decision Analysis, Amsterdam, New York 1984, pp. 209-241.

15. Ernst, Ch.J.: A logic programming metalanguage for expert systems, in: Kacprzyk, J., Yager, R. (edts.) 1985, pp. 280-288.

16. Farreny, H., Prade, H.., Wyss, E.: Approximate reasoning in a rule-based expert system using possibility theory, Proc. 10th IFIP World Congr., Dubl. 1986.

17. Fieschi, M., Joubert, M., Fieschi, D., Soula, G., Roux, M.: Sphinx: An interactive system for medial diagnoses aids, in: Gupta, Sanchez (edts.) 1982, pp. 269-282.

18. Gaines, B.R., Shaw, M.L.G.: Systemic foundations for reasoning in expert systems, in: Gupta et al (edts.) 1985, pp. 271-282.

19. Giles, R.: A computer program for fuzzy reasoning, in: Fuzzy Sets and Systems 4 (1980), pp. 221-234.

20. Gupta, M.M., Kandel, A., Bandler, W., Kiszka, J.B. (edts.): Approximate reasoning in expert systems, Amsterdam, New York, Oxford 1985.

21. Holroyd et al.: Developing expert systems for management applications, Omega 13 (1985), pp. 1-11.

22. Jones, P.L.K.: REVEAL: Adressing DSS and expert systems, in: Mitra (ed.) 1986, pp. 49-58.

23. Kacprzyk, J., Yager, R.R. (edts.): Management decision support systems using fuzzy sets and possibility theory, Köln 1985.

24. Kling, R.: Fuzzy Planner: Reasoning with inexact concepts in a procedural problem-solving language, in: J. of Cybernetics 4 (1974), pp. 105-122.

25. Mamdani, E.H., Gaines, B.R. (edts.): Fuzzy reasoning and its applications, London, New York, Toronto 1981.

26. Martin-Clouaire, R., Prade, H.: SPII: A simple inference engine capable of accomodating both imprecision and uncertainty, in: Mitra, G. (ed.) 1986, pp. 117-131.

27. Mitra, G. (ed.): Computer assised decision making, Amsterdam, New York, Oxford 1986.

28. Negoita, C.V.: Expert systems and fuzzy sets, Menlo Park, Calif. 1985.

29. Ogawa, H., Fu, K.S., Yao, J.T.P.: SPERIL-II: An expert system for damage assessment of existing structure, in: Gupta et al. (edts.), 1985, pp. 731-744.

30. Shafer, G.: A mathematical theory of evidence, Princeton, NJ, 1976.

31. Shafer, G.: Probability judgment in artificial intelligence, in: Kanal, L.N. and Lemmer, J.F. (edts.): Uncertainty in Artificial Inteligence, Amsterdam, New York 1986.

32. Stefik, et al.: The organization of expert systems, Art. Int. 18 (1982), pp. 135-175.

33. Togai, M., Watanabe, H.: A VLSI implementation of a fuzzy inference engine toward an expert system on a chip, in: Inf. Sc. 38 (1986), pp. 147-163).

34. Wang, P.P. (ed.): Advances in fuzzy sets, possibility theory and applications, New York, London 1983.

35. Wallstein, T., Budescu, D., Rappaport, A., Zweck, R., Forsyth, B.: Measuring the vague meaning of probability terms, in: J. of Exp. Psychology 115 (1986), pp. 348-365.

36. Werners, B.: Interaktive Entscheidungsunterstützung durch ein flexibles mathematisches Programmierungssystem, München 1984.

37. Whalen, Th., Schott, B.: Goal-directed aproxmate reasoning in a fuzzy production system, in: Gupta et al. (edts.), 1985, pp. 505-518.

38. Zadeh, L.A.: A computational approach to fuzzy quantifiers in natural languages, in: Comp. + Maths. with Appl. 9 (1983), pp. 149-184.

39. Zadeh, L.A.: The role of fuzzy logic in the management of uncertainty in expert systems, in: Fuzzy Sets and Systems 11(1983), pp. 183-227.

40. Zemankova-Leech, M., Kandel, A.: Fuzzy relational data bases - a key to expert systems, Köln 1984.

41. Zemankova-Leech, M., Kandel, A.: Uncertainty propagation to expert systems, in: Gupta et al. (edts.) 1985, pp. 529-540.

42. Zimermann, H.-J., Zadeh, L.A., Gaines, B.R. (edts.): Fuzzy sets and decision analysis, Amsterdam, New York, Oxford 1984.

43. Zimmermann, H.-J.: Fuzzy set theory and its applications, Boston 1985.

44. Zimmermann, H.-J., Zysno, P.: Quantifying vagueness in decision models, in: European Journal of Operational Research 22 (1985), pp. 148-158.

45. Zimmermann, H.-J.: Fuzzy sets, decision making and expert systems, Boston 1987.

46. Zimmermann, H.-J., Zysno, .: Latent connectives in human decision making, in: Fuzzy Sets and Systems 4 (1980), pp. 37-51.

47. Zwick, R., Carlstein, E., Budescu, D.: Measures of similarity between fuzzy concepts: A comparative analysis, GSIA WP #34/86/87, Pittsburgh 1986.

48. Zwick, R., Walsten, T.: Combining stochastic uncertainty and linguistic inexactness: Theory and experimental evaluation, GSIA Working Paper #37/86/87, Pittsburgh 1987.

Summary of a Panel Discussion

on

REPRESENTATION OF UNCERTAINTY AND IMPRECISION IN DECISION SUPPORT SYSTEMS

PANEL: Professors DEMPSTER (Chair and Rapporteur), ZIMMERMANN, WHINSTON, COOKE, KALL and SHAPIRO.

FORMAT: With the exception of the Chair each panelist made an introductory statement, which was followed by a discussion prompted by questions from the audience and concluded with a position summary from each panelist. After the session, panelists and others contributed references.

1 Introductory Statements

- ZIMMERMANN. The modelling of systems about which decisions are to be taken must be based on three key ingredients: a *language* in which the system can be described, a *calculus* by which the language can be manipulated to derive inferences and conclusions or induce causes and assumptions, and *representation* within the language of the specific system of interest. It is an empirical matter to choose amongst possible modelling *methodologies*, and it is by no means clear that a universal methodology will ever be at hand. However, each such *formal* methodology must involve both a consistent set of *axiomatics* and an (often considerable) *approximation* of the complexities of the system being modelled. *Natural* language is a powerful modelling and decision-making tool. The use of the *fuzzy system theory* methodology allows the modeller to take advantage of the power and deliberate *vagueness* of natural language in a consistent, replicable manner.

- WHINSTON. Regarding methodologies for introducing uncertainty and imprecision into modelling systems for decision support, two basic points should be made. First, the appropriateness of the modelling methodology depends on the *level* in the organizational hierarchy of the decisions to be informed by the model. The *higher* the decision making *level* in the hierarchy rising from operational to strategic, the *more abstracted, approximate*, and the *coarser* the "granularity" of *time* involved in the modelling can be. This is the concept underlying both computer-based *hierarchical planning systems* and *macroeconomics.* The second point concerns the necessity of a mechanism for *pooling*

NATO ASI Series, Vol. F48
Mathematical Models for Decision Support
Edited by G. Mitra

knowledge from different sources, e.g. experts, in any useful methodology. Within the framework of (subjective) *probability theory*, for example, this may be accomplished using the concept of *Bayesian dialogues*.

- COOKE. It should be stressed that there exist fundamental *axiomatics* for *probabilistic logic* in a finitely generated formal language. One such scheme is the *probability semantics* of Los. As a consequence of applying mathematical probability, such schemes are entirely internally *consistent*. Mathematical consistency is *not* unfortunately a property possessed by many *popular schemes* for probablistic reasoning currently implemented in expert systems. For example, while there is *initial* agreement between *certainty factors* and *probabilities* assigned to propositions in a first order logic, after *long* chains of deductive or inductive reasoning the consistent probabilities and the inconsistent certainty factors will *disagree* markedly.

- KALL. The *important* question is, indeed, what is the underlying axiomatic structure of a methodology for representing uncertainty? Probability theory has by now built up a great body of mathematical theorems to justify its practical use in a wide variety of situations in an *appropriate context*. Consider, for example, the use of *Gaussian* statistics in the *large sample* analysis of *stationary* time series. In the field of *subjective* probability, statistical decision analysis is another example. The following question must be asked of *fuzzy system* theory. What is the body of corresponding justifications for modelling uncertainty, imprecision and vagueness with fuzzy entities?

- SHAPIRO. In the context of this discussion it is important to recall the reasons commonly adduced to the success of the (deterministic linear and near-linear) *mathematical programming* (MP) methodology in real world applications. First and foremost is the *inductive understanding* of the system gained through the trial-and-error modelling process itself. Only second is the *prescriptive* value of the optimal model decisions themselves. Finally, the *specific* nature of the *domain* subsystem modelled usually makes the model decisions practically *implementable*. In many real world situations, *mixed integer programming* techniques extend the domain of applicability of the modelling. Further still, *dynamic stochastic programming with recourse* is a mathematical programming methodology incorporating uncertainty whose time for practice has come. *Decomposition* is a powerful tool for solving such models which allows massive use of *parallel processing*. Further, *expert system* (ES) software technology can be used to make computations with such mathematical programming models more *flexible* and *responsive*. Such ES/MP systems must incorporate model *generators* and *solvers*, together with an appropriate *database management system* (and/or *knowledge base*). Moreover, *learning* with model use in the real environment over time is easily implemented in such systems. Regarding the practicality of MP methodology, on the negative side is the fact that most models concentrate on *individual* decision-making at the cost of ignoring the decision taker's rôle in the *organization*. This was the biggest obstacle to implementation in the early days of mathematical programming. Again, expert system techniques can be used to implement MP modelling in an organizational context and undoubtedly the *organizational consequences* of the resulting systems are of primary importance.

2 Discussion

- GREENBERG. Why use only probability to model and reason with uncertainty, imprecision and vagueness?
- COOKE. Because only probabilistic methods are mathematically consistent.
- MURPHY. What can fuzzy set theory do that probability theory cannot?
- ZIMMERMANN. First, it should be noted that within fuzzy system theory it is Zadeh's *possibility theory* rather than *fuzzy set theory* that is analogous to the basic construct of probability, i.e. a *probability space*. In possibility theory, *events* are *not crisply formulated*—for example, a "mostly red" poker hand rather than a hand with "at least three red cards." Deliberate advantage is taken of the looseness of natural language using the *membership function* as the focal point. The promise of this approach is that the well-documented *inconsistent* use of *heuristics* by human experts can be directly captured in a computer-based fuzzy system and then consistency can be enforced by the computer system with a minimal distortion of the input for subsequent reasoning.
- COOKE. This promise may, however, be a chimera. Indeed, *fault diagnostic* support systems in the nuclear power industry based on probabilistic *Bayesian inductive inference* have so far proved a *failure* because of the *burden of data* which must be specified at input. Although the interpretation is different—and the question of internal consistency remains open—the *data requirements* of possibility theory are similar to those of Bayesian probability theory.
- GREENBERG. How does formal probability theory answer the question of differences in the *character of uncertainty*, such as the uncertainty of how much oil is in the ground versus the uncertainty regarding legislation defining proven reserves?

- DEMPSTER. This question misses a prior fundamental point mentioned before. The advantage of mathematical probability theory is that, however interpreted, it is a mathematically consistent theory with a large body of applicable results and inference schemes (mathematical statistics). In the fifties and sixties it became widely understood that both *subjective* (which incidentally includes the cases in question), *objective*, i.e. frequency based, and *algorithmic* interpretations of mathematical probabilities may be consistently *mixed* in the same decision modes in the situation when a decision *must* be taken on the basis of *current* information. The question of which of these interpretations—or, more generally, the interpretations of alternative consistent theories—are easiest to turn into numerical or symbolic data for a computer system in a given setting is in the end an *empirical* matter on which evidence is accumulating both *pro* and *con*. It is certainly clear that modern computer graphics can greatly facilitate this inductive process in practical situations.

3 Position Summaries

- DEMPSTER. The key to symbolic and numerical representation and manipulation of uncertainty, imprecision and vagueness in decision support systems is a *consistent* mathematical theory whose entities must then be *estimated* as input from the real world. At this point, probability theory is the best developed methodology from both points of view.

- WHINSTON. There is no good reason to suppose that various methodologies cannot be *mixed* in a given expert or decision support system. Some, however, such as *nonmonotonic logic*, must be ruled out on the grounds of producing absurd results. In fact there are a puzzling array of competing approaches. Internal consistency is the prime requirement for methodologies which go beyond the current ones to support the *unstructured* nature of decisions informed by decision support systems.

- KALL. My earlier question regarding justifications *within* fuzzy system theory for its use in modelling has gone unanswered in this discussion. I suspect that in many applications of fuzzy system theory probabilities have *not* been used merely as a matter of taste. In any event, it should be borne in mind that the best representing methodology in a given situation can never be *proven* mathematically.

- ZIMMERMANN. It is probably fair to say that fuzzy system theory has not *yet* been applied in contexts in which it is both entirely and *uniquely* appropriate. It is hard to convince a novice of its practical utility without his or her undertaking a real *study* of the subject—a property which it shares with probability theory!

- COOKE. I must be a browser into things fuzzy, because I am not yet convinced. However, inference within probability theory *can* illuminate two questions that have only been touched upon in this discussion: namely, the *combination* of, and *evaluation* of, *expert opinion*. Before concluding, it is perhaps worth answering the question, what is a *theory of inference*? It consists of a (usually finitely-generated) *language* (i.e. set of sentences), a set of *models* of the language (by which it is interpeted) and a set of *rules of inference* (e.g. $A \Rightarrow B$) valid in all models of the language. A *probability semantics* can be defined on such a system by defining a probability measure on the set of models (i.e. *possible worlds*) and lifting it to a measure on sentences and predicates.

- SHAPIRO. Are the various methodologies that have been discussed here at all *comparable*? The most important thing to remember is that decision support systems are designed for *practical* purposes. *Any* methodology that fits the situation at hand should be used. The important question is *which* methodology is important *when*?

4 References

Aside from the contributions of the panelists to this volume, the following references were suggested regarding the discussion.

- FUZZY SYSTEM THEORY

H.J. Zimmermann (1987). *Fuzzy Sets, Decision Making and Expert Systems.* Kluwer, Dordrecht.

Basic theory and applications of fuzzy system theory containing an extensive bibliography.

J. Kacprzyk & S.A. Orlovski, eds. (1987). *Optimization Models Using Fuzzy Sets and Possibility Theory.* Reidel, Dordrecht.

Basic theory and fuzzy optimization theory.

C.V. Negoita & D.A. Ralescu (1987). *Simulation, Knowledge-based Computing and Fuzzy Statistics.* Van Nostrand Keinhold, New York.

Contains a rudimentary, but nontrivial, fuzzy *analogue* of probability-based Gaussian (large sample) and Bayesian statistics.

[Although this monograph provides a partial answer to Professor Kall's open question, it is not clear what *modelling* advantage this theory has over the standard theory. Indeed, it would appear to be possible to rigorously derive and interpret the entire theory by using the concept of mixing *within* probability theory.]

The following books and papers concern the empirical foundations of, approximate reasoning with, and the relation with probability theory of, fuzzy system theory.

J.F. Baldwin (1986). Support logic programming. *Int. J. Gen. Systems* **1**, 73–104.

M.M. Gupta, A. Kandel, W. Bandler & J.B. Kiszka, eds. (1985). *Approximate Reasoning in Expert Systems.* North Holland, Amsterdam.

J. Kacprzyk & R.R. Yager, eds. (1985). *Management Decision Support Systems Using Fuzzy Sets and Possibility Theory.* Nijhoff, Köln.

E.H. Mamdani & B.R. Gaines, eds. (1981). *Fuzzy Reasoning and Its Applications.* Academic, London.

M. Mizumoto & H-J. Zimmermann (1982). Comparison of fuzzy reasoning methods. *Fuzzy Sets and Systems* **8**, 253–283.

A.M. Norwich & I.B. Turksen (1981). Measurement and scaling of membership functions. In: G.E. Lasker, ed. *Applied Systems and Cybernetics.* Oxford, New York, 2851–2858.

U. Thole, H-J. Zimmermann & P. Zysno (1979). On the suitability of minimum and product operators for the intersection of fuzzy sets. *Fuzzy Sets and Systems* **2**, 167–180.

R.R. Yager (1984). A representation of the probability of a fuzzy subset. *Fuzzy Sets and Systems* **13**, 273–283.

L.A. Zadeh (1968). Probability measures of fuzzy events. *J. Math. Anal. Appl.* **23**, 421–427.

H-J. Zimmermann & P. Zysno (1980). Latent connectives in human decision making. *Fuzzy Sets and Systems* **4**, 37–51.

__________ (1983). Decisions and evaluations by hierarchical aggregation of information. *Fuzzy Sets and Systems* **10**, 243–266.

__________ (1985). Quantifying vagueness in decision models. *Euro. J. O.R.* **22**, 148–158.

- ALTERNATIVE METHODOLOGIES

Representation and manipulation of uncertainty, imprecision and vagueness in knowledge-based systems.

R.I. Goodman & H.T. Nguyen (1985). *Uncertainty Models for Knowledge Based Systems.* North Holland, Amsterdam.

I. Graham & P.L. Jones (1988). *Expert Systems Knowledge, Uncertainty and Decision.* Chapman & Hall, London.

Comparison and effectiveness of current approaches to uncertainty.

L.N. Kanal & J.F. Lemmer, eds. (1986). *Uncertainty in Artificial Intelligence.* North Holland, Amsterdam.

__________ (1988). *Uncertainty in Artificial Intelligence 2.* North Holland, Amsterdam.

Relation of the (A.P.) Dempster–Shafer theory of evidence to Bayesian inference.

H.E. Kyburg, Jr. (1987). Bayesian and non-Bayesian evidential updating. *Artificial Intelligence* **31**, 271–293.

Small sample inference in uncertain situations.

J.B. Paris & A. Vencovská (1987). On the applicability of maximum entropy to inexact reasoning. Technical Report, Department of Mathematics, University of Manchester.

Logical approaches to uncertain knowledge.

M.O.L. Bacharach (1985). Some extensions of a claim of Aumann in an axiomatic model of knowledge. *J. Economic Theory* **37**, 167–190.

__________ (1986). The problem of agents' beliefs in economic theory. In: M. Baranzini & R. Scazzieri, eds. *Foundations of Economics: Structures of Inquiry and Economic Theory.* Blackwell, Oxford, 175–203.

R.M. Cooke (1986). Probabilistic reasoning in expert systems reconstructed in probability semantics. *1986 Proc. Philosophy of Science Assoc.* Vol. 1, 409–421.

H.S. Shin (1987). The logical structure of common knowledge. Technical report, Nuffield College, Oxford.

- OTHER TOPICS

The psychology of human information processing under uncertainty.

R.F. Hink & D.L. Woods (1987). How humans process uncertain knowledge: An introduction for knowledge engineers. *AI Magazine*, Fall, 41–53.

Varying requirements for representation and manipulation of uncertainty in hierarchical decision processes.

M.A.H. Dempster (1982). A stochastic approach to hierarchical planning and scheduling. In: M.A.H. Dempster, J.K. Lenstra & A.H.G. Rinnooy Kan, eds. *Deterministic and Stochastic Scheduling.* Reidel, Dordrecht, 271–296.

Y.M.I. Dirickx & L.P. Jennergren (1979). *Systems Analysis by Multilevel Methods: With Applications to Economics and Management.* Wiley, Chichester.

Probability risk assessment in the nuclear power industry.

S.H. Fistedis, ed. (1986). Special issue on 'The Role of Data and Judgement in Probabilistic Risk and Safety Analysis.' *Nuclear Engineering and Design* **93**, 121–378.

SECTION 8:

MATHEMATICAL BASIS FOR CONSTRUCTING MODELS AND MODEL VALIDATION

Validation of Decision Support Systems

Harvey J. Greenberg
Mathematics Department, Campus Box 170
University of Colorado at Denver
1100 Fourteenth Street
Denver, CO 80202 USA

1. Introduction

In science, the *validity* of a model refers to how well the model agrees with reality. On the surface this seems to be a precise definition, but one must deal with terms like "agrees with reality." As we move from natural to social sciences, the imprecision becomes more glaring. Indeed, models of natural phenomena assume a universal truth that does not vary; the scientists' job is to discover that truth. This is done with a model based on a theory, and validation is the process of observing the prediction error, that is, the difference between what the model calculates and what is observed. In social science, like economic decision-making, it is unclear whether there is an unchanging, universal truth; and, even if so, its observation seems impossible. This distinction is an uncomfortable, but important one. The fact that scientists' knowledge of truth is changing is not the same statement as the assertion that truth, itself, is invariant (this is called the *epigenic principle*, and it is fundamental to the scientific method). The importance of our distinction is that we can abandon attempts to apply the same meaning of validation as scientists apply to models (or theories) of natural phenomena. Here we consider social science models to include representations of social phenomena, including all human behavior, notably economic, that must necessarily be (perhaps tacitly) assumed in a decision support system (DSS).

We propose that the validation of a DSS is a process that addresses the question: To what extent does the DSS provide support that generally leads to "good" decisions, or at least steers the user away from "bad" decisions most of the time? It is, of course, an imprecise definition owing to the imprecision of validity that rests on subjective evaluation of "error." Despite the difficulty with precision, we can and shall consider approaches to this process of validation.

NATO ASI Series, Vol. F48
Mathematical Models for Decision Support
Edited by G. Mitra

At the heart of a DSS is some model of a world in which decisions must be made. Examples of worlds are corporate planning, government policy-making and institutional resource allocations. The scope of a DSS is rarely that broad, and for our purpose we shall restrict ourselves to *mathematical models*. Here we mean there is a collection of *objects* and *relations* among objects. Objects include variables, parameters and data elements; relations include numerical equations and logical expressions. The process of DSS validation includes a process of *model validation*: How well does the model represent its part of the world to support decision-making? The issue here is one of structure, not of particular numerical quantities.

A DSS contains more than a model; it also has a database, so we must consider *data validation* as part of DSS validation. There are occassions, however, where useful decision support is attainable without data, just by inferences drawn from the qualitative structure of the relations. Still, the process of DSS validation would not be complete without attention to data validation; and, in many cases even qualitative properties depend partly on data values (perhaps with some uncertainty, such as fuzzy or interval-valued representations).

Here we want to consider the incorporation of expert system technology in DSS design and use. We must therefore add another component: To what extent does the rulebase represent valid knowledge to support decision-making (in the particular world)? That is, we must also consider *rulebase validation* as part of the process of DSS validation. Fortunately, we enter an arena where recognition of invalidity--that is, the process of determining something is wrong with the DSS--leads to *learning* to overcome the unsuitable advice given. This becomes an important departure from the traditional concepts of validation, which are largely statistically based, owing to the tradition of measuring validity by agreement with numerical observations.

Because the total subject of DSS validation is vast and unchartered, this paper focuses on the last point: rulebase validation and how it can automatically lead to improvement in that part of the DSS. We shall draw heavily from the work of [Politakis, 1985] and attempt to apply some of the principles to other DSS components.

First, in the next section we briefly review approaches to validation that have been taken. In general, these seem to be tied to modeling disciplines. That is, the simulation community has a particular approach they have developed over the years, based in statistical testing. The mathematical programming community has a different perspective; and, we shall try to synthesize these as we develop a historical perspective of the validation process.

Second, we consider validation as a social process, using *peer review* as a legitimate method to arrive at validity assessments. This seems less scientific than statistically-based methods, but in fact even theorem proving has evidence of being a social process, as demonstrated in [DeMillo, Lipton and Perlis, 1979].

Third, we consider an artificial intelligence approach, which constitutes a learning model superimposed on the DSS. Here the social process is evident, for the rule refinements depend on someone expressing dissatisfaction with the advice given by the DSS.

Fourth, we briefly consider *fuzzy validation*, which is a new approach that combines features of traditional and AI approaches, drawing heavily from [Schmucker, 1984]. Due to limitations of space only a sketch of this approach is given here. A more detailed description is in preparation.

We conclude with a summary and suggest avenues for further research. Throughout this paper we have taken the position that validation is a process that addresses a question of degree, not of kind. Not everyone agrees with this premise; some believe a model, and hence a DSS, is either valid or it is not. The position here is based on a more realistic view of why DSS's exist and dissociates connections with issues of scientific validation about natural phenomenon, suggesting a fuzzy definition of validation for DSS's.

2. Traditional Approaches to Validation

Traditional approaches to validation are based on two concepts. The first is to compare model results with observed values and measure the error quantitatively. Often this is refined into an analysis of variance. The second is to draw inferences from the model, usually by sensitivity analysis, and compare these inferences with underlying theories. Both of these methods are used in validating models of natural phenomenon, and both have been applied to models used for decision support.

Divide validity into two parts: *internal* and *external*. Internal validity includes:

- consistency--no logical contradictions;
- algorithm validity--acceptable approximation errors;
- no biases--randomization richness.

External validity includes:

- agreement with empirical observations;
- consistency with underlying theory;
- delineation of scope;
- isolation of control factors.

Within the confines of statistical validation one could improve external validity at the expense of internal validity. For example, to help isolate control factors biases can be introduced [Keppel, 1973].

Another common example goes the other way by accepting some inconsistency with underlying theory in order to reduce approximation errors. That is, one might assume a Cobb-Douglas production function that yields a log-linear relationship between quantities and prices of commodities: log Q = E log P, where E is the price elasticity (matrix). Now suppose this is applied to many regions, yielding regional quantity estimates (say supply) as a function of regional prices. The total quantity, aggregated over N regions, is $Q_1+...+Q_N$, but the log-linear relation must fail for any price aggregation (e.g., simple or quantity-weighted average). Thus, the underlying Cobb-Douglas theory that implies the log-linear relation cannot hold simultaneously for the regions and for the aggregate. In practice, this invalidity is accepted by compromises in estimating the price elasticities.

Delineation of scope is sometimes overlooked when validating a DSS, even just its model component. Often one calibrates portions of a model with fine detail, then puts it into a reduced form for embedding into a larger model. One example is to use parametric programming to obtain I/O relations of a process model, like a refinery (with crude oil as input and petroleum products as output). Then, this may serve as an approximation within a large equilibrium model, like an international energy market. The validity of this approximation generally depends on how the model will be used to support decisions--that is, its scope. If, for example, one uses the model to analyze an extreme scenario, such as disallowing imported oil, the model's results are likely to be invalid.

The paradigm *What if...?* sensitivity analysis is an important traditional approach, which is still used as part of newer methods we shall consider. This includes testing agreement with numerical observations, such as a linear program's marginal prices versus observed market prices. It also includes structural analysis, such as implied relations from a system of equations. Combinations of flat-numerical and relational properties may also be tested, such as imputing price elasticities from scenario analysis. Specialized abstractions, like the multiplier analysis in [Challen and Hagger, 1983], often give insights, even without empirical testing.

Whether sensitivity analysis is done by abstraction or by empirical testing, the design and interpretation of the results still depend on some human, which we shall call an *expert*. This recognition leads to validation as a social process, the topic of the next section.

3. Validation as a Social Process

The notion of peer review, third-party assessment, independent assessment, or by some other name, appears to be particular to social science models in general and decision support systems in particular. However, as demonstrated in [Demillo, Lipton and Perlis, 1979], even mathematical proofs are really a social process in that the bottom line as to the validity of a proof rests with acceptance of peer mathematicians of the time. The same argument undoubtedly applies to natural science model validity; one example is how long it took for the special theory of relativity to replace Newton's model, even after recognizing its connection with the Michaelson-Morely experiment. (Probably, the much later, pragmatic goal of developing nuclear power mothered its validation.)

Although there have been hints at a formal approach of peer review, some couched in the Delphi method, the Model Assessment Group of the MIT Energy Laboratory appears to have been first to formalize this approach by openly accepting ad hoc practice and putting validation by peer assessment on a foundation that itself can be subjected to scientific scrutiny (see [Wood, 1980] and [Kresge, 1980]). The MIT approach is first to state the *model category* (e.g., Energy Model, used for economic policy analysis) and the *levels of assessment* (e.g., logical, empirical, comparative). They rely on literature reviews, sensitivity analyses, expert review of structures, and any combination of traditional approaches, controlled by peer evaluation.

The use of sensitivity analysis could be a matter of experimental design and hypothesis testing, but confidence in a model is rarely accomplished by statistical recipe. An insightful discussion is given in [Schweppe and Gruhl, 1980]. Often, part of the sensitivity analysis imputes abstract measures, like elasticities or multipliers. The validation study in [Keeping, 1983] reports a twist that opens yet further uses of sensitivity analysis to form a basis for peer evaluation.

Typically, this approach results in concrete suggestions for improvements with the team of validators available for consultation. An important aspect is that these experts state clearly the basis for their evaluations. This opens prospects for an artificial intelligence (AI) approach, where we might imagine an expert system designed to validate a model or, more generally, a decision support system. We are not quite there, and the MIT case studies are sufficiently complex that it will probably be a while before some such expert system exists. There is, however, a more specialized AI approach that we shall consider next.

Before proceeding, it may seem appropriate to separate validation into what may be regarded as *objective* processes, like the traditional internal and external validity criteria, from peer review. The position taken here, however, is that there is no objectivity. All validation in practice, however clothed, ultimately comes to some person or group deciding on how valid the DSS is for some problem domain. What we think of as objective validation is better viewed as part of the validator's tool kit (e.g., methods of sensitivity analysis).

4. An AI Approach to Validation

We now adapt a recent approach in [Politakis, 1985] where an invalidity suggests rule refinement. The interactive system called SEEK allows a knowledge engineer to:

1. obtain performance of rules on stored cases;
2. analyze the rules;
3. revise the rules.

Although this was designed for medical diagnosis, we shall apply the main idea to DSS validation, particularly for economic decisions. The idea is to see how the best advice (judged so by an expert) could have been given by the DSS after making certain changes in the rulebase. For our purpose this means an invalidity is recognized in the form of unsuitable advice given by the DSS, and we shall develop a revision in the DSS's rules to achieve validity. As such, we may properly view this as a learning component of the DSS triggered by the invalid case.

To help fix ideas consider a DSS designed to give advice on the selection of a project among a competing set. Each project is evaluated with a *selection rule* that yields three levels of selection confidence: *definite*, *probable* or *possible*. If no selection rule has its conditions satisfied for a particular project, that project is rejected from further consideration. In the final advice given, a project with the strongest selection confidence supersedes those with lower confidence. For example, if a definite selection is determined for a project, it is given as the recommended investment even if other projects have probable confidence. (We shall ignore the situation when the DSS selects more than one project due to equal confidence levels reached because our only aim is to develop an approach to learning (i.e., rulebase refinement) when the DSS advice disagrees with that of an expert.)

A selection rule is a conjunction of three parts:

1. Number of general criteria satisfied;
2. Specific requirements; and,
3. Specific exclusions.

General criteria are divided into *major* and *minor* ones (though this could be expanded to more categories). For our example we consider the following.

Major Criteria	Minor Criteria
1. Production technology is stable.	1. Able to borrow capital if cost overrun.
2. Demand forecasts are reliable.	2. Tax benefits are possible.
3. Raw materials are available.	3. Trade secrets are secure.
4. Market expansion is possible.	4. There is adequate corporate experience.

In addition, there are 3 measurable factors used in specifying requirements and exclusions.

G = Expected gain (e.g., profit or savings).

R = Risk of loss.

L = Labor availability.

The expected gain (G) and risk of loss (R) may be obtained by running a mathematical model (e.g., a mathematical program or simulation). In any case, we shall suppose they have been categorized by the following *descendingly ordered sets*.

G is from {GREAT, SOME, MARGINAL, NONE}.

R is from {HIGH, MEDIUM, LOW}.

L is from {ABUNDANT, ADEQUATE, MARGINAL, SCARCE}.

For example, suppose G is estimated (perhaps from a mathematical model). Then, its numeric value is mapped by:

$G > g$ ==> GREAT

$g \geq G > m$ ==> SOME

$m \geq G > 0$ ==> MARGINAL

$G \leq 0$ ==> NONE

where the threshold parameters g and m are presumed known.

Table 1 shows a tabular format for the DSS's selection rules. For example, the rule for concluding definite selection can be stated as follows. If the project satisfies all 4 of the major criteria, and its expected gain is greater than marginal (i.e., G equals SOME or GREAT), and its risk is low, and the labor availability is not less than adequate, then definitely select the project.

	Definite	Probable	Possible
	4 majors	2 majors 2 minors	3 majors
Requirements	G > MARGINAL R = LOW	G > MARGINAL	G > NONE
Exclusions	L < ADEQUATE	L < ADEQUATE	L = SCARCE

Table 1. Tabular Format for Project Selection Rules

Notice that a project may satisfy more than one selection rule. For example, a project may satisfy 3 majors, 2 minors and have G=SOME, L=ADEQUATE. Rule conflict resolution in this case is by strongest confidence--that is, the selection confidence would be probable. (See [Holsapple and Whinston, 1986] for alternatives to rule conflict resolution during chaining as well as final ranking.)

When the advice given by the DSS disagrees with that of an expert, we declare an invalidity and initiate a rule revision that constitutes a form of machine learning. For definiteness suppose we have the following two projects to consider.

P_1: open new plant in London.

P_2: open new plant in New York.

Further, suppose we reach the following situation.

DSS's advice: Probable open new plant in London.

Expert's advice: Open new plant in New York.

A single case analysis seeks a rule that has the expert's conclusion; and, if there is more than one, picks a strongest one.

Suppose, for example, the two competing projects have the attributes shown in Table 2.

	P_1	P_2
Major Criteria		
1. Production technology is stable.	YES	YES
2. Demand forecasts are reliable.	YES	YES
3. Raw materials are available.	YES	YES
4. Market expansion is possible.	YES	NO
Minor Criteria		
1. Able to borrow capital...	YES	YES
2. Tax benefits are possible.	YES	NO
3. Trade secrets are secure.	YES	YES
4. Adequate corporate experience.	YES	YES
Measured Criteria		
Gain	SOME	GREAT
Risk	MEDIUM	LOW
Labor	ADEQUATE	MARGINAL

Table 2. Attributes of Competing Projects in Example

For our example, suppose we have the *strongest rule for expert's conclusion*:

Rule 91: 3 or more majors for P_2

G > NONE for P_2

L is not = SCARCE for P_2

---> Possible P_2.

What we mean by *strongest* here is that the expert's conclusion (P_2) is not satisfied by any rule having stronger confidence than possible. (From Table 1 we see that L=MARGINAL is enough to exclude the stronger confidence levels.)

Now consider the *rule for the DSS's conclusion*:

Rule 70: 2 or more majors for P_1

2 or more minors for P_1

G > MARGINAL for P_1

L is not < ADEQUATE for P_1

---> Probable P_1.

Project P_1 may satisfy other rules, including rule 91, but the DSS fired Rule 70 because it yields the strongest selection confidence. (From Table 1 we see that R=MEDIUM violates a requirement for definite confidence level.)

The rulebase could be refined in two ways: weaken rule 70 so it would not override rule 91, or find a stronger rule that concludes probably (or definitely) P_2 to agree with the expert's choice. The former approach is discarded on the grounds that to modify a selection rule's confidence level is a drastic revision that may cause other invalidities. Instead, we shall pursue a more subtle revision by some combination of rule *generalization* and *specialization*.

Generalization of a rule is a weakening of its conditions, so it may be invoked more frequently. For example, consider a *rule for expert's conclusion with confidence stronger than that of the DSS's conclusion*:

Rule 72: 4 majors for P_2

G > MARGINAL for P_2

R=LOW for P_2

L is not < ADEQUATE for P_2

---> Definitely P_2.

We may weaken conditions in rule 72 to obtain a generalized rule satisfied by the expert's conclusion (P_2). Since, however, it suffices to find a confidence of probably for P_2, we would seek to generalize some other rule. Still, we may find that rule 72 is the closest one satisfied by P_2, perhaps due to P_2 having low risk of loss. The specific types of weakening could be:

- Change conditions in place (e.g., require only 3 majors);
- Add to list of majors, giving more opportunity for satisfaction;
- Refine categories of Gain or Risk, giving finer partition of requirements.

Details to find a rule of *best-fit*, like rule 72, and how to generalize it to eliminate the invalidity of the new case may be adapted from the methodology in [Politakis, 1985].

Specialization of a rule is a strengthening of its conditions, so it may be invoked less frequently. For example, we can achieve the expert's conclusion by specializing rule 70 so that it is not satisfied by P_1. This can be done by:

- Change conditions in place (e.g., require at least 3 minors);
- Strengthen criteria (e.g., change major #4 to require that market expansion is probable);
- Refine categories of Gain or Risk, giving finer partition of requirements.

Unlike medical diagnosis there are few, if any, binary tests (i.e., positive or negative) that yield much guidance in this kind of decision. Accordingly, methods of generalization and specialization are more complex. This apparent difficulty may be overcome by a broader-based methodology that uses fuzzy reasoning. One such approach is considered in the next section.

5. Fuzzy Validation

We suppose uncertainty is represented by fuzzy set membership functions, including the decisions themselves. The main issue is how we can synthesize the AI approach with approximate reasoning, like the fuzzy linguistics in [Schmucker, 1984].

To help fix ideas let C be a descendingly ordered set of *primitive confidence levels*. Typically, C will be:

{HIGH, MEDIUM, LOW}

or

{DEFINITE, PROBABLE, POSSIBLE}.

Now let H be a set of *hedge linguistic variables*, or simply *hedges*. An extensive list of hedges is in [Schmucker, 1984]; we may suppose H is simply {ALMOST, VERY, SLIGHTLY}.

In general, we let $m_A(x)$ denote the *fuzzy membership value* of x for the set A. We define this to be in the interval [0,1] with a degree of belief interpretation: $m_A(x)$ near 0 means we have very little belief that x is in the set A, and $m_A(x)$ near 1 means we have high belief that x is in A. Superficially, we want the fuzzy membership value, $m_V(S)$, to be near 1, where V is the set of valid DSS's, and S is the DSS we want to validate. This, itself, does nothing for us. We must instead return to the pragmatic goal of validation: isolate reasons for unacceptable advice given by the DSS. Then, this can initiate a learning model to improve the DSS's validity, that is, its quality of support.

We must begin to address such questions as these:

> To what extent can validation result in linguistic expressions like VERY PROBABLE or SLIGHTLY POSSIBLE?
>
> Can such expressions be obtained for rules or other DSS components, and will this lead to learning?
>
> Can this be done such that the traditional methods and the AI approach given in the previous section become special cases (i.e., by control settings governing the approximate reasoning)?

Consider the general expression: IF DSS is valid THEN P. Property P can be any consequence of the DSS as a whole or isolated to one of its parts. In the example of the previous section we can let P represent the concluding advice. Now when P disagrees with some validation criterion, like with the conclusion of an expert, an invalidity is declared and instantiates a *causal trace*. The goal of the trace is to isolate reasons for the DSS to imply P. Once the trace is complete, a self-correcting procedure may be invoked, or an interactive session may begin to achieve validity--i.e., revise the DSS so that P is no longer implied (and no new invalidities are caused by the revision).

Property P could also be a consequence of the DSS's model, not in the form of concluding advice. This is important to prevent poor advice. That is, one deficiency of the AI approach described in the previous section is that it corrects concluding advice only after disagreement with an expert. This might be mitigated by training sessions, but it still constitutes only a portion of DSS validation and may not prevent poor advice at a time when it matters.

To illustrate another use of this general rule consider a (simplified) linear program with the structure shown in figure 1.

	Provide				Generate		Substitute	
	PNGEL	POLEL	PNGIN	POLIN	GNGEL	GOLEL	SNGIN	
COST	s_N	s_O	s_N	s_O	g_N	g_O	f	= MIN
BNGEL	1				-1			= 0
BOLEL		1				-1		= 0
DELIN					1	1	-e	$\geq d_{EL}$
DNGIN			1				1	$\geq d_{NG}$
DOLIN				1			-o	$\geq d_{OL}$

Figure 1. An LP Structure with Fuel Substitution

According to the structure in figure 1 (which is say only a portion of the linear programming model), industrial demand for natural gas (d_{NG}) can be satisfied by shares of electricity and oil (e and o, respectively). The activity (SNGIN) cost is some "fudge factor" f, which we shall suppose has been imputed to ensure that the level of SNGIN becomes positive only when there is a shortage of natural gas. We see that when this occurs a price relation is imposed:

$$f + e\,p_{EL} + o\,p_{OL} = p_{NG},$$

where p_f = marginal price of fuel f (computed from the dual). A consequence of this is that the electric utility's dispatching decision--i.e., whether to use oil or natural gas to generate electricity--is affected by their relative prices. The relative prices are determined by industrial demands, so we can derive:

IF LP structure is valid THEN an electric utility's dispatching decision is affected by industrial demands for oil and gas.

We could sharpen this consequence by some numerical derivations, using intervals of uncertainty for the input costs. The main point is that we can apply validation to the DSS's model structure, not just the rulebase, and isolate causes of invalidities found.

Now let us consider uncertainties using fuzzy reasoning. Instead of the deterministic rule representation of a DSS's consequence, let $m_W(P)$ denote the fuzzy membership value of property P in the (real) world within the DSS's scope. Further, let $m_D(P)$ denote the fuzzy membership value of property P in the DSS--i.e., it is the degree of belief that property P is implied by the DSS. Let V(P) denote the *validity discrepancy* of property P, which may be defined as the absolute difference between $m_W(P)$ and $m_D(P)$. Essentially, we are considering the expression:

$$\text{IF DSS is valid THEN } m_D(P) = m_W(P)$$

and we regard the difference in their fuzzy values as *error*.

Now we fuzzify the validity measure to obtain a degree of belief that property P has valid membership, denoted (somewhat wrongly) by $m_V(P)$. This may simply be 1-V(P), so that when $m_V(P)$ is near 1 we have a high belief that the DSS is valid (relative to property P); and, when it is near 0, we have a low belief that the DSS is valid. In the latter case we also have a reason for the invalidity, namely P, to initiate learning.

The world fuzzy values, $m_W(P)$ for P in some set of properties *P*, may be obtained from observation or from expert judgement. The DSS's fuzzy values, $m_D(P)$ for P in *P*, is inferred from the validation process. Using fuzzy conjunction, we may define *DSS validity* as:

$$m_V(S) = \min\{m_V(P): \text{ P in } \mathit{P}\}.$$

To initiate learning, we collect only those properties P that bind the overall validity--i.e., P in *P* for which $m_V(P) = m_V(S)$ (or close). These properties comprise the input for the learning mechanism that improves validity by one of several methods:

1. apply a self-correcting rule, such as rule refinement in the AI approach or, more generally, fuzzy rule revisions;

2. initiate an interactive, training session with an expert;

3. delineate the DSS's scope by adding an exclusion with an explanation for why the exclusion has been added (i.e., the invalid property).

All of this is, of course, simplistic and much remains to be done to develop the ideas given. In the next section we cite several avenues for research to arrive at a useful approach to validation that leads to self-correction through learning.

6. Concluding Remarks

Traditionally, validation is a process to measure how well a model agrees with the world it models. The final result is often a statement of kind: either the model is valid or it is not. The same tradition applies to database validity (though here some people use the term validation when they really mean verification--i.e., that what is computer-resident is what is believed to be there). Even when validation is treated as a matter of degree the traditional approaches have little to say about improving it. (Exceptions exist in fragments.) The situation now is different because we define validation as a different process than its traditional one.

We propose that the validation of a DSS is a process that results in either (provisional) validity with no further action or in the detection of an invalidity in the form of an implied property that is deemed in too much disagreement with the world. One example of this is unacceptable advice given by the DSS to support decision-making, deemed so either by the user or by disagreement with an expert who is believed to be right. The result of invalidation provides input to a learning model, so the DSS subsequently becomes (provisionally) valid. One potential problem with this is whether it is possible to correct the cited invalidity without causing some other invalidity. Even recognition of this dilemma is an avenue for further research.

Learning models may vary, as may the validation form and content. One example that requires further study is the criterion that validation measures disagreement between the DSS advice and that of a human expert. We must also consider what happens when experts disagree. Although we could design a learning model around the idea of rulebase modification (e.g., use of generalization and specialization), this may not always be the best method of self-correction. When automatic self-correction cannot be done, an interactive training session may be initiated. One possible outcome is a constriction of the DSS's scope that eliminates the invalid case.

Fuzzy values may be the key to help unify approaches to validation as a process that initiates learning. Only a rudimentary foundation has been suggested here, and the main questions remain open. Even if the proposed propositional schema is appropriate, concepts of learning, well summarized in [Michalski, Carbonell and Mitchell, 1983], are inadequate. One critical avenue for research is sharpening the idea of causal trace. In a sophisticated DSS, using more than a simple rulebase, isolation of causal parts is unchartered, except in

special cases. Still, the proposed foundation seems to show promise for transferring some of the art (perhaps black) of validation into the realm of science.

Acknowledgement

The author gratefully acknowledges stimulating discussions with Drs. Weldon and Dora Lodwick, which helped to form the ideas expressed. Of course, the author is responsible for the positions taken and any errors or misconceptions.

7. Bibliography and References

[1] O. Balci and R.G. Sargent, 1980. "Bibliography on Validation of Simulation Models," Spring 1980 Newsletter-TIMS College in Simulation and Gaming, pp. 11-15.

[2] O. Balci and R.G. Sargent, 1981. "A Methodology for Cost-Risk Analysis in Statistical Validation of Simulation Models," *Communications of ACM* **24, pp. 190-197.**

[3] E.R. Carson, C. Cobelli and L. Finkelstein, 1983. The Mathematical Modeling of Metabolic and Endocrine Systems Model Formulation, Identification, and Validation, John Wiley & Sons.

[4] D.W. Challen and A.J. Hagger, 1983. Macroeconomic Systems Construction, Validation and Applications, MacMillan Press.

[5] C.R. Deeter and A.A.J. Hoffman, 1978. *An Annotated Bibliography of Mathematical Models Classified by Validation and Error Analysis Methods*, **Texas Christian University, Fort Worth, TX.**

[6] R.A. DeMillo, R.J. Lipton and A.J. Perlis, 1979. "Social Processes and Proofs of Theorems and Programs," *Communications of ACM* **22, pp. 271-280.**

[7] J. Felsen, 1976. Decision Making Under Uncertainty: An Artificial Intelligence Approach, CDS Publishing Company.

[8] B.R. Gaines, 1977. "Foundations of Fuzzy Reasoning," in Fuzzy Automata and Decision Processes, M.M. Gupta, G.N. Saridis and B.R. Gaines (eds.), Elsevier, pp. 19-75.

[9] S.I. Gass, 1980. Validation and Assessment Issues of Energy Models, Proceedings of a Workshop, NBS Special Publication 564, Washington, DC.

[10] S.I. Gass, 1983. "Decision-Aiding Models: Validation, Assessment, and Related Issues for Policy Analysis," *Operations Research* 31, pp. 603-631.

[11] J.S. Greenstein and M.E. Revesman, 1986. "Development and Validation of a Mathematical Model of Human Decision-making for Human-Computer Communication," *IEEE Transactions on Systems, Man and Cybernetics* 16, pp. 148-153.

[12] C. Hermann, 1967. "Validation Problems in Games and Simulations," *Behavioral Science* 12, pp. 216-231.

[13] C.W. Holsapple and A.B. Whinston, 1986. Manager's Guide to Expert Systems Using GURU, Dow Jones-Irwin.

[14] D. Kahneman, P. Slovic and A. Tversky (eds.), 1982. Judgement Under Uncertainty: Heuristics and Biases, Cambridge University Press.

[15] B. Keepin, 1983. "A Critical Appraisal of the IIASA Energy Scenarios," IIASA Working Paper WP-83-104, Laxenburg, Austria.

[16] G. Keppel, 1973. Design and Analysis: A Researcher's Handbook, Prentice-Hall.

[17] D.T. Kresge, 1980. "An Approach to Independent Model Assessment," in [Gass, 1980], pp. 183-203.

[18] W. Lodwick, 1987. "Fuzzy Linguistics in a Decision Support System," these proceedings.

[19] R. Michalski, J. Carbonell and T. Mitchell, 1983. Machine Learning: An Artificial Intelligence Approach, Tioga Press.

[20] T.I. Oren, 1981. "Concepts and Criteria to Assess Acceptability of Simulation Studies: A Frame of Reference," *Communications of ACM* 24, pp. 180-189.

[21] P.G. Politakis and S.M. Weiss, 1984. "Using Empirical Analysis to Refine Expert System Knowledge Bases," *Artificial Intelligence* 22, pp. 23-48.

[22] P.G. Politakis, 1985. Empirical Analysis for Expert Systems, Pitman.

[23] L. Rendell, P. Benedict and H. Cho, 1987. *Concept Acquisition from Examples: Measurement of System Performance and Suggestions for Improved Design*, Report No. UIUCDCD-R-87-1315, Department of Computer Science, University of Illinois at Urbana-Champaign, Urbana, IL.

[24] R.E. Schellenberger, 1974. "Criteria for Assessing Model Validity for Managerial Purposes," *Decision Science* **5, pp. 644-653.**

[25] K.J. Schmucker, 1984. Fuzzy Sets, Natural Language Computations, and Risk Analysis, Computer Science Press.

[26] F.C. Schweppe and J. Gruhl, 1980. "Systematic Sensitivity Analysis Using Describing Functions," in [Gass, 1980], pp. 497-513.

[27] R.L. Van Horn, 1971. "Validation of Simulation Results," *Management Science* **17, pp. 247-258.**

[28] D.O. Wood, 1980. "Model Assessment and the Policy Research Process: Current Practice and Future Promise," in [Gass, 1980], pp. 23-60.

[29] R.R. Yager, 1978. "Validation of Fuzzy-Linguistic Models," *Journal of Cybernetics* **8, pp. 17-30.**

[30] H.J. Zimmermann, 1982. "Testability and Meaning of Mathematical Models in Social Sciences," *Mathematical Modelling* **1, pp. 123-139.**

[31] H.J. Zimmermann, 1985. Fuzzy Set Theory and Its Applications, Kluwer Nijhoff.

[32] H.J. Zimmermann, 1987. "A Tutorial on Fuzzy Sets and Approximate Reasoning," these proceedings.

Panel Discussion on DSS Validation

Chairman: Dr. Harvey J. Greenberg
Panelists: Dr. Roger M. Cooke
Dr. Melanie L. Lenard
Dr. Andrew B. Whinston

After the lead paper was presented by Dr. Greenberg, each panelist gave opening remarks, as follows.

Roger Cooke. The question posed by Prof. Greenberg is this: What is a good DSS system? This is surely the big question, but given the short time available for preparation, I have nothing to add to his remarks. Instead, I would like to address the narrower question: How in principle can we externally validate the propositional output of a decision support system?

In posing this question one is not interested in the internal reasoning mechanism by which this output is generated, be it fuzzy logic, support logic, probability semantics or whatever. The following off-the cuff remarks are directed to this narrower question.

If the propositional output takes the form of simple declarative sentences, then we can in principle validate this output by determining the truth values of such sentences. If the output takes the form of (subjective) probability statements, then under suitable assumptions we can evaluate this output by the methods described in my paper [in these proceedings]. If the output takes the form of sentences-cum-certainty-factors, as in MYCIN-type expert systems, then external validation is not possible. Indeed, certainty factors cannot be interpreted as probabilities, and no one has clarified their meaning. It is therefore impossible to distinguish "good" from "bad" certainty factors. Similar remarks would seem to apply when the output takes the form of fuzzy membership values, or fuzzy truth values. If such statements are purely subjective, as Prof. Zimmermann suggests, then external validation is excluded. Fuzzy set theory is much poorer in this respect than subjective probability, as the theory of exchangeability provides a well understood link between the latter and observable relative frequencies. An expression like "real world fuzzy membership," as used by Prof. Greenberg, is one to which I can attach no discernible meaning.

Given the existing knowledge on expert opinion, Turing test type of comparisons between DSS output and human expert performance cannot be considered as external validation, interesting though such comparisons may be. It is the responsibility of the decision analyst to define and monitor external validation. The frequently heard comment to the effect: "I know it's a bag of wind but it sells" should be regarded as a breach of professional ethic. Such comments cannot even be made in jest, as they are not funny.

NATO ASI Series, Vol. F48
Mathematical Models for Decision Support
Edited by G. Mitra

Expert systems have the dangerous potential of compromising the personal accountability of human experts. Can one file a malpractice suit against an expert system? Obscuring personal accountability is not the way to improve the quality of expert opinion.

Melanie Lenard. Let me open with some points from a structured modeling perspective. (1) A comprehensible modular modeling format, like structured modeling, could be an aid to validation. (2) Measures of validity should be chosen early in the model life cycle. (3) Experts are not always right; they can and do learn from models. The results of models should agree with intuition, expert opinion, etc. most of the time, but the counter-intuitive results are perhaps more valuable. (4) When the output of expert models is deemed invalid, instead of trying to revise the rulebase with more rules or certainty factors, we should consider building a deeper model using an optimization or simulation paradigm for example. (5) I am curious about how to validate underlying structural assumptions of models (e.g., linearity, normality). How would we know when deviations from these assumptions invalidate the results?

Andrew Whinston. Suppose we think of a DSS as an assistant who we hope possesses intelligence and can give support to certain aspects of a decision problem. If the decision problem involved searching through a data base our assistant could be viewed as an algorithmic file processor. Validity could be based on the performance of the algorithm and the completeness and relevance of the data base. If we were to be faced with decision problems that would require analytic models as well as a data base, validity could be based on the quality and relevance of the results. As an example, the analysis of product routings in a network should be associated with a realistic representation of the transportation network as well as producing a low cost solution. The realism of the model may be somewhat dependent on how well the DSS software can translate the problem statement into an adequate model. The quality of the value of the cost function is dependent on the effectiveness of the algorithm.

The problem of DSS validation may be sufficiently complex and heterogeneous that the only feasible way of devising a solution is to decompose the DSS system into various components and develop a validation criteria for each component. In *Foundations of Decision Support Systems*[1] we have presented a framework for DSS that is based on three components. The validation of the knowledge base could be viewed as an empirical issue and handled statistically. Analytic techniques represented as procedures could be evaluated from a computational, algorithmic perspective. Is the algorithm correct? What about the complexity issues? The validity of the user interface or language system would be the purview of human factors specialists. Of course, the validity of the whole system is not the sum of the validity of the parts. How

[1]R.H. Bonczek, C.W. Holsapple and A.B. Whinston. Academic Press, New York, 1981.

to put a total validity measure together should be an interesting research problem and would lead to significant insights into DSS as a discipline. After all, the essence of DSS is in the integration of the subcomponents.

One point was clarified before proceeding to open discussion.

Harvey Greenberg. I do not know how to define external validity for DSS, and I agree it is fundamentally important. Let me clarify the point in my paper about "agreeing with an expert" since this was refuted by both Roger and Melanie as the definition of validity. I agree with the refutation, and I intended only to use this as an example in my paper. I suggest that this is <u>sometimes</u> an appropriate measure of DSS validity. In general, I believe that, unlike validation of natural science models, DSS validation is relative, based on goal-directed measures.

The discussion was then open. The following is a partial report of the comments made from the floor.

Hans-Jürgen Zimmermann. Validation will have to be defined better (quality, value, fit, reliability). There are different requirements for validation in [natural] science from those in technologies (OR, MS, DSS). Our goal in science is to find truth; our goal in technologies is to improve operations. Hence, costs of validation and improvements have to be compared to 9respective benefits. Empirical validation is very difficult, perhaps impossible, because peers (experts) might be very imperfect judges (limitations of human consistency and information processing capabilities). Plausibility (face-validity) might be a bad measure of validity because "optimal solutions" might be very implausible. What is required is a theory of validation similar to those theories in the philosophy of science.

Frederic H. Murphy. Models to be validated fall into two groups, operations models and policy models. Validation of an operations model is a relatively simple task. One verifies that it is implemented without major error and one runs the model in parallel with the current operations of the system and tests directly whether or not the model provides better decisions. Policy models cannot be run in parallel with the world to verify their results before they are used. One must then test the inputs instead of the output, checking the assumptions for consistency (that the results from parameter changes move in the direction predicted by theory) and auditing the model to make sure it is implemented as stated.

The other check is on the level of confidence one has in the model builder. The model builder should know the subject modeled at least as well as he or she knows the tools for modeling. The more one can trust the model builder the more one can trust the models. A critical dimension to this trust is the ability of the model builder to articulate the results of the model in terms,ms of the subject modeled as opposed to the mechanics of the model.

The track record of a policy model is not necessarily that useful an indicator of how the model will perform in the future. This is because a used policy model is typically revised substantially before the original forecast can be compared with actual experience. Thus, the comparison does not necessarily apply to the new model.

Gezinus Hidding. DSS validation is similar to correspondence. In order to establish external validity the assumptions underlying the specific DSS have to match the problem as perceived in reality. The assumptions have to be believable. (A counterexample is, however, the Capital Asset Pricing Model, whose assumptions seem to be far removed from reality, but the model is of great practical value.)

Freerk Lootsma. I am rather skeptical because the issue of validation appears at the end of the conference. Until now, it has not been an integral part of the discussions about decision support systems. So, we still have to consider the question of whether those systems support the decision maker or whether they violate his intentions. Do they really fathom his preferences? Do they lead him (faster than before) to the decision which is deeply hidden in the back of his mind, or do they lead him to new, unexpected decisions? Do they merely accelerate the decision process, or do they also optimize the quality of the final decision. These questions should have been on the agenda from the start.

Manfred Grauer. The role of decision support (making) could be characterized more explicitly as not only solving LP, MIP, and stochastic problems, but also including definite types of decision behavior as the utility paradigm or satisfying paradigm. It seems important to include the statements about the notions of "adaptation" and "learning," which contradicts the classical utility theory assumption that the decision maker must be consistent. Decision support seems to be a tool, which helps to manage complexity of a problem, to be consistent in the problem formulation and to recognize "good" alternatives as possible candidates for final decisions. In this sense it is a tool for learning what is a "good" alternative under given circumstances. The question of validation includes the evaluations of the above mentioned issues.

Michael Dempster. Validity of models, systems and theories may be established by attempting to use fundamental assumptions that fit reality and uses valid, consistent reasoning methods to reach decisions, recommendations and conclusions – often by a process of great complexity. This allows for the possibility of conclusions, etc. reached by models, etc. to improve upon currently existing decisions, etc. A concommittment is that several models, etc. may reach the same conclusions, etc. – some from absurd assumptions. Thus, a validation procedure should require improved conclusions, etc. by logically valid inference from verifiably realistic assumptions. To come to this ideal situation, a critical component – analogous to code debuggers – is an explanation facility for model, etc. reasoning.

Istvan Maros. Why do we call someone an expert? How did he prove his expertise? or How can we validate his expertise? If we knew the answers, we may be able to apply the same or similar validation process to the model. I am looking forward to a good definition of an "expert."

Leon Lasdon. Leaders of successful corporate or private sector OR/MS activities qualify as experts on DSS model validation.

Gautam Mitra. I consider decision support systems, such as an expert system shell, and modeling systems, such as CAMPS or GAMS, are in the realm of management engineering. Hence, we need to use an engineering approach to test and validate these. The concept of engineering validation is different from scientific validation: it is more in the nature of testing. For instance, from a scientific point of view it is easy to accept polynomial algorithms for LP, yet from an engineering point of view only by investigations of a carefully chosen test problem set can we establish average time performance of such methods. For these systems I would also like to take up the concept of model of models introduced [here] by Melanie Lenard. Hence, we need validation at two levels. In level 1 we validate the modeling system itself, and in level 2 we need to have mechanisms for validating the generated models. I think it should be possible to incorporate in level 1 consciously methods for validating models generated in level 2. Of course, the method of validation in level 1 is still a difficult problem.

The panelists made brief closing remarks, and we adjourned.

DSS Conceptualizers in O.R.: Should you apply AI?[1]

Gezinus J. Hidding,
Arthur Andersen & Cie.,
Tour GAN Cedex 13,
92082 PARIS LA DEFENSE 2
France

1 INTRODUCTION AND OVERVIEW

The task of designing Decision Support Systems (DSS) is becoming increasingly difficult for a number of reasons:

DSS potentially contain any combination of techniques from Artificial Intelligence (AI), expert systems, conventional data processing, Operations Research (OR), statistics, data base, etc. to solve business problems in practice. It depends on the problem on hand which techniques are appropriate.

New techniques to model and solve problems are rapidly becoming available, for example, parallel processing.

More and more DSS software products appear. Software packages to solve linear programming, to develop expert systems, to solve routing and distribution problems, to solve mixed integer linear programming, to solve facility layout problems, to develop conventional d.p. applications with greater programmer productivity, data base packages, etc. Software products for p.c., for minis, for mainframes, etc.

Specialized hardware (data base machines, LISP machines, etc.) plays an increasingly important role in solving business problems.

----

1. This paper has greatly benefitted from remarks and discussions on earlier drafts with Prof. C. Kriebel, and Prof. J. Williams, both from the Graduate School of Industrial Administration of Carnegie-Mellon University, and Dr. Bruce Johnson of Arthur Andersen & Co, as well as the participants to this NATO ASI Conference. I thank both Carnegie-Mellon University and Arthur Andersen & Co. for financial support to conduct this research.

NATO ASI Series, Vol. F48
Mathematical Models for Decision Support
Edited by G. Mitra

As a result, the following question is becoming increasingly important for DSS designers: "With more and more (very) different problem solving techniques available, which one(s) should be chosen to solve a specific business problem?"

This question is not only becoming more important, but, unfortunately, also becoming harder and harder to answer. For example, Artificial Intelligence and Operations Research have been "doing their own thing" and have developed more specific and detailed techniques that "grew" away from each other instead of towards each other [2]. For an excellent overview of the reasons for this separation and what we can be done to bring the field back together again, see Simon (1987).

It is becoming less and less likely that a single individual knows all, or even most, relevant problem solving techniques.

How would you help a DSS designer with this question?

Any attempt to support decision making should take the problem on hand as its starting point. Also, it should take into account the process of decision making, simply in order to be able to support that decision making process.

If you turn to the literature on Decision Support Systems design methodologies, however, you will find that the process of decision making is not incorporated explicitly in any DSS design and development methodology. See also Stabell (1983).

This paper attempts to remedie that deficiency and adopts Mitroff et al's (1974) view of the problem solving process, which takes the problem as perceived in reality as the starting point for solving that problem.

We identify a new type of system that addresses the designer's question: DSS Conceptualizers, which assist in selecting the important factors in the problem and in choosing an appropriate model class. We describe similarities and differences between DSS Conceptualizers and Model Management systems.

----

2. The seeds planted at the ORSA/TIMS Conference of October 1986, with its central theme "OR and AI" will hopefully reverse this trend. Also, the recently created Artificial Intelligence interest groups within TIMS and ORSA will work towards this end.

Section 3 presents a literature survey of a number of prototypes as well as completed DSS Conceptualizers.

Section 4 presents conclusions from the literature survey. An important conclusion is that DSS Conceptualizers should be based a model of models, which we call a meta model. Section 5 proposes such a meta model.

Section 6 presents issues that need to be adressed in further research and development of DSS Conceptualizers.

2 THE PROBLEM SOLVING PROCESS

2.1 Decision Support

2.1.1 Mitroff et al's view

As stated in the Introduction, the decision making process is not treated explicitly in the literature on DSS design and development methodologies. To explicitly consider the decision making process, we have adopted Mitroff et al's (1974) view of problem solving, see figure 1.

We adopted Mitroff et al's view of the problem solving process primarily because it:

- takes the problem as perceived in reality as a starting point
- explicitly takes into account the conceptualization phase of problem solving
- explicitly highlights that problem as perceived in reality and the model of that problem are different "things"
- highlights correspondence of a model to the real problem.

The stages in a problem solving process are[3] : "a PROBLEM AS PERCEIVED IN REALITY, a BASE MODEL, a MODEL SYSTEM, and a SOLUTION", see figure 1.

----

3. We use the terminology as presented in Bosman and Sol (1983), who have also used this model extensively for his work in DSS Development Methodologies.

These stages are connected by the activities of conceptualization, problem specification, solution finding, and implementation.

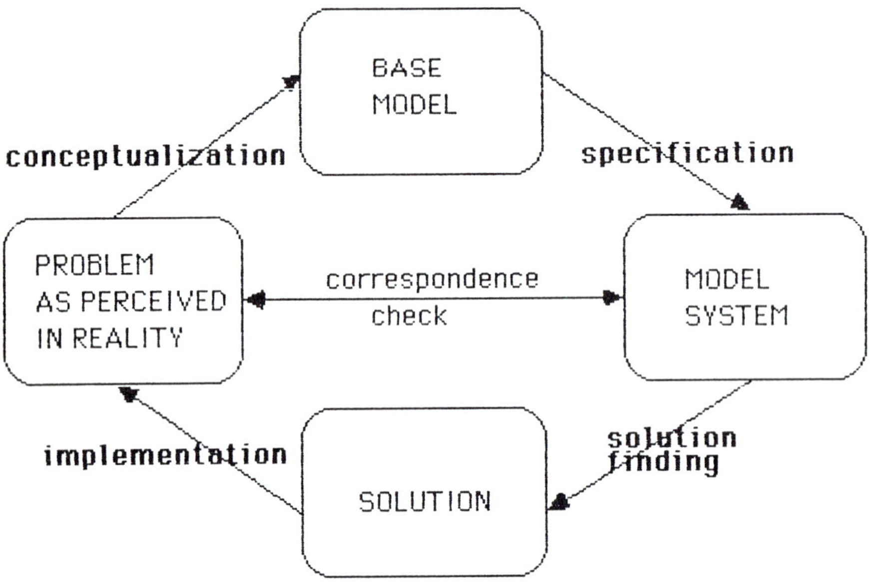

Figure 1: The process of problem solving[4]

Next, we will explain BASE MODEL and MODEL SYSTEM. We will use the word model short for model system, since this causes no confusion in the context of this paper. Also, we will explain the activities conceptualization and specification.

Although we do not perceive the other stages and activities to be unimportant, we will not discuss them in the rest of this paper, as we focus on the initial stages of model development.

The first step in solving a PROBLEM is PERCEIVED IN REALITY is "conceptualization". In the conceptualization phase you establish, see figure 2:

- What are the most relevant factors in the problem?

- Which "model class" is appropriate for the given problem?

----

4. This figure appears in Bosman and Sol (1983).

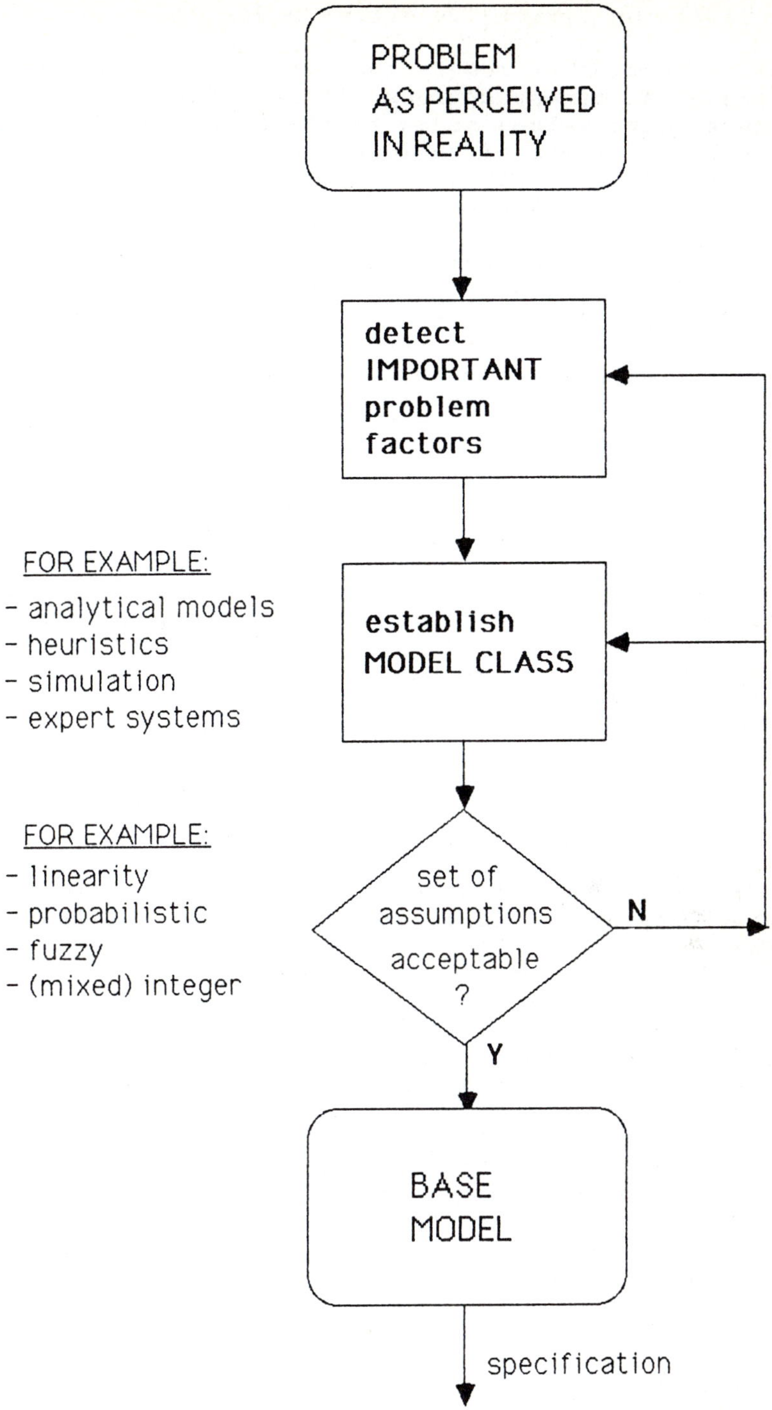

Figure 2: DSS Conceptualization

After Geoffrion (1986b) we define model class as:

> a collection of models that are based on a certain fixed set of assumptions; it is indefinite either as to data values or as to the identity or even number of items of various types, but otherwise is quite definite as to its form (e.g. the class of all Hitchcock-Koopmans transportation models).

This definition encompasses what Hayes-Roth, Waterman, and Lenat (1983, page 24) call conceptualization (explicate the key concepts, relations, and information- flow characteristics needed to describe the problem- solving process in the given domain) and formalization (mapping the key concepts and relations into a formal representation suggested by some tool or language).

The most relevant factors in the problem depend on the problem domain (Which function (production, finance, etc.) has the problem? In which industry is the organization a player? etc.). The factors also depend on the model that you use to describe the problem. For example, in scheduling problems, certain heuristics tend to focus on lead time of the jobs, or due date. Mathematical programming techniques may put more emphasis on the cost, accepting the lead time or due date simply as an input variable. Hence, what you call the most relevant factors depends on the problem domain and on the model class you apply.

In trying to establish which model class is appropriate for a given problem you would probably consider various "modeling paradigms" (a collection of similar model classes) and "modeling traditions" (e.g. O.R., database management, computer programming languages, and A.I.), see Geoffrion (1986b).

We note that the conceptualization phase relies heavily on testing whether or not certain assumptions (inherent to different model classes) hold, i.e. can be believed, given the problem as perceived in reality.

As a simple example, if the assumption of the variables being continuous corresponds to reality, linear programming (l.p.) may be applicable. For example, production volumes in continuous variables ("13.675 tons") makes sense in the petrochemical industry (where l.p. has been much applied). In contrast, in the context of scheduling, continuous variables often do not correspond to reality: "assign 0.5 men" is not meaningful; it is either 0, 1 or 2 etc. Hence, linear programming cannot be applied. One has to evaluate the applicability of integer programming or maybe heuristics.

The conceptualization activity results in the BASE MODEL which describes the relevant factors and their relations. For example:

> "We will employ a discrete event simulation model that describes the performance of the finance deparment as measured by 'adjusted net income'. The model will incorporate short term and long term cash needs, the scenario for borrowing and raising funds, credit line, and the company's expected cash generation."

Next, the activity "specification" takes the base model as a starting point. The specific variables to be included are defined (they represent the relevant factors that were identified in the base model). Also, the complete set of relationships is constructed. The result is the MODEL, which is thus an abstraction of the problem as perceived in reality.

For the example above, one of the relationships might be:

interest payable =
short term borrowing rate * short term debt +
long term borrowing rate * long term debt.

One of the variables, the short term borrowing rate, could be defined as:

> the short term borrowing rate as quoted by bank X on three month's loans, or as the prime rate of bank Y or as etc.

2.1.2 problem versus Model

A model should never represent each and every little aspect of the problem. If it does, an important objective of the modelling effort will not be achieved: Gaining insight in the problem situation, see Geoffrion (1976).

Note that when a model takes into account only a subset of the factors in the problem, it no longer adresses the complete problem as perceived in reality. It represents an artificially created problem that hopefully is very similar (in its relevant aspects) to the problem as perceived in reality. Clearly, "the problem as perceived in reality" and "the model" are really two different "things"!

Hence, we strongly feel that the terms problem and model should NOT be intermixed. Instead, the term "problem" should only be used to indicate the problem as perceived in <u>reality</u> with all its detail and nuances; the term "model" should only be used to refer to the <u>abstraction</u> of the problem. Such a separate terminology for model and problem is developed in further detail in section 5.

The difference between problem and model motivates issues that are well-known as part of common (sense) knowledge:

- Avoid "errors of third kind". An error of the third kind is "to solve the wrong problem". In other words, you want to avoid that irrelevant factors of the problem are included in the model as though they were relevant factors in the problem.

- Correspondence of the model to the problem. Although this notion is certainly not new as evidenced, for example, by Mitroff et al's article, Operations Research often does not treat correspondence of a model explicitly. Exceptions are, for example, simulation and social science, that both deal with the (external) validity of a model.

In another paper, which is under development, we elaborate on these and related issues.

2.2 DSS Conceptualizers

Two phases in Mitroff et al's view of problem solving generally enjoy computerized support in the form of what Sprague and Carlson (1982, Chapter 1 and 4) called "Specific DSS" and "DSS Generators".

Specific DSS support the solution finding phase. An example of a specific DSS is a production planning model for a specific department that is run each month.

The specification phase is supported by "DSS Generators". An example of a DSS generator is a linear programming package in which the previously mentioned production planning problem can be specified. Note that a DSS generator generally embodies only one model class: the models specified with it are based on only one fixed set of assumptions.

A third type of system now emerges, namely a system that supports the conceptualization phase. Such a system assists the DSS designer in determining the important factors in the problem and in selecting an appropriate model class. We call such a system "DSS Conceptualizer".

If you have an O.R. background you might think of a DSS Conceptualizer as an algorithm selecting aid. If you have an A.I. background you might think that a DSS Conceptualizers will help you choose an appropriate problem representation. Both these ideas are correct, but neither of them is complete. We view DSS Conceptualizers to select an algorithm (a search strategy, if you will) as well as to choose a problem representation (to select the model class, if you will).

DSS Conceptualizers do not exist yet, even though we have found several examples of systems and prototypes that resemble what we envision DSS Conceptualizers to be. The literature survey as well as the sections following it, should give you a good understanding of our ideas about DSS Conceptualizers.

An important advantage of DSS Conceptualizers will be that the DSS designer does not need a detailed knowledge of several different model classes in order to pick an appropriate one for the problem on hand.

Note that the distinction between DSS Conceptualizer and DSS Generator is not black and white. Rather, Conceptualizer and Generator represent two ends of a spectrum.

The systems at the Generator end of the spectrum allow the DSS designer to specify models based only on a certain fixed set of assumptions. Systems on the Conceptualizer end of the spectrum allow the DSS designer to choose among several model classes each based on a different fixed set of assumptions.

The grey area in the middle is indicated, for example, by this question: "Is a system that can generate Mixed Integer Programming formulations, as well as Linear Programming formulations, a DSS Generator or a DSS Conceptualizer?" On the one hand it can generate formulations that are based on different sets of assumptions, but on the other hand the sets of assumptions are not <u>that</u> different.

A discussion on such a topic is probably not very useful. The important question is: "Which model class should be applied and why?"; a question that DSS Conceptualizers can help to answer.

Research has already yielded systems and prototypes that come close to what we envision "DSS Conceptualizers" to be, see the literature survey further in this paper.

2.3 Relationship with Model Management

The advantage of DSS Conceptualizers, that the DSS designer does not have to have an intimate knowledge of a number of specific models in order to pick the appropriate one, is often quoted as an objective of Model Management Systems (MMS). See, for example, Dolk and Konsynski (1984, page 619).

In addition, Model Management Systems have been proposed to ensure the integrity of models used in several functions across an organization, to avoid unnecessary duplication of efforts in model building, to create a central unit where the expertise about different applicable models can be readily available to prospective users, and lastly as a solution to problems of interfacing different models (read: software packages or routines). See (Elam et al, 1980, pp. 97-98).

Structured Modeling, see Geoffrion (1986a), Lenard (1987) and Dolk (1987), is closely related to Model Management Systems. Geoffrion (1986a) lists a number of desirable features of a new generation of modeling systems. We quote the ones related to DSS Conceptualization:

- usefulness for most phases of the entired life-cycle associated with model-based work

- sufficient generality to encompass most of the great modeling paradigms that MS/OR and kindred model-based fields have developed for organizing the complexity of reality.

- A rigorous and coherent conceptual framework for modeling based on a single model representation format simultaneously suitable for managerial communication, mathematical use, and direct computer execution

- representational independence of general model structure and the detailed data needed to describe specific model instances

3 DSS CONCEPTUALIZERS: A LITERATURE SURVEY

3.1 Introduction

This section presents an overview of several systems or prototypes that resemble our notion of DSS Conceptualizers. This overview is not meant to be exhaustive, but it should give you a better idea of what we envision DSS Conceptualizers to be. In addition, it will give you some idea of the "state-of-the-art-in-operation" in DSS

Conceptualizers[5]. Other overviews of DSS Conceptualizers can be found in Hwang (1985), Hill (1986), and Turban and Watkins (1986).

We distinguish "paper" DSS conceptualizers, when they are not implemented as a running computer program, from "automated" DSS conceptualizers, when they are implemented as a running computer program.

Furthermore, we distinguish "free-standing" DSS Conceptualizers from "integrated" DSS Conceptualizers.

We call a DSS Conceptualizer "free-standing" when the generated base model (or parts of it) has to be input manually into the DSS Generator that will further specify the model. A DSS Conceptualizer is "integrated" when the base model can be input "automatically" into the DSS Generator.

3.2 DSS Conceptualizers in related disciplines

Apart from Operations Research, there are other disciplines that can tap into a vast array of numerical techniques developed over decades as well as into a smaller array of new Artificial Intelligence Techniques. Two of these disciplines are statistics, and engineering.

In both disciplines systems have emerged that are similar to DSS Conceptualizers.

3.2.1 statistics

An example of a system similar to an automated DSS Conceptualizer is NOSTRADAMUS, see (Weitz, Macgregor Smith, and Lesser, 1983). NOSTRADAMUS is an "interactive, knowledge-based consultation program to aid in the selection and user of appropriate forecasting techniques" . . . "The system is designed for use by people who are not experts at forecasting, but rather are knowledgeable regarding the environment in which the forecast is to be made."

Gale and Pregibon briefly describe their REX (Regression EXpert) system in (Gale and Pregibon, 1982):

> The strategy implemented focuses on checking the assumptions implicit in an initial model, and suggesting changes to data, model, and fitting method as may be appropriate when an assumption fails.

----

5. We recall our caveat that DSS Conceptualizers and DSS Generators represent two ends of a spectrum. Hence, you may consider some of the systems we present to be DSS Generators.

Portier and Lai (1983) describe a prorotype of their STATistical PATHfinder expert system that assists the user in "identifying an analysis appropriate for the data in hand". "The objective of the program is to narrow the field of possible analysis and point to appropriate procedures to be used".

For more Conceptualizers in statistics, see (Gale and Pregibon, 1985). Their assessment of the statistics discipline holds, in our view, also for Operations Research:

> Some of the knowledge developed by research statisticians is regularly taught for example the lore of the normal distribution, student's t-test, analysis of variance methods, and linear regression analysis. But some statistical knowledge is not yet so formalized specifically how these and other methods are chosen and applied to analyze data in practice (which process we call _strategy_[6]). ... The existence of extensive statistical packages suggests that AI contributions to data analysis will be intelligent _interfaces_[7], an area of little development. These interfaces could provide guidance, interpretation, and instruction, which are needed by novice users and are not available in current packages.

3.2.2 engineering

Rogers and Barthelemy (1986) describe an expert system called EXADS. It assists users of a general purpose optimization program called Automated Design Synthesis (ADS) in selecting one of the more than 100 optimization algorithms that are available in ADS. ADS is used in engineering design.

The algorithms encompass model classes such as sequential linear programming, sequential quadratic programming, various unconstrained minimization techniques, and various Golden Section methods.

----

6. emphasis by the original authors

7. emphasis by the original authors

3.3 "Paper" DSS Conceptualizers in O.R.

A simple, and excellent, example of DSS Conceptualizers in O.R. is presented by (Bolander, 1983). His article assists a reader in selecting an appropriate scheduling technique. He makes the following introductory remarks to which we fully subscribe:

> This presentation will present the position that all techniques are valid approaches. Each has its own strenghts and weaknesses and must be properly matched with the manufacturing environment to make it function effectively[8].

Bolander presents a production- inventory control framework that highlights the key issues that should be dealt with in a given manufacturing environment. Note that he thus tries to identify the most important factors in the problem, and thus tries to avoid errors of the third kind.

Bolander identifies many different scheduling techniques and subsequently shows how the production- inventory control framework suggests certain scheduling techniques that address the key issues for a given manufacturing environment.

Garg and Tsai (1986) present a case example for a wire and cable plant. They identified four different problem situations that the plant could face. One such problem situation is, for example, forecasted sales quantity is less than production capacity in a given period. They show that, dependent on the specific problem situation, different model classes are appropriate.

3.4 Automated DSS conceptualizers in O.R.

3.4.1 integrated DSS conceptualizers

We note that we have not found truely integrated DSS Conceptualizers. The examples presented below, however, will give you at least some idea what we envision integrated DSS conceptualizers to be.

----

8. The latter point means, in our terminology, that the assumptions of the model have to agree with the real-world situation.

The MITRE corporation has developed the AURORA system (Automatic Reasoning with Operations Research Applications), see Yu (1986). AURORA simulates the process that humans typically have performed: "recognize stereotypical subproblems, solve them with appropriate techniques, and use the subproblem solutions accurately within the global problem.

AURORA applies a mixture of A.I. and O.R. techniques in "extracting an O.R. subproblem from the overall planning problem, selecting an appropriate O.R. algorithm, and then use it to compute an optimal solution to the subproblem".

Recently, the PLANETS system surfaced that has been used by General Motors since 1974, see Breitman and Lucas (1987). PLANETS has been used for over 80 major corporate studies as well as numerous divisional and plant studies.

PLANETS is "highly elastic model-building system that can automatically generate unique mathematical models to support large and small, simple or complex business scenarios". It can be used to evaluate the following questions, either independently or simultaneously:

- What to make,
- When to make it,
- Which markets to satisfy,
- How to make it,
- Whether to make or buy,
- Where to ship,
- Where to make, and
- How to purchase.

The resulting models all belong to the Mixed Integer Linear Programming model class: PLANETS creates input data files and control files for MPSX or SCICONIC, that solve the models.

A similar model management system has been used at EXXON corporation since 1973, see Boudwin, Palmer, and Rowland (1984). The system is called PLATOFORM, PLAnning TOol developed in the DATAFORM language of MPS III. PLATOFORM contains several modules, the main ones being Data Management, Matrix Generation, Optimization, and Report Writing. These modules are structured around a relational - like data base.

The user interfaces with the system (actually with its data management component) through a very simple input syntax. All the internal data formats are transparent to the user. The user does not need to be an expert in problem formulation.

Using PLATOFORM, the user can solve numerous oil refining problems as well as related problems such as crude oil scheduling, product planning, inventory projection, contract evaluation, and manpower planning. PLATOFORM can solve models that belong to model classes like sequential linear, mixed- integer, and recursive nonlinear programming.

Another operational system is LOGS. LOGS assists in "streamlining the process whereby the manager's problems and relevant data are translated into correctly specified models". And also: "once the models have been optimized, output from the optimization package needs to be translated back into the manager's terms". See Brown, Northup and Shapiro (1985).

LOGS can be considered a front-end to the well-known IBM optimization package MPSX. With it, two types of model classes can be automatically instantiated, Linear Programming, or Mixed Integer Programming.

IFPS/OPTIMUM, see Waren, Lasdon, and Sarkar (1987), has characteristics of a DSS Conceptualizer in that it "automatically" classifies a model as belonging to an appropriate model class.

Using the well-known spreadsheet user- interface, the DSS designer first specifies a model in detail. IFPS/OPTIMUM then determines the appropriate model class among several of the Linear Programming and Non-Linear Programming variety, and automatically invokes the correct algorithm.

IFPS/OPTIMUM fails to be a DSS Conceptualizer, however, because it does not indicate at all whether or not a (non-) linear programming O.R. technique is appropriate for the particular problem on hand. Hence, the DSS designer still has to know (possibly assisted by a Conceptualizer of some sort) whether such techniques are appropriate or not.

3.4.2 free-standing DSS conceptualizers

The SAK-OPTIMALI expert system, see Ivanek (1986), recommends (mathematical) model classes adequate to a given problem in reality. This system encompasses the highest number (38) of different O.R. model classes of any DSS Conceptualizer that we know. Some of the model classes includes are: linear, integer, and nonlinear programming, network techniques, and inventory control techniques.

SAK-OPTIMALI asks the user certain questions (from a total pool of 35 potential questions), e.g. "Is the consequence of your decision evaluated according to a single criterion?" or "Are you looking for an optimal production plan depending on variable conditions in delivery of raw materials?". The user answers with a code on a seven-point scale, indicating a response ranging from "certainly yes" to "certainly no".

Based upon the user's answers, the system applies a rule set with 234 rules in order to determine which solution techniques, ranked by a certainty factor, are appropriate for the given problem.

Lee (1986) has developed a prototype model management system that contains two knowledge bases: one about different types of equations, e.g. less than or equal constraint or the sum of indexed variables equals one. The second knowledge "knows about" different model classes, e.g. knapsack model, assignment model.

The system is called ALESA (A Language for Equation Structure Abstraction). Lee wanted to attack the model storage problem first; he considers it "the core". This model base will eventually be able to provide a model builder with various model formulations in building a model. This design objective is based upon Lee's claim that "a model for a particular problem is usually built not from scratch but by modifying a prototype".

Murphy (1987) and Stohr (1987) are working on a system that uses template models to form the building blocks for a larger model.

4 CONCLUSIONS

Figure 3 schematically depicts, for a number of modeling paradigms, which operational DSS technology exists for the phases conceptualization, specification, and solution finding. Support for the conceptualization phase (and even for specification phase) is clearly lacking for several modeling paradigms.

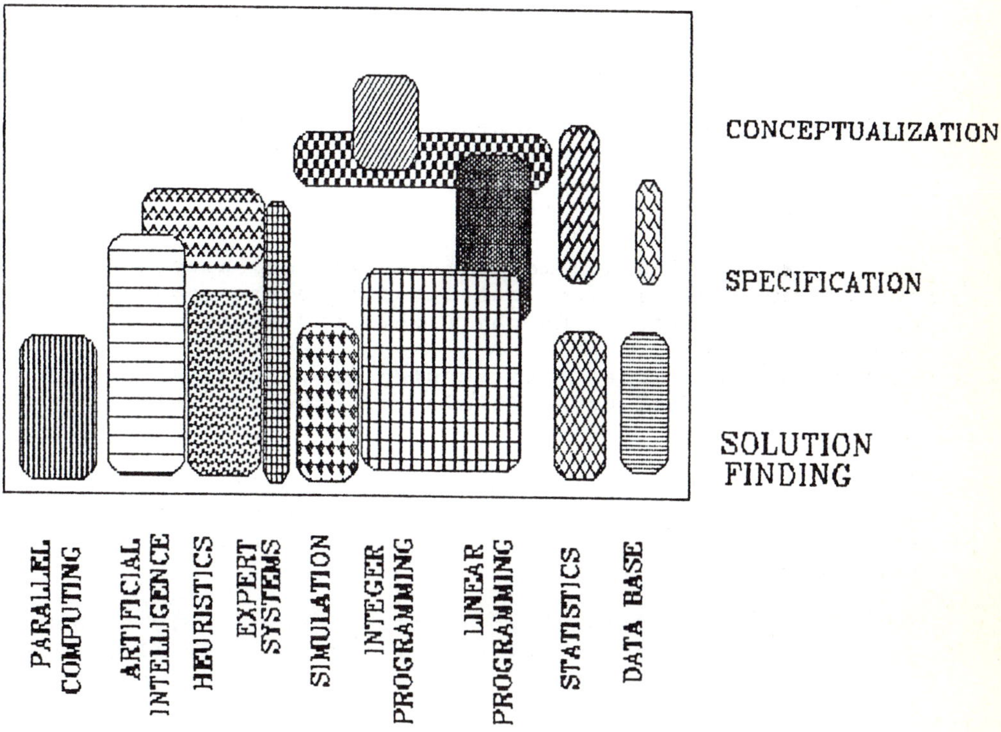

Figure 3: Status of DSS technology

4.1 Functionalities of DSS Conceptualizers

Synthesizing the literature survey, we conclude that DSS Conceptualizers should allow a DSS designer to:

1. Analyze the problem situation and define the important factors of the problem (as, for example, in Bolander (1983))

2. Classify the problem by identifying an appropriate model class (as, for example, in Ivanek (1986))

3. Search for an existing model in a model base, as performed by Model Base Management modules, (as, for example, in Geoffrion (1986), and Lee (1986))

4. If the model base contains only a model that is "close", modify that model so that it will correspond to the particular problem specification (as, for example, in Lee (1986))

5. "Assemble" a new model from existing pieces ("building blocks") that were retrieved from the model base (as, for example, in Murphy (1987) and Stohr (1987))

6. Specify a model from scratch (as, for example, in Breitman and Lucas (1987), or Boudwin, Palmer, Rowland (1984))

The functions "analyze", "classify", "modify" and "specify" have clear characteristics of DSS conceptualization, because they guide the DSS designer to consider (only) the important factors of the problem.

The "Search" and "assemble" functions are likely to be performed during the model specification phase also, when all the important problem factors will already have been translated into variables.[9].

4.2 DSS Conceptualization is more than Model Base Management

The current state of the art in Model Management is probably better indicated by the term Model Base Management, as (only) storage and retrieval of models appear to be the major topics.

----

9. Liang (1986, pages 95 - 96), for example, presents fourteen of such functions.

Unlike data in a data base, models in a model base are hardly ever reused in exactly the same form as they are retrieved from the model base. The focus of DSS Conceptualization should be on changing, adapting, and modifying existing models, as opposed to (only) storing and retrieving models.

Consequently, we view a Model Base Management System as a necessary subsystem of any DSS Conceptualizater.

4.3 Decision Support Systems should be based on a meta model

As we explained above, one the functionalities of Model Management Systems as a component of DSS Conceptualizers is to retrieve (and thus also store) models from a model base, see also Lee (1986). In addition, DSS Conceptualizers reason about models.

These two functionalities are similar to functionalities desired of a data base. A data base allows us to store and retrieve data and to reason about the data.

In order to be able provide these functionalities, data base theory developed a number of MODELS OF DATA.

Similarly, for model bases we need a MODEL of MODELS, in order to store and retrieve models and to reason about them. We call such a model of models a META MODEL. In the next section we propose a meta model for DSS Conceptualizers.

To be consistent, the meta model should underly not only the conceptualization phase, but also the other phases of the process problem solving. Hence, the meta model is a meta model for Decision Support.

5 A META MODEL FOR DECISION SUPPORT

Several researchers have, implicitly or explicitly, proposed different meta models, for example:

Liang (1986, page 90) claims that five categories of information are essential to MMS design: the output of the model, the input required to produce the output, the computational algorithms used in the model, the integrity constraint of the model, and the validity of the model.

The Meta Model that Dolk and Konsynski (1984, page 622) proposed for a "generic" linear programming model consists of: an objective function to be optimized, (subject to one or more) constraints, (evaluated over) parameters, (evaluated over) index-sets, and (yielding values for) decision variables.

The Meta Model of Geoffrion's Structured Modeling, see Geoffrion (1986a, page 10 and 15), consists of: functions (similar to objective functions), tests (similar to constraints), and attributes that can be variable (similar to decision variables) or fixed (similar to input variables).

The differences between these Meta Models are striking, especially if one realizes that quite standard O.R. models were implemented "under" them. But even more striking is what is not covered (at least explicitly): the assumptions.

The assumptions are probably the most important aspect to consider for a DSS. In our discussion on conceptualization, we stated that the conceptualization phase relies heavily on testing whether or not certain assumptions (inherent to different model classes) hold, given the problem as perceived in reality.

On the subject of conceptualization (in our terminology), Dahr and Pople (1986, page 16) argue that making assumptions about various parts of the problem domain "leads to situation decision makers can have significantly differing interpretations". "It is possible to generate several models that match some problem scenario". One practical use they envision for their system is that of reconciling these differing model interpretations by providing access to assumptions underlying them.

Dahr (1984, page 7) states: "In contrast to the parametric perturbation facility provided by existing modeling systems, PLANET provides the capability for systematic variations in the underlying model assumptions, with concomitant structural variations induced in the planning model that reflect the interdependencies of those assumptions. As a result, whenever previously held beliefs prove to be unjustified, the program has the potential to bring into focus new conceptualizations of the problem that account for the changed set of assumptions."

Hence, models are "shaped" by the assumptions underlying them. See also Gale and Pregibon (1982). Testing whether or not assumptions hold is of crucial importance in the conceptualization phase. Therefore, assumptions have to appear in any Meta Model that underlies a DSS.

We propose a Meta Model that integrates a systems theory view of input - process - output, the notion of decision variable, and assumptions, see figure 4.

Next, we discuss each element of the META MODEL in detail. Referring to section 2.1.2 we use a separate terminology to refer to either problem or (meta) model. The following table summarizes the terminology.

```
                     operationalization
PROBLEM ------------- based upon ----> (META) MODEL
                        assumptions
```

PROBLEM	(META) MODEL
controllable factor	decision variable
performance (criterion)	output variable objective function side result
restriction	constraint
uncontrollable factor	input variable
dependency	relation

Table 1: Terminology for problem and (meta) model

DECISION VARIABLES represent controllable factors in the problem. By manipulating the controllable factors, which are represented by the decision variables, the organization under study is assumed to be able to excercise control over performance. For example, by manipulating advertising an organization can be assumed to increase sales. The decision variable "monthly direct advertising costs", for example, could then represent the controllable factor advertising.

The OUTPUT VARIABLE provides a measure of performance that is relevant in the context of the problem. Performance might be measured by profit, cost of operations, market share, return on investment and similar variables that are relatively easy to observe objectively.

The output variable(s) can be thought of as the value of the objective function, e.g. a profit function that is maximized subject to certain constraints.

SIDE RESULTS are output variables that neither measure performance nor indicate decisions (like decision variables do, discussed above); side results are generated more or less as a "by- product" of the model. A good example of side results is shadow prices (dual values) generated by a linear programming optimization.

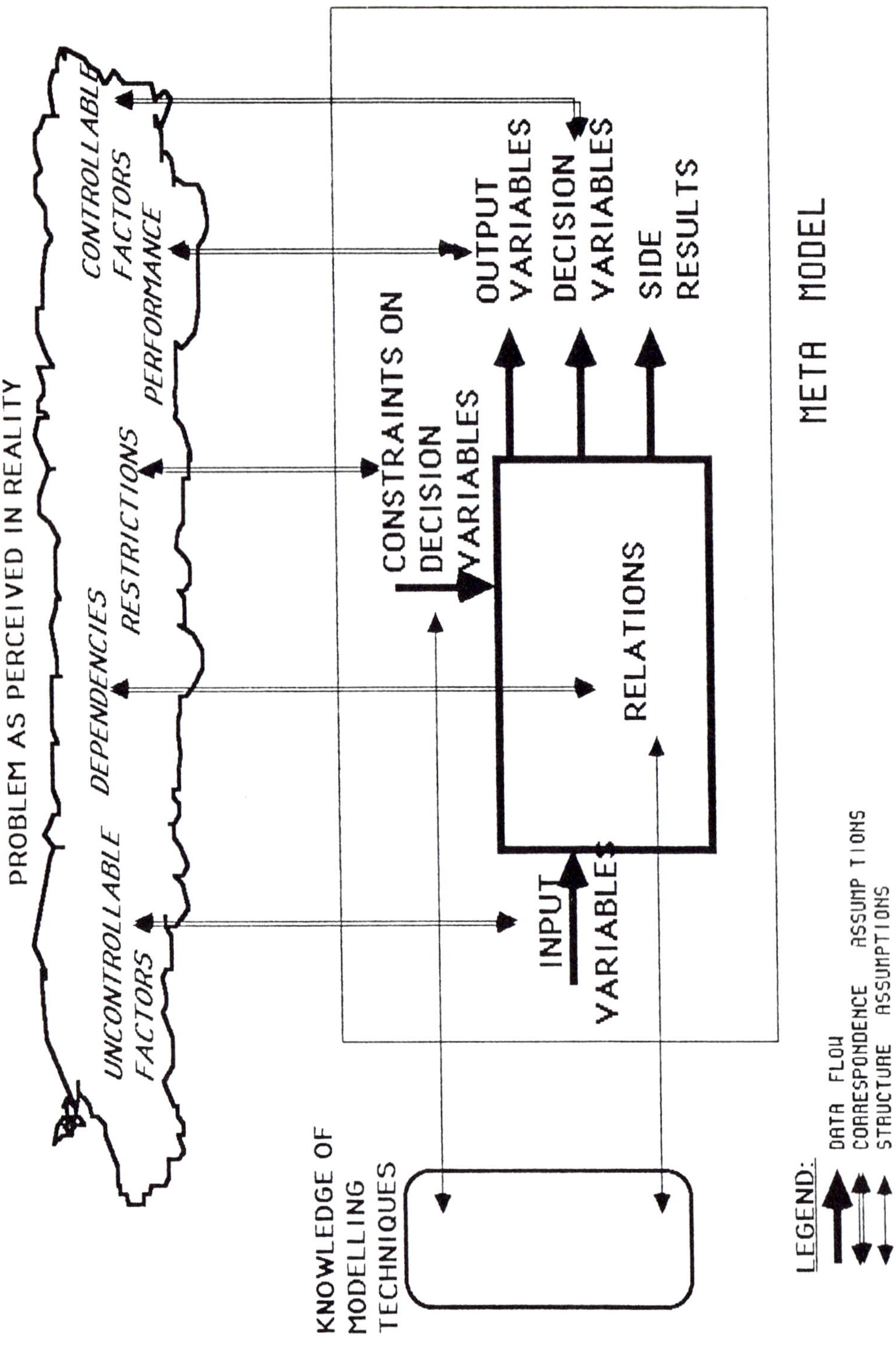

Figure 4: A Meta Model for DSS

CONSTRAINTS ON THE VALUES OF DECISION VARIABLES represent restrictions imposed on the values of decision variables. These restrictions may be "dictated" by the problem situation in reality (we call them "correspondence constraints") or by reasons having to do with the structure of the resulting model (we call them "structure constraints").

An example of correspondence constraints: Every factory has a production capacity that is limited. The resulting constraint will effectively restrict the values of the decision variable "amount to produce" to values that will not exceed the available production capacity.

As an example of structure constraints, consider spread-sheet models used for "what-if" analysis: The user imposes a severe constraint on the decision variable; namely, the value of every decision variable is restricted to one possible value. For this value the user wants to know the value of the objective function. ("What happens with profit if I set advertising expenditures (the decision variable) to twenty million (the one and only value)?"

Another example of structure constraints are heuristic decision rules in that they constrain the potentially possible values of a decision variable. Heuristics generate, usually through a quite simple IF ... THEN ... statement, the one and only value that the particular decision variable will have using that heuristic.

Consider, for example, the well-known Shortest Processing Time (SPT) heuristic in job-shop scheduling: IF this machine is available AND the list of jobs that still have to be finished on it is non-empty THEN assign this machine now to the job that has the shortest processing time.

If you use the SPT heuristic, the job that will be started at time t on this machine will **never** be the one with the longest processing time.

The distinction between output variables and correspondence constraints has since long been recognized as vague (maybe even non existent): Simon (1969) says:

> "In the decision- making situations of real life, a course of action, to be acceptable, must satisfy a whole set of requirements, or constraints. Sometimes one of these requirements is singled out and referred to as the goal of the action. But the choice of one of the constraints, from many, is to a large extent arbitrary. For many purposes it is more meaningful to refer to the whole set of requirements as the (complex) goal of the action."

Eilon (1972) claims:

> Essentially, all constraints are goals, since they all express desirable (or undesirable) modes of operation. If I state that in a particular situation overtime should not be used, then it is conventional to define such a statement as a constraint, but it is equally legitimate to regard such a statement as being an objective. Similarly, statements that are usually singled out as being objectives (...) may be regarded as constraints.

Zionts (1987) presents the ambiguity between output variables and constraints ambiguity in the context of Multi Criteria Modelling techniques.

This ambiguity between goals and constraints has been known for a long time in, for example, linear programming, where it is called duality. The primal model and the dual model represent exactly the same problem, but have radically different forms. Also, Lagrange multipliers clearly indicate the duality between output variables and constraints, as any constraint can also be modeled (together with its Lagrange multiplier) as part of the objective function.

In our terminology, the ambiguity of goals and constraints translates into: A given set of performance criteria can be operationalized into different combinations of output variables and constraints.

The way in which a given set of performance criteria is operationalized into a combination of output variables and constraints depends to a large extent on which modeling technique the DSS developer applies. For example, linear programming, constraint propagation and satisfaction techniques, goal programming, or heuristics would, for a given set of performance criteria, result in radically different combinations of output variables and constraints.

In earlier days, single- objective- function modeling techniques were generally the only techniques that were technically and economically feasible (given computer speed and memory size), well-known, and widely available.

Continued education as well as the advent of more powerful computers and software packages may enable widespread use of multiple- objective- function techniques. These techniques, interestingly, eliminate the need to translate a performance criterion into either an output variable or a constraint, it can be translated simply into an objective.

INPUT VARIABLES represent the relevant uncontrollable factors in the problem. These factors nevertheless have a significant impact on performance (represented by the output variables). A good example of an uncontrollable yet significant problem factor in ice cream sales, for example, is the weather. The factor "weather" may be translated into the input variable "day's maximum temperature" (or is it "hours of sunshine per day"?).

The RELATIONS represent the dependencies between the various factors in the problem. The relations are the manipulations of the values of the input variable(s) and the constraint(s) on the values of the decision variables to yield the value of the output variable(s) as well as the value of the decision variable(s).

A relation can simply be a mathematical objective function to be maximized over the decision variable. The relations can also contain thousands of equations and variables for a complicated optimization problem. Also, the relations can be logical relationships, such as a set of so-called production rules[10].

ASSUMPTIONS are statements that restrict the form of a model by indicating which variables should be included in the model and which form the variables and the relations between them should take.

Assumptions underlying a model can be implicit or stated explicitly. By assumptions we do not mean specific values for certain input variables. We distinguish two types of assumptions: "correspondence assumptions" and "structure assumptions".

The assumptions that indicate which variables are included in the model we call "correspondence assumptions". Correspondence assumptions indicate which input variables, output variables, decision variables, and which correspondence constraints are included in the model. An example of a correspondence assumption is: "The production department wants to minimize the sum of inventory carrying costs and production costs".

Correspondence assumptions represent beliefs about the problem as perceived in reality that can be stated without taking into account any modelling technique that might be

----

10. Simply put, production rules are clauses in the form IF condition THEN action. For example: IF interest on Eurobonds is lower than on american bonds THEN consider borrowing on the European capital markets.

applied. In other words, the beliefs that can be stated by looking at the problem only.

The assumptions that indicate which form the variables and the relations between them should take we call "structure assumptions". Structure assumptions also indicate which structure constraints are included in the model. An example of a structure assumption is: "All relations are linear, and deterministic".

Structure assumptions are the assumptions that are inherent to the model (class). For example, axioms underlying model classes are structure assumptions. Structure assumptions can be stated without looking at any problem at all.

The total set of assumptioms underlying a DSS thus consists of the union of the correspondence assumptions (representing beliefs about the problem) and structure assumptions (representing axioms about the model).

Assumptions act as a filter between the problem as perceived in reality and the model. They filter the important factors of the problem and determine the form of the variables and relations of the model.

The Meta Model described above thus provides us with a "language" with which we can describe and represent any model system. Note that this Meta Model does not presume that the variables are numeric. They can equally well be symbolic logic variables.

6 ISSUES FOR FURTHER RESEARCH

This section presents issues for further research and development of DSS Conceptualizers.

Issue 1: The META MODEL that is proposed in this paper must be evaluated. See the previous section.

Issue 2: An implementation for the META MODEL needs to be defined.

Issue 3: Choice between different modeling traditions must be provided

The DSS Conceptualizers surveyed in this paper do not take into account significantly different modeling traditions like, for example, A.I. and O.R. This will increasingly become necessary as several theoretical disciplines continue to develop new methods and techniques for similar types of problems.

Also, in situations in practice, consultants are often in a situation that they have to choose between theoretically rigorous techniques (in one discipline), e.g. Dynamic Programming, that may not be economically feasible, and simple techniques (in another discipline) that are economically feasible, e.g. heuristic decision rules. See, for example, Garg and Tsai (1986).

Issue 4: "Practical" factors must be taken into account

Factors that influence economic feasibility are, for example, available budget for development, maximum capacity of hardware and software that can run the model(s), maximum allowable response time, a cost - benefit analysis of the proposed Decision Support System, etc.

In practical situations, such factors always have to be taken into account. Therefore, any DSS Conceptualizer should take them into account.

7 REFERENCES

1. BOLANDER, S.F., "Selecting a Scheduling Strategy: The Alternatives", Proceedings of the American Production and Inventory Control Society Conference 1983, pp. 233 - 237.

2. BOSMAN, A., SOL, H.G., "Evolutionary Development of Information Systems", pp. 121 - 140 in Evolutionary Information Systems, edited by J. Hawgood, North-Holland, 1983.

3. BOUDWIN, N.K., PALMER, K. ROWLAND, A.J., "A Model Management Framework for Mathematical Programming", Exxon Monograph, John Wiley and Sons, 1984.

4. BREITMAN, R.L. and LUCAS, J.M., "PLANETS: A Modeling System for Business Planning", Interfaces, Volume 17, Number 1, January - February 1987, pp. 94 - 106.

5. BROWN, R.W., NORTHUP, W.D., and SHAPIRO, J.F., "LOGS: A Modeling and Optimization System for Business Planning" in Computer Assisted Decision Making, edited by G. Mitra, North-Holland, 1985.

6. DAHR, V., "PLANET: An Intelligent Decision Support System for the Formulation and Investigation of Formal Planning Models", Unpublished Ph.D. dissertation, University of Pittsburgh, 1984.

7. DAHR, V., POPLE, H., "An Approach to Knowledge Representation Based on Model Fragments Rather Than Rules: Maintaining Evolving Designs Via a Modular Encoding of Knowledge", Working Paper No. 128, Department of Information Systems, Graduate School of Business, New York University, June 1986.

8. DOLK, D.R., "Model Management and Structured Modeling", presented at this NATO ASI Conference.

9. DOLK, D.R., and KONSYNSKI, B.R., "Knowledge Representation for Model Management Systems", IEEE Transactions on Software Engineering, Vol. SE-10, No. 6, November 1984.

10. EILON, S. ,"Goals and Constraint in Decision-making", Operational Research Quarterly, Volume 23, No. 1, 1972, pp. 3 - 15.

11. ELAM, J.J., HENDERSON, J.C., and MILLER, L.W., "Model Management Systems: an approach to decision support in complex organizations", Proceedings of the First Conference on Information Systems, December 1980.

12. GALE, W.A., and PREGIBON, D., "An Expert System for Regression Analysis", in Heiner, K.W. (Ed.) "Computer Science and Statistics; Proceedings of the 14th Symposium on the Interface" New York: Springer Verlag, 1982.

13. GALE, W.A., and PREGIBON, D., "Artificial Intelligence Research in Statistics", AI Magazine, Winter 1985, pp. 72 - 75.

14. GARG, U. and TSAI, C-Y, "Modeling and Analysis of a Large Wire and Cable Plant Operation", Interfaces, Volume 16, Number 6, November - December 1986, pp. 77 - 85.

15. GEOFFRION, A., "The Purpose of Mathematical Programming is Insight, Not Numbers, Interfaces, Number 1, 1976, pp. 81 -92.

16. GEOFFRION, A., "An Introduction to Structured Modeling", Working Paper No. 338, Western Management Science Institute, UCLA, Los Angeles, Ca., June 1986.

17. GEOFFRION, A., "Integrated Modeling Systems", Working Paper No. 343, Western Management Science Institute, UCLA, Los Angeles, Ca., November 1986.

18. GEOFFRION, A, "Modeling Approaches and Systems Related to Structured Modeling", Working Paper No. 339, Western Management Science Institute, UCLA, Los Angeles, Ca., February 1987.

19. HAYES-ROTH, F., WATERMAN, D.A., LENAT, D.B., "Building Expert Systems, Addison- Wesley, Reading, MA, 1983.

20. HILL, T.R., "Toward Intelligent Decision Support Systems: Survey, Assessment and Direction", Working Paper, Graduate School of Business, Indiana University, Bloomington, Indiana 47405.

21. HWANG, S., "Automatic Model Building Systems: A Survey", Proceedings of the DSS 1985 Conference, pp. 22 - 32.

22. IVANEK, J., "An Expert System Recommending Suitable Mathematical Decision Method", Computers and Artificial Intelligence, Volume 5, 1986, pp. 241 - 251.

23. LENARD, M.L., "Fundamentals of Structured Modeling", presented at this NATO ASI Conference.

24. LIANG, T-P, "Toward the Development of a Knowledge-based Model Management System", Unpublished Ph.D. dissertation, Department of Decision Sciences, The Wharton School, University of Philadelphia, 1986.

25. MITROFF, I.I., BETZ, F. PONDY, L., SAGASTI, F., "On Managing Science in the Systems Age: Two Schemas for the Study of Science as a whole Systems Phenomenon", Interfaces, Volume 4, Number 3, May 1974, pp. 46 - 58.

26. MURPHY, F.H., "A Knowledge Base for Formulating Linear Programs", presented at this NATO ASI conference.

27. PORTIER, K.M. and LAI, P-Y, "A Statistical Expert System for Analysis Determination", Statistical Computing Section Proceedings of the American Statistical Association, 1983, pp. 309 - 311.

28. SIMON, H.A. "On the Concept of Organizational Goal", in: Business Strategy, H.I. Ansoff (editor), Penguin Books, 1969.

29. SIMON, H.A., "Two Heads Are Better than One: The Collaboration between AI and OR", Interfaces, Volume 17, Number 4, July - August 1987, pp. 8 - 15.

30. SPRAGUE, R.H., and CARLSON, E.D., "Building Effective Decision Support Systems", Prentice Hall, 1982.

31. STABELL, C.B., "A Decision-Oriented Approach to building DSS", pp. 221 - 260, in John L. Bennett, "Building Decision Support Systems", Addison-Wesley Publishing Co., Reading, Massachusetts, 1983.

32. STOHR, E.A., "Knowledge and Inference Techniques for Linear Programming", presented at this NATO ASI conference.

33. TURBAN, E. and WATKINS, P.R., "Integrating Expert Systems and Decision Support Systems", MIS Quarterly, June 1986, pp. 121 - 136.

34. WAREN, A., LASDON, L., and SARKAR, S., "Optimization and Decision Support", presented at this NATO ASI Conference.

35. WEITZ, R.R., MACGREGOR SMITH, J., and LESSER, V.R., "NOSTRADAMUS: An automated forecasting consultant", Working Paper, University of Massachusetts, Amherst, Massachusetts, April 1983.

36. ZIONTS, S., "Multiple Criteria Mathematical Programming", presented at this NATO ASI Conference.

FUNDAMENTALS OF STRUCTURED MODELING

Melanie L. Lenard
School of Management
Boston University
Boston, Massachusetts 02215
U. S. A.

1 INTRODUCTION

Rapid advances in hardware and software technology have fundamentally changed the environment in which mathematical models are used in support of decision-making. Decision-makers, accustomed to using personal computers, electronic spreadsheets, word processors, and on-line information retrieval from centralized databases, now expect the same kind of access to, and control over, the mathematical models which claim to predict, simulate, or optimize the consequences of their decisions.

Furthermore, the builders and purveyors of models and modeling expertise, otherwise known as management science/operations research (MS/OR) practitioners, want and need improved computer-based support for their work as well. Using traditional methods, model development is a costly and time-consuming activity. All too often, the final product is misused, under-used, or even not used at all, largely because of poor communication between the model builder and the model user.

The twin challenges then for the next generation of modeling software are: (1) to meet the rising expectations of decision-makers for powerful and easy-to-use modeling capabilities in decision support systems, and (2) to provide professional model builders with the means for achieving increased productivity and improved communication with model users.

Certainly, the evolution toward this next generation of modeling software in well underway. It has been recognized for some time [16, Chapter 2] that decision support systems must include subsystems for model management as well as data management and dialog management ("dialog" being the generic term for the user interface, whatever form it may take). There are now a number of software packages regarded as suitable vehicles for building decision support systems. However, most tend to be stronger either on the model management side (for example, a modeling language supplemented with some data management capability) or on the data management side (for example, a database management system supplemented with some modeling capability). Furthermore, vendors of long-established vehicles for model building, such as software systems for mathematical programming, simulation, and statistics, have been augmenting and upgrading their systems' capabilities for data and dialog management.

NATO ASI Series, Vol. F48
Mathematical Models for Decision Support
Edited by G. Mitra

Despite all this activity, there remains much to be done. A promising approach to addressing the as yet unmet need for modeling software is the recent and ongoing work in "structured modeling" by Geoffrion [8, 9, 10, 11]. As he puts it [11], "Structured modeling aims to provide the foundation for a new generation of modeling systems...[and]...to influence how model-based work is carried out..."

The purpose of these notes is to give an overview of the subject of structured modeling--what it is, how it works, what's happening now, what's likely to happen next, and what it all means.

2 WHAT IS STRUCTURED MODELING?

At its core, structured modeling is a conceptual framework for representing models based on a set of interrelated definitions of all the elements comprising a "model". This definitional system is, in effect, a "model of models" or a meta-model. It occupies the same position relative to model management as does any one of the major data models (e.g. relational, network, or hierarchical) relative to data management.

In this section, we describe the basic concepts of structured modeling and then two alternative representations for a structured model: the first being graphical, the second non-graphical.

2.1 Basic Concepts

Structured modeling identifies the basic components of models, the relationships among these components, and conditions under which a model may be termed "structured". In what follows, we will introduce the basic concepts of structured modeling in an informal manner based on examples. (For formal definitions, see Geoffrion [11, Appendix].)

A structured model is composed of three basic types of elements: entities, attributes, and functions. Thus, a model comprises, not only the entities and attributes generally recognized as the components of a database, but also a new kind of component, namely functions. There are in fact two types of entity elements: primitive entities and compound entities. Compound entities are those entities which are defined in terms of other entities (which may be either primitive or compound), while primitive entities are undefined. Also, logical-valued function elements are distinguished from all others kinds of functions and treated as a separate type called tests.

To illustrate these definitions, consider the familiar spreadsheet model. In structured modeling terminology, each row and each column of the spreadsheet is a primitive entity element. Each cell is a compound entity element, defined by the combination of two primitive entity elements, namely one row and one column. The labels a user might give to the rows and columns are attributes of those entities. If the content of a cell is some specified value, then the content of the cell is an attribute; whereas, if the content of a cell is determined by a formula, it is a function element.

Each element in a structured model (other than a primitive entity element) has a calling sequence or a set of elements on which it is definitionally dependent. For the spreadsheet model, each cell is defined by ("calls") one row element and one column element. The content of a cell, if it is an attribute element (that is, a value), is defined by ("calls") only that cell. However, if the content of a cell is a function element (that is, a formula), it is defined by the cell, of course, and also by the contents (be they attributes or functions) of the cells needed to evaluate the formula.

Now the general spreadsheet model has very little structure or meaning in and of itself. It simply provides the basic elements for model-building. To continue our discussion of structured modeling concepts, we need to consider a model constructed for a particular application or class of applications. The example we will use is the modeling of the classic transportation problem: fixed amounts of a given commodity are available at a number of supply points (say, plants) and fixed amounts of the same commodity are needed at a number of demand points (say, customers); the transportation links between the supply points and the demand points have different unit costs; the problem is to determine how much of the commodity should be shipped from each supply point to each demand point so that demand is met while minimizing the total cost of transportation.

For the Transportation Model, the supply points and the demand points are _primitive entities_; the transportation links between them are _compound entities_ (that is, each link may be represented as a combination of one supply point and one demand point). The unit cost of each transportation link is an _attribute_, as is the amount shipped on each link. Typically, the unit cost is a "fixed" attribute (that is, a value specified in advance) while the amount shipped is a "variable" attribute (that is, a value to be determined later, usually by "solving" the model). The total cost of transportation is a real-valued _function_ of the attributes; testing whether or not demand is satisfied is a _test_ defined on the attributes.

Each transportation link is definitionally dependent on ("calls") both the supply point and the demand point it connects. The unit cost associated with each link "calls" the compound entity element which represents the link itself. The function element for the total cost of transportation "calls" two groups of attribute elements: one representing the costs of every link and the other representing the amounts shipped on every link.

Structured modeling recognizes that model elements tend to occur in groups of similar elements: each group is called a _genus_ (plural _genera_). All elements within a single genus must be of the same element type and they must share a "generic" calling sequence. This property, called _generic similarity_, means that if, say, one element of genus A calls one or more elements of genus B and genus C, then _all_ the elements of A must call one or more elements of B and C (in the same order). For example, the collection of supply points constitutes a primitive entity genus, while the collection of the amounts available for shipping from the supply points constitutes an attribute genus. Each attribute element (amount) "calls" a primitive element (supply point), and so the attribute genus generically "calls" the primitive entity genus.

Finally, in a structured model, groups of conceptually related genera are called _modules_. For example, the transportation links, the amounts shipped on each link, and the unit costs associated with each link, taken together, could constitute a module. Related modules can be grouped to form even larger modules, thereby creating a hierarchy which has at the top a module which encompasses all genera in the model.

There are three levels of structure required in a structured model: elemental, generic, and modular. Elemental structure, applies to the definitional dependencies or "calls" between elements. It is required that there be no circular references in the elemental structure (that is, it cannot be, for example, that A calls B, B calls C, and C calls A). Generic structure, applies to the calls between genera. Because of the condition of generic similarity, it follows that there can be no circular references in the generic structure. Finally, modular structure refers to the hierarchical relationships among the modules.

In a structured model, the hierarchy of modules is required to have a monotone ordering; that is, it must be possible to represent the modular structure as an indented ordered list of modules and sub-modules (much like an outline of the model), so that none of the calls between genera in different modules involves forward references. The so-called default modular structure has one module for each genus and one module for the model as a whole. It always has a monotone ordering because there are no circular references in the generic structure. Requiring a monotone ordering thus effectively restricts only more complex and, of course, more useful modular structures.

This completes our discussion of the basic concepts of structured modeling. Next, we will consider how a structured model may be represented.

2.2 Graphical Representations

The definitional system of structured modeling described above is based on the mathematical theory of attributed acyclic graphs. At the lowest level, the element graph represents the elemental structure of a model, capturing all the details of a specific model instance. (Figure 1 shows the elemental structure of the Transportation Model.) The nodes of the graph represent elements; the arcs represent "calls" or definitional dependencies between elements. By convention, the arcs are directed from the "called" element to the "calling" element (otherwise stated, from the "defining" element to the "defined" element). In Figure 1, we have labeled each node with a code for its type--"t" for test, "f" for function, "a" for attribute, and "pe" and "ce" for primitive and compound entities, respectively. The nodes and arcs of the graph are further attributed with (i) values for non-entity elements, (ii) rules for function elements, and (iii) an ordering of the inbound arcs at each node. The graph is acyclic because circular definitions are disallowed.

A less detailed (but more comprehensible) graph, the genus graph, represents the generic structure of a model class (See Figure 2). It captures the definitional dependencies among the genera, while suppressing the details of a model instance. The genus graph is obtained by a condensation of the element graph in which all the elements of a genus are represented as a single node. (The property of generic similarity makes this condensation possible.)

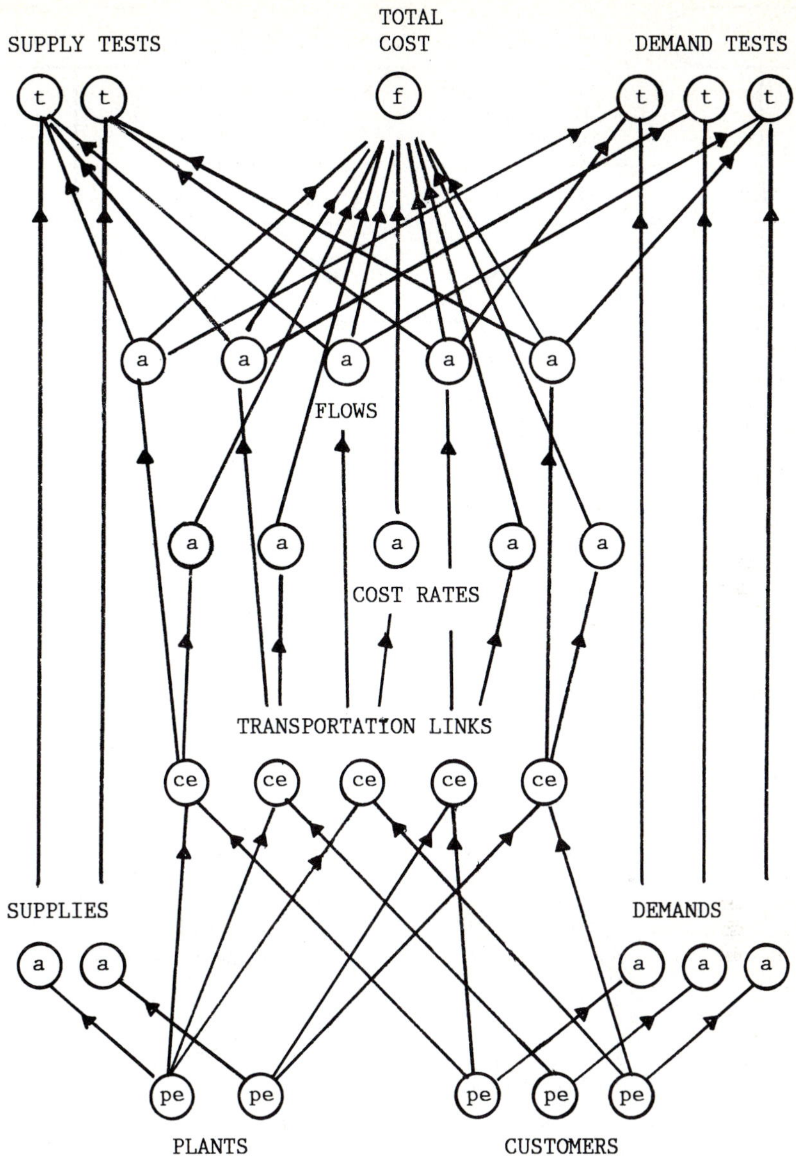

Fig. 1. Elemental Structure of 2x3 Transportation Model

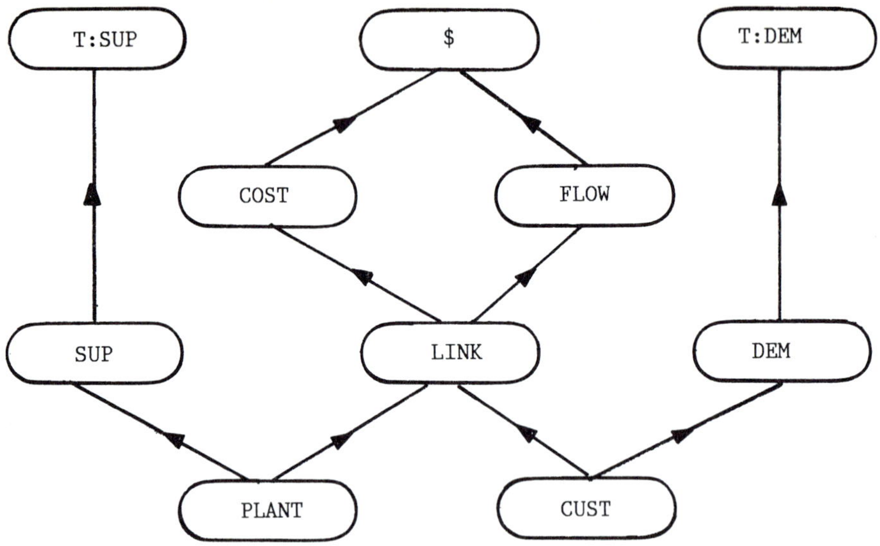

Fig. 2. Generic Structure of Transportation Model

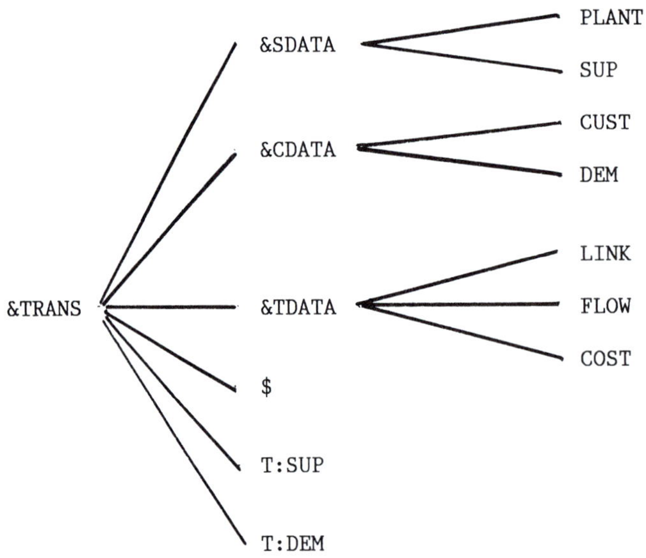

Fig. 3. Modular Structure of Transportation Model

Finally, modular structure is represented graphically by the modular tree (See Figure 3). Its root represents the entire model; its terminal nodes correspond 1:1 with the genera; all other nodes are modules containing their descendant genera. The arcs indicate that a node is "contained in" the module above it in the tree. (By convention, modules are denoted by names beginning with "&".)

2.3 Non-Graphical Representations

As useful as the graphical representation may be for some purposes, there is a need also for non-graphical representations, especially as the size and complexity of the model grows. In this discussion, in contrast to the one in Section 2.2, we begin with representations of the highest level of structure and progress to those at lower levels.

First the modular structure, as mentioned in Section 2.1, can be represented naturally in outline form. (See Figure 4.) Indentation is used to indicate a sub-module contained within a module. The items at the lowest levels in the outline are in 1:1 correspondence with the genera of the model (equivalently, the terminal nodes of the modular tree).

```
&TRANS
   &SDATA
      PLANT
      SUP
   &CDATA
      CUST
      DEM
   &TDATA
      LINK
      FLOW
      COST
   $
   T:SUP
   T:DEM
```

Fig. 4. Outline of Transportation Model

A more informative representation of the modular structure (and some aspects of generic structure) is the natural language summary, as shown in Figure 5. In this summary, every module and genus name is followed by an informal interpretation or comment written in natural language. Although there is no formal syntax requirement on the interpretation, the example follows the convention of having a key phrase which is capitalized and underlined. Any subsequent reference to a key phrase is capitalized.

Furthermore, in the summary, the name of each genus having more than one element is followed by its "indexing variable". In the example, PLANT is indexed by "i". Thus, individual elements in the genus (although they can also have individual names) can be referred to as PLANTi where i takes on a value in some allowed set. So, we may have PLANT1, PLANT2, ... or perhaps PLANTA, PLANTB, ... Continuing with the example, SUP is also indexed by i, (because the SUP genus has elements corresponding to the elements of the PLANT genus), but CUST has a different index, namely "j", and hence LINK is indexed by the combination "ij".

Because its content is almost entirely natural language, the summary is intended to facilitate communication with a non-technical audience. The summary is also useful to a technical audience (including the model builder) because it provides an overview of the model with the barest minimum of technical detail.

&SDATA SOURCE DATA

PLANTi There is a list of PLANTS.

SUPi Every PLANT has a SUPPLY CAPACITY (tons).

&CDATA CUSTOMER DATA

CUSTj There is a list of CUSTOMERS.

DEMj Every CUSTOMER has a nonnegative DEMAND (tons).

&TDATA TRANSPORTATION DATA

LINKij There are some transportation LINKS from PLANTS to CUSTOMERS. There is at least one LINK incident to each PLANT, and at least one LINK incident to each CUSTOMER.

FLOWij There can be a nonnegative transportation FLOW (tons) over each LINK.

COSTij Every LINK has a TRANSPORTATION COST RATE ($/ton).

$ There is a TOTAL COST associated with all FLOWS.

T:SUPi Is the total FLOW leaving a PLANT less than or equal to its SUPPLY CAPACITY? This is called the SUPPLY TEST.

T:DEMj Is the total FLOW arriving at a CUSTOMER exactly equal to its DEMAND? This is called the DEMAND TEST.

Fig. 5. Summary of Transportation Model

Next, to specify the generic structure of a model class, Geoffrion has proposed a text-based model schema, an example of which is shown in Figure 6. Each genus in the model corresponds to a paragraph in the schema. All of the information about a genus (including its "calls" on other genera) is encoded in the formal part of the genus paragraph. (For a more detailed description of the syntax, see Geoffrion [11, Section 2.2].) The last component of a genus paragraph is the informal "interpretation" as it would appear in the model summary discussed above.

Finally, to complete the specification of a model instance, it remains to supply the elemental detail, for example, the list of elements in each primitive entity genus or the values for the elements in each attribute genus. Geoffrion prescribes a set of data tables (See Figure 7.) to contain the elemental detail. The configuration of the data tables is determined by the generic structure specified for the model class in the model schema. (A more detailed explanation of the data tables is provided by Geoffrion [11, Section 2.2].)

Before leaving the subject of representing structured models, we should emphasize, quoting Geoffrion [11], that the "notational conventions used here ... do not 'define' structured modeling in any sense. Others may wish and, indeed, are encouraged to propose other notational conventions to embody the core concepts of structured modeling ...".

&SDATA SOURCE DATA

PLANTi /pe/
There is a list of PLANTS.

SUP(PLANTi) /a/ {PLANT} : R+
Every PLANT has a SUPPLY CAPACITY (tons).

&CDATA CUSTOMER DATA

CUSTj /pe/
There is a list of CUSTOMERS.

DEM(CUSTj) /a/ {CUST} : R+
Every CUSTOMER has a nonnegative DEMAND (tons).

&TDATA TRANSPORTATION DATA

LINK(PLANTi,CUSTj) /ce/ Select {PLANT}x{CUST} where i covers {PLANT}, j covers {CUST}
There are some transportation LINKS from PLANTS to CUSTOMERS. There is at least one LINK incident to each PLANT, and at least one LINK incident to each CUSTOMER.

FLOW(LINKij) /va/ {LINK} : R+
There can be a nonnegative transportation FLOW (tons) over each LINK.

COST(LINKij) /a/ {LINK} : R
Every LINK has a TRANSPORTATION COST RATE ($/ton).

$(COST,FLOW) /f/ ; SUMi SUMj (COSTij * FLOWij)
There is a TOTAL COST associated with all FLOWS.

T:SUP(FLOWi.,SUPi) /t/ {PLANT} ; SUMj (FLOWij) <= SUPi
Is the total FLOW leaving a PLANT less than or equal to its SUPPLY CAPACITY? This is called the SUPPLY TEST.

T:DEM(FLOW.j,DEMj) /t/ {CUST} ; SUMi (FLOWij) = DEMj
Is the total FLOW arriving at a CUSTOMER exactly equal to its DEMAND? This is called the DEMAND TEST.

Fig. 6. Schema for Transportation Model

PLANT

PLANT		INTERP	SUP
DAL		Dallas	20,000
CHI		Chicago	42,000

CUST

CUST		INTERP	DEM
PITTS		Pittsburgh	25,000
ATL		Atlanta	15,000
CLEV		Cleveland	22,000

LINK

PLANT	CUST		FLOW	COST
DAL	PITTS		5,000	23.50
DAL	ATL		15,000	17.75
DAL	CLEV		0	32.45
CHI	PITTS		20,000	7.60
CHI	CLEV		22,000	25.75

$

	$
	1,102,250

T:SUP

PLANT		T:SUP
DAL		TRUE
CHI		TRUE

T:DEM

CUST		T:DEM
PITTS		TRUE
ATL		TRUE
CLEV		TRUE

Fig. 7. Sample Data Tables for 2x3 Transportation Model

3 WORKING WITH STRUCTURED MODELS

In the previous section, we considered representations for structured models. However models are not static objects. Their purpose for being is to produce new information by inference from existing data. (For a model in MS/OR tradition, the inference is usually accomplished by a mathematical computation, involving evaluation, solving equations, or optimization.) Furthermore, models have a life cycle, during which they are created, grow and develop, are used to perform useful work, and eventually are retired to make way for the next generation.

Thus, a true test of the value of a modeling framework is an active one. How does it perform over the life cycle? How does it address the dual needs for enhanced productivity and better communication?

A fully functional computer implementation of structured modeling is still a ways off, so our comments in this section are of necessity somewhat speculative. However, structured modeling can be thought of as a style of modeling as well as a formal framework, so it makes sense to speak of "working with structured models" independent of any implementation.

3.1 Formulation

The various representations of a structured model can be useful at different times in the process of formulating a model. For example, a modular outline might be a starting point. It could be fleshed out with some interpretation to yield at least an approximation to the natural language summary. Perhaps at this point, looking at a graphical representation of the generic structure would elucidate the definitional dependencies. Then, the model builder would revise the outline and perhaps review the summary with the model user in preparation for the next step--fully specifying the genus paragraphs of the model schema. Finally, the elemental detail, possibly extracted from other data sources, would be entered into the data tables.

Of course, formulating a model is not a straight line process any more than writing a journal article is. However, outlines and summaries are familiar tools for keeping track of the overall structure of an article and can serve the same purpose for a model. These tools are particularly useful, given software that can automatically move from one level of abstraction to another.

Furthermore, the modular structure of a structured model should be especially helpful in increasing productivity during the formulation stage. With some judicious restructuring (see section 3.3 for examples) and the modification of the data tables, one could anticipate formulating a "new" model largely from "off-the-shelf" modules.

3.2 Solution

Because a structured model exists independently from the algorithms which "solve" the model, a given model can conceivably be processed by more than one "solver", or to use a more general term "problem processor" [1]. For example, the Transportation Model might first be processed by a function evaluator to determine the cost and the supply/demand consequences for some trial values for the amounts shipped on each transportation link. This requires only a forward pass through the model to evaluate all the function and test elements. Alternatively, the same model could be optimized by some linear programming procedure to find the quantities which would satisfy the supply and demand tests at minimum cost. Another option would be to optimize the model (in the interests of computational efficiency) using a network code.

The schema together with the data tables constitute a sufficiently unambiguous description of the model instance so that it can be automatically translated into whatever format is required by the problem processor. This property alone could be a major factor in productivity enhancement by relieving the model builder of the burden of constructing interfaces to problem processors.

Furthermore, some variations on the same model can be solved--for example, some tests ("constraints" in the common parlance of linear programming) might be added or deleted simply by adding or deleting the corresponding genera. Case studies using different values for projected demands, say, could be done by substituting a different version of the relevant data table, leaving the schema and the other data tables untouched.

ITEMi There is a list of ITEMS.

&ITEMDATA Certain ITEM DATA are provided.

Di Every ITEM has a DEMAND RATE (units/year).

Hi Every ITEM has a HOLDING COST RATE ($/unit/year).

Fi Every ITEM has a FIXED SETUP COST ($/setup).

Qi The ORDER QUANTITY (units/order) for each ITEM is to be chosen.

&OPCON OPERATING CONSEQUENCES following from ORDER QUANTITY choices.

FREQi Every ITEM has a SETUP FREQUENCY (average number of setups/year) equal to DEMAND RATE divided by ORDER QUANTITY.

SETUP$i Every ITEM has an ANNUAL SETUP COST ($/year) equal to the SETUP FREQUENCY times the SETUP COST.

CARRY$i Every ITEM has an ANNUAL CARRYING COST ($/year) equal to its HOLDING COST RATE times one-half of its ORDER QUANTITY (which estimates average inventory level).

ITEM$i Every ITEM has an ANNUAL ITEM COST ($/year) equal to its ANNUAL SETUP COST plus its ANNUAL CARRYING COST.

**TOT$** The TOTAL ANNUAL COST ($/year) is the sum of all ANNUAL ITEM COSTS.

Fig. 8. Summary of Multi-Item EOQ Model

3.3 Restructuring

In the course of model development, it may become necessary to add more detail, say about the sources of the data required in the model. To illustrate this process of "top-down refinement", consider the Multi-Item Economic Order Quantity (EOQ) Model, whose summary appears in Figure 8 and whose outline appears in Figure 9a. Suppose, for example, that the holding cost rate needs further elaboration. In that case, the H genus is replaced by the &H module, as shown below.

&H HOLDING COST RATE DATA

VALi Every ITEM has a UNIT VALUE (dollars/unit).

STORAGEi Every ITEM has a STORAGE COST RATE (dollars/unit/year) associated with physical possession.

Hi Every ITEM has a HOLDING COST RATE (dollars/unit/year) equal to a 12% opportunity cost of capital tied up (calculated on the basis of UNIT VALUE) plus the STORAGE COST RATE.

Then, the VAL genus might be further refined as a &VAL module:

&VAL UNIT VALUE DEVELOPMENT

DIRMATi The value of each ITEM includes a certain amount of DIRECT MATERIAL COST (dollars/unit).

DIRLABi The value of each ITEM includes a certain amount of DIRECT LABOR COST (dollars/unit).

VALi Every ITEM has a UNIT VALUE (dollars/unit) equal to the sum of DIRECT MATERIAL COST and DIRECT LABOR COST.

The combined effect on the outline is shown in Figure 9b.

Another useful restructuring operation is integration, in which two separate models are merged into one. As an example, consider integrating the Transportation Model with the Multi-Item EOQ Model.

If the Transportation Model is solved for the cost-minimizing "flows" or shipments on an annual basis, it remains to determine the frequency, or equivalently, the size of these shipments. For the customer, frequent small shipments incur high transaction costs; infrequent large shipments incur high holding costs. The EOQ model will suffice for determining shipment size with a few modifications:

(1) replace the ITEM genus by a copy of the LINK genus (since each transportation "link" plays the role of an "item" for which the economic "order" quantity must be determined) and correspondingly rename ITEM$ as LINK$;

(2) replace the D genus by a copy of the FLOW genus (since each transportation "flow" plays the role of a "demand rate");

(3) rename the SETUP$ genus as REC$ to reflect the re-interpretation of a setup cost as a shipment receiving (or transaction) cost; and

(4) rename the $ genus as TRANS$ to distinguish this cost as the cost of transportation.

Now the two models must be integrated into a single model if jointly optimal choices for FLOW and Q are desired. This can be accomplished by joining the two schemata as follows:

(1) concatenate the two schemata (either model can be first);

(2) delete the LINK and FLOW genera from the second model schema (all calls to them will be routed to the like-named genera in the first model schema);

(3) add a new function genus TOTCOST whose purpose is to add the costs calculated in the two models (now modules).

The outline of the integrated model is shown in Figure 10.

```
ITEM
&ITEMDATA
   D
   H
   F
Q
&OPCON
   FREQ
   SETUP$
   CARRY$
   ITEM$
   TOT$
```

Fig. 9a. Outline of EOQ Model Before Refinement

```
ITEM
&ITEMDATA
   D
   &H
      &VAL
         DIRMAT
         DIRLAB
         VAL
      STORAGE
      H
   F
Q
&OPCON
   FREQ
   SETUP$
   CARRY$
   ITEM$
   TOT$
```

Fig. 9b. Outline of EOQ Model After Refinement

```
&TRANS
   &SDATA
      PLANT
      SUP
   &CDATA
      CUST
      DEM
   &TDATA
      LINK
      FLOW
      COST
   TRANS$
   T:SUP
   T:DEM
&EOQ
   &ITEMDATA
      H
      F
   Q
   &OPCON
      FREQ
      REC$
      CARRY$
      LINK$
      TOT$
TOTCOST
```

Fig. 10. Outline of Integrated Model

3.4 Documentation

A critical part of the life cycle is documenting the model and communicating its content to users. The inherent structure of a structured model along with its various representations should help in this regard. The summary is particularly accessible to a non-technical audience. The outline (or its tree representation) is helpful in conveying the "big picture". Furthermore, by selectively displaying (or not displaying) lower levels of detail in different sub-modules, the outline can be tailored to the needs of a specific audience or occasion. For example, in the Transportation Model, some audiences might be interested in the detail of the module containing supplier data (&SDATA), content to know only that there is a module (&CDATA) containing data about the customers, and vice versa.

Finally, the graphical representation of the generic structure (or at least a portion of it) can help explain "where the numbers come from." For example, for the integrated model shown in Figure 10, the partial genus graph of Figure 11 shows the generic components of TOTCOST.

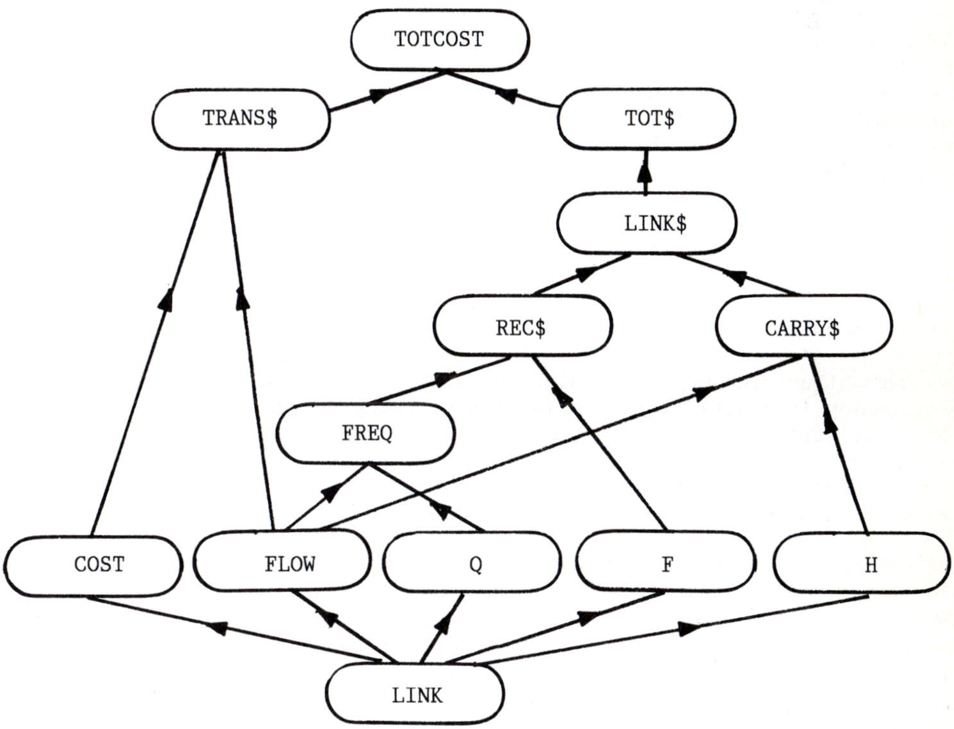

Fig. 11. Generic Cost Structure of Integrated Model

4 FUTURE DIRECTIONS

Taking the conceptual framework of structured modeling as a starting point, there are a number of avenues open to further research and development. Among them:

(1) Refining and extending the underlying theory;

(2) Implementing the framework as a "modeling environment" or as a model management system; and

(3) Evaluating the impact of structured modeling on model-based work.

Consideration of any one of these areas gives rise to a number of issues and questions, some of which are enumerated below. Wherever possible, we will make note of those topics which are, or recently have been, under active investigation.

4.1 Theory

There are a number of theoretical issues concerning the relationship of structured modeling to other conceptual frameworks. For example, Farn [7] has shown that any relational database as well as the Entity-Relationship data model [3] can be rendered as a structured model. What about other data modeling frameworks? Can SM be used for database design? Or, taking the opposite view, can the structured modeling framework be represented as a relational data base [7, 12] ?

Is structured modeling general enough to encompass the knowledge representation frameworks used in artificial intelligence (e.g. logic, production rules, semantic networks, or frames)? Chari [2] is investigating, in particular, the relationship of structured modeling to first order logic.

How does structured modeling relate to some of the newer paradigms for programming languages--for example, functional programming or object-oriented programming? (See Lenard [13] for some preliminary ideas on this.) Could structured modeling be used for program design? (Sanchez [15] is adapting structured modeling principles for use in writing requirement specifications for large-scale software development projects.)

Another set of issues involve extensions of the framework. How could stochastic models be included? How could continuous time models be included? How could infinite time horizons be modeled? What additions to the syntax and semantics would be helpful? desirable?

On a higher level of abstraction, is there a more general theory of modeling that would identify the elements common to the model-based fields of MS/OR, database theory, artificial intelligence, and programming language design?

4.2 Implementation

Three prototype structured modeling systems are complete or nearly so. One of these, LEXICON [4], was done in FORTRAN on a mainframe and is aimed mainly at supporting optimization for large linear programming problems.

The schema and data tables are entered and processed in batch mode, but otherwise the user interface with LEXICON is interactive. A second prototype, IIS [7], was done in KNOWLEDGEMAN (Trademark, Micro Data Base Systems, Inc.) for the IBM PC/XT and is aimed mainly at demonstrating the feasibility of a hybrid information and modeling system. The system is entirely menu-driven.

The third and most fully functional prototype is FW/SM [10] is being developed (at UCLA under Geoffrion's direction) in FRAMEWORK II (Trademark, Ashton-Tate) for the IBM PC/AT. FW/SM makes use of the full range of FRAMEWORK facilities: a menu-driven user interface, word processing, outlining, spreadsheets, flat file databases, graphics, telecommunications, and a built-in programming language (FRED). It will include interfaces to "problem processors" for data retrieval, as well as linear, non-linear, and network optimization.

A host of design issues arise out of the effort to implement structured modeling. For example, how could the language for describing the model schema be improved? What form should the command language for invoking "problem processors" or other operations on models take? How should the compiler or interpreter of these languages be built? What programming language(s) should be used?

Should the user interface be based on graphics, text, tables, "natural language", or all of the above? What internal data structures are appropriate? What existing software packages could be used for implementation? How could they be integrated?

Could a database management system be used as a basis for a "structured" model management system? Dolk [5, 6] has made a proposal along these lines and has developed in some detail the notion of an active information resource dictionary (that is, a dictionary of both data and models). "Structured" model management will also be the subject of another lecture [14] at this Institute.

Model management presents its own set of questions: for example, how can structured models be translated to and from other modeling systems? or, can we use a model schema to direct the process of extracting data from a variety of sources? Wright [17] is developing a prototype model management system specialized for marketing applications.

How can structured models be interfaced with, or translated for, a variety of "problem processors", including query languages, inference engines, evaluators of functions (and derivatives), and equation solvers? Can an "expert system" choose a problem processor based on the problem at hand?

4.3 Impact on modeling

As we have mentioned, it is possible to think of structured modeling as a style of modeling. Could it in fact be a means for developing principles for building "good" models? or even for identifying "good" models? Could structured modeling serve as a vehicle for teaching "good" modeling? Is there a "normal form" for structured models analogous to that developed for relational databases? Can model operations such as refinement and integration be formalized? Can any techniques for program or database design be adapted to model design? Can principles of good modeling be captured in an expert system?

Whether structured modeling is seen primarily as a conceptual framework, or a modeling language, or a style of modeling, the ultimate question is: How does structured modeling influence the way people interact with models? How do they create them, use them, indeed, think about them? Is this structured approach beneficial? and how do we measure that?

5 CONCLUDING REMARKS

In the foregoing, we have presented an overview of the fundamentals of structured modeling. As we have seen, the core concepts constitute a meta-model or a model of models. Thus, structured modeling provides a conceptual framework that clarifies our understanding of what a model is and what model builders do. As such, it can serve as the basis for a new generation of modeling software, be it an integral part of a decision support system or a stand-alone system. Furthermore, structured modeling prescribes a style and standard for working with models throughout their life cycle. Finally, and perhaps most importantly, it establishes a theoretical foundation which will make possible deep and ultimately fruitful connections with other model-based disciplines. Overall, structured modeling is likely to make a substantial contribution to the goal of this Advanced Study Institute: namely, a better understanding of the mathematical formulation of decision problems.

REFERENCES

1. Bonczek, R. H., C. W. Holsapple, and A. B. Whinston (1980), Future directions for developing decision support systems, Decision Sciences, 11, 616-631.

2. Chari, S. (1987), Knowledge representation using structured modeling, presented at Joint National Meeting, The Institute of Management Science/Operations Research Society of America, New Orleans, May.

3. Chen, P. P. S. (1976), The entity-relationship model: Towards a unified view of data, ACM Trans. Database on Database Systems, 1:1 (March), 9-36.

4. Clemence, Jr., R. D. (1984), LEXICON: A structured modeling system for optimization, Master's Thesis, Naval Postgraduate School, Monterey, CA, June.

5. Dolk, D. R. (1986a), Data as models: An approach to implementing model management, Decision Support Systems, 2:1 (March), 73-80.

6. Dolk, D. R. (1986b), Model management and structured modeling: The role of an information resource dictionary system, Dept. of Administrative Sciences, Naval Postgraduate School, Monterey, CA, August.

7. Farn, C. K. (1985), An Integrated Information System Architecture Based on Structured Modeling, Ph.D. Thesis, Graduate School of Management, UCLA.

8. Geoffrion, A. M. (1986a), Modeling approaches and systems related to structured modeling, Working Paper No. 339, Graduate School of Management, University of California-- Los Angeles, July.

9. Geoffrion, A. M. (1986b), Integrated modeling systems, Working Paper No. 343, Graduate School of Management, University of California--Los Angeles, November (also appears in Proceedings of the Conference on Integrated Modeling Systems, University of Texas, Austin, October).

10. Geoffrion, A. M. (1987a), An introduction to structured modeling, Working Paper No. 338 (Revised), Graduate School of Management, University of California--Los Angeles, February (also appears in Proceedings of the Conference on Integrated Modeling Systems, University of Texas, Austin, October, 1986).

11. Geoffrion, A. M. (1987b), An introduction to structured modeling, Management Science 33:5 (May), 547-588.

12. Lenard, M. L. (1986), Representing models as data, J. Management Information Systems, 2:4, 36-48.

13. Lenard, M. L. (1987a) An object-oriented approach to model management, Proceedings, Twentieth Hawaii International Conference on System Sciences, Volume I, 509-515, January.

14. Lenard, M. L. (1987b), Structured model management, Proceedings, NATO Advanced Study Institute, Mathematical Models for Decision Support, July-August.

15. Sanchez, J. (1986), Current status of a structured requirements methodology as applied to large scale real-time software development, presented at the Workshop on Structured Modeling, UCLA, August.

16. Sprague, R. H. and E. D. Carlson, (1982), Building Effective Decision Support Systems, Prentice-Hall, Englewood Cliffs, N.J.

17. Wright, G. (1987), An integrated marketing information system based on structured modeling, presented at Joint National Meeting, The Institute of Management Science/Operations Research Society of America, New Orleans, May.

ACKNOWLEDGEMENT

The author wishes to thank Arthur M. Geoffrion for the opportunity to read early drafts of his manuscripts and for many thought-provoking discussions.

This work was supported in part by National Science Foundation Grants No. RII-8310337 and No. SES-8520262.

Mathematical Basis for Decision Support Systems

James C. Moore, William B. Richmond and Andrew B. Whinston
Krannert Graduate School of Management
Purdue University
West Lafayette, IN 47907, U.S.A.

1. INTRODUCTION

In most real world situations, decisions are made under uncertainty. Uncertainty results from both a dynamic environment and a lack of information about parameters relevant to the decision. We assume the environment is given and look at reducing the uncertainty associated with a lack of information. In general, the less uncertainty a decision maker has, the better his/her decision. Because of this, the decision maker wants to acquire information to reduce his/her uncertainty. A computer system's, especially Decision Support System's (DSS), purpose is to aid people in making decisions by providing information relevant to the decision. Even though a computer system's primary purpose is to aid in making decisions, few computer systems or algorithms are designed from a decision theoretic standpoint.

We pursue the link between computing and normative, economic decision theory, and we try to develop a theoretical understanding of the appropriate support system for decision making. The decision model [8] decomposes the decision process into information-gathering and decision making, so a decision maker requires strategies for both acquiring information and making decisions. The information-gathering strategy can be viewed as executing a series of experiments such as running computer models, making computations or comparisons, querying the user, or taking environmental readings. Depending on the experiments used, the information-gathering strategy may correspond to a computer algorithm, an integrated decision support system, or a combination of both. A decision maker's goal is to determine an optimal strategy. Since executing computer models and taking environmental readings, etc., cost money and time, obtaining all of the possible information may not be worthwhile. The decision maker must decide if the expected value of the information from an experiment is worth the experiment's cost. What information to acquire, how much information to acquire, and in what sequence to acquire the information must be answered in determining the kinds of decision support models to be used and how to solve those models. Determining the optimal level of information for making a decision based on the tradeoff between the cost and value of

NATO ASI Series, Vol. F48
Mathematical Models for Decision Support
Edited by G. Mitra

information is largely ignored in algorithm and DSS development.

In the next section, we present the decision model, and in Section 2 we discuss some of its applications and interpretations. In Section 3 we discuss two extensions to the basic model, the work that has been accomplished in these extensions, and the goals we plan to pursue.

2. DECISION MODEL WITH INFORMATION ACQUISITION

A decision problem is a function of eight parameters:

$$\mathbf{D} = < \mathbf{X}, \emptyset, D, \omega^*, A, \{\mathbf{M}_a | a \in A\}, c, r >$$

where:

- $\mathbf{X}$ denotes the state space. It is the set of possible, mutually exclusive states of the world. We assume that $\mathbf{X}$ is finite.
- $\emptyset:\mathbf{X} \rightarrow [0,1]$ is the probability density function. $\emptyset(x)$ is the probability that x is the true state of the world, and we assume that $\emptyset(x) > 0$ for all $x \in \mathbf{X}$. $\emptyset$ defines the probability distribution function π: $P(Y) \rightarrow [0,1]$ by
  $$\pi(Y) = \sum \emptyset(x) \text{ for } Y \in \mathbf{X}$$
  where "P($\mathbf{X}$)" denotes the power set of $\mathbf{X}$.
- D is the (finite) set of available final decisions.
- $\omega: \mathbf{X} \times D \rightarrow \Re$ is the gross payoff function. $\omega(x,d)$ is the payoff from making decision d when x is the true state of the world.
- A is the set of initial (information-gathering) actions, or experiments. $A = \{0,1,2,...,n\}$, where 0 is the null action. For each action there are a finite number n(a) of outcomes or signals, y_a. $y_a \in \{1,2,...,m(a)\}$.
- $\mathbf{M}_a$ is the information structure associated with action $a \in A$. Each $\mathbf{M}_a$ is a partition of $\mathbf{X}$. $\mathbf{M}_a = \{M_{a1}, M_{a2}, ... M_{am(a)}\}$ where $M_{ay} = \{x \in \mathbf{X} \mid y$ is the outcome of experiment a when x is the true state of the world$\}$.
- $c:A \rightarrow \Re_+$ is the cost function; c(a) is the cost of utilizing action $a \in A$, and we assume $c(0) = 0$.
- r is a positive integer representing the maximum number of information-gathering actions that can be taken before a final decision is made.

An element, x, of the state space represents a state of the world (actually an equivalence class of states) that is relevant to the decision problem. In a medical diagnosis system, such as Mycin, $x \in X$ represents a disease; in a file search algorithm, x represents a record or a gap in the file. Choosing the correct formulation of the state space is crucial, since different representations of the same problem lead to different optimal strategies.

The probability density funciton, $\emptyset$, is difficult to assess. Often, objective statistics are unavailable and subjective probabilities must be used. For example, in the medical diagnosis area, $\emptyset(x)$ is the likelihood of a disease, x, occuring.

The payoff of the decision, ω, has been largely ignored in designing computer systems. It usually only enters the process in resolving the question of whether or not a system should be built at all. This is primarily because most computer systems obtain full information, and because choosing an appropriate payoff function is difficult. Using a payoff function to evaluate decision support systems aids in customizing the system for different environments. Consider an interactive medical diagnosis system implemented in the U.S. The doctor inputs the results of some initial tests and the diagnostics system either proposes a disease and treatment or asks for more information. The request for information may involve running more tests on the patient. Before the government placed a cap on charges for certain treatments, the payoff function for the diagnostic system should reflect the immateriality of the cost of information or experiments. A system used in the current environment, however, must take into account the cost of experimentation, and requires a different information-gathering strategy.

The set of available experiments, A, determines the level at which the problem is investigated, and controls the cost and flow of the information strategy. By assuming the experiments are computer models, we can investigate DSS integration. Assuming the experiments are computations leads to the investigation and design of a DSS algorithm. When working at the micro level, the choice of allowable experiments is crucial and is intimately related to the definition of the state space.

In deriving an information and decision strategy, we maximize Ω^*, the expected net payoff of the decision. Ω^* reflects both the value of the decision and the cost of acquiring information. We justify maximizing expected utility by reference to the economic literature [11]. Expected utility was developed for an individual, not a group. Is it appropriate when the model is used to develop a DSS to support multiple users? When the DSS supports multiple users, Ω^* becomes a social welfare function. Welfare economics and social choice investigate how to aggregate individual preferences to derive a social or group preference function. In general, a social welfare function must be Pareto efficient, but with regard to other criteria, no results are absolute. We skirt the social welfare dilemma by arguing that the organization has its own utility funciton (e.g., wanting to maximize profits) and ω^* can be designed to represent the organization's utility function.

3. RESEARCH AND RESULTS

Several researchers have applied the decision model to a variety of problem areas. Although research based on the Moore/Whinston decision model is in its infancy, it has resulted in some valuable insights into the relationship between decision theory and computing. In this section, we highlight some of the results. Most of the research on expert systems is largely empirical and centers on explanation systems, knowledge representation, inference methods, acquiring expert knowledge, and handling uncertainty. Hall et al. [3] use the decision model to formulate a theoretical basis for expert systems. They begin by characterizing an ideal process in which an expert (and correspondingly an expert system) arrives at a decision. They then show that constructing an information and decision strategy corresponds to constructing an expert system.

In a rule based expert system, the rule compiler, the rule processor and the information-gathering rules (rules of the form: If $\mathbf{b}_i$ then $\mathbf{a}_i$ where $\mathbf{b}_i$ represents a set of possible data base values, and $\mathbf{a}_i$ represents a request for further information) implicitly determine an information strategy and the associated final information structure. If the information strategy is both complete and consistent, then it can be represented by a decision tree with the leaves of the tree as decisions, interior nodes as information-acquisition actions, and branches as the possible results of the actions. The inference process is equivalent to searching the tree for an acceptable solution, and the path through the tree represents the sequence of rules executed.

Hall shows that the decision model framework provides an alternative method for implementing a decision making system (e.g., an expert system). The decision theoretic approach Hall uses differs from current expert systems by focussing on the efficiency of the decision process and on the tradeoff between the correctness of the decision and the cost of the decision.

At a seemingly opposite end of the type of problems studied in computer science, two related areas where the model has been successfully applied are in the computer file search problem and in the common index problem. In the file search problem, Moore and Whinston [8] show that the optimal file search algorithm developed in computing theory is a special case of an optimal information and decision strategy. The results obtained indicate that computer algorithms in general, and the file search algorithms in particular, model decision processes. The computer file search problem is a special case of the categorization problem. In solving this problem, computing theory implicitly assumes a payoff function that is positive iff there is an exact match between the record requested and the record returned and a constant cost function $c(a) = c$ where c is less than the expected payoff for any query. When these conditions do not hold, the optimal binary search tree does not provide an optimal information-gathering strategy.

Related to the file search problem is the common index problem. In the common index problem, a random individual wants to determine if a given element, the ideal element, from a universal set is present in the file. If the ideal element is not in the file, then the best available element is returned. Moore et al. [7] consider a special case of the common index problem where there exists an index over the set of alternatives that contains all of the relevant information for choosing between the alternatives. Each user's utility is a function of the index and the utility functions are single peaked and symmetric.

A dynamic programming algorithm is presented for constructing an optimal search algorithm, and an example is worked out for two payoff functions:

$$1. \quad \omega(x,d) = \begin{cases} \varpi > 0 & \text{if } v_u \in v_d \text{ or } v_u = y_{d-1} \\ 0 & \text{otherwise} \end{cases}$$

which implies there is a positive payoff if the best available element is returned, and a payoff of 0 if any other element is returned.

$$2. \quad \omega(x,d) = \frac{-|w_u - w_d|}{\varpi}$$

which reflects that the payoff depends on how close the returned element, w_d, is to the best available element w_u. In the example presented, the resulting information and decision strategies are significantly different. The first payoff function results in complete information; whereas, the second payoff function does not result in complete information. Sufficient conditions for obtaining complete information are presented for both payoff functions.

Rao [10] investigates resource allocation among members of a team. The team members can be thought of as processors in a concurrent or distributed environment. Each processor needs certain resources to perform its tasks, and these needs translate into a preference ordering over the set of possible resource allocations. The preference ordering is assumed to be a strictly increasing weak order, so each processor prefers more of a resource to less of a resource. The author assumes that there are a finite number of feasible allocations, and they define each processor's utility function as: u(x) is the number of x'such that x is preferred to x', where x and x' are feasible resource allocations. Each processor's individual preference ordering can be unique, but they all desire a resouce allocation that maximizes the sum of the individual utility functions.

To determine the optimal resource allocation, a meta-agent polls the processors for information on their preferences. Two polling procedures are investigated: pairwise comparisons and rank ordering. In both cases, each time the meta-agent polls a processor, the meta-agent gains knowledge of the group preference function (due to Marschak's cautionary note [5], the meta-agent estimates the group utility function directly rather than the individual preference functions). The decision model is used to develop a strategy for determining the group preference function, which accounts for the trade-off between the cost of polling the processors and the correctness of the final resource allocation.
The final area the decision model has been successfully applied to is model selection for operation research (OR) optimization problems. In OR optimization models, the level of detail must be balanced against the information and computation requirements. The trade-off is an economic one, and the solution equates the marginal value of the better decision with the marginal cost of increased information and computation. Balakrishnan et al. [1] investigate mode selection for

determining message routing in a computer network. The computer network consists of a set of n information processors (nodes) and m communication links (arcs). The problem is how to route messages from source nodes to sink nodes. Since real networks are susceptible to both traffic congestion and network failure, the state of the network at the time a node sends a message is unknown.

Two common classes of models exist for determining a message's route. In the static models, the route a message takes is solved before any message is sent. A message from node A to node B uses the same route regardless of changes in the state of the network. Dynamic models, on the other hand, recompute the best path from the source to the sink every time a message is sent. In computing the path, every arc in the network is tested to determine if it is operable.

The dynamic model uses complete information about the network in determining a message's route. The static model uses no information. Balakrishnan et al. look at selecting an optimal model based on partial information that balances the transmission costs against the information costs. They look at a special case of the message routing problem where there is a single source node, a single sink node and a single message (so there is no traffic congestion). Each arc, j, in the network fails with probability p_j, and arc failures are assumed to be independent. If arc j is operable, the cost of transmission along arc j is l_j. If arc j is inoperable, the cost of transmission along arc j is u_j.

The goal is to route the message from source node to the sink node at the least cost. If no information can be obtained before routing the message, then a static routing model is used and results in the shortest expected path. Assuming that accurate information on the status of arc j can be obtained at a cost c_j, determining the cheapest way to route the message must include the cost of gathering information on the status of the network.

The question is which arcs should be tested. Balakrishnan et al. use dynamic programming to determine the optimal information-gathering and decision strategy. The dynamic programming formulation, however, requires storage that is exponential in the number of arcs in the network. To alleviate this problem, an alternative representation of the state space is presented, which works if the number of paths from the source node to the sink node is small. In this formulation, each element of the state space represents a path from the source to the sink. Since each path can have several lengths depending on the status of its links, there is an element of the state space for each length of each path. With this formulation of the state space, the information actions now consist of acquiring information on the length of an entire path.

Since the alternative formulation of the problem will only work in special cases, two heuristics are presented. The first heuristic is the value of information (VOI) heuristic. To determine the information structure, compare the cost of each experiment with the expected value of the information resulting from the experiment. If the cost of acquiring the information is greater than the value of the information for all of the experiments, then no more information is gathered; otherwise, choose the experiment that maximizes the difference between the value of the information and the cost of the experiment. This is a greedy approach and will produce only a locally optimal strategy, since the experiment choosen at each step is chosen independently of what experiments may be executed later.

The second heuristic is called the Best Case heuristic. The Best Case heuristic assumes that all of the arcs are operable and computes the shortest path. It then checks the path to ensure that all of the arcs are indeed operable. If any arc on this path is not operable, then its cost is updated from l_j to u_j, and the shortest path is recalculated. This process continues until a true shortest path is found.

Balakrishnan et al. evaluated a total of 2000 networks to observe the effect of arc failure probabilities and information acquisition cost on the performance of dynamic programming, the VOI heruistic, and the best case heuristic, compared to the static and dynamic models. They looked at networks with 4 nodes and 6 arcs, 5 nodes and 10 arcs, 10 nodes and 45 arcs, 15 nodes and 105 arcs and 20 nodes and 190 arcs, and they compared the total cost of using the various models with failure probabilities ranging from .1 to .9 and with information costs ranging from 1 to 10, and in almost every case, using partial information was found to be superior to using either no information or complete information.

4. MODEL EXTENSIONS

In most decision problems, time is a crucial factor, impacting the payoff function directly or creating a deadline for reaching a decision. Time dependent payoff functions and time constraints are two reasons for delegating information-gathering actions in the decision process, and it is the value of time, which results from people's impatience and their need to get answers quickly, that is the basis for parallel and concurrent processing. By extending the decision model to incorporate the effects of time on the decision process, we can develop a theory for concurrent or parallel processing. Developing SIMD algorithms is equivalent to determining a concurrent information-acquisition strategy, where every processor has the same set of actions A, the same cost function c(a) and the same time function t(a). In MIMD algorithms, each processor has its own set of actions A_i, but the same cost function c(a) and the same time function t(a). In both MIMD and SIMD algorithms, parallel computing theory ignores the question of when parallel computation is justifiable. Computing theory takes a problem solvable in O(g(n)) time by a sequential algorithm and tries to construct a parallel algorithm that solves the problem in O([1/h(n)] g(n)) time with h(n) processors (and where h(n) is a polynomial in n).

Because computing theory uses an order-of complexity measure, it can ignore the added cost of the parallel algorithm. A sequential strategy allows each next move to be made on the basis of all of the current information; whereas, a parallel process must communicate information plus handle other overhead. To trade the optimality of the sequential algorithm for the increased speed of a parallel algorithm makes sense only when the value of the time saved exceeds the added cost of running the algorithm in parallel.

Jacob [4] has started investigating an extension of the decision model that explicitly incorporates time. In this extension of the decision model, a decision is a function of nine parameters:

$$\mathbf{D} = < \mathbf{X}, \emptyset, D, \omega^{*}, A, \{\mathbf{M}_a | a \in A\}, c, t, T >$$

where $t: A \rightarrow \Re$ is the time required to perform action a, $a \in A$, and T is the total time allowable for gathering information. He uses the model to investigate the effects of a time constraint in a decision environment.

Jacob investigates a two processor decision environment where the human and the computer, designated information processors IP1 and IP2 respectively, work to solve a common problem. There is a common state space, but IP1 and IP2 each has its own set of actions, A_1 and A_2, cost functions, $c_1(a)$ and $c_2(a)$, and time functions, $t_1(a)$ and $t_2(a)$. The human initiates the decision problem and makes the final decision, and the optimal strategy may be sequential, concurrent or a mixture, and it may involve one or both processors. If both processors are involved, then communication points and the cost of communication must be included in determining the optimal strategy. The communication actions are considered part of the information-acquisition actions A_1 and A_2. A communication action refines the receiving agent's information structure, but does not refine the sender's information structure. Jacob uses the model to provide a basis for constructing admissible (good) dual processor strategies and identifies, based on the problem's characteristics, a category of strategies that dominates all other strategies. He applies the extended model to the only correct guesses count problem, a special case of the categorization problem, and prove sufficient conditions for an optimal strategy.

In extending the model to incorporate the effects of time on the decision process, the model was extended to allow multiple agents. Within the multiple agent model, two reasons (other than time) for delegating information acquisition actions can be investigated:

1. Delegation of the information-acquisition process to a processor (agent) that can perform a class of actions less expensively than other processors.
2. Delegation of the information-acquisition process to a processor that has specialized actions, unavailable to the other processors (e.g., an expert). This can be viewed as a special case of Reason 1 by setting the cost of a specialized action to infinity, $c(a) = \infty$, for non-experts. Marschak and Radner [6] term this specialization of action (information).

Within the multi-agent framework, we can investigate organizational structure and, as a special case, distributed processing.

In the distributed environment, the processors work jointly to solve a common problem. Each processor has its own partition of the state space based on what it knows about the environment. The processors are allowed to communicate with each other, as well as perform experiments to obtain more information about the true state of the world. We distinguish three classes of decision problems: one, where a single, fixed processor makes the final decision; two, where a group (or all) of the processors must reach a common decision, and three, where each processor must make a decision and the payoff of the decisions depend on the decision made by the other processors. (Note, the second class of problems is a special case of the third class of problems).

The first class of problems naturally fits within the extended framework of the model. Determining the multi-processor information and decision strategy is equivalent to determining when to delegate parts of the information-acquisition process to the other processors. The second and third classes of decision problems require a broader view of the state space. The state space must include knowledge (or possibly beliefs) about other agents' knowledge. A simple way to represent the meta-knowledge is for each agent to have multiple partitions of the state space. Sets of partitions represent different levels of knowledge. The first partition represents an agent's knowledge of the state of the world. The second set of partitions, one partition for every other agent in the system, represents the agent's knowledge of the other agents' knowledge, etc.

The need for the meta-knowledge arises from the interdependencies among the decisions. An agent's decision, d_i, depends on what processor i believes processor j's decision, d_j, will be, which in turn depends on processor j's beliefs about processor i's decision, and so on. The limit of processor i knows processor j knows processor i knows etc. is called common knowledge. In distributed computing theory, the question of when common knowledge is attainable arises in protocol design for problems that require cooperation or mutual agreement (e.g., the Byzantine General problem). We feel that the focus should instead be on what level of knowledge is required to make economically good decisions. And the Moore/Whinston [8] decision model is an appropriate framework for investigating the economic and decision theoretic issues in a distributed environment.

5. CONCLUSION

The types of problems, both proposed and under investigation, depict the range of research areas open to a decision theoretic approach. These areas are not exhaustive. Other areas of interest to DSS include learning, repetitive decision, and default reasoning. Management science and artificial intelligence dream of creating systems that learn. Buchanan and Feigenbaum [2] and Veelenturf [12] use inductive inference to teach computer systems to infer "breakage rules" for chemical molecules and puzzle solving heuristics. What they do not address is how much learning should take place before making a decision. Related to learning is the repetitive decision scenario. Decision support systems face the same decision problem (e.g., what toothpaste to buy) in possibly different environments. How much information should the system gather each time the decision is made? If relevant aspects of the environment are static, how much information should be gathered before the first decision and carried over for the other decisions? If information is used in later decisions, how should the cost be amortized. A third related area is default reasoning. The purpose of default reasoning is to reduce the cost of gathering information by assuming the answer to unexecuted experiments, so when to use default reasoning is a decision problem.

6. REFERENCES

[1] A. Balakrishnan, J.C. Moore, R. Pakath and A.B. Whinston, "Information Acquisition for Model Construction: An Integrative Decision-Theoretic Framework," Working Paper, Krannert Graduate School of Management, Purdue University, West Lafayette, IN, 1987.

[2] B.G. Buchanan and E.A. Feigenbaum, "Dendral and Meta-Dendral: Their Applications Dimension," *Artificial Intelligence*, Vol. 11, 1978, pp. 5-24.

[3] H.K. Hall, J.C. Moore and A.B. Whinston, "An Economic Basis for Expert Systems," Working Paper, Krannert Graduate School of Management, Purdue University, West Lafayette, IN, 1985.

[4] V.S. Jacob, "A Model of Decision-Making for the Integrated Human-Computer Information Processor," Ph.D. dissertation, Krannert Graduate School of Management, Purdue University, 1987.

[5] J. Marschak, "On Adaptive Programming," *Management Science,* " Vol. 9, No. 4, July 1963, pp. 517-526.

[6] J. Marschak and R. Radner, *Economic Theory of Teams*, Cowles Foundation, 1972.

[7] J.C. Moore, W.B. Richmond and A.B. Whinston, "A Decision Theoretic Approach to File Search," forthcoming in *Computer System in Economics and Management,* 1988.

[8] J.C. Moore and A.B. Whinston, "A Model for Decision-Making with Sequential Information-Acquisition - Part 1," *Decision Support Systems,* Vol. 2, No. 4, 1986, pp. 285-307.

[9] J.C. Moore and A.B. Whinston, "A Model for Decision-Making with Sequential Information-Acquisition - Part 2," *Decision Support Systems*, Vol. 3, No. 1, 1987, pp. 47-72.

[10] H. Raghavendra Rao, "A Decision Theoretic Perspective of Multiple Agent Problem Solving: Application to a Resource Allocation Problem," Ph.D. Thesis, Krannert Graduate School of Management, Purdue University, December 1987.

[11] H.R. Varian, *Microeconomic Analysis*, W. W. Norton & Co., New York, 1984.

[12] L.P.J. Veelenturf, "Inference of Sequential Machines from Sample Computations, *IEEE Trans. Comput.*, Vol. C-27, 1978, pp. 167-170.

FUZZY SET THEORY - AND INFERENCE MECHANISM

H.-J. Zimmermann, RWTH Aachen, 5100 Aachen (F.R.G.)

1. INTRODUCTION

Most of our traditional tools for formal modelling, reasoning, and computing are crisp, deterministic and precise in character. By crisp we mean dichotomous, that is, of yes-or-no-type rather than more-or-less type. In conventional dual logic, for instance, a statement can be true or false - and nothing in between. In set theory an element can either belong to a set or not, and in optimization a solution is either feasible or not. Precision assumes that the parameters of a model represent exactly either our perception of the phenomenon modelled or the features of the real system that has been modelled. Generally precision also implies that the model is unequivocal, that is , that it contains no ambiguities.

Certainty eventually indicates that we assume the structures and parameters of the model to be definitely known, and that there are no doubts about their values or their occurrence. If the model under consideration is a formal model [Zimmermann 1980, p. 127], that is, if it does not pretend to model reality adequately, then the model assumptions are in a sense arbitrary, that is, the model builder can freely decide which model characteristics he chooses. If, however, the model or theory asserts to be factual, that is, conclusions drawn from these models have a bearing on reality and they are supposed to model reality adequately, then the modelling language has

NATO ASI Series, Vol. F48
Mathematical Models for Decision Support
Edited by G. Mitra

to be suited to model the characteristics of the situation under study appropriately.

The usefulness of the mathematical language for modelling purposes is undisputed. However, there are limits of the usefulness and of the possibility of using the classical mathematical language, based on the dichotomous character of set theory, to model, in particular, systems and phenomena in the social sciences. "There is no idea or proposition in the field, which can not be put into mathematical language, although the utility of doing so can very well be doubted" [Brand 1961]. Schwarz [Schwarz 1962] brings up another argument against the unreflected use of mathematics, if he states: "An argument, which is only convincing if it is precise loses all its force if the assumptions on which it is based are sligthly changed, while an argument, which is convincing but imprecise may well be stable under small perturbations of its underlying axioms". For factual models or modelling languages two major complications arise:

1. Real situations are very often not crisp and deterministic and they cannot be described precisely,
2. The complete description of a real system often would rerequire by far more detailed data than a human being could ever recognize simultaneously, process and understand.

Let us consider characteristic features of real world systems again: Real situations are very often uncertain or vague in a number of ways. Due to lack of information the future state of the system might not be known completely. This type of uncertainty (stochastic character) has long been handled appropriately by probability theory and statistics. The Kolmogoroff type probability is essentially frequentistic and bases on set-theoretic considerations. Koopman`s probability refers to the truth of statements and therefore bases on logic. In both types of probabilistic approaches it is assumed, however, that the events (elements of sets) or the statements, respectively, are well defined. We shall call this type of uncertainty or vagueness stochastic uncertainty by contrast to the vagueness concerning the description of the semantic meaning of the events, phenomena or statements themselves, which we shall call fuzziness.
Fuzziness can be found in many areas of daily life, such as in engineering [see, f.i., Blockley 1980], in medicine [see Vila, Delgado 1983], in meteorology [Cao, Chen 1983], in manufacturing [Mamdani 1981] and others. It is particularly frequent, however, in all areas in which human judgment, evaluation, and decisions are important. These are the areas of decision making, reasoning, learning, and so on. Some reasons for this have already been mentioned. Others are, that most of our daily communication uses "natural languages" and a good part of our thinking is done in it. In these natural languages the meaning of words is very often vague. The meaning of a word might even be well defined, but when using the word as a label for a set, the boundaries within which objects belong to the set or do not, become fuzzy or vague. Examples are words such as "birds" (how about penguins, bats, etc.?), "red roses", but also terms such as "tall men", "beautiful women", "creditwor-

thy customer". In this context we can probably distinguish two kinds of fuzziness with respect to their origins: Intrinsic fuzziness and informational fuzziness. The former is illustrated by "tall men". This term is fuzzy because the meaning of tall is fuzzy and dependent on the context (height of observer, culture etc.). An example of the latter is the term "creditworthy customers": A creditworthy customer can possibly be described completely and crisply if we use a large number of descriptors. These are more, however, than a human being could handle simultaneously. Therefore the term, which in psychology is called a "subjective category" becomes fuzzy. One could imagine that the subjective category creditworthiness is decomposed into two smaller subjective categories, each of which needs fewer descriptors to be completely described. This process of decomposition could be continued until the descriptions of the subjective categories generated are reasonably defined. On the other hand, the notion "creditworthiness" could be constructed by starting with the smallest subjective subcategories and aggregating them hierarchically.

1.2 Basic Definitions of Fuzzy Set Theory

The first publications in fuzzy set theory by Zadeh [Zadeh 1965] and Goguen [Goguen 1967, 1968] show the intention of the authors to generalize the classical notion of a set and a proposition (statement) to accomodate fuzziness in the sense described in paragraph 1.1.

Zadeh [Zadeh 1965, p. 339] writes: "The notion of a fuzzy set provides a convenient point of departure for the construction of a conceptual framework which parallels in many respects the framework used in the case of ordinary sets, but is more general than the latter and, potentially, may prove to have a much wider scope of applicability, particularly in the fields of pattern classification and information processing. Essentially, such a framework provides a natural way of dealing with problems in which the source of imprecision is the absence of sharply defined criteria of class membership rather than the presence of random variables".

"Imprecision" here is meant in the sense of vagueness rather than the lack of knowledge about the value of a parameter as in tolerance analysis. Fuzzy set theory provides a strict mathematical framework (there is nothing fuzzy about fuzzy set theory!) in which vague conceptual phenomena can be precisely and rigorously studied. It can also be considered as a modeling language well suited for situations in which fuzzy relations, criteria, and phenomena exist.

A classical (crisp) set is normaly defined as a collection of elements or objects $x \in X$ which can be finite, countable, or overcountable. Each single element can either belong to or not belong to a set A, $A \subseteq X$. In the former case, the statement "x belongs to A is true, whereas in the latter case this statement is false.

Such a classical set can be described in different ways; either one can enumerate (list) the elements that belong to the set, one can describe the set analytically, for instance, by stating conditions for membership ($A = \{x \| x \leq 5\}$) or one can define the member elements by using the characteristic function, in which 1 indicates membership and 0 non-membership. For a fuzzy set, the characteristic function allows various degrees of membership for the elements to a given set.

Definition 1:
If X is a collection of objects denoted generically by x then a fuzzy set $\tilde{A}$ in X is a set of ordered pairs:

$$\tilde{A} = \{x, \mu_{\tilde{A}}(x)) \| x \in X\}.$$

$\mu_{\tilde{A}}(x)$ is called the membership function or grade of membership (also degree of compatibility or degree of truth) of x in $\tilde{A}$ which maps X to the membership space M. (When M contains only the two points 0 and 1, $\tilde{A}$ is nonfuzzy and $\mu_{\tilde{A}}(x)$ is identical to the characteristic function of a non-fuzzy set.). The range of the mmbership function is a subset of the nonnegative real numbers whose supremum is finite. Elements with a zero degree of membership are normally not listed.

Example 2:
A realtor wants to classify the houses he offers to his clients. One indicator of comfort of these houses is the number of bedrooms in it. Let X = {1,2,3,4...10} be the set of available types of houses described by x = number of bedrooms in a house. Then the fuzzy set "comfortable type of house for a 4-person family" may be described as

$$\tilde{A} = \{(1,.2),(2,.5),(3,.8),(4,1),(5,.7),(6,.3)\}.$$

Definition 2:
The support of a fuzzy set $\tilde{A}$, $S(\tilde{A})$, is the crisp set of all $x \in X$ such that $\mu_{\tilde{A}}(x) > 0$.

Definition 3:
The (crisp) set of elements which belong to the fuzzy set $\tilde{A}$ at least to the degree α is called the α-level-set:

$A_\alpha = \{x \in X \| \mu_{\tilde{A}}(x) \geq \alpha\}$
$A_\alpha = \{x \in X \| \mu_{\tilde{A}}(x) > \alpha\}$ is called "strong α-level-set" or "strong α-cut".

Operations with fuzzy sets are defined via their membership functions. We first list those definitions which were already defined by Zadeh [Zadeh 1965] and which nowadays constitute the formal framework of what is called "Possibility Theory".

Definition 4:
The membership function $\mu_{\tilde{C}}(x)$ of the intersection of two fuzzy sets, $\tilde{A}$ and $\tilde{B}$, is defined by

$$\mu_{\tilde{C}}(x) = \min\{\mu_{\tilde{A}}(x), \mu_{\tilde{B}}(x)\}.$$

The reader should realize that the set-theoretic intersection corresponds to the logical "and".

Definition 5:
The membership function $\mu_{\tilde{D}}(x)$ of the union of two fuzzy sets $\tilde{A}$ and $\tilde{B}$ is defined by

$$\mu_{\tilde{D}} = \max \{\mu_{\tilde{A}}(x), \mu_{\tilde{B}}(x)\}.$$

This corresponds to the "inclusive or" in logic.

1.3 Special Fuzzy Sets

Within the last 20 years numerous special notions of fuzzy sets have been suggested. For our purposes two are of particular interest: Fuzzy numbers and linguistic variables.

Definition 6:
A linguistic variable is characterized by a quintuple $(x, T(x), U, \tilde{G}, M)$ in which x is the name of the variable; T(x) (or simply T) denotes the term-set of x, that is, the set of names of linguistic values of x, with each value being a fuzzy variable denoted generically by x and ranging over a universe of discourse U which is associated with the base variable u; $\tilde{G}$ is a syntactic rule (which usually has the form of a grammar) for generating the name, x, of values of x; and M is a semantic rule for associating with each x its meaning, M(x) which is a fuzzy subset of U. A particular x, that is a name generated by $\tilde{G}$, is called a term. It should be noted that the base variable u can also be vector-valued.
In order to facilitate the symbolism in the following some symbols will have two meanings wherever clarity allows this: x will denote the name of the variable ("the label") and the generic name of its values. The same will be true for X, and M(x).

The following example illustrates the notion of a linguistic variable:

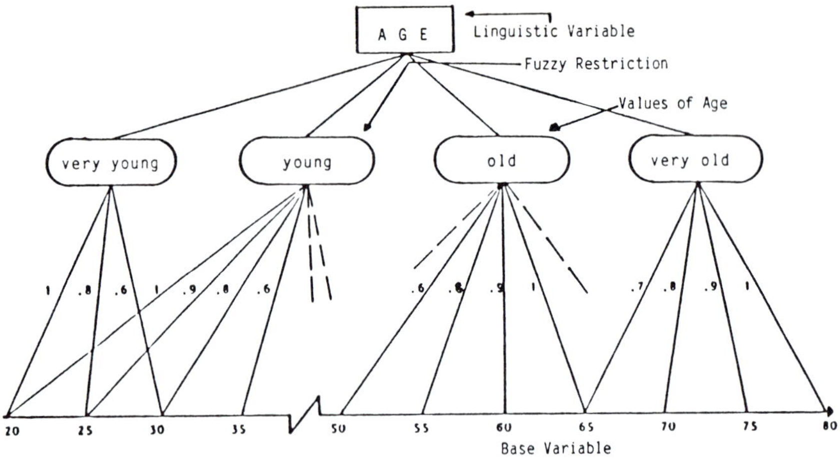

Figure 1: Linguistic Variable Age

<u>Definition 7:</u> [Zimmermann 1985, p. 51]
A fuzzy number $\tilde{M}$ is a convex normalized fuzzy set $\tilde{M}$ of the real line $\mathbb{R}$ such that

1. There exists exactly one $x_o \in R \mu_{\tilde{M}}(x_o)=1$ (x_o is called the mean value of $\tilde{M}$).
2. $\mu_{\tilde{M}}(x)$ is piecewise continuous.

The following figure illustrates the fuzzy number "approximately 5":

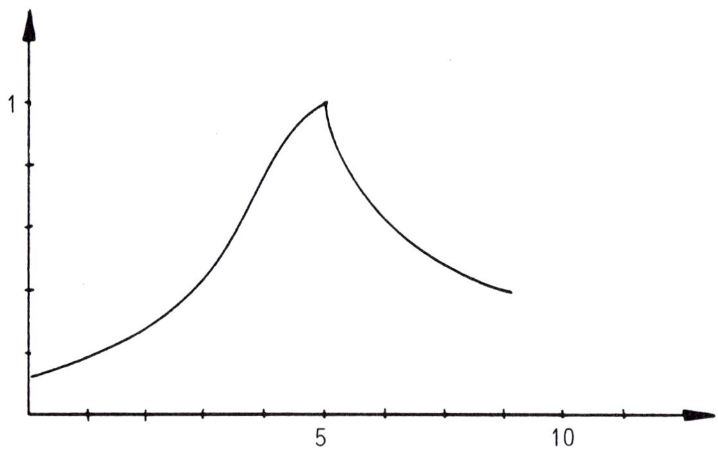

Figure 2: Fuzzy Number "approximately 5"

1.4 Operators and Membership Functions

Obviously the crucial element of a fuzzy set of whatever kind is the membership function. Methods have been designed to determine membership functions empirically [Zimmermann 1987 pp. 197]. Often they are computed on the basis of formal assumptions. It is important to realized which type of membership function is available. In some cases it is sufficient to know the grades of membership of the elements of discrete fuzzy sets, which cannot be interpolated. In other cases it is absolutely necessary to know the membership function analytically. For the second case the function

$$\mu_{\tilde{c}}(x) = {}^{o}\lceil ((1+e^{-a(x-b)})^{-1} - c)\, 1/d + \tfrac{1}{2} \rceil^{1} \qquad (1)$$

has proven to have particularly advantages properties [Zimmermann 1985, pp. 322].

At the beginning of section 1.2 it was mentioned that the possibilistic operators "min" and "max" as models for intersection and union, respectively, correspond to the logical "and" and "or". In the meantime numerous other mathematical models have been suggested as alternatives for "min" and "max" and it has also been shown empirically that "min" and "max" are not very suitable models for the linguistic "and" and "or", used in human communication. To illustrate the variety of suggestions we cite some other mathematical models for the intersection operator:

For the sake of space efficiency we only show definitions for the intersection (and-connective) and general connectives, including the logical "and" and "or". The union (or)-connectives are defined accordingly.

Let us denote the degree of membership of fuzzy set $\tilde{A}$ by x and that of $\tilde{B}$ by y.

The alternative definitions of the membership functions of $\tilde{A} \cap \tilde{B}$ for binary operations are:

$$\mu(\tilde{A} \cap \tilde{B}) = \min(x,y)$$

$$= x \bullet y \qquad \text{(Zadeh)}$$

$$= \max(0, x+y-1) \qquad \text{(Giles)}$$

$$= 1-\min(1, [(1-x)^p + (1-y)^p]^{1/p}) \quad p \geq 0 \qquad \text{(Yager)}$$

$$= \gamma \min(x,y) + (1-\gamma)\tfrac{1}{2}(x+y), \quad \gamma \in [0,1] \qquad \text{(Werners)}$$

$$= \frac{x\,y}{\gamma + (1-\gamma)(x+y-xy)} \qquad \text{(Hamacher)}$$

Empirical research indicates [Zimmermann, Zysno] that the "linguistic and" as expression of aggregation of information, evaluations etc. can be considered as an operator between the extremes of the logical "and" and the "inclusive or". It is, therefore, not particularly meaningsful to use different mathematical models for "and" and "or", but rather to model the aggregation operation as one parametrized expression. Models of that type which have performed particularly well empirically are:

$$\mu(\tilde{A} \cap \tilde{B}) = (xy)^{(1-\gamma)} (1-[(1-x)(1-y)])^{\gamma} \quad \gamma \in [0,1] \quad \text{(Zimmermann, Zysno)}$$

$$\mu(\tilde{A} \cap \tilde{B}) = \min(x,y)+(1-\gamma)\max(x,y).$$

These connectives are normally called "compensatory and".

2. MAJOR APPROACHES FOR REASONING

2.1 Dual and Multi-Valued Logic

Logic as bases for reasoning can be distinguished essentially by their three topic-neutral (context-independent) items [Mamdani, Efstathiou 1984], truth values, vocabularly (operators), and reasoning procedure (tautologies, syllogisms). In Boolean logic truth values can be 0 (false) or 1 (true) and by means of these truth values the vocabularies (operators) are defined via truth tables.

A	B	$\wedge$	$\vee$	(x)∇	=>	<=>	?
1	1	1	1	0	1	1	1
1	0	0	1	1	0	0	1
0	1	0	1	1	1	0	0
0	0	0	0	0	1	1	0

There are $2^{2^2} = 16$ truth tables, each defining an operator. Assigning meaning (words) to these operators is not difficult for the first 4 or 5 columns: The first obviously characterizes the "and", the second the "inclusive or", the third the "exclusive or", and the fourth and fifth the implication and the equivalence. We will have difficulties, however, interpreting the remaining 9 columns in terms of our language. If we have three statements rather than two, this task, assigning meanings to truth tables, becomes even more difficult.

2.2 Fuzzy Logic

So far it has been assumed that each statement, A and B, could clearly be classified as true or false. If this is no longer true, then additional truth values, such as "undecided" or similar, can and have to be introduced, which leads to the many existing systems of multi-valued logic. It is not difficult to see how the above-mentioned problems of two valued logic in

"labelling" truth tables or operators increase as we move to multi-valued logic. For only two statements and three possible truth values there are already $3^{3^{3}} = 729$ truth tables! The uniqueness of interpretation of truth tables which is convenient in Boolean logic disappears immediately because many truth tables in 3-valued logic look very much alike.
The third topic-neutral item of logical systems is the reasoning procedure itself which generally bases on tautologies such as:

modus ponens: $(A \quad (A \Rightarrow B)) \Rightarrow B$

modus tollens: $((A \Rightarrow B) \wedge \neg B) \Rightarrow \neg A$

syllogism: $((A \Rightarrow B) \wedge (B \Rightarrow C)) \Rightarrow (A \Rightarrow C)$

contraposition: $(A \Rightarrow B) \Rightarrow (\neg B \Rightarrow A)$

Let us consider the modus ponens which could be interpreted as "If A is true and if the statement "If A is true then B is true" is also true, then B is true". The above mentioned tautologies obviously depend on the character of the statements, the type of permissible truth values, the definition of the operators. They assume that, for instance, all A`s contained in one tautology are identical. The respective assumptions made in dual logic are gradually relaxed in fuzzy logic, approximate reasoning and plausible reasoning.

Fuzzy logic [Zadeh 1973a, p. 10] is an extension of the set-theoretic multi-valued logic in which the truth values are linguistic variables (or terms of the linguistic variable truth).

Since operators, like $\vee$, $\wedge$, $\neg$, $\Rightarrow$ in fuzzy logic are also defined by using truth tables, the extension principle can be aplied to derive definitions of the operators. So far possibility theory has primarily been used in order to define operators in fuzzy logic, even though other operators have also been investigated [see, for instance, Mizumoto, Zimmermann 1982] and could also be used. Here we will limit considerations to possibilistic interpretations of linguistic variables and we will also stick to the original proposals of Zadeh [1973a]. To the interested reader, however, we suggest to study also alternative aproaches such as [Baldwin 1979], [Baldwin and Pilsworth 1980], [Giles 1979, 1980] and others.
It was already mentioned above, that in the truth tables of fuzzy logic the truth values (in dual logic 0 or 1) are terms of the linguistic variable "truth". This variable has been defined differently by different authors.

Figure 3 shows graphically the definitions of Baldwin [1979, p. 316].

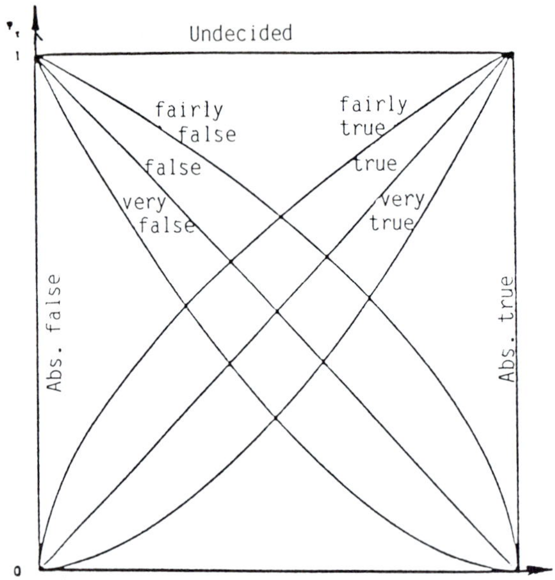

Figure 3: Linguistic Variable Truth

2.3 Approximate and Plausible Reasoning

Approximate and plausible reasoning are ways of drawing conclusions from hypothesis which relax even more assumptions of dual logic than fuzzy logic.

On the basis of what has been said so far two quite obvious generalizations of the modus ponens, for example, are:
1. to allow statements which are characterized by fuzzy sets
2. to relax (slightly) the identity of the "A`s" and "B`s" in the implication and the conclusion.

In approximate reasoning the statements in the antecedents are allowed to contain fuzzy sets rather than crisp statements.

In 1973 Zadeh suggested the compositional rule of inference for the above-mentioned type of fuzzy conditional inference. In the meantime other authors (f.i. [Baldwin 1979], [Baldwin and Pilsworth 1980], [Baldwin and Guild 1980], [Mizumoto et al. 1979], [Mizumoto, Zimermann 1982], [Tsukamoto 1979]) have suggested different methods and investigated also the modus tollens, syllogism, and contraposition. Here, however, we shall restrict considerations to Zadeh`s compositional rule of inference.

<u>Definition 8:</u>
Let $\tilde{R}(x)$ and $\tilde{R}(y)$, $x \in X$, $y \in Y$, be fuzzy sets in X, Y, and $\tilde{R}(x,y)$ a fuzzy relation in XxY, respectively. $\tilde{A}$ and $\tilde{B}$ denote particular fuzzy sets in X and XxY. The compositional rules of inference asserts that the solution of the system $\tilde{R}(x) = \tilde{A}$ and $\tilde{R}(x,y) = \tilde{B}$ is given by $\tilde{R}(y) = \tilde{A} \circ \tilde{B}$, where $\tilde{A} \circ \tilde{B}$ is the min max composition of $\tilde{A}$ and $\tilde{B}$.

Plausible reasoning goes one step further and relaxes slightly the identity of the elements in the facts and the rules and tries to still arrive at conclusions on the basis of the generalized modus ponens.

Let $\tilde{A}$, $\tilde{A}$\`, $\tilde{B}$, $\tilde{B}$\`be fuzzy statements, then the generalized modus ponens reads:

Premise	x is $\tilde{A}$\`
Implication	If x is $\tilde{A}$ then y is $\tilde{B}$
Conclusion	y is $\tilde{B}$\`

For instance [Mizumoto, Zimmermann 1982]

Premise	This tomato is very red
Implication	If a tomato is red then the tomato is ripe
Conclusion	This tomato is very ripe.

It should be mentioned, however, that the generalized modus ponens alone, which characterizes "plausible reasoning", does not allow to obtain conclusions from unequal premises. Such an inference presupposes or necessitates the knowledge about modifications of the premises and their consequences. (For instance, that increase in "redness" indicates an increase in "ripeness" (see [Dubois, Prade 1984, p. 325]).

3. FUZZY LANGUAGES

Fuzzy languages are formal languages on the basis of fuzzy logic and approximate reasoning. Quite a number of them have been developed in the meantime. They vary with respect to method and scope of treating fuzziness and uncertainty. They also differ from each other in their user friendliness, i.e. whether they constitute just a formal language or whether they are more an AI-tool. Without being exhaustive we mention a few: Fuzzy Planner [Kling 1973], FLIP [Giles 1980], LPL [Adamo 1980], FRIL [Baldwin 1985], SLOP [Baldwin 1986], FLOPS [Buckley 1986], and SPII-1 [Martin-Clouaire, Prade 1986]. One of them, VLSI, is even a hardware implementation on a chip [Togai, Watanabe 1986].

We shall restrict our considerations here to PRUF, a meaning representation language on the basis of possibility theory which was developed by Zadeh [Zadeh 1981].

PRUF may be employed as a language for the presentation of imprecise knowledge and as a means of precisiation of fuzzy propositions expressed in a natural language. In essence, PRUF bears the same relationship to fuzzy logic that predicate calculus does to two-valued logic. Thus it serves to translate a set of premises expressed in natural language into expressions in PRUF to which the rules of inference of fuzzy logic or approximate reasoning may be applied. This yields other expressions in PRUF which can then be retranslated into natural language and become the conclusions inferred from the original premises.

The main constituents of PRUF are

1. a collection of translation rules and
2. a set of rules of inference.

The latter corresponds essentially to fuzzy logic and approximate reasoning.

The former will be sketched in the following:

The following types of fuzzy expressions will be considered:

1. Fuzzy propositions such as "All students are young", "X is much larger than Y", and "If Hans is healthy then Biggi is happy".
2. Fuzzy descriptors such as tall men, rich people, small integers, most, several, or few.
3. Fuzzy questions.

Fuzzy questions are reformulated in such a way that additional translation rules for questions are unneccesary. Questions such as "How A is B?" will be expressed in the form "B is ?A", where B is the body of the question and "?A" indicates the form of an admissible answer, which can be: A possibility distribution (indicated as π); a truth value (indicated as τ); a probability value (indicated as λ); a possibility value (indicated as ω).

The question "How tall is Paul?" to which a possibility distribution is expected as an answer, is phrased "Paul is ?π" (rather than "How tall is Paul?π). Is it true that Katrin is pretty?" would than be expressed as "Katrin is pretty?τ" and "Where is the car?ω" as "The car is?ω".

PRUF is an intentional language, that is, an expression in PRUF is supposed to convey the intended rather than the literal meaning of the corresponding expression in a natural language. Transformations of expressions are also intended to be meaning-preserving. Translation rules are applied singly or in combination to yield an expression, E, in PRUF which is a translation of a given expression, e, in a natural language. The most important basic categories of translation rules in PRUF are:

Type I	Rules pertaining to modification
Type II	Rules pertaining to composition
Type III	Rules pertaining to quantification
Type IV	Rules pertaining to qualification.

Examples of propositions to which these rules apply are the following [Zadeh 1981, p. 29].

Type 1. X is very small
X is much larger than Y.
Eleanor was very upset.
The man with the blond hair is very tall.

Type II X is small and Y is large.
(conjunctive composition)
X is small or Y is large.
(disjunctive composition)
If X is small then Y is large.
(conditional composition)
If X is smal then Y is large else.
(conditional and conjunctive composition)

Type III Most Swedes are tall.
Many men are much taller than most men.
Most tall men are very intelligent.

Type IV Abe is young is not very true.
(truth qualification)
Abe is young is quite probable.
(probability qualification)
Abe is young is almost impossible.
(possibility qualification).

Of particular interest from the point of view of the contributions related to expert systems are the rules of type IV. They shall, therefore, be described here, even though they are not independent of the rules of type III.

In PRUF the concept of truth serves to make statements about the relative truth of a proposition p with respect to another reference proposition (and not with respect to reality!). Truth is taken to be a linguistic variable such as defined before. Truth is then interpreted as the consistency of proposition p with proposition q. If

$$p \hat{=} N \text{ is } F \rightarrow \pi_p = \tilde{F}$$

$$q \hat{=} N \text{ is } G \rightarrow \pi_q = \tilde{G}$$

then the consistency of p with q is given as

$$\text{cons}\ \{N \text{ is } \tilde{F} \| N \text{ is } \tilde{G}\} \hat{=} \text{Poss}\{N \text{ is } \tilde{F} \| N \text{ is } \tilde{G}\} =$$

$$= \sup_{u \in U} \{\min(\mu_{\tilde{F}}(w), \mu_{\tilde{G}}(w)\}.$$

The main purpose of this contribution is to provide the bases for the following other two presentations of the author on decision support systems and uncertainty in expert systems. There the reader will find some more justifications for notions defined here.

References:

Baldwin, J.F.: A New Approach to Approximate Reasoning Using a Fuzzy Logic, in: Fuzzy Sets and Systems 2 (1979), pp. 309-325.

Baldwin, J.F., Guild, N.C.F.: Feasible Algorithms for Approxi- Approximate Reasoning Using Fuzzy Logic, in: Fuzzy Sets and Systems 3 (1980), pp. 225-251.

Baldwin, J.F., Pilsworth, B.W.: Fuzzy Truth Definition of Possibility Measure for Decision Classifica tion, in: In. J. Man-Machine Studies I (1979), pp. 447-463.

Bellman, R., Zadeh, L.A.: Decision Making in a Fuzzy Environment, in: Management Science 17 (1970), pp. B141-164.

Blockley, D.I.: The Nature of Structural Design and Safety. Chichester 1980.

Brand, H.W.: The Fecundity of Mathematical Methods, Dordrecht 1961.

Cao, H., Chen, G.: Some Applications of Fuzzy Sets to Meteorological Forecasting, in: Fuzzy Sets and Systems 9 (1983), pp. 1-12.

Giles, R.: A Formal System for Fuzzy Reasoning, in: Fuzzy Sets and Systems 2 (1979), pp. 233-257.

Giles, R.: A Computer Program for Fuzzy Reasoning, in: Fuzzy Sets and Systems 4 (1980), pp. 221-234.

Goguen, J.A.: L-Fuzzy Sets, in: JMAA 18 (1967), pp. 145-174.

Goguen, J.A.: The Logic of Inexact Concepts, Synthese 19 (1969), pp. 325-373.

Mamdani, E.H.: Advances in the Linguistic Synthesis of Fuzzy Controllers, in: Mamdani, Gaines (eds.), 1981, pp. 325-334.

Mamdani, E.H., Efstathiou, H.J.: A Comparative Study of Applied Logics, in: Fuzzy Sets and Systems (1984)

Mizumoto, M., Fukami, S., Tanaka, K.: Some Methods of Fuzzy Reasoning, in: Gupta et al. (eds.), 1979, pp. 117-136.

Mizumoto, M., Zimmermann, H.-J.: Comparison of Fuzzy Reasoning Methods, in: Fuzzy Sets and Systems 8 (1982), pp. 253-283.

Schwartz, J.: The Pernicious Influence of Mathematics in Science, in: Nagel, E., Suppes, P., Traski, A. (eds.): Logic Methodology and Philisophy of Science, Stanford 1962.

Tsukamoto, Y.: An Approach to Fuzzy Reasoning Method, in: Guppta et al. (eds.) 1979, pp. 137-149.

Vila, M.A., Delgado, M.: On Mecial Diagnosis Using Possibility Measures, in: Fuzzy Sets and Systems 10 (1983), pp. 211-222.

Werners, B.: Interaktive Entscheidungsunterstützung durch ein flexibles mathematisches Programmierungssystem, Dissertation, Aachen 1984.

Zadeh, L.A.: Fuzzy Sets, in: Information and Control 8 (1965), pp. 338-353.

Zadeh, L.A.: The Concept of a Linguistic Variable and Its Application to Approximate Reasoning Memorandum ERL-M 411, Berkeley, October 1973 (a).

Zadeh, L.A.: Outline of a New Approach to the Analysis of Complex Systems and Decision Processes, in: IEEE IEEE Trans. Vol. SMC 3 (1973b), pp. 28-44.

Zadeh, L.A.: Test-Score: Semantics for Natural Languages and Meaning Representation via PRUF, in: Techn. Note 247, SRI, 1981.

Zadeh, L.A.: The Role of Fuzzy Logic in the Management of Uncertainty in Expert Systems, in: Fuzzy Sets and Systems 11 (1983), pp. 199-227.

Zimmermann, H.-J.: Testability and Meaning of Mathematical Models in Social Sciences, in: Mathematical Modeling 1 (1980), pp. 123-139.

Zimmermann, H.-J., Zadeh, L.A., Gaines, B.R. (eds.): Fuzzy Sets and Decision Analysis, Amsterdam, New York Oxford 1984.

Zimmermann, H-J., Zysno, P.: Decisions and Evaluations by Hierarchical Aggregation of Information, in: Fuzzy Sets and Systems 10 (1983), pp. 243-266.

Zimermann, H.-J., Zysno, P.: Latent Connectives in Human Decision Making, in: Fuzzy Sets and Systems 4 (1980), pp. 37-51.

Zimmermann, H-J.: Fuzzy Set Theory - And Its Applications, Boston, Dordrecht, Lancaster 1985.

Zimmermann, H.-J.: Fuzzy Sets, Decision Making and Expert Systems, Boston, Dordrecht, Lancaster 1987.

SECTION 9:

SUMMARY OF SOFTWARE PRODUCTS

LIST OF SOFTWARE SUMMARIES

1. Name of the System: CAMPS

2. Author/Developer: Cormac Lucas and Gautam Mitra
Brunel University, Kingston Lane
Uxbridge, Middlesex, UB8 3PH, UK

3. Brief Outline

Computer assisted mathematical programming (modelling) system: CAMPS is designed to support construction, investigation and analysis of linear, integer and nonlinear (special ordered sets) programming models. A number of model management functions covering data tables, generated models, output solution, analysis, reports, model documentation are also supported by CAMPS. FORTLP linear and integer programming system is used as the optimisation module within CAMPS to process the generated models. The primary aim of CAMPS is to provide assistance to the modeller so that he can develop and refine his model and present it to a computer with the minimum of inconvenience. Thus CAMPS allows the modeller to communicate his requirements via a set of menu options. The modeller is considered to possess quantitative modelling skills and is not necessarily an expert in computer programming. He conceives and states mathematically his model and the system assists him in communicating this to the computer.

4. Domain of application

Linear, discrete and (a restricted sub-class of) nonlinear optimisation problems. These problems may be modelled and solved.

5. Implementation Language

FORTRAN 77 and C.

6. Hardware and Operating System

The system is designed to be easily portable under PC-DOS, UNIX and other industry standard operating systems. Currently the system runs under PC-DOS, RT/PC-AIX, UNIX and VAX-VMS.

7. Special Features

The system may be used with other optimisers. For input CAMPS generates MPSX standard models. Internal model formats and solution formats can also be interfaced.

8. Price and Terms of Installation

(a) The user manual and a demonstration version can be purchased for £50.
(b) Different module prices and costs of upgrades are supplied on application.
(c) Academic discount is available, details on application.

9. Available from:

Europe:
Dr S Hague, NAG Limited, Mayfield House
256 Banbury Road, Oxford, OX2 7DE, United Kingdom

BCAMPS.CL

1. Name of the System: EXPERT CHOICE - version 5.2

2. Author/Developer: Decision Support Software Inc
1300 Vincent Place
McLean, Va. 22101, U S A

3. Brief Outline:

Expert Choice, a microcomputer software program, assists decision makers by organizing complex problems, communicating the results and justifying the rationale for decisions. It provides a logical and powerful framework for comparing many alternative courses of action when confronted with numerous conflicting criteria. Expert Choice is an expert support system that facilitates insight into a problem by amplifying the expertise of the decision maker. Designed to increase productivity, not to replace the decision maker, Expert Choice is a tool that enhances one's problems solving capabilities.

Expert Choice's structured approach to complex decisions accommodates both quantitative data and subjective judgments. It lets the decision maker graphically portray a complex problem in the form of a hierarchy. This structure has been proven to be one of the most natural and powerful ways for people to organize complexity. Expert Choice differs from conventional decision analysis techniques by not requiring numerical guesses. It reduces the decision process to its simplest terms - paired comparisons (comparing two items at a time with respect to some criterion).

4. Domain of application:

Expert Choice has been successfully applied to business decisions such as strategic planning, acquisitions and mergers, site selection, product mix decisions, marketing strategies and employee evaluation; to political and government decisions, such as tax policy, arbitration, international trade policy, evaluating proposals, and arms limitation agreements; and to personal decisions such as, career planning and marriage counselling.

5. Implementation Language: Complied Basic and Assembler

6. Hardware and Operating System:

Expert Choice runs on the IBM PC, XT, AT, and PS/2 series as well as 100% compatible, and requires IBM PC DOS 3.1 or later. If used on a PC or XT, Expert Choice requires two disk drives. Expert Choice can be installed on to a fixed disk and supports all printers. A graphics card is needed to view the sensitivity analysis.

7. Special Features:

Expert Choice enables the decision maker to structure a model consisting of a goal, scenarios, criteria and alternatives; then the decision maker provides judgments about the relative importance of criteria, about likelihood of scenarios, and about the preference for alternatives with respect to each criterion. Subjective judgments can be applied in a systematic way even when there is no tradional scale of measurement. The process is so natural that no time is wasted learning a new way of thinking.

Expert Choice synthesizes both quantitative information and qualitative judgments to produce a graphic display of the alternatives' rankings and priorities. Expert Choice also provides a measure of consistency which helps to validate the decision maker's judgments as well as the results.

The documentation produced by Expert Choice serves as an excellent vehicle for communicating a recommended decision. Lengthy reports and issue papers can be replaced by succinct Expert Choice reports. Thus, an executive can examine Expert Choice reports, quickly glean the reasoning that led to the decision, and request additional or substantiating information for those judgments deemed to be most critical or controversial.

When used in a group decision setting, Expert Choice facilitates communication and permits a full range of considerations to be taken into account succinctly and comprehensively. No longer will group discussions drift from topic to topic with little chance of reaching consensus. Because Expert Choice minimizes the bandwagon effect (dominance by a strong member of the group), discussions can focus in turn on each facet of a problem. Thos most knowledgeable about a particular facet of the problem will find it easy to share their expertise with others in the group.

Judgments can be expressed in any of three ways - numerically, verbally or graphically. Expert Choice has a unique method of using redundancy to derive weights that more accurately reflect the decision maker's perceptions than any other known approach. Expert Choice's features include what-if and sensitivity analyses, facilities for identifying and reducing inconsistency, and a ratings module for use when a large number of alternatives are being evaluated. There are extensive help screens, as well as facilities to create, modify, and combine models. Information from data bases and spreadsheet models can be organized and accessed with Expert Choice's "node pads". This facility is also useful for recording the rationale for the decision makers' judgments.

8. Price and terms of installation: $495.00 - purchase price.

9. Available from: Decision Support Software, Inc.
1300 Vincent Place
McLean, Va. 22101, U S A

enatosft.exp

1. Name of the System: FORTLP

2. Author/Developer:

Gautam Mitra and Mehrdad Tamiz
Brunel University, Kingston Lane,
Uxbridge, Middlesex, UB8 3PH, UK.

3. Brief Outline:

FORTLP is a linear programming system with integer and other nonlinear programming capabilities. It can be installed and run as an integrated optimiser or it may be used as a modular suite of subroutines. The system exploits super sparse data structures and dynamic storage management techniques. FORTLP is designed to be main memory resident and provides efficient and robust performance on 16-bit micros, minis and large main frames. It accepts problem data in the MPSX format and uses the simple upper bound representation implicitly. The algorithmic subroutines use many advanced features of sparse simplex solution methods. Reinversion of the basis matrix is carried out by using lower block triangular restructuring and an elimination form of the the inverse. Medium size problems (5000 rows, 10,000 columns and 90,000 non-zero elements) have been processed by the system.

4. Domain of Application:

Linear, discrete and nonlinear optimisation problems. Applications can be constructed by using the complementary modelling system CAMPS.

5. Implementation Language:

FORTRAN 77. Plan for revision using FORTRAN 8X is under construction.

6. Hardware and Operating System:

The system design takes into account 8-bit byte, 16-bit half word and 32-bit full word memory structure. It can run on any machine/operating system which has a suitable Fortran 77 compiler. Use of floating point processor is strongly recommended. The system runs under ICL 2980, PERQ, VAX under VMS or UNIX, PRIME under PRIMOS, IBM PC under PC-DOS, IMB RT/PC-AIX.

7. Special Features:

The system may be exploited in one of the following three modes:-

(i) stand alone optimiser,
(ii) optimiser sub-system within CAMPS,
(iii) as a suite of user callable subroutines driven by a main Fortran program.

8. Price and Terms of Installation

(a) The user manual and a demonstration version can be purchased for £60.
(b) Different module prices for annual licence will be supplied on application.
(c) Academic discount is available, details on application.

9. Available from:

Europe: Dr S Hague, NAG Ltd., Mayfield House
256 Banbury Road, Oxford, OX2 7DE, UK

US:

DFORTLEX.MT

1. Name of System: GAMS

2. Author/Developer: J J Bisschop, A Drud and A Meeraus

3. Brief Outline

The GAMS system offers a symbolic modeling language for the representation of large-scale mathematical programming models. The system is made up of seven sections, namely: SETS; TABLES; VARIABLES; EQUATIONS; MODEL EQUATIONS; SOLVE AGAMS MODEL; and DISPLAY. Exception handling can be done in almost any part of GAMS Model. It can be used to specify subsets, to specify which blocks of data are to be used, and to delete beforehand some redundant parts of an optimisation problem. The modeller can also formulate starting bases and has direct access to the optimisation results.

4. Domain of Application

Linear, discrete and non-linear optimisation problems may be modelled and solved.

5. Implementation Language

FORTRAN and Assembler.

6. Hardware and Operating System

The system runs on mainframes and PCs.

7. Special Features

The system provides an automated interface with several solution algorithms.

8. Price and Terms of Installation

9. Available from:

Dr A Meeraus
Analytic Support Unit
Development Research Department
The World Bank
1818 High Street, N W
Washington DC 20433
U S A

enatosft.jjb

1. System Name: GNO/PC Version 1.0
2. Author/Developer: Computer Aided Planning & Scheduling, Inc. 2900 Paces Ferry Road, Bldg. D, Atlanta GA 30339, USA.
3. Brief Outline:

GNO/PC is a state-of-the-art minimum cost generalized network flow optimizer. The package employs an innovative technology for manipulating data structures associated with generalized network flow problems. Its in-core out-of-core implementation of arc storage allows GNO/PC to solve large networks extremely quickly, while maintaining a high level of accuracy. Installations of GNO/PC on an IBM PC have solved networks with over a hundred thousand arcs, and installations on minicomputers have generated solutions with nearly three million arcs. GNO/PC has solved a randomly generated network of 3000 nodes, 50,000 arcs (with roughly 10% of the arcs capacitated) on an IBM PC-AT with a math coprocessor in 2 hours, 15 minutes. A variation of the GNO/PC code is used by the U.S. military to aid in crisis action deployment planning.

4. Domain of Application:

Generalized and Pure network flow problems.

5. Implementation Language:

GNO/PC is written in the "C" language. The code is available in stand-alone executable format, subroutine library format, or source code.

6. Hardware and Operating System:

GNO/PC runs under MS-DOS. Since GNO/PC is written in the highly portable C language, the source code should transfer with minimal effort to any computer supported by a C compiler.

7. Special Features:

(a) Maximum number of nodes 8,000 under MS-DOS (may be larger depending on computer and operating system). Number of arcs is limited only by disk availability. Each arc usually requires 20 bytes of disk space.
(b) All input files are flat ASCII files which may be created and/or modified using a variety of text editors and word processors. The use of ASCII files allows GNO/PC to be called as a subroutine from other programs.
(c) Five different output reports including Summary Report, Basic Arc Flow Report, Non-Zero Arc Flow Report, All Arc Flow Report and Node Report.
(d) Open file format for access of solution vector, dual variables, artificials, etc.

8. Price and Terms of Installation:

The MS-DOS executable version of GNO/PC is available as follows: Commercial - US $795, Academic - US $250. Both packages include complete documentation and two hours phone support. The source code may also be purchased for US $5000. Complimentary demonstration diskettes available upon request.

9. Available from: Computer Aided Planning & Scheduling Inc., 2900 Paces Ferry Road, Bldg. D, Atlanta, GA 30339, USA.

enatosft.lml

1. Name of System: IFPS Version 3.5
IFPS/Optimum Version 4.1.2

2. Author/Developer: Execucom Systems Corporation
Arboretum Plaza One
9442 Capitol of Texas Hwy. North
Austin, Texas 78759, USA

3. Brief Outline

Optimum is an extremely powerful optimization tool for models created in IFPS. Optimum transforms the ability to answer "What if?" questions into the ability to answer "What's best?" questions. In order to achieve this, all the user has to do is specify which variables in the IFPS model fall in the category of decisions, constraints and the objective respectively. Optimum will create implicitly the coefficient matrix, determine if the decision variable appear linearly or not, and then invoke the relevant solver automatically. The system has the capability of solving large linear and mixed integer optimization problems and medium-size nonlinear optimization problems.

4. Domain of application:

Linear, mixed-integer and nonlinear optimization problems.

5. Implementation language:

FORTRAN & ASSEMBLER PROGRAMS (for I/O routine).

6. Hardware and Operating System:

The optimization system runs only on mainframes on PRIME under PRIMOS, on VAX under VMS and on IBM mainframes under VM/CMS and MVS/TSO.

7. Special features:

(i) Stand alone optimization subsystem.
(ii) Completely integrated with IFPS.
(iii) Optimization problem can be completely data driven, thereby ensures proper model management.

8. Price and terms of installation:

Optimum is a standard feature of Execucom's Côrporate Decision Support System (CDSS). Pricing for CDSS varies according to the size of the machine it is installed on. Both quantity discounts and academic discounts are available. Contact the vendor for details.

Available from:

USA: Execucom Systems Corporation
Arboretum Plaza One
9442 Capitol of Texas Hwy. North
Austin, Texas 78759, USA

enatosft.ll

1. Name of System: LEONARDO

2. Author/Developer: Creative Logic Limited

3. Brief Outline: **LEONARDO** is a fully compiled, object orientated expert system development environment, available at three levels. All levels share the same structure and principal functionality, offering a powerful rule based language for knowledge representation and a frame structure for the storage of object related information. There is an inbuilt procedure language for computation, database access and complex report generation. The management of uncertainty is supported by multiple methods.

4. Domain of Application: Diagnostic, advisory, selection, configuration, planning

5. Implementation language: FORTRAN & ASSEMBLER

6. Hardware and Operating System: **LEONARDO** runs on all IBM PC XT, AT and compatibles under MS DOS and the full range of VAX machines running under VMS.

7. Special features:

(i) Multiple knowledge representation techniques (rules, frames, procedures)
(ii) Object class structure with multiple inheritance
(iii) Multiple inference methods (forwards and backwards chaining, cyclic execution)
(iv) Portfolio of optional toolkits (database/spreadsheet access, function libraries, screen/graphical design facilities)

8. Price and terms of installation:

LEONARDO prices range from £149 to £1995 for PC based implementations. Prices for the VAX start at £4000. Both quantity and academic discounts are available from the vendor.

Available from:

Creative Logic Limited
Brunel Science Park
Kingston Lane
Uxbridge
Middlesex UB8 3PQ

1. Name of System: MILP

2. Author/Developer: Istvan Maros and Antal Dobosy, Computer and Automation Institute of the Hungarian Academy of Sciences, H-1111 Budapest, Kende u. 13-17, Hungary.

3. Brief Outline:

MILP is a linear programming (LP) system designed to solve medium to large scale LP problems efficiently on professional personal computers. The systems can handle 4 types of variables and constraints. The solution algorithm is a variant of the revised simplex method with upper bounding technique and product form of the inverse (PFI). It is equipped with some known and some recently developed algorithmic tools. The most important features are multiple pricing, FEWPHI algorithm in Phase-I, reduction of error propogation, error recover procedures, sparsity technique, dump/restart (also from partial basis), dynamic scaling of reduced costs (optional), anti-degeneracy column selection strategy (optional), MPS input format, MILP own input format, user accessible run parameters, 4 levels of iteration report, short and detailed solution output, interactive user interface. The system is memory resident, triangular factors of PFI are not stored. MILP has several variants depending on the precision (simple, double) used, the presence of the math coprocessor, and the memory model (in the case of 16-bit micros). Minimum requirement is an IBM PC/XT or compatible with 256 KB of memory. Problems of 1000 rows and 1000 columns are solved on a routine basis within very reasonable time.

4. Domain of Application:

Any kind of optimization problems that can be expressed in terms of a general linear programming problem.

5. Implementation Language:

Portable FORTRAN77.

6. Hardware and Operating Systems:

It can run on any computer which has a standard FORTRAN77 compiler. Recent versions run on IBM PC/XT, AT and compatible machines.

7. Special Features: see 3

8. Price and Terms of Installation

Different prices for different versions. Academic discount is available, details on application.

9. Available from:

Dr I Maros, Computer and Automation Institute of the Hungarian Academy of Sciences (MTA SZTAKI), H-1111 Budapest, Kende u. 13-17, Hungary.

enatosft.im

1. Name of the System: XPRESS-LP

2. Author/Developer: Dash Associates, Blisworth House, Church Lane, Blisworth, Northants NN7 3BX, UK.

3. Brief Outline:

The system is in 3 parts: a) a symbolic model builder enabling the modellers to express his model in a natural formulation b) a state of the art super-sparse optimiser c) a solution browser. Efficient interfaces are provided to enable data to be exchanged with spreadsheet and database software.

4. Domain of Application:

Linear Programming modelling and optimisation on microcomputers. Integer Programming facilities available Q1 1988.

5. Implementation Langugage:

Fortran 77 plus Assembler.

6. Hardware and operating system:

Any MSDOS or PC-DOS computer. A numeric co-processor is recommended but not essential.

7. Special features:

Optimised for performance on Intel microprocessor systems. The system uses all available memory.

8. Price and terms of installation:

Dependant upon problem size. Typical prices are £1500 for both modeller and optimiser for 2000 row by 5000 column problems, £500 for 300 row by 500 column problems. Educational version £60.

9. Available from:

Dash Associates, Blisworth House, Church Lane,
Blisworth, Northants, NN& 3BX

(+44) 604 - 858993

enatosft.rd

SECTION 10:

LIST OF PARTICIPANTS

Dr J F Baldwin
Engineering Mathematics Dept
Queens Building
Bristol University
Bristol
UK

Dr Maurizio Bielli
National Research Council
Viale Manzoni 30-00185
Rome
Italy

Prof Meral Binbasioglu
School of Management
Purdue University
420 Krannert Building
West Lafayette, IN 47907
USA

Dr J J Bisschop
University of Twente, Univ
of Technical and Social Sci
PO Box 217
7500 AE Enschede
The Netherlands

Prof W Brauers
Uni Antwerpen, Rijksun Cent
Antwerpen, Coll Voor Ontwik
Middelheimlaan 1,
B-2020 Antwerpen
Belgium

Dr J Carmona
Rua Correia de Sa, 309
4100 Porto
Portugal

Dr J Cha
Nat Cent for Earthquake Eng
Rsrch, State Uni of NY at
Buffalo, Red Jacket Quadrangle
Buffalo, N Y 14261
USA

Mr W Nickels
Rsrch Assistant. RWTH Aachen
Lehrstuhl fur
Unternehmensforschung.
Templergraben 64 5100 Aachen
Germany

Mr J S Clohessy
Univ of Colorado at Denver
Dept of Maths
1100 14th Street
Denver, Colorado 80202
USA

Dr R M Cooke
TH Delft, Delft University
of Technology
PO Box 356
2600 AJ Delft
The Netherlands

Prof Ch. De Bruyn
Univ De Liege (-Bat. B31)
Bd de Rectorat
4000 Liege
Belgium

Dr H A Eiselt
Univ of New Brunswick
PO Box 4400
Fredericton N.B.
E3B 5A3
Canada

Dr M A H Dempster
Dalhousie University
Sch of Business Administration
6152 Coburg Road
Halifax, Nova Scotia
B3H 1Z5
Canada

Prof j Dias Coelho
Faculdade de Economia
Universidade Nova de Lisboa
Campo Grande 185
1700 Lisboa
Portugal

Prof D R Dolk
Naval Post Graduate School
Monterey
California 93943
USA

Prof A Drud
Analytic Support Unit, Dev Rch
Dept, The World Bank
1818 H Street, N W
Washington DC 20433
USA

Mr V Debroey
Instituut Voor Chemie
Ingenieurstechn
De Croylaan 2
3030 Heverlee
Belgium

Prof I J L D Faco
Computer Science Department
Instituto de Mathematica-UFRJ
Caixa Postal 68530
21945-Rio de Janeiro-RJ
Brazil

Mr A M Fakeih
Saudi Vegetable Oil & Ghee Co
PO Box 1202
Jeddah 21431
Saudi Arabia

Prof E Forman
George Washington University
Washington DC 20052
USA

Mr M Forster
Freie Universitat Berlin
Garystrasse 21
D-1000 Berlin 33
West Germany

Dr N Ghiaseddin
University of Notre Dame
Dept of Management
College of Business Admin
Notre Dame, Indiana 46556
USA

Prof H W Gottinger
Univ of Virginia, Sch of Eng
& Appl. Sci, Dept of Sys Eng.
Thornton Hall, Charlottesville
Virginia 22901
USA

Prof M Grauer
University of Hagen
Faculty of Economics
D-5800 Hagen
Postfach 940
West Germany

Prof H J Greenberg
Dept of Mathematics
University of Colorado, Denver
1100 Fourteenth Street
Denver, Colorado 80202
USA

Dr K Guner
Faculty of Natural Science
Hacettepe University
06532 Beytepe
Ankara
Turkey

Dr G Hidding
c/o Mr Patrice Ruchon
Arthur Anderson & Co
Tour Gan - Cedex 13
92082 Paris La Defense
France

Mr G W Hintz
RWTH Aachen, Lehrstuhl fur
Unternehmensforschung
Templergraben 64
5100 Aachen
Germany

Mr H Holm
Aalborg Boilers A/S
PO Box 661
DK-9100 Aalborg
Denmark

Prof A Idnani
Pace University
Computer Science Dept
Bedford Road
Pleasantville, N Y 10570
USA

Miss A Iyilikci
Dokuz Eylul Univ, Eng &
Architecture Faculty
Environment Engineering Dept
Bornova, Izmir
Turkey

Mr A Janisz
Mgr of Policy & Co-ordination
Petroleum Purchasing Dept
British Gas, Nat. West. House
326 High Holborn, London
W1V 7PT
UK

Prof E Jaquet-Lagreze
Univ de Paris, Lab D'Analyse Et
Modelisation: Lamsade, Place
Du Mal De Lattre De Tassigny
Cedex 16, 75755 Paris
France

Mr M Jeffreys
Jeffreys Systems Plc
Jeffreys House
134 North Lane
Aldershot, Hants
GU12 4QM
UK

Dr E L Johnson
IBM Watson Research Centre
PO Box 218
Yorktown Heights
N Y 10598
USA

Dr A Kalamatianou
20 Simandira
Athens 10445
Greece

Prof P Kall
Institut fur O R & Math
Meth der Wirtsch der Univ
Zurich. Moussostr. 15.
CH-8044 Zurich
Switzerland

Mr C Kuip
University of Twente
PO Box 217
7500 AE Enschede
The Netherlands

Dr L Lasdon
Coll & Grad Sch of Bus, The
Univ of Texas at Austin, Dept
of Mgt Sci and Info Systems
Room 5.202,Austin,Texas 78712
USA

Prof M Lenard
School of Management Science
Boston University
704 Commonwealth Ave, Boston
Massachusetts MA 02215
USA

Prof A Y Lewin
Programme Director, Decision,
Risk and Management Science
National Science Foundation
Washington, DC 20550
USA

Prof M L Rico
Prof. Dr. Univ. Complutense de
Madrid
c/o Moratin, 50-50I;
Madrid 28014
Spain

Prof W A Lodwick
Dept of Maths - Box 170
Univ Of Colorado - Denver
1100 14th Street
Denver, Colorado 80202
USA

Prof F A Lootsma
Dept of Maths and Infomatics
Delft University of Technology
PO Box 356
2600 AJ Delft
The Netherlands

Dr C Lucas
Maths & Stats Dept, Brunel Uni
Kingston Lane
Uxbridge
Middx
UB8 3PH
UK

Prof O B G Madsen
IMSOR
Building 321
The Tech Univ of Denmark
DK-2800 Lyngby
Denmark

Dr C Marco
National Research Council
Viale Manzoni 30 - 00185
Rome
Italy

Dr I Maros
Comp & Automation Institute of
the Hungarian Academy of Sci
PO Box 63
H-1502 Budapest
Hungary

Ms E Medova-Dempster
Tech Uni of Nova Scotia
PO Box 1000
Halifax, Nova Scotia
B3J 2X4
Canada

Dr A Meeraus
World Bank
1818 H Street
North West NW
Washington DC 20433
USA

Dr G Mitra
Department of Maths & Stats
Brunel University
Kingston Lane
Uxbridge, Middx
UK

Dr F H Murphy
Business School
Temple University
Philadelphia
PA 19122
USA

Ms M W Cooper
Southern Illinois University
of Edwardsville
Edwardsville
Illinois 62026 - 1653
USA

Prof I Or
Industrial Engineering Dept
Bogazici University P.K. 2
Bebek
Istanbul
Turkey

Ms M Pereira Leite
Universidade Do Minho
Pavilhoes De Engenharia
Av. Joao XXI
4700 Braga
Portugal

Ms P Rahnavard
6001 Arlington Blvd No 820
Falls Church
VA 22044
USA

Mr W Richmond
Purdue Univ, Sch of Management
Krannert Grad Sch of Mgmt
Krannert Building, West
Lafayette, IN 47907
USA

Prof P D'Alessandro
Dept of Electrical Engineering
University of L'Aquila
Monteluco 67100
L'Aquila
Italy

Prof M Rijckaert
Instituut Voor Chemie
Ingenieurstechn
De Croylaan 2
3030 Heverlee
Belgium

Mr D Rios-Insua
Isaac Peral, 5
28015 Madrid
Spain

Prof T Saaty
Graduate School
University of Pittsburgh
Pittsburgh
Pennsylvania 15260
USA

Prof J F Shapiro
M. I. T.
Operations Research Centre
Room 40-164
Cambridge, Mass. 02134
USA

Prof R Sharda
Associate Prof of Mgmt Science
Oklahoma State University
College of Business Admin
Stillwater, Oklahoma 74078
USA

Prof B Simeone
The State Uni of New Jersey
RUTGERS Centre for Oper Rsrch
Hill Centre for the Math Sci
New Brunswick,New Jersey 08903
USA

Mr J A Smith
US Dept of Transportation
United States Coast Guard
USCG R&D Center, Avery Point
Groton, CT 06340-6096
USA

Dr M Paolo
Dept. of Maths and Stats
Via Ridolfi, 10
Pisa
Italy

Prof E A Stohr
New York University
Grad School of Bus Admin
100 Trinity Place
New York, N Y 10006
USA

Dr M Tamiz
Maths & Stats Dept, Brunel Uni
Kingston Lane
Uxbridge
Middx
UK

Dr J Teghem Jr
Faculté Poytechnique De Mons
Dépt De Mathe Et Gestion
7000 Mons (Belgique)
Rue De Houdain
Belgium

Cpt F Tuna
Turkish Land Forces Command
Dept of Planning & Policy
Defence and Research Branch
K.K.K. P.P. Bskligi, Ankara
Turkey

Prof L Valadares Tavares
Dept of OR. CESUR
Instituto Superior Technico
Avenida Rovisco Pais
1000 Lisboa
Portugal

Mr S Wang
Dept Maths & Informs
Delft Univ Of Technology
PO Box 356
2600 AJ Delft
The Netherlands

Dr H S Weigel
Deputy & Tech Dir, Mnmt Sci Gp
General Rsrch Corp, 7655 Old
Springhouse Rd, Westgate Rsrch
Park, McLean, Virginia 22102
USA

Dr B Werners
Research Assistant
RWTH Aachen
Templergraben 64
5100 Aachen
Germany

Prof A Whinston
Management Information
Research Centre, Krannert Sch
Purdue University
West Lafayette, IN 47907
USA

Dr D Wijnmalen
Physics & Electronics Lab TNO
PO Box 96864
2509 JG The Hague
The Netherlands

Prof R T Wong
Purdue University
School of Management
Krannert Building
West Lafayette, IN 47907
USA

Prof H J Zimmermann
Director, Institute for Oper.
Research, RWTH Aachen
Templergraben 64
51 Aachen
West Germany

Prof S Zionts
School of Management
State University of New York
at Buffalo, N Y 14260
USA

Late Registration

Prof. R. Daniels
University of Buckingham
BUCKINGHAM
MK18 1EG

NATO ASI Series F

Vol. 1: Issues in Acoustic Signal – Image Processing and Recognition. Edited by C. H. Chen. VIII, 333 pages. 1983.

Vol. 2: Image Sequence Processing and Dynamic Scene Analysis. Edited by T. S. Huang. IX, 749 pages. 1983.

Vol. 3: Electronic Systems Effectiveness and Life Cycle Costing. Edited by J. K. Skwirzynski. XVII, 732 pages. 1983.

Vol. 4: Pictorial Data Analysis. Edited by R. M. Haralick. VIII, 468 pages. 1983.

Vol. 5: International Calibration Study of Traffic Conflict Techniques. Edited by E. Asmussen. VII, 229 pages. 1984.

Vol. 6: Information Technology and the Computer Network. Edited by K. G. Beauchamp. VIII, 271 pages. 1984.

Vol. 7: High-Speed Computation. Edited by J. S. Kowalik. IX, 441 pages. 1984.

Vol. 8: Program Transformation and Programming Environments. Report on an Workshop directed by F. L. Bauer and H. Remus. Edited by P. Pepper. XIV, 378 pages. 1984.

Vol. 9: Computer Aided Analysis and Optimization of Mechanical System Dynamics. Edited by E. J. Haug. XXII, 700 pages. 1984.

Vol. 10: Simulation and Model-Based Methodologies: An Integrative View. Edited by T. I. Ören, B. P. Zeigler, M. S. Elzas. XIII, 651 pages. 1984.

Vol. 11: Robotics and Artificial Intelligence. Edited by M. Brady, L. A. Gerhardt, H. F. Davidson. XVII, 693 pages. 1984.

Vol. 12: Combinatorial Algorithms on Words. Edited by A. Apostolico, Z. Galil. VIII, 361 pages. 1985.

Vol. 13: Logics and Models of Concurrent Systems. Edited by K. R. Apt. VIII, 498 pages. 1985.

Vol. 14: Control Flow and Data Flow: Concepts of Distributed Programming. Edited by M. Broy. VIII, 525 pages. 1985.

Vol. 15: Computational Mathematical Programming. Edited by K. Schittkowski. VIII, 451 pages. 1985.

Vol. 16: New Systems and Architectures for Automatic Speech Recognition and Synthesis. Edited by R. De Mori, C.Y. Suen. XIII, 630 pages. 1985.

Vol. 17: Fundamental Algorithms for Computer Graphics. Edited by R.A. Earnshaw. XVI, 1042 pages. 1985.

Vol. 18: Computer Architectures for Spatially Distributed Data. Edited by H. Freeman and G. G. Pieroni. VIII, 391 pages. 1985.

Vol. 19: Pictorial Information Systems in Medicine. Edited by K. H. Höhne. XII, 525 pages. 1986.

Vol. 20: Disordered Systems and Biological Organization. Edited by E. Bienenstock, F. Fogelman Soulié, G. Weisbuch. XXI, 405 pages. 1986.

Vol. 21: Intelligent Decision Support in Process Environments. Edited by E. Hollnagel, G. Mancini, D.D. Woods. XV, 524 pages. 1986.

Vol. 22: Software System Design Methods. The Challenge of Advanced Computing Technology. Edited by J.K. Skwirzynski. XIII, 747 pages. 1986.

NATO ASI Series F

Vol. 23: Designing Computer-Based Learning Materials. Edited by H. Weinstock and A. Bork. IX, 285 pages. 1986.

Vol. 24: Database Machines. Modern Trends and Applications. Edited by A.K. Sood and A.H. Qureshi. VIII, 570 pages. 1986.

Vol. 25: Pyramidal Systems for Computer Vision. Edited by V. Cantoni and S. Levialdi. VIII, 392 pages. 1986.

Vol. 26: Modelling and Analysis in Arms Control. Edited by R. Avenhaus, R.K. Huber and J.D. Kettelle. VIII, 488 pages. 1986.

Vol. 27: Computer Aided Optimal Design: Structural and Mechanical Systems. Edited by C.A. Mota Soares. XIII, 1029 pages. 1987.

Vol. 28: Distributed Operating Systems. Theory und Practice. Edited by Y. Paker, J.-P. Banatre and M. Bozyiğit. X, 379 pages. 1987.

Vol. 29: Languages for Sensor-Based Control in Robotics. Edited by U. Rembold and K. Hörmann. IX, 625 pages. 1987.

Vol. 30: Pattern Recognition Theory and Applications. Edited by P.A. Devijver and J. Kittler. XI, 543 pages. 1987.

Vol. 31: Decision Support Systems: Theory and Application. Edited by C.W. Holsapple and A.B. Whinston. X, 500 pages. 1987.

Vol. 32: Information Systems: Failure Analysis. Edited by J.A. Wise and A. Debons. XV, 338 pages. 1987.

Vol. 33: Machine Intelligence and Knowledge Engineering for Robotic Applications. Edited by A.K.C. Wong and A. Pugh. XIV, 486 pages. 1987.

Vol. 34: Modelling, Robustness and Sensitivity Reduction in Control Systems. Edited by R.F. Curtain. IX, 492 pages. 1987.

Vol. 35: Expert Judgment and Expert Systems. Edited by J.L. Mumpower, L.D. Phillips, O. Renn and V.R.R. Uppuluri. VIII, 361 pages. 1987.

Vol. 36: Logic of Programming and Calculi of Discrete Design. Edited by M. Broy. VII, 415 pages. 1987.

Vol. 37: Dynamics of Infinite Dimensional Systems. Edited by S.-N. Chow and J.K. Hale. IX, 514 pages. 1987.

Vol. 38: Flow Control of Congested Networks. Edited by A.R. Odoni, L. Bianco and G. Szegö. XII, 355 pages. 1987.

Vol. 39: Mathematics and Computer Science in Medical Imaging. Edited by M.A. Viergever and A. Todd-Pokropek. VIII, 546 pages. 1988.

Vol. 40: Theoretical Foundations of Computer Graphics and CAD. Edited by R.A. Earnshaw. XX, 1246 pages. 1988.

Vol. 41: Neural Computers. Edited by R. Eckmiller and Ch. v. d. Malsburg. XIII, 566 pages. 1988.

Vol. 42: Real-Time Object Measurement and Classification. Edited by A.K. Jain. VIII, 407 pages 1988.

NATO ASI Series F

Vol. 43: Sensors and Sensory Systems for Advanced Robots. Edited by P. Dario. XI, 597 pages. 1988.

Vol. 44: Signal Processing and Pattern Recognition in Nondestructive Evaluation of Materials. Edited by C.H. Chen. VIII, 344 pages. 1988.

Vol. 45: Syntactic and Structural Pattern Recognition. Edited by G. Ferraté, T. Pavlidis, A. Sanfeliu, H. Bunke. XVI, 467 pages. 1988.

Vol. 46: Recent Advances in Speech Understanding and Dialog Systems. Edited by H. Niemann, M. Lang, G. Sagerer. X, 521 pages. 1988.

Vol. 47: Advanced Computing Concepts and Techniques in Control Engineering. Edited by M.J. Denham, A.J. Laub. XI, 518 pages. 1988.

Vol. 48: Mathematical Models for Decision Support. Edited by Gautam Mitra. IX, 762 pages. 1988.

Vol. 49: Computer Integrated Manufacturing. Edited by I. Burhan Turksen. VIII, 568 pages. 1988.